# FREEDOM

# JUST AROUND

# THE CORNER

ALSO BY WALTER A. McDOUGALL

*Promised Land, Crusader State:*
*The American Encounter with the World Since 1776*

*Let the Sea Make a Noise . . .*
*A History of the North Pacific from Magellan to MacArthur*

*. . . the Heavens and the Earth:*
*A Political History of the Space Age*

*The Grenada Papers*
(coeditor, with Paul Seabury)

*France's Rhineland Diplomacy, 1914–1924:*
*The Last Bid for a Balance of Power in Europe*

# FREEDOM JUST AROUND THE CORNER

*A New American History 1585–1828*

WALTER A. McDOUGALL

HarperCollins*Publishers*

FIRST EDITION

*Designed by Joseph Rutt*

Printed on acid-free paper

Library of Congress Cataloging-in-Publication Data

McDougall, Walter A.
Freedom just around the corner : a new American history, 1585–1828 /
Walter A. McDougall.— 1st ed.
p. cm.
Includes bibliographical references and index.
ISBN 0-06-019789-7 (acid-free paper)
1. United States—History—Colonial period, ca. 1600–1775. 2. United States—History—Revolution, 1775–1783. 3. United States—History—1783–1865. I. Title.

E178.M47 2004
973.2—dc22        2003061094

04 05 06 07 08 NMSG/RRD 10 9 8 7 6 5 4 3 2 1

To the immigrant Barclays, Brueggemans, McDougalls, and Voltzes,
thanks to whom I am American

# CONTENTS

# MAPS

## JOIN or DIE

*The first American political cartoon appeared in Benjamin Franklin's* Pennsylvania Gazette *on May 9, 1754. During the run-up to the climactic French and Indian War, Franklin implored the American colonies to "Join or Die." In this version, which appeared in the* Boston Gazette *on May 21, 1754, the snake hisses a tempting corollary: "Unite and Conquer." (Courtesy of the Massachusetts Historical Society, Boston)*

*The rattlesnake motif graced any number of battle flags, standards, uniform buttons, posters, and pamphlets during the American War of Independence, not least the first U.S. Navy jack with its thirteen red and white stripes, snake, and warning, "Don't Tread on Me." This banner, carried by the First Virginia regiment of militia in 1775, added the equally popular slogan "Liberty or Death." (From Benson John Lossing,* Pictorial Field Book of the Revolution *[New York: Harper & Brothers, 1860])*

*Standing on the waters casting your bread*
*While the eyes of the idol with the iron head are glowing.*
*Distant ships sailing into the mist,*
*You were born with a snake in both of your fists while a hurricane was blowing.*
*Freedom just around the corner for you*
*But with truth so far off what good will it do?*

*Jokerman dance to the nightingale tune,*
*Bird fly high by the light of the moon,*
*Oh, oh, oh, Jokerman.*
—BOB DYLAN

# PREFACE

$\mathcal{T}$he creation of the United States of America is the central event of the past four hundred years. If some ghostly ship, some *Flying Dutchman,* were transported in time from the year 1600 into the present, the crew would be amazed by our technology and the sheer numbers of people on the globe, but the array of civilizations would be recognizable. There is today, as there was then: a huge Chinese empire run by an authoritarian but beleaguered bureaucracy; a homogeneous, anxious, suspicious Japan; a teeming crazy quilt of Hindus and Muslims in India attempting to make a state of themselves; an amorphous Russian empire pulsing outward or inward in proportion to Muscovy's projection of force; a vast Islamic crescent hostile to infidels but beset by rival centers of power; a dynamic, more-or-less Christian civilization in Europe aspiring to unity but vexed by its dense congeries of nations and tongues; and finally an Iberian/Amerindian culture in South America marked by relative poverty and strategic impotence. The only continent that would astound the Renaissance time-travelers would be North America, which was primitive and nearly vacant as late as 1607, but which today hosts the mightiest, richest, most dynamic civilization in history—a civilization, moreover, that perturbs the trajectories of all other civilizations just by existing.

One might object the most salient features of modern history have not been territorial and demographic, but intellectual and political: the invention and spread of enlightened ideas of human rights and democratic self-government on the one hand, and the scientific and technological explosions in human power on the other hand. That is so, but the rise of America goes far to explain the rapidity and scale of their triumphs. North America was simply the greatest prize in the world *circa* 1600, and the fact Britons won that prize rather than Spaniards, Frenchmen, Chinese, or Russians explains the shape of modern history more than anything else. I used to disparage American history as a relatively provincial field of research. I now realize trying to make sense of America is nothing short of heroic (unless it be foolish). For if historians aim to explain change over time, then the United States is the most swiftly moving target of all, because nowhere else has more change occurred in so short a span. America was not just born of revolution, it is one.

At an early stage I chanced to describe this new project to a distinguished senior scholar and mentor. I expected to receive a blessing from this man of goodwill that might relieve the anxiety I felt over the undertaking. Instead, he asked me a question: "Do we really need another American history?" My eyes fell to the pavement of the Lower Manhattan street, and I croaked, "I don't know. Probably not."

What, after all, did I have to say about the United States that had not already been written by Henry Steele Commager, Samuel Eliot Morison, Arthur Schlesinger, Jr., Richard Hofstadter, Oscar Handlin, Carl Degler, and others? How many times did the stories of Jamestown and Plymouth Rock, Valley Forge and the Constitutional Convention, the Erie Canal and the Civil War, the Progressive Era and the Great Depression, World War II and the Civil Rights Movement need to be told? What could I say about our national past that would be both original and defensible? What indeed, given I was not even formally trained in American history and thus risk whatever remains of my professional reputation? But the faith of others won out, for better or worse.

Cass Canfield, Jr., and Hugh Van Dusen of HarperCollins hatched the idea of a narrative history that would avoid the extremes of condemnation and celebration of the American past characterizing the Howard Zinn and Paul Johnson titles already on their list. They imagined a cool, objective book telling Americans candidly "who and why we are what we are." Steve Fraser suggested my name to them, and Gerry McCauley urged me to accept their offer. I thought it all over during a solo automobile trip to New Hampshire and back. Did I have some new notion of what made Americans exceptional, some additional insight into the American character? Perhaps not, but I had lots of ideas about specific eras and themes I wanted to test. For instance, existing U.S. histories, whatever their slant, display little appreciation (much less forgiveness) of the flawed human nature that makes Americans *un*exceptional. Perhaps that is why our great national narratives contain so little humor: whether they extol or condemn the American experience, they take it terribly seriously. I also realized while driving through upper New England how much I love the fifty United States (all of which I have lived, worked, or traveled in save North Dakota and Oregon). At length, I decided to learn the history of my country *whether or not* I had much to teach.

But I couldn't tell that to the editors. So I sent them upon my return a list of themes worthy of emphasis in a new U.S. history. First, *geography*, being the reconnaissance, conquest, and settlement of the North American continent, and the challenges and chances posed by its lands, woods, and waters. Second, *technology*, being the tools Americans fashioned to tame and develop the continent. Third, *demography*, being the ways in which the numbers, origins, customs, and values of those who peopled America expanded and sometimes restricted the nation's choices. Fourth, *mythology*, which is to say the construction of America's civic religion and its problematical coexistence with multiple forms of Christianity. Fifth, the *federative power*, a concept coined by Ambassador Robert Strausz-Hupé to describe the unique power of American institutions and ideology to knit together diverse territories and peoples while relieving the tension between their ideals of liberty and equality.

I also imagined special features that might justify a new U.S. history. I wanted to pay more attention to all *regions and states* so that Kansas, for instance, would not exist only when it was "bleeding." The Midwest, in particular, has received far less attention than it deserves in synthetic histories, while the "new Western history" demands a correction of traditional interpretations of the frontier. I hoped to be genuinely inclusive by making room not only for African, Asian, and Hispanic Americans, but for *European ethnic groups* such as the Germans, Irish, Italians (indeed, Catholics generally), Slavs, Scandinavians, and Jews. I meant to treat all these as *people rather than icons*, recognizing that no American is "just" a member of a group, but a person with loyalties to kinfolk, region, occupation, religion, and political party as well as ethnicity. Next, it seemed imperative to stress how the United States, despite its reputation for xenophobia and isolationism, grew on the strength of *immigrant labor, foreign capital, and imported technology*. Last but not least, I wanted to study the unique American experiment in *religious liberty*. As Bob Dylan wrote, in a striking poetic inversion: "I heard the Sermon on the Mount and knew it was too complex / It didn't amount to anything more than what the broken glass reflects." Of course, the Sermon on the Mount is not complex, but terrifying in its simplicity. Rather, the effects of Biblical religion, filtered through the lenses of American consciences and projected onto law, society, and politics, are what seem kaleidoscopic.

A good plan, or so it seemed to me then. But the moment I dove into the research, much less writing, I realized the plan was madly ambitious. Given how much exciting new scholarship in American history appears every month, trying to synthesize it all is like trying to dam the Mississippi River. What levees might I build just to channel the flood? Shall I portray Americans as individualists or community builders, pragmatists or dreamers, materialists or idealists, bigots or champions of tolerance, lovers of liberty and justice for all, or history's most brazen hypocrites? Did succeeding waves of immigrants make the United States what it is, or did the land make Americans of immigrants? Are words such as capitalism, republicanism, and democracy abstractions best not used at all, or can the lexicon of social and political science help us to shrink our own heads? Some of the answers emerged from the telling. But it quickly dawned on me that one of the book's major themes would be *none of the above.* It is the American people's penchant for hustling—in both the positive and negative senses. It emboldens me to call this book candid. It is novel enough to require a whole chapter of explanation.

A sabbatical year in 2001 permitted me to get a head start on what has become the first volume of a projected trilogy. For that leave I am indebted to the University of Pennsylvania's School of Arts and Sciences, the Earhart Foundation, the Marion Fund of the Foreign Policy Research Institute's Board of Trustees, and contributors to the FPRI Center for the Study of America and the West, especially the Lynde and Harry Bradley Foundation and the John M. Olin Foundation. I thank FPRI President Harvey Sicherman, Vice President Alan Luxenberg, and Business Manager Harry Richlin for granting me an office, a computer, and above all, privacy. Sicherman and David Eisenhower also deserve credit—or blame—for teaching me much about how politics really work. I treasure our sprightly conversation. Frank Plantan held the fort at Penn's International Relations Program during my absence, and managing editors Steve Winterstein and Trudy Kuehner eased my burden as editor of *Orbis: A Journal of World Affairs.* I thank Hugh Van Dusen, David Semanki, and an outstanding copy editor, John Yohalem, for shepherding this book through the press. I thank my wife, Jonna, and children, Angela and Christopher, for patience beyond measure. Above all, I thank Christopher M. Gray for invaluable bibliographic assistance, criticism of the text, and encouragement during my frequent funks. Indeed, if trying to write good history can be likened to golf (they are equally quixotic), then Chris is the best caddy of all—and like a good caddy will doubtless take blame for any "bad shots" I have made.

# FREEDOM

# JUST AROUND

# THE CORNER

# AMERICAN ARCHETYPES
## *What Some Great Novels Tell Us About Ourselves*

"At sunrise on a first of April, there appeared . . . a man in cream colors, at the water-side in the city of St. Louis. His cheek was fair, his chin downy, his hair flaxen, his hat a white fur one, with a long fleecy nap. He had neither trunk, valise, carpet-bag, nor parcel. No porter followed him. He was unaccompanied by friends. From the shrugged shoulders, titters, whispers, wonderings of the crowd, it was plain that he was, in the extremest sense of the word, a stranger." He and the crowd proceeded to climb the ramp onto the steamboat *Fidèle,* bound from St. Louis to New Orleans. The stranger, all eyes upon him, paused beneath a "Wanted" poster on deck warning of a "mysterious imposter." Not long before, notorious gangs of cutthroats terrorized travelers on western rivers. But the predators these days were swindlers: "Where the wolves are killed off, the foxes increase." The stranger then produced chalk and a slate and wrote for the crowd to read: "Charity thinketh no evil, Charity believeth all things, Charity never faileth." Two doors down, beneath the smoking saloon, a barber hung on his shop door a placard of contrary sentiments: "*NO TRUST.*"

Thus began a great American novel. It described one day—April Fools' Day—on board a Mississippi steamboat, and its publisher contrived, for publicity's sake, to release it on April 1, 1857. Reviewers panned the book (one called it nothing but "forty-five conversations held on board a steamer, conducted by personages who might pass for the errata of creation"). But some critics think *The Confidence-Man* to be the greatest novel by Herman Melville.[1]

Melville's satirical allegory holds up a mirror to the American people. They are "natives of all sorts, and foreigners; men of business and men of pleasure; parlor men and backwoodsmen; farm-hunters and fame-hunters; heiress-hunters, gold-hunters, buffalo-hunters, bee-hunters, happiness-hunters, truth-hunters, and still keener hunters after all these hunters." They include fine ladies, philosophers, and land speculators, soldiers, black slaves and quadroons, Mormons, Jews, Papists, and Baptists, jesters, teetotalers, and Yankee peddlers: "in short, a piebald parliament" of "that multiform pilgrim species, man."[2] All seek to hustle each other or, if charity gets the best of them, be hustled in turn. Melville doubtless got the original idea from a story run by the New York *Herald* in 1849. It told of a respectable-looking fellow who talked people into lending him their pocket watches for some innocent purpose, whereupon neither man nor watch would return. The reporter coined the term "confidence-man" for the rascal, likening him to the brokers downtown who urged passers-by to "take a flyer" touting some hot stock issue. "His genius has been employed on a small scale in Broadway. Theirs has been employed in Wall street. That's all the difference." A friend of Melville even suggested that the con-man's success "speaks well for human nature, that, at this late day, in spite of all the hardening of civilization, and all the warning of newspapers, men *can be swindled*."[3]

Ever since borrowing money against *Moby Dick*'s royalties, which proved disappointing, Melville was "damned by dollars" and in need of commercial success. At the same time, he was tormented by the disparity between Americans' acquisitiveness and the Calvinist values he acquired in youth. The economy in the 1850s boomed on the strength of the California Gold Rush, land speculation, railroad construction, and the Cotton South, but far from becoming the New Jerusalem of millenarians' dreams, the nation was a sink-hole of corruption. In northern eyes the southern slavocracy was almost Satanic, while Southerners were quick to believe that in the industrial north (as a New Yorker confessed), "public men are all rogues, honest men are driven from the polls—the ballot boxes are in the hands of ruffians—the very men who are elected . . . are so many swindlers, stock-jobbers, liars, even forgers and robbers." It was a "plundering generation."[4]

So Melville took the risk of telling the truth, as he saw it, about the tricks Americans played on themselves in their effort to worship both God and Mammon. His Confidence-Man, variously likened to a jester, traveling sales-man, "genial misanthrope," P. T. Barnum (who published his scandalous auto-biography in 1855), the Devil, an angel, and the Second Coming of Christ, is a master of disguise and persuasion. Though some passengers prove tougher to gull than others, he eventually employs their own fear, greed, or fancied virtue to pry open their wallets, exposing in the process every conundrum and lie— about slavery, Indians, business, industry, and frontier religion—Americans preferred not to acknowledge. In the opening scene the Con-Man is that silent prophet dressed in white and quoting St. Paul. In the next he impersonates a crippled Negro beggar, worse off in freedom than he was under slavery. In the next he gulls a Methodist clergyman into contributing to the Seminole Widow and Orphan Asylum. "I have not heard of that charity," says the preacher. "But recently founded," the Con-Man replies, and pockets his coins.[5]

As the day progresses the Con-Man appears as a global philanthropist aiming to quicken the missionary impulse "with the Wall street spirit,"[6] a director of the Black Rapids Coal Company whose "exclusive" shares passengers beg him to sell, an herb-doctor hawking miracle cures, an agent of the Philosophical Intelligence Office (an employment bureau), and a wounded veteran of the Mexican War. In each case the Con-Man's glib sophistry strips his victims of the psychological raiment cloaking their vanity, while the victims in turn have occasion to mock Emerson, Thoreau, and Poe, abolitionists and slavers, topers and teetotalers, industrialists and agrarians, Bible-thumpers and free-thinkers until all roads out of the human dilemma appear to circle back on themselves. Melville's Americans are uproarious, profligate exemplars of pride and cupidity—call it sin if you wish—stubbornly bent on denying the same. The Con-Man does not persecute them so much as assist their self-flagellation: he is accuser, prosecutor, judge, bailiff, and even redeemer insofar as the dupes can blame their misfortune on the *Con-Man's* bad faith. Can no one resist? Are none sufficiently holy or cynical to escape the urge to prove they are what they're not?

The final test comes after dark when "Frank Goodman" (the Con-Man) returns to the barber shop begging a shave—on credit, of course. He implores Mr. Cream to take down his sign and *trust*. "Sir, you must excuse me," the barber replies. "I have a family." Goodman assures Cream he is Philanthropos himself, but the barber replies he abets deception every day by shaving off beards and selling wigs. So the Con-Man offers to "put it in writing," drafting a contract whereby the barber will revoke his "no trust" policy for the rest of the voyage and Goodman will make good any loss suffered as a consequence. Cream signs, then demands a $50 bond from the Con-Man to be returned if no losses are suffered. Too late: to demand a bond at this point is to break his own agreement to trust! The Con-Man departs (having neglected to pay for his shave), while the barber is left to reflect on this curious "man-charmer—as certain East Indians are called snake-charmers."[7]

"And now abideth faith, hope, and charity, these three, but the greatest of these is charity," preached St. Paul. There is lots of hope, but no charity or faith on board the *Fidèle* as it paddles down river. "It is as if Melville were answering his country's millennial expectations in the spirit of the prophet Amos: 'Woe unto you that desire the day of the Lord! To what end is it for you?' "[8] Is *The Confidence-Man* rightly interpreted as an antebellum apocalypse or is it a judgment on "the Christian god as a religious confidence man"?[9] Both are characteristic American poses—Puritanism and its flip side. But whatever the state of Melville's tumultuous soul in 1857, his great American novel was rewarded in kind. Just weeks after its release the publisher Dix & Edwards went out of business. It seems one of the partners dipped his hand in the till. *NO TRUST.*

American histories invariably quote M. G. Jean de Crèvecoeur, who asked in his *Letters from an American Farmer* of 1782: "What then is the American, this new man?" He answered himself by defining Americans, first as people who have left behind old prejudices and manners and received new ones from the mode of life in the New World, and second as a mixture of many nationalities, hence "a new race." Few histories go on to report Crèvecoeur was not altogether smitten with New World manners. For all their virtues, he found Americans "litigious, overbearing, purse-proud." If their society was not quite a war of all against all, it was nonetheless "a general mass of keenness and sagacious acting against another mass of equal sagacity. Happy when it does not degenerate into fraud against fraud."[10] Who is this new man, this American? As Melville would certainly have it, he or she is a hustler.

That may strike readers as grossly unfair. Surely Americans are no more selfish, sly, or corrupt than others, and is not the artful dodger a stock character of every culture's folklore and mythology? In ancient Greece the god Hermes was patron of tricksters, while Aesop's fables celebrated the art of dupery. In classical drama the shifty slave was a comic perennial. Hebrew lore is replete with stories of the clever Jew outfoxing the muscle-bound Gentile. In medieval Europe only the jester had a standing at court on a par with kings and bishops. The deceptive strategist has a central place in Chinese, Japanese, and Hindu literature. The Uncle Remus stories attest to the African oral tradition of prey more cunning than predator. Most intriguing, perhaps, is the Winnebago Trickster Cycle passed down by Native Americans. The tales tell of a shape-changer whose sole mode of interaction with others is to dupe or be duped. He is "at one and the same time creator and destroyer, giver and negator. . . . He knows neither good nor evil yet he is responsible for both. He possesses no values, moral or social, is at the mercy of his passions and appetites, yet through his action all values come into being." In the Winnebago cycle the trickster seeks only wealth, power, and sex (he carries his penis in a pouch and calls it "little brother"), but through his adventures with animals, trees, rocks, and other Indians he calls into being a world rich in humor and irony.[11]

To suggest Americans are, among other things, prone to be hustlers is not to accord them a nature different or worse than other human beings. It is simply to acknowledge Americans have enjoyed more opportunity to pursue their ambitions, by foul means or fair, than any other people in history. In Europe and elsewhere the privilege of manipulating the system to one's advantage was either reserved to elites or severely constrained: the wily peasant could not go far. In America, by contrast, all white males enjoyed full freedom to hustle, white women had their own tricks, and even enslaved Africans (we now know) played the system as best they could. No wonder American English is uniquely endowed with words connoting a swindle:

VERBS (excluding obscenities): bait; bamboozle; beat the system; bilk; bite; blackmail; bleed; blindfold; blindside; blow smoke; bluff; buffalo; bullskate; burn; caboodle; cheat; cheek; chisel; clip; collude; con; connive; conspire; cook up; corner; counterfeit; cozen; cream; crib; crimp; cross up; cut; deacon; deceive; decoy; defraud; deke; delude; diddle; do a number on; doctor; double cross; double deal; duck out; duff; dupe; embezzle; entrap; fake out; fast talk; fix; fleece; fob; foist; fool; forge; fork; four flush; fox; fudge; gaff; gas; gin; give a raw deal, give the business, give the runaround; goldbrick; gouge; grift; gull; gum; gyp; have ("been had"); hoke; hoodwink; hook; hornswoggle; hose; hump; hustle; ice; ike; inveigle; jerk around; jive; job; jockey; juggle; kite; lead (astray); load (the dice); lure; mark (the cards); milk; mislead; mooch; mug; nick; noodle; outfox; palm off; palm on; parlay; pinch; plant; play; play the angles; play the system; play upon; pluck; poach; pratt; pull a fast one; pull one's leg; ream; rig (the system); rim; rinkydink; rip off; rook; rope in; salt (the mine);

sandbag; scam; screw; seduce; sell a bill of goods; set up; shaft; shake-down; shave; shortchange; shuck; shuffle; skim; skin; skip out; skunk; slice; slip (one) over; snake; snare; snatch; snooker; snow; soak; splash; stack (the deck); stiff; sting; string (along); strip; suck in; sucker; swin-dle; swipe; take ("got took"); take a dive; take in; take for a ride; take to the cleaners; throw; throw a curve; trick; trim; trip; trump up; two-time; vamp; victimize; wangle, wrong; yank. NOUNS (without corre-sponding verbs): blarney; booby trap; brummagem; catchpenny; chicanery; clout; cobweb; doberman; dodger; drag; fake; flimflam; fraud; grifter; hanky-panky; hoax; huckster; humbug; hurdy-gurdy; imposter; land shark; phony; pinchbeck; pretender; pull; racket; ringer; runaround; ruse; sea-lawyer; sham; shark; sharp; shell game; (on the) take; thimble-rig.

Americans meet each other and ask, "How's tricks?" or "What's your racket?" Americans take it for granted that "everyone's got an angle," except maybe themselves. Americans hold all politicians, lawyers, advertisers, bankers, mer-chants, mechanics, salesmen, and "non-profit organizations" guilty until proven innocent, holding all professions to be conspiracies against the laity. Yet far from despising flimflam artists as parasites or worse, American popular culture habitually celebrates rascals as comedic figures, from Broadway's *The Music Man* (set in Iowa) and *How to Succeed in Business Without Really Trying* (New York City) to radio's *Jack Benny Show* (an upscale white setting) and *Amos 'n' Andy* (a downscale black setting), to television's *Sergeant Bilko* (an army base in Kansas), *Maverick* (the Old West), and *Seinfeld* (post-modern Manhattan), to movies as diverse as *The Sting, A Fistful of Dollars, Beverly Hills Cop,* and *The Hustler,* with its classic performances by Paul Newman, Jackie Gleason, George C. Scott, and Piper Laurie. American dramas complete the tribute by depicting the difficulties of earnest doctors, lawyers, police, judges, and politi-cians attempting to *avoid* being corrupted by ubiquitous sleaze.

A country ballad popularized during the presidential campaign of 1884 said it all with characteristic American wit:

Oh, the candidate's a dodger, yes a well known dodger
Oh, the candidate's a dodger, yes and I'm a dodger, too.
He'll meet you and treat you and ask you for your vote
But look out, boys, he a-dodgin' for your note.

Subsequent verses warned listeners against the merchant who doubles the price when there is no competition, the lawyer who claims he's your friend but is "easy for to bend," the general who will march you around and then "put you underground," the preacher who tells you of your crimes because he's "dodgin' for your dimes," the doctor whose bill makes you sick, the girl who connives to snare a husband, and the man who escapes her by "dodgin' down the line." The minstrel even admits to being a dodger, while the chorus lets no one off the hook:

> "Oh, we're all a-dodgin', dodgin', dodgin', dodgin'
> Oh, we're all a-dodgin' out away through the world."[12]

Melville was stingingly right to portray Americans as hustlers in the sense of self-promoters, scofflaws, occasional frauds, and peripatetic self-reinventers. But if he meant that is all Americans are he was wrong.[13] They are also hustlers in the *positive* sense: builders, doers, go-getters, dreamers, hard workers, inventors, organizers, engineers, and a people supremely generous. Needless to say those qualities, not their baser ones, were what justified Americans' faith in themselves, their nation, and their nation's destiny among nations. Americans came to believe early in colonial times—and the belief was redoubled at various points in the nineteenth and twentieth centuries—that the ordered liberty they uniquely enjoyed naturally bred prosperity and reform, which in turn bred more liberty, which someday they would export to the world. This three-fold American Dream of individual "rags to riches" success, collective social progress, and national crusades overseas is usually associated with the Progressive Era around the turn of the twentieth century. But the trinity dated back to the creation of the American colonies, while its assumptions were challenged well before 1900. One of the doubters was Samuel Clemens.

"I am an American," said the curious stranger in England's Warwick Castle to a tourist bewitched by his knowledge of medieval arms and heraldry. They had toured the castle that afternoon and now sat before a glowing hearth in the tourist's room. The stranger continued: "I was born and reared in Hartford, in the State of Connecticut—anyway, just over the river, in the country. So I am a Yankee of the Yankees—and practical; yes, and nearly barren of sentiment. . . . My father was a blacksmith, my uncle was a horse doctor, and I was both, along at first. Then I went over to the great arms factory and learned my real trade; learned all there was to it; learned to make everything; guns, revolvers, cannon, boilers, engines, all sorts of labor-saving machinery. Why, I could make anything a body wanted—anything in the world, it didn't make any difference what; and if there wasn't any quick new-fangled way to make a thing, I could invent one—and do it as easy as rolling off a log."

Thus began Mark Twain's *A Connecticut Yankee in King Arthur's Court*.[14] The year is 1889, and the "Yankee Pedlar" of Melville's time has given way to "Yankee Know-How." The Connecticut man, Hank Morgan by name, gets into a fight, takes a blow to the head, and awakes in unfamiliar surroundings. He is promptly captured by a mounted knight whom he takes to be a fugitive from an asylum or circus. The knight means to drive his prisoner to a fell fortress in the distance. " 'Bridgeport?' said I, pointing. 'Camelot,' said he." Informed the year is A.D. 528, and this is indeed King Arthur's court, the Yankee records, "I made up my mind to two things; if it was still the nineteenth century and I was among lunatics and couldn't get away, I would presently boss that asylum or know the reason why; and if on the other hand it was really the sixth century, all right, I didn't want any softer thing: I would boss *the whole country* inside of three months."[15]

Morgan's deliverance comes from his knowledge that a total eclipse of the sun occurred that very year. So he pronounces himself a wizard who will extinguish the sun unless he is made Arthur's prime minister. Still, Morgan must contest with the envious Merlin. But after "calling down lightning" on Merlin's tower (dynamite, wire, and a lightning rod do the trick) he is given the run of the kingdom. Within a few years the Connecticut Yankee founds mines and factories, railroads and telegraphs, schools, hospitals, and a newspaper. The noblemen are given prestigious positions in the new economy to appease their vanity and keep them out of trouble. Sir Launcelot, for instance, becomes chairman of the stock exchange. But however much the Yankee despises feudalism, he needs a title himself to be accorded the respect he deserves. So he gives himself one: The Boss.

Morgan is now the most powerful man who ever existed. But his beneficent goals are to prosper medieval England and liberate its superstitious minions from the grip of the church and nobility. First, he removes children to a secret Man Factory ("I'm going to turn groping and grubbing automata into *men*"). Next, he determines to overthrow a system in which 994 people out of a thousand slave on behalf of the remaining six: "It seemed to me that what the nine hundred and ninety-four dupes needed was *a new deal.*" Finally, he dreams of deposing Arthur and teaching the people self-government. "A man is a man, at bottom. . . . Yes, there is plenty good enough material for a republic in the most degraded people that ever existed—even the Russians."[16]

As Morgan works to collapse a millennium of progress into a few decades, the church awaits a chance to strike back. At length the clergy conjure a false emergency calling Morgan abroad, then take advantage of his absence to place all his works under interdict. Morgan returns to find England laid waste, his remaining disciples besieged, and the people in thrall. Enraged, he calls for a revolution and holes up in a redoubt guarded by electric fences and minefields, Gatling guns, and a great moat he can flood at the turn of a lever. The flower of English chivalry, driven by king, church, and honor, defiantly charge the fort until all 25,000 are electrocuted, blown to bits, drowned, or riddled by bullets. Morgan and his boys feel nothing but pride until, the next morning, a mysterious intruder pronounces their doom. They cannot leave the fort since England outside is more hostile than ever. But they cannot remain without being poisoned by the rotting corpses around them. Pulling off his disguise the intruder cries: "Ye were conquerors; ye are conquered! . . . Ye shall all die in this place—every one except *him*. He sleepeth now—and shall sleep thirteen centuries. I am Merlin!"[17]

There is evidence Twain wrote the book for prosaic reasons: to savage *English* civilization in revenge for an anti-American diatribe by Matthew Arnold and to recoup his disastrous investment in a new typesetting machine.[18] Twain himself claimed his purpose in writing *A Connecticut Yankee* was to contrast medieval with modern civilization, "to the advantage of the latter, of course." But even if Twain, unlike Melville, knew how to sugarcoat satire and thereby sell books, his tale is a *post*-bellum apocalypse. Did the Missourian mean to suggest the industrial Union had poisoned itself by the carnage it visited on the feudal Confederacy? Did Twain instead have a premonition of the self-righteous zeal with which Americans would charge into the slaughter of World War I? Whatever the subtext, Twain had no illusions that wars designed to extinguish the past could usher in utopias or change human nature. The American hustler Morgan fairly boasts of his know-how, impatience, and lust for control. But no matter how godlike his powers, Morgan cannot win hearts and minds. His outward appeal (like that of his namesake sorceress Morgan le Fay) masks evils no different from those he longs to expunge. His tyranny dwarfs that of King Arthur, his violence surpasses that of the knights, his zeal to indoctrinate eclipses that of the church. We know Twain affirmed science and delighted in technology. But he discerned, as clearly as his contemporary Jules Verne did, the American potential for hubris.

In 1883, six years before *A Connecticut Yankee* appeared, yet another great American novelist moved to bleak south-central Nebraska. Willa Cather was just nine years old. But having been born in Winchester, Virginia, northern gateway to the Shenandoah Valley, she was baptized in the spirit of the frontier.[19] Her uncle, grandparents, and three aunts had already gone to Nebraska, suffering the shock all settlers (women especially) felt when they left the great forest behind and trudged into the featureless Great Plains.[20] The proximate cause of the move was simple enough: the Cathers' sheep barn burned down. Since they had to start over anyway why not do so where land was still plentiful, cheap, and promising? But deeper causes included Virginia's post–Civil War poverty, their kinfolk's prior migration, and the American farmer's canny instinct that land is ultimately more valuable than anything one happens to grow on it. Indeed, within a year of reaching "the Divide" (the watershed between the Republican and Little Blue Rivers), Mr. Cather quit farming to start up a real estate business in the town of Red Cloud.

After attending Nebraska's public schools and land-grant college, Willa found her calling as a celebrant of American hustling in the best sense of the word. Her most touching heroes were surely the French missionaries of *Death Comes for the Archbishop*, who suffered four decades on behalf of Indians, Mexicans, and "Anglo" pioneers in the Southwest. But her archetypal heroes were her own neighbors and kin.

"One January day, thirty years ago, the little town of Hanover, anchored on a windy Nebraska tableland, was trying not to be blown away. A mist of fine snowflakes was curling and eddying about the cluster of low drab buildings huddled on the gray prairie, under a gray sky. . . . The main street was a deeply rutted road, now frozen hard, which ran from the squat red railway station and the grain 'elevator' at the north end of the town to the lumber yard and horse pond at the south end. On either side of the road straggled two uneven rows of wooden buildings; the general merchandise stores, the two banks, the drug store, the feed store, the saloon, the post office. . . . On the sidewalk in front of one of the stores sat a little Swede boy, crying bitterly."

Had Cather's *O Pioneers!* been published in 1970 or perhaps 1940, this brief *mise en scène* would have caused Hollywood producers to drool. But in 1913 the film industry was an infant, while gatekeepers of American letters had no eyes for the heartland. "I simply don't care a damn what happens in Nebraska," wrote one New York critic, "no matter who writes about it."[21] Happily, many readers did care.

Cather's heroine is Alexandra Bergson, the mannish daughter of Swedish immigrants who arrived too late to grab some rich soil in Illinois or Iowa. For eleven years her father struggled to tame the sod, but made "little impression upon it." Blizzards killed cattle, horses broke legs in prairie-dog holes, hogs died of cholera, crops withered. Now he is dying at age 46, his sickly wife soon to follow. So he puts Alexandra in charge, urging her to prevent her two younger brothers from running off to some menial city job, and urging the boys "to keep the land together and be guided by your sister."[22]

All goes well until drought strikes the Divide and many neighbors abandon their farms. Alexandra is desperate until she studies how the settlers on good bottom land have learned to exploit new crops and methods. Having fallen in love with Nebraska, she sits her brothers down at the kitchen table and lays out a plan. "The [river] land sells for three times as much as this, but in five years we will double it. The rich men down there own all the best land, and they are buying all they can get. The thing to do is to sell our cattle and what little old corn we have and buy the Linstrum place. Then the next thing to do is take out two loans on our half-sections, and buy Peter Crow's place; raise every dollar we can, and buy every acre we can." The older brother objects: they cannot possibly work so much land. "You poor boy, you won't have to work it. The men in town who are buying up other people's land don't try to farm it. They are the men to watch, in a new country."[23]

Thirteen years have passed when the next chapter begins. Cather feels no need to describe the real estate deals or suggest Alexandra feels guilt over profiting from the bad luck and weak will of her neighbors. She is now a wealthy spinster reigning over family and servants, independent in every sense. The older brother is married and quite full of himself. He taunts their former neighbor, Carl Linstrum, back from New York on a visit, with the rising political power of the West. If men back east had backbones, he jibes, they would dynamite Wall Street. Carl cannot defend himself. "Freedom so often means that one isn't needed anywhere. Here you are an individual, you have a background of your own, you would be missed. But off there in the cities there are thousands of rolling stones like me. We are all alike; we have no ties; we know nobody; we own nothing. . . . All we have managed to do is pay our rent, the exorbitant rent that one has to pay for a few square feet of space near the heart of things."[24] The brothers suspect Carl means to marry their sister and grab all the land. She hotly declares she will do as she pleases with her land. What do you mean "your" land, the older brother retorts: all their acquisitions came from mortgages the boys helped to pay off. "What about my work?" asks Alexandra, reminding the brothers they opposed every investment she made. At length, the boys are reduced to muttering she is too old to marry without making a fool of herself.[25]

Carl joins the Klondike Gold Rush hoping to strike it rich in a manly pursuit. What finally unites him to Alexandra is an article he spies in a stray San Francisco newspaper reporting the only sort of news from Nebraska people elsewhere might notice: an adulterous couple has been shot by the cuckolded husband. The dead man is Alexandra's youngest brother. So Carl travels three thousand miles to comfort her. She, in turn, comforts the killer in jail. Arm in arm with Carl at last, she surveys her lands and confides, "I thought when I came out of that prison . . . I should never feel free again. But I do, here." Alexandra draws a long breath and gazes "into the red west."[26]

This little novel might have inspired a dozen ballads. Carl's lament about life in the city recalls Kris Kristofferson's "Freedom's just another word for nothing left to lose" and Bob Dylan's "How does it feel to be on your own, a complete unknown, like a rolling stone?"[27] But what does the author mean to say? Surely Cather tells of Nebraska's founding, hustlers speculating in land, and pioneer women proving more tough than their men. Recent scholars have also detected a feminist allegory that Cather smuggled into American literature by making her heroine less threatening than she might have been. An early twentieth-century reader could admire Alexandra without for a moment thinking "suffragette," much less "lesbian." She merely insists on her right to play the material and matrimonial markets, a subject, not an object, on a brave new frontier. The *New York Times Book Review* was therefore on target when its judged *O Pioneers!* "American in the best sense of the word."[28]

Melville's tapestry contains only faint threads of politics woven into the background. Twain's anti-hero is ruined by political subterfuge, but the schemers of church and court are just nemeses, off-stage and unchanging. In Cather's tale politics emerge only once as a sordid but distant game played by top hats back east. The authors were hardly remiss in ignoring politics—they had other stories to tell. But politics matter deeply, both as the intoxicated arena of those vying for power and the sober arena in which Americans' pursuits of happiness are either nurtured or choked. One additional novel tells how.

In December 1792, when the French Revolution's terror and war stoked passions among the rival Federalist and Republican factions in the United States, shocking papers come into the hands of Speaker of the House Frederick Augustus Muhlenberg. They suggest President Washington's Treasury secretary, the arch-Federalist Alexander Hamilton, has abused his office to enrich certain friends, including one James Reynolds, now jailed. Behooved to investigate, the Pennsylvania German enlists the aid of Senator James Monroe, protégé of the arch-Republican Thomas Jefferson. Reynolds, sprung from prison, has met with Hamilton and then disappeared. His lovely, high-busted wife, Maria, testifies vaguely in a way that protects both Hamilton and her husband. Finally, Hamilton himself confesses to an affair with Maria, after which Reynolds blackmailed him. "My crime is moral, not pecuniary," swears Hamilton.

Muhlenberg and Monroe, absent a "smoking gun," do not trouble Washington. But they do ask the clerk of Congress, John Beckley, to copy their letters and notes and return the originals to Virginia "for safekeeping." The fox Beckley makes secret copies for himself. Then he hurries down to Philadelphia's docks where two skilled polemicists are due to arrive from Britain.

"First to appear was Cobbett. He was a robust, six-foot-tall Englishman, with ruddy face and close-set eyes, the beginnings of a paunch, and redolent with confidence. He warmed his hands on a pot of tea and, to Beckley's 'tell me about yourself,' spoke proud and plain: 'I am charged with being a troublemaker. The charge is true.'" The second refugee, a lean, intense Scotsman named Callender, asks, "What sort of country is this?" Cobbett replies, "This country is good for getting money, provided a person is industrious and enterprising. In every other respect the country is miserable, exactly the contrary of what I expected. . . . And the people are worthy of the country—a sly, roguish gang." Asked what he thinks of the newspapers, Cobbett barks, "Tupp'ny [twopenny] trash. But the Americans who read, read nothing else."

So begins *Scandalmonger,* William Safire's hilarious novel of American politics as played at the start and still played today.[29] Callender joins the Republican ranks. By 1797 his inflammatory *Aurora* is the chief bane of Federalist President John Adams. Cobbett (a British agent in fact) edits the Federalist *Porcupine's Gazette,* shooting his quills at Jefferson. The rival journalists take their marching orders from the warring camps of the Founding Fathers, but they also know how to boost circulation. When Cobbett accuses Beckley of misconduct, the clerk leaks the damning Hamilton file to Callender. The climax arrives when the 1800 presidential election ends in a tie between Jefferson and rival Republican, Aaron Burr. That throws the election into the House of Representatives with Federalist congressmen holding the balance of power. While Jefferson's front men Monroe and Madison troll for votes, the wily but patriotic Hamilton persuades some Federalists to pick Jefferson over Burr, who is truly dangerous (and another of Maria Reynolds' old lovers). The pawns are all sacrificed. Jefferson rewards the despised Beckley by naming him Librarian of Congress at the wage of $2 per day. Callender, disillusioned by Jefferson, prints a new scandal screed in Virginia itself. That prompts the Republican press to print lies about Callender's personal life, whereupon Callender (now shacked up with Maria) publishes rumors about Jefferson's dalliance with his slave Sally Hemings. Soon the audacious Scot turns up dead in a river. Cobbett is forced into exile through a trumped-up libel suit. Burr, of course, kills Hamilton in a duel, ruining his own career. Who wins? Only Maria (whose name, story, looks, and lovers adjust to each twist of events), the Virginia junto . . . and the American people, who are delivered from the corruption of those bent on subverting the Constitution by the corruption of those bent on saving it.

Safire's history is bracing precisely because he takes the behavior of men and women as he finds it. Unlike revisionist prudes who pretend to be "shocked, shocked" upon learning the Founding Fathers committed politics, profit, and sex, Safire gleefully shows Americans knew how to play "hardball" from the very first inning.

Another observer who took the underside of democracy in America for granted was Alexis de Tocqueville. Asking simply how it differed from an aristocratic society, he concluded that aristocratic corruption tends to be limited to the high-born and wealthy, and involves prestige and power more than money. Democratic corruption, by contrast, aims at power in part because power is a means to wealth. "In a democracy private citizens see a man of their own rank in life who rises from that obscure position in a few years to riches and power; the spectacle excites their surprise and their envy. . . . To attribute his rise to his talents or his virtues is unpleasant, for it is tacitly to acknowledge that they are themselves less virtuous and less talented than he was. They are therefore led, and often rightly, to impute his success mainly to some of his vices; and an odious connection is thus formed between the ideas of turpitude and power, unworthiness and success, utility and dishonor."[30]

Does that make democracy or America bad? Certainly not, if by bad one means dysfunctional. No large nation on earth has provided more stability, prosperity, security, and liberty to more people than has the United States. Have Americans somehow managed to tame their continent, while more or less taming themselves, *in spite* of their pervasive corruption? Or is it possible the fraud Melville damned, the pride Twain tweaked, the cupidity Cather cheered, the skulduggery Safire sketched, and (one might add) the self-deception Frank L. Baum spoofed in *The Wizard of Oz* all help to *explain* America's sudden, stupendous success?

Harvard's Samuel P. Huntington hinted at that possibility in a 1960s rumination about Third World countries. Granting corruption is everywhere (nobody's perfect), he saw evidence that it is pervasive during eras of swift social change. First, any major mutation of technology or institutions challenges inherited values while encouraging (even necessitating) the bending, breaking, or reinterpretation of law. Such corruption may be creative, productive, even progressive. Second, corruption serves as a lubricant reducing friction between old elites and new ones demanding their "cut" of the spoils and status. Such corruption may be a source of social stability. Third, a nation rapidly growing, or growing more complex, generates new laws inviting people to influence, exploit, or circumvent the new rules of the game. Such corruption may help clear the path for emerging industries and business models. Indeed, corruption, as Edward Gibbon observed, is the most infallible symptom of constitutional liberty! The only ways to suppress corruption are to try to crush progress like a Chinese emperor or define it out of existence by blessing "honest graft" so long as it serves the public interest.[31]

Let us take Huntington a step further. What if the United States, as suggested in the preface, is a permanent revolution, a society in constant flux, a polity devoted by general consensus to fleeing as quickly as possible into the future? In that case, we would expect *every* period of American history to be washed by turgid, overlapping waves of old and new forms of "creative corruption" at the federal, state, and local levels.[32]

In a later book, Huntington examined the gap between the ideals of the American creed and the sometimes grotesque realities of American life. This gap is not to be wondered at; it is a natural consequence of ideals themselves. If Americans were dedicated to the proposition that men (and women) are endowed with no rights at all, with life a matter of getting all you can at others' expense, then no one would accuse them of hypocrisy. But given their high ideals Americans can cope with the gap in any of four ways. The hypocrite ignores the reality. The cynic dismisses ideals as, at best, useful myths. The complacent just admits the gap and moves on. The moralist seeks to narrow it through religious uplift or social reform. But whichever mood may be prevalent, every era of American history is defined by disharmony: "America is not a lie; it is a disappointment. But it can be a disappointment only because it is also a hope."[33]

What is novel about Americans, as their novelists repeatedly teach, is not that they are better or worse than peoples of other places and times (100 percent of whose genes they share), but that they are *freer* than other peoples to pursue happiness and yet are no happier for it. Therein lies the source of America's disappointment. Only free people can disappoint and be disappointed by the discovery that worldly ideals cannot be advanced except by worldly means. That raises the historical question: how did it happen that Americans managed to seize such freedom, conceive such ideals, achieve such success, yet grieve over such disappointment? Did they think themselves somehow exempt from the curses of Adam and Eve?

A short answer can be had by conducting a thought experiment based on a popular 1990s computer game. The player begins with an endowment of land, resources, and people, then plays God (or Caesar) in an effort to build up a civilization. Imagine a continent, heavily forested, plentifully watered, fertile, rich in metals and fossil resources, situated in the most benign latitudes of the north temperate zone. Imagine the continent vacant but for a few million neolithic tribespeople scattered over thousands of miles and vulnerable to diseases pandemic in the rest of the world. Imagine, too, a restless, advanced civilization across the sea, whose own population is starting to soar. Now introduce on the coasts of your continent tens of thousands, then millions of Britons, leavened by a mix of Germans, Frenchmen, and others, endowed with all the power, ideas, and ambitions of the Renaissance, Protestant Reformation, and Scientific Revolution. Having imagined all this, all you need do is cry "Let the games begin!" and you have your American Genesis.

That is the short answer. For the long answer you have to read on.

# SAINT GEORGE
# AND THE DRAGON
## *The Original Spirits of English Expansion*

*T*he United States grew out of thirteen colonies planted by England over the course of 125 years, beginning in 1607. Accordingly, those colonies bore the stamp of England's tumultuous history during the overlapping eras known as the Renaissance, the Age of Discovery, and the Protestant Reformation. In many respects England reflected patterns of social, economic, political, military, and religious upheaval that prevailed elsewhere in Western Europe during the smash-up of medieval Christendom. In other respects English development contrasted sharply with that of France, Spain, or the Holy Roman Empire. Those special facets of English history provide clues to the spirit—in fact, four spirits—that infused English colonization in North America. One was economic, one religious, one strategic, and one legal or philosophical. But they reinforced each other, every one helping to turn the English into a nation of hustlers: often corrupt but usually creative; usually aggressive but occasionally righteous; always ambitious, impatient, and practical even in their employment of myth. Honor or condemn them for their values and deeds, the English conceived what became at length the United States. What were those four spirits, and what conjured them?

In the century preceding England's overseas expansion something unique occurred there: the invention of the first free market or "capitalist" society. It was invented in the sense of being a human artifact, but also in the sense of not being inevitable. That assertion flies in the face of the Classical Liberal assumption to the effect that human beings are natural traders who needed only to be freed from the chains of feudalism to fashion a market society. It also flies in the face of the Classical Marxist assumption about bourgeois capitalism being a natural stage in the technical and social dialectic of history. It even appears to fly in the face of the evidence suggesting local and long-range exchanges of goods by profit-seeking merchants have characterized every known civilization. But the relevant fact is that at *no time and place*—not in the ancient Mediterranean, the Middle East, China, India, pre-Columbian America, or medieval Europe—was an entire society organized by market exchange. Likewise, although we associate the emergence of capitalism with cities such as Venice and Amsterdam and techniques such as joint-stock companies, banks, insurance, double-entry bookkeeping, and floating debts, such mercantilism involved small numbers of people dealing mostly in luxury goods. A true market *society* could only emerge in the countryside, where over nine out of ten people lived and earned their daily bread.[1]

Why an increasingly free rural market in land, labor, and basic commodities occurred first in England is a matter of debate in which cause and effect are unclear. The English Common Law tradition, unknown on the continent, was surely one necessary condition. Anglo-Saxons carried over from northern Germany the habit of resolving disputes by appeal to local customs as interpreted by judges according to precedent and case law rather than statutory laws imposed by distant, capricious rulers or diets. After their conquest of England in 1066, the Norman kings introduced feudal law and dispatched royal clerks (clerics, or churchmen) to administer it. But they left in place the Common Law, defined by the eighteenth-century juridical scholar Sir Henry Blackstone as "the custom of the realm from time immemorial." Thus, the Statutes of Westminster enacted in 1275 and 1285 under Edward I (the "English Justinian") made Common Law jury trials compulsory in criminal cases, codified Common Law norms for tort and damage cases, and declared land previously frozen under Frankish law to be legal tender for the payment of court judgments in England. Finally, the *Quia Emptores* statute of 1290 barred new feudal land grants except by the crown, making all property held in "fee simple" (that is, in exchange for a fixed annual fee) liable for transfer to third parties. Edward I also restricted the jurisdiction of clerks to canon (church) law, thereby creating the secular professions of lawyer and judge. All that meant England uniquely enjoyed a flexible system of civil justice based on contracts, traditional notions of fairness, adversarial jurisprudence, equal access to courts, and property rights no king or bishop could sweep away with a simple decree. To be sure, the state-building Tudor and Stuart monarchs did set up chancery courts under their executive authority, but defenders of the Common Law such as Sir Edward Coke (in his *Institutes of the Lawes of England*, 1628–44) resisted royal impositions, and the Parliamentary rebellion against Charles I swept them away. Finally, the kingdom of England possessed no internal barriers to trade. Unlike other European realms it was a ready-made national market for goods.[2]

The felicitous emergence of the legal basis for a free market economy does not by itself explain why landed gentry, the social class privileged under the feudal system, allowed it to wither away. That very different story runs roughly as follows. During the High Middle Ages (c. 1000 to 1350) villeinage, or serfdom, was on the decline throughout Europe. But England's feudal landlords still controlled an unusually large percentage of the land. Thanks to economic and demographic growth they also enjoyed generally rising income from the fees, dues, and shares of the harvest exacted from peasants. The English landed nobility was also unusually cohesive, as demonstrated by the barons' success at Runnymede (1215) when they imposed the Magna Carta on King John. But the good times ended abruptly after 1348, when bubonic plague carried off a third of the people of Western Europe and continued to depress population for a century. Faced with a grave labor shortage, landlords attempted without success to revive serfdom; peasants, knowing their value, just fled. To make matters worse, the nobility fell into a series of civil wars in the 1400s over the royal succession.

Finally, after generations of falling rents and incomes, the lords hit on a means to exploit the only leverage they retained—feudal control of the land—to replace feudalism altogether in a bid to maximize revenue. It happened slowly, unevenly, and with numerous local variations, but around 1500 landlords began to push cottagers without clear titles or rights off their domains, enclose common fields and pastures for cultivation or sheep-raising, and experiment with farming out land to "farmers" under competitive leases and rents. Productive, hardworking farmers, in turn, might bargain with lords for lower rents and longer leases, or else offer higher rents than neighbors could afford to increase their holdings and turn larger profits through more efficient husbandry, cost-cutting, and specialization. As the new techniques spread, lords and farmers had ever more incentive, not to sit back and collect dues imposed by custom or law, but to expand and improve as much acreage as could be salvaged from swamp, fen, moor, and commons. A whole society began to move from a system based on communal rights and responsibilities to one based on property rights and contracts.[3]

The elimination of common lands climaxed in the great Parliamentary enclosures of the late 1700s and early 1800s. But partition and fencing had already reduced common lands by as much as a third in the Midlands and southern counties by the turn of the seventeenth century. The transition was not gentle. Since proprietors of whatever rank had to concur in the disposition of commons, lords intimidated, bought out, or found reason to dispossess as many rights-holders as possible, then negotiated the terms of enclosure with the rest.[4] Neighbors were pitted against neighbors, even those linked by marriage or kinship. But by hook, crook, or pocketbook the proud Anglo-Norman knighthood itself dismantled feudalism until, in 1660, the legal abolition of feudal tenure was confirmed and all land and labor put up for sale. This agricultural revolution both sustained and was hastened by the stunning recovery of England's population from about 2.8 million in 1541 to 4 million by 1600 and 5.3 million by 1650. Farmers had all the more reason to expand acreage planted to cereals, while brisk exports of woolens made it profitable to convert meadows into sheep runs.

Farming for the market placed a premium on productivity and cost-cutting. The printing industry, barely a century old, met the growing demand for useful knowledge with books and pamphlets until "[m]en were imbued with the conviction that everything could and should be employed and improved." How to put more land under cultivation through drainage, how to improve pastures and increase herds, how to manure and till for larger harvests, how to plant fruit trees along every hedgerow, how to make use of sandy, marshy, or mossy soils and moors overrun with heath. How to make and mend ploughs, barrows, clodding beetles, drags, rollers, forks, weedhooks, scythes, sickles, pitchforks, rakes, flails, sleds, seedlips, dung carts, and corn carts. How also to *minimize* dependence on hired labor since "small fear of God is in servants, and thou shalt find my counsel just and most true," as one planter wrote in 1610.[5] From Thomas Tusser's *Five Hundred Points of Good Husbandry* (1557) to Gervase Markham's *The English Husbandman* (1613), the English knighthood, once expert at little besides bashing heads, learned to match crops to soil and climate, fertilize, plant, and graft, dress vines, prune fruit trees, breed livestock, and prescribe for sick animals.[6] It all added up to the greatest surge in agricultural knowledge since the thirteenth century. But the ethic of improvement also spoke to the issue of property itself because many enclosures of dubious legality were justified by it. Land did not exist to lie idle, hence any claims on it made by indigent peasants were forfeit.

A final stimulus for England's expansion of market agriculture was the fourfold increase in prices for foodstuffs between 1540 and 1640. Symptomatic of the great inflation stoked by the flood of Spanish silver and gold from the New World, the surge in prices far outpaced wage rates, impoverishing the losers in the transition. They, of course, were the cottagers. Accustomed for centuries to eking out humble but secure livings through free use of common fields, forests, pastures, and private gardens, they were reduced to itinerant farmhands selling their labor on a daily or seasonal basis, or else forced off countryside their ancestors had inhabited since Anglo-Saxon times.[7] Their complaint was that "whereas the ancyent tenantes kept ploughes . . . the nowe cotagers do lyve . . . but barely, only by theire day labor."[8]

So massive was the internal migration of cottagers that only one-fourth of English men and women in the early seventeenth century remained in their parish of birth. They might move a few villages away in search of work and a spouse, and get lucky. But the burgeoning towns absorbed—and in the case of London, a sinkhole of filth, crime, and disease, often *killed*—tens of thousands per decade. The percentage of people living in communities of more than 5,000 people rose from about 5 to 13 percent by 1600. London quadrupled in size to more than 200,000. Many of the displaced poor found employment in the new coal mining industry, which expanded output sevenfold over the century ending in 1630. The reason for increased use of coal in this pre-industrial era was another consequence of the agrarian revolution. England was by then largely deforested, so coal replaced wood in all manner of trades, especially metallurgy. Other migrants entered the woolen trade, domestic service, carting, or shipping. But thousands of "masterless" men and women became vagabonds, beggars, or prostitutes. Parliament and the crown, alarmed over protests against enclosure, demands for a living wage, and dangerous vagrants, enacted England's first Poor Laws in 1598 and 1601. Controls on the grain trade, workhouses for the unemployed, and a parish dole for widows and orphans relieved the worst suffering, but the trend toward free markets in land, labor, and produce could not have been reversed even if anyone had wanted to do so. And no one did, as Bishop Hugh Latimer ironically noted in a sermon of 1548: "What man will let go or diminish his private commodity, for a common wealth? Who will susteine any damage for the respect of a publique commodity?"[9]

A growing and mobile population, surplus production in the countryside, burgeoning urban markets, and the ubiquitous profit motive encouraged the growth of regional and national markets in England well in advance of most continental states. Bulky, low value commodities such as coal from Newcastle could only be shipped profitably by sea and river, but goods of low weight or high value, ranging from flour and cattle to linen and wool, might be carted to ports or internal markets. That required a network of roads, bridges, and fords. By Queen Elizabeth's time counties and towns were admonished to contribute money and labor to their upkeep, while publishers sold maps and tables (often grossly inaccurate) for the use of merchants and teamsters. Itinerant peddlers also took advantage of new byways to hawk wares of all sorts from town to town. Dishonest ones earned the enmity of farmers and villagers, while honest ones earned the enmity of local tradesmen who lost customers. But numerous bills introduced in Parliament to ban itinerant peddling failed to pass. They would in any case have been impossible to enforce.[10]

If rapid change breeds corruption and vice, one would expect this first embryonic market society to be awash in them—and it was. At the high end, officials plundered the government's coffers and courted bribes, while merchant-adventurers and lawyers skinned wealthy investors beguiled by visions of fortunes from overseas trade. Not surprisingly, two prevalent features of English commerce became the family firm and the network of business ties based on kinship or religious affinity, the better to foster trust. Inheritance across generations also hastened the accumulation of capital and transfer of skills and experience, while children provided cheap, disciplined labor. Thus, "kinship and capitalism complemented and reinforced each other; their relationship was not antagonistic but symbiotic."[11] Beyond one's trusted circle, however, the English Common Law principle of *caveat emptor* (let the buyer beware) prevailed.

At the low end of the social scale corruption took familiar forms. Enterprising older women stocked bawdy houses with girls, tavern-keepers hosted crooked gamblers and pickpockets for a share of the take, and the royal monopoly could not keep pace with unlicensed alehouses. Drunkenness and its offspring—crime, fights, and promiscuous sex—seemed out of control. Vagrants accosted travelers, footpads haunted London, gangs of rootless toughs of both sexes lived off the land like brigands. When Berkshire constables captured one such gang in a rustic sheepcote, they surprised six boys and six girls "dauncing naked" while other couples "lay about." Parish records reveal that at least one-fifth of English brides were pregnant upon marriage. But given illegitimate children accounted for one-sixth of all baptisms, the illegitimacy rate was probably more like 40 percent.[12]

Finally, in the "respectable" middle ranks of society, numerous shopkeepers, tradesmen, and artisans took advantage of strangers with false weights and measures, skimped on the quality of materials, and skipped town to escape debts, threats, spouses, or paternity suits. There is no way to quantify such behavior, but it is suggestive that between 1570 and 1606 the number of property and debt cases under litigation increased by a factor of seven, while the ratio of lawyers to people grew by a factor of five. Contemporary observers were unanimous in their belief a "general corruption hath overgrowne the vertues of this latter times" and (as a character in the 1609 play *The Gull's Hornbook* put it) "to cosen and be cosen'd makes the age."[13]

Did the English simply carry these traits to the New World, in which case "Americans had been 'capitalists' since the first colonial settlements"? Did England's flight from feudalism mean liberalism was bred in the bones of its American offspring?[14] The story is more complicated than that. Since the inequity and insecurity of a free-wheeling market society seemed demoralizing and potentially perilous, English philosophers spent the seventeenth and much of the eighteenth century trying to reconcile the new economy with an ethic of public good. Indeed, English Puritans, long identified with the capitalistic "Protestant ethic," were among the most strident *critics* of individualism and acquisitiveness throughout much of England's transition. But Roger Coke summed up the empirical evidence of England's first capitalist century in 1675, when he wrote in *England's Improvements*, "I will never believe that any man or Nation ever will attain their ends by forceable means, against the Nature and Order of things."[15] Once upon a time, hierarchical feudalism and the communal village seemed to reflect the natural order. England's demonstrable success over the past hundred years proved instead that the natural order arose from the free interplay of men and nations in markets. And if it was natural, how could it not conform to God's will?

In sum, a tool of unbelievable power was under research and development in Tudor England—capitalism, or the market economy. For not only did landlords turn their domains into agribusinesses, they invested their profits in all manner of other enterprises, from mining and textiles to overseas trade, blurring distinctions between noble and commoner, prestige and wealth, and merging their interests with those of farmers, merchants, and ultimately the crown.

Meanwhile, the general population, rapidly growing and increasingly displaced, had to adjust to new notions of freedom that meant, among other things, bowing to the "dictates of the market." They had to learn how to hustle themselves to get their piece of the action in agriculture or trade. That was the first spirit in which the English embarked on colonial enterprise.

Empire, however, required a national state to bless, protect, and promote it, and a concept of national interest to justify it. Enter the Tudor kings and queens, who had the good fortune of ruling England during its lengthy initial takeoff. Henry VII laid the foundations by defeating Richard III in battle and killing all other possible claimants to the throne. He rationalized administration, financing the state through taxes acquiesced in by Parliament. He also codified and imposed the king's justice on all corners of England and Wales. By the time his son Henry VIII was crowned in 1509, the only medieval institution left to defy the "new monarchy" was the church, and it was ripe for plucking. For a thousand years the Roman Catholic church functioned as glue holding European civilization together. But over that ocean of time it inevitably suffered severe inflation of its responsibilities, offices, benefices, involvement in all spheres of life (not least politics), as well as indulgences the papacy offered as rewards for penitence, service, obedience, or cash.[16] Indulgences were what drove the earnest monk Martin Luther to protest, but the church's inflated wealth and influence were what annoyed kings and emperors grasping for unchallenged authority in their realms.

In the centuries before Henry VIII's coronation the church's prestige was in free fall. The Avignon "captivity" of the papacy by the kings of France after 1309 gave rival monarchs no incentive to honor the church's authority. The scandalous schism among rival popes from 1378 to 1417 mocked the church's claim to inerrancy. The succession of decadent fifteenth-century popes eroded the church's spiritual pretensions. By the end of that century Renaissance kings seeking to build centralized states determined as a matter of course to ensure their national clergy's highest loyalty was to them, not the pope. Henry VII repeatedly invoked the Statute of *Praemunire* to establish the supremacy of Common Law over canon law and Parliament's jurisdiction over the pope's. Therefore, when Henry VIII later petitioned the pope to annul his marriage to Catharine of Aragon, he was in fact showing scruples. Once the pope refused, however, Henry instructed asking his national churchman, Archbishop of

Canterbury Thomas Cranmer, to grant his divorce and remarriage to (the now pregnant) Anne Boleyn.

Clement VII snubbed Henry's appeal not only because it challenged papal authority on an incontestably ecclesiastical issue, but because an army of Catherine's nephew, Habsburg Emperor Charles V, held the pope under house arrest. So Clement reluctantly excommunicated Henry, whereupon Parliament passed an Act of Supremacy in 1534 naming Henry the head of the Church of England and England itself an "empire" bowing to no other authority on earth. A few centuries earlier the papal ban might have driven Henry to his knees or into the hills since excommunication released all his vassals from their fealty. But he got away with the coup because Lords and Commons were composed mostly of Tudor-appointed nobles and bishops, country squires greedy for church properties or royal bribes, and university men and merchants already sympathetic to Lutheran ideas.[17] Reinforcing these carrots was Henry's stick: ruthless use of chancery courts to condemn opponents and even supporters who fell into disfavor, including Sir Thomas More, Cardinals Wolsey and Fisher, Thomas Cromwell, and Anne Boleyn.

In his own day Henry VIII made the crown unassailable and, it must be said, popular. But his bold expansion of royal prerogative in fact limited the potential for absolute monarchy in England for the simple reason that he made legal all that he did through *acts of Parliament*. What one compliant Parliament granted another obstreperous one might take away.

Now head of the church, Henry wasted no time liquidating its assets. First he closed minor religious establishments, including scores of provincial hospitals, schools, and alms houses. Next, when the Pilgrimage of Grace, a pro-Catholic resistance, emerged in the north, the king declared all monasteries traitorous havens of gluttony, drunkenness, and promiscuity (his own favorite vices). In truth, most of England's monastic establishments were moribund, having failed to participate in the market revolution and devoting just 5 percent of their income to charity. Still, their revenues were triple that of the crown, tempting Henry at first to annex all church property to the royal estate. But the cost of his wars and flamboyant court forced him instead to sell monastic lands for immediate cash. The hand-picked agents of his Court of Augmentations predictably enriched themselves in the process, but disposed of vast properties at close to real market prices. What is more, few buyers had qualms about gobbling up land once donated to the service of God, an indication of how holy "the very idea of property" had become.[18] By 1603, three-fourths of the church's holdings had passed into the hands of gentry and farmers, accelerating the trend toward a free market in land.[19]

Of equal importance was the "nationalization" of religious doctrines and prejudices. The king might have been interested only in siring a dynasty, and his collaborators only in high office and wealth. But they recognized the need to drape their murders (judicial or otherwise) and theft (legislative or otherwise) in patriotic clothing. They were able to do so thanks to the English *people*'s resentment of the church's wealth and legal immunities ("benefit of clergy").[20] Accordingly, Tudor propaganda echoed Luther's own earthy tracts denouncing the Roman church as the Whore of Babylon, the Pope as Anti-Christ, and all who served them as damned or enslaved. A growing number of English people of all ranks were prepared to believe this message, while the more zealous reformers itched to abolish the mass, priestly vestments, "idolatrous" icons, and doctrines such as transubstantiation, purgatory, and clerical celibacy. When Henry's nine-year-old son Edward succeeded him in 1547, the zealots got their chance.

William Tyndale and Miles Coverdale had already translated the Bible into English. But the greatest achievement of the English Reformation was Thomas Cranmer's *Book of Common Prayer* in its 1549 and 1552 versions. A stylist of surpassing genius, Cranmer did as much to codify and edify vernacular English as Luther's Bible did for High German. The task he appointed himself was to retain what seemed good and true in Catholic doctrine and practice, add what seemed good and true in Protestant doctrine and practice, and express it all in cadences so sublime English folk across most of the religious spectrum would be comfortable praying in common. But precisely because of his "enterprisingly ecumenical" methods the Prayer Book introduced theological ambiguities that still plague Anglicans 450 years later. For example, the communion rite merged the Catholic understanding of the eucharist as "the Body and Blood of our Lord Jesus Christ" with the Protestant admonition "Take and eat this in remembrance that Christ died for thee, and feed on him in thy heart by faith." The Gospels provide ample proof texts for both interpretations, but whereas the first affirms the real presence of Christ and consecration of the host by an ordained priest, the latter treats the Lord's Supper as a commemoration that any lay congregation might perform by faith alone.[21] Such ambiguity seemed a prudent way to cool sectarian passions, especially apt given the Church of England was established as a *political* institution. Who cares what people in pews believe so long as they are loyal to throne and altar? Unfortunately for the crown many people in the sixteenth and seventeenth centuries cared deeply about what they and their clergy thought they were doing in church, hence the liturgical compromise satisfied no one. What triumphed in the interim, with tremendous importance to England's political future, was a taste of reaction in the person of Mary, who became queen when young Edward died of consumption in 1553.

Bloody Mary, the daughter of Catherine of Aragon, won the throne on the strength of a pro-Catholic uprising in East Anglia, part of a counteroffensive the Roman church had recently launched all over Europe. In 1540 Ignatius Loyola founded the Society of Jesus devoted to learned refutation of Protestant claims and the rollback of Protestant political power. In 1545 Paul III, first in a series of reforming popes, summoned the Council of Trent that condemned the sale of indulgences and church offices (simony), raised standards for priestly education and discipline, reaffirmed justification by faith and the importance of Scripture, and called dissidents back to the true and cleansed church. Mary was riding this Catholic- or Counter-Reformation when she expelled married clergy; restored the mass, high altar, and vestments; and appointed a Catholic to the see of Canterbury. She also authorized the burning of nearly three hundred Protestants, Cranmer included, on charges of heresy. In fact, that purge was modest by contrast to continental persecutions and entirely in line with the 1555 Peace of Augsburg, which declared princes free to impose their religion in their own realms (*cuius regio eius religio*). But the blood of Mary's victims, sanctified for generations of readers by John Foxe's *Book of Martyrs,* and the welcome she gave to Spanish and Italian Jesuits both inflamed English nationalism and identified it with Protestantism. Worst of all, Mary wed a son of Charles V, made an alliance with Spain, and dragged the nation into a war that resulted in the loss of Calais, England's last foothold on the continent. No wonder churchbells tolled England's glee when Mary died childless in 1558. No wonder Protestant pastor John Aylmer returned home from exile crying, "God is English!"[22]

The throne passed to Elizabeth, who, being the daughter of Henry VIII and Anne Boleyn, had no choice but to be Protestant. But her true calling was just to survive as a twenty-five-year-old virgin thrown into a snake pit of courtly intriguers, threatening foreigners, and a fractious, confused population. Her lodestone was the curious Greek word, *adiaphora,* meaning indifference toward imponderable mysteries of dogma in the interest of pragmatic statecraft. Thus did Elizabeth anticipate by four decades the "politicians" (*les politiques*) who ended France's religious wars by persuading Henri de Bourbon to display a genial indifference toward Catholics and Calvinists alike. But the Elizabethan compromise embodied in the 39 Articles of Religion proved only marginally more successful than Cranmer's. First, Scotland was scorched by the fiery Presbyterian preacher John Knox, forcing the Catholic Mary Stuart, Queen of Scots, to seek refuge with her cousin Elizabeth. That was especially provocative inasmuch as Mary, a grand-niece of Henry VIII, was presumptive heir to the English throne should the queen die childless. But Elizabeth knew her marriage to anyone, Protestant or Catholic, might provoke civil war. Still, she was too tenderhearted, risk-averse, and irresolute to have Mary killed. Soon Jesuits plotted on Mary's behalf in London and Edinburgh, Protestant spies rooted them out with the same Machiavellian tactics they denounced in their enemies, and English politics took on the "paranoid style" that character-ized it for over a century.[23]

Equally dangerous for Elizabeth was the revolt of the Calvinist Dutch against Spanish rule in the 1570s because it drew the imposing armies and fleets of Spain's Philip II into the English Channel. Finally, England's own Cal-vinists began forming seditious-sounding "cells" dedicated to purifying the Church of England of the episcopacy and all trappings of popery. Dubbed Puritans by their detractors in the 1560s, they soon relished the sobriquet.

Passions, conspiracies, and threats thus combined to wreck Elizabeth's peace of indifference. In 1585 she grew sufficiently alarmed by the propinquity of Spanish arms to offer military aid to the Dutch. In 1586 a popish plot to assassinate her was exposed, in 1587 Elizabeth finally ordered Mary beheaded, and in 1588 the Spanish Armada sailed to make England Catholic by force. The upshot was fifteen years of war as total as sixteenth-century resources permit-ted, during which Anglican and Puritan Englishmen alike came once and for all to equate Catholicism with treason, regard England as the Providential instrument of true religion and virtue, and resolve to slay the Spanish beast as England's patron St. George slew the dragon. That was the second spirit in which Englishmen embarked on colonial enterprise.

Every pupil used to know that in 1494, two years after Columbus sailed, the Treaty of Tordesillas divided the Atlantic world between Spain and Portugal. In 1529, following Vasco da Gama's crossing of the Indian Ocean for Portugal and Magellan's crossing of the Pacific for Spain, the line of demarcation was extended around the globe. Less known is that well before Columbus, in 1479,

Castile and Portugal agreed to recognize each other's exclusive control over any islands and coasts they discovered. That principle meant European imperialism was from its inception akin to a great game of Monopoly®. The first to land on a square got to purchase the property and could lose claim to it only through bankruptcy. The game board proved far larger than anyone dreamed.

Christianity neither mandated nor inspired imperialism, nor did Europe's monarchs need any excuse beyond their own material ambitions. Rather, Christian morality was something to be dodged or made an excuse for conquest, and it was easily done. To Europeans around 1500, there were only four categories of people in the world: Catholic Christians, heretics (including Muslims), Jews, and pagans. Whereas some clerics in the colonial world later pled for humane treatment of foreign peoples, no higher law bound Christian states to respect heretical or pagan rulers, religions, or institutions. Indeed, the idea Europeans ought to *tolerate* the seemingly diabolical customs they observed on exotic shores was as yet inconceivable.

So in terms of international law the *res gestae* posed by European discovery was whether Christians were obliged to respect the claims of other Christians. As early as 1497 and 1508, English merchants in Bristol sponsored the voyages of John and Sebastian Cabot, the first Europeans since the Vikings to spot the North American mainland. But Henry VIII did not follow up, and Bloody Mary forbade her subjects to violate the Spanish New World. It was left to Bretons, who began to fish the Grand Banks off Newfoundland in 1508, and their French sovereign Francis I to issue the first challenge to Spain and Portugal: "The sun shines for me as for the others. I should like to see the clause of Adam's will which excludes me from a share of the world." A long war ensued during which France made abortive attempts to colonize Florida and Canada. But at the peace talks of Cateau-Cambrésis in 1559, the Spaniards refused to discuss any relaxation of their monopoly in "the Indies," conceding only that French ships sailing west of the first meridian did so at their own risk. This "no peace beyond the line" principle and "doctrine of two spheres"—one law for Europe and another (or no law) for the Americas—added two more rules to the Monopoly game.[24]

England was not a player, but was beginning to acquire the tools. One of the first large convents seized by Henry VIII was turned into an armory. William Levett, a parish priest turned weapons czar, pioneered the art of casting iron cannons. Until then bronze was preferred because iron tubes had a nasty habit of blowing up in the gunners' faces. But English iron did not, probably because Sussex ore was rich in phosphorus and low in sulfur. As a result, Henry and his successors could exploit cast iron's greater rigidity to make longer barrels that imparted more range and velocity to cannon balls. By the 1570s English guns were in such demand at home and abroad that nine foundries in Sussex and Kent were going "full blast."[25] Henry VIII also began mounting cannons on the ships of England's first sailing fleet, helping to make a naval revolution. The older Mediterranean practice was to deploy oared galleys or caravels outfitted with "fighting castles" and masses of soldiers in expectation of boarding and defeating enemy ships through swordplay. The new Atlantic practice was to build pure sailing ships with guns mounted on the main deck or below, and fired through portholes. The English flagship *Harry Grace à Dieu* with 186 guns seemed a veritable *Dreadnought* when launched in 1514. Such leviathans were, however, ill-suited to oceanic voyages and running fights in which speed and maneuver were decisive.

So Henry VIII's technological bequest was promising, but by the end of his reign only twenty or so English masters dared to sail beyond sight of land. That forced England's merchant adventurers to rely on an old 1496 treaty with Spain, the *Intercursus Magnus,* for access to the woolen markets of Flanders. But under the press of the market revolution within and the tension with Spain without, English merchants went into frenetic motion in the mid-sixteenth century. The Muscovy Company, trading with Russia, arose in 1554 to be followed under Elizabeth by the Eastland, Levant, Barbary, Africa, and finally East India Companies (1600). The governors of these national start-up firms realized worthy vessels and guns were of little use without daring, skilled captains provided with up-to-date maps and navigational tools. So they ordered their agents to purchase or steal maritime intelligence from the Iberians, French, and Dutch. A Muscovy Company pilot scored the biggest coup when he returned from Seville with a copy of Spain's textbook for sailors. Translated in 1561 under the title *The Arte of Navigation,* it was probably "one of the most decisive books ever printed in the English language. It held the key to the mastery of the sea."[26]

Merchants also hired mathematicians such as John Dee and Edward Wright of Cambridge to prepare texts on trigonometry and celestial navigation, and help cartographers prepare accurate Mercator maps with rhumb lines. Meanwhile Oxford's Thomas Hariot provided mariners with the finest instruments, celebrating his work in doggerel: "Three Sea Marriadges here are made / one of the staffe & sea Astrolabe / Of the sonne & starre is an other / which agree like sister & brother / And charde and compass which at bate / will now agree like master & mate."[27] Finally, England's fighting captains spurned the great galleons, relying instead (as a Spaniard lamented) on "vessels very light and very well gunned."[28]

Hustling merchants made England, in just a few years, into a mighty sea power through investment, science, and industrial espionage. But the world did not notice until Elizabeth dared copy the French by sending off privateers to plunder the Spaniards in their own balmy seas. John Hawkins was among her most celebrated freebooters, but none of his victories aroused England so much as one crushing defeat. Spaniards lured Hawkins into a West Indian port under a flag of truce only to torture, kill, or imprison a hundred of his "heretical" crewmen. One of the survivors was young Francis Drake, whose circumnavigation of the globe from 1577 to 1580 and fabulous capture of a half million pounds sterling in Spanish bullion made England's maritime reputation. However, Elizabeth's Lord Treasurer had not approved the expensive voyage; Drake had sailed secretly on her say-so alone. That is why his first shout, upon returning at last to Plymouth Sounds, was, "Is the queen alive?"[29]

The queen was alive, Drake was a hero, and the Spanish ambassador lodged vehement protests. That forced the English to render their first legal opinion regarding the colonial game. According to Elizabeth, "the Spaniards have brought these evils on themselves by their injustice toward the English, whom, *contra ius gentium* [against international law], they have excluded from commerce with the West Indies. The Queen does not acknowledge that her subjects and those of other nations may be excluded from the Indies on the claim that these have been donated to the King of Spain by the Pope, whose authority to invest the King of Spain with the New World she does not recognize. . . . Prescription without possession is not valid. Moreover all are at liberty to navigate . . . since the use of the sea and the air are common to all."[30]

That last principle derived from Common Law, but in the next century Hugo Grotius would make "freedom of the seas" a cardinal principle of international law. Elizabeth's first principle concerning English rights to trade refuted Spain's "doctrine of two spheres" to the effect that European treaties did not apply to America. But buried in the middle of Elizabeth's response was the most salient of English principles: effective possession alone confers ownership. That meant all America beyond existing Spanish settlements was *res nullius* and up for grabs by anyone who could plant colonies and make them stick. In England's emerging free market in land, those who enclosed and improved property possessed eminent domain. So far as England was concerned, those were the rules of the New World market as well. That was the third spirit in which the English embarked on colonial enterprise.

No one expected colonization to be easy. In 1564 the French tried again to penetrate Florida only to be expelled by soldiers from Spain's new military colony at St. Augustine. But England did not lack for energetic promoters who believed, or were soon persuaded, American colonies far north of Florida would be safe from Spanish reprisals. Foremost among them were Sir Humphrey Gilbert, who judged England too small for his ambitions; Gilbert's half-brother Sir Walter Ralegh (or Raleigh), a heroic Protestant soldier the queen fancied; Ralegh's friend Thomas Hariot, a navigational expert; Dr. John Dee, the queen's science adviser; and two men named Richard Hakluyt. The elder of these cousins was a lawyer with close ties to London merchants. The younger was a devout parson. Fascinated by his father's map collection, he reinvented himself as Oxford's first lecturer in geography and devoted his life to chronicling *The Principal Navigations, Voyages, Traffics and Discoveries of the English Nation* (first edition 1589). So prodigious were his geographical *cum* spiritual exhortations that by his death in 1616 he not only did more than anyone to promote England's imperial destiny, he enriched English prose as much as Shakespeare, who died the same year, enriched poetry. A mere prebendary in the Church of England, Hakluyt is buried in Westminster Abbey.

At Ralegh's urging young Hakluyt drafted a *Discourse of Western Planting* in 1584 and placed it, on bended knee, in Queen Elizabeth's hand. A masterpiece of promotional literature, it explained in detail the economic, social, political, and strategic advantages that North American colonization offered nation and crown. Timber, fish, furs, and perhaps precious metals would enrich England and reduce its dependence on imports. Colonies would provide burgeoning markets, especially for England's now depressed woolen trade. Emigration would open a safety valve draining off vagrants, criminals, the unemployed, and religious dissenters such as the Puritans. Above all, colonies over the water would make the North Atlantic an English lake while providing bases from which to strike at the Spanish Main.

Lest all this appear too "Machiavellian," however, Hakluyt opened his litany of boons with a moral appeal. Could English souls ever know peace if they chose to do *nothing* while Popery imposed its cruel and superstitious regime on America's unfortunate Indians while black-hearted conquistadors killed and enslaved them? Was England not called to bestow on those heathen the liberty of Reformed Christianity? Nor need the queen challenge Spain, because "it is well known that the Spaniards, for want of people of their own country, have not been able now in the space of ninety-two years to inhabit a third or fourth part of those exceeding large and waste countries, which are as great as all Europe and Africa." In any event, North America was discovered first by the Cabots sailing for England, so Spain lacked all claim to the continent. But, Hakluyt stressed, England must act quickly lest Spain, France, or the Netherlands preempt her. It was imperative her Gracious Majesty place the power and wealth of the state behind colonial ventures.[31]

Elizabeth was probably impressed by all Hakluyt's points except the last. The wily monarch encouraged her gentlemen adventurers, but she also knew that all large public works were invitations to patronage, bribery, price gouging, creative bookkeeping, and theft. She often railed against "the insatiable cupidity of men."[32] With total war against Spain about to break out and England targeted for invasion, she would do no more than lend her blessing and nickname (Virginia) to *privately* financed colonization. The first such effort dated from 1578, when the crown granted a patent to Sir Humphrey Gilbert to explore and settle all lands not in European possession. It contained some prescient prescriptions. First, it implied the entire American coast north of Florida was potentially English territory. Second, it freed Gilbert to establish whatever forms of government he deemed best, albeit his colonists would remain English subjects endowed with inalienable rights. Third, the colonists were free to retain all the profits and fruits of their labor save for the crown's 20 percent share of any gold and silver discovered. Finally, the colonies were granted unconditional rights to self-defense against all enemies (implicitly, other Europeans and Indians alike). Gilbert's enterprise aborted. His captains never got beyond coastal reconnaissance, and he himself perished in a shipwreck. But the patent he bore was a template for the future Anglo-America.[33]

Ralegh assumed leadership of the promoters, investors, and strategists intrigued by America, duly receiving an identical patent with one notable excision. Whereas Gilbert's charter envisioned a quasi-feudal system of grants under his proprietorship, Ralegh's contained no such boon. The task of recruiting emigrants, it was thought, would prove easier if they had reason to hope for abundant land. And not just any land, but a *paradise,* because Ralegh evidently believed in a terrestrial Garden of Eden, which divines deduced from the Bible lay somewhere at 35 degrees North Latitude. They assumed, of course, Eden lay to the east. But the hope was widespread and by no means absurd that similar conditions might exist in the New World. After all, Spaniards spread tales of a Fountain of Youth and El Dorado (Ralegh later sailed to the Orinoco in search of it); early reports from offshore observers confirmed subtropical America was a land of lush palms. So Virginia might well prove to be so blessed a land as to release mankind from the curses of work and disease. Indeed, one of the greatest sources of excitement was the 1577 publication of *Joyful News out of the New Found World*. The translation of a treatise by a Spanish physician, it claimed American herbs, oils, and plants (including tobacco) cured every human affliction.[34]

Ralegh has been dubbed a "proto-American" in that he combined energy, ambition, greed, swagger, and a certain idealism.[35] But he was not an American, proto- or otherwise: he was a sixteenth-century Englishman eager to place his stamp *on* America. Born of an old noble family that lost most of its wealth during those "hard times" suffered by landlords before they invented capitalism, young Walter knew he was brilliant, believed he deserved much more from life, and was impatient to get it. Following Gilbert's lead he studied at Oxford, fought for the Protestant cause in France and Ireland, commanded a ship reconnoitering North America, and learned how much careful planning colonization required. Unfortunately, he also shared Gilbert's bad luck.

The famous Roanoke tale needs little telling. In 1584 Ralegh sent out two ships to explore the coast for a likely landing. They discovered a channel through the Outer Banks of what is now North Carolina, and returned to tout the advantages of Roanoke Island. The following spring Ralegh dispatched seven ships under his kinsman Sir Richard Grenville, the soldier Ralph Lane, and the scientist Hariot. Storms, Spanish attacks, and dissension dispersed the fleet, but eventually Grenville deposited Lane and a hundred men on Roanoke. The colonists did little over the winter but fight and beg food from the Indians, so Lane evacuated them the following year. In 1587 Ralegh tried again. This time the 114 men and women planted by captain John White were cut off from home altogether when every English ship was requisitioned to fight the Spanish Armada. Not until the summer of 1590 was White able to cross over to Roanoke, by which time nor hide nor hair of the people remained, just the cryptic carved word CROATOAN.[36] Whatever their fate—death by Indian treachery or life by assimilation into the local Hatteras tribe—the Roanoke colonists may be likened to a first wave of marines told to storm a hostile beachhead before their supply line is secure. They were eulogized in advance, so to speak, by England's poet laureate, Michael Drayton, who wrote of "brave heroic minds, worthy of your country's name, that honour still pursue, go and subdue, whilst loitering hinds lurk here at home with shame. . . . And cheerfully at sea success you will entice, to get the pearl and gold and ours to hold, Virginia, Earth's only Paradise."[37]

Virginia was England's to hold, but not right away, and not because the Gilbert and Ralegh debacles discouraged colonization. Rather, the Spanish war absorbed England's energies, diverted her sea dogs into piracy, and raised a danger closer to home that influenced English imperialism as much as Hakluyt's geopolitics. That danger was Ireland.

The remotest bastion of the Celtic fringe to which Romans, Angles, Saxons, Norse, and Normans had chased the Gaelic folk, Ireland seemed to Elizabethans as much a relic of a bygone age as Camelot seemed to Twain's Connecticut Yankee. The Irish were lazy, brawling, oppressed, irrational, self-defeating: in short, all the English liked to believe they were *not*. Even the so-called Pale of English settlement—twenty miles west and north of Dublin—had largely succumbed to local customs; Gaelic was heard more than English. The mere existence of Ireland at England's back, as it were, annoyed and sometimes enticed. But what made its independence intolerable was the Reformation and consequent threat of Spanish-Irish collusion. So Henry VIII reasserted the English crown's old claim to sovereignty over the island, insisted the Irish Parliament disestablish the Catholic church, and demanded clan chiefs surrender their land in exchange for fiefs granted by royal prerogative. This was typical Renaissance state-building, but it betrayed a total misunderstanding of Irish practice, whereby land belonged to the septs, or clans, and chiefs received life tenures only by dint of the popular will. When English officials and Irish tenants accused each other of betrayal, the chiefs were caught in the middle. Henry, damning all Irish as bandits, undertook the long, bloody work of subduing them.

What his soldiers and settlers found in the interior appalled them. By all accounts Irish people were handsome and gay, with a gift for blarney, humor, and horsemanship. Their country, too, was green and fair, well-watered and -wooded. But how little the Irish had done with their gifts! Peasants could not so much as hitch an ox to a plow, and instead just tied the instrument to the poor animal's tail. They believed in harvesting wheat before cutting the hay, by which time late summer rains had spoiled it. They thought it unlucky to cleanse buckets used to hold milk, so they deposited fresh milk in vessels an inch deep in filth. They practiced transhumance, the seasonal migration of whole villages with all their kit and caboodle into the highlands to pasture their flocks. They knew nothing of improved agricultural methods, relying instead on amulets, spells, and enchantments to protect their crops and herds. They seemed to have more feast days than work days. They were lascivious even by sixteenth-century English standards. Above all, they were Catholic and—unlike the Scots—evidently immune to Protestant preachments.

Under Elizabeth the power vacuum in Ireland became a source of acute anxiety. When private colonizing efforts again proved inadequate she dispatched many of her best soldiers to pacify the "barbaric" Irish interior. After initial defeats and atrocities on both sides, the English learned to fight in the skirmishing Irish style. But they were hindered by terrain, poor intelligence, the damp climate, poor supply trains, and desertions. Of the 3,500 men sent over in 1596 only a thousand returned. In 1600 Elizabeth placed another army under command of the able Charles Blount, Lord Mountjoy. This time Tyrone, charismatic chief of the O'Neills, the chief of the O'Donnells, and a leavening of Spanish infantry took the offensive. In 1601 their combined force of perhaps 9,000 men pinned down the 6,000 English, threatening them with annihilation. But on Christmas Eve, Mountjoy struck first with a cavalry charge that broke Tyrone's infantry and drove off the Irish horse. O'Donnell chose to retreat rather than relieve O'Neill, at which point the Spanish commander cursed the Irish and surrendered. A much relieved Queen Elizabeth authorized Mountjoy to pardon rather than execute The O'Neill in hopes of reconciling the Irish to English rule.[38]

Instead, pacification of Ireland beyond the Pale took centuries and the people never did abandon Catholicism. But after 1601, Ireland was more or less doomed to fall under English landlords, officials, and bishops, suffer serial waves of Scottish immigration to Ulster, and (in Sir Thomas Smith's words) be reduced "to civilitie and the maners of England." Ireland was England's first colonial laboratory, and the English brought to America the attitudes and experience gained there, not least a contempt and honest fear of uncivilized neighbors. Hariot himself said the Irish were like to the Indians of Roanoke. Another Englishman quipped, "We have Indians at home—Indians in Cornwall, Indians in Wales, Indians in Ireland."[39]

John Locke provided the classic formulation of the English theory of property in his *Second Treatise of Government.* "In the beginning all the world

was *America*," by which he meant *not* that the natural world was free, but unde-
veloped and thus no one's property. Asia and Europe had long since advanced
in civilization, but America remained in a primitive state in which "the
Inhabitants were too few for the Country, and want of People and Money gave
Men no Temptation to enlarge their Possessions of Land, or contest for wider
extent of Ground." Hence, American Indians "exercise very little Dominion,
and have but a very moderate sovereignty." It was only when men mixed their
labor with the land that they could name it their own.[40] Although the Irish and
later the Indians may be excused for missing the point, what is surprising about
the English is not that they were predatory, but that—unlike the Huns,
Mongols, Turks, or (they liked to believe) Spaniards—the English felt it necessary to *justify* their predations to themselves and others with appeals to
Common and natural law. The displacement of savagery by civilization was the
fourth spirit in which the English embarked on colonial enterprise.

What about liberty? Did not the love or quest for liberty inspire English
colonists to brave the perils of the Atlantic crossing and American wilderness?
Yes, in a sense, but so varied and contradictory were the meanings of liberty
borne by British settlers any use of the word now might mislead. Certainly no
one could predict how those four original spirits of English colonization—the
improvement ethic, the holy war against Catholics, the competition for empire,
and the mission to expel or reform the uncivilized—would lead in time to the
spirit of 1776. So perhaps the best way to put the matter is this: "Liberty was
not the goal toward which the Europeans becoming Americans set forth, but a
continent inadvertently discovered in the search for another destination."[41]

# PLANTERS, PATROONS, AND PURITANS
## The Chesapeake, New Netherlands, and New England, 1607–1660

*T*he imperial contest for North America began in earnest when the English settled the James River in 1607, the French founded Québec on the St. Lawrence River in 1608, the Spaniards founded Santa Fe on the Rio Grande in 1609, and the Dutch built Fort Nassau on the Hudson River in 1614.[1] But the Netherlands was a small nation still struggling for independence. Spain, hard-pressed to defend the vast empire it already had, lacked the population and resources to do more than plant a few forts in Florida and New Mexico, and did not reach Alta California until the 1760s. Frigid Canada's main appeal was the fur trade rather than farming, and French kings made matters worse by prohibiting religious dissenters to colonize. Even the energetic English numbered a mere 2,400 in Virginia and 1,400 in New England by 1630. Why, therefore, did the Native Americans east of the Appalachians, who numbered some 400,000 in 1600, not overwhelm the starving white beachheads on the Atlantic seaboard?

The reasons are easily stated. First, Europeans concentrated around fortified villages supported by a monopoly of sea power and firearms. To be sure, Indians quickly developed a lust for muskets, which they used to hunt game or rival tribes. But guns only made the Native Americans dependent on Europeans for ammunition, powder, and repair of weapons, while causing them to lose their skill with a weapon actually better suited to sylvan conflict, the bow. One frontier war ended in 1641 when the proud Iroquois sued for peace to regain access to French firearms.[2] Second, colonists pinned to the coasts and rivers had more incentive to fight tenaciously once there were too many of them to evacuate over a summer. Indians, by contrast, had the option to retreat inland rather than fight desperate wars with the white men. Third, the English drew on inexhaustible reinforcements from a single national "tribe," whereas the Indians strewn across a thousand-mile front were more crippled by tribal feuds than the Scots and Irish.

Fourth and most important were the "invisible armies" fighting on the Europeans' behalf: infectious diseases such as influenza, chicken pox, smallpox, measles, and plague against which Native Americans had no genetic immunity. Upward of 90 percent of the Algonquin, Wampanoag, Massachusetts, and Pawtucket tribes on the New England coast were carried off in the years just before the Pilgrims arrived. Between 50 and 75 percent of the Hurons, Iroquois, and Mohawks in the eastern Great Lakes died in the 1630s and 1640s. Perhaps 90 percent of the Powhatan, Susquehannock, and other tribes around Chesapeake Bay disappeared by 1670. The first English outposts on the Connecticut River were saved when "it pleased God to visit these Indians with a great sickness and such mortality that of a thousand, above nine and a half hundred of them died, and many of them did rot above ground for want of burial." Such mortality occurred whenever Native Americans first met Europeans, its effects magnified by the Indians' own low fertility (resulting in part from their habit of breast-feeding infants for three or four years) and the high death rate of children. Early Virginia colonists also knew wholesale death from malaria, saline poisoning, and other maladies of the tidewater, while their birth rate was also tiny due to the sheer lack of females. But Virginians soon moved out of the fetid estuaries while being supplemented by an average of 8,500 newcomers per year in the 1630s and 1640s. In comparatively healthy New England the Puritan families were not only reinforced, but reproduced at a rate close to the biological maximum. As a result, English colonists may have outnumbered all the eastern Indians combined as early as 1690.[3]

A final reason for the Indians' defeat was their failure to realize they were engaged in a demographic and economic war until far too late. Small bands of whites come to trade or till on the coasts and rivers hardly seemed threatening, and indeed were positive boons insofar as they paid for land and furs with muskets, iron tools, useful or showy curiosities, and liquor. They might also extend friendly Indians decisive military aid against rival tribes, if only to make more room for themselves.[4] English colonists did not come to America intent on killing, enslaving, or for the most part converting or consorting with Indians at all. They just wanted them out of the way, and thanks to their microbes, technology, organization, and agriculture they swiftly displaced the indigenous people in what amounted to a Darwinian contest for an ecological niche. There is simply no plausible "what if" scenario for a successful Indian defense of the continent once Europeans determined to make their colonies stick.[5]

Why did the English found colonies and make them stick? For most the goal was material, whether they were poor and hoping for a chance at a better life, or rich and hoping to build personal empires. For some the goal was spiritual, whether they hoped to escape religious uniformity or establish their own uniformity on virgin soil. But all the colonists who suffered perilous voyages and risked early death in America were either hustlers or hustled. That is, they knew the hardships beforehand and were courageous, desperate, or faithful enough to face them, or else they did *not* know what lay ahead but were taken in by the propaganda of sponsors. Most of the 30,000 Puritans who flooded into New England after 1630 were of the former sort; most of the 120,000 indentured servants and adventurers who sailed to the Chesapeake in the seventeenth century were of the latter sort. In every case colonists left a swarming, competitive country that heralded self-improvement but offered limited opportunities for it. Indeed, when Englishmen made the voyage to Ireland, the West Indies, or mainland America it was often just the last leg of an odyssey leading from village to town to port city in a search for upward mobility.[6]

Less than half of the seventeenth-century English emigrés in fact chose mainland America, but those who did came for land, wood, and water. The ubiquitous bays, harbors, inlets, and rivers offered navigators a plethora of sheltering anchorages and avenues "so Convenient for Exporting and Importing goods into any part . . . that no Country can Compare with it." The deciduous forests blanketing the eastern seaboard amazed refugees from deforested England. Virginia looked "like a forest standing in water"; a Maryland pioneer said "we are pretty Closely seated together, yet wee cannot see our Neighbours House for Trees."[7] Their first sensory impression of the New World was often the scent of evergreen conifers borne out to sea on a westerly breeze, and the panorama of hard pine, live oak, maples, elms, and willows was transformed in settlers' imaginations into warehouses of lumber, furniture, fuel, bark for tannin to make leather, charcoal for smelting metals, and masts, pitch, rope, and hulls

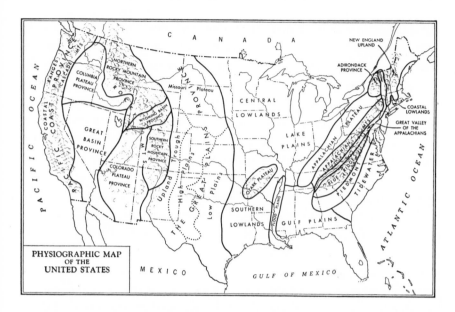

PHYSIOGRAPHIC MAP
OF THE
UNITED STATES

for numberless boats and ships. Wood was more precious than gold, its harvest requiring no more than axes and willing shoulders.

Moreover, the forests were often partially cleared thanks to the Indian practice of killing trees by stripping them of a ring of bark (girdling) and burning underbrush to plant corn or attract game. Many of the first sites of white settlement were thus patches of forest cleared and either abandoned or sold by Indians. But in every case the land seemed so infinite as to allow every man to dream of becoming a baron. That was the dream promoters encouraged, because their own tracts of American land were worthless until settlers invested their labor and possibly lives in what amounted to audacious real estate schemes. As in all new industries "shake-outs" were bound to occur in which a few profited grandly and many lost everything. But the colonies had to display enough overall progress to lure still more investors and settlers and drive up the value of property. "In other words, the American venture had acquired at the very outset some of the qualities of a gigantic land speculation."[8]

The first decade of the seventeenth century was a moment, to cite Shakespeare, for frighted peace to pant. Ireland was subdued, the war with Spain ended, the crowns of England and Scotland united in the person of King James I (VI of Scotland). Accordingly, London merchants led by Thomas Smythe and

Richard Hakluyt, and a Plymouth group including Sir Ferdinando Gorges and Raleigh Gilbert breathed new life into dormant colonial projects. In 1606 a royal charter granted the London and Plymouth companies overlapping rights to plant colonies between 34 degrees and 41 degrees North Latitude and 38 degrees to 45 degrees respectively. Plymouth's first effort was another flop—its expedition to glean fish and furs in what is now Maine quit after one brutal winter. London's colony, located at Jamestown upriver from the Chesapeake Bay in April 1607, looked likely to fail as well. Everything about the expedition was botched. The 105 colonists were all soldiers of fortune who wasted their first year hunting for lucre and either skirmishing with or begging food from the Indians. Their chain of command was confused, quarrels were constant, and orders ignored. One George Kendall was shot for treason after plotting against the colony's council, thereby making disloyalty to one's employer America's inaugural crime. Jamestown itself was a mosquito nursery, so disease joined with famine to reduce the colony to a mere forty souls by the time the next contingent arrived in January 1608. Worst of all, the region's Indians formed a threatening if fragile confederation. Their *weroance* Powhatan assumed a decidedly suspicious stance toward the newcomers.

Jamestown might have gone the way of the Roanoke colony had Captain John Smith not maneuvered himself into leadership. Like Ralegh, Smith has been dubbed an American prototype due to his energy, vision, and unabashed self-promotion (the story of how his perfect love for Pocahontas cast out all fear between Indians and English is undoubtedly bogus). But Smith is more correctly described as "the first Englishman to leave the imprint of his personality and character on a distinctively American scene."[9] In the summer of 1608 he cajoled Jamestown's survivors into cutting timber instead of looking for gold, into trading with Indians for corn, planting forty acres themselves, and tending the livestock brought in the first resupply. He also dodged Powhatan's ploy to lure the Englishmen upstream where they were sure to collide with the Monocan tribe. Still, disease and poor nourishment again shrank the colony to just fifty-eight men by the end of year two.[10]

Back in England, the investors attempted to rally. A new charter in 1609 provided the Virginia Company with an elected board of directors and "one able and absolute governor" advised by a council. Most important, the company offered stock certificates redeemable in land to all who went to Virginia and worked seven years. So successful was the new dispensation that interim governor Sir Thomas Gates led a fleet of nine ships bound for Jamestown in May

1609. A hurricane beached Gates in Bermuda for the winter, but some four hundred people completed the voyage, thereby quintupling the colony's population. That was *another* massive mistake since the emaciated hosts were barely able to feed themselves. When Smith took a gunpowder burn and returned to England in October, the colony lacked leaders as well. Consequently, when Gates finally arrived in the spring to find only sixty people and no livestock alive, he decided to call it quits. But fate, chance, or providence intervened. The colonists embarked and were on course for the sea when they spied a captain's gig bearing none other than the Company's newly appointed permanent governor, Lord De La Warr (Delaware). Becalmed a few miles behind him was a ship bearing another 150 recruits, livestock, and firearms. But far, far more important, its hold also contained axes, adzes, hammers, chisels, knives, saws, pliers, scythes, shovels, spades, augurs, shears, vises, hoes, utensils, blacksmith equipment, millstones, and vegetable seeds. De La Warr chased everyone back to found three new, healthier settlements, then left the colony in 1616 in the able hands of Gates and marshal Thomas Dale, whose *Lawes Divine, Morall, and Martiall* disciplined Virginia's horde of young men. "Dale's Laws" decreed death for the theft of a boat, slaughter of an animal, or unauthorized trade with Indians. They made church attendance mandatory, outlawed swearing, and specified tortures to be inflicted on rebels. They also obliged men (on pain of having their rations cut off) to build wharves, warehouses, stables, churches, blockhouses, and forts, as well as to plant private plots of maize, beans, potatoes, carrots, and cucumbers. Deer, turkeys, and soon domestic chickens, hogs, and cattle yielded vital protein.

But Virginia was still a commercial enterprise with prodigious sunk costs and little chance of quick profits. The London Company found new money hard to raise, while hearsay and published accounts of the colony's travails made recruitment a hard sell. So the dogged directors obtained another change in the charter permitting the company to stage lotteries, in effect financing a gamble through gambling. Next, the dynamic director Sir Edwin Sandys launched an advertising campaign bolder than any of Hakluyt's or Ralegh's. Whereas the latter targeted only the crown, merchants, and educated opinion, Sandys' "demographic" included men and women of all social strata. His hirelings posted placards and tracts proclaiming the glorious opportunities in Virginia in every village and town, and reached the illiterate through hawkers, minstrels, and preachers. Unscrupulous agents called "spirits" haunted taverns and markets in search of beached sailors, drifters, journeymen, and farmers' sons hoping to set up on their own. They even hung around church congregations tempting youth at the moment they might take an offer of passage to America as a sign from above. Finally, the directors leaned on fellow gentry and Anglican bishops to tout the purchase of shares in Virginia as a patriotic duty.[11]

The campaign succeeded thanks to John Rolfe's fortuitous discovery in 1612 that the way to profit in Virginia was by raising tobacco. The native species was acrid and raw, but Rolfe experimented with an aromatic Spanish variety that flourished in the Chesapeake. By 1618 the colony was shipping 50,000-pound crops of tobacco, but still not growing enough corn. So some leading shareholders formed a subsidiary, the Magazine, to broker tobacco and send food to the colony. That ploy started a feud among rival directors that propelled Sandys to leadership.

It is tempting to name Sandys yet another archetypal American since he believed in popular sovereignty, representative government, and social equality. But he was really an English businessman who happened to understand better than his fellow investors the company must give colonists a serious stake in their enterprise. His most effective political theory was "What's in it for me?" So Sandys wooed colonists with talk of "a grand charter of liberty" replacing Dale's Laws and authorized Virginians to elect an assembly to share legislative and judicial authority with the governor and his council. It first met at Jamestown's church in August 1619 to pass a law obliging tobacco-mad colonists to plant a certain acreage to food crops. Another great boon was the company's transport that year of more than ninety young *women,* one of whom a freeman might take to wife for the cost of her passage (125 pounds of tobacco). Sandys also laid plans for an iron foundry and school. Finally, he persuaded King James, notorious for damning the diabolical weed, to grant the Virginia Company a tobacco monopoly in exchange for one-third of the business.

The bottom line was that 4,500 new settlers arrived during the years of Sandys' presidency—and that was what ruined the Company! Powhatan suffered the presence of the English, but he died in 1618. Opechancanough, the new *weroance,* faced a frightening new reality. These English were no longer just replacing their dead, they were swarming, pushing up rivers, planting tobacco wherever they went. Opechancanough quietly prepared his tribes to exploit the vulnerability of the now scattered English plantations until the murder of an old chief gave him a pretext to strike. On Good Friday, 1622, Indians killed 347 whites and condemned another 500 to slow starvation by destroying their crops and animals and driving them back into their fortifications.

As far as the crown was concerned that was the last straw. Of the thousands of English subjects who had removed in good faith to Virginia, only 1,132 remained alive in America. Surely this amounted to criminal mismanagement. Company lawyers pleaded extenuating circumstances, noting as evidence the £100,000 its investors had plunged into the venture. But the attorney general sued for abrogation of the company charter and won a judgment in 1624. The following year, James's successor, King Charles I, established a privy council for colonial affairs, made Virginia a royal province, and appointed a governor.

Would America's first elected self-government survive under a royal regime? Virginia's burgesses took matters into their own hands. In 1629 the assembly boldly declared inasmuch as the crown took no steps to defend the colony, Virginians would undertake to cleanse the peninsula between the James and York Rivers of Indians and assert their right to legislate. The king's ministers were careful to defend royal prerogative, but as a practical matter acquiesced in home rule and representative government. Ten years later, after another inquiry, the crown formally divided the assembly into a lower House of Burgesses and an upper house composed of the Governor's Council, stipulating annual meetings and passage of any suitable laws not contravening those of England itself. Burgesses then established a regular system of courts and jettisoned the English township basis for local government in favor of counties, each with its sheriff and council. Thus did Virginia adapt to the geography of a spread-out plantation society.

The governor's duties included command of the militia. In 1644 Sir William Berkeley was obliged to act in that capacity when the aged Opechancanough launched a final assault on the English. He could not hope to "win" at this point, but may have sent his eager young braves to kill over five hundred whites (and be killed in turn) in hopes the governor might at least acknowledge some *limit* to Virginia's expansion. If so, his victory was pyrrhic. For even though Berkeley agreed to a treaty in 1646 that recognized inviolable Indian territory, the war destroyed any lingering chance of peaceful co-existence. After burying their mutilated women and children, whites deemed Indians incorrigibly savage, adopting almost unconsciously a policy of "mobile apartheid." Indians might do as they pleased in the woods, but they had better get out of the way of English expansion. All Indians could do to enforce their treaty rights in the face of white violations was to engage in spasmodic massacres that reinforced the whites' fear and hatred, hastening the Indians' extinction.

By 1650 Virginia's population passed eighteen thousand and its settlements stretched far up the James, York, and Rappahannock Rivers, and Chesapeake Bay. "First families" such as the Byrds, Carters, Randolphs, and Masons began to found great plantations, add the first wings to their "big houses," and buy up the contracts of scores of indentured servants. They were joined by investors rewarded with 1,250 acres for transporting 250 settlers and by cronies on whom Governor Berkeley bestowed handsome grants. Many of them were "distressed cavaliers": noblemen who lost all back in England fighting on the King's side in the English Civil War of the 1640s. Whatever the provenance of their master's plantation, Virginia's indentured servants (still overwhelmingly English) dragged or floated their masters' hogsheads of tobacco to river wharves where merchants came to trade textiles, furniture, and manufactures from England. But overland trails began to link rivers and settlements, hence Virginia's horse culture was also in healthy gestation by the later seventeenth century. The more numerous minor planters and farmers labored alongside their servants, made extra cash when tobacco prices were high, and lived far better than they could have in England. Even indentured servants might expect to become freemen, voters, and landowners after seven years' labor, assuming they survived their initial "seasoning" with grit and good health. Other newcomers got a leg up because family members in England armed their young men with loans or bequests and young women, much in demand, with dowries. To be sure, the radical imbalance between sexes still depressed natural growth, especially since most female indentures could not marry until completing their contracts. But under Governor Berkeley the colony thrived sufficiently to attract new blood, while its medium of exchange—tobacco, not money—sufficed to import its other needs.

What had the Virginia Company wrought? Aside from old tales of pioneer courage and new tales of expropriation and racism, Virginia's story was a real estate speculation in which thousands lost their lives and the promoters were forced out of business. No wonder one might conclude the very "cheapness and precariousness of life lent a tone of macabre lunacy to colonial undertakings" such that the Chesapeake seemed "a grotesque parody" of English society.[12] But the colony was no parody: it was a legitimate offspring displaying many of the genes of its parent society, above all the improvement ethic born of rural capitalism. Nor were its founders macabre lunatics: their keen insight into America's tremendous potential was proven by the fact Virginia took off *in spite of* undercapitalization, faulty, contentious management, false advertising, and false starts. It just turned into something different than the company (or crown) had in mind: a largely autonomous civil society in which every free subject, not just the "sirs," might make it big through hustle and luck.

Meanwhile, Virginia acquired a neighbor that at first glance and in subsequent myth seemed to belie the spirit of English colonization. Whereas the Anglican church was established in Virginia, the colony of Maryland was founded by English Catholics in the name of freedom of conscience. Whereas planters in Virginia might obtain land in freehold, or subject at most to quit rents, Maryland was self-consciously feudal. Whereas Virginia was initially a commercial venture and later a crown colony, Maryland was subject to a sole proprietor with perpetual, inheritable rights. But all that was in theory; in practice rural capitalism, anti-Catholicism, home rule, and the tobacco culture quickly turned Maryland, too, into something its sponsors never intended.[13]

The Irish peer George Calvert, First Baron Baltimore, dreamed of developing vast American estates for himself and his children. He owned shares in the Virginia Company and fell in love with Chesapeake Bay on a visit in 1629. As a Catholic convert, however, he could not openly practice his faith in Virginia, so he petitioned his friend Charles I for a new grant diplomatically named after the king's wife. Virginians howled in protest, but Baltimore's charter (which he drafted largely himself) awarded him all the land between 40 degrees North Latitude and the Potomac River "in free and common soccage," which meant the proprietor enjoyed all the prerogatives of a feudal lord without the restriction of inalienable tenure. He could sub-grant any of the 10 million acres at his personal disposal, or rent it, or sell it in a market of his own making.[14] All the crown asked was the usual 20 percent of any silver and gold found in the colony.

Upon Calvert's untimely death in 1632, his son Cecilius, Second Baron Baltimore, wasted no time coming into his kingdom. Learning from the Virginia experience, he launched an advertising blitz before, not after, planting the first colony, wisely including in his promotional tracts a list of the tools, weapons, supplies, seeds, and livestock a colonist needed. He also attracted planters with an offer of 2,000 acres for every five men they transported and an annual quit rent of just two shillings per hundred acres (the going rate in Virginia). The first 1634 contingent dropped anchor in February—another wise move since that gave settlers a full season to plant and harvest before facing a winter. They chose a Potomac River site they called St. Mary's, traded with the Yoacomaco tribe for cleared land, and set about raising corn and tobacco.

Maryland was thus self-sufficient from its inception, and thrived under the governorship of the younger Calvert brother, Leonard.

It was not, however, a Catholic colony, since the Calverts attracted few co-religionists, apart from seventeen gentlemen and their wives expecting to form a Catholic aristocracy. Most of the two hundred pioneers were Anglicans, while almost all the indentured servants deposited in Maryland in decades to come were Protestants ready to hate Catholic lords from the moment they stepped off the boat. No sooner did the governor try to appoint Maryland's first colonial assembly in 1638 than settlers rose in protest. Proprietor and people bickered for years, but as no one would get rich without willing labor, the people gradually won the right to elect representatives until, in 1650, Maryland embraced Virginia's model of a governor's council sharing power with a popular assembly.

The original religious vision of the Lords Baltimore lasted no longer than their political one. Calvert made no move to establish his church, but he did invite Jesuit missionaries to move among the Indians, which inflamed the Protestants because the hated Jesuits behaved as if this were a Catholic empire, claiming the right to church lands, tax exemptions, and legal privileges. In the interest of tranquillity the proprietor sent them packing. But the pot boiled over in 1642 when the English Civil War broke out back home, the Puritan-dominated Parliament taking up arms against the Calverts' patron, King Charles. A Virginian named William Claiborne took that opportunity to declare a private war against Maryland. Years before he set himself up as a trader on the Chesapeake island of Kent only to be dispossessed by an English court under the terms of the Maryland charter. Now the vengeful Claiborne returned with a band of roughnecks to seize Kent Island while another anti-popery zealot, Richard Ingle, attacked St Mary's. Governor Calvert had to flee to Virginia where Berkeley remained loyal to King Charles. He arrived just in time to be caught up in the colony's second war against Opechancanough. (Indeed, the old *weroance* may have attacked in 1644 in the wild misconception that Maryland's whites might ally themselves with the Indians against Virginia.)

Further threatening the Maryland proprietor's rule was a sudden influx of Puritans who founded Providence (later Annapolis). They rejected out of hand the governor's Act of Toleration for Christians of all sorts and, once in command of a majority in the assembly, repealed it. The proprietors sued on the grounds that Lord Baltimore's charter mandated toleration, eventually winning in English courts. But forever after Catholics were wise to keep their faith private and by no means carry it into the political sphere. Compared to other English colonies, not to mention those of Spain and France, this was "religious freedom" of a sort, but hardly the harmonious diversity of Maryland legend.

All that remained of Baltimore's original vision was the manorial system which did spawn some sixty estates encompassing much of the colony's best land. Hence, while well over half of the earliest colonists did acquire land of their own and a few "attained a level of wealth and social standing unthinkable for men and women of humble origins,"[15] most settlers and indentures who arrived after 1645 lived out their lives as tenants or hired hands. Maryland's social structure was thus more hierarchical than that of any mainland American colony—except New Netherlands.

The worrisome presence of Dutchmen not far from Chesapeake Bay may help to account for the crown's locating the Baltimore grant north of Virginia. Back in 1614 Amsterdam merchants took advantage of a Twelve Years' Truce in the Dutch war of independence against Spain to build Fort Nassau and other strong points near the mouth of the Hudson River. Their goal was to monopolize trade with the great Iroquois confederacy. Monopolize against whom? Against rival *Dutch* firms that poached on their turf in defiance of the "pretended charter" Amsterdam "cunningly obtained" from the States General, Netherlands' parliament.[16] But in 1621, when the Spanish truce was close to expiring, the States General chartered an omnibus West India Company to unite the Netherlands' contentious capitalists and admonish them to stir up no trouble with England's American colonies.

The company never intended a large agricultural colony, but it still needed labor and advertised, in the usual way, the fabulous opportunities in New Netherlands. Their first takers learned, in the usual way, that no opportunities were permitted under the company's own rules. When settlers either went home or refused to work, the company's factors pleaded for skilled and industrious colonists. Some arrived in 1625 under Peter Minuit, who purchased Manhattan Island from the Indians for sixty guilders in goods, put men to work on "bouweries" (farms) outside New Amsterdam on the East River, and tried to turn a profit for the shareholders. He also made feints toward the Delaware River, where Dutch fur traders shadowboxed with the English. But New Netherlands had a mere three hundred people by 1629, when a hustling commissioner, Amsterdam jeweler Kiliaen Van Rensselaer, persuaded the company to launch a new promotion. This Charter of Privileges to Patroons offered any patron who paid passage for fifty people a fifteen-mile stretch of Hudson River frontage and a guaranteed cut of the Indian fur trade. Not surprisingly, Rensselaer himself took advantage of the new dispensation by sending his sons over to "boss" (a Dutch word) the sprawling domain of Rensselaerswick. But his was the only patroonship to thrive because other stockholders suspected the patroon system was a scam to shave their own profits. They voted to retract the fur trade provision. That did not work either, because bevies of *bosch-lopers* (forest-runners, equivalent to the French *coureurs de bois*), sometimes employed but usually out for themselves, journeyed far up the Hudson by canoe and portage to trade with Indians for beaver pelts, which they then smuggled past the West India Company's factors. So prevalent were these first American frontiersmen that it seemed to one visitor in New Netherlands "every boer [farmer] was a merchant."[17]

Cheated of the profits they expected to cheat from the Indians by way of cheating their stockholders, the Dutch commissioners sent out a series of governors, each more imperious than the last. But all their harsh methods accomplished was to turn New Amsterdam into the odd spectacle of a lawless, bustling harbor town occasionally punctuated by official torture and summary judgment. Ships from many nations and colonies, legal and illegal, stood at anchor. After the company set up the first American brewery (another attempt to fashion a lucrative monopoly) drunken sailors and Indians careened down the streets every night until a curfew was imposed. Sooner or later the company's tactics were bound to endanger the colony, and it happened in 1643 when Governor William Kieft provoked a war with the local Algonquins. The Indian warriors proceeded to slaughter close to half the white population in the Hudson Valley, forcing the beleaguered burghers to huddle behind their defensive wall (Wall Street). Kieft also set the terrible precedent of paying bounties for scalps. The Native Americans soon returned the favor. (Before that time forest tribes preferred to remove the whole head for a trophy.)[18]

In all, the West India Company suffered a net loss of over half a million guilders and stood in the same position as the Virginia Company back in 1622. But the Dutch firm was able to carry the colony, given its profits from other endeavors, and no royal government existed to revoke its charter. So the company repopulated New Netherlands by opening it up to immigrants from all nations, the first American jurisdiction to do so. This stunning stroke of liberality had equally stunning results. By 1650, the colony grew to over four thousand; by 1664 over ten thousand, of whom a third or more were Huguenots (French Calvinists), Catholic Walloons (from present-day Belgium), English Puritans, Sephardic Jews, or aliens of other varieties. Finally, the company turned to the crippled war veteran Peter Stuyvesant in 1647 in hopes of good government and profits at last. But Stuyvesant saw the colony's salvation, not in reforms giving people more of a stake in Dutch rule, but in expansion of the company's trade far beyond Manhattan, Long Island, and the Hudson.

Ten years earlier the Kingdom of Sweden, heavily engaged in Germany's Thirty Years' War but still at the height of its power, granted its own West India Company a charter to found New Sweden at Fort Christina (the future Wilmington, Delaware). By 1648 about four hundred colonists fanned out from the fort to plow the first farms along the Delaware and Schuylkill Rivers. The colony displayed remarkable energy, given that its governor Johan Printz weighed over four hundred pounds and its main contingent was composed (in Printz's estimation) of "lazy Finns" recruited or impressed on Sweden's eastern frontier. But those Savo-Karelian Finns sent home such glowing accounts that "America fever" reached the far corners of the Baltic Sea. Suffice it to say that when William Penn arrived in 1681 he counted over a thousand fecund families. Finns were skilled woodsmen and eager to learn what additional lore the Indians could teach. They also bequeathed to American pioneers a technology of surpassing importance: the log cabin.[19]

Stuyvesant could not abide Swedish interlopers. His colony's inland prospects were already circumscribed by French traders moving south from the St. Lawrence and English ones moving west from the Connecticut Valley. So he targeted the weakest of his neighbors and ordered a rival fort built on the Schuylkill in 1648. The Swedes watched until the Dutch finished their sweaty work, then burned the fort down. Stuyvesant nursed the insult until 1655 when he mounted another offensive and forced the Swedes to capitulate. But the absorption of New Sweden did nothing to make New Netherlands more defensible. Just nine years later Stuyvesant himself would be forced to surrender when he called his polyglot people to arms only to find none were willing to fight for a Dutch company's balance sheet.

It was said of the Virginia Company that it created a country only to destroy itself in the process.[20] New Netherlands was a country that destroyed itself because it never escaped from its company. The most successful of all the early colonies, by contrast, was founded by people clever enough to dupe their sponsoring company before they ever set foot in America. They were the Puritans.

In 1606, one year before Jamestown, a young man named William Bradford trudged ten miles from the village of Austerfield to the manor house at Scrooby on the high road from London to Edinburgh. There, in the chapel, some fifty or more Protestants gathered to beg the Lord's guidance in troubled times. Most were mere farmers, but they had leaders in William Brewster and the scintillating preacher John Robinson, both of whom studied at Cambridge. These Separatists, soon to be called Pilgrims, broke away from the Anglican church because Elizabeth's 39 Articles of Religion traduced their simple creed. It was enough for them to believe all human beings are sinners, but all are offered the free gift of salvation through the sacrifice of the Son of God known through Scripture, prayers, and the sacraments. To them, anything beyond such mere Christianity, especially church hierarchy and elaborate liturgy, only subtracted from the faith.

When the Scrooby congregation was denounced in 1607, Bradford and Robinson led their flock into exile in the Netherlands. The families got on well enough in Leyden, but worried about the resumption of war against Spain and by their children's tendency to "go Dutch" on them. The Separatists wanted to live as English men and women, but could not do so in England itself.

Captain John Smith had an answer. Following his salvific exploits in Virginia he led a whaling expedition to northeastern American waters in 1614, returning to publish a book that gave the region its name: *A Description of New England.* It created a sensation because of the style, fame, and promotional skill of its author, but in substance it only repeated the praise Edward Hayes, a veteran of Gilbert's 1583 expedition, had lavished on the region two decades before. At those latitudes, Hayes wrote, the climate was "Well agreing with the Constitution of our boddies." The distance from England was short and "the trade alewayes open & free from restraynt by forren princes." The coasts were fair and the excellent harbors "apt to be fortefyed." The soil was exceedingly good for maize and the mighty trees of "Fyrr, pyne & cedar abell to Mast the greatest shypps of the world." The land abounded with fur-bearing animals and such quantity of game as to "sustayn armies of men wyth varietie of Beasts, fysh & fowle to content every tast."[21]

In 1617 two Pilgrim agents traveled to London to seek permission to settle in this blessed land. King James I abominated their sect, but pronounced himself willing to "connive" in the national interest. It was the Virginia Company that dithered and bickered until Edwin Sandys, playing America's godfather once more, gave the new Plymouth Company its blessing. The Pilgrims still needed financing and while merchant Thomas Weston offered to provide it, he insisted that the colony be run as a joint-stock company in which the Pilgrims would each have one share and the investors many. After seven years the colony's accrued assets would be divided accordingly. The Pilgrims pleaded in vain for private ownership and may have accepted Weston's terms in the belief that they might do as they liked over the water. But in the end just thirty-five of their number found the courage to embark for the unknown, which meant only a third of the passengers boarding the *Mayflower* in September 1620 were Pilgrims.

The captain chose not to sail south to the Azores, pick up the trade winds, then coast northward to their planned destination in Long Island Sound. Instead, he beat his way due west across the rough North Atlantic and after two trying months made landfall at Cape Cod. The season was very late, but the unknown shallows, currents, and rocks made a fight back to open sea risky. So the company huddled, and decided to stay even though they were beyond the Virginia Company's patent. Colonists who had signed on in London promptly mutinied, which inspired the improvisation known as the Mayflower Compact. All but one of the Pilgrim fathers made a covenant to form a "civill body politick" and obey such "just and equall lawes" as they may establish. They had, in effect, made a solemn pledge to *violate* the terms of their charter by settling outside its boundaries and under laws of their own making. And as the captain was determined to wait until spring to attempt his return crossing, the malcontents had no choice but to throw in their lot with the Pilgrims.

Governor Bradford thanked God on his knees for bringing them safely to that "firm and stable earth." But he spent the first winter praying over the corpses of half his colonists while the few men able to work dragged logs through the snow to build shelters. As everyone knows, they received vital assistance from Squanto, who had learned English from fur traders and watched his Wampanoag people die from European diseases. In 1621 the survivors planted twenty acres of Indian corn, fished, and gathered enough furs and timber to please the ship captain who arrived just after the Pilgrims' Thanksgiving feast that autumn. The Pilgrims were not pleased, however, when the captain deposited thirty-five new settlers to feed. Two more hard winters ensued during which the merchant Weston sent no supplies. So Plymouth's leaders decided in 1623 to ignore their contractual obligations again by parceling out private plots to each family. Experience, Bradford wrote, had proven "the vanity of that conceit of Plato's . . . that the taking away of property and bringing community into a commonwealth would make them happy and flourishing." In fact, "the young men that were most able and fit for labour and service did repine that they should spend their time and strength to work for other men's wives and children without any recompense. . . . Let none object this is men's corruption . . . all men have this corruption in them."[22] The trick was to make men's corruption creative, and the way to do that was to give each man responsibility for his own property and dependents.

The Pilgrims' final deliverance came in 1624, when the despairing stockholders simply dissolved the company on the condition the Pilgrims pay off their debts. After Bradford's agent settled with the company for a sum of £1,800, the governor exhorted his now hustling colonists to raise the money through exports of furs, fish, and timber. The Pilgrims' economic and moral universe was brazenly challenged, however, when one Thomas Morton and a godless band of indentured servants from a failed colony to the north squatted at "Merriemount" (now Braintree). They not only cut into the Pilgrims' fur trade, but erected an eighty-foot-tall antlered Maypole around which they drank, danced, and fornicated with Indian girls: "Drinke and be merry, merry, merry, boyes, Let all your delight be in Hymen's joyes!" In June 1628 Bradford dispatched his militia (armed with muskets, not blunderbusses) under hired soldier Miles Standish to expel the intruders and ship Morton back to England.[23] Their trade restored, the Pilgrims paid off the whole debt by 1630 to win a free and clear patent to Plymouth colony.

That same year marked the start of the Puritans' Great Migration, which means it is time to examine that particular form of Calvinism so important to American history. For fifteen hundred years the Roman Catholic Church had articulated doctrines and rituals drawn from Scripture, tradition, deduction, and custom designed to meet the psychological needs of Christians both simple and sophisticated. The annual rhythm of penitential and celebratory seasons in the ecclesiastical calendar, the seasonal rhythm of work days and saints' days, and the daily rhythm from lauds to vespers redeemed the time in what for most people was a short and uncertain life. Through the sacraments even illiterate peasants gained mystical access to grace, and if they chose to believe in relics and charms, what was the harm? Of course the church was often corrupt, but all men are sinners and it was expected the devil paid special attention to clergy. What is more, every time the church fell into prolonged decadence, the Holy Spirit renewed it through great reforming orders such as the Benedictines, Augustinians, Franciscans, Dominicans, and lately the Jesuits. The one, holy, catholic, and apostolic church both expressed and redeemed human nature because it was the very Body of Christ. To be at peace *outside* the church was unthinkable.

Then new sorts of Europeans appeared: Renaissance humanists and reformed Protestants of great erudition and a new sense of history. They studied the Bible in its original languages, noted mistakes made in translation and changes over the centuries in the meaning of words. They questioned ancient claims made on behalf of the papacy, arguing many Roman doctrines and practices lacked biblical or patristic authority. As self-conscious creatures of reason finding themselves in the presence of error, they asked, "What must *I* do to be saved, what does *God* (not the priesthood) require of me?"[24] The holy grail of their quest was whatever characterized the primitive church. Jesus denounced the legalistic priests and formulaic ritual of that day, instructing disciples to love God and each other and obey His commandments. So, too, must devout Protestants reject the grotesque Pharisaism and worldliness into which Rome had fallen and recapture the faith of the first century.

But for every pietistic Protestant sect that preached humility and charity in the presence of sin, another sect insisted whole societies conform to what they took to be Biblical norms. That sort soon replicated the very things it denounced. Thus, the Roman church was often "Erastian" in that it courted favor with secular rulers. But Luther positively offered up his churches to princes willing to shelter him, while Henry VIII made his church a personal fief. Alternatively, the Roman church at times tried to dominate secular states and societies. But Calvin presided over a virtual theocracy in Geneva, as did Knox's disciples in Scotland, and many of Cromwell's supporters hoped for the same in England. The Romans seemed to encourage belief in salvation through works, as if souls could earn their way into heaven. But Puritans not only made church attendance and tithes mandatory, they imposed rigorous rules over personal behavior, mandated inquisitory public (not private) confessions, and visited corporal punishment, excommunication, banishment, and even death upon heretics. Calvin*ism* (as opposed to the faith and order of the scrupulous Calvin himself) seemed often to turn into a parody of "popery" without the forgiveness and absolution the Catholic church offered to all. To be sure, the best of the Puritans exhibited love and humility because of their own deep introspection. But they only learned what Catholic ascetic saints knew all along from their having really *tried* to live without sin in thought, word, deed, or omission. Nobody could do it for five minutes. However, those Puritans who could not bring themselves to forgive human foibles, and who continued to believe in the possibility of a heavenly city on earth, had no way to bridge the awful gap between a holy God and a fallen race. They wavered between self-righteousness and self-condemnation.

Who was saved? Another problem Catholic theologians had long put to rest, but which Calvinists (not Calvin) revived, was predestination. Since God by definition knew no limits, He must know from eternity whose names are written in the Book of Life and whose are not, and there is nothing anyone can do about it. Yes, humans are saved by faith, but since humans cannot be the authors of their own salvation their faith must have been planted in them by prevenient, irresistible grace. How then could divine omnipotence and human free will co-exist? Augustine of Hippo, Thomas Aquinas, and numerous rabbis had observed that God is beyond time whereas man is trapped in time, so the mystery of free will is not worth fretting about. But Calvinists fretted because they believed the "elect" must display their status through a life of piety and good works and be blessed in turn with material fruits ("seek ye first the kingdom of God and all this shall be added unto you"). Such people composed the "visible church" and indeed were the only ones permitted full membership in a Puritan congregation and voting rights in the community.

Such logic, and logic it was, placed a great onus on those who were convinced of their salvation to demonstrate sanctification each waking hour and indeed in their dreams. It placed an even greater onus on those who had not had a wrenching conversion. They asked what they could do to escape eternal damnation, and had to answer nothing at all. Strict Puritanism, when not terrifying, all but invited hypocrisy. But few theologies display such power to inspire godly commitment from women and men to their families, congregations, and communities.

The radical wing of English Protestantism was fortified under Elizabeth by the return of the "Marian exiles" from the continent where their theology had been honed by contact with Lutherans, Zwinglians, and especially Calvinists. But far from celebrating Elizabeth's moderation, Puritans rejected the Anglican Prayer Book, a church run by the monarch and bishops, and

England's High Renaissance culture which they deemed thoroughly decadent. It has become commonplace to point out that the Puritans were not "puritanical": from Calvin to Cotton Mather they enjoyed food, drink, and dancing in moderation, and begat scads of babies.[25] But they nonetheless damned the plays of Marlowe and Shakespeare as immoral, the science of William Gilbert and Sir Francis Bacon as idolatrous, and the sacred music of William Byrd and Orlando Gibbons as distracting. The Puritans were "at war with nearly every form of the beautiful" and the raucous, ribald, curious, grasping spirit of the age only proved to them that the human mind was "a foul sink of all atheism, sodomy, blasphemy, murder, whoredom, adultery, witchcraft, buggery."[26]

The Puritans placed their hopes in Mary Stuart's son, King James I, who inherited both the Scottish and English thrones and coined the term Great Britain to describe his joint realm. Raised in his mother's absence by Scottish tutors, he was given a rigorous, mostly Calvinist education. Hence the Puritans' excitement over his coronation. But once in power James revealed his preference for the trendy new theories of royal absolutism being touted in France. He also grasped the political function of the Anglican church established under the Tudors. A Protestant English church with a Presbyterian polity meant doing away with bishops, hierarchy, and, by implication, the monarchy. Thus, when no less than a thousand Puritans petitioned the king for the right to worship openly in defiance of Anglicanism, James hurled back his famous equation "no bishops, no king," warning Puritans to "conform themselves" or be harried out of the land. Unfortunately, while he was prepared to renounce both his mother's Catholicism and his own Calvinist upbringing in the name of the Anglican compromise, the rigid Scotsman had no sense at all of how Henry VIII and Elizabeth had governed by making the monarchy a popular, charismatic institution. James and his even more determined son Charles made no friends, but a great number of enemies, by cracking down on "non-conforming" Puritans. Tens of thousands repaired to the New World, certain that divine wrath was soon to be visited upon England.

The Puritan colony's story began with another company, in this case a Massachusetts Bay Company that obtained a royal charter in 1629 to the land three miles north of the Merrimac River to three miles south of the Charles River. Though hoping to profit, this company was formed mostly by Puritans. One was John Winthrop, a lawyer and lord of Groton Manor in Suffolk, who shared the ambition of purifying the Church of England and worried whether he would be serving or betraying God's cause if he left for America. At length he reached the prayerful conclusion that building a holy community in America might serve as an example and so redeem England. He justified this "errand into the wilderness" according to all four spirits of English colonization: to "raise a bulwark against the kingdom of anti-Christ" (that is, Catholicism), tend and improve the Lord's garden which is "the whole earth," defend the New World against England's enemies, and convert (or dispossess) the heathen Indians.[27] But shrewd lawyer that he was, Winthrop knew the colony could not perform its special "errand" unless it emerged as a self-governing commonwealth independent of the English crown, Anglican church, and its own company. So even though his supporters were minority shareholders, they made secret preparations to sail, maneuvered Winthrop into a leadership role, and hid the Massachusetts Bay Company charter in their America-bound baggage.

They pulled off this magnificent coup in only six months, for by April 1630 four ships and four hundred settlers were at sea. They arrived, exhausted, at Salem, whereupon Winthrop made his first command decision. Two settlements had already been planted at Salem without success, and location is everything in real estate. So he re-embarked the whole expedition for the Charles River, ordering his people to disperse in search of previously cleared land. Boston, Charlestown, Newtown (Cambridge), Watertown, Roxbury, and Dorchester were soon under construction. Still, half the settlers perished from hunger, scurvy, or frostbite the first winter. Spring brought a second wave of colonists and supplies, but many others went home to tell wretched stories. That might have defeated the colony were it not for King Charles I's and Archbishop William Laud's determination to be "thorough" in their imposition of High Anglican uniformity. Every year in the 1630s a dozen or more ships carried to Boston families equipped with money, guns, tools, and seed. Nor was available land a problem since the Puritans readily purchased it from the Indians, as confident as Virginians about their right to do so. As Winthrop wrote: "As for the Natives in New England, they inclose noe Land, neither have any setled habytation, nor any tame Cattle to improve the Land by, and soe have noe other but a Naturall Right to those Countries, soe as if we leave them sufficient for their use, we may lawfully take the rest, there being more than enough for them and us."[28] That probably strikes contemporary ears as cant, but he was only telling the truth. Another smallpox epidemic struck the Indians after 1633, renewing the "providential" die-off that preceded the Pilgrims. There was indeed land to spare which tribal chiefs were pleased to sell, especially since contracts of sale invariably reserved to the Indians the right to hunt, fish, and sometimes even plant on land they gave up. Boundary disputes were rare as well for "The Natives are very exact and punctuall in the bounds of their Lands."[29]

Under Winthrop's tireless guidance early Massachusetts was a paragon of tranquillity by comparison to Maryland or New Netherlands. But the Puritan notion of peace required rigid conformity. That was because Winthrop, "first and foremost a fanatic," found fanaticism worked, at least for a while.[30] Puritans no more believed in democracy than did the Stuarts, for their notion of government as a covenant between the magistrates and people was an earthly reflection of the greater covenant between God and man under which people promised to obey their heavenly king in return for His blessings in a Promised Land. Such positive freedom meant to escape the slavery of sin born of one's own corrupt soul and thus be at liberty to do what was right—the exact opposite of a libertarian's negative freedom from external constraints. As Winthrop summed it up in his "little speech" of 1645, men must fulfill their part in the covenant because they enjoyed "a liberty to that only which is good, just and honest," which is "maintained and exercised in a way of subjection to authority" for the good of all parties.[31]

Since Winthrop was the company's governor and had purloined its charter, it was his responsibility to summon the other Puritan leaders to a General Court, elect officials, and establish a civil regime that conformed to Biblical prescriptions as they understood them. The body first met in October 1630 and within a year transformed the company into a commonwealth in which all adult male freeholders could vote so long as they were members in good moral standing of the established Congregational church. Still, so many residents challenged Winthrop's right to govern at all that he found himself forced to produce the mysterious charter in 1632. Caught out in the sleight of hand his own faction had performed on the company, Winthrop acquiesced in direct election of representatives to General Court by every township. Sixteen years of more or less bitter debate ensued, but by 1648 General Court had codified the Laws and Liberties of Massachusetts from Biblical, local, and Common Law sources.

The Laws and Liberties established a commonwealth, which did not mean a commune but rather a covenant based on willing obedience to God's natural laws which by definition served the interests of all in common. To the extent all were obedient, this Zion in the wilderness formed a pyramid of "peaceable kingdoms" with families at the base, congregations and towns in the middle,

General Court and the synod of clergy at the apex.[32] That the whole structure was paternalist goes without saying: this was a seventeenth-century culture founded on Biblical precepts with a heavy Old Testament bias, a culture in which most women believed as (or more) devoutly than men. How many women felt repressed is unknowable, but those who left a record behind either affirmed the system, like the romantic poet Anne Bradstreet, or protested it on theological grounds, like Anne Hutchinson. In any event, New England women worked at least as hard as the men to build their Puritan commonwealth, for in addition to sharing toil in household and fields they gave birth (according to Andover's statistics) to an *average* of 8.3 children.[33]

Given that birth rate on top of the immigrant tide, one of General Court's most critical functions was administering the founding of towns. On other American frontiers controlled growth under uniform institutions and a rule of law was often just a fond pretense, but in New England it was reality. To obtain approval to plant a new town, some fifty or sixty heads of households had to show proof that all Indian claims were retired and title to the land was clear. Next they had to present a plan endowing each founder with a town lot and fields, plenty of room for new settlers, a common, church plot, parsonage, town hall, and school. Indeed, General Court made Massachusetts the first jurisdiction in history to require universal primary education. It also founded Harvard, the first American college north of New Spain, in 1636. But the purpose of education was to train orthodox ministers and indoctrinate lay people, as the Rev. Nathaniel Ward insisted: "God does nowhere in His word tolerate Christian States to give toleration to such adversaries of His truth, if they have power in their hands to suppress them. . . . Poly-piety is the greatest impiety in the world."[34]

The civil code accordingly restricted the right to vote and even to speak at town meetings to church members. The code forbade vices such as gambling, public lewdness (including kissing one's spouse in public), work or travel on the Sabbath day and idleness any other day. It made church attendance and tithing compulsory, while clerical synods beginning in 1637 enjoined the state zealously to enforce orthodoxy. The colony was not quite a theocracy in the sense that clergy controlled the state. But it was an oligarchy of the devout. As one pastor put it, "a speaking Aristocracy in the face of a silent Democracy."[35]

Under Charles I the crown made two futile efforts to crack down on the Puritan plan to make New England a judgment on Old England. First, it tried to suppress the great migration by requiring emigrants to register with royal officials. Puritans got around that by using assumed names or phony contracts identifying them as humble indentured servants. Next, the crown created a Commission for Foreign Plantations in 1633 and appointed old Ferdinando Gorges governor of New England. But he resigned when his ship foundered on launch, and was never replaced. By 1640, of course, King Charles had a rebellious Parliament on his hands, so he ignored the colonies. At the same time, however, the English Civil War orphaned New England by ending the Puritan exodus and making the colony's "errand" redundant. Not only did England itself become a Puritan commonwealth, but its Lord Protector Oliver Cromwell seemed more interested in perfecting his New Model Army than perfecting souls and society. Thus, at the very moment their influence should have been greatest, New World Puritans "lost their audience" and were "left alone with America."[36] Or rather that part of America was left alone with them, because the Puritans looked to themselves and their new continent from the start regardless of what happened in England.

Most of the Kentish and East Anglian Puritans, indentured servants, and miscellaneous freemen who poured into Massachusetts Bay in the 1630s and 1640s were not farmers. One ship's register of forty-two emigrants in 1637 numbered only eleven yeomen, but eight weavers, four cordwainers, four carpenters, two joiners, two tailors, two coopers, two mariners, and one brewer, shoemaker, grocer, locksmith, minister, butcher, and calender. If that was normal it helps to explain both the indifferent yields of early New England farmers and the rapidity with which they exhausted the soil. It also explains the rapidity with which trades, crafts, and industry sprang up.[37] But all colonists eagerly attacked the American forest with their brittle and heavy English axes. (Not until the eighteenth century was the sturdy, contoured, and balanced "American ax" designed.) In the first instance, they did so because woods were a source of fear and vexation. Foliage blocked the rays of the sun and inhibited planting. Damp undergrowth spawned swarms of mosquitoes, gnats, and other insects that caused more complaints than anything else. Poison ivy, sumac, and oak plagued men and women trying to clear land or gather berries and nuts. Forests harbored wolves, cougars, and Indians, all of whom preyed on the pigs beloved by the colonists precisely because they could forage rather than eat precious corn. Rattlesnakes were a fearsome novelty. Even the cacophony of frogs, crickets, birds, and arboreal mammals frazzled Puritan nerves. So a war of attrition ensued in which colonists drove back the biomass, felling trees and pulling up roots and stumps with oxen a few acres per man-year of labor.

On the other hand, the harvested timber provided raw material to build a new civilization, America's "wooden age." At first the settlers dwelt in earthen dugouts, wigwams, or daub-and-wattle cabins, but as time permitted they clove tree trunks into boards and erected frame cottages. Since nails were expensive (when available) Puritan carpenters fastened boards with notches and pegs into walls that would break under the weight unless made very thick. As a result, several tons of timber might have to be cut and shaped to build a single small house. Needless to add, New England was cold, and the yawning fireplaces in the center of each dwelling consumed huge amounts of wood. So, too, did fencing, which became a veritable obsession of the early General Courts since free-ranging pigs trampled fields and caused endless disputes with the Indians. Finally, wood was New England's primary export. As early as 1640 coopers prepared thousands of barrels and staves for the wine-growing Madeira and Azores islands and the sugar islands of the West Indies, plus masts and other ship stores for England. But if land and wood were plentiful, labor was not. So American colonists sought from the start to increase production through technological means. In 1634 John Mason built the first American sawmill on the Great Works River (in present-day Maine); by 1650 a dozen were operating. Indeed, some of the first patents issued in the New World went to Joseph Jenks for his innovative sawmills and scythes.[38] Finally, the Puritans were so assiduous in their own advancement that within a decade of their arrival they exported wheat to the West Indies, fish and cattle to the Chesapeake, and furs and fish to England and the Canary Islands in return for sugar, tobacco, salt, wine, and citrus.

That commerce, however, was carried in English (or sometimes Dutch) ships because New England lacked carpenters and joiners able to do more than fashion one-masted shallops and pinnaces for fishing and the coastal trade. John Winthrop's *Blessing of the Bay*, launched on the Mystic River in 1631, was the first. But the shipbuilding industry's takeoff—and in fact the coming of age of Massachusetts' economy—occurred after 1640, when English captains informed the Puritans they had exhausted their credit in London. Prices for New England exports and land collapsed, and America's first economic crisis (not counting the "starving times") was at hand. Why was the colony indebted if it made all the progress outlined above? First, because developing free economies need prodigious input of capital goods just to build infrastructure, and the faster they grow the bigger their deficit. Second, because New England was chronically short of money. The colonies lacked specie and any mechanism for issuing their own bonds, credit, or paper currency, hence their need to rely on credit from English merchants to finance trade, investments, and even local exchange.

General Court reacted at once and with savvy, putting in place America's first economic stimulus package. To ease the currency shortage, it declared wampum legal tender for all transactions. Probably invented by the Narragansett Indians, wampum consisted of strings of beads carved from white periwinkle or blue quahog shells (the latter were rarer and worth twice as much). The Indians literally "made money" during the winter by cutting, shaping, polishing, drilling, and stringing shells, more or less three hundred to a fathom, then joining strands width-wise to make *wampumpeage* one to five inches wide. As one English trader marveled, "With this wampumpeage they pay tribute, redeeme captives, Satisfy for murders and other Wrongs, purchase peace with their potent neighbors as occasion requires; in a word it answers all occasions with them, as gold and silver doth with us." It was also the medium of exchange in the fur trade and thus "the magnet which drew the beaver out of the interior forests."[39] Once wampum became legal tender in Massachusetts, counterfeiters inevitably tried to palm off adulterated, inferior, or undersized fathoms, but colonists soon learned from the Indians how to avoid being "suckered." By the 1650s, commerce with the Indies grew sufficiently for Spanish pieces of eight and other coins to replace wampum in the colonists' dealings with each other. But it tided them over for a decade.

General Court also met the emergency by reducing New England's dependence on imports through subsidies on production of textiles and iron, and boosting exports through bounties for shipbuilding under strict quality controls. Shipwrights in Salem and Boston, often working for deferred wages, responded with eight seagoing ships, one over four hundred tons, in just five years. New England was still dependent on imported cordage and sails, but its domestic merchant marine helped it through the lean years of the English Civil War and founded an industry that produced 170 ships by century's end in Massachusetts alone. Such precocious mercantilism on the part of General Court was not exactly a declaration of independence, but it loudly proclaimed the Puritan colony was ready and able to become self-reliant.[40]

Demographic and economic momentum also propelled geographical expansion in the form of sub-colonization into what became Rhode Island and Connecticut. The stories of those colonies are usually organized around Roger Williams, Anne Hutchinson, Thomas Hooker, and their respective disciples, portrayed as martyrs to Winthrop's crabbed and tyrannical spirit, champions of toleration and democracy, or both. Some of them *were* some of those things, if only in a seventeenth-century sense. But Massachusetts refugees included two other sorts: inveterate malcontents and hustlers looking for new opportunities.

Roger Williams was both. Born to a London shopkeeper in 1603 and educated at Cambridge under the patronage of the great legal mind Sir Edward Coke, Williams fled from Archbishop Laud to Boston in 1631. Being a Separatist, he promptly ran afoul of the authorities. But after moving to Plymouth Colony he got into trouble again. The Pilgrims, he noted, disgracefully allowed their people to attend Prayer Book services during visits to family in England! Next Williams made for Salem, where he called the whole Massachusetts Bay Colony a fraud since its charter derived from the criminal English crown. He also protested its laws on compulsory church attendance, tithes, and the swearing of oaths. But Williams' worst sin in the eyes of Boston was to win popularity; Salem even elected him pastor! In 1635 he was tried and banished according to Nathaniel Ward's famous principle that a dissenter's liberty is the "liberty to keep away from us." But Williams defiantly stayed until he heard rumors of his arrest, whereupon he sneaked out of Salem with part of his flock and settled near Indians he had befriended on Narragansett Bay.

Another troublemaker who refused to shut up was Anne Hutchinson. Witty, nimble of tongue, and a model goodwife who eventually gave birth to a dozen children, her meditations on the sermons of Boston preacher John Cotton caused her to question whether sanctification (outward piety) was really proof of justification (inward grace). If not, then by implication anyone, even Winthrop, might be deluded or hypocritical: who could tell? She also claimed one must obey when the Holy Spirit spoke to one's conscience even if it meant one must defy church authorities. She claimed such revelations herself. Worst of all, she acquired a following for her Antinomian views. Winthrop, persuaded that the voices she heard were demonic, expelled Hutchinson's coterie. They repaired to Aquidneck Island, while Samuel Gorton and William Coddington, two other dissenters, settled the towns of Warwick and Newport. But contrary to myth, these settlements were not composed only of victimized outcasts forced to trudge through the woods in search of Roger Williams' asylum. Their migrations were minutely planned and financed according to the latest English models of agricultural capitalism. Indeed, most of Rhode Island's first settlers came not on foot but by coastal pinnaces from Cape Cod, and they purposely chose their destinations to maximize production for export from Narragansett Bay.[41]

Williams certainly deserves notice for his enlightened constitution (the Twelve Articles of 1640) which separated church and state, eschewed religious tests, and established assemblies elected by all heads of families (bachelors excluded) and a weak central government. He also protected his creation by obtaining a Parliamentary charter in 1644. But since Rhode Island was damned by its neighbors as a refuge for scoundrels and a model for no one, its true legacy was commercial. Rhode Island attracted a polyglot population of entrepreneurs who grew rich (Williams and Coddington most of all) on bustling trade with the Dutch and the Indians. As early as 1645 a visiting English agrarian expert marveled that Aquidneck "abounds with corne and cattle, especially sheep, ther being nigh a 1000 on the Isle"—due in good part to the absence of wolves, a bane elsewhere in New England. Newport, of course, was destined to be a prosperous entrepôt.[42]

Meanwhile, a more powerful pattern of expansion was set on the Connecticut River, where "Go West, young man" was the motto as early as 1635, and Hooker, John and William Pynchon, and John Winthrop, Jr., exhibited "Yankee" qualities usually pinned on much later New Englanders. Hooker, who sailed on the same ship as John Cotton, was another pastor chased out of England by Archbishop Laud. He settled in Newtown in 1633 and within a year petitioned General Court for permission to head for the Connecticut Valley. Perhaps he was envious of the fact that Cotton proved the more popular preacher. But his petition cited as motives the inadequate, tired farmland of the Charles River, the richness of the Connecticut Valley, the danger posed by Dutch expansion, and "the strong bent of our spirits to remove thither."[43] After another year spent prosecuting Roger Williams, Hooker departed with a hundred settlers and 160 cattle to settle the town of Hart's Ford (Hartford). Simultaneously, William Pynchon, a Yorkshireman who sailed in Winthrop's first contingent, received license to settle twenty-five miles upriver from Hartford. Naming his colony Springfield after his English hometown, Pynchon exploited the lush valley grass to raise horses, sheep, cattle, and pigs for export to Barbados. For seventeen years he expanded his lands, herds, workforce, and commerce, and governed the frontier like a marquess. General Court far away indulged Pynchon's independence until he published a "heretical" memoir, ceremoniously burned on Boston Common in 1652. Pynchon resigned his offices in disgust, retired to England, and left his empire to his son.

John Pynchon, possessed of the same pioneer spirit, was Anglo-America's first cowboy. He learned growing up how difficult it was for even skilled riders to herd cattle running free on pasture or common land. Bulls "bullied" their cows and keepers; stallions injured each other in fights over the mares. But according to English folk wisdom animals stabled for long periods stopped giving milk and might even take sick and die. Hence, colonists slaughtered in late autumn when animals were fattest, depending on cured meat to tide them over until the following year. Pynchon, however, learned from sailors about certain West Indies roughnecks called *boucaniers* (buccaneers, from the French word for smokehouse), famous for their beef *charqui* (jerky). They kept their livestock in barns and stables, the males separated except for breeding or exercise, and fattened their beasts on fodder. So he tried an experiment over the winter of 1654–55. He built barns and fed some of his cattle on Indian corn until they were plump and docile, while those left to forage in the snow grew rangy and mean. When spring arrived he organized a hundred-mile cattle drive along the Old Bay Path to Boston. It is not known how large a profit Pynchon turned because he kept his accounts in code, but the cycle of winter feeding and spring drives became the norm. It also gave a great fillip to horse breeding in the Narragansett (famous for its pacers) and Connecticut valley, which became the breadbasket of New England and grocer to the West Indies. Soon New England exported hundreds of horses per year to the Caribbean in specially designed ships known as "jockeys."[44]

A third Puritan sub-colony at the mouth of the Connecticut River was just one of the many achievements of John Winthrop, Jr. He was an observant enough Puritan and, like Ralegh in the previous century, volunteered to fight in the Calvinist cause in France. He then toured the Mediterranean and Levant until sailing to America to join his father in 1631. But John, Jr., could not stay in one place. He left Boston to found the town of Ipswich in 1633, sailed back to England when his wife and child died the next year, remarried, and returned to New England in 1635 to oversee the new fortress town of Saybrook, Connecticut. By then he decided what this new civilization really required was science and industry. So he crossed the sea yet again to spend the next five years touring Europe in search of the latest technical and medical knowledge. Back in New England in the 1640s, Winthrop, Jr., helped start the Puritans' first foundries and chemical plants (to make gunpowder), then at last settled down to become Connecticut's greatest early statesman, medical doctor, promoter, and land baron.[45]

The lesson of these pocket biographies—and more could be told—is that "declension," a theme often used to interpret early New England, is at best of marginal value.[46] According to that theme the first generation of Puritan migrants was zealous and fixed on a heavenly mission, whereas succeeding generations became more interested in exploiting the resources, land, and trade of the New World for worldly gain: they gradually turned into Yankees. The generalization has some merit in the realm of theology, but obscures the obvious fact that New England could not have expanded and prospered at such a frenetic pace unless a hustling spirit were present at its creation. Perhaps that spirit was an expression of the Puritans' tendency to make the human career itself into a sacrament, the outward sign of an inward grace. But Winthrop and the others also selected New England as the site of their holy experiment because they knew its land, wood, waters, and fish offered *material* opportunity. "Where was ever Ambition baited with greater hopes than here," asked a Puritan promotional tract, "or where ever had Vertue so large a field to reape the fruits of Glory, since any men, who doth goe thither of good quality . . . shall have as much Bounds as may serve for a great Man, whereupon he may build a Towne of his owne, giving it what forme or name he will." That was the optimists' view. Pessimists such as Roger Williams expected "the common trinity of the World—Profit, Preferment, Pleasure" was bound to eclipse the holy trinity until "God Land will be as great a God with us English as God Gold was with the Spaniard."[47]

As in Virginia, New England's rapid expansion and insouciance toward the native peoples made war on the frontier just a matter of time. Only about twenty-five thousand Indians were left in New England after the epidemics, and Wampanoag sachems such as Massasoit were at first pleased to court the English as allies against the more numerous Narragansetts. But depopulation also attracted the notice of the Pequots ("Destroyers"), a belligerent tribe that aimed to monopolize trade on the Connecticut River, exploit or ally with weaker tribes, and block further English expansion. When in 1636 colonists demanded retribution for the apparent murder of two ship captains by Indians, the sagamore Sassacus made it a pretext for war. The infant Connecticut towns could field only ninety militiamen, so the outcome hinged on whether the Narragansetts and Mohegans sided with the Puritans or the Pequots. Both chose the English side, serving Captain John Mason as warriors, trackers, and guides. After raising a siege at Saybrook, Mason attacked in spring 1637, taking a Pequot encampment by surprise. A swift, confused melee ensued that might have gone either way, since the Pequots outnumbered the allies and some forty of the colonists' Narragansett allies were wounded by "friendly fire." At the critical moment Mason set fire to the Indians' dwellings while his soldiers and Indians formed a circle to kill or capture hundreds of braves, women, and children fleeing the flames. An enraged Sassacus later arrived with the rest of the Pequot warriors and might have slaughtered the exhausted militia in turn but for Mason's cool head. He rallied a rear guard that drove off the Pequots with disciplined musket fusillades. When reinforcements arrived a few weeks later from Massachusetts, Mason resumed his offensive and, thanks to his Indian scouts, surrounded the Pequots in a swamp.[48]

Under the peace treaty concluded at Hartford in 1638 the Pequot survivors were melded into the victorious tribes and their lands opened up to Puritan settlement. Thomas Hooker now had the chance, with Massachusetts' approval, to summon a Connecticut General Court and draft his Fundamental Orders of 1639. What makes them interesting is the attempt Hooker made to learn from Massachusetts' brief history. Thus, the Orders forbade governors to hold consecutive terms lest another John Winthrop arise to lord it over the colony (a delightful irony since Connecticut soon repealed "term limits" to allow John Winthrop, Jr., to succeed himself!). They also eliminated the religious test for citizenship, substituting instead the court of public opinion (a delightful novelty since one's neighbors rather than pastors became the judges of character). Though democracy of a kind, it too ensured a large dose of conformity, therefore hypocrisy.

Rounding out the Puritan empire were New Hampshire's first towns and the logging and fishing posts in the Maine District, all pleased to be governed from Boston since the Puritan fathers granted those outlying regions religious liberty (proof positive that they were at least as hungry for timber as souls). Finally, the Puritan colonies of Massachusetts Bay, Plymouth Plantation, New Haven, and Connecticut first displayed Americans' federative genius by forming a New England Confederation in 1643. Admittedly a reaction to the appalling Pequot War, this was still a surprising innovation in light of the jealousy and competition among colonies. What is more, the confederation began to act as a sovereign entity when it concluded treaties of trade and navigation with the French colony of Acadia (Treaty of Boston, 1644) and New Netherlands (Treaty of Hartford, 1650).

Did such behavior indicate the colonists were beginning to think of themselves as "Americans"? No, that would be a severe anticipation. But by 1650 it was surely the case that two English societies in America (the Chesapeake and New England, each with about twenty-two thousand settlers) and one multiethnic society (New Netherlands, with about four thousand people) were beginning to define their interests independently of their mother countries' laws, churches, and merchants. New England had no use for the crown and even stood aloof from Cromwell's Commonwealth. Virginia had escaped its founding company and refused to recognize the authority of Cromwell's Long Parliament. Maryland was torn between a Catholic proprietor and a dissenting populace, both anathema to the Anglican royal establishment. New Netherlands residents opposed both English regimes as well as their own chartered company. All the colonies engaged in illegal commerce with the West Indies and ignored metropolitan laws that impinged on their "liberties." To be sure, such acts might be interpreted as a function of England's chaotic politics rather than colonial self-consciousness. But that was certainly not the case after Parliament executed King Charles I and Cromwell undertook to bring the colonies to heel.

History texts often associate the economic model of mercantilism with monarchies and free enterprise with the bourgeoisie, Protestantism, and republics. In the English case almost the reverse was true. A market economy grew up with the Tudors, while colonization was a private initiative enjoying little more than the crown's blessing. The first attempts to impose mercantilist monopolies, restrictions, and taxes, by contrast, were made by Cromwell's republic. In the Declaratory Act of 1650, Parliament asserted its total supremacy over colonies that "are and ought to be subordinate to and dependent upon England." It pronounced them "subject to such laws, orders and regulations as are or shall be made by the parliament of England" *even if* such laws contradicted a colony's privileges under its charter. The act prohibited all trade whatsoever with "rebellious" colonies such as Virginia and Maryland whose governors recognized the Stuart pretender. Finally, the act banned all colonial commerce with foreign ships not licensed by the English government (especially Dutchmen hoping to exploit England's Civil War to take over the tobacco trade). A Navigation Act followed in 1651 in which Parliament stipulated all goods shipped to England or her colonies must be carried in English bottoms.

To write "in all the colonies there was a failure to observe this act" is a wonderful understatement.[49] The colonists had long since learned (if they needed to learn) to be scofflaws. Moreover, the New England Confederation had just made that free trade treaty with New Netherlands, while Virginians were not about sit on their hogsheads of tobacco just because the ship on the river flew the wrong flag. So Massachusetts, Rhode Island, and Connecticut positively forbade their inhabitants to *obey* the Navigation Acts, while in 1660 Virginia legalized what Parliament deemed to be smuggling by concluding its own trade agreement with the Dutch. These episodes were short-lived and only the first chapter in a very long story. But it is worthwhile to note, at that early date, how the American colonists' duly constituted authorities nullified great acts of Parliament and dared London to do something about it. Those were the true "proto-Americans."

# BARBADIANS, YORKERS, AND QUAKERS
## *The Carolinas, Middle Colonies, and New England, 1660–1689*

*A*merican colonists wisely remained aloof from the English Civil War, but they followed its twists and turns with keen interest. One way or another its outcome was bound to alter the political, legal, economic, and religious character of the entire empire. Had King Charles I and Archbishop Laud become English equivalents of Louis XIII and Cardinal Richelieu, who established royal absolutism in France, then statutory law would doubtless have rolled back Common Law, the Anglican Church would have been established everywhere, and overseas colonies would have faced the choice of becoming royal satrapies or else bidding for independence long before they were strong enough to prevail. Nor was English absolutism as unlikely as two centuries of Whig (Liberal) historians subsequently assumed. Centralized royal administration was the *progressive* trend in the early seventeenth century as monarchs attempted to eradicate the vestiges of feudalism in their realms. The Stuarts successfully expanded the system of arbitrary courts such as the infamous Star Chamber begun by Henry VII. Mercantilism was the hot new economic theory, and High Church (more Catholic) practices were increasingly popular among Oxford and Cambridge seminarians. Puritanism seemed the wave of the past. Even the make-up of Parliament in 1639 revealed a striking generational gap between the youthful king's party and the relatively older opposition. Had Charles managed to stave off confrontation with Parliament for just another decade or so, the Great Rebellion or English Civil War might not have happened.[1]

Instead, the Stuarts bungled their way to ruin because James I and his son Charles I did not grasp the political sea-change conjured by their Tudor predecessors. In order to make and defend the Reformation, Henry VIII and his daughter Elizabeth appealed directly to public opinion, governed "in" Parliament rather than above or against it, and trumpeted the monarchy as chief protector of the public good.[2] The Stuarts, by contrast, showed little interest in politicking at Westminster or in the country, incurred public suspicion by flirting with Spain and France, and tried vainly to impose religious conformity. When Charles I proceeded to botch two military campaigns in rebellious Scotland, he was forced to summon Parliament in hopes of raising new revenues. Clashes over representation, religion, money, and the military escalated until Parliament passed (by a mere eleven-vote majority) the Grand Remonstrance of 1641, whose long list of grievances against royal abuses inspired Thomas Jefferson 135 years later. When at length Charles called out his soldiers, Parliament raised its own army in 1642.

The Parliamentary cause triumphed, but far from upholding Common Law and the rights of Englishmen, the victorious general Oliver Cromwell trod them underfoot in the name of natural law as ordained by a Puritan God. A king captured and executed for treason; Parliament purged of all but Erastian Presbyterians; freedom of conscience extinguished for all but a handful of acceptable sects; heresy and adultery made capital crimes; Scotland and Ireland brutally crushed; England divided into eleven military governments: such were the fruits of millenarian revolution. But regicide and Commonwealth did not lack for apologists. Most prominent was James Harrington, whose *The Commonwealth of Oceana, The Excellency of a Free State* (1656) drafted a blueprint for republicanism ("the good old cause") in the English-speaking world. As Harrington saw it, the Rebellion was not at all like the medieval conflicts between the crown and barons in Parliament because feudalism itself had disappeared. England was now a country in which people owned their own land, weapons, and persons, where (as he put it) "king people" were sovereign. Harrington imagined a republic of free citizens exhibiting both the classical civic virtues venerated in ancient Rome and Renaissance Italy, and the Christian virtues to which only a propertied, hence morally free, people could aspire. That vision, born of deep reflection on the meaning of history, failed in its day. But it helped to persuade a later generation across the sea that the only proper regime for a free, English, and Protestant people was a republic founded on virtue and property.[3]

By the time the self-styled Lord Protector of the Commonwealth died in 1658, the British people were heartily sick of Cromwellian war, persecution, and prudishness. A newly convened Parliament in 1660 invited the dead king's oldest son to take up his throne. Presbyterians knew this meant re-establishment of the Anglican church, but once again hoped a Stuart might tolerate them. Instead, Charles II and his "Cavalier Parliament" banned all but Anglicans from holding office while imposing the 39 Articles and 1662 Book of Common Prayer on all clergy. Non-Conformists and Dissenters of all sorts were forbidden even to assemble in numbers greater than five. They were also banned from professions such as law, education, and politics. That, more than the famed Protestant ethic, may explain why so many Dissenters went into business. Catholics fared no better. In the spooky year of 1666 ("666" being the mark of the beast in the Biblical book of Revelation), Britain suffered a recurrence of plague and London was consumed by a fire widely attributed to Catholic arsonists. Twelve years later the outrageous liar Titus Oates stirred up an even greater panic by swearing to evidence of a Popish Plot to assassinate the king. Shopkeepers boarded their doors, constables stretched chains across streets against mobs, neighbors spied and informed on each other, twelve hundred people suspected of Jesuit sympathies were prosecuted in London, and another Test Act banned Catholics from public life.[4] In sum, politics under the Stuart Restoration continued to display a paranoid style even as the government pursued science, exploration, commerce, and colonial expansion with a vigor recalling Elizabethan times. Both the paranoia and vigor caused a crisis of authority in the American colonies that finally ended, against all expectation, in a new equilibrium.

The restored English king could well have been dubbed Charles the Penniless. He returned from exile without means even to keep up royal appearances, much less reward those who had stuck with him during the interregnum. So he revived the tactic pioneered by Henry VII, which was to squeeze the profits of merchants. Charles set up councils for trade and foreign plantations, consolidated in 1675 into a committee called the Lords of Trade. Their job was to enforce new Navigation Acts of 1660, 1663, and 1673, which granted English ships a monopoly of all imperial trade, required most foreign goods bound for the colonies to pay duties in English ports first, and even taxed intra-colonial cargoes to induce Americans to "buy English" instead. New Englanders above all hated the impositions, but beginning in 1671 the crown stationed customs officials in American ports and obliged colonial governors to assist them. Not surprisingly, many colonial merchants took to smuggling, bribes, and fraudulent bookkeeping, while governors tried to make a good show of enforcing statutes contrary to their own constituents' welfare. Finally, insofar as the Navigation Acts either fostered or harmed this or that sector in the English economy, they spawned a bevy of lobbies eager to bribe members of Parliament to pass or annul laws affecting their trade. Since colonial trade more than doubled from £800,000 to £1,750,000 per year between 1660 and 1690, royal revenues rose, but so did Americans' contempt for laws they had no hand in making.[5]

Yet England's New World empire also expanded rapidly under Charles II because one of his methods of paying off debts of gratitude or cash was to parcel out the still vacant properties remaining on his portion of the colonial Monopoly board. The first and largest such grant embraced the buffer zone between Virginia and Florida. Only a few Virginians had trickled into the Albemarle Sound region south of the Dismal Swamp, and they were such ruffians that planter William Byrd of Westover called the place Lubberland, the "Rhode Island" of the Chesapeake. The Outer Banks, a maze of hiding places and tricky channels sheltered from the sea, became mainland North America's premier haven for pirates. At the southern extreme of the buffer zone the French tried to plant a mission near the Savannah River, but were chased off by Spaniards, who were chased off in turn by Indians in 1661. Then Virginia's Governor Berkeley, Anthony Ashley Cooper, president of the king's council for foreign plantations, and John Colleton, a planter from Barbados, formed a consortium. Their plan was to fill the void with a new colonial province, dubbed Carolina to flatter the king. In 1663 they received, together with five other investors, a royal grant modeled on that of Maryland. The proprietors enjoyed full feudal rights to American land between 36 degrees 30 minutes and 31 degrees (soon extended to 29 degrees to include Spanish St. Augustine, if they could conquer it). Their first two expeditions went to Cape Fear in northern Carolina, but the sandy soil and a hurricane discouraged the colonists. Some sailed off to New England; others made their way overland to Virginia. So Cooper and his house intellectual, John Locke (yes, that Locke), turned the proprietors' eyes to South Carolina, assembling a third company of colonists from England, Bermuda, and most important of all Barbados.

The English colony on that sub-tropical island ninety miles east of the Antilles chain dated from 1627 and grew rapidly during the Puritan Great Migration. Numbering about 9,000 whites in 1640, Barbados grew to 22,000 whites plus 33,000 enslaved Africans by 1660. But the total human flow to Barbados may have reached 150,000 over the century. What happened to the missing persons? Many returned to England with a new appreciation for its green hills and cold rain, but most died of yellow fever or other diseases, poisonous vermin, malnutrition, exhaustion, or violence both domestic and foreign. Suffice it to say the British West Indies' only seventeenth-century celebrity was the infamous pirate Henry Morgan. Immigrants to Barbados were also 95 percent male, hence what offspring they had were overwhelmingly mulatto. At first planters tried to grow tobacco there, relying on white indentures. By the 1640s they had learned sugar cane was their true money crop and Africa their best source of labor.[6]

Much more will be said about slavery in the context of the mainland colonies, but it first took firm root in the West Indies for two generic reasons and one local motive. The generic ones explain how true-born Englishmen, jealous of their own liberties, could have so little regard for those of others. The "others" quite simply had no rights in English eyes because they were *not* true-born Englishmen, thus had no standing under Common Law. It may seem ironic that the least arbitrary legal system in Europe entertained the most discriminatory judgments, but it is not. Common Law was a product of centuries of legal renderings by courts that appealed to precedent and only warily adjusted to novel conditions. Universal human rights had no place in English jurisprudence save to some degree in the church's curtailed jurisdiction. Thus, Englishmen had the right to keep Africans in bondage for the simple reason no other Englishmen had the right to forbid it. In the Spanish and Portuguese empires clergymen such as Bartolomé de las Casas agitated for humane treatment of Indians and Africans (especially if baptized), and courts occasionally entertained suits from aggrieved servants—but not in the English empire.

A second generic reason for English slaveholding was racial. Historians have debated at length whether the institution of slavery caused (or magnified) racism or whether *a priori* racism caused (or justified) slavery. Whatever the case, seventeenth-century English people associated blackness with barbarism and evil, displaying no qualms about the purchase of African slaves.[7] Protected by law and encouraged by prejudice, slavery thus became a matter of economics alone. Hence the local motive: West Indian planters could not induce white indentured servants to sweat and risk death chopping cane in the jungle, nor could paid labor compete with the slave gangs already employed on French and Dutch islands. So England's West Indian colonies came to depend on slavery fifty years earlier than the Chesapeake. In fact, so stratified did crowded Barbados become that just 7 percent of its whites came to own over half the island's acres and slaves. That left a large population of frustrated small planters, younger sons, artisans, and women looking for ways to move up or else out. When Cooper's agents arrived to tout the limitless land and comparatively temperate climate of Carolina, first twenty, then hundreds of Barbadians leaped at the chance.[8]

England's first colonial promoters were mostly merchant adventurers arguing the worth of their ventures to the crown. Ashley Cooper, Earl of Shaftesbury after 1672, epitomized a new sort of promoter: a courtier exploiting his political clout with the crown to increase his own worth. So boldly did Cooper stand out among the other Machiavellians of Charles II's "merrie reign" that John Dryden named him "For close designs and crooked counsels fit / Sagacious, bold, and turbulent of wit." One of Cooper's standard ploys was to procure female companionship for toadies and co-conspirators (a practice *de rigueur* in English and American politics ever since). Even the king teased him for being "the greatest whoremaster in England." In time, Cooper would obtain the exalted post of Lord Chancellor only to end his life in exile for opposing the royal succession of James II. But he earned the immortality he craved through a colony planted at the spot where, South Carolinians joke, the Ashley and Cooper Rivers merge to form the Atlantic Ocean.[9]

It turned out differently than Cooper expected, however, because men who use devious means, even (or especially) for utopian ends, have no defense against those who use devious means to confound them. For all his corrupt traits, Cooper put Locke to work on Fundamental Constitutions of Carolina (1669) meant to establish the perfect mix of authority, property, and liberty imagined by Harrington in his *Oceana*. Two-fifths of all Carolina land was to endow a hereditary nobility and three-fifths to be distributed among commoners, thereby fashioning a balance between aristocracy and democracy. The eight "sovereign" proprietors were to appoint the governor and his council. But they were empowered only to propose laws to a popularly elected assembly. Locke's scheme also provided for local courts with grand and petit juries, but in a clause that reflected the era's contempt for lawyers (and the proprietors' desire to limit liability), monetary pleas were forbidden. These Fundamental Constitutions have often been mocked as absurd and unworkable. They were unworkable, but by no means absurd. Rather, they represented the most enlightened political thought of the post-Cromwellian era. They included shrewd, commercial incentives as well, including an established church for Anglicans, toleration for Non-Conformists, land for all who paid passage for settlers, voting rights for all freeholders, and impartial selection of juries by children drawing names from a hat. In several respects Carolina was more liberal than any colony save Rhode Island. But the proprietors also stipulated in writing the right to hold slaves as chattel property.

Ashley's Barbadian recruits were told to shun northern Carolina in favor of the Port Royal region. But Captain John West was loath to debark "in the very chops of the Spaniards," choosing instead the Kiawah (renamed Ashley) River where friendly Indians sought European help against the Savannah River's bellicose Westo tribe. So West and Governor William Sayle founded the first Charles Town, sixty-five miles upstream, in April 1670. Thanks to its inland location and immediate planting of food the colony suffered little morbidity. But its hustles began the moment old Sayle died. Sir John Yeamans, his successor as governor, arrived from Barbados determined "to convert all things to his private profit." The disgusted proprietors deposed him in 1674 in favor of Captain West, whereupon a running fight began between the proprietors and the Barbadians staking out their plantations along the banks of Goose Creek. The latter espoused republican principles and demanded more power for the elected assembly. In fact, they wanted no laws at all that they were bound to respect. The governor's council tried to enforce land provisions; the Goose Creek Men squatted wherever they wished. The governor tried to keep peace with Indians; the Barbadians exterminated the Westos in order to grab the deerskin trade. The proprietors tried to honor the Navigation Acts; Goose Creek encouraged smuggling and piracy.

Despite or because of the scoffing of laws the colony flourished. In 1679 the capital was relocated to the magnificent site of present-day Charleston at the tip of the peninsula between the Ashley and Cooper Rivers. Hundreds of religious dissenters from England, Scotland, and France (where Louis XIV would expel all the Huguenots in 1685) responded to the proprietors' hype about "The Fertility of the Earth and Waters; and the great Pleasure and Profit" awaiting the emigrant to fair Carolina. One flyer even anticipated the sexual subtexts of twentieth-century advertising by claiming the Carolina air made men "apparently more lightsome, more prone, and more able to all Youthful Exercises, than in England, the Women are very Fruitful, and the Children have fresh Sanguine Complexions."[10]

The mostly Calvinist newcomers to Charleston were soon at loggerheads with the Goose Creek Men whose leader they described as a "Metchivell Hobs and Lucifer" with the "soul of a mosquito." But the Barbadians gradually wore down resistance to their version of popular government. The brother of one proprietor, Governor James Colleton, was harried out of the colony. Seth Sothell found as governor he could not get anything done, such as road and pier construction or regulation of Indian trade, except on the sufferance of his fellow Barbadians. So he governed through bribery, arbitrary arrests, and connivance in piracy until his fellow proprietors sacked him. Finally, in 1691, the would-be "sovereigns" gave up on Locke's constitution, opened the governor's council to elected members, and expanded the powers of the lower assembly.[11]

If one sees the Fundamental Constitutions as authoritarian it is easy to depict the struggle against them as proto-democratic. But Locke was far more concerned with individual rights under a rule of law than were the Barbadian populists. Their notion of government reduced it to machine politics, intimidation, nullification, and plunder masquerading as freedom. Needless to add, they also made South Carolina the only American colony dependent from its inception on chattel slavery. It was a stunning success. Beginning in 1690 the planters discovered their likeliest cash crop was rice, which flourished in the aqueous Low Country and which their own slaves already knew how to plant, tend, and harvest. Corn, livestock, dairy products, and timber were soon in rich supply for local consumption, not to mention shrimp, crayfish, crabs, and other delicacies, while exports of rice and deerskins made Charleston the premier port on the southern seaboard. By 1700 more than sixteen thousand acres of land had been sold. Plantation houses began to appear on riverbanks from the Savannah to the Santee, and elegant townhouses on the Charleston strand where the children of squirrely Barbadians turned into ladies and gentlemen.[12]

One year after Charles II issued the grant to found Carolina he gave away his richest colonial plum—richest because it was already partly developed at others' expense. The plum was Stuyvesant's New Netherlands empire; the recipient the king's brother James, Duke of York. Now, England's merchants had long ago lost patience with Dutch interloping in the American trade, and New Netherlands was an especially obnoxious trespass on what the English considered their slice of America. So no sooner did the Netherlands finally win formal independence from Spain in 1648 than Cromwell began treating England's old Protestant ally as a rival. So much for Puritan solidarity, one may smirk: trade and empire trump faith once again. But the English characteristically justified their first war against the Netherlands in 1652–54 by arguing that the *Dutch* forfeited their Protestant, republican virtue by trading with Spaniards instead of preying on them. That made them "allies of the Whore of Babylon."[13] After the Stuart Restoration the crown's Council on Foreign Plantations cited Dutch violations of the Navigation Acts to justify a second war against the Netherlands in 1664.

The Duke of York, Lord High Admiral of the Royal Navy, was no mean strategist.[14] He knew New Amsterdam's defenses were feeble, the Dutch company unpopular, and the English had a fifth column among Puritan subcolonists on Long Island and the Hudson River. So after his brother granted him a proprietary estate to the entire region between the Connecticut and Delaware Rivers (with Maine, Nantucket, and Martha's Vineyard tossed in as *hors d'oeuvres*) he ordered Colonel Richard Nicolls to invade New Netherlands with four ships and four hundred soldiers. Nicolls began the campaign with some psychological warfare in the form of a promise to honor the rights and property of the people of New Amsterdam. Then he landed on Long Island and marched toward Breucklyn (Brooklyn). Stuyvesant bluffed and blustered before his town council, but the Dutch burghers only puffed on their pipes and looked to their pocketbooks. In September 1664, New Amsterdam was surrendered and rechristened New York.

James might, if he wished, have ruled as an absolute viceroy. Instead, he upheld the freedom of conscience allowed by the Dutch, respected existing property rights, allowed New York City self-government, and opened new lands to settlers. Nicolls, his first governor, carried out this program with tact, intelligence, and a feel for public relations (one of his initiatives was to establish America's first race track complete with pari-mutuel betting). However, the old enemies of the Hudson River colony—Indians, French, and New England Puritans—interrupted this peaceful transition in serial fashion. In 1666 French Canadians invaded the Mohawk Valley in a bid to discipline the Iroquois and monopolize the fur trade, thereby inaugurating an on-again, off-again border war that lasted a century. After 1668 Connecticut and Massachusetts challenged the duke's boundaries, harassing all "Yorkers" who contested land between the Connecticut and Hudson Rivers. Rhode Island laid claim to islands awarded to James. The Maryland proprietors filed suit challenging the duke's southern boundary. The Swedes on the Delaware rebelled. The Puritans on Long Island refused to pay taxes without representation. Worst of all, a third war with the Netherlands brought a Dutch fleet to the East River in 1672, whereupon New York became New Amsterdam again for a year and a half. When peace restored the colony to England, James got tough, naming as governor Sir Edmund Andros, a stern career soldier and Stuart loyalist. By all accounts Andros was that rare thing, an obedient, honest man under authority, which is why his presence sparked conflicts—analogous to those in Carolina—between the proprietorship and all manner of political, commercial, ethnic, and religious factions. So great was the turmoil New York soon acquired a reputation for being ungovernable. "Am sure if the Roman Catholicks have a place of purgatory," wrote a later governor, "its not soe bad as [this] place under my Lords Circumstance."[15]

Nonetheless the colony attracted numerous Britons, New Englanders, and Huguenots (thus New Rochelle) looking for a place to get rich and worship freely, or just to get rich. New English patroons received grand estates on the Hudson from their friend the duke. Others, such as the notorious Robert Livingston, hustled to take over existing estates. His father, a Scots Presbyterian pastor, quit Britain for Rotterdam when the Stuarts returned. So Robert Livingston grew up fluent in Dutch and, thanks to an apprenticeship in a countinghouse, versed in sharp business practices. In 1674 he decided to seek his fortune in America, briefly in Boston, then in Albany, center of the lucrative fur trade. He was just twenty years old and his pockets were empty. But Livingston made himself indispensable as a "linguister" (interpreter) helping to negotiate deals in English, Dutch, and Iroquois. Winning appointment as secretary to the governor's Indian commission and clerk of the Albany court, Livingston cut deals on his own account that multiplied many times his official salaries. But money did not begin to sate this gogetter's ambition, which was to become a patroon.

So the smart, handsome, red-headed Livingston practiced in the wilderness the ancient art of social climbing. But how could a lowborn Scottish clerk, however talented or newly rich, move among the haughty Hudson Valley patroons? The first goal was access to their households, which Livingston accomplished when Nicolas Van Rensselaer appointed him family clerk in 1675.

The second step was to woo surreptitiously the wife of his own employer. Legend has it when Livingston was summoned to the family yacht lying at anchor the aged and ill Rensselaer rose from his deathbed to croak: "Anyone but you, for you will marry my widow!" Sure enough, the twenty-two-year-old Alida Van Rensselaer, *née* Schuyler, wed Livingston in 1679 as soon as her year of mourning was over. If anything, the other *jonkheers* now resented Livingston more than before, but watched helplessly while he accumulated, through marriage, purchase, and ambiguous gubernatorial grants which he drafted himself, some 160,000 acres. At the center of the colony's politics, commerce, and Indian diplomacy for fifty years, Livingston propelled himself through perseverance and grit to the pinnacle of New York society. He was even elected speaker of the assembly. Thanks to the six surviving children Alida bore him, he also fathered a dynasty.[16]

For every high-roller who came, saw, and conquered New York, hundreds of industrious farmers settled in the Hudson Valley or Long Island to produce cereals, vegetables, and cheese for export. The fur trade made fortunes for those deft, rugged, and ruthless enough to charm the Iroquois while dodging the French and each other. New York City grew ever busier and more cosmopolitan, the only American port with close ties to the West Indies, Iberia, France, the Low Countries, and England. Thanks to its geographical location, it was also an ideal entrepôt for commerce among New England, the Mohawk Valley, Canada, the Delaware, and the Chesapeake. So while Livingston did manage to become a patroon, New York was the first spot in America where a man could aspire to status and wealth without large holdings in land.[17]

If proprietor James Stuart and Governor Andros were vexed by the "factious" Yorkers, they were driven to distraction by their subjects across the Hudson in New Jersey. At the start, in 1664, James sub-contracted the development of East and West Jersey to two more Stuart loyalists. The first, Sir George Carteret, purchased four hundred thousand acres from Indians, swamped the Dutchmen at Bergen and Elizabethtown with New England sub-colonists, and dispatched his cousin Philip Carteret to govern them and collect their quit rents. The assiduous Puritans fulfilled the Carterets' expectations by founding new towns all over the Meadowlands, including Piscataway, Middletown, Shrewsbury, and an intensely pious community called Newark. They also confounded their landlords by refusing to pay quit rents on the grounds they were denied the elected self-government New Englanders considered their birthright. Jerseyites also got the Carterets in trouble by sneaking ship cargoes past the royal customs house in New York

Harbor. Meanwhile, Lord John Berkeley, the second Jersey proprietor, found himself strapped due to some other bad investments, and in any case loathed having to deal with self-righteous deadbeats as tenants. So he sold the western portion of Jersey in 1674 to the prominent Quaker, Edward Byllynge, who sold it in turn to three other Quakers eager to promote a righteous colonial experiment under "Laws, Concessions, and Agreements" drafted back in 1665.

Matters grew still more complicated when, after the brief Dutch reconquest, the crown reaffirmed the Duke of York's charter in language that seemed to revoke the Carterets' rights. So New York's stolid Governor Andros asserted his own authority over Jersey, seized ships bound for Elizabethtown, and even arrested Philip Carteret on charges of smuggling and resisting lawful authority. Manhattan jurors, who loved a smuggler, thrice nullified the prosecution. But since all Yorkers agreed they should rule New Jersey, the jury also ordered Carteret to cease and desist from exerting authority. Only the Duke of York himself could save New Jersey now. For reasons of court politics he did so in 1680 by briefly recalling Andros and conceding the rights of the original Jersey proprietors. Philip Carteret beamed. Then he, too, had the rug pulled from under him when his cousin George died in debt. His estate lawyers, needing to liquidate, sold his stake in East Jersey to a new company dominated by Quakers. They in turn named a Quaker attorney, Thomas Rudyard, to the post of deputy governor with orders to grant the colony all the rights contained in the "Laws, Concessions, and Agreements" in force in *West* Jersey. The Concessions, as they were called, surpassed even the liberal Rhode Island and Carolina codes by mandating freedom of religion, trial by jury, election of judges, easy purchase of land, an elected assembly with power over taxation, and an elected executive commission.[18]

Although conflicts between Jersey's proprietors and people persisted, the liberality of its Quaker regime might have earned it a central place in the story of American self-government. The reason New Jersey in fact gets only passing mention in most history books is due to the fact that one of those "three other Quakers" who purchased West Jersey was named William Penn. His creation on the opposite bank of the Delaware River overshadowed West Jersey as much or more than New York overshadowed East Jersey.

Not only was Penn made into a figurative marble man by numerous Quaker or admiring non-Quaker biographers, his countenance literally presides over his commonwealth from the peak of Philadelphia's late-nineteenth-century City Hall. Biographies tell how Penn, born in London in 1644 to the wife of an English admiral, was expected to grow up a good Anglican royalist. But the boy happened to hear one of the first itinerant preachers of the Society of Friends (nicknamed Quakers) at his father's Irish estate. He dissolved into tears. Fluent in Greek and Latin, young William was also expected to shine at Oxford. But his refusal to honor its Anglican rituals led to his being "sent down" at age seventeen. The frustrated admiral next tried to break his boy of such unnatural piety by leading him into temptation on a grand tour of the continent. But William forsook fleshpots in favor of a French Calvinist college. Finally, his father obliged him to read for the law at Lincoln's Inn. But that, too, came to nought when London's 1666 fire forced him home to Ireland. Providentially, he encountered there the same Quaker preacher as before, this time accepting his challenge to practice a faith that overcomes the world rather than being overcome by it. Penn's Quakerism landed him four times in prison, but far from recanting he composed some forty-two books in his sect's defense, most prominently *The Great Case of Liberty of Conscience Once More Briefly Debated and Defended by the Authority of Reason, Scripture, and Antiquity* (1671). He also married, sired four babies (only one of whom survived infancy), and thanks to his father's prominence found friends and protectors in high places. At last Penn found his ultimate calling in a "holy experiment." He would plant a Quaker colony in America devoted to freedom of conscience. Thanks to his friendship with James, Duke of York, he obtained a charter for Pennsylvania in 1681, forever shaping the course of American history.

That heroic account, accurate as far as it goes, fails to explain why Charles II and his brother James chose to indulge the Quakers, whose views could not have been more hostile to their own views and interests. It portrays Penn as an innocent, whereas he must have done some heavy politicking to gain title to a New World empire under the noses of suspicious royal officials and competing colonial promoters. Above all, it makes Penn's father a mere stumbling block to be overcome by his son's stalwart faith. The truth was far more complex.[19]

The father, Sir William Penn, was not only a military leader of daring and skill, he was a political survivor of the first order. When the English Civil War broke out he faced the usual dilemma confronting patriotic generals and admirals when their old regimes topple. Initially he chose Parliament's side and rose rapidly to command during the time young William was born. But as Cromwell's rebellion turned increasingly radical Admiral Penn secretly trimmed his sails. In 1648, suspected of secret contacts with the Stuarts, he even landed in the Tower of London for a spell. Rehabilitated at the start of the first Dutch war in 1652, he fought with distinction again, but evidently considered defecting with his entire fleet to the pretender in exile, Charles II. Cromwell dispatched him to the West Indies (most likely to be rid of him) where he captured the sugar island of Jamaica, only to be imprisoned again upon his return. After the Restoration the admiral's secret contacts with the royal camp bore fruit. Charles knighted him and James named him his naval commander during the second Dutch war. But even though Sir William was rarely at home during these decades, he nonetheless paid loving attention to his son's education and prospects. He also taught him by example how to endure persecution and play both sides of the street in pursuit of higher loyalties. In the father's case, those were patriotism and the navy; in the son's case, patriotism and faith. William *père*, as he lay on his deathbed in 1670, asked the royal Stuarts to look after his dissident son's welfare. William *fils*, in gratitude, named Pennsylvania after his father.

Still, a promise to show royal favor to Penn hardly required Charles II to bestow on him lands as extensive as England itself. Nor is it obvious why James, the Catholic heir to the throne, went out of his way to bless George Fox's Quaker disciples. They were, after all, fiercely egalitarian, opposed to monarchy and nobility, and pacifist almost to the point of treason. The Friends abominated established churches, dispensing in their own meetings with clergy, liturgy, hymns, even preaching. Though influenced by the German Pietist movement, they went far beyond Martin Luther's "priesthood of all believers" to assert every man and, significantly, every woman, harbored the Holy Spirit within. Thus, all human beings might converse with, even speak for, God, if they kindled their inner light and knew "peace at the center." It may not be too wild to suggest Quakers were Protestant equivalents of the gentle Franciscans. But just as Catholic states could never have tolerated the spread of Franciscan ideas among the *general public*, neither could an Anglican state tolerate the dissemination of Quaker ideas.

That suggests the Stuarts might have granted the charter for Pennsylvania just to lure Quakers across the ocean. But there is no evidence for that motive. In any case, the exodus did not dissuade Friends from continuing to proselytize throughout Britain. A second theory, popular perhaps because cynical, has Charles granting Pennsylvania in lieu of a £16,000 gambling debt owed to Penn's father's estate. There is no hard evidence for that motive either. What is more, the Stuart treasury owed so much more to so many creditors it seems unlikely the king would part with such a great asset for that sum. Still others suggest Penn whisked his petition for a charter through government channels without anyone taking much notice. In fact, the Lords of Trade and the other concerned agencies studied his petition for four months, carefully adding to it detailed restrictions protecting the interests of the crown, merchants, and the Anglican church. What one is left with is the prosaic explanation: while Penn's ties to the royal family no doubt helped grease the skids, issuing the charter for Pennsylvania was a premeditated act of statecraft. First, a strong colony on the Delaware would surely be of strategic and commercial value to the empire. Second, putting a proprietor in charge of it kept the cost of developing the new colony off the government's books. Third, naming Penn the proprietor ensured James, proprietor of New York, a friendly neighbor. So what to Quakers seemed providential also made sense in worldly ways.[20]

Penn's 1681 charter made him sole proprietor of all land extending five degrees of longitude west of the Delaware River, bounded on the north by the 43rd parallel, on the south by an arc twelve miles above Newcastle, Delaware. Westward from there, the southern boundary of Pennsylvania overlapped with Maryland's claim, prompting the famous dispute not settled until the survey by Mason and Dixon in 1760. Penn tapped wealthy Quaker merchants and his own inheritance to finance the most elaborate colonial preparations to date. They paid off handsomely for Quakers such as Thomas Holme. He purchased a large tract in the planned capital of Philadelphia, then sailed over to survey the town and plot infrastructure certain to make his property's value soar. Holme went to work four miles above the confluence of the Schuylkill and Delaware Rivers, sketching out a vast grid of streets to be centered halfway between the rivers. More than a century passed before the city grew the fourteen blocks inland to Broad Street, but Holme's plan suggested Philadelphia was destined for greatness, thus achieving the speculator's principal task.

Penn arrived in 1682 on one of eighteen large ships bearing gentry, artisans, yeomen, and sailors, the vanguard of eleven thousand settlers who came the first decade alone. That no immediate conflict with Indians ensued was due in good part to Penn's courtship of them through feasts, entertainments, gift-giving, trade for furs and food, and formal purchases of land. Penn also left the holdover Swedes and Dutch in possession, even though they had staked out many coveted riverfront lots. Thanks to these wise preparations the peopling of Pennsylvania was an orderly land rush. Quakers were Penn's natural constituency, of course. But the promise of religious freedom helped his agents in France and the Rhineland lure Huguenots and German Pietists. As early as 1683 Francis Daniel Pastorius purchased fifteen thousand acres on which to build Germantown for his company of Rhenish Quakers and Mennonites. An influx of Welshmen left their place-names all over Pennsylvania's first counties. Scots-Irish, Swedes, and Dutch added to an ethnic mix as cosmopolitan as New York's. But religious liberty alone did not spark the rush. What closed the deal was the promise of good soil, cheap land, plentiful wood (hence *sylvania*) the fur trade, a fine harbor, and a central location rivaling that of New York—all of which Penn stressed in his promotional tract, *Some Account of the Province of Pennsilvania.*

Moreover, it would be wrong to laud Pennsylvania for its diversity without noting the resulting society was a mixture more than a solution. The Welsh and Germans, for instance, preferred to huddle together, maintain their customs and languages, and govern themselves to the extent permitted. Indeed, their brokers insisted their purchases be contiguous blocks far removed from English communities. Assimilation gradually occurred over generations, but was not the intent of Quakers or foreigners. On the contrary, Anglicans and Presby-terians despised the proprietorship and the Quaker elite. Quakers looked down on everyone else, expecting them to defer to their rule. Germans shunned all English ways. But grudging toleration prevailed because it proved a commer-cial boon. Just look, Penn wrote, at the Netherlands, a tiny bog whose people made it the wealthiest spot on the globe because they worked free from fear of expropriation.[21]

Penn was as fastidious as Cooper and Locke in his pursuit of the perfect constitution. He rejected no less than thirteen drafts before declaring himself satisfied with his "frame of the government." It began by quoting St. Paul: "The powers that be are ordained of God: whosoever resisteth the power, resisteth the ordinance of God." But unlike John Winthrop, for instance, Penn displayed no certainty about which political party or philosophical school claimed God as a member. Monarchy, aristocracy, and democracy all had their merits and drawbacks, the success of each depending on the rule of law and willing adherence of the people. "Governments, like clocks, go from the motion men give to them, and as governments are made and moved by men, so by them they are ruined too." To this conflation of theology and physics Penn added lessons from history taught by Harrington, Locke, and perhaps Thomas Hobbes. He came up in the end with a hybrid designed to encourage the best in human nature while checking the worst. The frame of government thus provided for two elected houses: the upper to propose laws; the lower to vote on them and administer justice. The franchise was broad, all trials were by jury, and prisons were meant to rehabilitate rather than punish. Education was to be universal and religion a matter of personal conscience for all who believed in "the one Almighty and eternal God."[22]

Pennsylvania was an instant success, especially for the Free Society of Traders who brought with them to Philadelphia a hefty stock of capital and a trans-Atlantic network of Quaker business connections. Within thirty-six *months* they began taking fur exports away from the Hudson and shipping grain and meat to Barbados. By 1700 Philadelphia was already America's second city (behind Boston). But proprietorship over this diverse, energetic population earned Penn himself nothing but trouble. He expected his fellow Friends to respect his authority while elevating community interests above personal ones. Instead, the Quaker elite flouted Penn's efforts to suppress land speculation, accused his officials of corruption, and used its majority in the lower assembly to agitate against the proprietor. Juries nullified cases he brought against malfeasants. Smuggling and piracy mocked Penn's efforts to enforce the Navigation Acts. Meanwhile Maryland, the Delaware counties, and New York all contested Pennsylvania's boundaries. In 1684 Penn had to sail to England to fight lawsuits that prevented him from setting foot in his colony for fifteen years. His absence emboldened the obstreperous Quakers. Finally, in 1688, Penn went so far as to appoint as lieutenant governor a *Puritan* disciplinarian from Massachusetts, but that *ausländer* was beset by such protests (non-violent, of course) he lasted only a year. Thereafter, the proprietor had little choice but to propitiate his unruly colonists.[23]

Penn's success as a promoter but failure as a Quaker patriarch bear comparison to the Puritan and Catholic experiments in New England and Maryland, while Pennsylvanians' prosperity but hostility to their proprietor echoed the behavior of Barbadians and Yorkers. But rebelliousness in their case expressed the peculiar Quaker hostility to *any* human authority. The doctrines of the inner light and obedience to a higher law would in time make Quakers some of the boldest critics and social reformers in America. But those same principles, as one of their number confessed, were simply "destructive or repugnant to Civil Government."[24] Most absurd of all to outsiders was the Quakers' stubborn pacifism. When in the 1690s England went to war, Pennsylvania just refused to participate. What kind of polity is that? asked the crown, not to mention other American colonies threatened by Indians and Frenchmen.

.  .  .

The Stuart Restoration, it should now be clear, brought a renewed burst of colonization: indeed, twelve of the original thirteen American states were creatures of Stuart policies, a fact unappreciated by later Americans hostile to the royal and Catholic causes upheld by the two Jameses and Charleses. But the later Stuarts also presided over a general crisis of imperial authority which their accustomed methods—consolidation and centralization—could not surmount. The crisis was not of their making, at least not at the start, and varied from colony to colony. But the crown's efforts to bring order out of America's evident chaos forced all colonists to react. In so doing, they began to think deeply about what it meant to be English subjects resident in America.

The crisis began in the oldest colonies (Virginia and Massachusetts) at the same time (the terrible year of 1675) and for the same reason (frontier conflicts with Indians). Virginia had by then grown to over thirty-five thousand people, organized into sixteen counties spreading from the Tidewater up rivers some fifty to a hundred miles. Virginia had no major towns, its economy utterly dependent on the exchange of tobacco for manufactures and commodities from Europe or other colonies. That was why Governor Berkeley, though a royal official, fiercely protested the Stuarts' decision to stiffen rather than relax the Navigation Acts. Of course, Virginians might get around them through smuggling, but they could not get around the falling price of tobacco due in great part to their own overproduction. The House of Burgesses tried repeatedly through laws and parlays with Maryland to form a producers' cartel and "stint" production. But since that depended on mutual trust among hundreds of remote and competing plantations it never had a chance. Tobacco exports to London rose from 1.2 million pounds in 1640 to 10.5 millions by 1672, the price dropping from three or four pence per pound to a penny. Back in Europe the glut made tobacco a poor man's luxury and a mass market, but in the Chesapeake it made tobacco a poor man's crop. To make matters worse, the second Dutch war of 1672–74 interrupted the trade, a series of poor harvests made even food more expensive in Virginia, and the flow of indentured servants dried up, to be replaced by enslaved Africans only wealthy planters could afford. The upshot was a depression during which large landowners swallowed up smallholders who had little choice but to head for the frontier and start over. But even that was problematical because of the promises Berkeley made to respect Indian lands after the last Powhatan war in 1646. English America thus faced its first social crisis as Virginia was rent by conflicts pitting rich against poor, whites against Indians, and settled folk against lawless frontiersmen.[25]

Tidewater gentry might forget their burdens of debt while hunting the fox or betting on their new sport, quarterhorse racing. But up the Potomac skirmishes broke out between displaced planters and the Indians they meant to displace. In July 1675, a self-appointed militia attacked the Doeg tribe, killing fourteen Susquehannocks for good measure and murdering five chieftains lured by a sign of truce. When the furious Indians took their revenge, frontier planters blamed Berkeley. The governor proposed building defenses on the frontier. What pioneers really wanted were offensives to drive Indians off the land. As for the burgesses, they were loath to assume any military burdens on behalf of up-country rabble.

That was where matters stood when shocking news arrived by ship from Boston: New England's Indians had declared total war on the colonists. Frontier Virginians either feared the same in their neck of the woods or else hoped for the same in order to conquer more turf. They found their champion in the enigmatic twenty-nine-year-old Nathaniel Bacon. A rake and a rambler sporting long moustaches and a goatee, he left England after his plans to defraud a neighbor were exposed and his wife was disinherited by a father who rued her taste in men. Bacon bought a Virginia estate, but quickly gave up on tobacco in favor of a scheme to monopolize the fur trade. When that also failed he held Berkeley responsible. Finally, Bacon concluded the way to make it in America was by igniting an Indian war, a rebellion, or both. Soon the dashing and skillful rabble-rouser attracted a following among the poor, aggrieved, and frightened in several counties, even winning a seat in the House of Burgesses. His plan was to obtain Berkeley's permission to punish the Pamunkey tribe (not the Doegs, but then Indians were "all alike," Bacon said). Instead, Berkeley had him arrested in June when he arrived in Jamestown to serve as a burgess. Bacon groveled to win his release and a promise he would at least be made a militia commander. But Berkeley procrastinated. Bacon, sensing betrayal, defiantly mustered his own militia on the frontier. But for what purpose? If at this point he had marched off to kill Indians, Bacon might have become a popular hero, won over the burgesses, and unmanned the governor. Instead, Bacon led his men back to the coast, put Jamestown to the torch, and ransacked "loyalist" plantations. That more than convinced Tidewater residents these "well minded and Charitable Volunties" were in fact a "Rabble Crue" composed of "the basest sort."[26] But it all ended in farce when Bacon up and died—whether of dysentery, a fever, or something more sinister nobody knows. Most of his rebels skidaddled, but Berkeley captured and hanged twenty-three. Alas, his apparent mismanagement of the affair also resulted in the governor's recall, ending his thirty-five years of loyal service to the crown and the Old Dominion.

Was Nathaniel Bacon a premature patriot and hero of the little people? Might an American revolution have occurred a century earlier if Bacon had lived to make war on Indians and royal authority? Some say maybe, citing reform legislation passed by the burgesses while he was still at the height of his influence. Or was Bacon a spoiled brat and bully imagining himself an American Cromwell? Whatever the case, Bacon's Rebellion inaugurated a conflict that proved in time as much a solvent of Anglo-American empire as the Navigation Acts: the British desire for peace with the Indians versus the colonists' demand for land at the expense of the Indians. So it was that Virginia, in the wake of the rebellion, became the first mainland colony to suffer English troops in its midst, the first to suffer imposts for royal administrators (through a tax on tobacco of two shillings per hogshead), and the first to have its assembly's power rolled back by the crown.[27] Those emergency measures, in turn, gave *all* white Virginians cause to resist the royal regime and, in the fullness of time, justify their resistance with some of the most innovative political theory in history.[28]

By contrast, New England's ambiguities regarding authority might be said to date from its inception. After all, Winthrop's whole plan was to set up a colony beyond English oversight, while the founders of Rhode Island and Connecticut meant to escape Massachusetts. But ambiguity did not become crisis until the Stuarts returned to power, the colonists blundered into a big Indian war, and the crown's remedies made New Englanders more politically self-conscious than ever before.

Charles II's new colonial and commercial administrators meant to fashion an orderly New World empire through enforcement of royal charters and the Navigation Acts. Far from imperious, however, they bent over backward to accommodate New England's "radical" Protestants. In 1662, the indefatigable John Winthrop, Jr., won a generous charter merging the New Haven and Hartford colonies into a unified, precociously democratic Connecticut polity. The following year the crown also blessed with a charter Rhode Island's "livelie experiment" in religious toleration.[29] But Massachusetts was another matter entirely. Leaders of the Bible Commonwealth, proud of their prior resistance to the Stuarts and Cromwell alike, refused to court English favor. When royal commissioners arrived in 1664, Boston gave them the coldest of shoulders, refusing even to provide information on the colony's population and trade. The commission reported the Massachusetts General Court seemed to think it was a law unto itself. The Puritans' political discrimination against all non-Congregationalists was certainly illegal under English law. What is more, Massachusetts merchants competed with English firms in violation of the letter or spirit of the Navigation Acts. For a decade the Lords of Trade patiently asked Massachusetts to negotiate amicable terms. Having received no satisfaction they finally dispatched Edward Randolph to recommend ways to rein in the colony. Randolph docked in Boston in 1676. He found all of New England aflame.

By that date the white population of New England numbered some sixty thousand. The surviving Native Americans grew desperate. Not that they were desperate to maintain some pristine prior lifestyle: Indians had long since chosen to base their livelihoods on trade for European tools, guns, and liquor. But many were desperate to maintain any control over their future whatsoever. Could not Indians have done so over the previous fifty-five years by settling down to farming and herding themselves? Was not one of the Puritans' original missions to convert Indians to Protestant civilization? Theoretically yes, but in truth few Puritans showed an interest in missionary activities (more evidence the Yankee materialistic spirit was there from the start). Only John Eliot, a preacher from Roxbury, devoted his life to domesticating Native Americans. In 1651 he founded Natick, the first town for "praying Indians," and subsequently translated the Bible into Algonquin. By 1675 about eleven hundred Indians resided in fourteen agricultural villages, but sadly they met with contempt from most whites and unconverted Indians alike. So when the *modus vivendi* established after the Pequot war broke down, "praying Indians" were caught in a crossfire.

Massasoit, the Pilgrims' old friend, died in 1661, making his son Metacom the new Wampanoag sachem. Not much is known about his early life, but his conversations with whites, who called him King Philip, suggest anger over white encroachments, while pressure from his own warriors drove him to suicidal resistance. "I am determined," he told a Rhode Island official, "not to live until I have no country." The turning point evidently came in 1671 when the white colonies tried to oblige Indians to surrender their guns and open new lands to settlement virtually on demand. For four years Metacom tried to build a war coalition with other tribes, including the Narragansetts, his father's ancient enemy. He was not successful. As in most other "Indian" wars some tribes sided with the whites and many just tried to stay neutral. But tensions peaked early in 1675 when a converted Indian, John Sassamon, warned the governor of Plymouth about King Philip's intentions and then was found murdered. A Plymouth court condemned three Indians for the crime while whites made their own preparations to fight. Metacom was not deterred. In fact, he was emboldened by a shaman's prophecy: if the English were guilty of firing the first shot, they would be beaten. That might also have been in the minds of some Pakanoket braves who slipped into Swansea in June and looted some buildings. Then, on a day of prayer and fasting when most Swansea residents were in church, a boy guarding his family's farm spied Indians slitting the throats of grazing cattle.[30] The boy fired a musket—the first shot—wounding a brave. A few hours later Indians returned in force to assault the town's men, women, and children as they rode back from church. Whether or not Metacom had a hand in it, the incident escalated into the war he desired.[31]

Practicing their traditional methods of skulking and ambush, the Wampanoags and their allies terrorized Plymouth, then Massachusetts, then all of New England. In per capita terms, this was the bloodiest, most destructive war in American history. Over fourteen horrific months Indians attacked fifty-two towns, destroyed twelve thousand buildings, and slew more than six hundred whites and eight thousand cattle. New Englanders rallied in spontaneous, unprecedented unity. In western Massachusetts, where Deerfield, Northfield, and Springfield were overrun, John Pynchon outfitted a sizable militia which he skillfully commanded himself. In Connecticut, Governor John Winthrop, Jr., died at age seventy in 1676, but not before he organized a draft of twenty-three hundred militiamen, a rotating tenth of whom were obliged to be ready to fight "upon an hour's warning." They also provided their own weapons, supplies, and horses, all for a mere 1 shilling, 4 pence per day. But men were willing, one veteran said, to risk their lives "in so good a cause, being both the cause of God and of the republic." In eastern Massachusetts Indians reached within twenty miles of Boston until Captain Benjamin Church formed a crack force of militia and friendly Indians—the first American rangers—to hunt down Metacom himself. The war's outcome might seem foreordained given the colonists' numbers and guns. The belligerent warriors, however, had the advantages of stealth, surprise, forest sanctuaries, and intimate knowledge of the terrain. They would have not been run to ground nearly so soon had white commanders not adopted the Indians' tactics at the urging of their own Indian scouts. In fact, Indian scouts enabled Church to corner Metacom in August 1676 on the Mount Hope peninsula where an Indian dealt "King Philip" his mortal wound.[32]

So Metacom got his wish not to live until his country was entirely lost. Nor did four thousand other Indians—40 percent of the native population—killed in King Philip's War. Still more Indians fled across the Hudson River, where New York's governor Sir Edmund Andros welcomed the refugees. Andros also brokered the sole positive result of the war when he invited to Albany Mohegans, Mohawks, Iroquois, and delegates from Massachusetts and Connecticut. Their agreement to act in concert on matters of land, migration, and the fur trade began the famous Covenant Chain alliance that served the Anglo-Americans well in coming conflicts with the French. Otherwise, Metacom's war destroyed the "praying Indian" communities, either wiped out by Indians who considered them traitorous or whites who considered all Indians "the same." The English population was traumatized: free now to expand its civilization at will yet tortured by doubt and guilt that obsessed a generation of Congregational clergy. Most shocked of all, however, was English commissioner Randolph. He observed how colonists ignored London's authority, but could not maintain law and order themselves except by vicious application of force. Randolph soberly reported that if Massachusetts' insubordination were tolerated, not only might the empire unravel, but the aggressive Americans might prove more dangerous rivals to England than the Spaniards or Dutch.[33]

Even then the Lords of Trade trod gently, expecting a much humbled Massachusetts to accept royal authority and, by implication, protection. New Englanders were indeed humbled, but being Puritans they humbled themselves before God, not before men and certainly not before kings. Their pastors already detected several signs of divine wrath provoked in their view by slackening faith. The first was the infamous compromise known as the Half-Way Covenant. Since no one could be fully admitted to a church without persuading ministers they had experienced a genuine conversion, a growing number of parents were dying outside the church, leaving their children in unbaptized limbo. Traditionalists called for no watering down of the covenant, but a majority of pastors, fearing their congregations might dwindle to a handful of aged zealots, voted in the synod of 1662 to create a second class of laymen who might claim God's redemption and have their children baptized while remaining unsanctified and unworthy to take communion. No sooner was the Half-Way Covenant approved, however, than a drought seared crops and smallpox carried off hundreds of people. Michael Wigglesworth was widely believed when he wrote of God having a "controversy with New England."

A second sign of divine wrath was the plague of Quaker missionaries who arrived over these same years. Like Roger Williams and Anne Hutchinson before them, they preached what Puritans regarded as heresy and they refused to shut up. Indeed, they kept coming back as if courting martyrdom. So a series of Quaker men, women, and teenagers were imprisoned, whipped, starved, chained, and hanged (all after due process, of course) until some Puritans began to weary of spiritual warfare. When Baptists, too, began to invade Massachusetts, General Court threw up its hands.[34]

Yet a third sign the Commonwealth had earned God's disfavor was the grasping for money and land prevalent among the second generation of saints. Not that prosperity or worldly success were bad things, but they were supposed to be understood as God's blessings upon faithful children. The children seemed now to expect the blessings while spurning the faith, even to the point of parading the latest London fashions and hosting licentious entertainments (the third generation Winthrops were among the leading playboys). King Philip's War, therefore, was only the fourth, if most unmistakable, plague on a stiff-necked people. So the response of the Puritan fathers led by Increase Mather was not to make political concessions to London (how beside the point was that?), but to get right with God by calling another synod to reform Congregational churches and reimpose moral discipline. In 1679–80 the synod condemned disrespectful language and comportment, sabbath-breaking, public displays of emotion and pride, dancing, elegant hair styles, and revealing dress. Puritanical blue laws that banned all manner of things in Boston could not, of course, rekindle hearts or suppress the appetites of English men and women on the make. But they were not just religious phenomena, because the same impulses causing pastors to combat the tyranny of sin from within emboldened secular leaders to combat the sin of tyranny from without.[35]

Accordingly, when the Lords of Trade suggested the good people of Massachusetts might cease being naughty and obey English law, General Court's agents replied that Parliament's laws had *no force* in New England. Boston even set up its own rival customs office in 1681 to funnel duties on cargoes to the colony's treasury rather than the crown's. English patience ran out. The Lords sued in chancery court to revoke the charters of Massachusetts Bay, Plymouth, Connecticut, and Rhode Island, and by 1687 won every case.

What sort of government would the crown now impose on New England?

The decision fell to the former Duke of York, who became King James II upon the death of Charles II in 1685. James much admired the centralized colonial systems established by his fellow Catholic sovereigns in Spain and France. So he consolidated all colonies from New Jersey to Maine in a Dominion of New England to be ruled, like a Spanish viceroyalty, by the stern Governor Andros of New York. New Englanders were incensed to learn an appointed council would replace their elected assemblies, town meetings would be restricted, royal customs officials would choke and tax their trade, Anglicanism (including the "popish" celebration of Christmas) would be established, and Maypoles rise on Boston Common. Worst of all, Andros arrived in Boston in December 1686 with the intention of making New England pay in the manner of Virginia for royal administration. He raised the quit rent for new grants to 2 shillings 6 pence per hundred acres and undertook to review existing land titles with an eye to raising their rates. All told, the king's plan and governor's policies threatened to efface not only the autonomy, but the personalities, ambitions, and values of the New England colonies.[36]

Local crises of authority disrupting the colonies from Charleston and Jamestown to Philadelphia and New Jersey to New York and Boston all reached a climax between 1686 and 1688. Would Andros and two or three other viceroys, backed by soldiers and fleets, remake the English empire in the image of the Spanish empire the colonies were founded in part to contest? Or would Americans rise in the spirit of Bacon's rebels and New England militias?

Those questions were not answered. In April 1689 a ship docked in Boston bearing glorious news: King James had fled into exile; the Protestants William of Orange and his wife Mary ( James' eldest daughter) were to be crowned king and queen. The Stuarts had done the American colonies yet another great service, this time by undoing themselves.

James II might have reigned for life if only he *lacked* the virtue Puritans and Quakers claimed to cherish most highly: a faith the world cannot overcome. Instead, he refused to sacrifice his Catholicism to expediency, baptized his baby boy in the Roman church, and named co-religionists to high office. The baptism threatened to saddle Britain with Catholic monarchs in perpetuity, while the appointments, by violating the Test Acts restricting office to Anglicans, elevated the royal prerogative above Parliament. To be sure, James issued two Declarations of Indulgence to reassure Protestant dissenters, but those only won him more enemies because the Church of England opposed toleration. Finally, since nobody wanted another civil war, even Stuart sympathizers stood aside when leaders in Parliament, the army, and church, backed by public opinion, invited James to depart and William of Orange to invade. The latter, a Dutch patriot eager for England's assistance against a looming threat from Louis XIV of France, landed with a Protestant army in November 1688.

That was the news that ignited Bostonians the following spring. A mob charged the governor's residence, arrested Andros and Randolph, and seized a royal ship in the harbor. A Council for Safety served as interim government until the General Court and officials chosen prior to the king's "usurpation" of power could reconvene. Plymouth, Rhode Island, Connecticut, and New Hampshire did the same even before news of the coronation of William and Mary reached America on May 26.[37]

Copycat rebellions spread down the coast. Thanks to riders on the Boston Post Road (another boon bequeathed by the Stuarts) Yorkers got wind of the Boston revolt a week later. The Dutch and Puritans were delighted to learn their respective mother countries were now allies. For its part, the New York militia mutinied against Andros' lieutenant Francis Nicholson under the command of Jacob Leisler. A Dutch Reformed deacon and merchant, Leisler wrapped himself in an anti-papist banner but characteristically stood to profit as well. He refused to pay a hefty £100 tariff on a cargo on the grounds the customs official was Catholic. The luckless Nicholson, his authority hollow, took ship in June 1689. Chaos ensued for twenty-one months during which Leisler imposed martial law under a Committee of Safety and New York's many factions sided for or against him. Since Albany's fur traders led by Livingston were among his opponents, Leisler did nothing when some two hundred Frenchmen in league with Indians tramped through the snow to test New York's frontier defenses. They fell upon Schenectady on a dark night in February 1690 to kill or capture eighty-seven men, women, and children. Enraged Yorkers cried for Leisler's neck and got it when William and Mary's new governor arrived. Leisler was convicted of treason and hanged.[38]

In Virginia the governor and Tidewater elite cheered the Glorious Revolution in England, but feared the spreading colonial uprisings might inspire some new "Bacon" to rouse the rabble and "betake themselves to Armes to plunder and robb just and good men." So the governor doubled his guard until William and Mary were crowned, then "celebrated" the event by parading English troops and loyal militia. By contrast, Maryland's Protestants, eager as always to challenge the Baltimore regime, took up arms behind one John Coode. Posing as a champion of liberty, he was in fact a mad Anglican parson given to outbursts of atheism. But Coode's paranoia (he believed in a Catholic-Indian conspiracy to slaughter all Protestants) won him a following sufficient to storm St. Mary's and expel Maryland's governor for a season. Finally, more or less popular uprisings occurred in Carolina's northern Albemarle County and in Charleston, where the Goose Creek Men had a last hurrah.

What came of it all? Many historians say nothing much, because in most cases the colonies returned to something like the status quo prior to James' abortive experiment with rigid consolidation. Massachusetts, despite the diplomacy of Increase Mather, did have to swallow a new charter in 1691 providing for a royal governor with veto power over General Court and abolishing the Puritans' religious qualification for voting. It also confirmed separate colonial status for New Hampshire towns. On the other hand, Massachusetts absorbed the Plymouth colony and retained sovereignty over Maine. As for Connecticut and Rhode Island, English courts simply overruled the chancery court's revocation of their charters. The Pennsylvania, New Jersey, and Carolina proprietors had some nervous moments awaiting the new regime's decisions, but by 1694 their colonies, too, returned to the *status quo ante* with the exception that North Carolina was formally spun off. In all cases American colonial governments now consisted of a governor, governor's council, an elected lower assembly, and more or less independent courts, the only major distinction being governors were elected in Connecticut and Rhode Island, named by the proprietor(s) in Pennsylvania, New Jersey, and the Carolinas, and appointed by the crown in the rest. Finally, but significantly, William and Mary's advisers continued the Stuarts' centralized control of trade under a Board of Trade (the old Lords of Trade) and drafted another Navigation Act in 1696 provocatively entitled "An Act for preventing Frauds and regulating Abuses in the Plantation Trade."[39]

Nevertheless, while on the surface the Glorious Revolution seemed to change little, it had portentous effects on Britain, the colonies, and the relationship between them. First, it crushed once and for all any conceivable Catholic or even High Anglican influence in the empire. Second, it de-legitimized (at least in colonists' eyes) any future attempts to set aside the colonies' charters or otherwise impinge on their liberties. Third, it confirmed the now hoary precedent of shared and balanced power within the colonies and between each and the metropole. Fourth, it reinforced the tight connection between politics and religion, self-government and Protestantism, dating from the earliest decades of the English colonial enterprise. Fifth, it implicitly endowed English subjects who happened to reside in America with the inalienable rights to life, liberty, property, the bearing of arms, freedom of worship, and due process of law enumerated in the 1689 Toleration Act and Bill of Rights agreed to by William and Mary.[40]

The greatest effect of the crisis of authority climaxing around 1688 was nevertheless none of those listed above. The greatest effect was wrought by John Churchill, chief plotter and military commander of the coup of 1688–89, because his motive for ousting James II was not just to defend the Protestant or Parliamentary cause. He meant also to ensure England leaped into William of Orange's war against France, expecting it to end in the conquest of all North America. Alas, Churchill underestimated the time and effort that project required, with the result that wars and preparation for wars shaped American colonial history for the subsequent seventy-five years.

# PAPISTS, WITCHES, SCOFFLAWS, AND PREACHERS

## Colonists at War, Business, and Prayer, 1689–1740

*O*n a cloudy summer day in 1534, the year Henry VIII broke with Rome, Jacques Cartier dropped anchor off the Gaspé Peninsula at the mouth of the St. Lawrence River. A delegation of curious Native Americans watched as Cartier's sailors planted a thirty-foot-tall wooden cross bedecked with *fleurs-de-lys* and the inscription "*Vive le Roy de France.*" The apparent chief of the Indians soon paddled out to the ship where he delivered "a long harangue, making the sign of the cross with two fingers; and then he pointed to the land all around about, as if he wished to say that all this region belonged to him, and that we ought not to have set up this cross without his permission." Cartier seized two of the chief's companions, whom he took to be sons, dressed them in Breton garb, and indicated he would return with them the following year. The chief in turn signaled he would not uproot the cross. Both promises were kept.[1]

A century later the Jesuit Jean de Brébeuf included in his annual report a "guide to good manners" for missionaries to Indians on the St. Lawrence. When beginning a canoe voyage, he wrote, never keep the natives waiting, embark and debark nimbly at their command, do not chatter, paddle heartily, carry a load during portages, and always provide match tinder or a magnifying glass to make fire. Likewise, eat their native salmagundi with gusto, however disgusting its taste and appearance. Always have a supply of knives, fish hooks, and beads. Tuck in your cassock lest you trip in the canoe and never don the broad Jesuit hat, which will only blow off your head or block the view of your companions. Such "little services will win their hearts." Many Indian customs, he concluded, will appal you. But do not try to "civilize" them: just bring their souls to Christ and you "will find roses among thorns, the sweet in the bitter, and all in nothing."[2]

Self-congratulatory Canadian authors and self-critical American ones have long contrasted the relatively dignified relations the French established with Indians with the predatory or fearful treatment meted out by English colonists. If there is truth in that caricature (and there is much), it was not because French were more tolerant in a twenty-first-century secular sense, but in a seventeenth-century Catholic sense. English colonists, after all, were motivated by the spirits of agricultural capitalism, crusading Protestantism, an imperial destiny, and displacement of backward peoples. *Nouvelle France,* by contrast, meant feudalism, popery, and willing alliance with any Indians prepared to trade and, better yet, fight the English. Worse still from New England's perspective, intrepid French explorers were first into the Great Lakes and Mississippi valley regions, so it seemed on the map France's empire encircled and choked the English colonies clinging to the Atlantic coast. Consequently, English and French colonists feared and hated each other to the depths of their souls regardless of the state of Anglo-French diplomacy back in Europe.

By most objective measures, France should have won the contest for North America. It was the richest and most populous kingdom in Western Europe, its long civil wars ended in the triumph of the dynamic, state-building Bourbon dynasty, and France's long coastlines bred seamen every bit as skilled as the English. But French monarchs and royal officials often stifled rather than released their nation's commercial energies. The very scale of the resources at their command tempted them to pursue land and sea power alike, dividing their forces among too many objectives in Europe and overseas. They never fully appreciated the potential of North America. They positively forbade their subjects most likely to become eager colonists—the Calvinist Huguenots—from emigrating. But all that is hindsight. To New Englanders, Yorkers, and later Pennsylvanians and Virginians the presence of French papists on "their" continent was intolerable. To be sure, they greatly outnumbered the French. But the seventeenth and eighteenth centuries were an amazing era in which the fate of a continent might hinge on a few hundred men, a dozen cannon, or a flotilla of ships being in the right place at the right time.

The contest began in 1613 when Captain Samuel Argall set sail from Jamestown, Virginia, to raid Port Royal, a French settlement founded eight years before in Acadia (Nova Scotia). Thus began more than a century of irregular warfare by land and sea between Acadians and their "Bostonnais" rivals to the south. French occupation of the St. Lawrence basin began in 1608 when Samuel de Champlain sailed a pinnace upriver to the point where the channel narrowed and a rocky promontory covered with butternut trees dominated the river. The Indians called it the Point of Québec. Only eight of Champlain's party of twenty-four survived the first frigid winter. But they were soon reinforced and learned the lay of the land. The Indians in the neighborhood were Hurons, Montagnais, and Algonquins, all bitter enemies of the Iroquois confederacy that once controlled the St. Lawrence, but had recently left or been driven out. The Five Nations of the Iroquois (Mohawks, Oneidas, Onondagas, Cayugas, and Senecas) now controlled a broad swath between the Hudson River and the lake of the Eries. They were formidable when united in purpose.[3]

So the fledgling French colony had no chance to survive if it antagonized the Hurons and their allies, but no means of ingratiating itself with those tribes except by adding their arquebuses and swords to the Hurons' campaigns against Iroquois. Accordingly, Champlain's soldiers served as valuable auxiliaries in a series of Indian wars, both as a matter of self-defense and to extend the French fur trade as far south as possible. Since the Dutch and English were starting to paddle up the Hudson, the Iroquois were in danger of being squeezed. Their attempts to exploit that middle position by playing the whites off against each other would dominate intra-American strategy for 150 years.

Champlain repeatedly begged Paris to send him more soldiers, settlers, and priests in hopes of subduing the Iroquois and confining the English and Dutch to the coast. At stake, he reported, was a monopoly of the fur trade and the rich deposits of copper, iron, and silver his scouts ascertained lay to the west. What is more, "the cost of 120 men is little to His Majesty, and the enterprise as honorable as can be imagined, and all is for the glory of God."[4] But as eager as Louis XIII and his prime minister Cardinal Richelieu were to promote empire, their first priority was always to check Habsburg ambitions in the Mediterranean, Low Countries, and Germany. So Richelieu took a page from the English colonial book by chartering a company to develop America with

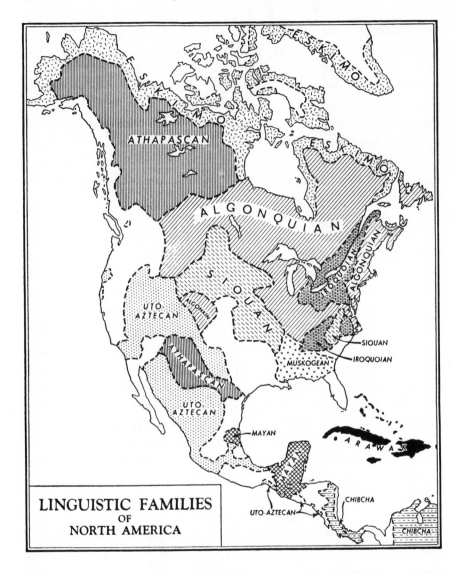

**LINGUISTIC FAMILIES**
OF
**NORTH AMERICA**

private capital. In 1627 the Company of New France, known as the "Hundred Associates," was granted exclusive rights to all North America from the Arctic to Florida and westward to the "seas" (the Great Lakes) reached by Champlain. In return for its monopoly the company was to transport four thousand settlers and priests and make loyal French subjects of all Indians who converted. But English privateers captured several of the company's ships and occupied Québec itself until a peace treaty restored it to France in 1632.[5]

The company then took a page from the Dutch colonial book, offering feudal land grants to anyone transporting settlers. There were some fifteen takers, but the patroon system proved no more successful on the St. Lawrence than on the Hudson, with one exception. The Sulpician Order of Paris was deeded the great island on which Montréal rose in 1640. Within a decade its monks and nuns presided over schools, a hospital, warehouses for furs, and the first urban community north of Boston. From Montréal the famous *coureurs de bois* explored west and north to trap or trade for pelts. From Montréal the Jesuits fanned out to evangelize among Indians in their own villages. Accounts of the missionaries' adventures, published in the annual *Jesuit Relations* back in Paris, advertised the colony to potential donors and recruits. Running forty-one volumes in the original, the *Relations* were one of America's earliest great works of literature, predating Cotton Mather's *Magnalia Christi Americana*, a 1702 history of New England, by half a century. How many Indians the Jesuits converted is disputed. Protestants ridiculed the notion that an illiterate savage became a genuine Christian by virtue of just being baptized. But it is undeniable the Jesuits brought a modicum of French civilization to numerous Indian communities. They were aided, perversely, by the alacrity with which French soldiers and traders fathered mixed offspring.

Still, *Nouvelle France* contained no more than about three thousand Europeans when disasters descended. In 1639–40 the inevitable smallpox epidemic killed up to half of the twenty thousand Hurons, causing many survivors to blame "Jesuit witchcraft." Then Iroquois armed with Dutch weapons struck the weakened Great Lakes tribes in a bid for empire, monopoly, or more likely security.[6] They killed hundreds of Huron braves, forced many more to retreat back toward Québec, and absorbed the rest into their own tribes. At a blow the French lost their military buffer and most of their fur trade to the Five Nations and their Dutch allies in Albany. The Jesuits (three of whom had been tortured and killed by Iroquois) tried to put the best face on events. But the flow of colonists, missionaries, and investment dried up.[7]

Then, in 1661, King Louis XIV reached his maturity. He at once ordered finance minister Jean-Baptiste Colbert to revive French fortunes in Canada by dissolving the Hundred Associates and making *Nouvelle France* a crown colony. Colbert appointed a vigorous new intendant to settle landlords and tenants, supply tools and livestock, even provide wives for the soldiers deployed to contest the frontier with the Iroquois. Their commander, the Sieur de Tracy, proved equally energetic. He marched a Franco-Indian force to the Mohawk River, burned

Iroquois villages, and imposed a treaty favorable to the French. The Comte de Frontenac, the able governor based in Québec, then presided over such rapid expansion that the population grew almost fourfold by 1690, to fifteen thousand self-supporting whites and thousands more of mixed race. Indeed, under Colbert it became official state policy to promote miscegenation to "civilize the Algonquins . . . and the other savages who have embraced Christianity, and dispose them to come and settle in community with the French." Meant to relieve Canada's numerical disadvantage vis-à-vis New England, the policy reflected an assimilationist ethic unknown in English America.[8]

The governor, intendant, and bishop predictably quarreled over law, Indian policy, the spoils of the fur trade, and their respective powers. But the late seventeenth century proved to be the only sustained period of peace and prosperity in the history of French Canada. Not long before the Iroquois had boasted the *coureurs de bois* could not "goe over a door to pisse" without fear of ambush. Now they roamed the interior rivers and lakes at will, returning each year or two to the Montréal Fair where they cashed out, got drunk, and coupled with Indian maids. So attractive was this wilderness life many French colonists deserted the farm at their first opportunity. One was Pierre Esprit Radisson, who said of his years in the north woods, "We were Caesars, there being none to contradict us." This extraordinary adventurer was captured in youth by a Mohawk party and adopted into the tribe. He murdered his overseers and escaped only to be recaptured and tortured before escaping again. Radisson then made for the Hudson Bay region, returning with a fortune in pelts. But French factors seized his cargo since he lacked a license to trade. So Radisson turned traitor, made for Boston, and ultimately helped British merchants found the Hudson's Bay Company. At length he retired in London to live comfortably off the company's annuity and dividends until his death in 1710.[9] The French had their hustlers, too.

More important, officially sponsored explorers fiercely loyal to throne and altar headed into the lake country, or *pays d'en haut*. Fathers Claude Allouez and Pierre Marquette charted Lake Huron, founded Sault Ste. Marie in 1669, and planted a mission at Green Bay in the land of the Wisconsins. Louis Joliet explored Lake Superior, finding there rich copper deposits. Then, in 1673, Joliet and Marquette teamed up to follow the water route Allouez had discovered to the Mississippi, the fabulous "river to the sea" of Indian lore. They floated south as far as the Arkansas River before stopping in fear of Spaniards. But from 1680–82, Robert de la Salle explored as far as the Gulf of Mexico, laying claim to the whole Mississippi basin. Forts and missions arose at Niagara, Détroit, Michilimackinac, Kaskaskia, and Natchez to sustain a far-flung network of new Indian alliances. All this was accomplished before a single Anglo-American explorer, trader, or pioneer even breached the Appalachians. The threat the French posed to the English colonies made for endemic violence from Hudson's Bay to Acadia, Maine, the Mohawk Valley, and soon the western frontiers of Pennsylvania, Virginia, and Carolina.

The Iroquois' response to the peripatetic French and prolific English was intensive war and diplomacy masterminded in part by Daniel Garacontié. This Onondaga "prince and orator" was a statesman on a par with governors Andros and John Winthrop, Jr., for like them he had to foster cooperation among jealous members of an ethnic confederation and defeat implacable enemies on the frontier, all the while paying obeisance to London's overlordship. Garacontié was also one of the few converts won by the Jesuits among the Five Nations. He warned the chiefs and shamans the Indians would never survive unless they quit making decisions on the basis of "dream-guessing" and instead practiced European-style strategy. So it was that Garacontié joined with Andros at Albany in 1677 to make the omnibus Covenant Chain alliance. Through it the Iroquois obtained peace on their southern flank, higher prices for furs, and ready access to firearms which they promptly used to blunt the French threat in the west. Beginning in 1680 the Five Nations launched furious assaults on the Illinois, Miami, Shawnee, and other tribes whom the French proved powerless to protect. The Iroquois confederation and their English colonial allies were invincible.[10]

Or so it seemed in 1685 when James Stuart ascended the English throne and Louis XIV refocused his foreign policy on the goal of expanding his kingdom to the Rhine and beyond. The two Catholic monarchs rued the chaotic combat of their respective American colonists and Indian proxies. So they concluded the Treaty of Whitehall of 1686, pledging to maintain peace in America and resolve any disputes between their colonial subjects through arbitration. This forgotten document is of the utmost importance because it gives the lie to later American complaints to the effect the colonies were constantly dragged against their will into Britain's imperial wars. In fact, American colonists *abhorred* James II's toleration of the French empire in America. So they did what they always did when obnoxious orders descended from London: they scoffed at them. Raids continued and even escalated all along the northern frontier until, following the accession of William and Mary, they got what they wanted: a full-scale war to destroy Catholic power in North America once and for all. Increase Mather's son Cotton was moved to decry all "Popery and Arbitrary Government" and rejoice that King William was "a Hook in the nostrils of that French Leviathan. . . . War with none but Hell and Rome!"[11]

To the consternation of New England Puritans, however, the War of the League of Augsburg—King William's War the Americans called it—did not follow their script. In 1690 Frenchmen and Indians razed the town of Schenectady and struck forts on the coast of Maine, sending a frisson of fear through New York and New England. The English colonies planned a two-pronged counterattack against Canada. But the naval expedition under Sir William Phips ascended the St. Lawrence only to find it lacked the cannon and infantry needed to storm Québec's fortified heights. An overland offensive via Lake Champlain and the Richelieu River never got started. New England and New York failed to deliver the militia they promised, while the Iroquois were distracted by smallpox and *la petite guerre* (guerrilla war) waged by the French on their frontier. No soldiers arrived from England. Nor had the colonists even restored effective governments in the wake of the Glorious Revolution. New York was still convulsed by Leisler's Rebellion, and the leaderless, unpaid Massachusetts militia was near mutiny. That deplorable military situation and the panic it caused provided the context for one of the most infamous episodes in colonial history: the Salem witch trials.

Salem Village, now called Danvers, was a small farming community north of Boston whose residents were so prone to feuds and disputes it was known as a graveyard for pastors. But the vexations that began in late 1691 emanated from the household of the Rev. Samuel Parris himself. His daughter and niece, aged nine and eleven, began screaming and rolling as if in horrible pain, and were tongue-tied when admonished to pray to the Lord for relief. Parris consulted a doctor and fellow clergy, but their ministrations availed nothing. A calm, if worrisome, month passed until more teenaged girls began to display bizarre symptoms. "Who torments you?" they were insistently asked. At length they blurted out "Tituba," a young Carib-African servant who enjoyed telling tales of sorcery, and the names of two older women they accused of conjuring spirits determined to make them cavort with Satan. The women denied the charges, but Tituba confessed to being a witch. She described the devil as "a thing all over hairy," and bragged nine others in town had "signed the witches' book."

The numbers of those jailed increased geometrically as the accused in turn accused others, but still the hysteria spread. Now, in a Catholic land the bishop, canon lawyers, and exorcists might have been summoned (for better or worse) to fight "principalities and powers" with spiritual weapons. But under English law witchcraft was a crime punishable by the civil authorities. Only there *was* no civil authority at the moment because the Stuarts had revoked Massachusetts' charter only to be overthrown themselves. So the panic continued until the new governor bearing the new charter arrived in Boston on May 14. He only made matters worse. Rather than exert executive authority he appointed a special Court of Oyer and Terminer "to hear and dispose of" the backlog of mysterious cases. In the course of its hearings some of the accused seemed persuaded by the charges against them, told blood-curdling stories, in one case even cried to the devil to come and rescue his servants. Others confessed in the hope (often justified) of being released on grounds of repentance. The great majority were female, but one man accused of being a warlock refused to recognize the court's authority. He was pressed to death under stones. In all, hundreds were interrogated, nineteen executed.

What put a stop to it all was the clergy. Boston pastors had communicated doubts to the governor as early as June, but not until October did Increase Mather preach and publish a sermon on *Cases of Conscience Concerning Evil Spirits Personating Men*. His argument was devastating. First, the very fact witchcraft was a capital crime ("thou shalt not suffer a witch to live") meant evidence of guilt must be unimpeachable. Second, evidence from the mouth of accused persons was untrustworthy since the devil could make the innocent appear guilty and the guilty appear innocent. Third, the use of "spectral evidence"—signs, tests, and omens of folk vintage—was especially abhorrent because it sought to root out the occult by occult means. Finally, there was almost no way of discerning, from the *effects* of a diabolical agency, the *motives* of the afflicted. Was the person in the dock a willing ally of the devil or his pitiable victim? Only material evidence from two or more witnesses might serve to convict, said Mather, and "it were better that ten suspected witches should escape, than that one innocent person should be condemned." The governor, who not incidentally owed his appointment to Mather, was persuaded a gross mistake had been made. On October 29 he prorogued the court and released most of the prisoners on bail. The following May he issued a general pardon.[12]

Americans ever since have been transfixed by the drama at Salem Village.

From Nathaniel Hawthorne's chilling stories such as "Young Goodman Brown" to Arthur Miller's play *The Crucible* to dozens of books analyzing the events from every conceivable angle, Americans expect the witch craze to teach them something deep and enduring about their national soul. Certainly issues of race, class, and patriarchy were present at Salem, as well as generational clashes, adolescent and adult psychology, repressed sexuality, and the Puritans' peculiar hunger for signs of the invisible world breaking into the visible one. A few years before the outbreak Cotton Mather himself had written an *Essay on Illustrious Providences* in which he catalogued cases of divine and demonic intervention. He thought disbelief in witches led inexorably to disbelief in angels and finally in God. For some historians the tale, while tragic, may be celebrated as a big step away from superstition in the direction of science and reason. For others, it is cautionary inasmuch as "witch hunts," conspiracy theories, and irrational credulity have continued to flare up in American life down to the present day.

But however beguiling the arguments made by those who see deeper meaning in the Salem affair, they often ignore some hard historical questions. Why, for instance, did it occur where and when it did? Why did this single prosecution of witchcraft (out of some 234 that occurred in the colonies) get thoroughly out of hand? Why did the governor abdicate his authority? Why did the highly educated and presumably prudent judges and clergy entertain outlandish testimony? Why was it left to the most conservative, traditional, and mystical elder—Increase Mather—to see madness for what it was?

Plausible answers emerge from the military context described above. For whatever else the witch trials might have been they were surely a war scare—a panic over "fifth columnists" on the home front that occurred while duly constituted authority was freakishly absent. To be sure, the mob and merchants in Boston installed a provisional government in 1689 after the Glorious Revolution. But it was of dubious authority and lost all sympathy by running up debts of £50,000 to pay for the abortive invasion of Canada while failing to defend New England itself. By 1691 pamphlets and sermons lamented the "Rage and Fury of the People" over the fact "we have no Magistrates, no Government, And by consequence no Security." By fall of that year rumors raced through Essex County, including Salem Village, warning of enemy soldiers advancing just twenty miles north. That was when the disturbed girls began to confess, and what did they say? That witches were not only in league with the devil, but held secret meetings in the forest with Frenchmen and Indians. As Cotton

Mather recorded, "One who was Executed at Salem for Witchcraft had confessed that at the Cheef Witch-meetings, there had been present some French canadians, and some Indian Sagamores, to concert the methods of ruining New England." Given that generations of English Protestants were told from the cradle that popery was of the devil and Indians the children of Satan, their conflation of spiritual and temporal threats should not be surprising at all.[13]

At length the new governor arrived and under different circumstances might have exerted a steadying influence. But that governor was none other than Sir William Phips, the very man who had just bungled the invasion of Canada. He was probably afraid to look "soft" on security and surely needed to buy time to establish his authority. So he let the local notables deal with this decidedly local affliction until, in October, the fear of invasion subsided and Increase Mather gave Phips the *political* cover he needed to call a halt to the craze.[14]

Finally, why was it Mather who interceded and not some more "rationally minded" critic? The answer is there were no "rational" critics, if by that one means a scientific materialist for whom the whole idea of supernatural beings was hogwash. Virtually all seventeenth-century Europeans, not to say all cultures on earth, believed in invisible forces, magic, occult powers, and evil spirits. For pious Christians, Protestant and Catholic alike, the reality of the devil and his fallen angels and human servants was an incontestable Biblical fact. Even Sir Isaac Newton and John Locke considered empirical, scientific method just one way among many (including, in Newton's case, alchemy, numerology, and astrology) to comprehend God's creation. So the intellectual contest at Salem Village did not pit superstition versus enlightenment, but rather naiveté versus sophistication regarding the full power and nature of evil. Mather saw how the judges' own efforts to gather and weigh evidence, to prove guilt or innocence on the basis of hallucinations, specters, and signs, made them susceptible to every trick played on the witnesses whether by demonic suggestion or their own fragile psyches.[15] Mather pointed out their mistake, the trials ended abruptly, and far from being a great turning point, "the intellectual history of New England can be written as though no such thing ever happened."[16]

The greatest irony of the Salem witch trials is the whole affair was triggered by a false alarm. French Canada never fielded enough soldiers to conquer densely populated parts of New England, while Paris never considered shipping over enough for that purpose. Indeed, so futile were all the war's offensive operations that France and England simply agreed in the 1697 Treaty of Ryswick to return the odd islands and forts they had captured and stop fighting. But there was no restoring the *status quo ante bellum* in America. The Iroquois suffered casualties on the order of five hundred warriors and eleven hundred noncombatants and got nothing from Britain in return. Some sachems repaired to Montréal to beg terms. In the Grand Settlement that followed in 1701, the Five Nations promised the French—and warned the English—they would remain neutral in future white men's wars. Hence the English colonies had to look all the more to their own resources should war break out again.

It did, almost at once, when Carlos II, last Habsburg monarch of Spain, died without a clear heir in 1700. The European courts had made provision for this two years before by agreeing peaceably to divide up Spanish possessions in Europe and America. But Carlos' will bequeathed his whole realm to Philip of Anjou, who happened to be a grandson of Louis XIV. The Sun King could not resist a chance to merge the domains of France and Spain into a grand Bourbon empire, so he pressed Philip's claim and provoked the War of the Spanish Succession (Queen Anne's War in America). Once again French and Indians sacked upper New England towns. In a massacre at Deerfield in 1704 they killed forty people and took over a hundred hostages. "Many of us are driven from our homes," mourned a farmer. "Much of our stock is killed by the Heathen. . . . and we daily grow more and more feeble and deplorable; daily walking and working with fear, trembling, and jeopardy of life."[17] Another English assault on Québec ended calamitously when eight ships ran aground and seven hundred soldiers perished. But an Anglo-colonial force did manage to capture and hold Acadia, much to New Englanders' joy.

On the southern front the French invested heavily in the fortification of Natchez, Biloxi, and Mobile, hoping to win the allegiance of the Choctaw, Chickasaw, and other tribes between the Mississippi River and Carolina. But the most powerful nation, the Creeks, sided with the South Carolinians. Together they killed or enslaved hundreds of French- or Spanish-leaning Indians in the southeast. In North Carolina belated white expansion inland from Albemarle County put similar pressure on the Tuscarora tribe with equally tragic results. That story began in Germany where thousands of farmers in the Rhenish Palatinate were ravaged by French invaders and a series of bitter winters. In 1709 a Swiss company led by the pietist Baron Christoph von Graffenried stepped in to purchase 17,500 acres in North Carolina, found the town of New Bern, and settle four hundred of these "healthy, industrious people" out of harm's way. This influx provoked the Tuscaroras, who complained whites "cheated the Indians in trading, and would not allow them to hunt near their plantations, and under that pretense took away from them their game, arms, and ammunition." Fearing violence, Graffenried and the colony's surveyor-general John Lawson set off upriver to placate the chiefs. Instead, the Indians proceeded to torture and kill the unfortunate Lawson whom they evidently mistook for North Carolina's despised Governor Edward Hyde. The pacifist Graffenried looked on helplessly while the Tuscoraras fell on white settlements to kill 140 people, half of them innocent Germans and Swiss.

After his release, Graffenried still urged the governor to appease rather than fight the Indians. But Hyde called out the militia, the assembly voted a £4,000 war chest, and South Carolina pitched in as well. In January 1712 Colonel John "Tuscarora Jack" Barnwell led thirty-three whites and five hundred friendly Indians over three hundred miles of woodland and swamp. Their surprise attack on the Tuscarora took fifty-two scalps and many prisoners whom the victorious Indians enslaved. At length a truce was negotiated, but it broke down in the summer when Barnwell complained the assembly had not fully compensated him for his service. So he sold a number of Indians into slavery to line his own pockets. The furious Tuscarora determined again to destroy the abomination whites called North Carolina. Disease, this time, sided with them. A yellow fever epidemic carried away many colonists, including Governor Hyde. But in 1713 a handful of militiamen, reinforced again by tribes hostile to the Tuscaroras, overran the enemy's stronghold to scalp, capture, or burn nearly a thousand men, women, and children. The surviving Tuscaroras gave up. They undertook a great trek northward to central New York where they joined the Covenant Chain as the Sixth Nation of the Iroquois. In North Carolina the industrious Swiss and Germans went back to work at New Bern, contributing mightily to the still fledgling colony of North Carolina.[18]

The global war also ended in 1713 with the grand Peace of Utrecht. The first treaty to put into writing the principle of the European balance of power, its signatories granted the Bourbon claim to the Spanish throne on condition that neither Philip nor his heirs ever unite the kingdoms of Spain and France. But the treaty's American provisions were just as momentous. First, the French surrendered all trading privileges in Spanish America and Portuguese Brazil. Second, the Spaniards contracted never to transfer American territory "to the French or to any other nations whatever" (one of the key principles of the Monroe Doctrine 110 years later). Third, the French recognized British sovereignty over Nova Scotia, Newfoundland, Hudson's Bay, and the Iroquois lands. Fourth, Spain awarded to Britain its valuable *asiento,* which meant the right to import forty-eight hundred slaves and one cargo of merchandise per year into Spanish America. Needless to say, English and American captains regarded that foot in the door as a license to smuggle at will.

At least as important was the fillip the warfare from 1690 to 1713 gave to American government. Although every colony possessed some sort of representative assembly (New York, in 1683, being the last to achieve one), only in New England did the lower houses display much authority or competence prior to England's Glorious Revolution of 1688. The others tended to meet irregularly, keep sloppy records, and either approve or protest whatever measures their governors or proprietors proposed. To the extent the assemblies did take independent initiatives they had mostly to do with local matters such as incorporation of towns, regulation of markets, and public morals. International war, however, obliged governors to raise soldiers and taxes, which they had no hope of doing without the sufferance of the people as expressed through their assemblies. The pace differed from colony to colony, but by the end of Queen Anne's War in 1713 all the colonial governments began to display sovereign attributes.

The first was the issuance of paper currency. No source of economic hardship was more prevalent and acute in the colonies than the virtual absence of money. As we know, the Chesapeake colonies used tobacco as a medium of exchange, and New England for a time employed wampum, gunshot, or bushels of corn. But most local transactions had to be done on the basis of barter and most long-range transactions on lines of credit in London. A floating supply of Spanish silver and gold—pieces of eight and thalers (dollars)—reached American ports, but such specie just as quickly gravitated to England to cover outstanding accounts.[19] The shortage of money was always a drag on the economy, but became a crisis upon the outbreak of war. Massachusetts, in the forefront as usual, issued the first paper bonds against future revenue in 1690 to finance the campaign in Canada and by 1715 had almost £500,000 in circulation. All the other non-tobacco colonies followed suit except for Pennsylvania, where pacifist Quakers sat out the war. One predictable result was inflation since the value of colonial paper fluctuated according to the confidence creditors had in its eventual redemption. So scorned was profligate Rhode Island's funny money that it traded at 1/32 of par. Most impatient with the practice were English merchants. They pressured the crown to forbid governors from approving currency laws without a suspending clause or a strict ceiling on the amount. But governors were hard put to enforce such injunctions without incurring the wrath of their constituents.[20]

A second attribute of a sovereign state is the raising of armies and waging of war. To be sure, colonial militias fought under the British banner (which became the Union Jack after the permanent merger of England and Scotland in 1707) and the command of their royal governors. But colonists whose homes, families, and futures were threatened by French, Spaniards, or Indians fought voluntarily, and their paymasters were their own elected assemblies. The New England towns were the first to require militia duty, but all except Pennsylvania had some sort of military regulation on the books by 1715. The weapons American colonists carried were still mostly of European manufacture, but colonial gunsmiths proliferated during Queen Anne's War on the strength of a domestic iron industry that produced fifteen hundred tons per year by 1700 and was doubling each decade. War so stimulated colonial shipbuilding that Philadelphia and Boston boasted fifteen shipyards apiece by 1720. Since American ships, thanks to the abundance of timber, were 60 percent less expensive than English-built ones, while England's merchant marine was subject to requisition in wartime, New England alone sold 187 vessels abroad during the War of the Spanish Succession. Such competition from their own colonies soon provoked British manufacturers to demand restrictions on American industry. But so long as colonial production contributed to a joint war effort Parliament could hardly object.[21]

Self-governance is a third sovereign attribute. Clearly the most profound political trend of the early eighteenth century was the growing power exercised by colonies' lower assemblies in at least four broad areas. One was financial power extending from the right to propose and/or pass laws bearing on taxes and money to control over appropriations and budgets. Another was administrative power over public employees, not excluding the governors themselves, and the salaries and fees they received. A third was the liberty of assemblies to make their own rules regarding elections, representation, and membership. Whereas seventeenth-century governors and proprietors sometimes prorogued obstreperous legislatures or forbade discussion of certain issues, assemblies after 1689 claimed for themselves the privileges enjoyed by Parliament, including free speech and debate, and immunity for members while the house was in session. Finally, assemblies assumed executive power over such functions as the appointment of tax collectors, public printers (an important and lucrative benefice), Indian agents, and church offices.

Colonial assemblies were especially eager to assume control over public works such as the building of fortifications, roads, bridges, lighthouses and port facilities, maintenance of ferries, clearing of rivers and creeks, and appointment of harbor pilots. Such activities spurred overall growth and enhanced the value of nearby real estate. It also meant tidy profit for contractors, hence ample chances for assemblymen to engage in kickbacks, log-rolling, and patronage. Lower houses in most of the colonies even began to usurp such apparent royal prerogatives as military and judicial appointments. The pace varied from colony to colony, with Massachusetts usually leading the way in the north and South Carolina in the south. But the process was everywhere similar, because all colonists drew on the same English precedents and all faced similar problems.[22]

What were British authorities to do? The initial response of officials under William and Mary and Queen Anne was to try to centralize control over the colonies in the same manner as James II. They insisted colonial assembles vote permanent revenues to support their royal governors and officials, tried to unify military command in New York and New England, and even re-appointed Stuart officials such as Randolph and Andros. But the "Whig" monarchs and officials who had overthrown James II did so in the name of English liberties. How could they then deny British subjects who happened to live in the colonies the same rights and privileges they claimed for themselves? Only through *force majeure*. But Parliament had no stomach for the expense and conflict that would entail, and in any event trying to bully the colonies was silly so long as they were engaged in a common war effort with Britain. So the crown gave up on "unified military command" in 1701, and by 1702 attempts to oblige assemblies to pay the salaries of royal officials failed everywhere but Virginia.[23]

The old proprietors had no more luck controlling their colonists than did royal appointees. William Penn lost his charter in 1692 due to the Quakers' refusal to fight for king and country. But recovery of his charter in 1694 only condemned Penn to prolonged negotiations with Pennsylvania's assembly. The resulting Charter of Privileges of 1701 was in effect a surrender. Government in Pennsylvania and Delaware was to reside in a single elected assembly endowed with "all other Powers and Privileges of an Assembly, according to the Rights of the Freeborn Subjects of England, and as is usual in any of the King's plantations in America." Penn retained a nominal veto power to which the assembly paid lip service so long as he never dared wield it. After Penn died in 1718 and his son reverted to the Anglican church, proprietary influence became even viler to the Quaker majority. In Carolina the heirs of Ashley Cooper and his associates lost what little deference they had enjoyed by failing to lift a finger during their colonists' struggles against Spaniards, Frenchmen, Tuscaroras, or, for that matter, the ferocious pirate Blackbeard.[24] When another war scare erupted in 1719 the South Carolina militia took the occasion to depose the governor, declare itself a constitutional convention, and petition the crown to dispossess the absentee proprietors. The Board of Trade was not displeased by this latest American revolution. It sent out a royal governor and in 1729 bought out the proprietors on behalf of the crown.[25]

Suffice it to say the twelve mainland American colonies were now largely self-governing and willing to recognize British authority so long as it was not really enforced. Nowhere was that mentality more pronounced than in matters of trade, because Whig officials after 1689 maintained the mercantilist policies inherited from Cromwell and the Stuarts. What is more, they made a serious attempt to enforce the Navigation Act of 1696 by creating a centralized colonial customs office supported in turn by Admiralty courts and royal advocates-general. No longer would enforcement of Britain's commercial laws depend on the colonists' voluntary obedience, or impotent royal governors, or anodyne promises made by proprietors. No longer would the Board of Trade virtually beg Massachusetts to respect Parliamentary acts and turn a blind eye to smuggling and illegal competition. At least, that was the theory.

In fact, American colonists resisted by all manner of means, from legal challenges and lobbying to outright violence against officers of the crown and the courts. British customs officials, in turn, were asked to police a thousand miles of serrated coastline, without naval or military assistance, at an ocean's remove, all the while dependent on the colonists themselves to provide information about ship movements and cargoes, and prosecute, testify, or serve as jurors in court. A few examples illustrate what the hapless customs officers faced.[26]

In 1715, the earnest Maurice Birchfield assumed responsibility for the Chesapeake. He found Maryland's port records especially chaotic. Cases against colonial merchants charged with evasion of duties or illegal imports had piled up for decades. He tried to pursue them only to learn that convenient fires had destroyed the bonds and depositions supporting the crown's cases. In one instance an accused merchant had long since died, but not before making a sizable bequest to the Maryland attorney-general responsible for suing his estate!

When Birchfield persevered in litigating the backlog of claims, the annoyed colonial assembly simply passed a statute of limitations on mercantile suits.

Up in Boston comptroller William Lambert learned the American brigantine *William and Mary,* allegedly carrying a legal cargo of salt from Lisbon, dropped anchor first at Piscataqua to unload contraband wine, oil, and leather. He filed suit against the captain and owners and summoned the crew to testify. Just two sailors responded, and irate Bostonians subjected them to such violent threats they had to be put in protective custody. When Lambert persisted in the prosecution, the townspeople took to jostling British officials in the streets. The distraught governor even pleaded for troops to discourage "the many Riots and Disorders that have been Committed in the Town." Thus, customs agents learned early on no colonial assembly, official, witness, or jury could be trusted.

In 1724 the merchant ship *Fame* docked in Philadelphia on a mission of mercy to deliver Palatine refugees to Penn's haven. But hidden deep in her hold was a cargo of goods from Europe and the Dutch East Indies worth over £20,000. John Moore, British customs agent, seized the ship and placed four guards on board. It was no good. During the night some sixty Pennsylvanians approached the vessel in disguise, seized it "in a tumultuous & violent Manner," floated it downriver, and smuggled the cargo ashore. All Moore earned for his trouble was a reprimand for failing to recapture the ship before the evidence vanished. He would have done better to have taken a bribe and entered false accounts, as many of his colleagues did as a matter of course. Lord Bellomont, dispatched to investigate one such case of official abuse, simply concluded: "a Collectors is the most ungratefull Office in these plantations that can be—if he is Just to his trust in looking into their Trade they hate him mortally."[27]

Colonial mischief was one thing, but the Navigation Acts also proved nugatory because Britain's administration in these decades was a confused tangle of ministries and agencies all claiming an interest in the colonies. In 1721, the Board of Trade tried to streamline the imperial service by recommending its president be given cabinet rank, direct access to the monarch, and sole control over policy and appointments. Nothing came of that sensible suggestion because a "confused tangle" of rival interests was exactly what the ruling Parliamentary faction wanted.

What the Whigs' Glorious Revolution bequeathed to Britain was not "liberalism," much less a two-party system, but patronage and corruption. Everyone aspiring to wealth, power, and influence in eighteenth-century Britain had to be a Whig of one sort or another, for to oppose the regime implied sympathy for the exiled Stuarts. But the Whigs themselves were divided into *juntos* of back-scratching peers and merchants from country or town, representing themselves, their families and friends, and various economic interests in a House of Commons still a century away from the first democratic Reform Bill. The job of cabinet ministers and other power brokers, therefore, was to patch together Parliamentary majorities through the deft dispensing of patronage, benefices, and bribes.[28]

Chief among brokers were Robert Walpole, first minister, lord of the treasury, and chancellor of the exchequer from 1721 to 1742, and Thomas Pelham-Holles, Duke of Newcastle, who ran the department responsible for colonial affairs from 1724 to 1748. They knew the Board of Trade's 1721 recommendations, however sensible from an administrative point of view, were political madness. An honest, centralized colonial service would deprive various ministries of patronage over forty plum appointments in the colonies. Few of them carried large salaries, but all provided ample opportunity for personal enrichment through the courting of bribes, sweetheart deals, and insider trading. Control over patronage also endowed cabinet members with political capital to bestow on the friends and family of key figures in Parliament.[29] So Walpole's choices were either to wink at the colonists' peccadillos while preserving the colonial service as a political pork barrel, or else to forge an efficient colonial service backed by the navy that would eliminate patronage, cost a great deal, and surely enrage the Americans. There was really no choice to be made.[30]

So Walpole and Newcastle made *quieta non movere* and "Salutary Neglect" the mottoes of their colonial policy. This meant losing revenue to Americans' illicit trade, but not so much as to hurt because the real money to be made in the colonies came from West Indian sugar. Indeed, the only time Walpole considered suspending Salutary Neglect was when Americans' bad behavior damaged the sugar interest.

The problem was rum. Americans consumed, per capita, over four gallons of rum per year. After 1700 they also distilled for export from Philadelphia, Boston, and Newport over a million gallons per year. Hence, the northern colonies especially were a large, growing market for West Indian molasses. But a customs official was alarmed to discover New Englanders purchased about half their molasses from French, Dutch, and Spanish islands rather than British ones. So members of Parliament, many personally interested, passed a 1733 Molasses Act, slapping a prohibitive tariff on foreign sugar sold in the British empire. Receipts from the tariff rose over the following year, then fell

precipitously as Americans resorted to the usual dodges. Pressured by West
Indian planters, Parliament considered a bill to enforce the tariff in 1739, but
rightly judged it "penny wise and pound foolish."

The implications for imperial unity were dire. As William Knox, a British
official with long experience in the colonies, surmised, "the seeds of disunion
were sowed in the first plantation in every one of them, and that a general disposition to independence of this country prevailed throughout the whole."[31]
Since the Whigs' own constitutional principles struck from their hands any justification for discriminatory regulations, the only ways out of their quandary
were to grant the colonists their own representation at Westminster or else recognize the colonial assemblies as coordinate parliaments. But those were as yet
unthinkable ideas, and in any case would have had dire implications for the
British empire elsewhere, especially Ireland.

Thanks to Salutary Neglect, new flows of immigration, the colonists' energy
and fertility, the richness of climate and land, the increasing exploitation of
slave labor, and the fact the colonists were the least taxed people on earth,
British North America developed at a galloping pace. New England's population more than tripled from about 87,000 in 1690 to 289,700 by 1740, that of the
middle colonies sextupled over that period from about 34,800 to 220,500, the
Chesapeake population quadrupled from 75,500 to 296,500 (of whom 84,000
were enslaved Africans), and Carolinians multiplied almost ten times from
11,500 to 108,000 (of whom almost half were African). The mainland American
colonies as a whole approached 1 million by 1740, a figure more than one-sixth
the population of England and Wales.[32] Men still outnumbered women everywhere but New England, but the grotesque sexual imbalance of the seventeenth century had disappeared. Children under sixteen accounted for almost
*half* the entire population, while more than two-thirds of the population made
their livings from agriculture. Further demographic expansion, therefore, dictated geographical expansion. By 1740 southern New England, the Hudson
River Valley, Long Island, and the New Jersey corridor from New York to
Philadelphia were all (as the charming New England road signs still read)
"thickly settled." So, too, were the southeastern counties of Pennsylvania as far
west as Lancaster.

Virginia's growth beyond the fall lines of its rivers into the foothills of the
Blue Ridge is linked in legend and fact with Governor Alexander Spotswood.

Fired by visions of "a new English nation" spreading out to claim the whole continent, he led an expedition in 1716 of sixty-three horsemen from the capital (since 1699) of Williamsburg to the first crest of the mountains. From there Spotswood's riders, dubbed the Knights of the Golden Horseshoe, gazed east toward the century-old commonwealth of Virginia and west to pine-covered mountains that might soon belong to the French if the British did not get there first. Most breathtaking, however, was the valley beneath them cut by a river the Indians called Shanando, "daughter of the stars": Shenandoah. With solemn ceremony Spotswood buried a bottle on its banks containing his claim to the valley and mountains beyond in the names of Virginia and King George I. Then the party made camp to toast the future with "Virginia red wine and white wine, Irish usqubaugh, brandy, shrub, two sorts of rum, champagne, canary, cherry, punch, water, cider, &c." Spotswood left the next day (presumably not very early), but ordered a company of rangers to remain and explore. What they found amidst the tangle of laurels alive with squirrels, woodpeckers, rattlesnakes, and mosquitoes was a well-worn Indian trail marked by hatchet-chops made on trees. It proved to be nothing less than the Great Warriors' Path that stretched southward into the Carolinas and north across the Potomac into western Maryland, central Pennsylvania, and finally the Iroquois strongholds in central New York. This great route, the first "interstate highway" in eastern North America, had served the Indians in war and commerce for centuries, and Spotswood determined it must serve the English as well. So he attended another great conference at Albany in 1722, joining the governors of New York and Pennsylvania in a renewal of the Covenant Chain. The elaborate parlay dragged on almost three weeks since every governor and sachem insisted on rehashing the others' past abuses, the better to justify their own present demands. For his part, Spotswood promised the Indians perpetual liberty to travel the Great Warriors' Path in return for their promise never to come east of the Blue Ridge or south of the Potomac. At length the governor's gifts of guns, wampum, and alcohol induced the chiefs to cry "O-ha, O-ha," indicating their approval. At least so far as the northern tribes were concerned, Virginia could expand unmolested.[33]

As the colonies grew spatially they developed internally. Economic histories generally stress foreign trade, and for good reasons. All the colonies relied heavily on imports of manufactured goods and exports of commodities, whether timber, fish, and furs in the north, grain and other foodstuffs in the middle colonies, or tobacco, rice, indigo, tar, turpentine, and deerskins in the south. Statistical data on the early American economy deal mostly with trade and scarcely at all with household or local production, consumption, and barter. Finally, trade was important because mercantilist restrictions were a constant source of tension between the colonists and the mother country. But the place to begin seeking the origins of America's precocious prosperity is the farm, not the wharf.

Since land, wood, and water were available in abundance, American farms were generally much larger than those in Europe, often exceeding one hundred acres. Production was thus a function of the labor supply in the forms of children and other kin, indentured or chattel servants, and tenants. If enough hands were available, the farmer could raise ample amounts of grain for human consumption, devote over half the crop to livestock feed, let some fields lie fallow, and still have acres to set aside for orchards, vegetables, pastures, and forest. In one Maryland county, around 1700, the average household counted twenty cattle, twenty pigs, thirteen sheep, and three horses. Data also show a high rate of tenancy rather than ownership, but that is not necessarily evidence of rural poverty. Renters were often owners of neighboring farms seeking additional acreage, or younger sons leasing a farm until such time as they could purchase their own. Farmers blessed with rich soil in Pennsylvania or the Chesapeake also had expectations their land might appreciate as much as 300 percent over a lifetime. Sons, immigrants, and farmers on marginal land had the option of moving west where land was still cheap. Only in New England did poor and exhausted soil, erosion, a shorter growing season, and a denser population make "subsistence farming" the rule. Indeed, colonial husbandmen and their wives were so productive that after meeting their own needs and those of their animals, putting aside next year's seed, and provisioning local markets, they provided the British West Indies, Ireland, and England with tens of thousands of hogsheads in corn, flour, rice, flaxseed, hemp, indigo, and tobacco, the price of which recovered sufficiently by 1719 to make it generally profitable again to Chesapeake planters.[34]

What is more, Anglo-American farmers "made it" without significant innovations. Iron-plated moldboard plows were still a luxury as late as 1700, few farmers of English origins bothered to fertilize, and only slowly did they grasp the need for contoured fields to resist the erosion caused by "nor'easter" storms.[35] They did, however, adopt the windmill from the New Amsterdam Dutch, sawmills based on Danish designs, and three inventions of their own. The first was the Z-shaped crisscross fence, which could be built of split rails without any nails at all. The second was the tapered, flat-headed American axe that allowed them to fell trees and split rails at three times the clip of English axemen. The third, thanks to the sawmills, was standardized building material. By the 1720s carpenters in Philadelphia and Boston began to sell everything a home builder needed from seasoned crossbeams to pre-glazed window frames. Most of all, Americans invented themselves. Freedom of movement and freedom from guilds meant an enterprising youngster might set himself up, if not here then there, as a smith, cooper, skinner, saddler, shoemaker, tailor, fuller, miller, apothecary, or perhaps more than one trade with a farm on the side for good measure.

The colonies were as yet far from self-reliant, but the nature of their imports from Britain began by the 1720s to show a subtle change toward specialty goods and luxuries, and away from basic tools, clothing, and capital goods they were increasingly able to make for themselves. American farms, especially over the winter, doubled as little textile works turning out clothing of wool, linen, and leather. Generally men sheared the sheep, skinned the cattle, and teased the flax, while women cleaned and spun fibers. But that was only the beginning. Raw wool had to be scrubbed in tubs, then dried (in the shade, not sun), then beaten, then carded by hand through tiny wires embedded in a paddle, then disentangled, then spun on a spindle or wheel whose rotation speed had to be delicately controlled. The making of linen from flax was an even more elaborate and time-consuming matter involving warp, woof, weft, heddles, and treadles. But the most taxing occupation of all was the tanning of leather. First, hides must be soaked in vats of lime for months in order to loosen the animal's hair. Second, hides must be beamed, which meant scraping them clean of hair on the outside and clinging fat on the inside, by means of a double-handled curved knife. Third, they must be washed again and rubbed with a stone. Fourth and finally came the tanning itself, when hides were soaked from four months (for a calf or buck skin) to a full year (for a tough old cow skin) in solutions of tannin, the powdered bark of a hemlock or oak. After chemistry did its work the tanner dried the leather and beat it until it was soft enough to be sewn into a girl's shoes or a frontiersman's jacket.[36]

Labor—backbreaking labor—was just as necessary to the colonies' development as land and raw materials. It is all very well to note that whereas only twelve ironworks were founded in the seventeenth century, ten were established in the Chesapeake and twenty-two more in Pennsylvania just during the years 1715–40. That meant the colonies were achieving a capacity to supply their own markets with horseshoes, tools, plowshares, nails, needles, and gun barrels and still export two thousand tons of pig iron per year to Britain. Indeed, the American colonies' share of the *world*'s iron production rose from 2 to 15 percent over the years 1690 to 1775. But those statistics do not begin to convey the prodigious effort metallurgy required under pre-industrial conditions. The first chore was locating a rich deposit of ore in a bog or an outcropping because, without power tools, no amount of manpower made it worthwhile to extract ore from a poor vein. Second, since most deposits lay inland in the wilderness, food and other supplies had to be shipped out to workers and defense provided against Indian raids. It often made sense to surround the ironworks with an agricultural plantation, build a fort, and ask laborers to double as militiamen. Next, colliers went to work felling hundreds of trees and gathering flux, usually limestone, whose chemicals help molten metals to fuse. Logs were then piled in a gigantic mound, with a "chimney" hole in the middle, and cooked more than burned as slowly and evenly as possible. Colliers achieved this by tossing dirt on the smouldering mound and digging vents in order to reduce or increase the flow of oxygen. A week's worth of such sweltering, around-the-clock labor yielded a hillock of charcoal. After several more days to allow for cooling, the charcoal was hauled to the bloomery to be mixed with ore and flux and heated by bellows until the iron melted into blobs. Then the smithies took over, removing the blobs with tongs, pounding them, reheating and pounding them again until iron was finally wrought.

Bloomeries only sufficed to supply local needs. Large-scale iron production required a blast furnace, which looked like a stone pyramid twenty-five feet tall lopped off at the top and punctured at the bottom by a horizontal shaft. The shaft led to a tapered interior chamber where hell would be kindled by blasts of air shot through a porthole by a twenty-foot-long bellows driven by stone counterweights moved in turn by a huge waterwheel. As iron melted into the crucible, forgers drew off the floating slag and opened a plug in the bottom to allow the molten iron to flow into molds made of clay. From there the molds or bars were hauled to the finery where excess carbon was burned away. Then they were pounded by a gigantic hammer raised high in the air by water-powered levers. So much time, effort, and wood was required to heat up a blast furnace to the necessary temperature the forgers might tend it for as long as nine months before letting it cool down for maintenance.[37]

Thanks to the abundance of good land, the moderate climate, the seemingly inexhaustible animal, fish, and tree life, and not least the improvement ethic and market orientation colonists brought with them from England, Americans achieved, at some point in the early to mid-eighteenth century, the highest per capita standard of living of any people on earth. With the exception of the enslaved, their prosperity was also remarkably egalitarian. Thus, while even the richest colonists were pikers compared to Europe's grand nobles or merchants, poor colonists enjoyed diets, dwellings, and opportunities far beyond the reach of Britain's lower classes. That is why colonial militiamen were on average two inches taller than British soldiers sent over to fight the French.

The colonies' expanding production of guns, ships, furniture, paper, glass, wood products, textiles, and metals did not escape notice in Britain, where merchants and manufacturers rued the competition and strategists feared the day the colonies would become self-sufficient. But so long as British exports to America continued to rise with the growth of the colonies' population and wealth, the practitioners of Salutary Neglect were content. What is more, their exports did continue to rise because Americans, by the second third of the eighteenth century, were busy embracing something else hustling Britons invented: consumerism.

In 1660, the year of the Stuart Restoration, a thirty-two-year-old Calvinist named John Bunyan was arrested for preaching against the Church of England. Since he refused to desist Bunyan spent much of the ensuing twelve years in jail. It was there he began *The Pilgrim's Progress,* one of the classics of English literature and one of the first bestsellers among New England's Puritans. Bunyan's tale is an allegorical dream sequence in which a young man named Christian confronts every diversion, temptation, and threat that a fallen race and its master the devil can throw at him by way of impeding his pilgrimage to the Heavenly City. All Christian's adventures illustrate some poignant and usually humorous truth about man's self-delusion. But the one most likely to pierce American hearts was that of Vanity Fair, Beelzebub's grand market town where all the world's finery is displayed and all the inhabitants are buyers and sellers. Christian and his companion Faithful avert their eyes from the shops and stalls. That refusal to join in the acquisitive orgy lands them in prison. Faithful is placed in the dock before Judge Hategood while Misters Envy, Superstition, and Pickthank testify that he is a "disturber of trade." That being a capital offense in Vanity Fair, Faithful is scourged, lanced, pierced, stoned, and finally burned at the stake. Christian escapes only to fall in with a pilgrim from a similar town called Fair-Speech. It, too, is a covetous beehive, but unlike Vanity Fair it preserves an aura of sanctimony under the Rev. Mr. Two-tongues and Milords Turn-about, Time-server, and Fair-speech. His own grandfather, says the pilgrim, "was but a waterman, looking one way and rowing another: I got most of my estate by the same occupation."[38]

How to feel good about doing well was a central psychological concern of British Protestants and their American offspring. To be sure, they believed material success was no sin—love of money, not money per se, being the root of all evil. Puritans (and Quakers) also believed worldly blessings were a sign of God's favor. But how could that concept of justice, perfectly logical in the abstract and supported by Biblical texts, be reconciled with the fact that apparently pious and orthodox Christians often suffered cruel reverses in life while blasphemers and cheaters "made out like bandits"? Why did the mere acquisition or inheritance of wealth so often turn children into pilgrims in search of Vanity Fair rather than the Heavenly City? Cotton Mather's pithy lament about New England's decay said it all: "*Religion* brought forth *prosperity*, and the *daughter* destroyed the *mother*."[39] There were (and still are) just three ways out of the dilemma confronting a culture awash both in faith and material wealth. The first was to reject Vanity Fair in the manner of Faithful and accept, if not persecution, then the ostracism of one's community. That is a hard choice that only a handful of people (for example, Amish and Oneida communities; Catholic monastics) have tried in America. The second was to worship God on the Sabbath day and Mammon the other six. But easy hypocrisy, though the popular choice, came at the cost of an uneasy conscience. The third way out was to design a uniquely American brand of Protestantism that made the pursuit of happiness sacred, that commercialized religion and sanctified commerce, that freed people to choose whatever faith helped them feel good about doing well.

The "twin gospels of Christ and commerce," to anticipate an American cliché of the 1850s, were implicit in the original spirits of English colonization. If England was the vanguard in the war against popery, and development of idle soil from Ireland to Virginia a means of waging that war, then empire was *ipso facto* a holy endeavor and the "cult of commerce" an important part of what it meant to be British.[40] And if that were so in the British Isles, how much freer were American colonists to sanctify getting ahead for the glory of God?

If we believe the accounts of New England divines and travelogues of Anglican visitors to the Chesapeake, American colonists around 1700 were either lax in religious observance, torn by dissension, or unchurched altogether.[41] Virginia, where the Anglican church was established, was duly divided into parishes with glebes (grants of land) to support clergy. Nor, contrary to an old canard, were Virginia's clergymen any less educated than those of England. But most parishes were rural and vast, their congregations spread out miles from chapel or church, and their vestrymen (being planters) often resistant to rectors who nagged them about morals or money. In Maryland, Catholics were driven underground while the Protestants scattered about rural plantations remained largely unorganized. In South Carolina, by contrast, church life was both orderly and socially respectable. The elegant St. Philip's Anglican Church rose in Charleston as early as 1681, to be followed by a dozen more with generous glebes. State-funded missions ministered to the back country.

Among the middle colonies New York was by far the least churched. The Dutch Reformed, the oldest and best organized sect, had a mere seven pastors for thirty-four congregations in 1700. The Quakers of Pennsylvania, Delaware, and New Jersey were as untamed in religion as in politics, especially when the "Keithian schism" erupted after the death of George Fox, founder of the Society of Friends, in 1691. George Keith launched a public assault in Philadelphia against what he deemed the laxity, worldliness, and neglect of doctrine and scripture among Quakers. The outraged town fathers appealed the dispute all the way to the Yearly Meeting in London and succeeded in having Keith denounced. Most of his followers drifted off to the Baptists, leaving American Quakers free, as the saying went, to subordinate meetinghouse values to those of the countinghouse.[42]

New England's churches remained the most organized in the colonies, but as we know they suffered from demoralization and theological discord. The Half-Way Covenant was meant to reverse the decline in church membership, but as is often the case such watering-down of doctrine and discipline only increased defections. Many congregations counted as members less than half the families in town. Solomon Stoddard, pastor at Northampton, Massachusetts, from 1672 until 1729, thought the solution lay in completely "open communion" just to get people through the church doors. He sparked five local revivals between 1679 and 1718, suggesting declension, Mather's gloom notwithstanding, was reversible. Stoddard also proposed a hierarchical Presbyterian-style polity to enforce uniformity and more rigorous training of ministers. That idea bore fruit in 1701 when New Haven chartered Collegiate School, the future Yale University.[43]

Cotton Mather adamantly opposed all these Connecticut valley innovations from his father's pulpit in Old North Church, Boston. Cotton overcame a bad childhood stutter through prayer and discipline to become the youngest boy ever to matriculate at Harvard. The eventual author of 469 publications, he was obviously a man of extraordinary energy, not to say ego. He had opinions about everything and believed all of them right. But Cotton Mather was not "The Last Puritan," as he is often called, if that implies a throwback to the early days of the Bible Commonwealth. An avid reader of Newton and Locke and member of the Royal Society, he showed keen interest in the new science. In *The Christian Philosopher* he argued natural philosophy could only help to reveal the perfection of God's handiwork. His historical works, the *Magnalia* above all, are infused with a precocious objectivity and skepticism. He believed that "to learn all the brave Things in the world is the bravest Thing in the world." He excoriated masters who withheld the gospel from slaves on the grounds they were not fully human. As husband to three wives and father to fifteen children (thirteen of whom died in his lifetime), Mather also meditated at length on the mysteries of sex and child-rearing. But he was also a mystic who meticulously recorded natural disasters, wars, and supernatural phenomena in search of apocalyptic omens of the millennium, the thousand-year reign of the saints on earth prophesied in St. John's Revelation. Moreover, he firmly believed New England was destined to play a teleological role in that "end of history," which is why he was vexed (or hexed) by social discord and wickedness, which he attributed to Satan. So far from symbolizing the end of an era, therefore, Mather's life and musings anticipated both the Enlightenment and the Christian revivalism—each with its own millenarian tones—that the colonies embraced soon after his death in 1721.[44]

How should one characterize Americans' spirituality *circa* 1720? Tepid, by comparison to their Puritan grandparents? As tepid as Queen Elizabeth intended Englishmen to become? Distracted by material needs and ambitions? Simply unchurched as one would expect on an overseas frontier? Evidence exists to support all these generalizations. But it would be wrong to conclude more than a very few colonists were purposely *irreligious*. Deistic, much less atheistic, views were still very rare in Europe itself, and it is safe to conjecture almost all Americans would pray like a Spaniard if a fever, hard birth, failed crop, or Indian attack threatened. What the colonists lacked was instruction, organization, and above all *choice* in matters of faith. Hence, it seems more accurate to describe the early eighteenth century as a time of spiritual resurgence and mutation that did not "revive" some old-time religion so much as create a marketplace of new or adapted Protestant sects.

The resurgence that turned religion into a marketable commodity began, ironically, with initiatives from the established church. With the crown safely in Protestant hands after 1689, the Church of England finally took an interest in the colonies, and the Bishop of London sent commissaries to report on their needs. The first, James Blair, founded the College of William and Mary in 1693, and remained pastor in Williamsburg until his death at eighty-seven in 1743. Even more prominent was Thomas Bray, who inspired the Society for the Propagation of Christian Knowledge (1698) and the Society for the Propagation of the Gospel (1701). In the ensuing decades the S.P.C.K. and S.P.G. dispatched over six hundred clergymen to the colonies, filling most of the vacancies in the south and planting more than three hundred Anglican parishes in the middle colonies and New England.[45]

Anglican initiatives provoked a vigorous response from the growing Scots Presbyterian communities. In 1706 their convention in Philadelphia formed an American presbytery, the first intercolonial civic body of any kind. But while all adhered to the Calvinist Westminster Confession, Presbyterians quarreled over issues of governance and ordination, especially after the colonies' first religious entrepreneurs set up shop. In 1726 William Tennent, Sr., ordained Anglican but married to the daughter of a Presbyterian preacher, founded a tiny seminary in Neshaminy, Bucks County, Pennsylvania. He instructed a score of preachers, including three sons, in Hebrew, Latin, Greek, and a fervent "experimental" style of evangelism. Traditionalists mocked Tennent's "Log College" and the urgent, emotional sermons of its graduates, not least Gilbert Tennent. But neither Presbyterians nor other denominations had any means or authority to keep spiritual freelancers from ordaining ministers and proselytizing among churched and unchurched alike. A close friend of Gilbert Tennent, the Dutch Reformed pastor Theodore Jacob Frelinghuysen, shocked all New Jersey clergy in the years after 1720 by urging their flocks to transcend denominational niggling in the name of Christ and their personal bliss.[46]

A new spirit blew and listed in the Connecticut valley as well. Stoddard showed the way by opening pews not just to sanctified Puritans, but to *sinners*. He left his grandson and successor at Northampton, Jonathan Edwards, a rich field to harvest. A fourth-generation clergyman and the only boy among ten sisters, Edwards lived up to the expectations placed on him. At thirteen he matriculated at Yale; at twenty-one he was named Yale's head tutor; at twenty-eight, in 1731, he was invited to deliver the great Thursday Lecture at Harvard. Edinburgh philosopher Dugald Stewart said of Edwards he did "not yield to any disputant bred in the universities of Europe." He was also extremely handsome and so conscious of pride he kept a diary of his sins until he escaped that "abyss" by accepting God's unmerited grace.[47]

From 1729 until his death in 1758 from a smallpox inoculation gone wrong, Edwards wrote dozens of metaphysical and psychological treatises affirming original sin, not just as dogma but as empirical fact, and Trinitarian Christianity as God's rational mechanism to restore mankind's "original righteousness." He began with Locke's postulate to the effect that all human knowledge is sensory and subjective. He concluded with St. Augustine's observation to the effect that God's light must shine within fallen creatures for them to desire and grasp objective truth at all. It therefore followed, if God's Spirit is indeed present in receptive men and women, they do possess free will to choose among motives and do have moral responsibility for the choices they make. Thus did Edwards sweep away all the Puritan pother about predestination, Arminianism, and Half-Way Covenants.

Edwards' philosophical genius would have longlasting effects on American high culture, leading others in directions he would have disdained. But his homiletic genius lay in getting simple farmers and townspeople to look at themselves from the perspective of eternity, reifying for them the choice they could not escape. His most famous sermon, "Sinners in the Hands of an Angry God," likened the complacent man to a loathsome spider hanging by a thread over the flame. It reduced many congregants to weeping on hands and knees. But Edwards did not employ fire and brimstone to terrorize sinners into repentance: that would only indulge the selfish instincts he meant to purge. He just wanted people to *feel* how truly abhorrent sin is in the eyes of a holy God so they might appreciate the boundlessness of God's love and the "excellency" of Christ's sacrifice. Above all, he wanted to free them from tempters, including "unconverted clergy," who denied them their freedom. He wanted them to grasp that they sinned precisely because they were free—free to ask God to remake their lives to His glory, which is the sole end of existence. Edwards, like Mather, also believed the earthly millennium when God "shall take the

Kingdom" was imminent, and that what was happening "in America, especially in New England, may prove the dawn of that glorious day."[48]

The result, beginning in 1734 in Northampton, was a "Surprising Work of God" that caught up young people especially and filled the town with "love, joy, and distress." Edwards' published sermons and accounts of the revival soon flooded neighboring colonies, inspired other preachers, and reached across the ocean to England.

The success of these first evangelists—emotional, extra-institutional, but by no means anti-intellectual—suggests early eighteenth-century Americans were *not* spiritually moribund. They had just been wanting a faith that spoke to the hopes and fears of a hustling but insecure people hostile to established churches and jealous of liberty—a faith that blessed their material dreams and offered them heaven, too.

No initiative combined the goals of developing America while saving souls more explicitly than the founding of Georgia in 1733. British imperial strategists (not to mention South Carolinians) long desired a military buffer against Spanish Florida. But politics merged with piety when James Oglethorpe and John Percival requested a charter to found a utopian colony between the Savannah and Altamaha Rivers. These wealthy, pious Parliamentarians were devoted to rehabilitation of criminals and education of Negroes. They dreamed of making Georgia a haven for the poor of all sects except, of course, Roman Catholics. They advertised it, from pillar to post to pulpit, as the "greatest social and philanthropic experiment of the age," and raked in contributions including £10,000 from Walpole himself. Oglethorpe led the first contingent of a hundred settlers (not convicts, as myth has it, but yeomen). He chose a site on the south bank of the Savannah River about eighteen miles from the sea, surveyed a grid of boulevards amply punctuated with parks, and started to raise a most elegant town. Like Penn, he also powwowed at once with Indians for the peaceful purchase of land.[49]

The first year was nonetheless awful. Half the pioneers fell ill; most of the rest displayed what Oglethorpe called "Petulancy." They flouted authority, refused to work, demanded extra rations to trade for contraband rum. "By degrees," he wrote, "I brought the People to Discipline, but could not revive the Spirit of Labour: Idleness and Drunkeness was Succeeded by Sickness." In fact, the English villagers and Scots highlanders who settled on the Altamaha could never be disciplined so long as they were obliged to work for the common good, stand guard against Spaniards, and pay hefty quit rents to reimburse the trustees' expenses. Nor could they be induced to obey prohibitions against the boons that made life in South Carolina jolly and prosperous, which is to say rum and slaves. So the first Georgians nullified Oglethorpe's high-minded statutes one by one until, after war with Spain became a reality (in 1739), they won Parliament's ear. By 1742 rum, slavery, and a free market in land were legal de facto; by 1750 de jure. Two years later the philanthropists bowed out, leaving Georgia another crown colony under a royal governor, his council, and an elected assembly.[50]

So yet another holy experiment fell apart, this time the moment its unholy colonists hit the shore. But Georgia nevertheless made an enormous contribution to American religiosity because a young English preacher inspired by Oglethorpe sailed there in 1738. He believed his calling lay in America. By the end of his life he did as much as any one person to give Americans *their* calling.

George Whitefield was born in Gloucester in 1714, the son of an innkeeper who died when he was two and a mother who expected great things of him. An indifferent student, all he learned growing up were tall tales, mimicry, and japes from the gamblers, drunks, prostitutes, pickpockets, sailors, and more "respectable" dodgers frequenting the family tavern. By the time he reached his teens, George was out of school, out of work, and spending his time reciting theatrical scripts in the dialects of the characters. He also admired Anglican liturgies, but when he began winning parts in stage plays he assumed he would make a career in that "devil's workshop," the theater. One day he blurted out to his sister, "I think God will provide for me some way or other that we cannot apprehend." The way appeared almost at once. His mother learned poor boys might attend Oxford if willing to valet for gentlemen's sons. "Will you go?" she asked. "With all my heart," he said. At Pembroke College George quit playing the rake, excelled in his studies, and fell in with a group of young "methodists" led by John and Charles Wesley. He read *The Pilgrim's Progress* over and over, imagining himself on a similar trip through the Slough of Despond and Vanity Fair. He inflicted such mortifications and fasts on himself the college doctor even sent him home for a while to regain his strength.[51]

In 1736 Whitefield was ordained in the Church of England and got into trouble at once. He was too good. After his debut in London the bishop heard complaints the young man had driven fifteen parishioners "mad." Doubtless he envied Whitefield as well after his first published sermon, "The Nature and Necessity of Our Regeneration or New Birth in Christ Jesus," flew out of bookstalls. When the bishop rebuked him for enthusiasm, Whitefield, just twenty-two, rebuked the bishop in public. He had a gift, a technique, and a message that latitudinarian place fillers of an established church could not tolerate. His gift, of course, was theatrical. In the pulpit Whitefield delighted listeners with impressions of sinners, scoffers, and stodgy old parsons. He drove home theological points with humor, suspense, and pathos. Almost always he broke into tears upon offering sinners the free gift of God's grace. He was also cross-eyed in a hypnotic sort of way that transfixed an audience (mockers dubbed him Dr. Squintum). In short, Whitefield was a spellbinder and knew it.

His technique, by contrast, was acquired. Whitefield grew up in an inn in a bustling commercial town during the very years the English were becoming a consumer society.[52] Middle- and upper-class incomes were rising thanks to Britain's commercial expansion and agricultural revolution. Merchants and manufacturers learned to reach national and international markets. The growth of advertising made possible "brand names" and products such as Wedgwood china that "no good household should be without." It was only a matter of time before the methods of market capitalism spilled into the cultural sphere. Whitefield, assisted by some wealthy Methodist patrons, was among the first to post placards announcing upcoming appearances, much to the discomfort of local clergy. He also adopted the Welsh practice of preaching in open fields. Not only did that allow for much larger audiences than a church or hall, it added to the mystique, encouraged the added intoxication of beverages, and pointedly separated the service from any church or authority except heaven above.

Finally, there was Whitefield's message, which almost always stressed the Lord's answer to the inquiring Nicodemus: "Unless a man is born again he cannot see the kingdom of God" (John 3:3). While rebirth was stressed by every denomination, most Catholic, Anglican, and Calvinist treatments of it were theological and linked to the sacrament of baptism. Whitefield, the Wesleys, and the other "experiential" preachers stressed, indeed evoked, the sinner's emotional response to the gospel. They endeavored, that is, to create customer demand for the ecstatic *feeling* of being born again. That is not to say they were hucksters—on the contrary, they themselves had undergone intense conversions and were eager to share that joy. But they did market religion in the same way a parfumerie or couturier marketed fashion. Why should the devil have all the good tunes?

Buffeted by Anglican resistance, Whitefield asked again for a sign and got two. The first was an impromptu invitation to preach in December 1737, which worried him because he had no prepared notes. Then he remembered the Biblical promise "Lo! I am with you always." When the extemporaneous sermon proved a hit, he lost all doubts about his ability to take the show "on the road." The second sign was the Wesleys' decision to carry the gospel to England's new colony Georgia. They urged Whitefield to follow them.

What he found was a ragtag outpost united in nothing but contempt for Oglethorpe's rules, which the Wesleys sternly endorsed. Whitefield, by contrast, won his first Georgia converts by *blessing* both rum and slavery, asking only that slaves, too, be permitted to hear the gospel. He reached out to folks of all backgrounds, including German Lutherans, whose customs and liturgies he accepted. All he asked of people was to hear the call to rebirth and support his plan for an orphanage school. He stayed in Georgia just three months, but preached twice a day, founded churches and charities, won a land grant for the orphanage, and in all things was "received as an angel of God."[53]

The frenetic Whitefield spent the next year touring England. His crowds grew enormous, some said twenty thousand, and his celebrity crossed the ocean. Thus, when Philadelphians learned he was sailing to their town in October 1739, the result was a sensation. Whitefield and his advance man William Seward deliberately chose Philadelphia because it was large, diverse, centrally located, and tolerant. It was also a center of publicity thanks to its equally energetic printer and publisher, Benjamin Franklin. Everything went according to plan. Pennsylvanians, well prepared by the Tennents and Freylinghuysen, turned out in droves to hear the evangelist's call to repentance in the name of no particular church. Still, Franklin suspected Seward of exaggerating the crowds, so he performed an experiment. Indeed, up to twenty-five thousand people could hear an outdoor oration. The skeptical Franklin even professed to be so moved by Whitefield he "emptied his pockets" into the collection plate. Ben neglected to mention he himself promoted the preacher's crusade because it earned him windfall profits from printing and selling religious books and tracts. But the lifelong friendship between the two men was more than a matter of mutual backscratching. Each respected the sincerity of the other's public spiritedness, each learned from the other how to manipulate one's popular image, and each appreciated (perhaps with a wink) the other's genius for self-reinvention.[54] In their own ways, Whitefield and Franklin were never off stage. Both hustlers for good causes, they also felt good about doing well.

After departing Philadelphia, Whitefield preached his way across Jersey to New York, while Seward rode ahead distributing placards, placing advertisements, and writing dozens of letters per day to editors, preachers, converts, anyone who might feed the buzz at subsequent stops.[55] But Yorkers were unmoved by the message however much they may have admired Whitefield's marketing skills. Shaking the dust off his feet, the evangelist left behind a printed attack on Manhattan's "unconverted ministry," thereby ensuring his name stayed on everyone's lips. In 1740 the show proceeded through Newport to Boston, where Whitefield was lionized to the consternation of cold Congregrationalists. One offended Bostonian even suggested General Court pass a law "for the discouragement of Pedlars in Divinity."[56] Whitefield, knowing there is no such thing as bad publicity, returned the favor by lambasting the faculties of Harvard and Yale.

To make a long story short, Whitefield's career honed and hawked the techniques of revivalism. He made fifteen tours of Scotland, three of Ireland, and seven of the colonies, where he was named the American St. Paul. From 1740 to 1770 he visited all the colonies more than once, especially his beloved Georgia, where the orphanage thrived thanks to the £12,855 he raised for it. While on tour he either traveled or preached for fifty or more hours per week; a conservative estimate of his sermons exceeds eighteen thousand. Orthodox critics questioned whether the excitement he inspired in converts survived their next pub crawl. In any event revivalism tapered off sharply by mid-century as war and politics pushed religion aside and genuine frauds such as the book-burning John Davenport sullied the reputations of itinerant preachers. Boston's Charles Chauncey, looking back on the whole business, called it "a small Thing" in the end. He was wrong. The social, ecclesiastical, and political effects of the revivals led by Whitefield and his imitators proved indelible. Up and down the coast American congregations split asunder as evangelical "new lights" (or "new sides") took over churches from "old lights" or left to found new churches. Some two hundred schisms occurred in New England alone. Old denominations exploded and new ones arose, not because colonists *rejected* authority but because they insisted on choosing the authority under which they would live. In many cases people left lax congregations for more rigorous ones. But whether old or new light, churches now had to adjust to the marketplace. New colleges such as Princeton (1746), Brown (1764), Rutgers (1766), and Dartmouth (1769) sprang up to train evangelical ministers. Social distinctions grew fuzzier as some Americans, at least, flocked together on the basis of faith rather than class or ethnicity. Frontier folk gained a new sense of dignity and independence from coastal elites.[57]

Last but not least, the message that individuals enjoyed free will under God and bore responsibility for their own destiny encouraged and justified the colonists' habitual defiance of external control. Whitefield baptized slavery, but preached to blacks as well as whites.[58] He baptized commerce, but preached a higher calling wealth could help serve. He baptized appetite and celebrity, but preached humility and service to others. He exemplified frenetic labor, utter impatience, and insouciant tolerance. He offered the colonies a cause: liberty under God and before men.

So what was the "First Great Awakening," as these events are called in the history books? First, that term is anachronistic because it was coined a century later (in 1840) by another evangelist hoping to promote a similar revival. Nor was it really a revival, because that word implies resuscitation of something old and near death. What the experiential preachers of the eighteenth century really did was construct novel Protestant variations and employ novel methods to market them. Had there been no prior need among the American (and British) masses for a new line of spiritual products the movement would never have taken off. But it is true the movement grew so large so quickly thanks to conscious promotion of the idea of "revival" itself.

Jonathan Edwards started it all by publishing—in London—his account of the Northampton conversions, *A Faithful Narrative of the Surprizing Work of God*, in 1737. That helped to inspire the Wesleys and Whitefield. Then colonial journals prepared the way for Whitefield by publicizing the excitement he created in Britain. Then Seward and Franklin sensationalized Whitefield's success, prompting a bevy of fired-up preachers to ape him. Then, in 1743, Boston's Thomas Prince founded a magazine, *Christian History*, whose sole purpose was to stoke revivals by reporting revivals. How much it was based on wishful thinking, credulity, or sheer invention is moot since most of the details about revivals originated with their preachers and press agents. But it is telling that Edwards was turned out of his own church when the frenzy finally abated. While "there was a glorious work of God wrought," he surmised in 1751, "false appearance and counterfeits" did their work as well, such that "the number of true converts was not so great as was then imagined."[59]

Should the term "Great Awakening" be purged in favor of some complex sentence to the effect that the 1730s witnessed new forms of mass evangelization that may or may not have quickened the spirituality of one generation of American colonists? Not quite—and not only because of the revival's effects, listed above. Rather, the very fact the "Great Awakening" *was* partly a social construction suggests something profound about the gestation of American culture. By praying for the land to be scorched by the Spirit, but at the same time acting as if God *needed their help* to do His surprising works; by calling the country to emotional, transcendental rebirth, while at the same time blessing its rational, material order, preachers and converts alike were living the millenarian hopes entertained by Mather and Edwards. They were, if only subconsciously, thrusting their clutches skyward to pull down heaven itself—down to America. You can't help but do well and feel good about it, in heaven.

# Germans, Four Sorts
## of Britons,
## and Africans
### *Peoples and Cultures*
### *of the Thirteen Colonies to 1750*

*T*he 2000 census revealed that more American citizens trace part of their ancestry back to Germany than to any other nation, England included. Not only did Germans reinforce their eighteenth-century migration with two more immigrant floods after 1848 and 1890, they included Protestants, Catholics, and Jews hence intermarried with Americans of almost all other backgrounds. Yet synthetic histories usually underestimate the importance of the first German American communities. They might mention the Palatines and Swiss in North Carolina, or the Lutherans and Moravian Brethren that Whitefield encountered in Georgia. They are bound to mention the sixty thousand Pennsylvania Dutch (*Deutsche*) who arrived between 1710 and 1760, if only to illustrate that colony's reputation as "the best poor man's country" or to explain Benjamin Franklin's initial American cry for immigration restrictions.[1] But if that is all textbooks impart they ignore the full story of this prominent American ethnic group—a story of desperation, exploitation, and death, but also of determination, discipline, and priceless gifts which the Germans and their adopted land gave each other. The German experience was the template for all European "ethnics" to come.

"Hail to Posterity! Hail, future men of Germanopolis!" wrote Francis Daniel Pastorius upon his arrival in Philadelphia. "Farewell, dear Germany!

Forevermore, farewell."[2] He hoped Germantown would become a magnet drawing more and more of his countrymen from an old country plagued by feudalism, persecution, and war. Had he known what they would go through, perhaps the gentle pastor would have hoped otherwise.[3]

The mass migration of "Palatines" began in 1709 after a second consecutive year in which thousands of families on the upper Rhine lost their crops and livestock to French army foragers and icy cold.[4] When spring arrived some fifteen thousand of the stricken farmers (*Bauer* in German, *boer* in Dutch, hence the English slur "boor") fled down the Rhine to the Netherlands. The first to arrive in Rotterdam were received with pity. As their numbers grew the Dutch shipped them over to England just to be rid of them. The first to arrive there also knew charity, especially from tenderhearted Queen Anne. But as their numbers swelled the Board of Trade hatched a plan to transport the refugees to America, where they might be employed gathering timber and pitch for the Royal Navy. As it happened, some Mohawk sachems on an embassy to London offered to settle the Palatines in New York. Preparations took time, during which British goodwill dried up. Germans stood accused of bringing disease and (worse yet) popery into England. Some five hundred Catholic Palatines converted to please their hosts, but thirty-five hundred who refused were deported. Hundreds more went to North Carolina or Virginia, where Governor Spotswood used them to found the Spotsylvania ironworks. But the largest group, about three thousand, trusted in the Board of Trade's plan. They meekly boarded ships bound for New York in 1710.

A fifth of the adults and almost all the children died at sea, and more perished from disease or hunger soon after arrival. But New York's governor and Robert Livingston, the Scottish patroon on the Hudson, allowed the survivors to build towns and plant crops at what are now Saugerties, Germantown, and Rhinebeck. Over three hundred Palatines fought in the 1711 British expedition against French Canada. But since their struggling villages shipped no naval stores over two years, the Board of Trade withdrew its subsidy, whereupon New York evicted them. Mohawks tided the hungry, uncomprehending Germans over another winter, allowing hundreds of families to settle in the Schoharie valley. Again the governor (and Albany fur traders) cried no: the Germans were trespassers and might stir up trouble. At length they scraped together funds to send Johann Weiser and two others to England to plead their case. But pirates captured their ship, robbed them, and flogged two to death. Weiser finally reached London penniless, only to languish in debtors' prison. The irony in that is considerable, given that England's king at the time was the former Elector of Hanover, Georg Ludwig von Braunschweig-Lüneburg (King George I).[5] Five years passed before Weiser carried back to his people three simple words of advice: go to Pennsylvania. In 1723 hundreds of families put all they owned on their backs—for the *fifth* time—and followed Indian guides through the woods to Tulpehocken Creek. Theirs was the first white settlement in what became Berks County.[6]

The Quaker elite had already grown crotchety over Germans arriving by ship. In 1710 Mennonites in wooden shoes and plain bonnets settled Lancaster County, soon to be joined by Dunkers and Moravians. Year by year more sects arrived until the Penns' colonial agent, James Logan, wrote in 1717 "Our Countrey People are inflamed" over foreigners. They insist "we are to sell them no more Land." Happily, existing German communities petitioned for extensions of their grants to make room for the newcomers. But ten years later Rotterdam merchants disembarked thirteen hundred Germans in one month and reported five thousand more were booked for the following year. Fearing "these Colonies will in time be lost to ye Crown," Logan and the governor asked the Duke of Newcastle for permission to ban immigration while the Pennsylvania assembly imposed a 40 shilling tariff per head on importers of aliens. But once again the panic subsided, the law was repealed, and the German exodus continued. By 1750 Pennsylvania became the first colony in which a majority of the white population was no longer of English stock.[7]

Why did the nativist panics subside? Not because the Quaker oligarchs had an extra dose of altruism. Rather, their debates and deeds reveal considerations that would echo in many subsequent American tiffs about immigration. First, they had to admit most of the Germans were industrious and law-abiding; they even paid Logan their quit rents! The Germans improved land and increased demand for it, raising the value of everyone's real estate. The German pietist sects shared the Quakers' pacifism and could be counted on not to provoke the Indians. Above all, perhaps, the naturalized Germans happily voted for the Quaker party, permitting the oligarchy to maintain its majority in the assembly long after Quakers were outnumbered by Presbyterians and others in Pennsylvania.

The Germans' political value was strikingly proven in the election of 1742. Back in London, the Board of Trade had recently ruled that Pennsylvania's liberty of conscience statute pertained only to private religion, not affairs of state. Hence it disallowed the Quakers' "conscientious objection" to defense measures.

The Presbyterian backwoods party hoped to ride this decision to victory, but the wily Quakers spread spurious rumors among Germans about the dangers of "military government." Their opponents accused them of stuffing the ballot box with votes cast by illegal aliens and intimidating voters by forming a human gauntlet outside the polls (which the Quakers habitually did). It came to a head in an election day riot. Rowdy sailors stormed Philadelphia's polling place crying "down with the plain coats & broad Brims" and "knock those Dutch Sons of Bitches off the Steps." But crowds of Germans beat back the sailors while the Quaker slate swept the election. Thus were American ethnic politics born.[8]

Bigotry was the least of the Germans' problems, however. Most of the sixty thousand who crossed the ocean in the mid-eighteenth century did so as "redemptioners," a variety of indentured servant. That is, they redeemed whatever they owed on their families' fares by renting themselves out as laborers through brokers in Philadelphia. But inasmuch as the emigrants had first to traverse numerous principalities in the Holy Roman Empire, each extracting its tariffs and fees, just to reach port, then had to beg or bribe some cold-hearted Dutch or English bursar for the right to be squeezed aboard an America-bound vessel, then had to sell years of their lives in a market glutted with new arrivals, redemptioners were geese ripe for plucking. Shipping firms such as the notorious Rotterdam Stedmans often made families wait for a booking just to exhaust their money and supplies. Other families found upon boarding a ship their "fare" entitled them to no more than hammocks, hence their chests of clothing, tools, and food were confiscated or sold back to them for cash. The ships were foul; disease and malnourishment took a terrible toll. Heinrich Keppele, first president of the *Deutsche Gesellschaft* (German Society) in Pennsylvania, counted 250 dead on his own ship. The Society estimated some two thousand of its countrymen's corpses were hurled into the sea from 1750 to 1755 alone. A teacher and organ master from Württemberg, Gottlieb Mittelberger wrote an exposé of the "wretched and grievous condition of those who travel from Germany." He condemned the "outrageous and merciless proceeding of the Dutch man-dealers and their man-stealing emissaries" who seduced Germans with tales of America then auctioned their bodies to merchants and planters as if they were African slaves. Most cruel of all, parents had to work double or triple the normal term of indenture to pay off the passage of their "worthless" children and old folks. Only in 1765 did the German Society's lobbying—and Philadelphians' concern about hygiene—induce the assembly to impose regulations on importers of human cargoes.[9]

Germans who survived their voyage and term of indenture eventually earned the respect, if not amity, of their English hosts. Thus, even as the Society for the Propagation of the Gospel yearned to teach the Germans good English religion, the Mennonites, Lutherans, and Moravian Brethren founded churches and schools in all their communities, including America's first school for girls at Bethlehem (1742). Conrad Weiser built missions and schools for Indians. The Ephrata community, founded by a stern Heidelberg pietist named Conrad Beissel, achieved such acclaim Voltaire remarked upon it in Paris. Beissel preached utter rejection of all worldly things, including sex (even though his community was open to women). At its height Ephrata's three hundred people, all dressed in white habits like monks, mesmerized visitors with their polyphonous chants and published some of the most elegant books of the colonial era. German craftsmen carved many of the colonies' earliest violins (the fiddles of frontier fame), keyboard instruments (including the Old Organ at Grace Church, New York), and church bells that began to serenade American landscapes by the mid-eighteenth century. Germans also added the exquisite hymnody of the Lutheran Reformation to England's buoyant hymns and carols, thus making the panoply of American church music as rich as any in Christendom.[10]

Nor, despite the language barrier and separatist tendencies of sects such as the Amish, did the Germans shun the affairs of the larger colony. Lutheran pastor Henry Muhlenberg, whose son Peter became a prominent general and politician after 1776, pestered Benjamin Franklin and the Quaker assembly constantly in defense of the Germans' interests. So did Lutheran pastor Christoph Sauer and his son, who printed the first American Bible and founded a newspaper, the *Pennsylvanische Nachrichten,* that rivaled Franklin's *Pennsylvania Gazette.* Another journalist, John Peter Zenger, came to New York a threadbare orphan in the Palatine odyssey, learned the printer's trade, and by 1735 was such a fierce critic of the royal governor he was tried for libel. Philadelphia lawyer Andrew Hamilton's eloquent defense of Zenger's right to print the truth persuaded the jury to acquit.[11]

Most of the German settlers, however, were farmers and their contributions to agriculture extended far beyond Pennsylvania. Their contoured fields, advanced methods of crop rotation, and copious use of manure brought them enviable yields. Their capacious "Holzsteiner" barns, with large wooden forebays for extra storage and numerous doors for livestock, put the plain "shed" barns of Virginia and New England to shame. As one English admirer noted,

"The German was sure to build a large, fine barn before he built any dwelling house for himself except a rude log cabin." Thanks to the barns animals could be kept warm and well fed all winter long, and in spring the matted straw and leftover fodder were spread on the fields to enrich the soil and protect the young plants.[12] Needless to say, Rhinelanders also introduced to the colonies such nutritious, caloric foods as pretzels, pickles, rye breads, cheeses, wines and beer, cakes and pastries, and all manner of hams and sausages. Two measures of the Germans' productivity and keen eye for soil are the average inventories of the acreage, livestock, and capital goods on Lancaster County farms, which doubled between 1730 and 1760, and land prices, which quadrupled over that period.[13]

Once their ordeals were over, therefore, the Germans ate very well, fed the growing Philadelphia market, and provided its merchants with export commodities. But Lancaster County lay some sixty miles west of the Delaware River, so as early as 1718 some "Inhabitants of & near Conestogoe" asked the proprietors for permission to lay out a road. Within fifteen years that first segment of what became the Great Philadelphia Wagon Road was complete, whereupon another German wonder appeared for English to emulate: the broad, covered Conestoga wagon rigged to four or six sturdy horses controlled by a single "jerk line" or by shouts of *gee, haw, geh-auf* (giddy-up) and *ho* (whoa) for right, left, go, and stop. By 1753 an estimated seven thousand Conestoga wagons were already in use. A Quaker reported: "Every German farmer in our province almost has a Waggon of his own" to serve as "their Bed, their Inn, their everything. Many of them will come 150 miles without spending one shilling."[14] In time Conestoga wagons and horses would carry thousands of pioneers across the continent. But they were first employed for bulk inland transport, and their importance to the early American economy was immense.

Many Germans shunned violence, but self-defense was another matter. Their excellent gunsmiths soon realized English muskets were too unreliable, slow, and inaccurate. They also knew of a prototype weapon with just the characteristics needed on the frontier—the *jaeger* (hunter's) rifle. As early as 1725 Lancaster County artisans such as Martin Meylin perfected what became known overseas as the American Rifle and later at home as the Kentucky Rifle. It is more properly called the Pennsylvania Rifle. Its very long forty-four-inch barrel, finely rifled with spiraling lands and grooves, imparted a much higher muzzle velocity to a ball, resulting in very long range, as well as a predicable spin that kept the projectile on track. To be sure, the spin caused the ball to curve in flight, but even a novice marksman soon learned to adjust his sights to allow for that "Kentucky windage."[15]

Draft horses, great wagons, frontier rifles, new farming techniques, and a road: thanks to the Germans, pioneers in the middle colonies now had all they needed to plunge deeper into the interior. Once again, Germans showed them the way by exploring southward until they happened upon the same Great Warriors' Path through the Shenandoah Valley that Governor Spotswood had found. So the Philadelphia Wagon Road was rapidly extended by sheer use into western Maryland and Virginia where William Byrd II billed his western reserves a "*Neu-Gefundnes* [new-found] Eden." Finally, in 1743, two Moravian Brethren trekked from Philadelphia all the way to Georgia. But if Germans opened the door to the Appalachian back country, most of the people who walked through it were Ulstermen and lowland Scots, some seventy thousand of whom followed the Germans to America between 1730 and 1763.

The Ulstermen were descendants of the Protestant Scots whom England encouraged to populate northern Ireland only to betray them when merchants talked Parliament into outlawing the export of Irish woolens. Thousands thus ruined made their way to America. In 1740 an Irish famine boosted the migration to twelve thousand people per year. The lowland Scots' economic lot had always been harsh, but worse still was the plight of highlanders after 1746 when the clans took up arms on behalf of the Stuart pretender only to be decimated at the Battle of Culloden. The vindictive English disarmed and outlawed the clans, confiscated their land, and drove out Scottish crofters to make room for sheep. Tens of thousands of Scots moved into towns to become abject mill hands, but ten thousand more found their way to America. As a result, it turned out to be rough-hewn British border folk, not quiescent, mind-your-own-business Germans, who placed an indelible stamp on the American West.

These last two migrations completed the *dramatis personae* on the American colonial stage. By 1750 descendants of Puritans populated New England, Quakers nestled in the Delaware Valley, Anglican planters and children of former indentured servants dominated Virginia and the Carolinas, and Scots-Irish borderers leapfrogged the German counties to lay claim to the frontier. Where did these people come from? What folkways and beliefs did they bring to America? How did life in America change them? What, if anything, bound them together?[16]

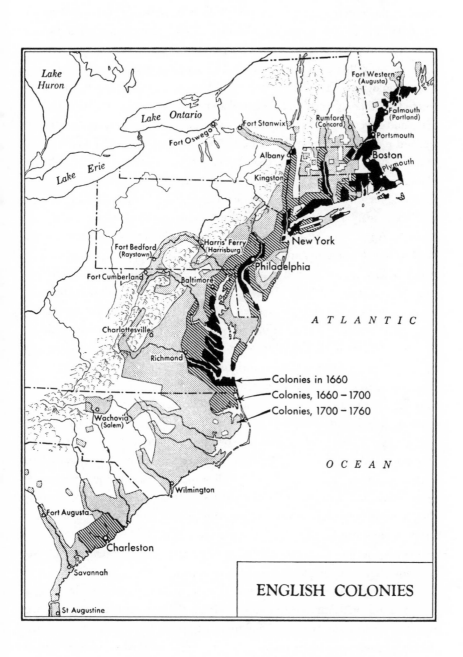

Colonies in 1660

Colonies, 1660 – 1700

Colonies, 1700 – 1760

*ATLANTIC*

*OCEAN*

**ENGLISH COLONIES**

Let us begin in New England, some 60 percent of whose founders originated in the eastern counties of Essex, Suffolk, Cambridge, Lincolnshire, and Kent. Most of the rest of the early Puritan families came from England's West Country, and perhaps 10 percent from London. They were largely crafts- and tradespeople rather than farmers, East Anglia's cloth industry being their most likely employment. The Puritans counted few indentured servants in comparison to the other colonies, and were well above the English norm in terms of literacy and education. Women outnumbered men in their churches by a ratio of 3:2, and most of the emigrants came to New England as part of a family unit. What they found there was a cold, rocky, stormy land unsuited to cash-crop plantations. Hence slavery did not catch on with them for economic as much as for moral reasons. Instead, New Englanders displayed a strong bias in favor of free labor organized around family and town units.

East Anglians bequeathed the broad, twangy "Down East" accent that survives to this day among native New Englanders. They tended to add an "r" to words ending in vowels (thus "Ameriker"), soften long vowels (thus "paahk" for "park"), and elide syllables ("Haav'd" for "Harvard"). They dotted their new environs with East Anglian names such as Boston, Cambridge, Groton, Braintree, Hingham, Weymouth, and Sudbury, and filled them with "saltbox" and "gabled" frame houses. However, the Puritans' social customs were as much sectarian as regional in their origin and began and ended with the family. They deemed marriage a covenant between goodwives and husbands who, like Old Testament patriarchs, were called upon to seed the commonwealth with a great and godly multitude. One result of that faith (or conceit) was the genealogical fixation or "ancestor worship" characteristic of later Boston Brahmins and "blue bloods." Puritans made pariahs of bachelors, considered spinsters cursed, and were in horror of all sexual expression other than marital intercourse (itself banned on the Sabbath). New England women, even though they married on average at the relatively advanced age of twenty-three, bore as many as eight or nine children.[17] On the other hand, since Puritans conceived of marriage as a civil contract rather than a sacrament between persons God hath joined, they tolerated divorce, shameful though it be.

Hard work, large families, a harsh climate, and the belief that sin, temptation, and sudden death were omnipresent made the Yankees long-suffering people. The best means of rearing children, they believed, was through religious instruction and severe constraints to break a child's original selfish will. Parents might even farm their children out to other households (in the manner of later

New England boarding schools) because authority figures other than parents would be less inclined to spare the rod. Children were also made to observe sickness and death, the better to teach them the brevity of life and the need for faith and salvation. Finally, these people were stoic. They learned to repress their emotions (especially in public) and sat through Sabbath day services lasting six to eight hours, often in unheated churches. They shunned proud clothing and loud colors. They ate pease porridge, pumpkins, and cornmeal with their pork, beef, or fish, often cooked all in one pot (the New England boiled dinner). They also had few holidays since Congregational pastors abolished the "Romish" feasts of Christmas, Easter, Pentecost (Whitsunday), and saints' days. What they did celebrate were Election Day, Commencement Day, Training Day to honor the militia, and Thanksgiving Day, whose regular observance dates from the aftermath of King Philip's War. Of course, New England authorities eventually gave up trying to suppress Christian holidays, but their own tradition of setting aside days to celebrate *the polity, the community, the armed forces, and the people's prosperity* survived to become major expressions of Americans' civic religion.

Were New Englanders always good capitalists, as their Yankee trader and pedlar image later suggested? Not if that is taken to mean individualists competing against one another for material gain. Hustlers and speculators, merchants and developers were there from the start—after all, East Anglian clothiers were hardly immune to the profit motive. But a Calvinist religious calling was supposed to temper greed and subordinate individual needs to those of the commonwealth. With the exception of premeditated commercial developments such as Newport, New Haven, and Springfield, relative land holdings and wealth in New England were unusually egalitarian. The pure Yankee creed extolled hard work and prosperity, but defined the first as a duty and the latter a blessing, while enjoining all who were blessed to give back to their communities. Public service thus joined education at the top of the Puritans' roster of values, and respect for both would survive the gradual loss of faith in the creed that inspired them. Perhaps the best illustration of the New England ethic was a fondness for town ball, the so-called New England game that evolved at length into baseball. It was an orderly sport in which every action was a personal contest (pitcher versus batter, runner versus fielder) occurring within an overall communal context. Whatever players' individual skills, they won or lost as part of a team.[18]

The political theories spawned by this Puritan culture formed an ellipse around the foci of freedom and order. There was no contradiction in that because liberty to a New Englander did not mean license, nor did order imply oppression. Rather, liberty was of four sorts: first, public or collective liberty from outside coercion, such as that of the Lords of Trade, the Anglican church, or the French; second, liberties as privileges, such as liberty to fish the Grand Banks or hunt in the woods; third, Christian liberty, which meant being free to worship and serve God without fear of sin, death, or earthly impediment; fourth, freedom from deprivation as expressed in the Bay Colony's poor laws for widows and orphans. None of these forms of liberty could be realized without public order and private discipline, while any "order" that trampled on liberty was really its opposite: moral anarchy.[19] These were values ingrained in such children as Samuel Adams (born 1722), John Adams (born 1735), and John Hancock (born 1737).

Quakers, by contrast, considered New England as oppressive and militaristic in its way as Old England was in its way. It was said of Fox's Society of Friends that it made a theology of the absence of theology. They also dispensed in their meetings with all liturgy, clergy, vestments, icons, and music. Believing all men and women imbued by a divine inner light, they were egalitarian—one might say "non-judgmental"—in external behavior. Quakers addressed everyone as "thee" and "friend" without regard to temporal status or wealth. Most early immigrants to Pennsylvania and West Jersey, moreover, derived from the lower-middle part of the English social spectrum, so they had little to be proud about. Indeed, English meetings often helped pay the way of poor brethren to America. However, the Quakers (unlike the Puritans) encouraged importation of indentured servants, thus elevating social mobility above social equality.

The Society of Friends made converts all over the British Isles, but the ones who placed their stamp on America came mostly from the Midland counties of Yorkshire, Derby, and Nottingham, with minorities from London and Wales. Thus, except where they adopted Indian names, Pennsylvanians chose place names from home, such as Lancaster, York, Swarthmore, Darby, and Chester, or else Biblical names such as Providence, Salem, and Philadelphia. (The Welsh, of course, inspired the "y" towns such as Cynwyd, Wynnewood, Bryn Mawr, and Bryn Athyn.) The Quakers likewise bequeathed to the Delaware valley a curt and earthy Yorkshire dialect long on slang (bamboozle, brat, by golly, chock-full, flabbergasted, thingamajig, wallop) but short on style by comparison to the syntax of a Harvard-trained minister or the Ciceronian phrases of an educated Virginian. Midlands immigrants were also used to building in stone, and Pennsylvania fieldstone was the best. But whether in architecture, speech, dress, food, or religion, Quakers made an affectation of plainness.

Like the Puritans, Quakers placed great value on family, children, and education, but treated them all as a personal rather than communal pursuit. Thus, where Puritans set up public schools and obliged attendance, the Friends established private schools and left children's attendance up to the parents. Where Puritans saw children as naturally naughty and treated their discipline as a village affair, Quakers appealed to a child's inner light as they would to an adult's. Where Puritans affirmed romance and a healthy physical bond between spouses, Quakers considered all sex not for procreation to be sinful and sometimes made couples wait years before approving their marriages. They also denounced alcohol, shunned team competitions, and encouraged exercise only for reasons of health.

Passive and pacifist, earnest and equable, William Penn's protégés claimed to deplore all distinctions of rank based on birth, wealth, sex, or age. They distrusted ambition, damned avarice, and promoted private philanthropy. Yet no colony save for early Massachusetts was dominated for so long by so small an oligarchy. The first Quaker merchant families of Philadelphia, dubbed "our mob" by one of its matriarchs, intermarried to such a degree 85 percent of the members of the town corporation were related well into the mid-eighteenth century.[20]

An oligarchy so steeped in Quaker values, so incestuous, and so jealous of its leadership understandably distrusted change—any change—which helps to explain eastern Pennsylvania's reputation for cultural conservatism. Henry Adams later observed that while his Boston forebears had been "ambitious beyond reason to excell," Pennsylvanians were too democratic and humane to do much of anything in the public sphere. It was "as though political power were aristocratic by nature, and democratic power a contradiction in terms."[21] Suffice it to say the list of colonial Boston's civic institutions was long, distinguished, and associated with many founders, whereas the comparable list for Philadelphia was short and overwhelmingly the work of one man: Benjamin Franklin, a native Bostonian. It seemed as if Quakers, trusting mankind, distrusted institutions, whereas the reverse was the case with the Puritans.[22]

Not surprisingly, the political culture of Pennsylvania contrasted sharply with that of New England. Quaker liberty, as symbolized by the great Liberty Bell cast in 1751, was less a condition of mankind than a reciprocal relationship between human beings, a relationship based on the Golden Rule. Thus, even though Friends believed their piety conformed most closely to New Testament teaching, they affirmed the freedom of others to believe, or not, as they chose, and denied the right of any to impose their beliefs on others. A simple enough proposition, but its corollaries could be complex, including the Quakers' fierce resistance to taxes imposed for the waging of war or any taxes and regulations imposed by a non-representative body. But by the same token their "fierce resistance" could never be martial given their "do unto others" pacifist ethic. No wonder Pennsylvanians *shouted* for liberty as loudly as anyone, yet drove other colonists to distraction by their reluctance to *act*.[23] Such were values ingrained in John Dickinson (born 1732), Clement Biddle (born 1740), and Thomas Mifflin (born 1744).

The original and most widespread colonial culture was so at variance with those of New England and the middle colonies that an observer ignorant of English history might not have believed it stemmed from the same country. Tidewater Virginia was comfortably Anglican, aristocratic, hierarchical, slave-holding, almost entirely rural, enamored of horses and gambling, and everywhere lusty, sporting, and deeply in debt.

The indentured servants who made up the base of Virginia's population originated from all over England, but a majority hailed from the vicinities of Bristol and London in England's southwest and south. This regional bias was strongly reinforced by Governor Berkeley, who bestowed estates and high offices on dozens of "distressed cavaliers," the royalist gentlemen uprooted by Cromwell. As many as two-thirds of Virginia's "first families" had roots in England's south and southwest, precisely the regions that were still wooded, largely manorial, and heavily Anglican. Thus, whether he was an indentured servant or petty nobleman, the fortune-seeker who sailed for Virginia dreamed of becoming a grand country squire.[24]

These were the emigrés, needless to say, who gave America its first "southern accent." They spoke in languid rhythms, softened consonants (especially the "r") and elongated syllables ("Guuuhv'nah Baah-kly"). They employed solecisms such as "I be" and "ain't," dropped the "g" in "-ing," and imported a lexicon of terms from Sussex and Wessex such as chomp, flapjack, grit, pekid, yonder, and book-learning. Like New Englanders, they placed great store in the family, ancestry, and patriarchy, but in fundamentally different ways. Where Yankees thought in terms of the nuclear family, southerners identified with the extended family, many members of which might live in proximity and in which even servants might be included. Where prominent Yankees imagined themselves Old Testament patriarchs in a prophetic sense and labored to pass on their values to children, southern gentry imagined themselves passing on their genes in the manner of a prize stallion. They also identified patriarchy with individual freedom as when William Byrd II rhapsodized in 1726: "Like one of the Patriarchs, I have my Flocks and my Herds, my Bond-men and Bond-women, and every Soart of Trade amongst my own servants, so that I live in a kind of Independence on every one but Providence."[25] A Puritan might consider such lordliness prideful, but to a Virginian lordliness enjoined one to be responsible for all who lived in one's domain and hospitable toward all who did not. So great a political and social pillar was patriarchy, in fact, that a wife who cuckolded her husband was considered guilty of *treason*. After all, female adultery might "adulterate" the family bloodline; male philandering did not.

Philander they did, at least those randy cavaliers with means, motive, and opportunity among servants, slaves, and widows. The secret, coded diary of William Byrd II provides ample evidence of the dalliances that a vigorous planter might enjoy on his own estate, among neighboring ones, and especially while visiting London.[26] But sex was only one outlet for aristocratic *joie de vivre*. Thus, New Englanders ate (or "et") their food, but wealthy Virginians and Carolinians dined on the pork, beef, and chicken they seasoned and fried in the "Dorset style" carried from England. They smoked their tobacco and drank wine and punch with equal gusto, considered a dancing master at least as valuable as a tutor, prided themselves on elegant clothes, and flirted in ways that would have landed a Puritan in the stocks. Virginians loved sports, but their competitions invariably tested the prowess of individual men and their animals, above all in horse races and cockfights. They also gambled incessantly over races, card games, and dice.

Nor was that just *noblesse oblige*, because life itself was a gamble in early Virginia and later on the frontier. Tobacco prices fluctuated unpredictably; bankruptcies and early deaths caused property to change hands at a rapid rate. Speculators went for the quick turnover rather than the long-range investment, and wealth was something to be enjoyed, not squirreled away for a rainy day. No wonder "the colonial Virginian so often appears to have been something of a hustler."[27] Likewise, since the past seemed no guide to the future, Virginians came late to an interest in history which New Englanders displayed from the start.[28]

The cliché has it that male Virginians were sexual predators and regarded women as breeding stock. But women, too, knew how to exploit such advantages as they had to get what they could. In the seventeenth century they were in such short supply that female indentured servants brought a price six times that of males. Free women enjoyed a signal advantage in the marketplace of marriage and might live to combine estates inherited from serial husbands.[29] Wives and daughters of poor planters earned a certain equality just by their indispensable labor and child-bearing, while ladies of breeding shared the same ambitions and pretensions as their men. Dames presided over the household and sometimes its finances, wielded immense power in the competition for social prestige, "put on airs" toward people of inferior rank, and in some cases claimed the "rights of Englishmen" for themselves. Thus did Sarah Harrison shock the parson and guests at her wedding (to James Blair, founder of William and Mary College) by agreeing to love and honor but refusing three times to obey.

It is amusing, given their own reputations, that Yankees and Quakers disapproved of the hauteur on display in the southern colonies. Thus did a clergyman remark upon meeting a Virginia gentleman on his "lofty elegant horse": "I never beheld such a display of pride in any man. . . . His countenance appeared as bold and daring as satan himself." It is perhaps closer to the truth to observe that Virginians did not try to cloak their pride beneath a fig leaf of piety or plainness. They wore their coats of arms, not their religion, on their sleeves, while their religion in any case was easygoing. In the plantation South, perhaps more than anywhere in England itself, Queen Elizabeth I's Anglican latitudinarianism prevailed. Virginians might attend church on a Sunday, consult their prayer books regularly (William Byrd II, between bouts of fornication, prayed morning and night), and cherish their family Bible. But they did not pry into what, or how fervently, their neighbors believed. In the same manner southerners of all but the highest ranks placed little store in education. In 1671 Governor Berkeley even wrote the Lords of Trade: "I thank God there are no free schools nor printing . . . for learning has brought disobedience, and heresy, and sects into the world, and printing has divulged them, and libels against the best government."[30] In fact, William Byrd II read Greek and Hebrew and owned more books than Cotton Mather, while Thomas Jefferson's two libraries (the first burned) are legendary. But whereas Boston had five newspapers in the mid-eighteenth century, Virginia had only one. Its literacy rate was also a fraction of that in New England.

Aside from Anglican texts, the books most likely to find place in a planter's parlor were manuals on agriculture, husbandry, and good habits and manners. Puritans might spank their children and Quakers reason with them, but Cavaliers put children to work memorizing long lists of "dos" (fear God, honor the King, revere parents, bow to superiors, show courtesy to all) and "don'ts" (abuse inferiors, laugh raucously, stare, boast, give offense, or be selfish). In addition to teaching comportment, such books taught the value and praxis of the honorable life. Honor obliged a man to fight in defense of his kin, serve his country without hesitation or hope of reward, respect one's betters, command respect oneself, and never betray a trust.

The politics spawned by this Cavalier culture expressed yet a third distinct understanding of liberty, one based on hierarchy and independence. What did it mean to be free? It meant not to be dominated *by* others—which is slavery—and thus to exert authority *over* others, be it a wife, children, or servants. Such "hegemonic liberty" may seem repugnant today, but it was not some sophistry contrived to prop up a plantation culture. Rather, it was a direct descendent of the aristocratic definition of liberty that inspired the Magna Carta, the English Parliament, and the Bill of Rights of 1690. There is no liberty at all in egalitarianism, because people are not naturally equal and can only be made to appear equal through coercion (in which case *everyone* is a manner of slave), or pretense (in which case society pretends to be all chiefs and no Indians). To a planter the most salient question in politics was not "who should govern" but rather whether the natural aristocracy of prominent gentlemen governed with honor, justice, and wisdom.[31] Children such as George Mason (born 1725), George Washington (born 1732), Thomas Jefferson (born 1743), and James Madison (born 1751) learned to cherish such freedom.

The fourth British culture transplanted to America was unique in a far different way. It despised order and hierarchy on principle, scoffed at all authority, and appeared simply barbarous to Virginians, Pennsylvanians, and Yankees alike. The ruffians bearing that culture were, of course, the "Scotch-Irish," and so numerous were they that estimates of their migration into the colonies range from a minimum of 125,000 between 1700 and 1775 to a quarter million.[32] Like the people who came to New England and the Delaware basin, they were religious non-conformists, in this case Presbyterians or New Lights caught up in the Whitefield revivals. But, as with the people who came to Virginia, the motives of these textile workers, farmers, and wives (about 40 percent of the influx was female) were almost wholly material. They were not abjectly poor, because most paid their way to America, but they feared falling lower in life in the old country and hoped to rise higher in life in the new one.

The term "Scotch-Irish" is American shorthand. This fourth cultural group was really composed of Scots, whether from Ulster or southern Scotland, extreme northern English, and a few southern Protestant Irish. Those from Ulster tended to be more educated, urban, and community-minded than their rural cousins from Scotland.[33] But what justifies lumping them together are the facts that almost all spoke a dialect of English rather than Gaelic and all were fleeing chaotic and bloody borderlands. The Scots who crossed the Irish Sea to colonize Ulster, displace the primitive Catholics, and improve the land were the first shock troops of English imperialism. As for the Scottish-English frontier, its history of feuds, war, cattle rustling ("reiving"), and outright banditry dated back to the eleventh century. All but three English kings or queens until 1750 fought at least one war on their northern border. To the Scots, the English were oppressors and plunderers come to steal their meager possessions, force their church down Catholic or Presbyterian throats, break up the clans, and in effect castrate them. To the English, the Scots were savages who had advanced little since the days when their Pictish ancestors painted their naked bodies blue and fell in a bloodlust upon Roman encampments. Worse still, the Scots, for centuries, had a nasty habit of seeking aid from the French.

The human beings who had to live on either side of these borders, for all their deep-seated hatreds, nevertheless shared identical fears, hardships, and duties, chief among them being always on guard, fiercely protective of family, loyal toward friends, and ruthless toward enemies. They were proud and clannish, distrustful of outsiders, hungry as sheep for security, yet ferocious as wolves for their next meal. No wonder the settled communities on the Atlantic seaboard were appalled when these newcomers poured onto the docks in their thousands, then relieved when they moved to the frontier where they could endanger no one but Indians.[34]

The largest cohort of these northern Britons trod the Great Philadelphia Wagon Road westward in search of vacant land. Fanning out in the Appalachians they placed names such as Cumberland, Galloway, Derry, and Durham on the frontier. Their dialects became a main source of the country-and-western speech patterns associated ever since with hillbillies ("git offa mah prah-pitty"). From the English-Scots border came the frequent subject-verb disagreements ("them gals is buck nekkid"), double negatives ("I ain't fixin' ta wrassle no critters"), and double positives ("he done did it, jedge, Ah seen him mah own self") which later leather-stockings and buckskins carried to the Mississippi and beyond. More elevating to American culture were the Scots, Irish, and north English ballads telling tales of love, loss, injustice, and death, thereby spawning American folk music.

Of course, the Scots-Irish also brought with them a clan system, not least because an entire extended family might take ship and squat together in central Pennsylvania, the Shenandoah Valley, or the Carolina uplands. Hugh Jackson, an Irish weaver, led a boatload of "kith and kin" to America in 1765, transplanting the clan that later produced Andrew Jackson. Patrick Calhoun arrived with wife, Catherine, and four sons in 1733, followed the Wagon Road to Lancaster County and thence to South Carolina. No less than twenty-three Calhouns would be killed in wars against the Cherokees, but the clan multiplied until, four generations on, it spawned John C. Calhoun, the leading statesman of the antebellum South. All the border people married extremely young and had scads of offspring. Some youths abducted their "honeys" in old-country fashion. Others were forced into shotgun weddings after a pregnancy or formed Common Law marriages in the absence of clergy. Still, their illegitimacy rates were far higher than anywhere else in the British Atlantic save for the Scots-English border itself.

Virginians, though sensual, preserved a certain decorum. Border people did not, as Anglican missionary Charles Woodmason was shocked to observe among the cabins dotting Virginia's foothills. Everyone slept in a family pile, children ran naked, and girls who had barely reached puberty pulled up their skirts (especially while dancing) and pulled down their shifts to display buttocks and breasts.[35] Even topographical names contained the familiar "four letter words."[36] One might imagine such libertine habits were a function of remoteness, lack of social constraints, and the libidinous influence of the pungent valleys of the Blue Ridge and Smokies. But the seeds of these sexual habits were planted back on the borders of Ireland and Scotland. Moreover, the seeds were well watered with another north British import: whiskey. Scots and Irish carried with them their thirst for the wee dram, or pint as the case may be. Even children at table were given a glass of whiskey sweetened with sugar. Over time, their experimentation with local mashes, stills, and the aging of liquors in various casks perfected those backwoods masterpieces called Kentucky bourbon and Tennessee sippin' whiskey.[37]

For a' that, as the Scots would say, life on the frontier was made harsh by relatively poor soil, Indian wars, intramural feuds, and familial strife. The border folk brought with them a customary division of labor whereby men fought and women worked, a code of honor whereby men protected and women obeyed, and a hierarchy whereby males governed the clan and wives were absorbed into it. Their sports, such as "no holds barred" wrestling and marksmanship contests, were blatantly martial, and "frontier justice" was a blend of vigilantism, lynching, and "eye for an eye" retribution. All these folkways, practiced so often under the influence of alcohol, made community and family life a capricious mix of violence and laxity.

Since few civil authorities policed the Appalachian foothills, the main source of social discipline was personal conscience quickened by itinerant preachers. Thus, while the "Great Awakening" touched all the colonies, the revivals may have had the profoundest impact on the frontier. So numerous and idiosyncratic were the evangelical preachers who worked the frontier that no generalizations are possible except to observe that they were highly emotional, given to field-preaching in the manner of Whitefield, hostile to organized churches, and focused on the born-again, life-changing experience. Those were features bound to appeal to a rural Celtic population already romantic, suspicious of authority, and jealous of independence. "Repent, ye sinner, and be saved"—especially when cried at dusk in a torchlit meadow littered with jugs— was a simple message that blamed the frontiersman alone for his sordid condition and put his future entirely in his own hands. The preacher was the medium, but the message was that man and God are alone with each other, free to make their own peace. So when more disciplined denominations such as the Methodists arrived on the frontier, they did not just scour the glens and dales for bodies to fill little white churches. They, too, staged enthusiastic field meetings and competed for audiences with the spoken word. After all, much of their flock was illiterate.[38]

As primitive as this Scots/Ulster/north English culture may seem today, its politics expressed a familiar conception of liberty. Having known nothing but oppression and suffering for centuries at the hands of all manner of governments and churches, these were people infused with a pure libertarian spirit for whom freedom meant individual choice. These were people who hated taxes because they reckoned all who imposed or collected them to be glorified thieves. These were people who hated boundaries because they reckoned all who drew or enforced them to be glorified jailers. These were people who, as a German traveler observed in 1768, "shun everything which appears to demand of them law and order, and anything that preaches constraint. They hate the name of a justice, and yet they are not transgressors. Their object is merely wild." On the American frontier they could achieve that object as they never could back on the Irish and Scottish marches. Should obnoxious officials impinge on them, why, a whole continent lay beyond the Appalachian ridge in which one could find "elbow room."[39] That was the freedom precious to Francis Marion (born 1732), Daniel Boone (born 1734), Daniel Morgan (born 1736), and Patrick Henry (born 1736).[40]

Liberty, independence, and virtue were dear to the people of all four British-American cultures, however their definitions varied. Three of the cultures were paternalistic; one was not (the Quakers). Three were tolerant; one was not (the Puritans). Three were egalitarian; one was not (the Cavaliers). Three were orderly; one was not (the Scots-Irish). But what of the last great colonial culture, that numbered no less than 20 percent of the non-Indian population of British America? We cannot know what liberty meant to them because almost all those West Africans were enslaved. Just a handful of slave narratives and the flawed perceptions of European contemporaries survive to provide glimpses into the mental, physical, and emotional anguish they suffered or the sources of the grit and genius that helped them survive, multiply, and fashion American cultures of their own. But the very existence and scale of the institution of slavery forced colonists of European stock to make such tortuous adjustments in their notions of liberty and justice that one might argue the colonies (especially in the south) were Africanized as much as slaves were Americanized.[41]

Slavery was, of course, universal. It has existed in almost all cultures in almost all eras of history. Mainland American slavery was itself but a minor offshoot of a much larger phenomenon that has been termed the "plantation complex." This was born in the Eastern Mediterranean as early as the fourteenth century, when Arab and Turkish overlords learned that the most efficient way to plant, cut, and process large quantities of raw sugarcane was on plantations worked by slave gangs. The Portuguese and Spaniards simply extended this system to the Azores, Canary, and Cape Verde islands in the fifteenth and sixteenth centuries, then to Brazil and the Caribbean. But as late as the 1640s there were many more Englishmen held in slavery by Muslims than there were Africans held in slavery by the English. Only in the late seventeenth and eighteenth centuries did Dutch, French, and English slavers tempt North American colonists to meet their own labor shortages in like fashion. The planters of the Chesapeake and the Carolinas succumbed.[42]

Thanks to dogged and imaginative scholarship, the volume of the Atlantic slave trade is now known within surprisingly narrow parameters.[43] Over 27,000 slave-trading voyages, estimated to be about two-thirds of the total, have been catalogued for the years 1519 to 1867. Hence European ships made roughly 40,000 trips to the West African coast over 350 years, and three-quarters of them succeeded in delivering human cargoes to American ports. The total number of people taken in Africa was about 11 million, and about 9.5 million survived the journey. Since Brazil was far and away the largest market for chattel slaves, Portuguese captains accounted for 46 percent of the traffic; English captains just 28 percent. The total number of slaves carried to mainland North America was 361,100 or just 3.8 percent of the overall forced migration of Africans. Of these, only 2,300 arrived before 1675 and 9,800 between 1675 and 1700. So the slave economy of the American south was overwhelmingly an eighteenth-century phenomenon: 37,400 enslaved people were imported between 1700 and 1725; 96,800 between 1726 and 1750, and 116,900 between 1751 and 1775, for a "thirteen colonies" total of 263,200 prior to independence.[44]

Most of these people originated in regions of West Africa inland from Guinea, Dahomey, and Benin, and came from cultures (such as the Ibo, Ewe, and Biafada) that were settled rather than nomadic and either too few or too weak to defend themselves. The powerful Ashanti, Yoruba, Dahomey, and Mandinga nations, by contrast, yielded up few captives. Slavery was the usual fate of prisoners of war in African conflicts, and some chiefs disposed of undesirables among their own subjects in like fashion. But the arrival of Europeans eager to trade guns, alcohol, and manufactures for slaves prompted African coastal kings to raid villages and kidnap people simply for sale. The captives were chained together and marched, sometimes hundreds of miles, to gathering pens on the coast. Many perished, some committed suicide, some tried to escape. But most ended up the objects of palaver between white captains and *compradors*, the African middlemen who knew coastal pidgin and the ways of the whites.

The ways of the whites, whether sadistic or coldly commercial, are notorious. Terrified by the prospect of revolt and sickened by the ordure, disease, and odor of hundreds of chained, squatting blacks, slavers must have struggled to kill their own humanity even as slaves struggled to retain theirs. On about one in ten voyages Africans did stage revolts, and about 1 percent of all transported people, or one hundred thousand, were killed in them. But mortality on the three weeks to three months voyage (depending on winds, currents, and destinations) was determined far more by diseases such as dysentery. About 1.5 million, or an average of 15 percent of the Africans, *and an equal percentage of crewmen,* perished during the Middle Passage. Only in exceptional cases of epidemic did ships bearing German redemptioners or English soldiers or convicts reach that level of mortality.[45] Once delivered to colonial ports, the surviving Africans were again held in pens until examined at auction by prospective buyers. Judging from notices in eighteenth-century Charleston newspapers, a few newly arrived slaves fled into the forest at their first opportunity only to be recaptured, perish, or be enslaved by Indians. But so weak, ill, and disoriented were most new arrivals that they fell into a sullen and obstinate funk until broken by white, or in many cases black, overseers. They had, after all, lost home, family, culture, status, and identity, and had to adjust to a new climate, environment, and diet. All the Africans could lean on, ironically, was a familiarity with slavery itself and the sort of agricultural and pastoral work they were given to do.[46]

Unlike English colonists in Barbados, however, planters on the American mainland showed little interest in purchasing slaves prior to 1650 and displayed a certain equanimity toward the few blacks in their midst. To be sure, a first contingent of Africans had been shipped to Virginia as early as 1619 and lifetime bondage was the norm from the start. By the 1640s the Virginia and Maryland assemblies were already so worried about revolts that they forbade masters to arm slaves while requiring them to arm white servants. Nevertheless, a surprising number of blacks either earned or were granted freedom in these decades. A few ex-slaves even owned slaves themselves. One manumitted African named Anthony Longo became sufficiently versed in English values to resist a summons to testify in court on the grounds that it was unwarranted, and anyway he had a harvest to bring in.[47]

Nor did it profit tobacco planters to purchase a slave at a cost five times or more that of an indentured servant's contract. As a result, the plantation complex matured in the Chesapeake—and there alone—on the basis of voluntary white labor. Large spreads had all the features of a slave system, including separate dwellings, corporal punishment, labor gangs, and the risk of revolt, but without lifetime bondage or racism. It is worth speculating, therefore, whether the mainland colonies might have avoided the bane of slavery altogether had not the terms of the financial equation subtly changed around 1660. The English economy stabilized after the Stuart Restoration at the same time the tumbling price of tobacco made Virginia less attractive to emigrants. Hence the flow of indentured servants began to dry up. Finally, the decline in the death rate among newcomers to the Chesapeake meant it was now a good bet a healthy young slave would provide decades of productive labor. So the Virginia assembly abolished tariffs on slaves imported by Dutch skippers in 1660. The English Parliament tried in turn to tax the slave trade, while the crown chartered the Royal African Company in 1672 in hopes of establishing a monopoly.[48]

A slight tilt in the balance sheet in favor of slave labor, therefore, bequeathed to North America an intractable racial divide. By 1708, when half the field workers in the Chesapeake were of African origin, there was no going back to a contractual system. Nor did planters want to go back because slavery had the unanticipated but welcome effect of relieving Virginia's social class tensions. The main problems with indentured servants, after all, were getting the whites to work (since they were already "paid in full" by being transported to America) and providing opportunities for them after their terms of labor were up. Resentment among the growing numbers of frustrated young men and women seeking land of their own was a root cause of Bacon's Rebellion. The use of African labor reduced the "army of poor whites" problem even as it united all whites against a new racial group occupying the lowest rung on the social scale.[49] The obvious downside was the danger of rebelliousness among blacks, who had nothing more to lose but life itself. So beginning in 1661, Virginia and the other southern colonies began to pass slave codes authorizing masters to inflict punishments up to and including castration and death. Terror was presumed necessary to deter violence and flight among slaves and was *ipso facto* judicious since no "prepensed malice (which alone makes murther Felony) should induce any man to destroy his own estate." One case against a homicidal master in Barbados did reach the English high courts. However, the Lords of Trade dismissed it on the grounds that Negroes were brutish, commonly regarded as chattel, and posed a threat to English subjects in the islands. The color bar was thus written into law, as in 1705, when Virginia outlawed public, naked lashing of white servants, but upheld that humiliation for black ones.[50]

South Carolina was the first colony to rely on slave labor, but Chesapeake planters opened the floodgates. Some 30,000 enslaved Africans worked there by

1710, their numbers increasing to 50,000 by 1730, 145,000 by 1750, and 250,000 by 1770. The initial burst may be explained by the shift of existing plantations from white to black labor, but the persistently high rates of growth are evidence of the territorial spread of plantations into the Piedmont, where forty-two new counties were organized between 1721 and 1776. Given that increases in black populations significantly outran the numbers of new imports, the numbers also indicate that the increasingly healthy blacks' own procreation did more to add to their numbers than slavers plying the Middle Passage. What is more, life in the Chesapeake, while undeniably hard, was not insufferable and resistance to it at most episodic. Slaves on a large plantation might sleep in unfurnished, unheated hovels and perform sweaty labor on a diet deficient in calories. But they might also work under their own supervisors and form unofficial families and communities across plantations. Except at peak labor times they enjoyed leisure on Saturday afternoons and Sundays, alcoholic holidays on Christmas and the king's birthday, and funeral days when they celebrated the return of a dead slave's spirit to Africa. Slaves on small farms also lived poorly, but might share the same roof, meals, and labor as their master and mistress. In terms of privacy, command of one's time and whereabouts, food, amusements, and tedium, slavery fell somewhere between hard prison labor and rugged army life—but without parole, pay, advancement, or discharge.[51]

The initial reason colonists purchased an army of slaves was tobacco, the cultivation of which is arduous, unceasing, artistic, and anxiety-laden. A brief description of it may offer a sense of the rhythm of life among Chesapeake slaves and their masters. To begin with, the production of tobacco (or "tobo" as the planters nicknamed it) was not seasonal work, but a year-round cycle in which falling behind schedule or foolishly trying to get ahead of the schedule might ruin an entire year's crop. The cycle began (weather permitting) on the Twelfth Day of Christmas when a seedbed of perhaps a fourth of an acre was manured, seeded, and sheltered with pine fronds against frost. Still, the loss of seedlings from cold, disease, and insects was such that ten times more seeds were planted than the fields would have room for. By April the seedlings were ready for transplant, but exactly when was a judgment call depending on the strength of the plants and the weather. What is more, the soil had to be just moist enough to allow the young plants to be safely pulled up by the roots. Negro boys and girls then carted the seedlings into the fields and dropped them at intervals where adult slaves carefully planted them one by one. That skilled but stoop labor might last two months since large landowners such as Landon

"King" Carter boasted over one hundred thousand plants. They were then repeatedly weeded, hoed, and debugged until, by mid-summer, they had eight to twelve leaves. The next chore was "topping" which meant cutting the top portion so the plants would not flower. But topped plants sprouted "suckers" or new shoots that had to be clipped as well. Finally, sometime in September, the planter or overseer studied the crop's moisture, maturity, aroma, and color, and judged it ready to cut. The harvest had to be swift lest the plants get overripe or an early frost blight them.

Harvest time, however, was only the halfway point because cut leaves had to be hung in curing barns to dry out. If packed while too damp the tobo would rot during transport; if too dry it would crumble. The leaves had to be cured until "case," at which point slaves stripped the stalks and stems off tens of thousands of leaves, "prized" them in hogsheads, and carefully mashed them down until one barrel might weigh a thousand pounds. Finally the hogsheads were pushed down "rolling roads" to warehouses on the river. If rolling was done before Christmas the holiday was especially gay. But two weeks later a new nervous year began.

Planters prided themselves on the quantity and especially the quality of their crop because they bespoke a man's character. Bad weather or luck was always in play, but it was part of the Cavalier's philosophy that consistently bad tobo could only be due to stupidity or negligence. So foreign to the planters was the notion that all was in God's hands that Whitefield despaired of them. He thought "the greatest probability of doing good in Virginia is among the Scots-Irish, who have lately settled in the mountainous parts of that province." In sum, the Chesapeake plantation system was a rational market activity in the spirit of English rural capitalism and improvement ethic. The price a given planter's tobo commanded in London determined both his bottom line and his place in the pecking order of the Tidewater elite. But it all depended on slaves, which is why a wise master tried to manage his workers as deftly as he treated his plants, being neither too harsh nor too lenient, too distant nor too familiar. Enslaved Africans, in turn, knew how to "discipline" a cruel planter or overseer through slovenly work or sabotage. It is safe to conclude master-slave relations in the American south were the product of an elaborate, unspoken negotiation.[52]

Patterns of life in South Carolina, where over half the population was black as early as 1708, differed from those in the Chesapeake. Rice, timber, cattle-raising, and indigo were not conducive to the gang system. Instead, labor in the southernmost colonies was based on a "task" system that left workers free once their assigned daily tasks were done. Hustling Africans, who completed their chores quickly, might well have a few hours per day plus Sundays to tend poultry or a vegetable garden, go fishing or crabbing, and sell their own produce. The drivers themselves were often experienced blacks who knew as much or more about the crops and cattle as their white bosses (not least the skilled African herdsmen to whom the term "cowboy" may have first been applied). African drivers were also valuable as "drill sergeants," assimilating blacks newly arrived from Africa or the West Indies. Finally, many landlords were absentees who resided in London or at least summered in Charleston and Savannah. All these conditions meant there was more separation between masters and field hands, more autonomy for the latter, and more surviving West African folkways in Carolina and Georgia than in the Chesapeake.[53]

What those folkways were is a matter of educated guesses based more on anthropological studies of Low Country descendants than on contemporary sources. But two remarkable eighteenth-century narratives by high-born West Africans caught up in the slave trade provide clues. Their authors remembered their native societies as patriarchal and polygamous, highly protective of women, communal, hardworking, and joyously ceremonial: "We are almost a nation of dancers, musicians, and poets." Africans were animists, but also believed in a creator god who dwelt in the sun and governed all things including captivity and death. Births, funerals, harvests, and special events were occasions for song and dance accompanied by the *molo* (banjo) and *quaqua* (drum), which they crafted as ornately as their rugs, baskets, and garments. Of course, the Africans represented many tribal traditions, including those of voodoo and conjuring patronized by the snake god of the Whydah and Ewe tribes. Moreover, African customs generally were reinforced in Carolina by a high volume of new arrivals in every decade except the 1740s.[54]

Why that one recess in the Charleston slave market? Because of the greatest slave revolt of the colonial era. Like the Salem witch trials it was in part a war-induced panic because Spain declared St. Augustine a haven for fugitive slaves in 1738 and an Anglo-Spanish war broke out in September 1739. It might have seemed like a "now or never" chance to a defiant Angolan named Jemmy, because he aroused a score of followers and seized guns and powder from a store in Stono, fifteen miles south of Charleston. They repaired to a nearby camp, mounted a standard, and beat African drum messages that rallied another fifty or seventy-five freedom seekers. But as luck would have it, the lieutenant-governor observed Jemmy's band on the road and sounded the alarm. In two brief but violent encounters, one at the camp and the other on the road to St. Augustine, colonial militia killed or captured the rebels. In the aftermath of this Stono Rebellion the South Carolina assembly passed a rigorous new slave code, but not of the sort one might expect. First, it levied a punishing tariff on new imports of slaves lest whites become dangerously outnumbered. Second, it prohibited masters from killing, maiming, or overworking slaves, and stipulated a "minimum wage" in terms of the food and clothing provided for slaves. Third, it prohibited whites from teaching slaves to read and established patrols to enforce curfews and examine slave quarters for weapons. In other words, South Carolina, again in advance of the other southern colonies in political insight, acted to constrain any white as well as black behavior that put the social system at risk. The enslaved were made to know their station in life was permanent and inalterable, while slave masters were obliged to make that station more or less tolerable, at least in physical terms.[55]

But enslaved Africans were not animals interested only in less work and more fodder. Nor were their masters just accountants. Black or white, all were creatures of spirit, psychology, and philosophy who had somehow to reconcile their humanity with an economy that assaulted it. To the extent that was possible the solution could only derive from religion. But the Africans had been torn from their religious supports, while the planters professed a religion that made slavery at best problematical. What was required, therefore, were two more American adaptations of Christianity sufficient to comfort slaves and masters alike.

Spirituality among early African Americans is also a mystery because whites either ignored or condemned the "idolatrous dances and revels" that occurred around the slave quarters' campfires. Fearing evangelization of slaves might put ideas into their heads, however, the planters also protested the missionary work of the Anglican Society for the Propagation of the Gospel. Virginia's burgesses even reported in 1699 the "Gros Barbarity and rudeness" of the Africans, "the variety and Strangeness of their Languages," and the "Shallowness of their minds" disqualified them for conversion. Still, Anglican clergy on the scene were often called upon to parse the obligations slaves owed their masters, and masters, in good conscience, their slaves. Bishop William Fleetwood, a church reformer and SPG stalwart, endeavored to meet the needs of colonial clergy and planters in a mammoth 1705 treatise, *The Relative Duties of Parents and Children, Husbands and Wives, Masters and Servants*. Not surprisingly, he took as his text the apostle Paul's dicta in Ephesians about servants obeying their masters and masters showing forbearance to servants. But Fleetwood, true to his Whiggish politics, distinguished between English servants, who were obligated to *resist* unjust masters (that is, Stuart kings), and "downright Slaves" who must accept their fate regardless. To be sure, he scolded masters who denied the gospel to slaves, but construed the gospel so as to support, not corrode, the slave system. His justification for that was wonderfully English: "We are a People who live and maintain ourselves by *Trade;* and if that *Trade* be lost, or overmuch discouraged, we are a ruined Nation; and shall our selves in time become as very *Slaves.*"[56] English liberty thus required African slavery.

Fleetwood's formulations, accepted and disseminated by two generations of Anglican clergy, reconciled the Chesapeake and the Carolinas to the evangelization of their African populations and influenced revivalists beginning with Whitefield himself. As for the other major Protestant denominations, none of them—not even Quakers—took a religious stand against the institution of slavery prior to American independence. That is a fact of unappreciated significance. For even though slavery is rightly associated with southern plantations, it was legal in all thirteen colonies and slaves could be found in almost every sector of the economy, from shipyards in New England to farms in New York (the biggest northern slave state) to ironworks in the middle colonies to crafts and domestic service everywhere. As of 1730 only a third of enslaved Africans worked in tobacco and a tenth in rice, which meant over half labored in farming, trades, and service.[57]

If the British empire thus declared Christian liberty to be exclusively spiritual, requiring only that planters and their wives display a modicum of mercy toward minions, how did the uprooted Africans fill their spiritual void? The process and timing of their inventions are uncertain, but the results of them are clear. By the end of the colonial era African Americans blended traditional rituals and practices such as chants, dances, and healings with the faith preached by white evangelists, especially Baptists and Methodists, into a vibrant religion of consolation and hope. It did not condone slavery—quite the contrary—but it helped slaves endure their "exile in Egypt," their "Babylonian captivity," their "time on the Cross" until the blessed day of deliverance when "the last shall be first." Thus did black Christianity inject its own millennial expectations into American religion.[58]

But "massah" did not get off so easily. For if slaves might spend part of the

Sabbath praising the Lord with their hands, feet, and voices, they also spent evenings composing, singing, and swaying to songs expressing their hardships, mocking the folly or damning the cruelty of their overseers, and extolling runaways and other dissenters. As a white observer in Maryland wrote, the slaves' songs "generally relate the usage they have received from their Masters and Mistresses in a very satirical stile and manner."[59] African Americans were already inventing the work songs, field hollers, ironic laments, and gospel calls that would evolve, a century later, into the blues.

Puritans, Quakers, Anglican planters, Presbyterian Scots on the frontier, pietist and Lutheran redemptioners who did not even speak English, and a large underclass of Africans not permitted to share in the others' American dreams: what possible sources of unity existed that might allow these people to coalesce into a nation? The first such source, the one that made unity physically possible, was a growing infrastructure of transportation and communications linking the colonies' major ports. The 1760 populations of Boston (15,500), Newport (7,500), New York (18,000), Philadelphia (23,700), Baltimore (9,800 including 2,000 slaves), and Charleston (8,000) were still small in absolute terms and contained less than 5 percent of the overall colonial population. But almost all the colonies' political, intellectual, and commercial activities occurred in or through them, and their modest size and compactness ensured that everyone of substance knew everyone else. The fact most of the colonies' thirteen thousand Roman Catholics and all five of their small Jewish congregations were nestled in major ports also tested the limits of tolerance. In the war years of the 1740s, St. Joseph's, the first Catholic church north of Maryland, was attacked by mobs in Philadelphia, Jewish cemeteries were desecrated in New York, and in most places Catholics and Jews remained ineligible to hold public office.[60] But by comparison to conditions in Europe the colonial towns were relative havens. They soon became laboratories to test whether being a good Protestant was a requirement for being considered a good American.

The eighteenth-century colonial towns were not pleasant places to live. To begin with, they were exceedingly crowded, which might appear strange given the abundance of land. As late as 1770 the settled portion of Philadelphia covered a mere six-tenths of a square mile, that of New York just 1.1, and that of Boston about 1.2; hence seven to nine people occupied each dwelling and population densities ranged from thirteen thousand (Boston) to thirty thousand (Philadelphia) per square mile. One reason was the habit of tradesmen, their families, and their employees to live together above their own workplaces. Another was the paucity of residents sufficiently wealthy to buy or build houses. Still, the failure of real estate speculators to develop new blocks is a mystery. Evidently it was just more cost-effective to add stories and outbuildings to existing structures in the high-rent blocks of Boston Harbor, lower Manhattan, and Penn's Landing than it was to extend streets and build lower-rent housing on the edges of towns. It may also seem strange that colonial townspeople suffered from a shortage of firewood, but that was an inevitable consequence of growth as all the nearby timber was hewn. Fuel prices were accordingly a hot political topic, especially since wood mongers and even official "corders of wood" jacked up prices in winter and cheated customers with short stacks. Unpaved streets became sluices of mud and manure in wet weather and garbage dumps all year round. Thus did the 1707 town meeting in Newport decry the waist-high sewage that kept the streets "continually Dirty and Mire, and ye Stincks that issueth out of ye houses is not only noisom but is dangerous . . . especially in ye Night when people cannot see to shunn them." Human scum in the form of footpads also lurked in the darkness of night, smallpox and yellow fever were frequent summertime visitors, and fire a constant danger.[61]

Slowly but surely municipal and colonial assemblies took steps to clean up and pave old streets and grate new ones, regulate food markets and public health, ban tanneries and slaughterhouses in residential neighborhoods, dig sewers, draw clean upriver water through pipes, and draft or tax citizens to construct bridges, piers, government buildings, and other public works. Boston boasted America's first subterranean sewer in 1704 and lighthouse in 1716. John Headley of Newport installed the first indoor plumbing in 1723. The clever Germans of Bethlehem, Pennsylvania, installed the first pumped waterworks in 1755. Almost without exception municipal governance was apt to be contentious, corrupt, and dilatory. But coping with the day-to-day nuisances of crowded urban life probably taught American elites at least as much about the art of self-government as did the loftier business of colonial assemblies.

Above all, the towns were dissemination centers for news, advertising, and opinion thanks to the growth of publishing and the postal system. There was nothing inevitable about either development. First, a printing press was an expensive and cumbersome import, paper and ink were hard to obtain, and small markets and limited means for distribution made publishing risky.

Second, one or another colonial authority—be it the governor, proprietor, or assembly—was bound to fear the power of the press and try to suppress free speech even as England itself did until the 1770s. Thus, the English colonies' first press was set up in Cambridge in 1638 under the Puritans' aegis, but only sixty-two years later did General Court permit a private printer to set up shop in Boston. Even then authorities kept a close and censorious eye on private publications such as *Publick Occurrences, Both Foreign and Domestick,* a monthly (1690), and the *Boston News-Letter,* the colonies' first newspaper (1704). All the earliest colonial journals were in fact founded by printers who doubled as editors, publicity agents, and authors. Their purpose was to turn a profit, mostly through advertising, hence printers were chary of gratuitously offending authority.

Indeed, the best means of assuring a steady income was to win appointment as Publick Printer, postmaster, or both. Boston editor John Campbell held both positions, as did Connecticut's first publisher and Pennsylvania's Benjamin Franklin, who asked a London friend to pay a bribe of £300, if necessary, to get himself named deputy postmaster. That allowed him to fix postal rates for his own and competitors' journals and circulate his wares through the mail, not to mention pocket a tidy £1,859 for his public service. As a prolific writer, publisher, bookseller, and deputy postmaster for all the colonies from 1753 to 1774 Franklin became America's first media mogul. But he was not the prototype of the independent and fearless publisher. That mantle belongs to William Goddard and his wife, Mary Katherine, two Yankees driven by ambition and a mission. Son of the postmaster in New London, Connecticut, Goddard knew what power that office imparted and determined to break it. In 1762, after apprenticing with a printer, he set up shop with his wife in Providence, Rhode Island. But without patronage the Goddards could not make ends meet, so they moved on to New York, then Philadelphia. Everywhere they protested the post office monopoly and everywhere got into trouble. Finally they landed in the young town of Baltimore. Since bashing the proprietors was Maryland's pastime the Goddards' message was well received. But their greatest achievement was to gather the news themselves and distribute their *Maryland Journal and Baltimore Advertiser* (1773) through a privately financed post-rider network, the ancestor of the Associated Press and United Parcel Service alike.[62]

Public and private printing, intercolonial trade stoked by advertising, post roads and coastal packets between major towns, and a postal service linking

Savannah River plantations to New Hampshire towns: thanks to all that, the colonies became linked more closely to each other than to London. Thus, while the number of ships clearing Boston Harbor for England doubled between 1690 and 1740, the number bound for other colonial ports increased *sevenfold.* Those coasting ships, not to mention the busy traffic on the Boston Post Road, New York–Philadelphia Stage, and the Great Wagon Road, carried something far more mighty than cargoes. They carried people, American people whose heads were loaded with news, opinions, schemes, and ideas. One of them, the notorious Tom Bell, may have been America's first nationwide criminal. Assuming various names and the guise of a gentleman, he swindled men and seduced women throughout the colonies in the 1730s and 1740s.[63] But far more important, communications and transport acquainted the colonists with each other while diluting somewhat their original cultures. Slowly but surely the otherwise jealous descendants of Puritans, Quakers, Dutchmen, Germans, Cavaliers, Barbadians, and Scots-Irish borderers learned of the ambitions and enemies, which is to say, greed and fear, they possessed in common. American colonists (excepting always the Africans) shared a great deal of both greed and fear over the quarter century starting in 1739 when the Anglo-French contest for North America touched off world war.

# SOLDIERS, SPECULATORS, AND SAVAGES

## The French and Indian Wars Turn Britain into the Enemy, 1740–1763

*T*he American colonies lived in relative tranquillity for twenty-five years after the Peace of Utrecht of 1713. But it would be wrong to assume the peace was normal and to everyone's liking. The colonists were pleased to mind their own affairs, but had not abandoned the seventeenth-century imperial spirits any more than their quaint seventeenth-century accents. Nor had a rising generation of British politicians and merchants forgotten England's old missions to improve new lands, slay Catholic dragons, and dispossess any "savages" who got in the way. An expansionist "patriot party" in Parliament, therefore, deemed Walpole's pursuit of amicable relations with France and Spain anything but normal. Rather it seemed a sort of self-containment and betrayal of Britain's imperial destiny: two of the sins for which James Stuart was forced off the throne.

A recent book styled the United States "a country made by war."[1] So it was, but since the book in question begins in 1775 it neglects to observe how the war of American independence was only the last phase of a protracted conflict whose earlier phases go by the names of the War of Jenkins' Ear, the War of the Austrian Succession, or King George's War, the French and Indian War, the Seven Years' War, or Great War for the Empire, not to mention the Cherokee War, Pontiac's Rebellion, and other episodic conflicts with Indians. Nor did those wars simply pit the British and colonists against French and Indians.

Rather, the wars were fought out among at least six distinct groups of combatants: the French imperialists based in Québec; the Indians who sided with them because they feared the British more; the "war party" imperialists based in London; the Indians who sided with them because they feared the French more; the American colonists struggling to defend lands they already possessed; and the American colonists rivaling each other for conquest of lands none yet possessed. Four of the groups had limited aims, but the two that triumphed in the wars of 1739–1763—the British war party and colonial expansionists—were those with unlimited aims. They meant to control the St. Lawrence basin, the Great Lakes, the Ohio Valley, indeed the whole continent. Accordingly, the moment the French, Spaniards, and Indians laid down their arms, the victors began to quarrel over the spoils and court support from the other four. They quarreled over land, money, power, and principle, but also over which of them still truly embodied England's original imperial spirits.

The hexagonal war for the continent began in the 1730s in the side halls of Parliament and the parlors of England's great country houses. There various Tories and ambitious young Whigs gathered to share their contempt for the patronage-driven political machine run for so long by Walpole and Newcastle. But aside from the usual "anti-corruption" plank, these landed gentlemen, merchants, bankers, and military officers were too disparate to form a credible domestic policy platform. So they plotted to topple Walpole over foreign policy by wrapping themselves in the flag and accusing the government of coddling Spain. After 1713 British merchants smuggling goods in and out of Spanish Caribbean ports habitually howled in protest whenever Spaniards dared try to enforce their own navigation acts and the terms of the treaty Britain herself had ratified. Especially obnoxious was Spain's employment of *guarda costas*, freelancing captains licensed to capture and seize foreign vessels suspected of contraband. British merchant houses called that "piracy," but Walpole persevered in negotiating outstanding claims. So the war party cried "Freedom of the seas!" ever more loudly until, in 1738, they pulled off a propaganda coup by parading ship's master Robert Jenkins in Parliament. Spanish buccaneers, he alleged, had stolen his cargo eight years before and, for good measure, cut off his ear. Jenkins kept it pickled in a jar and now displayed it to great effect. Still Walpole tried to adjudicate matters with Madrid, but so feverish had public opinion become that Newcastle feared further appeasement might topple the government. So Walpole, against his better judgment, insisted that Spain cease and desist from seizure of foreign vessels. When the proud Spaniards refused,

Britain declared war in October 1739. "It is your war," Walpole grunted to Newcastle, "and I wish you well of it." Within three years Walpole, Britain's longest-serving first minister, quit public life.[2]

The true character of this Anglo-Spanish War is often obscured by its merger the following year with the War of the Austrian Succession. In that continental conflict a coalition led by Prussia and France fought to wrench provinces away from the new Habsburg empress of Austria. With predatory armies on the loose in the German states, King George II understandably feared for the security of his ancestral province of Hanover. He took Britain into the war on Austria's side.[3] But the pre-existing Anglo-Spanish conflict had nothing to do with central Europe and everything to do with the British war party's lust to plunder Catholic possessions in America. Several months before war was declared the British government granted colonial governors leave to issue letters of marque to American captains desirous of attacking Spanish ships and ports. The Admiralty also pre-positioned a fleet in Jamaica with orders to descend upon Panama. Its surprise attack netted 10,000 Spanish dollars in gold. A royal proclamation of April 1740 offered any person or company full title to any Spanish lands or wealth they might seize in expeditions they mounted themselves, while even the lowliest volunteer for the royal service was entitled to share in 50 percent of the proceeds from captured enemy prizes. A simple soldier or sailor might hope to become rich if he signed on "to singe the king of Spain's beard."[4]

As was the case with King William's War back in 1690, however, the War of Jenkins' Ear disconcerted cocky American colonists. Georgia was the scene of the initial campaign both because of its proximity to Spanish Florida and because James Oglethorpe, acting on a false rumor, declared the colony at war a month early. He prepared at once to attack St. Augustine. By May 1740, a Royal Navy squadron arrived to blockade the coast and more than two thousand Georgia and South Carolina militia marched with some Indians and redcoats. But St. Augustine's one thousand Spanish defenders not only refused to submit, they had the effrontery to launch a lethal sortie against a party of Georgia scouts. When the militiamen realized they were in for a long siege in the swamp rather than a quick raid for silver and gold, they forced Oglethorpe to retreat in July. Eighteen months later the tables turned totally when a Spanish fleet of fifty-six ships and seven thousand soldiers left Cuba for Georgia. Oglethorpe prepared to mount a vigorous defense, but instead saved Savannah through guile. He arranged for a Spanish prisoner to obtain (false) intelligence about the imminent arrival of a great British fleet, then let him escape. The nervous Spanish commander accordingly turned tail for the open sea the moment sails appeared on the horizon. Thus emboldened, Oglethorpe took another crack at St. Augustine in 1743. But his motley colonial force lacked the cannons needed to reduce the Castillo de San Marcos. All Oglethorpe earned for his troubles was a court martial in London and eventual loss of his trusteeship over Georgia.[5]

The major British initiative in the war was a campaign against Cartagena on the Colombian coast. The prospect of sharing loot from this greatest port and treasury of the Spanish Main attracted thirty-six hundred colonial volunteers, especially from Virginia where the governor Sir William Gooch proudly raised a regiment known as Gooch's American Foot. What these greedy but innocent boys and their Cavalier officers received for their service was unrelieved misery. Transported in a state of constant seasickness to the heat and humidity of the tropics, they were placed under the incompetent command of General Thomas Wentworth and either used as drudge laborers aboard British ships or folded into contemptuous British regiments. Camped in the jungle outside Cartagena, the invaders had no means of storming its stone palisades or resisting the fevers that carried off a dozen men every day. After one futile assault the campaign aborted. But so rampant were infectious diseases less than half the American volunteers returned to their homes. Those who did were lauded as heroes and victims of British stupidity throughout the colonial press.

Even more eye-opening than the Cartagena defeat was a victory New Englanders appeared to have won at Louisbourg on Cape Breton Island. That French fort, situated on a fine natural harbor, served as a base for raids against New England ships and trading posts as well as a haven for French fleets in the western Atlantic. Accordingly, when France and Spain joined forces in 1744 to defend each other's empires against British aggression, Governor William Shirley of Massachusetts persuaded General Court to launch a campaign against Louisbourg. The real authors of the plan, however, were two intrepid hustlers named John Bradstreet and William Vaughan. Bradstreet grew up in Nova Scotia, joined the British regiment there, and augmented his meager pay with illicit trade with the French. When hostilities broke out he was captured and spent five months in Louisbourg. Released on *parole* (meaning he gave his "word" as an officer not to re-enter the fighting), Bradstreet made straight for Boston to spread the word that Louisbourg's defenses were shoddy. He made a believer of Vaughan, a Harvard graduate who rejected the ministry in favor of a fishing and timber business in Maine. Vaughan was ambitious for glory as well as money. He hoped to follow the path of his father, who was named lieutenant-governor of New Hampshire after helping to capture Port Royal in 1710. So Vaughan rode through every village and town in upper New England selling Bradstreet's idea. Louisbourg could be taken—by New Englanders alone—to the consternation of papists and the profit of Protestants! Among his converts was Governor Shirley. But when he proposed the plan to a secret session of General Court in January 1745, the sourpuss Puritans were "struck with amazement." Fearing another expensive debacle such as their grandfathers' attempt on Québec, the Bay Colony assemblymen refused. Vaughan remounted his horse to circulate petitions among Marblehead fishermen and Boston merchants in favor of razing Louisbourg. One can only imagine the private calculations, bargains, and lobbying that must have ensued. For when Shirley put a revised war plan up for a vote, General Court approved it by a margin of one.

New England sprang to life in the usually dead months of February and March. Some three thousand volunteers stepped forward while local merchants, artisans, farmers, and fishermen made windfall profits outfitting the expedition. They liked to believe their cause was holy. George Whitefield himself blessed the amateur army, whose officers were mostly church deacons. One captain brandished an axe for the purpose, he said, of smashing the crucifixes and icons in Louisbourg's chapel. As early as April 4 an armada of small coastal craft delivered the militia, William Pepperrell of Maine in command, to the Cape Breton coast. After making rude camp two miles southwest of Louisbourg, Pepperrell ordered cannons placed on high ground in range of the fort. Cold fog and marsh made it hard work for horses and men alike, but at length the New Englanders laid siege to the town. Back home, colonists hungered for news. This was an *American* cause that excited people as far south as Philadelphia, where Benjamin Franklin wrote, "My shop is filled with thirty inquiries at the coming in of every post . . . as if forts are as easy taken as snuff." In fact, Louisbourg's acting governor Louis de Chambon fought tenaciously even after the Royal Navy blockaded the harbor. But Pepperrell's men were just as determined. First, thanks to another tip from Bradstreet, the New Englanders captured the defenders' Grand Battery which lay outside the fort. The French had spiked its thirty large cannons, of course, but Yankee blacksmiths drilled out the blocked touch holes and one by one trained the guns on Louisbourg. Then the New Englanders tried to assault the active French battery located on an island in the midst of the harbor. Their first amphibious attack ended in farce: "This Night about Eight hundred of us went to Tak the Iseland. But our head offiser Being a Couard we Rowd a Bout all Night and Never Landed." Their second attack ended in disaster with some two hundred militiamen captured or killed. Finally, Pepperrell ordered cannons muscled all the way around the bay to a spot within range of the island battery. Chambon now saw no reason to prolong Louisbourg's agony and sued for terms in mid-June.[6]

Fireworks and boozy celebrations exploded in Boston, Newport, New Haven, and Philadelphia when news of the victory arrived.[7] But the victors themselves knew little joy. Not only did the British admiral permit the French *habitants* to retain their property, thus "cheating" Americans of their plunder, he tricked out his own ships in French colors and picked up easy prizes for himself and his sailors as French ships unknowingly entered the harbor. Worst of all, when the colonial and European wars ended with the Treaty of Aix-la-Chapelle in 1748, the British restored Louisbourg to France. To be sure, Parliament reimbursed most of the colonies' expenses for the expedition, but the whole point of it had been to drive out the papists and take what they had. Thanks to the British the Americans were allowed to do neither. Meanwhile, the last years of the war reminded New England and New York of the danger of having Frenchmen as neighbors. In November 1745, a force of five hundred Canadians, French regulars, Hurons, and Abnakis fell upon Saratoga, thirty miles north of Albany. In one freezing, terror-filled night they killed or kidnapped over one hundred inhabitants, stole all they could carry, and torched every structure. The following summer Pepperrell's own Maine and New Hampshire frontier was exposed to predation, and Boston panicked at news of a French armada en route to their waters. When an on-board epidemic forced the French captains to turn back, New England's clergy made much of the fact that Providence, not the Royal Navy, was what saved them.

The war of 1739–48 left five powerful legacies, all of which spelled trouble for the British empire. The first was a new edginess in relations between the colonies and the mother country. The British lorded it over the provincials, made light of their contributions, begrudged every penny spent to repay the colonies, and wasted American blood in botched campaigns. The second legacy was an awareness among the colonies of discord between and within them. Beleagured Georgia and South Carolina got little help from anyone else. Only Virginia met Britain's expectations of colonial support for the Caribbean campaign. The Quakers kicked in £4,000 "for the king's use," but insisted it be spent on Pennsylvania foodstuffs. Of course, their assembly steadfastly refused to raise troops, leaving it to Benjamin Franklin to found a volunteer militia funded by lotteries.[8] New England chipped in for the Louisbourg effort, but wealthy Rhode Island merchants spared no more than one aging sloop. New York did nothing at all. Connecticut's merchants refused to fulfill their assembly's generous pledge of supplies unless the British paid cash on the barrelhead. Colonial officials also insisted on dictating who would control provisions and the uses to which they were put. Thus, even after the Saratoga massacre the defenders in Albany were denied needed supplies because Yorkers could not agree on whether the governor, commander, or militia captains ought to dispose of them.

In short, each colony asked "What's in this for us?" But so, too, did people within each colony learn to ask "What's in this for *whom?*" Merchants favored with government contracts or clever enough to anticipate supply and demand might make more profit in one wartime year than in ten years of peace. One of them was Boston's Thomas Hancock, who began life as a humble bookseller and grew prosperous as a trader in whale oil and bone. But war made him rich. In 1739 he sold his ships at inflated prices rather than risk having them captured, then invested the proceeds in gunpowder. He also won a plum British contract to supply meat for the Cartegena invasion fleet. Flush with profits, Hancock teamed up with other entrepreneurs to outfit privateers and a prominent London merchant house to share intelligence and political influence. He also won appointment as a major supplier of British forces in Canada. All the while his firm continued to smuggle tea and trade illegally in Dutch ports. The 1739–48 war thus added £20,000 to the family fortune Hancock bequeathed to nephew John. In 1742 another war profiteer, Peter Faneuil, bestowed upon Boston the grand market hall that still bears his name. New England and Hudson River traders continued to do business with their French Canadian contacts even as war raged, and ships from all the colonies traded with Dutch and French islands in the West Indies when not busy plundering Spaniards.[9]

Inasmuch as the insurgent "patriots" in Parliament claimed to be warring against patronage and corruption as much as against Spain and France, it is not surprising the British government rued the dilatory, uncoordinated, and often venal behavior of the colonies. Hence a third legacy of the war was Britain's determination to replace "salutary neglect" with a vigorous, centralized imperial policy. Such a policy was bound to exacerbate frictions between Britain and the colonies even if carried out by honest and circumspect ministers. But British belligerence triumphed in the *absence* of reform at home thanks to a fourth legacy of the war: the rise to power of William Augustus, Duke of Cumberland and younger son of King George II. It was Cumberland's army that suppressed the Jacobite (pro-Stuart) revolt of the Highland clans in 1746, subjecting Scotland to systematic spoliation and slaughter. He returned in glory to London, where his father the king made him Captain-general (commander-in-chief) of all British armies and the most influential voice in court politics. Cumberland meant to deploy those assets to achieve three ambitions: control of the cabinet, control of the colonies, and war *à outrance* against France.[10]

He had no difficulty achieving the first goal. By 1748 one of Cumberland's friends, John Russell, Duke of Bedford, was made secretary of the "southern department," hence colonial minister. Another of Cumberland's friends, George Montagu Dunk, Earl of Halifax, was made head of the Board of Trade. They went to work on their patron's second goal by sending the able official Thomas Pownall on a fact-finding mission to America while drafting plans to impose a centralized rule on the colonies.[11] Finally, the colonists themselves abetted the efforts of Cumberland and Halifax to provoke a resumption of war by engaging in a riot of land speculation. From upper New England to North Carolina the schemes of land companies turned American colonists against Indians, the French, and each other. That was the fifth legacy of the war of 1739–48.

The U.S. government later called it the Northwest and we know it today as the Middle West. But the original name for the forested empire south of the Great Lakes between the Alleghenies and the Mississippi was the Ohio Country. This well-watered masterpiece carved in the final Ice Age encompassed over three hundred thousand square miles (an area half again larger than France) and boasted "the finest and most fertile Country of America." That was the rhapsody sent Franklin's *Pennsylvania Gazette* by Colonel Henry Bouquet. He concluded with the insightful prediction the Ohio Country "may prove richer than the Mines of Mexico."[12] Land—land to be claimed and improved by a free and prolific race of Britons—was ultimately worth far more than all the metals dug from the ground or acquired through trade in sugar or pelts. That was the stroke of genius that inspired English capitalism in the first place and inspired American colonists long after mercantile interests and bean-counters monopolized economics in London.

The Scots-Irish frontiersmen who first settled the hilly interior thought little about grand imperial schemes. But planters in Virginia and the Carolinas, the proprietors of Pennsylvania, and far-sighted speculators in New York and Connecticut thought much about grand financial schemes. They competed furiously to establish claims to vast portions of the frontier. To do so, they had to obtain grants from one or another British authority, manipulate the numerous, contentious Indian tribes into ceding lands that may or may not "belong" to them, and above all keep out the French, whose explorers, traders, soldiers, and priests were already present around the Great Lakes. In the 1744 Treaty of Lancaster, Virginia's Lieutenant Governor Gooch persuaded the Iroquois to recognize Virginia's dubious western claims based on its seventeenth-century charter. Between 1745 and 1749 the Virginia governor's council proceeded to grant one hundred thousand acres each to the Greenbrier and Wood's River companies, eight hundred thousand acres on the Carolina border to the Loyal Company, and five hundred thousand acres of western Pennsylvania to the Ohio Company on condition it plant a fort and one hundred families there within seven years. That never happened, but the company did send out explorers, one of whom, Dr. Thomas Walker, was the first European to cross the Cumberland Gap in 1750.

Virginians had to contend, however, with the intrepid George Croghan, who emigrated from Ireland with an empty purse to Carlisle, Pennsylvania. Croghan quickly learned Indian tongues, wheedled loans from Quaker merchants on little more than blarney, and got rich in the Indian trade during the war. The British blockade meant French traders ran short of the guns and supplies Indians wanted. Croghan, just twenty-three years old, filled the vacuum. He built the first post at Cuyahoga (the future site of Cleveland), and even took Indian business away from the French near Détroit. The Penn brothers named the daring Croghan their Indian agent, whereupon he and interpreter Conrad Weiser made pacts with the Delawares, Shawnees, and Mingos. This first tug of war for the West climaxed in the spring of 1752 in a grand meeting at Logstown (now Ambridge), Pennsylvania. Virginia sent three delegates, but they were at cross purposes because one represented the Ohio Company and the others rival speculators in the House of Burgesses. Weiser and Croghan, representing the Penns and the Quakers' Friendly Association, refused to assist the Virginians. So complex was the tangle of personal, company, colonial, and tribal interests at Logstown, the conference seemed "to have more conspiracies than people." In the end, the Iroquois sold out the neighboring Delawares by opening portions of central Pennsylvania to whites in exchange for four canoes loaded with gifts. The treaty left unresolved, however, *which* whites were to come out on top.[13]

It was all a fantastic charade. Virginia's Ohio Company, Connecticut's Susquehanna Company, Pennsylvania's proprietors, and other investors (including some in England) were neither willing nor able to finance the settlement and defense of vast, virgin lands. So if their claims to empire were to pay off in cash the real work needed to be done by government-funded expeditions and armies. But even if the land-jobbers successfully bribed their governors and assemblies into footing the bill for westward expansion, no single colony could hope to subdue all its rivals alone—especially when the French made so bold as to defend their own claims to Ohio after the peace of Aix-la-Chapelle.

In 1749, Captain Pierre-Joseph Céleron de Blainville led an expedition of more than two hundred Canadians to the forks of the Ohio at the confluence of the Allegheny and Monongahela Rivers and thence downstream. His orders were to expel British traders such as Croghan, repair relations with Indians, and claim the Ohio Valley for France, which he did by planting lead plates at intervals on the shore. But back in Québec he warned that the *coureurs de bois* could never maintain the Indians' allegiance so long as they had to charge up to four times the number of pelts as the English for a comparable shipment of goods. France's only hope of securing the Ohio Valley was physical occupation. Céleron further warned French Canada would lose the Great Lakes and Mississippi Valley as well if its communication lines in the Ohio Valley were severed. Accordingly, Québec requested and Paris granted permission to construct a *glacis* of forts stretching from Ticonderoga (Lake Champlain) to Rouillé (Toronto), Presqu'ile (Erie), and Le Boeuf and Machault on the Allegheny River. By 1752 rudimentary stockades and nominal garrisons were in place at all those points, and the new governor-general of Canada, the Marquis Duquesne de Menneville, itched to complete the network with a grand fortress at the forks of the Ohio itself.

Virginia's new lieutenant-governor, Robert Dinwiddie, was a crony of Halifax and Cumberland. He meant to bring the pot to a boil. "I hope you will think it necessary," he wrote back to London, "to prevent the French from taking possession of the lands of the Ohio." Four months later the postal sloop docked at Yorktown with the reply he yearned for: an order signed by the king himself to meet the French threat by measures of his own choosing. Dinwiddie summoned the House of Burgesses and obtained its approval for a bold escapade. First he would send a messenger to Fort Le Boeuf to assert Virginia's western claims and invite the French to depart. Presumably the French would report to Québec and waste time drafting a counter-claim. In the meantime, Virginia militia companies would rush to fortify the Ohio forks. Since the latter was the more important task, Dinwiddie assigned it to his top frontier scout, William Trent. An erstwhile friend of Franklin and Thomas Penn, Trent had twice been in business with Croghan, twice betrayed him, and then defected to the Virginians. But with Trent put in charge of fort building, whom might the governor send as emissary to the French? Not by coincidence, an eager young officer lingered outside the hall awaiting the chance to volunteer. He did not know the way to Fort Le Boeuf, but was sure he could fake it just as he had spent the previous nine months pretending he knew more about soldiering than the militiamen he was hired to train. Dinwiddie soon rued his hasty choice of George Washington.

When Washington's father Augustus died in 1743, he left his sizable Potomac plantation, according to custom, to his eldest son, Lawrence. To eleven-year-old George and his mother (Augustus' second wife), he left only the modest Ferry Farm on the Rappahannock. George learned his letters and the ways of a gentleman, but had little prospect of advancement, adventure, wealth, or honor unless others gave him a leg up. Lawrence was his first likely patron, and George worshiped his older half-brother, especially after he returned from the Cartagena campaign to rename his estate after Admiral Edward Vernon. Lawrence, an early investor in the Ohio Company, no doubt regaled George with stories of fortunes to be made in western land speculation. But that was a sport for Cavaliers with capital and connections, and a teenager without means could enter the arena only as a squire to one of the knights. That may explain why George seized on the surveyors' tools he found in a shed on Ferry Farm and taught himself the science of measuring the earth. "For the rest of his life he would regard land as a jeweler inspects a gemstone, with minute attention to its flaws, facets, and values."[14]

The surveyor's chain, level, compass, and angle, like their seafaring cousins the knotted rope, compass, chronometer, and sextant, were vital tools of European expansion. They made possible accurate mapping and navigation, aided in construction of roads, told artillerymen the bearing and range to a target, and most important if prosaic, established the unimpeachable boundaries that made private property a meaningful concept. Surveys could be pedestrian work—measuring, triangulating, and doing trigonometry problems over and over again—and the frontier workplace rugged, risky, exposed. Starting on a promontory the surveyor would establish a benchmark and baseline on magnetic north, then proceed down into wild forests and fields, methodically laying out tracts no more than twelve miles across lest the curvature of the earth come into play. Predators both feral and human might lurk, especially squatters and snipers in the pay of rival speculators who hated the sight of a surveyor. The weather could always turn suddenly. Accordingly, Washington learned from his youthful work patience, precision under stress, and a knack for observing the ripples of Nature with an almost mathematical eye. He never much mastered military maneuver, but his surveyor's training must have imparted the good eye for ground, coolness in the midst of confusion, and "back to square one" stubbornness that eventually earned Washington the greatness he longed for.

George first encountered greatness four miles from Mount Vernon at the Belvoir manor of William Fairfax, whose older cousin Thomas was the Sixth Baron Fairfax of Cameron and the first British peer to relocate to America. Since Thomas' deceased father had squandered the family fortune, he was reduced to seeking government patronage. That door closed when Walpole took a dislike to him. In 1728 he fell back on his last asset: a huge tract of land granted to his mother's Culpeper family by King Charles II. But its legality was in doubt by dint of its size—all the land between the Potomac and Rappahannock—and its uncertain boundaries because no one knew where those rivers began. So Lord Fairfax came to Virginia in 1735 to collect decades' worth of quit rents, survey his territory, and fight rival claimants, including none other than Robert "King" Carter. At length a judgment in London upheld Fairfax's claim to the entire Shenandoah Valley. The baron resolved to spend the rest of his life there even if it meant dressing in buckskin and living in a log cabin.

The baron's cousin William, and William's son George Fairfax, however, were wedded to the gay life at Belvoir where they danced, drank, raced, and gambled. It was there Lawrence Washington met and married William's daughter. George Washington accordingly earned a social *entrée* that paid off in March 1748. The baron asked him to accompany George Fairfax on an expedition to survey the back country. The boys slept on straw mattresses, picked lice out of their hair, ate with their fingers, and sweated out encounters with Indians. But the experience impressed upon Washington how priceless this land would become over time. He racked his brain for ways to accumulate capital. Surveyor fees only bankrolled a few small real estate purchases. Then in one eventful year, over 1751–52, his brother Lawrence died of a lingering fever, eliminating George's chance for cash from that quarter, and a young heiress rejected his proposal of marriage (she preferred a wealthier suitor), eliminating his chance for cash from that one. So Washington decided, for reasons unrecorded in his otherwise thorough journals, to pester Lieutenant Governor Dinwiddie for a major's commission in the militia. At least it would pay him £100 per year.[15]

Washington spent most of 1753 in the steamy low country south of the James River teaching himself and his recruits how to soldier. He was probably looking for relief from the boredom when he begged to serve as Dinwiddie's envoy to the French. The 450-mile trek Washington made from Williamsburg to the Erie country was cold, wet, tedious, and wholly inglorious. He could make little sense of the politics among the Indian tribes he encountered and all too much sense of French intentions. At Venango, a day's ride short of Fort Le Boeuf, his besotted French hosts bragged of "their absolute Design to take Possession of the *Ohio,* and by G— they would do it." At Le Boeuf itself on December 11, Washington delivered Dinwiddie's ultimatum. The commander replied, "I do not think myself obliged to obey it." Washington turned around and trudged home, having accomplished nothing in "as fatiguing a journey as it possible to conceive."[16]

When the snow melted in April, French troops easily chased Trent's Virginians away from the forks and began work on their own Fort Duquesne. But Dinwiddie and the Ohio Company were not about to surrender the portal to the American West. They put men to work building a military road and dispatched Washington with thirty-three militiamen and some Indians as guards. At a place called Great Meadow he came upon a French scouting party sprawled around campfires in front of a cliff that would block any retreat. Washington gave the order to fire. His men shot down a third of the party and captured the rest while Indians scalped the French corpses. They were found to include the commander, Joseph Coulon de Jumonville. Washington, thinking he had won a great victory, advanced. He did not know one Frenchman had escaped to cry "Murder!" back in Duquesne. Within a month a vengeful French force tracked Washington down. He rallied his men into a ramshackle fort named Necessity, and on July 3, 1754, held fast while the French and their Indians battered away for nine hours awaiting a sign of surrender. The French officer concluded British reinforcements must be on the way. How else to explain Washington's mad resistance? So he offered the Virginians free passage home in exchange for a capitulation. Washington accepted the terms, not knowing (he claimed) that the paper he signed included a confession of guilt for the death of Jumonville. But unless Washington did not glance at the paper at all he could hardly have missed the French words *l'assassin* and *l'assassinat.*[17]

On the way home the Virginia militiamen deserted, compounding the ignominies of Washington's first command. But Dinwiddie refused to surrender his dreams of western empire even though he now recognized Virginia alone could not conquer it. So he sent another frantic dispatch to inform London he had "acted with all possible Precaution in this Affair" but that "We are now in a State of War, begun very unjustly by the French Forces." Nor was that all the bad news the British cabinet and Board of Trade had to digest in the summer of 1754. The Carolinas warned of Cherokee threats to go on the warpath. From New York came the shocking report that Albany's failure to mount an effective defense had caused the Mohawks to declare the Covenant Chain broken. From Massachusetts the ever belligerent Governor Shirley reported new French fortifications on Nova Scotia; he had already dispatched a reconnaissance-in-force up the Kennebec River to prevent a surprise attack.

But bad news from America was *good* news to Cumberland and Halifax, who were searching for pretexts to pressure Newcastle into approving aggressive initiatives. He had already agreed to send Dinwiddie £10,000 and a credit for £10,000 more to support *defensive* measures, but a vigorous debate erupted in Parliament and the press over whether to risk *offensive* measures in America. Merchants opposed an expensive war to conquer more trees; they wanted to focus on the navy and trade. At the other extreme, Cumberland and the hawks wanted to send over the army and "expel the French neck and crop." Newcastle was betwixt, advocating deterrence not war—until Washington's rout undercut him. Cumberland took the chance to make multiple demands: the despatch of two regular army regiments to America to retake the Ohio forks; the raising of two more regiments in New England to attack Nova Scotia; the imposition on the colonies of a unified British command; and the establishment of a common war chest to be filled by the colonies but controlled by the British. Finally, to ensure no eleventh-hour diplomacy forestalled war, Cumberland leaked news of the planned deployments to the official press, inflaming opinion in Paris. Neither George II nor Louis XV wanted to fight. The hawkish propaganda in London, however, made it impossible for Britain to acquiesce in French domination of the American interior, while the French were hardly going to retreat from land they had fortified and defended with arms. As Lord Shelburne later concluded, "the war was contrived by the Duke of Cumberland underhand [and] Newcastle was frightened, bullied, and betrayed into it."[18]

War or not, the arrival on American soil of large formations of redcoats changed the nature of the British empire. For if Cumberland intended those soldiers to expel the French—something the colonists devoutly desired—he also intended them to uphold British authority and make the provincials pay for the privilege—something the colonists hated. The only way the American colonies might have forestalled Cumberland's plan was to unite themselves before the crown did it for them. That is why many historians have styled the Albany Conference of 1754 a tragic missed opportunity.

A short account of the conference might run like this. Agents from all the northern and middle American colonies, cognizant of the growing French danger, deterioration of Indian relations, and their need for coordination, assembled at Albany to put all to rights. Benjamin Franklin, far-sighted as always, arrived with an extraordinary plan for a colonial federation led by a President-general and Grand Council empowered to raise money and troops for the common defense. After some tinkering, the delegates at Albany accepted the plan. But unfortunately the colonial assemblies were jealous of their autonomy, and the British of their authority, so the plan was rejected. Franklin later thought if his plan had been adopted, the British empire would have been strengthened and the later clash between the colonies and mother country either prevented or long delayed. John Adams later cited the plan as premature, but proof of the inevitable union of the colonies. In any event, historians have judged the Albany Plan "one of the most significant documents in American history."[19]

That's as may be. But to argue the Albany Conference was also a missed opportunity ignores the following facts. It was *not* a colonial initiative. It was *not* convened to promote colonial union. Its main business was *not* frontier defense, but—once again—land speculation. Accordingly, Albany is more important for understanding what *did* happen in the mid-1750s than what *might* have happened or *would* happen in the mid-1770s.

What precipitated the meeting in June and July 1754 was the breaking of the Iroquois Covenant Chain.[20] That was the worst blow the northern colonies could absorb, and it was made worse by French penetration into the Ohio. No doubt the Mohawks calculated their leverage over the British was at a maximum, so why not force them to return to the "middle ground" and engage in wholesale renegotiation of arrangements for land, trade, and defense? The surprising news spread quickly to Britain where the Board of Trade at once ordered the relevant American governors to summon the tribes and repair the damage. The crown's agents thus had one official purpose for staging the meeting, and that was to renew the Covenant Chain. All Six Nations sent sachems to Albany to protest the encroachments of Virginia, Pennsylvania, and the French, to protest New York's broken promises of powder, bullets, and guns, to request the usual lavish gifts that symbolized the alliance, and to insist William Johnson, the crown's trusted Indian agent, be the sole intermediary between the Iroquois and the colonies. The royal commissioners eagerly granted these wishes since they accorded with the ministry's plans for centralized royal authority. So the Covenant Chain was renewed, not between the Iroquois and New York or New England, but between the Iroquois and the crown.

That was the official business at Albany. The unofficial and (to the colonial delegates) more pressing business was conducted every day "in the bushes." Agents from Pennsylvania, Connecticut, and New York gave Indians alcohol and haggled, bribed, and cajoled in hopes of obtaining great swaths of land from the Mohawk and Pennsylvania's Wyoming valley to the Ohio. Only Virginia was unrepresented since its Ohio Company hoped to treat with local tribes behind the backs of the Iroquois. The result was a spectacle: in public sessions Indian spokesmen voiced plaintive grievances against fraud; in private they vied with each other to cut the best deal they could, often betraying each other. Why? First, Indians knew they no longer had much choice in the matter. If British soldiers should come to police the frontier and prevent new white encroachments, all well and good. But unless and until that occurred, the best the tribes could hope for was to "sell" land they were bound to lose anyway for the highest price they could get. To the whites, after all, it was not a matter of whether they or the Indians would win control of the west, but only which group of whites would control it, and no legal brief was complete without some sachem's mark on a bill of sale.[21] Second, Indians were perfectly willing to part with some land in return for muskets, powder, tools, and luxuries. Third, they had hopes a transfer of part of their land might shelter the rest from white penetration, at least in the short run. Fourth, Indians were quite capable of hustling themselves, for instance by selling distant territories for which they had only vague claims and no need. The Iroquois, thanks to their mighty confederacy and leverage over the whites, were especially adept at asserting dominion over lesser tribes and selling their birthrights. Thus did Conrad Weiser, interpreting for John Penn and his agent, the Rev. Richard Peters, bargain for all the land from Lake Erie to the Ohio River even though it was occupied by the French. He was frustrated at first because Hendrick, a Mohawk chief, counseled the Oneidas, Tuscaroras, and Cayugas to offer no land west of the Alleghenies. But Weiser, suspecting Hendrick of holding out for his own piece of the action, replied "all or nothing." Sure enough, the Indians decided to deal. More than a score of chiefs met with the Penn delegation and British commissioner Pownall to relinquish their claim to western Pennsylvania in exchange for 2,000 Spanish pieces of eight.[22]

What then of the famous Albany Union Plan? That issue arose only because the British government had already hatched the idea of making the colonies pool their resources. Accordingly, when New York Lieutenant Governor James DeLancey proposed building new forts on the Hudson, the British commissioners interceded. Good idea, they said, but since colonies are no longer to pursue their security in piecemeal fashion such measures must await a plan for "effecting the Union between the Colonies." That was Ben Franklin's cue.

After 1746, when he won popularity for creating the voluntary militia, Franklin decided to enter public service. As if being postmaster and founder of Philadelphia's library, fire department, police force, insurance company, college (the future University of Pennsylvania), hospital, Freemason lodge, and American Philosophical Society were not enough, Franklin also won election to the provincial assembly in 1751 and served as its Indian agent. In all things he opposed Thomas Penn, damned "stiff rump" Quakers, and had little use for the Germans or Presbyterians either. But he maintained personal friendships with people in every camp and devoted himself to the cause of *unity:* within Pennsylvania, among the colonies, and between them and Britain. Franklin's overriding loyalty was to the same Whig imperialism that moved Cumberland and Halifax. He simply believed the best way to pursue it was through a voluntary association among autonomous colonies, not an involuntary one imposed from London.

Franklin had elaborated his views on imperial reform in two striking essays in 1751. Such was the demographic growth of the colonies they would soon cease to be children. That would require the British to treat Americans as partners rather than wards. But they would never do so if they foolishly lumped the colonists of British stock together with African slaves and Indians, who truly were children, or with aliens such as the Germans. Franklin might have been inspired by a foremost imperialist of the Scottish enlightenment, William

Douglass, whose *A Summary, Historical and Political, of the First Planting, Progressive Improvements, and Present State of the British Settlements in North-America* (1749–51) called for imperial unity and full citizenship for all British subjects in the colonies.[23] Franklin, far from anticipating independence, was making a similar "transatlantic critique of the colonial system" in hopes of "reforming it in a way that would advance Britain's empire building but not at the expense of American liberties." Thus did his famous "cut-up snake" illustrations of May 1754—the first American political cartoons—invite the colonies to "Join, or Die," but also to "unite and Conquer."[24]

When the British commissioners called for colonial unity at the Albany Conference, Franklin immediately tabled his plan for a presidency-general, intercolonial council, and common defense policy. One of his purposes was to bypass penurious or pacifist colonial assemblies, Pennsylvania's above all, so Americans might marshal the force needed to defeat the French and open up western lands. Massachusetts delegate Thomas Hutchinson certainly envisioned offensive operations. He seconded Franklin's plan by calling for the conquest of the Ohio Valley lest France surround and crush the English colonies in a great fist.

Since the Covenant Chain was renewed and the speculators' last deals had gone down, the Albany delegates saw no harm in just endorsing the Union Plan and heading for home. No one, including Franklin, had much hope the colonies would act on it. Indeed, only Massachusetts General Court showed a real interest. The other governors and assemblies suspected "colonial union" was a ruse to extort taxes and power, while London's officials had their own plan for imperial union to be imposed by Cumberland's generals. So Franklin's postmortem was disarmingly simple: "The Assemblies did not adopt it as they all thought there was too much *prerogative* in it; and in England it was judg'd to have too much the *Democratic*."[25]

What the Albany Conference did underscore was the American colonists' lust to control the frontier and the British imperialists' lust to take frontier matters out of the colonists' hands. In that sense, the events of 1754 did presage the colonies' later rebellion, but it offered no model for unity vis-à-vis Britain. Nor could it have so long as the French still had to be fought.

The Seven Years War (1756–63) began early in America just as the War of the Austrian Succession (1740–48) had done. It is dated from 1756 because that was when the Prussians and Austrians renewed their armed struggle and the other great powers joined in. Only this time the alliances were reversed in a manner of the utmost importance for Britain and thus for America. What kicked off the "diplomatic revolution" was Tsarina Elizabeth's ambition to expand Russia's sway west along the Baltic coast in the direction of East Prussia. To this purpose her ministers sought an accord with the British, whose fleet might otherwise intervene, promising in return to supply mercenaries to defend George II's homeland of Hanover. Needless to say, Frederick II of Prussia was alarmed by a gambit that threatened to put Russian armies to his east and west, so he made his own overtures to London. Newcastle jumped at the chance to detach Frederick from his French alliance. In the Convention of Westminster (January 1756), Britain and Prussia contracted to defend the German states against all foreign invaders. That seeming betrayal of their previous alliances provoked Austria and France to end their ancient rivalry. Together with Russia they formed a grand alliance to gang up on Berlin and London. This complex diplomacy shows that melodramatic accounts of how Washington's musket volley sparked the Seven Years War are myopic in the extreme.[26] The Seven Years War was continental and global, and while America was a major stake in it, no British minister dared avert his eyes from Hanover without incurring the wrath of the king.

Few colonists saw the big picture. All they knew was two under-strength regiments of redcoats, disgraced in their last engagement, had been pulled out of Irish occupation duty and shipped to America, where they caused nothing but trouble. Cumberland ordered colonists to quarter the troops in their homes, and his North American commander, John Campbell, Earl of Loudoun, carried it out. When residents of Albany, Philadelphia, and Charleston challenged the constitutionality of the practice, Loudoun threatened to place the towns under martial law. He also expected the colonies to raise enough militiamen to bring his regiments to full strength, which bordered on conscription. Everywhere British quartermasters dueled with colonial assemblies and merchants over supplies and the prices paid for them. In short, all the problems experienced in the earlier war reappeared on a grander scale. But this time colonial foot dragging could sometimes be met by British coercion. So if redcoats did not forgive the colonists their ingratitude, neither did colonists forgive the soldiers who *in extremis* marched into their barns, warehouses, and homes to requisition supplies, bunk down, and doubtless flirt with their daughters.[27]

In victory, of course, all might be forgotten. But no victories were forthcoming. General Edward Braddock, picked by Cumberland to lead the offensive against Fort Duquesne, was so appalled by Pennsylvania's lack of magazines and storehouses he began to make excuses before his army even marched: "The jealousy of the people, and the disunion of many colonies are such that I almost despair of succeeding." He had mustered a mere tenth of the twenty-five hundred horses and two hundred wagons his army required when Franklin intervened personally to persuade Pennsylvania Germans to "lease" Braddock wagons and horses before he wrathfully seized them. Franklin also talked the assembly into voting funds to extend the wagon road west. George Washington also came to Braddock's aid after writing his aide-de-camp sycophantic letters begging for a royal commission.[28] But a wagon train, road, and experienced guides only hastened Braddock's defeat because he not only refused assistance from Indians he bluntly told them that Britain, not they, would possess all the land after the war.[29] As a result, Braddock received no warning of the one thousand Indians and Frenchmen lying in wait on his route. They caught his marching redcoats in a murderous fire on July 9, 1755. Some soldiers froze, many tried to flee, and others who ached to counterattack were held in place by Braddock himself until the army disintegrated. At the cost of 23 dead, the French and Indians killed 63 of 86 British officers (including Braddock), 914 out of 1,373 soldiers, and captured the British cannon, war chest, and secret papers.[30] The demoralized survivors straggled back to Philadelphia and refused to budge. That left frontier settlements naked before the *beaucoup de ravages* Canada's governor Pierre Rigaud de Vaudreuil encouraged Indians to inflict on the English. Streams of refugees—most of them furious Scots-Irish—followed the defeated regulars into eastern settlements with tales of tomahawks, fire, and torture. Franklin feared anarchy, while Washington, who survived a hail of bullets in Braddock's debacle, returned to warn Dinwiddie there soon would "not be a living creature in Frederick-County, and how soon Fairfax, and Prince William [counties] may share its fate is easily conceived." Panic spread through the Tidewater. Draft riots erupted in Petersburg and Fredericksburg as Virginia's poor objected to fighting on behalf of rich speculators. Planters feared a slave revolt might erupt if the entire militia went west. In such circumstances Dinwiddie begged Washington to reassume his colonial commission and construct forts to serve as refuges, at least, for terrified families on the frontier.[31]

The northern colonies were spared invasion, but Shirley's New England militia failed to reduce Fort Niagara and William Johnson's Yorkers were bloodied south of Ticonderoga (Johnson himself took a ball in the groin). British forces did secure Nova Scotia, but even that proved a vexation when the governor decided, on his own authority, to cleanse the island of its fifteen thousand "perfidious" French Catholic residents and dump them on the thirteen colonies. "If you find that fair means will not do with them," he ordered the army, "you must proceed by the most vigorous measures possible, not only in compelling them to embark, but in depriving those who shall escape of all means of shelter or support, by burning their houses and destroying everything." Hundreds of Acadians perished. Hundreds more began the fantastic inland odyssey that at long length carried them to Louisiana and bestowed on them the name Cajun. But upward of eleven thousand men, women, and children were just dumped on American docks to be sold into indentured servitude and stripped of their religion. Even so, Bostonians hated the presence of "a colony of French bigots" who were doubtless "ready to cut our own people's throats whenever the priest shall consecrate the knife."[32]

In 1756 Louis Joseph, Marquis de Montcalm, arrived in Canada with two regiments of French regulars. He dealt the colonials and redcoats a new series of defeats at Fort Oswego on Lake Ontario and Fort William Henry on Lake George (where Abnakis massacred a score of disarmed British prisoners). Still none of the colonial assemblies showed any eagerness to place their militias under British command or vote credits unlikely to be reimbursed.[33] Cumberland's confidence that the French and American colonists alike could be easily mastered was clearly mistaken. The war must be waged on an entirely different basis, or lost.

It is safe to say a majority in Parliament resented and feared the Duke of Cumberland. He was the king's favorite, schemed to enhance the royal prerogative, and was hardly the military genius his reputation suggested. Moreover, the American setbacks over which he presided were compounded by Admiral John Byng's loss of Minorca, the deaths by suffocation of 113 East India Company prisoners in the Black Hole of Calcutta, and the march of French armies toward Hanover. Old Newcastle knew changes had to be made, if only to pry funds out of Parliament to prosecute the war properly. So he choked back his distaste for the leader of the opposition and brought William Pitt into the ministry in December 1756.[34]

Pitt was a commoner who pried his way into politics with money inherited from his merchant grandfather, "Diamond Pitt," and his own charisma and grandiloquence. In 1735 he purchased a seat in Parliament from a rotten bor-

ough, attached himself to the patriot party, and fulminated against the evils of
Spain and France. Appointed paymaster to His Majesty's forces in 1746, Pitt
showed acumen for administration, but only in 1755 did he begin to formulate
the "gospel of empire and commerce" for which he is famous. There is no question he was a gifted politician and war minister, but to dub Pitt "the Winston
Churchill of the eighteenth century" is exaggerated as well as anachronistic. He
did not take singlehanded charge of Britain's war effort, did not have a strategy,
and did not lead Parliamentary opinion so much as follow it. Nor did his
appointment result in a sudden turnaround in the fortunes of war since Pitt was
stricken with gout at the time and suspected by George II of being insuffi-
ciently committed to Hanover's defense. Cumberland fed that suspicion. In
April 1757, just prior to assuming command of an "army of observation" in
Germany, the duke talked his father into dismissing Pitt. An appalling hiatus
ensued as three factions struggled for power. The first, the king's party, gave
priority to the European war. The second, Pitt's, stressed naval power and
commerce. The third, Newcastle's, believed the two might complement each
other. Much later Pitt claimed to have conquered North America in Germany,
but it was Newcastle who told Parliament as early as 1749, "I have always maintained that our marine should protect our alliances upon the Continent; and
they, by diverting the expense of France, enable us to maintain our superiority
at sea."[35] In June 1757 Newcastle and Pitt managed to form a new ministry, but
Pitt's own pet projects were an amphibious assault on the French coast and the
recapture of Minorca, not new attacks in America.[36]

What finally swept away the impediments blocking the British war effort
was the self-destruction of Cumberland. He was under strict orders to protect
Hanover and solidify Britain's alliance with Prussia. But in September he blundered into a French trap, obliging him to sign the Convention of Kloster Zeven
that virtually gave the French free passage through Hanover. George II was
livid. When Cumberland slunk home to Kensington Palace, the king turned to
the ladies at the card table and said, "Here is my son who has ruined me and
disgraced himself."[37] Cumberland resigned all his offices and went into a prolonged pout. The British war cabinet swung into action. First, Newcastle and
Pitt kept Prussian armies in the field with generous subsidies from the British
treasury. Second, they asked Parliament and The City, London's financial district, to raise unprecedented sums to outfit British armies and fleets. Third,
they shifted the war effort to the wide world, especially India and North
America. Fourth, the new captain-general of the armies, Sir John Ligonier,

sacked Loudoun and divided the American theater among three energetic commanders: Jeffrey Amherst, James Wolfe, and John Forbes (the latter assisted by Swiss Huguenot Colonel Henry Bouquet, who mastered frontier warfare more quickly than anyone). Fifth—and this was Pitt's most important initiative—the cabinet began treating American colonists as compatriots. He promised equal imperial rank to all provincial officers below full colonel and reimbursement of every shilling the colonies spent on the war effort.[38]

Morale in America soared over the winter of 1757–58 as new British generals arrived with bold offensive plans and bulging war chests. Massachusetts had mustered a pitiful eighteen hundred militiamen in 1757, but its 1758 militia manual began with an exhortation—"As it is the essential Property of a free Government to depend on no other Soldiery but it's own Citizens for it's Defence; so in all such free Governments, every Freeman and every Freeholder should be a Soldier." Volunteers poured forth.[39] Pitt judged up to half the fifty-one thousand troops needed for the 1758 campaign must be raised in America, and colonial governors answered his pleas by meeting between 75 and 90 percent of their enlistment quotas. American merchants now pressured colonial assemblies into voting funds for supplies, since Britain promised to foot the bill, while assemblies such as Connecticut's ceased to requisition goods at low fixed prices and instead approved markups ranging from 12 to 50 percent. To be sure, wrangling between British officers and tight-fisted colonials continued, as revealed by a plaintive message Bouquet sent to Forbes from Carlisle, Pennsylvania:

"One is not through with one difficulty before falling into another. The pork for our stores, which was bought in Maryland or Carolina, is worthless. . . . We got 98 horses yesterday which are better or, rather, not so bad as I was expecting. . . . We are waiting for the saddles and pistols. . . . Until tents can be obtained for the new recruits, nothing can be done with them. . . . At Winchester there were 40 barrels of powder and 170 boxes of bullets, which would still not be enough. . . . As I am obliged to make much of the country folk on the one hand, while I scold them on the other, I cannot avoid recommending a trifle, which is to find some way of paying . . . the cost of that cursed horse which was drowned last year in the service of the second battalion of the [Royal Artillery]. That will have a very good effect, and will smooth over many difficulties."[40]

But thanks to Pitt's new incentive structure such petty frictions were eased and the thirteen colonies went on to spend more than £2.5 million on the war.[41]

The familiar campaigns of the French and Indian War, exciting though they remain, need only be summarized.[42] After an initial setback at Ticonderoga, where the British learned the futility of European tactics, the Anglo-Americans rolled up French defenses almost at will. Amherst besieged Louisbourg with an army of redcoats and Yankee militia, receiving its surrender in July. The next month Lieutenant Colonel John Bradstreet's army, 95 percent of which were militiamen, captured Fort Frontenac and cut Canada's communications with the Ohio Valley. That meant Fort Duquesne, the French bastion at the forks of the Ohio, could expect no reinforcements when Forbes' English, Scottish, and Virginia regiments marched into western Pennsylvania in the autumn. The French and their Mingo and Shawnee allies tried twice to abort the offensive as they had Braddock's. But their attack on Fort Ligonier was repulsed by colonial troops and their rout of an advance party of Scots and Virginians outside Duquesne did not deter Forbes. When at last he was ready to move on the fort, a column of smoke told his scouts the campaign was over: the French had burned down their log palisades and retreated. Forbes began work at once on an imposing new structure, christened Fort Pitt, and won over the Indians by suggesting the British would evacuate the Ohio Country following victory.[43]

In the spring of 1759 French armies remained heavily engaged in Europe while the Royal Navy blockaded the entrance into the St. Lawrence. Short of a miraculous reversal of fortune, Montcalm and his officers in Canada saw little hope of resisting the forty-five thousand British regulars in America, especially now that the resources of the vastly more populous British colonies were effectively tapped. Still, no one expected the French defeat to be so swift and complete. In July, William Johnson's colonial troops captured Fort Niagara and Amherst's advance drove the French from Fort Ticonderoga. Meanwhile Wolfe sailed his army up the St. Lawrence to lay siege to Québec and await Amherst's arrival. What transpired there became so legendary that fact and fantasy both collide and collude. But whether one judges Wolfe a hero or madman, and Montcalm a knight or a fool, the fact is they would never have dueled in the manner they did had Pitt and Ligonier not consulted an engineer named Patrick Mackellar beforehand. While a prisoner of war in Québec he had made detailed notes that convinced him the place could be taken. Yes, the cliffs protecting the fortress and town made frontal attacks impossible, but a rear attack might succeed, especially because the fortifications on the town's upper (western) side were not yet complete. The problem was how to get an army on to that spot. Mackellar suggested an initial landing on the Isle d'Orléans in the river. From there an army might bombard the town while probing for landing sites on the north bank. Perhaps his most valuable intelligence concerned the navigability of the St. Lawrence. It was not a problem, he said: in most seasons warships went up and down the river with ease, while boats with skilled coxswains could ferry soldiers between banks. Ligonier decided to gamble. He approved an assault on Québec and named experienced brigadiers to serve under Wolfe.[44]

Still, as everyone knows, chance, personalities, and blunders shaped the outcome. Wolfe carried out Mackellar's instructions, with some variations. But Amherst was late in arriving, so Wolfe laid siege to Québec and took out his frustration by scorching the farmland round about. That was just stupid if he intended his army to winter there, hence Montcalm concluded the British meant to retreat. By mid-September Wolfe indeed faced the choice between ignominious withdrawal and a reckless thrust that might end in glory, death, or both, depending on the enemy's parry. When a rocky trail leading up a ravine to the Plains of Abraham was discovered, Wolfe personally led a party of scouts, one of whom spoke excellent French to bamboozle the enemy's pickets, and gradually deployed his army before the rear gates of the fortress. The incredulous Montcalm made no effort to foil the maneuver, then a foolish effort to undo it, as if the mere presence of crimson lines beneath his ramparts was an intolerable affront. He could have sat still, or sent word to the French forces in Montréal to advance on Wolfe's rear, or even withdrawn his own army upriver where the harvest had been early and bounteous. If he nevertheless chose to attack he might at least have drawn up his full army, two-thirds of which was deployed east of the city. Montcalm rejected all those good choices. Instead, he ordered his garrison of about fifteen hundred men to march outside the walls and engage an equal number of redcoats in a calamitous frontal assault. Both generals lost their lives to their folly, but the disciplined British musket volleys ripped the French lines apart and drove the survivors down into the city. When five days later Québec surrendered, it was Protestant bells, not Catholic *Te Deums*, that heralded victory. The British, now under General James Murray, did not feel like victors over the cold, hungry winter when scurvy killed or incapacitated a third of the army. But the arrival of a British fleet on the St. Lawrence in 1760 resupplied Murray and ended French hopes for a reversal of fortune. When Montréal at last fell to Amherst, the governor of *Nouvelle France* lowered the Bourbon flag.[45]

Pitt, his job done, immediately came under pressure at home. His supporters in the financial community adored the colonial triumphs (not least because of the boost they imparted to the value of bonds) but had no desire to continue a war that was adding £12 million per year to the national debt. Unfortunately, Pitt could not force a peace so long as the war raged in Germany. Worse still, France finally pried Spain out of her neutrality in August 1761. Worst of all, the king died in 1760 and the crown passed to his grandson, George III, who had a head full of ideas. He was the first of the Hanoverian line to be born and raised wholly English and, of course, considered himself a Whig. But all he had heard growing up were the royal family's rants about the indignities suffered at the hands of wily politicians. He meant to assert the king's prerogative by cleaning house, making peace, and seizing control of patronage. American colonists would learn of his stubborn will soon enough, but George III's first victims were Pitt and Newcastle, obliged to resign in October 1761 and May 1762 respectively. Then peace was finally achieved after an Anglo-American amphibious force occupied Havana, deflating Spanish ambition, and Russia pulled out of the war against Prussia, deflating the Austrians and French. In the resulting Treaty of Paris of 1763, more properties on the American "Monopoly board" changed hands than at other moment in history. France ceded Canada and all its claims east of the Mississippi River to Britain (except for two small islands near the Grand Banks fisheries). Spain ceded Florida to Britain in order to regain Cuba. France compensated Spain with the port of New Orleans and the Louisiana Territory west of the Mississippi. Britain returned the sugar islands of Guadalupe and Martinique to France. That the French swallowed such a lopsided trade was a measure of Britain's military achievements, but also the extent to which Paris remained in thrall to mercantilist calculations. Sugar islands were cheap to administer and yielded big profits. Huge land masses like Canada were expensive to defend and yielded no profit.

Many in London still thought that way, too, which is why the British peace delegation was criticized by some denizens of The City for failing to keep the islands. Other prescient critics did not want to annex Canada, since eliminating the French threat to the thirteen colonies might make them more independent of Britain.[46] But for the moment the Treaty of Paris turned the North Atlantic into an English lake, thus realizing the dreams of imperialists dating back to Hakluyt and Ralegh. How did "little England" achieve it? By vision, boldness, self-righteousness, courage, and skill in war on land and sea, by more effective colonial policies than those pursued by the French, and by belated mobilization of colonial support in the climactic war. But what enabled those immaterial agents to bear on the outcome was the very material agent of money. Subsidies for the Prussian army tied down French forces in Europe, large appropriations and loans financed the projection of British power overseas, and a blank check to the American colonists temporarily united the empire.

Where did all that money come from? Why were the British able to lay hands on it when the comparatively richer kingdom of France could not? The answers to those questions are to be found in the same institutions and principles that girded agrarian capitalism, the monarchy after Henry VIII, the chartered companies that planted overseas colonies, and the constitution that evolved spasmodically in the rebellions against the Stuarts. To be sure, England had an "old regime" resting on the pillars of the monarchy, church, and aristocracy. But whereas few checks existed on the power of those institutions elsewhere in Europe, the growth of landed, commercial, and financial interests *not* dependent on the crown and represented in Parliament obliged British monarchs to compromise and appease elites and even the "middling orders" if they wanted to get anything done. The whole imposing apparatus of state was impotent without money, hence those who approved and paid taxes had to be cut in on the political as well as the economic action.[47]

Never did the crown need money more than when it found itself at war, and the British imperial mission ensured it would be often at war. The Stuarts tried to find a lasting *modus vivendi* with Spain and France, and were overthrown in part for that treason. But not until the final suppression of the Irish in 1690 and the Act of Union with Scotland in 1707 were English energies fully released for overseas expansion. The Whig establishment was pleased to allow the landed gentry to look after the internal administration of the British Isles. That left Walpole and Newcastle free to devote their attention to the navy and merchant marine, whose tonnage tripled between 1700 and 1765, and trade, which expanded 250 percent over those decades. But their very success in building Britain's maritime power convinced more and more moguls in Parliament and The City that greater glory, power, and wealth were there for the taking. To the war party British patriotism meant bellicosity toward Britain's mercantile and colonial rivals, not Walpole's pacifism or recondite Hanoverian concerns on the continent. So long as France and Spain had to divide their energies while insular Britain focused on overseas power, the latter had a tremendous advantage.

Equally important was the gradual realization among Whig leaders and the "interests" they served that borrowing was a more economical, not to say popular, way to raise money than taxes. Of course, continental monarchs were profligate borrowers, but the debts they incurred were personal and had to be repaid out of revenue. The English, beginning with the Whig coup of 1689, developed the practice of a floating national debt that theoretically never had to be repaid so long as the state remained liquid and economic growth brought new buyers of bonds into the market. In so doing, they created the first large-scale "fiscal-military state," supported by an invisible army of clerks. Thus, even though the eighteenth-century British market economy was remarkably laissez-faire by comparison with most of the continent, contemporary critical literature abounded with complaints of an overbearing government putting English liberties at risk! What made the Whig mobilization of state power more tolerable than that of would-be "absolute" monarchs was that its measures were voluntarily approved by Parliament, benefits as well as costs were distributed through elaborate lobbying by interest groups, and the whole enterprise ran increasingly on borrowed money. The Bank of England was founded in 1694 for the purpose of juggling the national debt. A series of reforms in 1717 established a gold standard for British currency and permitted refinance of the national debt through long-term, low interest bonds. Finally, in 1751, government debt was consolidated into fully liquid bonds that could be redeemed at par, held for interest, or bought and sold as speculative instruments. What is more, the "fiscal-military state" encouraged the keeping of statistics and new mathematical methods of analysis that extended the "improvement ethic" born in the country to administration and finance in the city. Such methods made governance a science as well as an art, and policy a matter of prediction, not guesswork. Those institutions and expertise permitted the Pitt-Newcastle cabinet to tap wealth accumulated over sixty years, expand Britain's floating debt to the unimaginable sum of £140 million, and double the size of the British empire.[48]

What of the American colonies in the aftermath of the stunning victories won by their militias and merchants in league with the crown's financiers, soldiers, and governors? What did the apotheosis of British imperialism mean to them?

New England's predictable reaction was to consider it all Providential. "Quebec, after repeated struggles and efforts is at length reduced," preached Boston's top pastor Jonathan Mayhew, "QUEBEC, I had almost called it that Pandora's box, from whence unnumber'd plagues have issued for more than an hundred years, to distress, to enfeeble, to lay waste, these northern colonies; and which might, perhaps in the end have proved fatal to them." Throughout the conflict Calvinist ministers construed the war as a holy cause, called the French vassals of Antichrist, and served as chaplains to lead militiamen in prayers and psalms while enjoining them to live spotless lives worthy of God's protection. Righteousness no doubt was a force multiplier, but it could also unleash heinous cruelty, as when the otherwise dauntless colonial Rangers slaughtered a pacific Abnaki community at the St. Francis Mission in New Hampshire for the crime of being converted by Jesuits. Righteousness also served as a fig leaf draping less pristine motivations. Like soldiers everywhere, many Massachusetts militiamen signed up to fight out of peer pressure, duty, or the fear of being labeled a coward by the town fathers and womenfolk. Many enlisted out of personal loyalty to the captain under whom they would serve. But another undeniable motive for New England enlistments was booty seized in French forts and, for officers, western land grants or imperial rank and preferment.[49]

Personal motives, not excluding plunder, informed the war aims of all the colonial cultures. Scots-Irish frontiersmen, of course, fought their own running wars with the Indians both to defend their homesteads and open new western valleys. The Quakers were too proud to fight, but even before General Forbes took Duquesne, the Friendly Society and the governors of Pennsylvania and New Jersey met at Easton with representatives from fifteen tribes to divvy up land. Once again, the Iroquois traded away the pathetic Delawares' claim to the Wyoming valley in Pennsylvania's northeast in exchange for suzerainty over the Ohio Country. No sooner did Forbes capture Duquesne, however, than the Pennsylvanians tried to renege on the Ohio cession. In the meantime, Connecticut's Susquehanna Company sent settlers of its own to squat in the Wyoming valley. In 1763 they went so far as to burn down the Delawares' cabins and murder their "king" Teedyuscung. Back in Philadelphia, Franklin celebrated the end of the Seven Years War by plotting with Quakers to persuade the crown to terminate the Penns' proprietorship as punishment for their land frauds. Their purpose, of course, was to clear the way for their own land speculations. Most frenetic of all were the Virginians. Having shed blood with

Forbes to secure the west, they were not about to let Pennsylvanians and Iroquois freeze them out with pieces of paper. So Washington arranged for Virginia's authorities to grant him title to two hundred thousand acres of western land, ostensibly to reward Virginia's war veterans. Washington, as commander, emerged with the largest share of what he described as "the cream of the Country."[50]

The colonists' resumption of this war of all against all in the west guaranteed a renewal of Indian troubles. But what most threatened Indian security was the totality of Britain's triumph. From the Six Nations in the north to the Cherokees in the south the tribes had learned to play British and French off against each other. Now that was no longer possible, and Native Americans were forced into a terrible choice: trust the white man, or unite against him and fight.

In the southern colonies the powerful Cherokees, perhaps twelve thousand strong at mid-century, formed a buffer between the coastal colonies and the warlike Creeks and their Spanish and French friends based on the Gulf of Mexico. So important was this Cherokee version of a "covenant chain" that Carolinians reacted violently when a mystical German pietist, Gottlieb Priber, appeared among the Cherokees in 1736. He taught the Indians to read, use weights and measures, and practice Machiavellian diplomacy with the whites. His message, in short, was "No Trust." South Carolina put out a warrant for Priber's arrest. He was captured by Creeks in 1743 and later died in Oglethorpe's prison in Georgia. But the Cherokees had their own prophecies, such as the Vision of Eloh, instructing them the "white stranger was from the opposite pole of the heavens and put on his white skin for the purpose of deceiving." So the Cherokees deceived in return by accepting some bountiful "gifts" from Carolina and the crown in exchange for an alliance they failed to honor when war broke out. Only a handful of Cherokees signed on to help Virginia in 1757, then ravaged Virginia's back country when their services went unpaid. Scots-Irish pioneers put a bounty on scalps. Finally, full-scale war broke out between South Carolina and the Cherokees in 1759–60. Amherst himself was dispatched, but failed repeatedly to run the Indians to ground. So he resorted to burning their fields and villages. The Cherokees cried for help from their old enemies, the Creeks, but receiving none they were forced to give up more land for peace. Then the Creeks perversely made war on the whites and asked other tribes for help. Not surprisingly, the Cherokees, Choctaws, and Chickasaws preferred instead to parlay with four southern governors and a royal agent. In

1763 they all agreed peacefully to resolve conflicts over boundaries and trade. Thus, rather than Indians playing off French and British, the British and colonials now played off rival tribes to the ultimate detriment of all Native Americans.[51]

Far to the north, the Ohio tribes and Six Nations in western New York were deeply disturbed by the British sweep. They were led to believe that once the French were expelled the British, too, would go home and confirm Indian rights to their lands. Instead, the British army garrisoned all the frontier forts and began treating Indians as enemies. Amherst, fresh from his undistinguished Cherokee campaign, abruptly ceased deliveries of food and arms to the Indians, took some choice land from the Senecas to reward his staff, and threatened recalcitrant tribes with extermination. To be sure, George III tried to bring peace to the frontier through a grand proclamation in 1763 that forbade new white settlements west of the Alleghenies without royal approval. But since American colonists had no intention of honoring this Proclamation Line, the king's gesture only added to the tribes' disillusionment.

That was the background to the most promising movement for Native American unity. It was inspired by a prophet of the Delawares named Neolin, whose syncretic mix of frontier Christianity and traditional dream-guessing called on Indians to forsake alcohol and fight as one against "the dogs clothed in red." Thus did Neolin inspire "Pontiac's Rebellion," named for his disciple, the Ottawa chief Pontiac. In fact, the Senecas cheated by Amherst did the most damage. After killing seventy-two redcoats in battle above Niagara Falls they massacred two thousand white settlers. But the uprising quickly turned into a stalemate since Pontiac failed to capture Detroit or Fort Pitt, while Amherst was impotent to make good his vow to extirpate the savages once and for all. The whites' old ally, disease, broke the deadlock. After a smallpox epidemic decimated the Ohio tribes Pontiac agreed to powwow with the British on "the middle ground." Trusted veteran William Johnson brokered a settlement in 1766: the British resumed their gift-giving and ensured peace on the frontier would be guaranteed by their common "father," King George. Two years later the Iroquois came in as well. In a council at Fort Stanwix, New York, they agreed to cede lands in exchange for a British promise to enforce the Proclamation Line against white pioneers.[52] These two treaties were not defeats for the Indians: they amounted to a fair renegotiation of the Covenant Chain to fit the new post-war realities. But by turning redcoats in frontier forts

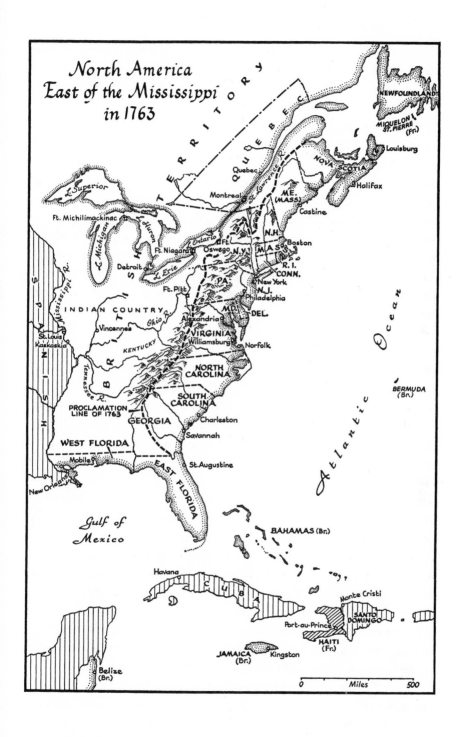

North America
East of the Mississippi
in 1763

QUEBEC

TERRITORY

NEWFOUNDLAND

MIQUELON
ST. PIERRE
(Fr.)

Louisburg

NOVA SCOTIA

Quebec

St. Lawrence

Montreal

Halifax

L. Superior

ME.
(MASS)

Castine

Ft. Michilimackinac

N.H.

Boston

Ft. Niagara

Ontario

MASS.

L. Michigan

L. Huron

Ft. Oswego

N.Y.

R. I.
CONN.

Detroit

L. Erie

New York

PA.

N.J.
Philadelphia

Ft. Pitt

Mississippi R.

INDIAN COUNTRY

Ohio

MD.

DEL.

Alexandria

St. Louis
Kaskaskia

Vincennes

KENTUCKY

VIRGINIA

Williamsburg

Norfolk

S P A N I S H

B R I T I S H

Tennessee R.

NORTH
CAROLINA

BERMUDA
(Br.)

Atlantic Ocean

PROCLAMATION
LINE OF 1763

SOUTH
CAROLINA

GEORGIA

Charleston

WEST FLORIDA

Mobile

EAST FLORIDA

Savannah

St. Augustine

New Orleans

Gulf of
Mexico

BAHAMAS (Br.)

Havana

C U B A

Monte Cristi

Port-au-Prince

SANTO
DOMINGO

HAITI
(Fr.)

JAMAICA
(Br.)

Kingston

Belize
(Br.)

0        Miles        500

into friends of the Indians, the new dispensation *ipso facto* turned redcoats into enemies of the American colonists.

In 1761, when New Englanders were still praising the names of Wolfe, Amherst, and Pitt, and toasting the coronation of King George III, an eloquent lawyer from Plymouth, Massachusetts, rose to deliver a brief in Boston's Superior Court. His name was James Otis, and his purpose was to protest with passionate logic the Writs of Assistance recently passed by Parliament. These amounted to a blanket warrant for British customs officials to enter any American warehouse or home to search for smuggled merchandise without having to show probable cause. In England, the mere fact that Parliament so decreed made the act legal—such was the legacy of the English Reformation and Glorious Revolution. But Otis invoked a higher law, the natural law whence English liberties derived, and denied Parliament's right to infringe them. John Adams was in the gallery that day. He later recalled how Otis seemed touched by "a flame of fire" like the apostles on Pentecost: "Then and there," Adams judged, "the child Independence was born."[53]

Conquest of Canada transformed the British empire. It had to, because the very act of defeating the French and annexing the American frontier meant the enterprise was no longer a matter of English Protestant colonies within and evil Catholics and savages without, but rather one of British colonists, Catholics, and Indians *within*. The British could not "cleanse" their empire of their former adversaries, so they had to accommodate them one way or another. Likewise, defeat of the French *did* make the colonies less dependent on Britain, so London resorted to sterner enforcement of its restrictions on manufactures and trade. Likewise, defeat of the French proved very expensive, so British taxpayers naturally expected the colonists to pay their fair share of the cost. George III heartily approved of the changes in the imperial system necessitated by victory. So did Parliament and the Bank of England. Even Pitt, before leaving office, was imagining ways to tighten controls over the colonies.

Altered circumstances required new policies; that was a truism to forward-looking, statistically minded, mercantilist statesmen after 1763. But American colonists cared not a whit for ledgers in London and looked to their own bottom lines. They were surely forward-looking in the sense that they imagined a continental destiny for themselves. But the colonists were very old-fashioned insofar as they persistently clung to the original spirits of English expansion:

improvement of land and pursuit of new markets; the anti-Catholic crusade; the contest for empire with Spain and France; and the removal of savages who got in the way. No wonder Americans were shocked when the crown turned apostate by proposing to choke colonists' pursuit of new land and markets, tolerate Catholicism in Canada, make lasting peace with France and Spain, and forbid removal of Indians! The English became heretics in their own church. The English betrayed their own cause. The English hustled for world power only to deny their most eager offspring the freedom to hustle.[54]

Adams indulged in poetic hindsight when he credited Otis with the immaculate conception of Independence. But his timing was sure. By 1761 the French and Indian phase of the struggle for North America was nearing its end, and the next, Anglo-American, phase was beginning. For not only did the war change British policies, it changed attitudes on both sides of the ocean. England's aristocratic officers remembered the provincials they had been obliged to put up with as wild, crude, untrained, insolent, greedy, stubborn, conniving, surly, obstructionist, cowardly, and ungrateful. Without regular army support, they believed, the colonists could not have done anything. For their part, American veterans remembered the redcoats they had been obliged to put up with as haughty, imperious, condescending, inflexible, destructive, wasteful, immoral, cowardly, and ungrateful. Without support from the wilderness-wise colonials, they believed, the British soldiers could not have done anything.[55] To be sure, the empire pulled together for a few years under Pitt, and no one yet imagined it flying apart. But when the British decided that Americans could no longer be allowed to go their own way, as they had for most of the previous 156 years, they put the colonists in the same position vis-à-vis Britain that Indians now occupied vis-à-vis colonists: trust or fight, and if fight, then unite.

# SONS OF LIBERTY AND "TWO-BOTTLE" TYRANTS

## Why Independence Became an Imperative, 1763–1775

*H*idden among great stands of elm and willow in the rustic county of Buckinghamshire lay the dilapidated Cistercian abbey of Medmenham. Secluded, but just a comfortable coach ride northwest of London, it suited the purposes of Sir Francis Dashwood. He was a typical young English nobleman with money to burn, political influence, and a dilettante's interest in satirical Enlightenment skeptics, especially Voltaire. He was atypical only in the pains he took to live out his Rabelaisian motto "Do your own thing" (*fais ce que voudras*). Dashwood acquired Medmenham around 1752 to make of it a palace of pleasure. His landscapers speckled its sumptuous gardens with erotic statuary and clipped the shrubbery to resemble sexual organs. Inside the abbey stained-glass windows depicted the twelve apostles *in flagrante delicto*. The ceiling's heavenly frescoes were painted over with scenes of orgies. The monks' cells contained instruments to suit every sexual taste. The library was a pornography trove. At least twice a year members and guests of Dashwood's "monastic order" convened at Medmenham for binges of dining, drinking, and debauchery. Donning friars' robes they recited profane liturgies and toasted the staff of nude girls who served them wines from the abbey's bursting cellars. Members included some of the top power brokers of Georgian England. Dashwood himself was Chancellor of the Exchequer in the very years, 1762–63, when the government began looking for ways to pry revenue out of the American colonies.[1]

That old rogue Benjamin Franklin, who wrote paeans to the joys of the flesh, is the sole American known to have visited Medmenham. During his lengthy sojourns in London, Franklin befriended the "whimsical" Dashwood. They even collaborated on a bowdlerized Book of Common Prayer shorn of all reference to sin, hence the need for redemption, hence the resurrection of Christ. But many other Americans, whether from personal experience or broadsides in pulpit and press, were aware of their mother country's merriment. Some, like William Byrd II, were delighted to discover that whereas Williamsburg sported no brothels, London's "Hell Fire clubs" advertised in the newspapers. Masquerade balls were especially popular occasions for the swapping of mistresses and wives. Booksellers offered sex manuals and tracts proclaiming the medical benefits of frequent indulgence. In private correspondence randy lords and ladies made intimate references to each other's privates, noting especially those of unusual size and stamina. Thus Major Thomas Gage, destined to command British forces in Boston, congratulated a fellow officer that his "Mr Slap Bang is so well and has got into such good Business." A friend of the earl of Lincoln (heralded as the "Joy of Womankind") even waxed patriotic: "With what Pow'rs art thou indue'd! . . . With Whores be Lewd, with Whigs be hearty / And both in Fucking and in Party / Confess this Noble Race."[2]

Lincoln's friend was merely candid when he conflated carnality and party politics, ennobling vigor in both pursuits. The whole Whig establishment rested on manipulation of political, commercial, and familial ties, which determined the distribution of the spoils of patronage. Parliamentary debates and votes might grace decisions of state with a patina of public spiritedness, but the decisions themselves were often made in private multi-course banquets over cases of madeira, port, and brandy. That made an ability to hold one's alcohol another point of pride; most of their lordships strove to be known as "two-bottle men." William Pitt, to his honor, was a "three-bottle man." The business conducted by these hard-drinking ministers, courtiers, and merchants amounted mostly to reciprocal bribes, while members of Parliament in turn bribed their voters. In 1754 young John Dickinson of Delaware, a law student in London, was shocked to observe raucous and drunken scenes around polling places. Over £1 million, he learned, was habitually spent to manipulate election results. "It is grown a vice here to be virtuous," wrote Dickinson to his father. "People are grown too polite to have an old-fashioned religion, and are too weak to find out a new, from whence follows the most unbounded licentiousness and utter disregard of virtue, which is the unfailing cause of the destruction of all empires." That last observation would soon be the theme of Edward Gibbon, who began *The Decline and Fall of the Roman Empire* with British *tempora et mores* very much on his mind. But the first critic to discern what British decadence meant for America may have been the Maryland law student Charles Carroll of Carrollton. In 1760 he wrote his father that Britain was so given over to immorality that "a change in our constitution is I think near at hand. Our dear-bought liberty stands at the brink of destruction."[3]

This portrait of English society as a noisome sink of hedonism, corruption, and ostentation (such as the Italianate "macaroni" fashion spoofed in "Yankee Doodle") was a caricature, to be sure. These same decades witnessed the spread of respectable middle-class values in Britain and the notion of the English as a "polite and commercial people." But England's elites were the ones on display, and the elites were indeed proud as peacocks during the decades of their empire's ascendancy—as proud of their vice as their virtue. A Swiss visitor observed, "I do not think there is a people more prejudiced in its own favour than the British," who "look on foreigners in general with contempt, and think nothing is as well done elsewhere as in their own country." Only at the stock exchange, joked Voltaire, did toleration triumph in London: "There a Jew, a Mohammedan, and the Christian deal with each other as if they were of the same religion, and give the name of infidel only to those who go bankrupt." The Pilgrim's Progress seemed risible as "the well-tempered pursuit of happiness in the here-and-now became a leading theme of moral essayists." Even the dour Scotsman James Boswell gloated in 1772, "I felt a completion of happiness. I just sat and hugged myself in my own mind."[4]

One would imagine a society whose top layer fairly paraded its privilege would have its share of unrest, and it did. In 1769 Benjamin Franklin recorded: "I have seen, within a year, riots in the country, about corn; riots about elections; riots about workhouses; riots of colliers; riots of weavers; riots of coal-heavers; riots of sawyers; riots of Wilkesites; riots of government chairmen; riots of smugglers, in which custom house officers and excisemen have been murdered, the King's armed vessels and troops fired at."[5] By far the most worrisome malcontents (besides the Irish) were those Wilkesites to whom Franklin referred. They were numerous, drawn largely from the urban middle classes, especially popular in London, and led by a poison-penned critic both highly placed and implacable. John Wilkes, elected to Parliament in 1757, gained national fame in 1763 when the ministry evaded the customary Parliamentary debate over no less an issue than the peace treaty ending the Seven Years War.

In "Number 45" of the journal *North Britain,* Wilkes called the ploy "odious" and threw in for good measure a slur on the king's personal life. George III ordered Wilkes imprisoned for treason, but a judge released him on grounds of his Parliamentary immunity. So the government carried a motion to expel Wilkes from the House of Commons then, when his constituency returned him, expelled him again. Wilkes fled to France, but later returned to write venomous tracts calling for Parliamentary reform. "Wilkes and Liberty!" became the slogan, and "Number 45" the talisman, of popular sovereignty and freedom of the press on both sides of the Atlantic.

The Wilkes phenomenon was of tremendous importance because it popularized in English towns the rural critique of the Whig establishment made earlier in the century. That "country-party" ideology, elaborated by polemicists such as John Trenchard and Thomas Gordon, and popularized by satirists such as Jonathan Swift and Alexander Pope, lambasted Walpole's plutocratic "court-party." Far from being old Tories, the critics were rather extreme Whigs disillusioned by the results of the Glorious Revolution of 1688. They had expected the overthrow of the Stuarts to restore traditional values based on religion (including civil rights for Dissenters), agrarian virtue, and England's ancient rights and liberties. Instead a new in-group seized power at court and in Parliament, and polluted the nation with its greed and vice. To be sure, the "patriot party" eventually toppled Walpole, but his successors perpetuated the patronage system and piled up new taxes and debt in wars that seemed only to benefit special interests. In 1746 James Burgh's *Britain's Remembrancer,* a book widely read in the colonies, chastised a nation awash in "luxury and irreligion . . . venality, perjury, faction, opposition to legal authority, idleness, gluttony, drunkenness, lewdness, excessive gaming, robberies . . . a legion of furies sufficient to rend state or empire." In one sense, these country-party moralists were reactionaries disgusted by the rise of the fiscal-military state and mercantilist empire. But in another sense they were progressives demanding reform and accountability, a Parliament reflecting the will of the people, and no taxation without representation. When Wilkes carried this message to the urban masses only to suffer persecution, his constituents leaped to the conclusion George III and his ministers were engaged in a plot against liberty. So they called the court party "Tories"—a dirty word that re-emerged after the last Stuart revolt of 1745 to connote anyone in cahoots with the *new* "old regime."[6]

Literate colonists gobbled up this country-party critique because it seemed even more applicable to America than to Britain. Colonists had no representation at all, suffered from policies imposed for the benefit of British interests, and were massively in debt to British merchants and manufacturers who beguiled them with vain luxury goods. Country-party ideology thus provided the colonists with a ready-made vocabulary in which to voice their outrage over new British impositions after 1763. It also gave them false hopes that Wilkes might succeed in promoting reform. Alas, the colonists did not know the man. Their Lancelot was in fact a grotesque, lisping rake without a scintilla of republican virtue. His father, a liquor distiller, gave the boy a chance for respectability by enrolling him in Leyden's prestigious Calvinist college. Wilkes spent his stipend on nightly visits to brothels. Back in England he married a country heiress ten years his senior only to squander her money on bacchanals in London. It was there Wilkes fell in with Thomas Potter, son of the archbishop of Canterbury and an even more accomplished satyr. Potter introduced Wilkes to Dashwood, who initiated him into the mysteries of Medmenham Abbey. Soon he was delighting the "monks," not least the earl of Sandwich, with his blasphemous wit. Most celebrated was Wilkes' *Essay on Woman*, an obscene takeoff on Pope's philosophical *Essay on Man*. Sandwich and Potter later arranged Wilkes' first election to Parliament. As for his famous "45" pamphlet, it was nothing more than a scurrilous overreaction. But when the king overreacted in turn, Wilkes saw instantly how valuable was the appearance of victimhood. He even cleared £800 while under indictment by reprinting his *North Britain* papers for a middle-class market hungry for scandal. Those proceeds financed his subsequent "exile" spent in the bawdy houses of Paris.

What then to make of John Wilkes? It is true he became a people's tribune of sorts during the turbulent decades of the American crisis and the French Revolution. He was certainly an important figure in the prehistory of the British Reform Bill of 1832. But Wilkes' personal philosophy was summed up in a famous couplet: "Life can little else supply / But a few good fucks and then we die." His most important legacy, perhaps, stems from the fact he was the first English or American politician to make a *business* of posing as the people's tribune so as to sustain a life of corruption through *attacks* on corruption. It helped that George III hated his guts, but even admirers confessed Wilkes was "an undoubted rascal."[7]

The "school for scandal" that was English politics would be unremarkable had it not been so unabashed. Joseph Butler professed not to understand it. "It is now come, I know not how," he wrote in 1736, "to be taken for granted that Christianity is . . . discovered to be fictitious . . . and nothing remained, but to set it up as a principal subject of mirth and ridicule, as it were by way of reprisals, for its having so long interrupted the pleasures of the world." But Butler, the queen's chaplain and a future bishop, knew very well how it happened and fought back in *The Analogy of Religion, Natural and Revealed, to the Constitution and Course of Nature.*[8] Butler was an Anglican version of Jonathan Edwards, his purpose being to refute Deists who concluded from Newton and Locke that human beings can know nothing of God except by observing Creation. Deists might themselves be high-minded, but their rejection of divine revelation gave lesser spirits an excuse to mock Biblical morals and embrace the occult as a style of play. If, Butler reasoned, they wished to call themselves atheists in the manner of some French *philosophes,* so be it. But if they held, as even the classical pagans had done, that the proper goals of philosophy were happiness, freedom, and virtue, then Biblical precepts from the Ten Commandments to the Sermon on the Mount were demonstrably rational. The fruits of disbelief were just as demonstrably the addiction, disease, and bankruptcy (through gambling) afflicting the highest and lowest classes in Britain. Butler's reasonable theology had little effect on the Anglican church until well after his death. But the emotional revivals of Whitefield, the Methodists, and the Baptists likewise equated British corruption with slavery and Christian virtue with liberty, and carried that message across the Atlantic. By the 1760s, evangelical Protestantism imbued British corruption with political as well as spiritual meaning, providing Americans with a second ready-made vocabulary in which to express their outrage.

Why this lengthy preface on public morals in Britain? Cannot the colonists' gradual drift into rebellion be explained by their material and political grievances over the years from 1763 to 1776? Yes and no, because none of the various grievances, however important to one or another group in the colonies, is sufficient to explain their bloody and risky challenge to the British empire. Thus, colonists reacted violently to new British taxes, but remained the least taxed people on earth. They hated the Navigation Acts, but the costs imposed by them were no more than 3 percent of the volume of trade. The colonies' gross domestic product by the 1770s was already about 40 percent that of England, and white Americans probably enjoyed the highest per capita standard of living of any people on earth.[9] Why revolt, then? American nationalist historians of the nineteenth century described the conflict simply as a clash between stupid, oppressive British authorities and colonists clinging to genuine Whig principles. But such history ignored the deep divisions within the colonies and caricatured Britain's serious efforts to adjust to the new challenges the empire faced after victory over the French. By contrast, a so-called imperial school of historians found Britain's attempts to reform the empire reasonable, if maladroit, but as a result had even more difficulty explaining the colonies' violent resistance. A third, progressive school of historians interpreted colonial resistance to Britain as the product of a revolt among the lower orders in American society. Thus, "home rule" was really about "who would rule at home." But if that were so, why did numerous members of the colonies' social elite join, indeed lead, the rebellion? More recently, a neo-Whig school of historians reaffirmed the role of ideas, especially country-party ideology, that persuaded colonial elites of a conspiracy against their liberties. But that failed to explain why so many colonists became "Tories," while skirting Americans' material and spiritual aspirations. Hence, two more schools arose to stress the importance of religion on the one hand and sheer ambition on the other. According to the first, the Great Awakening reinforced the colonists' rebelliousness against established authority and made civil and religious liberty a godly cause worth dying for. According to the second, land speculators and impatient expansionists seized control of colonial politics in order to replace Britain's mercantile imperialism with American continental imperialism.[10]

The nationalist and progressive historical schools are defunct: the American republic was not the product of a spontaneous uprising of instant democrats against tyranny, nor the product of bourgeois versus proletarian class conflict. Otherwise, contemporary historians agree the colonists' anger over taxes, restrictions on commerce, colonial assemblies, and new western settlements, and perceived threats to religious liberty were all necessary conditions for revolt, but none by itself was sufficient. Nor do any of the historical theories answer two mysterious questions. The first is why colonists, *especially* some of the wealthiest, risked their lives, fortunes, and sacred honor over a thrup'penny tax or mere point of principle. The second is how the colonists managed to set aside their provincial, religious, and social divisions so that—as John Adams put it—"thirteen clocks were made to strike together."[11]

Those questions cannot be answered by reference to material or legal interests alone. Or rather, they can be so answered only if one grasps that most Puritans, Quakers, Cavaliers, and Bordermen, Old Lights, New Lights, and rational skeptics, invested their material and legal complaints against Britain with moral and spiritual meaning. Was the American rebellion caused by conflicts over wealth or ideology, a backward-looking Whig mentality or a future-oriented American dream, a secular discourse of human rights and equality or an evangelical discourse of corruption and virtue? The answer is all of the above, because the whole experience of the colonists dating back to 1607—and the twin vocabularies they used to interpret that experience—made self-government, religious freedom, economic opportunity, and territorial growth *inseparable*. Almost everyone from Massachusetts to Georgia could agree that: civil and religious liberty went hand in hand; liberty could not long survive without virtue; an exploding population could aspire to no liberty at all if its territorial and commercial expansion were artificially choked. Of course no two colonies, or social groups within each colony, translated their commitment to liberty into laws and institutions exactly the same way. But by 1776 all American patriots called the cause of liberty "sacred" and endowed their glorious cause with the attributes of a religion, including a creation myth, a theology, a moral code, a martyrology, and a teleology promising a limitless "empire of liberty" (in Jefferson's words) if Americans snapped the chains of Old World corruption and made themselves worthy through abstinence, courage, faith, and community. In other words, while many colonial patriots interpreted their struggle in Protestant terms and others in secular terms, all patriots made *America itself* a sort of religion—and that made resistance to Britain and Tories at home into a holy war.

Palimpsests of rebellion against British and Anglican evil mottled the face of imperial unity even before the French and Catholic evil was vanquished. One was Massachusetts' outcry against the Writs of Assistance that made the name of James Otis. Another was Virginia's outcry against the Parsons' Cause that made the name of Patrick Henry. It was precipitated by the burgesses' Two-Penny Act of 1758, which stipulated the Anglican clergy's tobacco stipend was to be priced, for one year, at 2 pence per pound rather than the market price of 4 pence. The reason for this halving of parsons' pay was economic distress. The war, high taxes, planters' debts, and a drought hit the Chesapeake hard, so it was expected the sometimes lazy and in any case "kept" clergy would share the sacrifices made by their flocks. One angry rector appealed to the archbishop of Canterbury, who in turn persuaded the Board of Trade this Two-Penny Act was the opening shot in a colonial assault on throne and altar. So the king exercised a rare veto over the act of a colonial assembly, enabling Virginia parsons to sue for back pay. In one Hanover County case, Judge John Henry, citing the veto, instructed the jury simply to determine the damages owed. But that decision stank inasmuch as the judge's brother was one of the clergy affected. It especially infuriated Scots-Irish Presbyterians and New Lights in the Piedmont who hated the Anglican establishment on principle. So the county sheriff retaliated against the judge by appointing a jury from the "vulgar herd," while the defending church vestry hired the very lawyer needed to stampede that herd. He was young Patrick Henry, the son of the judge on the bench!

Henry was a natural leader of back-country Virginians, although he did not realize it for years. His father, a native of Aberdeen, Scotland, sailed for the New World in 1727. He enjoyed the patronage of a Scottish friend already established in the new county of Hanover, and began his ascent in typical fashion by marrying a widow with a plantation. They prospered, speculated in land, and had eleven children. The second eldest, Patrick, was apprenticed to a local merchant at age thirteen and set up his own store the next year. It flopped. At eighteen he married and received three hundred acres and six slaves as a dowry. The farm flopped as well, so Patrick sold his slaves and set up another store. When it promptly failed, he tried life as a tavern-keeper, but his penchant for "fiddling, dancing, and pleasantry" earned him more friends than money. By 1760 the twenty-four-year-old Patrick Henry figured there was nothing else for it but to become a trial lawyer. Two of his examiners at Williamsburg, the great legal minds Peyton and John Randolph, held their noses when they signed Henry's license to practice; Thomas Jefferson considered the lad's legal training "not worth a copper." But everyone granted Henry's theatrical skills. Like the revivalist Whitefield he was "a perfect master of the passions of his auditory, whether in the tragic or comic line." Even opposing counsel in the Parsons' Cause confessed that when Henry rose to speak he laid down his pen and listened.

Was the Two-Penny Act, Henry asked the jury in December 1763, a good law that served the people's interests in a time of travail? Yes, it was. Could the king simply annul a good law without breaking his own compact with his subjects? No, he could not, because "a King, by disallowing Acts of this salutary nature, from being the father of his people, degenerates into a Tyrant, and forfeits all right to his subjects' obedience." Thus did Henry elevate a lowly case over a parson's purse to the acme of constitutional law. Shouts of "Treason!" were hurled at Henry, but after they died down, the knee-slapping jurors effectively nullified royal authority by awarding the plaintiff one penny in damages. Within days all Virginia was toasting Patrick Henry and propelling his career as a lawyer, land speculator, and champion of colonial rights.[12]

Yet a third hint of rebellion dated from 1758 when rumors spread that the archbishop of Canterbury and the bishop of London (who had responsibility for the colonies) were plotting to plant bishops in America. That furor made the reputation of Jonathan Mayhew, latest in Boston's long line of great Puritan preachers. As early as 1755, Mayhew denounced the court-party Whigs and their accomplices in the Anglican Church for having made Britain a nation of "infidelity, irreligion, corruption and venality, and almost every kind of vice." Following Jonathan Edwards he reasoned the purpose of Christ's divine mission is "the happiness of man: but that happiness can only result from Virtue, and virtue is inseparable from Civil Liberty." Accordingly, Mayhew went ballistic when an agent of the Church of England showed up in Boston in 1758, hinting the mansion he was building would soon house a bishop. Were throne and altar scheming to enforce uniformity in the manner of Charles I and Archbishop Laud? Did they mean to extinguish freedom of conscience, force Anglican tithes out of Puritans, and visit upon the colonies plagues of corruption? If so, asked Mayhew, what new Columbus might discover some new America so that freedom might survive? No bishop appeared, but as John Adams recalled, "apprehension of Episcopacy contributed . . . as much as any other cause to arouse the attention not only of the inquiring mind, but of the common people, and urge them to close thinking on the constitutional authority of the parliament over the colonies." Even Virginia's Anglicans grew alarmed over rumors of bishops. Nor was it an accident Anthony Gavin's *A Master Key to Popery* (1724) was reprinted in the colonies in 1773. A masterpiece of titillating propaganda, it claimed to tell the truth about the evil machinations of prelates, the hypocrisy of licentious priests, and the suffering of martyrs wherever established churches held sway.[13]

In each of these preliminary rebellions—the Writs of Assistance, the Parsons' Cause, and the Bishops Affair—American colonists began to fuse issues of liberty, religion, and money. But officials in London either paid no attention or else dismissed the colonists as disobedient children in need of parental discipline. Certainly the king's new first minister, George Grenville, had no notion of the fury he was about to unleash when he announced his plan to "raise a revenue" in the colonies. The justification seemed clear enough; indeed, it was the same justification Virginians used to dock the pay of their parsons. Britain had emerged from the wars greatly indebted and faced ongoing expenses, not least support of colonial officials and garrisons on the Indian frontier. It only made sense for the king's American subjects to chip in with taxes, not to mention cease their inveterate smuggling and customs evasion. To be sure, the old Whig principle held no Englishman could be taxed without his consent, but Parliament's word had been law for more than seventy years, and, thanks largely to Whig one-party rule, statutory law gradually took precedence over Common Law. In any case, argued Grenville, the colonists did enjoy "virtual representation" insofar as all members of Parliament were assumed to speak for all British subjects, not just their local constituents. New industrial cities such as Manchester and Birmingham, he noted, had no seats in Parliament, but the voice of their textile interests was nonetheless heard in Westminster.[14]

The Sugar Act of 1764 accordingly levied a 3 pence per gallon tax on imports of foreign molasses and forbade the colonies to export certain goods to any country but Britain. In addition, Grenville tried to tighten up on enforcement. He ordered patronage appointees to take up their posts in America rather than subcontracting their duties to corrupt or incompetent underlings. He transferred cases against accused malefactors from colonial courts to British vice-admiralty courts. He even stationed naval vessels on the approaches to North American ports. Suddenly New England merchants such as the Brown family of Providence found it far harder to offload contraband under shadow of night. Frustrated merchants in Newport went so far as to fire a shore battery at a royal cutter, then were appalled when the new customs agent turned down their customary welcoming bribe. Several prominent firms, including that of Boston stalwart Nathaniel Wheelwright, went bankrupt, and a devastating contraction in credit ensued. The Sugar Act provoked no open rebellion; only New York and South Carolina challenged Parliament's right to tax the colonies at all.[15] But all Americans suffered from a severe post-war depression and shortage of money. That is why Grenville's next blow, the 1764 Currency Act, prepared the ground for an alliance among the three most populous colonies all the others were likely to follow: Massachusetts, Pennsylvania, and Virginia.

It may take some effort for twenty-first-century Americans to summon sympathy for a caste of extravagant slave-owning tobacco planters who hoped to get out of debt by bribing officials and despoiling Indians. But recall the values of their Cavalier culture, including honor and hierarchical liberty, and one may appreciate the shame they suffered when tobacco prices fell 75 percent after

1760. For a century planters had struggled with the uncertainties of a trans-Atlantic commodity market even as they succumbed to the blandishments of British merchants hawking the latest furniture, finery, and fashion no lord or lady could do without. Even in flush times most were in debt because they had to accept whatever prices their Glasgow factors were willing to pay, while they borrowed against next year's crop for capital and consumer goods. In hard times their debt grew so ruinous it seemed they were *slaves* to moneylenders, peddlers, and British authorities. Planters also faced challenges in their own bailiwick. Baptists alone founded ninety new churches between 1760 and 1776, despite prohibitions against their preaching in public (not least, in taverns, where they spoiled everyone's fun). Electoral politics became a tug of war between the Tidewater elite and Scots-Irish settlers whom William Byrd II likened to "the Goths and Vandals of old" (a sentiment shared by George Washington). By 1770 so-called Regulators on the Carolina and Virginia frontiers threatened to march on their capitals if their demands for representation, protection, and debt relief were not met. Even in long-settled counties, complained Landon Carter, a gentleman now had to "kiss the arses of the people" to win a seat in the assembly. But Virginia gentlemen soon realized they could not resist the new impositions from Britain so long as they faced a sullen Scots-Irish frontier in their rear. Those were the conditions under which a new, distinctly American, politics gestated: a politics of mutual deference between leaders and masses, a politics of religious toleration, and a politics preached to the masses in the revivalist idiom of a Patrick Henry.[16]

Planters were less successful in dealing with their financial woes. The most drastic solution, adopted by "King" Carter and George Washington (after he took up residence at his dead brother's Mount Vernon in 1759) was to abandon tobacco altogether in favor of grain. Other planters followed their lead until grain exports through the new port of Norfolk rivaled Philadelphia's. Another obvious reaction was to cut back on imports by redefining honor in terms of frugality rather than showy display. In the meantime, however, some of the biggest lords of the Chesapeake had to stage humiliating lotteries to raise cash (Patrick Henry managed several of them) or else call in debts owed by neighbors and tenants. That not only besmirched a Cavalier's honor, it outraged back-country settlers to the point where some vowed to shoot bill collectors on sight. Of course, many planters still hoped to recoup through western land speculation since nobody took the Proclamation Line of 1763 seriously. But Virginia's old Ohio Company, now managed by George Mason, and a host of start-up companies looking as far afield as Mississippi and Illinois failed to get royal approval.[17]

The most obvious way to restore solvency during a slump was to increase the money supply. But there again British restrictions on colonial currency choked the colonists. Royal governors were obliged to retire all paper notes used to pay taxes, the purpose being to hold down inflation in deference to British merchants and creditors. So Virginians resorted to public embezzlement through the medium of the portly, jocund John Robinson who served for three decades as Virginia's Treasurer and Speaker of the House. During the 1760s Robinson ceased to destroy paper money and instead secretly loaned no less than £100,000 to distressed friends. When the scandal broke after his death, Virginians contrasted his loyalty to the "treachery" of British creditors. Jefferson even imagined a royal conspiracy to make colonial planters "a species of property annexed to certain mercantile houses in London."[18]

Grenville's Currency Act of 1764, therefore, could not have come at a more damaging moment. It extended to all colonies an existing Massachusetts prohibition against colonial currencies, bonds, and land banks. Planters were hard hit, but so too were American merchants, artisans, sailors, and farmers, all of whom lacked cash to conduct local trade, much less finance an overseas deficit surpassing £4 million. A Philadelphia paper rued, "The Times are Dreadful, Dismal, Doleful, Dolorous, and DOLLAR-LESS." Poverty and unemployment increased in colonial ports after 1763 even as their populations soared anew with the coming of peace. In the 1760s alone the population of the thirteen colonies grew by more than a third to 2,148,000, reaching 30 percent that of England and Wales. New York grew by 64 percent in that decade; relatively vacant North Carolina and Georgia by 100 and 189 percent. A half million of these new Americans were native born, but another 158,000 were immigrants—mostly poor, young, male, and hungry for opportunity. Concentrated initially in the crowded ports, their arrival in a time of depression made colonial societies even more volatile.

In Boston, gangs from the north and south ends had hitherto contented themselves with Catholic-baiting and brawling on "Pope's Day" and "Guy Fawkes Day." Now they became shock troops for agitators such as Samuel Adams. In New York, the rival DeLancey and Livingston factions competed for the support of the street. In Philadelphia, feuds escalated among Quakers, Presbyterians, pro- and anti-Penn factions. In almost all the colonies friction between frontier and town increased. In 1764 Franklin had to broker a deal with the "Paxton Boys," who murdered Indians and threatened to invade Philadelphia if pioneers were not given more protection and representation. But a new source of tension just barely visible in 1764 soon transformed or transcended internal cleavages. That was the conflict with Britain, which separated American colonists into three groups: the few who benefited from British rule in some fashion, the few who resented British rule but had much to lose from rebellion, and the many who both hated British policies that hampered American growth *and* had little to lose from a conflict. The challenge faced by the colonies' habitual leaders in Virginia and elsewhere was either to contain or *mobilize* the anger of urban and rural "mobs" lest they lose control of events altogether.[19]

It almost happened in 1765, when the colonies' pleas for repeal of the Currency Act were overtaken by furor over the Stamp Act. Grenville decided to tax colonists directly by requiring them to purchase notary stamps for every sort of printed matter and document, ranging from pamphlets and newspapers to diplomas, licenses to practice a profession or trade, deeds, wills, insurance policies, and playing cards (a popular medium of "transactions"). The fees, in some cases as high as £6, restricted the ability of cash-poor Americans to get on in life. This time a Parliamentary opposition did arise. Isaac Barré, a veteran of the Battle of Québec, fulminated against the prevalent fiction to the effect the colonies were children planted by a nurturing mother country. "They planted by your Care? No! your Oppressions planted em in America. They fled from your Tyranny to a then uncultivated and unhospitable Country. . . . And yet, actuated by Principles of true english Lyberty, they met all those hardships with pleasure." All the mother country did, said Barré, was send "the Deputies of Deputies to some Member of this house" to spy against the colonists' liberty and cause "the Blood of those Sons of Liberty to recoil within them." Barré only challenged Parliament's wisdom, not its legal right to tax. But reports of his speech, arriving in tandem with news of Wilkes' persecution and protests by Irish "sons of liberty," were cattle prods to the colonists. Sons of Liberty chapters sprang up. They pledged to stop, by violence if necessary, any attempts to put the Stamp Act into effect.[20]

One example may stand for many local variations: that of Alexander McDougall of New York. His parents and two brothers were among an expedition of Highlanders that embarked in 1738 intending to found a Presbyterian farmer-militia community on the Mohawk. When war began in 1739, making that impossible, the family remained in Manhattan. During the years Alexander grew into manhood, his adopted city doubled in size and fattened itself on wartime trade. He went to sea, rose quickly in rank to ship's master, then command of a privateer in the West Indies. By 1763, when peace returned, McDougall was worth more than £7,600. Alas, his father and wife died that same year, so he gave up the sea to devote his life to his children (whom he educated at Princeton), his community (by affiliation with New York's Livingston faction), and his country (through fierce resistance to the Navigation Acts and Anglican church). McDougall was one who had much to lose. Even so, he took to the streets with New York's Sons of Liberty, rallying his old crews and cronies down on the docks to protest the Stamp Act. As it happened, the DeLancey faction proved more successful than Livingston at winning mass support. Still, McDougall sacrificed his local ambitions to the larger American cause. In a veritable military action he led the defense of the Liberty Pole against British soldiers bent on tearing it down. He went to prison for penning a pamphlet, "To the Betrayed Inhabitants," in which he called an aroused populace the only check on abusive authority. In all things he earned the sobriquet "the Wilkes of America."[21]

The Sons of Liberty included workers of various sorts, but were not led by them. As the movement spread north and south from New York, the instigators were mostly professionals and merchants like McDougall. Being mostly religious dissenters, they took inspiration from Whitefield's revivals. Never a secret conspiracy, they publicized their proceedings, advertised their "field meetings," and crafted their political speeches after fiery sermons. Their purpose, after all, was to bring sheer numbers to bear against any official trying to enforce the Stamp Act *or any colonial betraying a willingness to abide by it.* As yet no one looked beyond the immediate goal of Stamp Act repeal, but by 1765 colonists were already being pressured to take sides.

Virginia's burgesses were reluctant to take sides when they convened in May to consider resolutions proposed by their newest member, the sensational Patrick Henry. He made another treasonous speech, warning that as Caesar had his Brutus and Charles I his Cromwell, so might George III. . . . He prudently climbed down from that precipice, but his resolutions stated boldly that Virginians had always enjoyed the same liberties as the people of Britain. Hence, any effort to tax them except through their own assembly "has a manifest Tendency to destroy British as well as American Freedom." Randolphs, Carters, and other cool old heads shared this view. But they were sufficiently worried about the influence of hot young heads that they just argued for caution and went home. In their absence, a rump house of 39 burgesses (out of 116) passed Henry's resolutions. Once published throughout the colonies they were taken as evidence Virginia had spoken.[22]

In neighboring Maryland the eminent lawyer Daniel Dulany added an effective attack on Grenville's theory of "virtual representation" in Parliament. If the colonists' needs and desires were *not* met in Parliament, he asked, was there one single member they might cast out at the next election? And if Americans were in fact not represented in Parliament then *ipso facto* they could not be taxed because they lacked any means of expressing consent. Dulany stopped short of inciting a constitutional crisis, but he implied one was possible when he called on colonists to cease "moping, and puling, and whining" and instead "bid Defiance to Tyranny."[23]

Throughout the summer of 1765, Sons of Liberty in Rhode Island, Connecticut, New York, and the Carolinas did what Dulany asked by destroying the hated stamps, picketing royal offices, and burning British officials in effigy. What is more, the indignation was righteous. On Connecticut's day of fasting and prayer, Stephen Johnson attributed the Stamp Act to a "selfish and venal spirit of corruption" that required more revenue solely "to add fuel to ungodly lusts . . . all manner of unrighteousness and oppression, debauchery, and wickedness." But no resistance was more violent than that of Boston, thanks to John Hancock's money, Sam Adams' mobs, Jonathan Mayhew's zeal, and Lieutenant Governor Thomas Hutchinson's mulishness. Hancock, the town's richest merchant, all but dared British authorities to prosecute him for violating the Navigation Acts or make a conviction stick in the teeth of Boston opinion. He was a large contributor to the Sons of Liberty. Sam Adams was an enigmatic forty-two-year-old failure who never forgave the British for closing the Bay Colony's Land Bank in 1740, thereby ruining his father. Sam went to Harvard, but rejected the ministry in favor of politics. A stint as town tax collector ended badly: Sam was an honest but clumsy accountant and left owing Boston £8,000. In 1763 he discovered, like Wilkes, his talent for propaganda while working behind the scenes for the Loyal Nine, a committee of agitators soon to merge with the Sons of Liberty. Adams' ideology was distinctly old-fashioned in that he saw himself as a simple Puritan rebelling against sin and corruption. He imagined Boston as a "Christian Sparta" and often signed his anonymous articles: "A Religious Politician."[24]

Mayhew, by contrast, was a political preacher. He likened the Stamp Act to the manacles placed on men destined for slavery and reminded his fellow

New Englanders how "ye have been called unto liberty." Boston mobs may not have required ministerial blessing. They had already pulled down the tax collector's office and hanged him in effigy from a Liberty Tree. But on August 26, the day after Mayhew's "liberty" sermon, the mobs reassembled around a bonfire on King Street, lubricated themselves with rum punch, and plundered the homes of customs agents. Their last stop was Hutchinson's elegant house.[25]

The most distinguished American-born official in royal service, Hutchinson was intelligent and (by his lights) judicious and forthright. He was also proud and roundly distrusted, not least because he patronized his family and business associates in the English manner. He was especially despised by James Otis and John Adams, who accused him of ambition, avarice, and a false commitment to public service: the worst public sins in the Puritan catechism. But Hutchinson's greatest misdemeanor was his insistence on taking instructions from London against the interests and will of his own compatriots. Such "treason" made him a delicious target for the mob, which labored all night to raze his house and burn or steal everything from books and furniture to children's clothes and £900 in cash. The town fathers apologized and made some reimbursement, but Boston's point was made. "Authority rests in the populace," Hutchinson grumbled, and "no law can be carried into execution against their mind."[26]

A quieter, but even more threatening assemblage made the same point in October. For the first time colonial assemblies—nine of them, anyway—sent representatives to a congress charged with concerting their action. In October this Stamp Act Congress convened in New York and quickly agreed to petition the king and Parliament. The delegates were careful to pledge fealty to the crown and implicitly recognize Parliament's right to regulate external matters such as trade. But they took a strong stand against internal taxes in the absence of representation. That petition might be considered the first American public document.

The ministry did not get the message. Neither did George III, whose decision to dump Grenville in favor of the opposition "Rockingham Whigs" was due to his anger over—what else?—some patronage decisions not to his liking. But the marquis of Rockingham's faction included Barré, Pitt, Edmund Burke, and others who sympathized with the colonists' arguments and urged repeal of the Stamp Act. Lest Parliament seem to relinquish its authority, however, it paired the repeal of March 1766 with a Declaratory Act asserting its right to legislate for the colonies "in all cases whatsoever." That was ominous because a similar act passed in 1719 was employed to subjugate Ireland. Mayhew knew that, which is why he urged Bostonians on Thanksgiving Day to stay vigilant against "that ugly Hag Slavery, the deformed child of Satan."[27] Sure enough, the following spring Charles Townshend, Chancellor of the Exchequer in the new Grafton ministry, won passage of a new Revenue Act. This one levied duties on colonial imports of such staples as glass, paint, paper, and tea, and established vice-admiralty courts in Boston, Philadelphia, and Charleston. To add insult to injury, the ministry intended to use the funds raised to pay the salaries of royal officials in America.

Townshend did not expect resistance any more than Grenville had. After all, duties on imports were external taxes that the colonists, not least their principal agent Benjamin Franklin, agreed Parliament had a right to impose. But Americans, who knew a dodge when they saw one, denounced the Townshend duties as transparent taxes. What is more, they were right: Townshend had scoffed that the distinction drawn between internal and external taxes was "ridiculous in everybody's opinion except the Americans." So another pamphlet war erupted and another colonial spokesman emerged who combined the learning of Dulany, the guile of Franklin, and the mass appeal of Sam Adams. The very title of John Dickinson's *Letters from an American Farmer in Pennsylvania* contained two felicitous falsehoods and a half-truth. They were not letters in the sense of real correspondence, but a series of tracts. Dickinson was not a farmer, but an accomplished lawyer trained at Middle Temple in London. He did have a residence in Philadelphia, but he was born in Maryland and raised in Delaware. He also affected a false humility, professing to be a simple man "as happy without bustle, as with it." Between his investment in two large estates, additional business interests, law practice, and seats in both the Delaware and Pennsylvania assemblies, his life was bustling indeed. In sum, Dickinson no more resembled the man of his letters than Franklin resembled "Poor Richard" or John Adams "Humphrey Ploughjogger," his own rustic *nom de plume.* But he knew the best way to influence mass opinion on both sides of the ocean was to pose as a simple yeoman "conscious of my defects," but taught from infancy "to love humanity and liberty." Dickinson's letters instructed a large and sympathetic readership that the Townshend Acts were of more than fiduciary concern. If Parliament were able to fix duties on exports to America, then it might tax products the colonists were prohibited to manufacture themselves, in which case "the tragedy of *American* liberty is finished." To submit to the Townshend duties was to sit still for extortion. "We are therefore—SLAVES."[28]

Colonial assemblies responded with resolutions denying Parliament's right to impose internal and external taxes alike. Sons of Liberty rallied merchants, preachers, artisans, farmers, and distressed southern planters to boycott British goods, especially those that were taxed. That, of course, meant Americans must redouble their efforts to build basic industries and become self-sufficient, while shunning British luxury goods as immoral as well as expensive. No one except possibly Sam Adams yet thought of self-sufficiency as a prerequisite to independence—certainly not Dickinson, who described the empire as an indivisible whole and bowed to the Quaker pacifism of his mother and wife. Rather, the colonists expected non-importation to hurt British merchants enough for them to persuade Parliament to repeal the Townshend duties. But the colonists' resistance to external as well as internal taxes elevated their quarrel with Britain to yet a higher constitutional plane. That obliged all parties to confront sticky questions they had managed to ignore or put off for 160 years. Just what was the British empire anyway, and where did sovereignty reside within it?

Ireland, the first arena of English imperialism, was clearly a special case because (although a kingdom with its own parliament) it was conquered and governed by force. Scotland, under the 1707 treaty ratified by its own parliament, was merged into the United Kingdom and granted representation at Westminster. Several New World colonies, such as Jamaica, Nova Scotia, Québec, and Florida were conquered in war by royal forces paid for by Parliament. The thirteen colonies, however, made a stark contrast. They all originated as *private* commercial enterprises blessed by the crown, but in no way supported by Parliament. As Franklin reminded London readers, the colonies were planted in an era "when the powers of parliament were not supposed so extensive as they are become since the Revolution [1688]" and in "countries where the parliament had not then the least jurisdiction." They also differed from Ireland in that they were far away from the metropole and populated overwhelmingly by British subjects bearing their native traditions of law and governance as if they were the Ark of the Covenant. Moreover, those émigrés to America were originally dissenting Protestants, or became dissenters through the revivals, making them all the more resistant to hierarchy. As early as the 1650s colonists defied Cromwell's Navigation Acts. In 1688 they rose up against James II's attempted viceroyalty in the empire. Throughout the eighteenth century they treated the Whigs' Navigation Acts with equal contempt. Finally, while they did not need to articulate a theory of popular sovereignty during the pleasant decades of Salutary Neglect, they practiced it in their own assemblies, town meetings, and church congregations. The colonists still regarded the king as sovereign, but they viewed their relationship to the crown in the same way Parliament did, as a compact which neither party could alter without the consent of the other.[29]

That the constitutional relationship between the thirteen colonies and the mother country was ambiguous became obvious to all in 1768, when Parliament presumed to make laws for the empire as a whole. To grant the mainland American colonies fair representation in Parliament would set a dangerous precedent for Ireland, not to mention Wilkesites at home. Proportional representation was in any case out of the question. Franklin's demographic projections showed how Americans' numbers and trade would, in no distant future, outweigh those of England. When that day arrived the children would come to govern the parents; the tail wag the dog; the world turn upside-down. British colonial expert Thomas Pownall fretted over that possibility. Dean Josiah Tucker of Gloucester cathedral jested that Britain ought to "declare independence" from her colonies. The earl of Buckinghamshire asked the House of Lords whether Britons "were to be free, or slaves to our *colonies.*" Merchants and customs officials did not need to peer into the future. Treasury statistics on Americans' clandestine commerce with the French, Dutch, and others proved they had already ceased to be "British" colonies; colonial manufactures were capturing markets from British firms. Meanwhile, 6 million British subjects paid £6 million per year to support the armed forces and national debt while 1.6 million (white) Americans rioted rather than chip in £150,000. Parliament could always pass more stringent laws and attempt to enforce them at gunpoint. But the cost of such measures would surpass the revenues gleaned, while magnifying colonial outrage.[30]

What was to be done? Acquiesce in the colonists' demands for self-government so long as they maintained a loose, sentimental attachment to the crown? That might serve in the short run, but what ideas would it put in the heads of Irish, Canadians, for that matter Bengalis? To most ministers and MPs it seemed the British had no choice but to try to impose their will on America lest the whole empire fly apart.[31]

Colonists, of course, interpreted the imperial crisis altogether differently. Taxes were annoying, but trivial compared to the economic damage done by the Currency Act, the ban on western settlement, and prohibitions on manu-factures. Those laws (to the extent they could not be evaded) were in turn triv-ial compared to Writs of Assistance, vice-admiralty courts, the Quartering Act, and rumors of bishops, all of which violated rights to property, due process, pri-vacy, and freedom of conscience. Yet even those legal abominations might prove trivial compared to what Parliament might impose in the future once it jettisoned Common Law rights in favor of statutes it alone had the power to make. No wonder colonial pamphleteers wrote feverishly of conspiracies. Like Wilkes, they saw themselves upholding British as well as American freedoms. They began to call themselves true Whigs, damning London's court party for a cabal of Tories. They rolled out the same rhetorical cannons so recently fired at the French king and the Catholic church and trained them instead on the English king and the Anglican church.[32]

Rioters in colonial ports did not cite John Adams' *A Dissertation on the Canon and Feudal Law* (1765), much less William Blackstone's magesterial *Commentaries on the Laws of England* (1765–69). At most they read—or had read to them over pints in a pub—inflammatory tracts and newspapers that made the whole business a fight between good and evil. But educated colonists from New England to the Carolinas read and wrote intensely and with utter self-consciousness, which is one reason their steps toward independence were gradual and in every case reactions to British actions. What they were trying to do was to understand history, apply its lessons to their own thorny problems, and arrive at conclusions that would not create worse problems in the future. For instance, educated Americans knew the broad outlines of the corruption and collapse of the Roman Republic. But they knew also that the murder of Julius Caesar solved nothing. They knew licentious excess and corruption sub-verted the Roman Empire from within. But they knew also that the fall of Rome only ushered in the Dark Ages. They praised the rebellions against Charles I and James II. But they knew also those episodes only ushered in Cromwell's dictatorship and Walpole's patronage system. How might the colonists reason themselves into methods of resisting tyranny that did not pro-duce new forms of tyranny?

Adams, Franklin, Mason, and all other erudite colonists believed history was the best school of politics and the very essence of law. They read history in their own libraries, exchanged books with neighbors, and frequented the lend-ing libraries existing in all colonial capitals and collegiate towns. They read the Ancients, but the history most relevant to their needs was written by British legal commentators and country-party Whigs. We know now that Whiggish history was far from accurate, and that in any case American readers selected from it only what suited them. But the burden of it was a "creation myth" that ran roughly as follows.

In the beginning, Anglo-Saxons carried to Celtic Britain a spirit of natural liberty and consensual habits of property and governance. Their lands were widely distributed and held in personal title; their kings were proclaimed, even sometimes elected, by the people. Alas, all that disappeared with the Norman conquest of 1066 and the imposition of Frankish feudalism. But being "extremely jealous of their liberties" (in Mayhew's words) Englishmen fought back, throughout the medieval era, to recover their rights through the media of Parliament and the law. That they succeeded was proven by the successful revolts against the Stuarts, who were lawless tyrants and thus "unkinged themselves" even before the people dragged them from the throne. But freedom always fled just around the corner. After 1688 an even worse threat than the Stuarts arose: lawless kings *in league with* corrupt Parliaments conspiring against Englishmen's rights in the colonies and at home. Many variations of this argument appeared in colonial writings, perhaps most purely in the Novanglus papers of John Adams, who argued the king above all is subject to the "ancient constitution"; any who abuses it "forfeits his title." Franklin even teased British friends that if Americans erred in making such arguments "your most celebrated writers on the constitution . . . have reasoned them into this mistake."[33]

The British court and Parliament had little patience for mincing logic and abstruse history lessons. In fact, American rejection of the Townshend duties on top of the Stamp Act made the whole issue refreshingly clear: either British sovereignty over the empire was real or it was not. For if Parliament's authority was denied in a single instance (as one government pamphlet argued), then it could be denied in all instances and the imperial union must dissolve. Is that what the colonists wanted? This sovereignty question returned the ball to the Americans' court, for however loudly they proclaimed loyalty to their "sovereign" King George, the fact was the king backed Parliament to the hilt. Colonists could not defy one without the other; sovereignty could not be divided. Edmund Burke understood the colonists' logic and applied it to his native Ireland. But he also saw how close to the rocks the ship of empire had already drifted. In 1769 he told Parliament: "The Americans have made a discovery, or think they have made one, that we mean to oppress them; we have made a discovery, or think we have made one, that they intend to rise in rebellion against us. . . . We know not how to advance; they know not how to retreat. . . . Some party must give way."[34]


In the event neither party gave way the result could only be a spiral of reciprocal provocations discrediting moderates on both sides. That may have been just what Sam Adams hoped to provoke, but he was ably assisted by the bumbling British. Under Sam's prodding, General Court dispatched a Circular Letter in 1768 to its sister assemblies urging them to cooperate against the "illegal" acts of Parliament. The British colonial minister ordered Massachusetts' General Court to rescind the letter and dissolved the assembly when it refused. Then customs commissioners seized one of John Hancock's ships (with the symbolic name *Liberty*), thereby giving Sons of Liberty ample excuse to riot. British officials in Boston cried out for protection. In September the first contingents of two redcoat regiments disembarked. That provoked Massachusetts town meetings to convene a convention that denounced both the customs regime (deemed "parasitical insects") and standing armies, a sure sign of tyranny. Parliament, appalled by this effrontery, invoked a law dating back to Henry VIII for extradition of suspected traitors to England. The colonies, appalled by this coercion, considered new circular resolutions calling for resistance and a boycott of British goods.

By the turn of 1770, some four thousand "lobster backs"—a soldier for every four citizens—camped out at Faneuil Hall or Boston Common. They were hated by all, but especially by poor workers because in their off hours the soldiers competed with townsmen for jobs. On March 5, 1770, a motley crowd flung volleys of "dirt" (read: excrement), vile epithets, and possibly death threats at a British column, provoking some soldiers to level their muskets and fire. The Sons of Liberty immediately canonized the five American martyrs and turned March 5 into an annual holy day. The soldiers were tried, and John Adams bravely volunteered to defend them. But the defense he offered was skillfully crafted to suit his political purposes. First, he exonerated the soldiers by characterizing the mob as "saucy boys, Negroes and mulattoes, Irish teagues, and outlandish jacktars" asking for trouble. Next, he exonerated the mob by blaming their anger on Britain's decision to quarter troops on its own subjects. In short, he acquitted everyone except Parliament. Adams later recalled this "exhausting case" as "one of the best pieces of service I ever rendered for my country."[35]

Sympathy for besieged Massachusetts swelled in the wake of the Boston Massacre. The coincidental death of George Whitefield nearby within days of the bloodshed even draped Massachusetts in a heavenly light. (The theme of the great evangelist's final tour had been "the corrupting influence of consumption" and the morality of the American cause.[36]) Committees of Correspondence sprang up in all the colonies to share information, send alms to Boston, and coordinate action. But the sense of urgency ebbed in late April when colonists learned Parliament had backed down again. The duke of Grafton was out, Lord North was in, and a solid majority repealed all the Townshend duties save the one placed on tea. That exception was retained by a 5 to 4 vote in the cabinet, again for the purpose of paying lip service to Parliament's right to make law for the empire. But by a curious twist, it brought the empire down. It seemed the grand British East India Company, once a cash cow and rich source of patronage for its stockholders and friends, was in need of a government bailout. When Lord North learned the company was sitting on unsold inventories of tea worth £17 million, he imagined a way to kill two birds with one stone. The Tea Act of 1773 granted the company a monopoly in the colonial market while waiving all duties on tea in British ports. That allowed the East India Company to sell tea in the colonies for a lower price, undercutting Dutch competition and presumably pleasing American consumers. All the plan proved was how much court-party Whigs (now called the "King's men") still missed the point. The colonists' Committees of Correspondence had no trouble depicting the Tea Act as another usurpation of power, albeit masquerading this time as a bribe. Did Lord North expect Americans to sell their birthright for a few pence savings in the price of tea? If Parliament claimed the right to create a tea monopoly in the colonies, what commodity or industry might it *not* monopolize?

At that juncture, thanks to some nifty and still mysterious espionage, Boston leaders were fingering what they took to be ironclad evidence of conspiracy. It was a packet of letters exchanged between Massachusetts' royal governor Hutchinson and Grenville's secretary William Whately concerning means of addressing unrest in the colonies. Did the confidential missives pass through the hands of a sympathetic imperial official, perhaps Thomas Pownall? Did Philadelphia physician Hugh Williamson pilfer them from the British archives, as claimed by his eulogist after all parties were dead? Nobody knows. But whatever their provenance, the letters were "leaked" to none other than Benjamin Franklin.[37] He had resided in London since 1764, taking full advantage of his *entrée* to scientific and philosophical circles, the halls of government,

and Medmenham Abbey. Franklin's official business was to promote speculative land companies and serve as official agent for four colonial governments,
Massachusetts among them. His grander business was to preserve the unity of
the British empire precisely because he expected its leadership must someday
pass to North America. When that occurred, America might benefit from continued ties with a strong "Protestant nation" in Europe.

Upon reading the purloined letters, Franklin hatched a plot of his own.
Inasmuch as Hutchinson made frequent reference to British desires to relieve
transatlantic tensions, they might allay New Englanders' suspicions about ministerial plots and thus foster reconciliation. So he posted the letters to the leaders in General Court, requesting only the letters not be published. But when
they arrived in March 1773, irate Bostonians not only insisted on publication,
they read the worst into them. By way of meeting the British halfway,
Hutchinson had acquiesced in plans to limit colonial self-government and even
agreed to the use of troops in extreme situations. Sam Adams spied in that a
design "to overthrow the constitution." John Adams pronounced his distrust
confirmed, the only surprising thing about the letters being "the miracle of their
acquisition." To make matters much worse, Hutchinson declared his intention
to enforce the Tea Act through concessions he awarded to his own sons.[38]

The Tea Act begged for non-importation with a vengeance. New York,
Philadelphia, and Charleston either turned away East India ships or
impounded their tea. But Hutchinson steeled his will. He insisted the cargoes
of three ships standing at anchor be offloaded. As everyone knows, Bostonians
tricked out as Mohawks "offloaded" 340 chests of tea into the harbor on the
night of November 30, 1773, while their compatriots howled in mirth on the
wharves. Up to that point the English had suffered abuse, nullification, tax evasion, and even assaults on their officials and ships. But wanton destruction of
*property* on such a scale (more than £10,000 worth) was insufferable. Colonists
knew it, especially merchants, and the British might have taken advantage of
their contrition and apprehension. Instead, they exploited their status as hurt
party to lash out in every direction and drive colonists together more closely
than ever, beginning—fatally—with Benjamin Franklin. He was the colonies'
spokesman. He was the one who suggested indirect taxes. He was the one who
leaked the Hutchinson letters and now had the temerity to present
Massachusetts' petition for the governor's recall. So he was the one summoned
to answer for Americans' crimes in the dreaded Cockpit of the king's Privy

Council on January 29, 1774. The thirty-five members—peers of the realm—joined by the archbishop of Canterbury and the bishop of London in their popish "fish hats," the earls of Dartmouth and Sandwich, Lord North, Lord Amherst, and numerous other two-bottle tyrants stared Franklin down for over an hour while Solicitor-General Lord Wetterburn verbally scourged him for the sins of the people. He named Franklin a traitor, liar, knave, insurrectionist, worst of all a colonial parvenu. Then, having humiliated him publicly, lords approached Franklin privately with offers of bribes.[39]

Franklin had dined, drank, and debauched with these men. He had doubtless heard several boast of their own deceits. He relished his status as the most famous and admired American and tried mightily to overcome the negative stereotypes the British and colonists held of each other. But he knew now how thoroughly he had failed. In the months to come he was slapped with a lawsuit over the Hutchinson business, lost his postmaster position, and saw his ripening scheme for a western land grant die on the vine. Fearing arrest, Franklin did not tip his hand, but he gave up on the empire and made secret preparations to flee. "When I consider the extream Coruption prevalent among all Orders of Men in this rotten old State . . . I cannot but apprehend more Mischief than Benefit from a closer Union." To remain united with Britain "will only be to corrupt and poison us also." The British refused even to listen to colonists (that is, himself) much less treat them as equals. It was not that Franklin repented of his own machinations and pursuits of pleasure—he simply drew a distinction between the wasting corruption practiced by an aristocratic one-party elite and the creative corruption practiced by an expansive, egalitarian people. So he determined henceforth to devote his Machiavellian talents to the American cause, unknowingly doing it an enormous service even before he left England. Franklin advised young Tom Paine to seek his fortune in Philadelphia, and gave him letters of introduction.[40]

The British establishment made the Boston Tea Party a pretext to punish New England so severely the other colonies would surely knuckle under to avoid the same fate. Lord North dutifully pushed through Parliament a series of bills to close the port of Boston, shut down Massachusetts' provincial and even town governments, make all its offices appointive, and implicitly place it under martial law by naming General Thomas Gage its new governor. There was still more to come. In June 1774, Parliament's Quebec Act established another *authoritarian government* in Canada, extended its boundaries to include *all western lands* north of the Ohio River, and permitted the *Catholic Church* to practice and expand freely throughout. A separate decree severely limited grants of new land *within the boundaries* of the thirteen colonies and imposed outrageous quit rents.

These Intolerable Acts, as the colonists dubbed them, violated every spirit of English colonization and ground underfoot everything the colonies stood for and dreamed of achieving in harness with Britain. Worse still, British rule now stood for all the perils the colonists had so recently identified with the French, as illustrated by Paul Revere's engraving of bishops dancing around the Quebec Act to the approval of king, Parliament, army, and Antichrist. The colonial assemblies' first instinct was to call for days of fasting and prayer. Their second instinct was to prepare to fight, and if fight, then unite. For Boston's cause, as George Washington wrote, "now is and ever will be considered as the cause of America (not that we approve their conduct in destroy'g the Tea)." The alternative was to become "tame and abject slaves, as the blacks we rule over with such arbitrary sway."[41]

Washington recorded those judgments while preparing to ride to the First Continental Congress in Philadelphia. In that remarkable conclave Puritans devoted to ordered liberty under God, Cavaliers wedded to hierarchical liberty, Quakers resentful of all civil and religious authority, and libertarian Scots-Irish first gathered together. It is a wonderment no great stage play has been written about the Congress in Carpenter's Hall, the evening debates in City Tavern, the whispered conversations in parlors and streets, and their irresistible cast of characters. From New England came dour John Adams, volatile Paul Revere, and Connecticut's slippery Silas Deane. Virginia sent "dignified" Washington, "noble" Peyton Randolph, "masterly" Richard Henry Lee, and the "Cicero of his age," Patrick Henry. Pennsylvania's Joseph Galloway and John Dickinson, predictably cautious, tried to exploit their status as hosts to discourage belligerence. Judicious John Jay and businesslike James Duane led New York's delegation. Christopher Gadsden and Edward and John Rutledge spoke for South Carolina's bastion of white liberty and black servitude. How much posing and playacting went on is best left to the imagination, but it is safe to speculate the delegates were extremely curious about each other, eager to impress, and anxious to learn who might be allies or adversaries.[42] The Marylanders were headed by future Supreme Court Justice Samuel Chase, but the fifty-five congressmen were most intrigued by Chase's legal colleague Charles Carroll of Carrollton. He was the richest man in Maryland, "a most flaming Patriot," and a Catholic. So even as Congress considered Revere's petition protesting toleration of Catholics in Canada, it was discovering Catholics in the thirteen colonies were potential allies in the struggle for liberty.[43]

The First Continental Congress met for just over seven weeks in September and October 1774. Its stated purposes were to define and assert the colonies' rights and decide on joint measures to defend them. But Galloway feared a Massachusetts-Virginia alliance might stampede Congress into precipitous acts, so he formed a moderate coalition to resist the "sedition, nay treason that is daily buzzed in our ears."[44] His plan, like the Albany Plan two decades before, is often described as a missed opportunity and precursor of federalism. It called for an American government composed of a governor-general appointed by the crown and a council chosen by the assemblies. Any Parliamentary act concerning America must be approved by this council. On paper that seemed ingenious, but think: under the Galloway plan the colonies could not govern themselves at all without approval from the hated and distrusted Parliament, and would have no recourse should the British bribe or subvert the colonial council. In any event, even if the colonies had approved the plan unanimously, it was likely to be a dead letter in London because it was based on a theory of *divided sovereignty*. The plan consumed a month of public debate and private intrigue, but in the end only five colonies voted in favor. It deservedly died.

Congress then turned to the issues of rights and resistance, for which the more militant members had plans in their pockets. The first was a Declaration of Rights inspired by Virginia's Fairfax Resolves and Massachusetts' Suffolk Resolves. It rejected Parliamentary authority over internal colonial affairs and asserted each colony's right to see to its own defense. (Redcoats Go Home!) The colonies also agreed to support Boston if the British imposed the Intolerable Acts by force. The second was a petition designed to go over and under the heads of Parliament by asking the British king and people to defend colonists' rights. The third, and most grave, established a Continental Association calling on every colony and town to form local associations to enforce an absolute boycott of British imports and (except for South Carolina's precious rice) exports to British possessions. A total embargo seemed doubly apt because it both hurt the venal British and called on Americans to practice the self-denial Calvinists and Deists alike knew was the bedrock of liberty.

Article 8 of the Continental Association went beyond abstention from luxuries to "discountenance and discourage every species of extravagance and dissipation, especially all horse-racing, and all kinds of gaming, cock-fighting . . . and other expensive diversions and entertainments."[45] Many New England and southern associations cleansed themselves of other offenses such as dancing or bribing voters with money or drink. Quakers, too, admitted the depth of their declension and promoted a revival of piety, one expression of which was the founding of an anti-slavery movement. Americans craved salvation, but salvation required repentance.

The colonists counted on British merchants and the colonies' "friends" to oblige a third Parliamentary climb-down. One of those friends was Pitt, now earl of Chatham, who told the House of Lords in January 1775, the cause of America was identical to that of every true Whig and alluded to the danger of an aroused Ireland and watchful France. Did Britain wish to bring on a disastrous war simply to score a point of pride? If so, what were her chances of winning against "three millions in America: who prefer poverty with liberty, to gilded chains and sordid affluence; and who will die in defence of their rights as men, as freemen. . . . To such united force, what force shall be opposed? What, my lords? A few regiments in America, and seventeen or eighteen thousand men at home! The idea is too ridiculous to take up a moment of your lordships' time."[46] Chatham moved a resolution to withdraw British soldiers from Boston. It was defeated, 18 in favor, 68 opposed.

Two months later Edmund Burke rose in the House of Commons to deliver a three-hour-long evening speech whose details, logic, and insight are compelling even today. Like Chatham, he insisted the proposition before them was not a fine point of law, theory, or party politics, but simple peace that could not be achieved through coercion or "the labyrinth of intricate and endless negotiations." Yes, Britain must govern America, but she could govern only by consent. Indeed, the colonies' population, agriculture, fisheries, manufactures, and commerce were growing at such a rate that coercion was not even an option. But more salient than numbers was character. These colonists were Englishmen born with a free spirit, what is more Englishmen in whom religion "is in no way worn out or impaired; and their mode of professing it is also one main cause of this free spirit. The people are Protestants; and of that kind, which is the most adverse to all implicit submission of mind and opinion . . . the dissidence of the dissent; and the Protestantism of the Protestant religion." Northern colonies professed various denominations, but communed in the same spirit of liberty. As for the southerners, their leaders were mostly Anglican but their spirit of liberty was "still more high and haughty." That was because they were slave-holders, and "where this is the case in any part of the world, those who are free are by far the most proud and jealous of their freedom. Freedom to them is not only an enjoyment, but a kind of rank and privilege." Next, Burke explained, no country in the world made so general a study of law, which "renders men acute, inquisitive, dexterous, prompt in attack, ready in defence, full of resources." But even if the colonists were less numerous, less loving of liberty, less steeped in religion, less proud, they would still be irrepressible for the simple reason that they were "full of chicane" and took whatever they wanted. In any event, Burke concluded, "An Englishman is the unfittest person on earth to argue another Englishman into slavery."[47]

The purpose of the oration was to argue for six motions repealing the Intolerable Acts and leaving taxation up to the colonies' own assemblies. Like Galloway's plan it sounded ingenious, but would amount to an admission of error by Parliament and the previous three ministries, not to mention the king, and a grant of home rule and renunciation of force in the colonies. The implications of all that for the empire seemed suicidal. At 11 P.M. the House divided, Burke's motions failing 78 in favor to 270 opposed.

Few in Britain expected war because King George's generals thought the colonies' military potential contemptible. Nor did the large majority backing Lord North and the king want to hear talk of "true Whiggism," which was at best a code word for a politics two generations dead and at worst a slogan for rabble-rousers like Wilkes. When General Gage reported how Massachusetts persisted in governing itself through illegal town meetings, a convention, and a committee of safety empowered to raise the militia, Lord North declared the province "in rebellion." That meant all its ships trading with foreign countries or even fishing the Grand Banks became subject to seizure. A naval blockade was within Britain's means, but General Gage commanded nothing but Boston itself. Everywhere else Minutemen, like their fathers and great-great-grandfathers of old, turned out on town commons and drilled.[48]

Nor were they alone. Virginians convened in St. John's Church, Richmond, far from their governor's reach, to consider preparations for self-defense. It was there, on March 23, 1775 (one day after Burke addressed Parliament), that Patrick Henry delivered his greatest political sermon. He rebuked false prophets who cried "peace, peace" when there was no peace, and warned they would be consumed by sword and famine like Judah of old, once

3 million Americans "armed in the holy cause of liberty" stood up to claim "temporal salvation" under a God who is just. His volume rising, his cadence perfect, Henry finished: "Why stand we here idle? Is life so dear, or peace so sweet, as to be purchased at the price of chains and slavery? Forbid it, Almighty God! I know not what course others may take; but as for me, give me liberty, or give me death!" Melodramatic we may think it now, but Henry's appeal persuaded Peyton Randolph and other planters they had better get ahead of public opinion lest they be trampled beneath it. Henry's military measures, slightly watered down, were approved. A famous anecdote about Henry's speech tells of Colonel Edward Carrington, who listened at a window outside the packed nave. "Right here," he cried, "I wish to be buried" (and was). Far more important was the thrill felt by Peter Muhlenberg, a young Lutheran minister moved by Henry's speech to join the militia. He assumed he would be a chaplain; Washington made him a colonel and sent him home to raise a regiment. Muhlenberg's farewell in the pulpit—"There is a time to pray and a time to fight"—helped mobilize Germans in support of the patriot cause.[49]

It was now clear to the British that only a clarifying act of force might cool the colonists' ardor. Given his isolation in Boston and limited strength, General Gage was in no position to make it, but the new minister for the colonies, the earl of Dartmouth, insisted he march out and arrest the ringleaders in Massachusetts. Gage figured the most useful and feasible mission he could perform was to seize the powder magazine in Concord, thereby hindering the militia's ability to perform its own clarifying act of violence. Just a few years later he might have disguised some soldiers in mufti or recruited Tory saboteurs to sneak in and blow up the magazine. But at this early stage guerrilla tactics did not occur to the gentleman general. So the well-organized Bostonians knew at once when his seven-hundred-man force stepped into boats to cross the Charles River. Paul Revere and William Dawes rode inland to shout the alarm. Early on the morning of April 19 a freezing, tired, and ornery British column marched onto Lexington green to encounter an impertinent line of Minutemen. Somebody fired, eighteen militiamen fell, and the remainder took to their heels. The British marched on to Concord, only to find most of the munitions had been removed overnight, so they turned back to Boston, mission unaccomplished. By afternoon Minutemen appeared from several towns and skirmished, Indian-style, along the whole route. When the redcoats reached Boston, just 430 remained.[50]

Virginia Governor Lord Dunmore succeeded in seizing that colony's arse-
nal. But Randolph, Washington, and their lieutenants pledged to take up arms
against any "unjust and wicked invasion" of their own or a sister colony. New
Englanders did the same. Massachusetts' commander, the elderly, ill Artemus
Ward, was touched by the reinforcements marching swiftly from Connecticut,
New Hampshire, even Rhode Island, where Jewish merchants helped outfit the
troop. As early as May 1775, Ethan Allen's Green Mountain Boys seized Fort
Ticonderoga ("in the name of the great Jehovah and the Continental Congress")
and Connecticut militia under Benedict Arnold captured Fort Crown Point to
pre-empt a British invasion from Canada. The forts themselves were in terrible
repair, but thanks to the prodigious efforts of Henry Knox, a Boston bookseller
and amateur artilleryman, fifty-nine of Ticonderoga's large cannon were later
hauled by oxen and frostbitten men across the mountains to the colonial army
outside Boston.

In the meantime, Ward and his staff made an amateurish mistake. They
decided to fortify Charlestown Heights rather than the more imposing and
defensible Dorchester Heights. The militiamen also blundered when they
bypassed Charlestown's Bunker's Hill and dug in instead on Breed's Hill, which
was lower and potentially within range of British batteries. Gage, insulted by
such effrontery, determined in the same manner as Montcalm to fight a needless
battle with less than his full force. The fact that newly arrived generals William
Howe, Henry Clinton, and "Gentleman Johnny" Burgoyne were kibitzing may
help to explain Gage's rare brashness. But the risk seemed minor. Surely, these
"Minutemen" could not stand for a minute against professional soldiers.

How was it they did? They were farmers, mostly, commanded by silk-
stockinged doctors and lawyers. They were certainly moved by hatred, patriotism,
and faith, their fear of being shamed competing with fear of death or (what's
worse) maiming. They may also have shared with the British the foolish thought
prevalent at the start of every war: win here and now and the other side will go
home. But none of that can explain the remarkable discipline and fire control displayed at Breed's Hill on June 17, 1775. The redcoats advanced, bearskin hats and
bayonets bobbing, to within fifteen yards of the colonial line before the
Minutemen fired. The British reeled back, then charged twice more until almost
half their force of twenty-two hundred was dead. Late in the afternoon they
finally captured the hill, but only because the militiamen ran out of ammunition
and slipped away, again in good discipline. Gage then turned his command, still

besieged and twice bloodied, over to Howe, whose own later timidity may have stemmed from the carnage he witnessed on the banks of the Charles.[51]

Five weeks earlier the Second Continental Congress convened in the Pennsylvania Statehouse. It was a feistier lot than in 1774 because the delegates were chosen mostly by *ad hoc* conventions and Committees of Safety rather than broad-based colonial assemblies. They were also emboldened by the presence of Franklin, who arrived on May 5 and was immediately added to Pennsylvania's contingent.[52] But feisty or not, the delegates were forced by events either to leave New England to its fate—in which case their own colonies might be next to face British steel—or else begin to act like a provisional government. Once again, Congress resolved unanimously to request the colonies join in a common day of "publick humiliation, fasting, and prayer." Its stated hope was that "we may with united hearts and voices unfeignedly confess and deplore our many sins, and offer up joint supplications to the all-wise, omnipotent, and merciful Disposer of all events; humbly beseeching him to forgive our iniquities, to remove our present calamities, to avert these desolating judgments with which we are threatened." Virginia's burgesses made a similar appeal to the Almighty (absent the abject confession) and eminent clerics throughout the colonies issued pamphlets and sermons naming armed resistance a righteous duty. Even Philadelphia's ministers, John Adams noted, "thunder and lighten every sabbath" against Lord North and the crown, while Landon Carter's meek Anglican parson dispensed with the usual "God Save the King" in favor of "God Preserve all the Just rights and Liberties of America." Indeed, almost all sermons published in the 1770s cited Scripture to justify resistance and promise divine help if the colonists proved worthy of it.[53]

Having said its prayers, Congress debated how to respond to New England's desperate plea for soldiers and officers. John Adams knew what needed doing. He also knew (as in the Boston Massacre trial) how to "spin" his proposal so doubters could not murmur about overwrought Yankees dragging them to disaster. Adams recused Massachusetts from leadership of the cause, humbly requested advice from the other colonies, and placed in nomination a man whose name he reserved for an eloquent climax. There was among them that day, Adams said, the very man needed to lead a truly American army; a man whose experience, fortune, talent, and character recommended him above all others; a man from *Virginia*. . . . George Washington caught the drift and demurely slipped out of the hall. Two days later (don't we wish we had a transcript of those debates!) Washington was unanimously chosen commander of the Continental Army. Quakers might wring their hands at the prospect of fighting at all, and New Yorkers curse war's effects on their trade, but thanks to Adams, Virginia and the entire south lined up with New England. The middle colonies now had no choice but to get with the program.

Congress appointed four lieutenant generals to serve under Washington and began to raise a war chest by issuing paper money. It also named commissioners to seek treaties with Indians on the colonies' western flanks and set up an American post office under Franklin. In all these ways Congress bestowed on itself the attributes of a sovereign regime. It did appease moderate opinion by sending King George an Olive Branch Petition drafted by Dickinson and a loyal request for redress of grievances. But it also appeased zealots by approving a plan to conquer Canada before 1775 was out.

What was the king to make of this "olive branch"? His subjects not only made war on him in their own provinces, they even prepared to invade other provinces. He did not grant this "Congress" the dignity of a reply. Instead, he gave Lord North to understand the rebellion was to be crushed. In August, Howe was ordered to treat New England militias as enemies. In December, Parliament passed a Prohibitory Act declaring all American ships on the high seas fair prey for capture. Lord Dunmore recruited a loyalist militia, threatened to arm Virginia's slaves to fight for the king, then burned Norfolk on January 1, 1776. Most insulting of all, colonists learned of King George's intention to hire mercenary soldiers from Germany to ride herd on his subjects.

A war was on, but what sort of war was it? In one sense it was an imperial civil war since the colonies claimed sympathizers in the British Isles and the crown claimed "Tory" sympathizers in the colonies. But since Americans scarcely imagined sailing over to England to topple the king the war was more in the manner of a provincial revolt against a perceived tyrant. Still, that begged the question of what Americans were fighting *for*—a dangerous question bound to carry them beyond old, comfortable ground of Whig ideology and into new, treacherous ground. Indeed, had Americans been obliged to debate in advance what they meant to do with a victory over the British they might never have made common cause. But in January 1776, Thomas Paine addressed the question "What next?" in rhetoric exactly suited to unite American patriots. His manifesto spoke in lofty generalities about what "we" are for and in forceful detail about what "we" are against.

Paine was a thirty-seven-year-old ne'er-do-well when he landed in Philadelphia in November 1774. The rudely educated son of a Quaker father and an Anglican mother, he had failed in two marriages and numerous jobs ranging from corset-maker to collector of taxes on tobacco and liquor. His sole achievement in life was a broadside he published against corruption among excise officials, which he blamed on the low wages they received. Armed with Franklin's recommendation, however, he caught on with the *Pennsylvania Magazine*. Dr. Benjamin Rush noticed. Seeing in Paine a fearless man of Wilkesian talents, he urged him to weigh in print the arguments favoring independence. Rush also suggested a title: *Common Sense*. Paine did far more than weigh arguments: he wrote a fifty-page choleric indictment of British oppression targeting the king, not misguided advisers or Parliament. He rammed home the conclusion that any colonists who shrank from a declaration of independence lacked not only common sense, but courage, virtue, manhood itself. To say he touched off a frenzy barely conveys the power of Paine. So many printings were made so quickly that 150,000 copies of *Common Sense* were in circulation by spring, most copies read or heard by multiple people. In Washington's estimation the "unanswerable" tract worked a magnificent change in the minds of men and women. It tapped both the vocabularies Americans knew—country-party ideology and moral evangelism—to call for separation from Britain before the colonists were corrupted beyond reformation. Its sublime aphorisms, exhortations, and jeremiads thrilled and horrified, accelerating the already swift progress toward a mass politics. Paine did in print what Patrick Henry did with his voice.

Most people do not know, however, that *Common Sense* was a remarkably conflicted document.[54] Paine foresaw a continental union of limitless potential, yet warned of its glasslike fragility. He damned governmental authority, yet called for its relentless exercise lest the American cause abort. He told Americans they were like Noah's family, free to begin the world over again, yet suspected they lacked the virtue that task required. He preached liberty, yet called on patriots to expose and repress enemies in their midst. He extolled equality, yet feared "the mind of the multitude." He foresaw great prosperity, yet knew how materialism bored and corrupted a people. He praised Americans' rebelliousness, yet chided them for their lawlessness. He pleaded for reason and common sense, yet played on a keyboard of emotions ranging from hatred, anger, and self-righteous vengeance to self-love, fear, and self-doubt. The pamphlet lacked any sustained philosophical argument and its extremely "democratical" implications so alarmed John Adams he hurriedly wrote a rebuttal. But Paine, who had been in America just over one year, somehow intuited more about the mind of the colonists than Adams. Above all, he managed to appeal to Calvinists as well as Deists even though he himself was a bitter religious skeptic. Congregationalists, Presbyterians, and Baptists easily nodded in agreement when Paine labeled vice the great solvent of liberty and defined established churches and overbearing states the *symptoms* of sin, not its correctives. Deists and skeptics easily nodded in agreement when Paine employed Biblical allusions to make *secular* political points. "Ye that oppose independence now, ye know not what ye do" made independence itself the Messiah and faint-hearted colonists the Roman soldiers on Calvary. In sum, Christians reading *Common Sense* found in it the God of the Bible and a politics derived from religion. Deists just as readily found in it the God of Nature and a religion derived from politics. Paine even foresaw the three ways by which the colonists might achieve nationhood: "by the legal voice of the people in Congress; by a military power; or by a mob." He hoped for a combination of all three, which is precisely what Pennsylvania, Virginia, and Massachusetts proceeded to make.

Paine's remarkable pamphlet cemented the alliance between the Awakened and the Enlightened, summoned them to a just war, and promised a kind of heaven on earth if they won. That is why some historians miss the point when they denigrate the role of religion in the American rebellion. Perhaps religious language was just "window-dressing" for colonists primarily engaged in a political or economic struggle. Perhaps some clergy did climb on the bandwagon of what was otherwise a "profoundly secular event." But to stress the absence of Biblical language in the documents of the American founding while dismissing the torrents of religious rhetoric in the speeches, sermons, and tracts exhorting rebellion and war can only lead to a false conclusion. The American cause was profoundly religious for Protestants and Deists alike because both identified America's future with a Providential design and both entertained millenarian hopes. Even Deists believed in God, after all—that is what the word Deist means.[55]

Did Tom Paine help to create American mass politics, or must such politics have already existed for his pamphlet to be such a smash? Whatever the lines of causation, the author of *Common Sense* became all things to all men and the tract itself a template for American political rhetoric to come. Unity, unity, unity being the measure of all things, Paine united most Americans in common hatred and fear of outside oppressors as well as inside dissenters. After Paine, to be lukewarm, much less cold toward the glorious cause was sacrilege. Paine invited—nay, commanded—colonists to feel themselves part of his "*we*," adding always the not-so-veiled threat that "*we*" will get all of you who don't. As for devising a new form of government, the "noblest, purest constitution on the face of the earth"—that could wait. The first task was to wrest power to make laws away from the two-bottle tyrants. That could only be done by winning the war, and that could only be done by declaring independence. Only then would Americans be forced to hang together lest they be hanged as traitors. Only then—and this was Paine's parting shot—could Americans gain the French and Spanish help needed to prevail in the war, and so enlist monarchy in a holy war against monarchy.[56]

# PATRIOTS, TORIES, SLACKERS, AND SPIES

*The Not~So~United States, Hustling to Be Born, 1776–1783*

*I*n August 1780 the burly Baron Johann de Kalb died defending the American flank in the Battle of Camden, South Carolina. A Bavarian in the service of France, de Kalb was prominent in the pantheon of European professionals so valuable to the Continental Army. But de Kalb may have performed his greatest service thirteen years before as a spy. His paymaster was Étienne-François, duc de Choiseul, who became minister of war and foreign affairs after saving Louis XV's powerful mistress, Madame de Pompadour, from a court cabal. Choiseul's obsession was to reverse the verdict of 1763 by rebuilding the French army and navy and probing for chinks in Britain's imperial armor. By far the most interesting intelligence reports he received were de Kalb's. Britain's American colonies, he wrote, were more bounteous and energetic than heretofore imagined. Everywhere one went there were "children swarming like broods of ducks," large, fertile farms, flourishing industries, and harbors barely able to hold the merchant and fishing fleets. "Whatever may be done in London," judged de Kalb, "this country is growing too powerful to be much longer governed at so great a distance."[1]

The philosopher Montesquieu also predicted a new nation would rise on American shores, while Voltaire admired the Quakers' toleration. But prior to the late 1760s, French *philosophes* mostly deduced themselves into absurd and belittling generalizations about America. Montesquieu was partly responsible.

His famous 1748 treatise *The Spirit of the Laws* argued that human mentalities, passions, and institutions varied according to climate. Since America's environment differed markedly from that of Europe, seat of the world's greatest civilization, Indians and even those Europeans who migrated overseas must therefore be inferior. Rousseau was also partly responsible because his contrary claim that "noble savages" were superior to decadent Europeans begged for rebuttal. Thus did Georges-Louis Buffon argue, in his encyclopedic *Histoire naturelle* (1761), American animals and people were smaller and more sickly than those of the Old World. Cornelius De Pauw reasoned the American climate stunted the brain as well as the body. The Abbé Raynal asked why America had produced no artist, savant, or scientist worthy of notice in Europe. No wonder Montesquieu advised Europeans to "stay where they are" and Voltaire chided the crown for fighting wars over "a few acres of snow." If France were to resume competition for empire, that climate of opinion had to change. Choiseul knew the man who could do it. In 1767 he instructed the French embassy in London to shower Benjamin Franklin with "letters of recommendation to the Lord knows who" and spirit him over to Paris.[2]

At that early stage Franklin was not about to let scheming French diplomats "blow up the coals between Britain and her Colonies." But neither was he one to reject an invitation to become the toast of Paris and salesman for America. In 1767 and another visit in 1769, he made full use of his reputation as a scientist, man of letters, humorist, and philosopher to enhance French respect for the achievements of British Americans. He flattered Physiocrats, an influential school of economists, by attributing American prosperity to the agriculture, low taxes, and free trade they advocated. He published a translation of *Letters from an American Farmer* and circulated the journal of his American Philosophical Society. He showed off Dr. Benjamin Rush and other learned Americans in Parisian salons. His own social panache (especially with women) exploded the prevalent notion of Americans as primitives trying to build a city of God.[3] On the contrary, Franklin informed the powdered heads of Paris, Americans were busy building a great city of Man filled with libraries, schools, hospitals, and newspapers everyone read and discussed. Thanks to his advertising barrage, French opinion lurched (as it so often does) to the other extreme. Voltaire, Diderot, Lavoisier, and lesser savants now lauded the American colonies as proof of what natural man, unencumbered by superstition and oppression, could accomplish. Buffon hastily exempted North America from his theory of debilitating environments; Raynal wrote of a new Athens rising in

Boston and Philadelphia. By 1770 Paris was mad for America, had "its eyes fixed upon the quarrel which now divides England and her colonies," and rhapsodized about a continent founded on a liberty "inseparable from the soil, the sky, the forests and the lakes of that vast and virgin land." Franklin thus embellished upon de Kalb's sketch of British America, alerting French elites to the potential value of an alliance if and when the colonists needed one.[4]

By November 1775 they did. The Continental Congress named Franklin, Jefferson, Dickinson, Jay, and Benjamin Harrison to a secret Committee of Correspondence with Foreign Powers. The committee's initial hope was to contact "friends of America" in England, Ireland, perhaps the Netherlands. But within weeks it recognized, as did Tom Paine, that the most likely and potentially effective ally was France. Did sheer cynicism or realpolitik lead American colonists to court the "most Catholic" kingdom they heretofore loved to hate, or had subtle changes occurred in their image of France? The answer is a good deal of both. Now that French threats to North American liberties were quashed and replaced by new threats from Britain, a reversal of alliances was logical. In early 1776, Congress put out the word that agitation against Catholics in Maryland and Pennsylvania must stop. It even sent Charles Carroll of Carrollton and his priestly cousin John Carroll to Canada in hopes of wooing the Québecois.[5] But the more cosmopolitan colonists were also coming to realize France was not the horned beast of popery they imagined. Rather, it was home to the most advanced Enlightenment rationalists. Under Louis XV those *gens de raison* even influenced policy. In 1762 Choiseul looked the other way when the judicial *Parlement* of Paris outlawed Jesuit activity; in 1773 the kings of France, Spain, and Portugal prevailed on the pope to disband the order. Wise heads like Franklin knew French statesmen had never taken their orders from Rome, while suppression of the pope's own "black regiment" made it difficult even for a John or Sam Adams to justify snubbing Catholics on principle. Of course, the French would pursue their own *raison d'état* and could only be trusted up to a point. But so long as their interest overlapped with America's, religious and political differences could be safely ignored.

Choiseul fell victim to political intrigue, and Louis XV died in 1774. But Louis XVI's foreign minister, Charles Gravier, comte de Vergennes, shared Choiseul's thirst for *révanche*. Intrigued by reports of fighting in Massachusetts, he slipped a spy across the ocean in September 1775. Another secret agent, the Anglophobe playwright Caron de Beaumarchais, met with Arthur Lee of Virginia in London. Both spies thought the colonists' resolve was genuine, but warned they might seek reconciliation with Britain unless France shipped them the guns and powder they needed to fight. Accordingly, two wars of nerves played out in agonizing isolation from each other over the winter and spring of 1776. In Philadelphia, Congressmen fretted in hushed tones over how to get help from the French without becoming their pawns. Must the colonies make a formal declaration of independence to allay French doubts and enable America to treat with foreign powers? In March the Secret Committee of Correspondence sent Silas Deane to Paris to find out. Simultaneously, Vergennes lobbied the king to assist the Americans lest they *shrink* from declaring independence. His great opponent was finance minister Turgot, who feared aiding the colonists would provoke war with Britain and bankrupt the crown. The Parisian war of nerves climaxed on May 2, 1776, when the weak-willed Louis XVI agreed to support the Americans so long as it was clandestine. Deane, Lee, and Beaumarchais wasted no time setting up a bogus merchant house, Roderigue Hortalez et Compagnie, to launder French money and ship arms and powder to America. In the process Deane skimmed off sums for himself—the first of many procurement officials to do so. But Hortalez & Cie. eventually put a dozen ships into service and smuggled in 80 percent of the powder used by the Continental Army during the critical years 1776–78.[6]

Philadelphia's war of nerves climaxed two weeks after King Louis' decision. The Continental Congress instructed the thirteen colonies to suppress all royal authority and reconstitute themselves as autonomous states. That made a declaration of independence seem just a matter of time. The resolution of May 15 was a year in gestation. Since British authority ceased to exist beyond Boston after April 1775, the Massachusetts convention asked Congress for "the most explicit advice" regarding a new civil government. Other colonies did the same until, by early spring 1776, all had conventions or committees at work designing provisional governments. The conventions were, for the most part, in the hands of radical Patriots (who called themselves Whigs) because they were appointed or elected by bodies that prohibited voting by Loyalists (called Tories). They justified their insurrections in local declarations of independence, and since they borrowed freely from each other's language they displayed remarkable similarities. Almost all cited the king's use of mercenaries as the last straw, justified separation by appealing to natural law or the law of Providence, and named as their purpose the preservation of liberties. Thomas Jefferson described the defense and preservation of liberty as "the whole object of the present controversy." He even rued having to go up to Philadelphia in May 1776 because it meant he would be absent from Virginia's constitutional convention.

The colonists nonetheless knew the survival of the thirteen new sovereignties depended on the success of a united people acting "in Congress." Hence the May 15 resolution called on colonies to fashion governments that were not only "sufficient to the exigencies of their affairs" but conduced to the happiness and safety of *America in general* and provided "for defense of their lives, liberties, and properties against the hostile invasions and cruel depredations of their enemies." Congress thereby proclaimed the existence of an American people, lurched into instant republicanism, and echoed Paine's call for vigilance against Tories, traitors, and pacifists as well as the king's troops. Some delegates protested the haste, but on the same May 15, down in Richmond, Edmund Randolph authorized Virginia's delegation to propose that Congress declare the colonies "free and independent states" so they could make foreign alliances. The Carolinas and Georgia, menaced by a British invasion fleet, likewise instructed their delegations to concert in all measures necessary to defend America and win foreign allies.[7]

On June 7, Richard Henry Lee moved that Congress declare independence, seek foreign alliances, and unite under a constitution. Such audacious steps would be worse than useless if not passed unanimously, and foot-draggers argued that the middle colonies were still undecided about independence. Proponents retorted "the people" of the middle colonies were in fact pro-independence even if some of their delegates frustrated the popular will. So Congress agreed to postpone a vote until July 1, which gave both sides three weeks to bully, bribe, cajole, or persuade wavering delegates from Pennsylvania, Delaware, New Jersey, and New York. Meanwhile, a committee chaired by John Adams was charged with preparing a text. Since the other members, notably Franklin, had more *important* chores to perform, they asked their cerebral young colleague Jefferson to scribble out a first draft.

"Long Tom," just thirty-three years old, inherited every advantage a Cavalier could desire. His father was a grand tobacco planter in the Piedmont county of Albemarle; his mother a Randolph. Land, slaves, money, prestige, and connections fell into Thomas' lap. Tall and handsome, his bashful manner and distaste for the ruder male pastimes made him all the more attractive to ladies. He also received every educational advantage at hand and, to his credit, took full advantage of private tutoring, two years at William and Mary, and legal studies with the learned George Wythe. What is more, he inherited the plantation at twenty-one and soon married the daughter of a wealthier planter whose father ultimately bequeathed them forty thousand more acres of land and 135 more slaves. Even so, Jefferson's lifelong indebtedness would oblige him to sell most of his land; the slaves he retained to serve as collateral for his many loans. Where did the money go? Above all else, into Monticello, the hilltop mansion he first planned as a teenager, and the furniture, *objets d'art*, scientific and musical instruments, French wines and liqueurs, and books to grace each new room or wing. Jefferson's milieu was a peacock's display, and he might have been ruined had his growing political power not made lenders eager to do him favors. As it was, his character flaws were of the sort that harmed others more than himself. For instance, Jefferson was as curious and learned as Franklin, but unlike Ben he took himself with utter seriousness and had little patience for the frailties of others. He was as gentlemanly as Washington, but unlike George he shrank from combat whether martial or verbal (often claiming illness to avoid public debate) and repeatedly let others down. He was as idealistic as Adams, but unlike John he lacked an introspective, self-critical soul, and thus had difficulty forgiving others' faults or confessing his own. Jefferson was a consumer of life, the living answer to Dr. Johnson's query, "How is it that we hear the loudest yelps for liberty among the drivers of negroes?"[8]

Jefferson later wrote he took up the quill in his parlor on Market Street in 1776 not to discover "new principles, or new arguments," but simply to state "the common sense of the subject." Fair enough—but the fact remains the original passages in Jefferson's draft declaration were not good, while the good ones were not very original. The text's lofty philosophical introduction, bill of particulars against King George, and syllogistic conclusion calling for independence were a pastiche of phrases lifted from Paine, the "little declarations" issued by colonies, and above all Virginia's magnificent Declaration of Rights, written by George Mason and published in Philadelphia on June 12. It was Mason who based Virginia's plan for self-government on the premise that all men are "born equally free and independent." Mason included among the inherent rights of man the "enjoyment of Life and Liberty, with the Means of acquiring and possessing Property, and pursueing and obtaining Happiness." Mason attributed those rights to a power "by God and Nature, vested in, and consequently derived from the People." Mason went on to call for abolition of privilege, separation of legislative and executive power, an independent judiciary, a bill of rights, a free press, and "the fullest Toleration in the Exercise of Religion, according to the Dictates of Conscience."[9]

Jefferson did indeed compose the declaration's elegant preamble: "When in the course of human events . . . ," tighten Mason's list to "life, liberty, and the pursuit of happiness," and conclude with the moving pledge of "our lives, fortunes, and sacred honor." But in between those majestic heights lay a murky swamp of complaints that stick to a reader's boots even today. One that especially troubled Congress was Jefferson's diatribe against the British *people,* whom he accused of being "deaf to the voice of justice and consanguinity" despite "our former love for them" and necessitating "our everlasting Adieu!" Its false sentimentality aside, the passage shifted the focus of American ire away from the crown while gratuitously insulting the very people Congress hoped might pressure Parliament to change course. More bizarre still, Jefferson embarrassed American merchants and planters alike by blaming the British crown for the slave trade. Since he cannot possibly have believed this nonsense he must have been groping for some way to explain away the grotesquery of his postulate "All men are created equal." Congress retained that phrase for its ring, but otherwise saw the wisdom in taking a stand on the basis of Common Law, not embarrassing universals. So it deleted a full fourth of the draft, tweaked the rest, and inserted an appeal to Providence at the end—all to good effect. Jefferson maintained his text was "mangled" and went into a funk that lasted all summer. But as Richard Henry Lee put it, so long as the declaration did no harm to the cause, its wording was less important than "the Thing itself." Decades later the Declaration of Independence was canonized as American scripture, but in 1776 it was generally read once—in army camps, taverns, and village greens—cheered, and forgotten.[10]

"The Thing itself" was far from certain during the days Jefferson worked on the draft. The New England–Southern alliance appeared to hold firm, although South Carolinians expressed doubts, and delegates from New York, a Tory stronghold, pleaded a lack of instructions. Most doubtful were delegates from the Delaware Valley, where the stakes were gigantic. For if Pennsylvania's Quakers, pietist Germans, and Tories carried a "nay" on independence, chances were New Jersey, Delaware, and New York (soon to be under British occupation) would follow suit and the American edifice collapse for want of its keystone. Exactly how that was forestalled will never be known, but the story began in 1774. When Governor John Penn forbade the Pennsylvania assembly to name delegates to the First Continental Congress, Dickinson called an ad hoc convention to do so. Dickinson later rued the precedent he had set, but at the time he was eager to resist the Intolerable Acts. This convention, which met in the same Carpenter's Hall as the Congress, declared voting would take place by counties, not population, so that the seven interior counties might override the four Quaker-influenced counties near the Delaware River. Penn hastily summoned the regular assembly into session to restore his authority, hence Pennsylvania, alone among the colonies, had *two* representative bodies speaking in the name of the people. As late as May 1776 elections to the assembly returned a majority opposed to independence. That suggests John Adams' May 15 call for the suppression of authority "under the crown" was, among other things, an invitation to militants to disperse Penn's assembly by force. The soldiers and officers in Pennsylvania's military associations did not go that far, but in mid-June they resolved to ignore any orders issuing from the assembly. The atmosphere in steamy Philadelphia could thus hardly have been more electric.[11]

War news also weighed on the wafflers in Congress. Back in autumn 1775, a militia force under Richard Montgomery struck north via Lake Champlain in hopes of re-enacting Wolfe's capture of Québec. Washington supported him with a second detachment under Benedict Arnold. But a winter campaign in Canada was madness: the two columns lost half their men to exposure, disease, hunger, and desertion before reaching the citadel on the St. Lawrence. Still, Arnold and Montgomery determined to make a do-or-die effort. On December 31, under cover of a blizzard, a thousand ragged and freezing Americans charged into Québec's lower town, unleashing a maelstrom of close-quarters fighting in which Montgomery was killed, Arnold was wounded, and young Aaron Burr was heroic. But the British garrison rallied to force the surviving Yankees back to their lines. When spring arrived, British reinforcements pushed the Americans back to Ticonderoga and menaced New England with invasion. Elsewhere, the news seemed better. In North Carolina, militia routed a band of Scots Loyalists at Moore's Creek in February. In New England, General Howe, intimidated by the heavy cannons dragged by Henry Knox's men over the Berkshires, evacuated Boston by sea on March 17. Finally (though Congress did not know it yet), the citizens of Charleston, South Carolina, led by Christopher Gadsden and Colonel William Moultrie, pummeled a British squadron from their palmetto forts on James and Sullivan Islands. But even good news portended bad. Yes, those crazy Highlanders were cut down, but they proved how easily Loyalist militias might organize in the Patriots' rear. Yes, Howe had left Boston, but was free to return in greater force at a time and place of his choosing. Yes, Charleston had humiliated the Royal Navy, but what vengeance might its proud captains exact elsewhere?

Indeed, by the first of July, when Congress resumed its debate on Lee's motions, hundreds of sails had already been sighted at sea off Long Island. Was this the right moment to declare independence, or the worst possible moment? Would a clean break with King George end equivocation, energize the war effort, and secure an alliance with France? Or would it unleash civil wars in the states, steel British resolve, and condemn members of Congress to the gallows? Dickinson suspected the latter. He spoke of the folly of tearing down one's house in winter before a replacement was built, warned that the British lion had barely begun to roar, and imagined Indian scalping parties rampaging down Market and Wall Streets. John Adams turned no magic phrases, but made a sincere and logical case that no alternative to independence remained, while freedom was worth any risk. The vote was a letdown for both. Nine colonies favored independence, but Pennsylvania and South Carolina delegates split narrowly against it, Delaware deadlocked (with one member absent), and New York abstained. What happened next is uncertain except that many comings and goings were made that thunderous summer evening. Caesar Rodney, the missing Delaware delegate, rode all night through rain and lightning to cast an exhausted, asthmatic "aye" on July 2.[12] The South Carolinians were probably brought into line by Virginians. But what turned Pennsylvania around is a mystery. All we know is that two dissenters, Dickinson and Robert Morris, failed to attend the caucus the following day. Had Hancock, the wealthy president of Congress, bought them off in some fashion? Were they threatened in dark corners by Patriot goons? Or did they just shrink from taking responsibility for aborting the majority cause? Whatever the reason, Pennsylvania's delegates divided 3 to 2 in favor of independence instead of 4 to 3 against, and Congress "unanimously" (New York still abstaining) declared itself the voice of the people of the United States of America on July 2, 1776.[13]

The text of the Declaration, of course, was approved on the fourth. But a more important event occurred on the third, when General Howe landed the first of thirty-two thousand redcoats and Hessians on Staten Island, just sixty miles from Philadelphia. No wonder Congress refrained from distributing official *signed* copies of its treasonous Declaration until the military situation improved, at least for a while, in January 1777.

David Hackett Fischer has described the War of American Independence as a sequence of conflicts fought in serial fashion by the four folk cultures transplanted from England. Phase one was the Puritans' war of 1775–76, a people's uprising egged on by Congregational clergy. Phase two was the Cavaliers' war of 1776–81, during which regular armies led by gentlemen fought conventional campaigns. Phase three was the Bordermen's war of 1779–81, waged mostly in the southern back country. This was a bloody civil feud in which partisans and their Indian allies gave no quarter to combatants and non-combatants alike. Phase four from 1781–83 was, if not the Quakers' war, then at least a peacemakers' affair in which financiers and diplomats from the middle colonies, such as Robert Morris, John Jay, and Franklin, helped the nation survive and negotiate a favorable peace. Later, in 1787, the various strengths and understandings of liberty across the four cultures balanced and leavened each other to enable Americans to frame one Constitution despite glaring regional differences.[14] To grasp Fischer's point, imagine almost *all* American colonists had been rigid Puritans, or slave-holding Cavaliers, or pacifist Quakers, or lawless Bordermen, and ask yourself whether the colonies could have won independence at all.

This makes for a fetching schematic. However, elements of all four "wars" popped up in all phases and regions. The commanders of the Minutemen yearned for professional status. Few of Washington's generals were true Cavaliers. Partisan warfare tore through every theater and phase, while the climactic southern campaign was a cooperative effort by frontiersmen and regulars. The financial and diplomatic work of the non-combatants was vital throughout the conflict, not just at the end. What is more, all American regions were more or less divided among Patriots, Tories, and fence-sitters. Indeed, those divisions made it all the more critical for some omnibus institution transcending regions and states to sustain the fact (and sometimes the fiction) of a new nation still fighting for life. That indispensable institution was the Continental Army—and the activities of partisans, militias, moneylenders, diplomats, spies, and foreign allies possessed meaning only insofar as they helped keep the army in being. But even that was not the whole story, because the army needed to prevail without substituting itself for the *civil* cause. It must subordinate itself to the Congress even when civil authorities slandered its officers and starved its soldiers. That the Continental Army did prevail seemed, to George Washington, a miracle attributable only to Providence. That the army never subverted the civil cause was just as astounding, and is attributable mostly to Washington.[15]

A focus on the army—the only national institution besides feeble Congress—suggests a different chronology and different themes, including the relationships between Patriots' ideals and actual deeds, between the army and the civilian population, between the army and Congress.[16] In the early stages of the rebellion, say from Lexington Green to the Declaration of Independence, patriotic fervor obscured the tensions in those relationships. After all, this was a holy struggle in which defeat equated to slavery, victory depended on communal sacrifice, and indifference, as Nathanael Greene put it, was "spiritual suicide." The British might scoff that the American militias were "a vagabond army of Ragamuffins" and boast a mere thousand redcoats would suffice to "geld all the males" in the colonies. But Americans believed themselves chosen by Nature or Nature's God to prove self-government worked and bequeath it to posterity. In the exciting rush of 1775 a veritable *rage militaire* swept over them. Farm boys and mechanics enlisted as soldiers; planters, lawyers, merchants, and preachers took commissions as officers. Some were veterans of the French and Indian War. Most were amateurs who learned military science on the job and by reading books. Among the self-taught were Greene, Benedict Arnold, Alexander McDougall, Alexander Hamilton, Benjamin Lincoln, Peter Muhlenberg, Henry Lee, and Henry Knox, the father of the U.S. artillery corps.[17] In theory, every American male was a potential soldier, as Boston pastor John Allen bragged in 1773: "Where his Majesty has one soldier, America can produce fifty free men, and all volunteers." His brag was made good in 1775 when John Adams gushed all must become soldiers now. A people's army imbued with republican virtue would defeat an evil king's conscripts and mercenaries as surely as the ancient Greek hoplites defeated the Persians.[18]

Naive enthusiasm was cresting in May 1775, when Washington arrived to command the New England forces besieging the British in Boston. Every town turned out to cheer him, and he in turn was impressed by the volunteers marching in from neighboring colonies. But Washington also knew an easy patriotism would melt into disillusionment, cynicism, even cries of betrayal once the casualties, retreats, delays, requisitions, thefts, atrocities, bribes, kickbacks, and jealousies characteristic of all wars began to sully the glorious cause. He was not familiar with New England folk, but he knew they despised standing armies and would be quick to resent his own presence once the British were pried out of Boston. These people wanted no troops quartered on them, resented every penny of tax, defied centralized command, elected or appointed their own officers, and considered each general a tyrant-in-waiting. How then could Washington keep men under arms after their six-month enlistments ran out, drill and whip them into proper soldiers, and keep them supplied without alienating the people he was there to protect? American generals were compelled to answer that question over and over again in New England, the middle colonies, and the south, because (assuming they avoided catastrophe on the battlefield) their success in keeping the grudging support of the people would determine the outcome of the war.

The vigorous forty-three-year-old Washington had long since outgrown the impatient craving for glory that tarnished his first military career. For fifteen years he had squired wife Martha, managed Mount Vernon, and served in the House of Burgesses, both courting and deserving the image of a dignified, honest gentleman. Yet almost as if he suspected what life held in store, Washington scripted a role for himself beyond Virginia, an American role that no one besides Whitefield and Franklin had played before. His first performance was at the Continental Congress of 1774, where his tall, martial bearing, excellent horsemanship, and ecumenism impressed everyone. He socialized with delegates from all over, paid special attention to those from the middle colonies and New England, and modestly confirmed tales of his adventures in the French and Indian wars. He was reserved but in no way aloof, and was pleased to propose a toast, share in a song, or buy a round of drinks in the City Tavern. He spoke seldom, but gravely and always to further a common rather than provincial interest. Tellingly, Washington made a point of attending Quaker, Presbyterian, Anglican, and even Catholic services. In every way he presented himself—consciously, but not falsely—as a master of his emotions, a delegate above party or province, a military man with civilian values, a personification of the American cause. John Adams called him "noble and disinterested," Benjamin Rush thought there was "not a king in Europe that would not look like a *valet de chambre* by his side," and Virginians, who knew him best, all agreed.[19]

Effective leaders in any field must be actors, none more so than military leaders, and no military leaders more than supreme commanders of democratic armies. That the aristocratic eighteenth century produced such a commander is amazing, but not inexplicable. Unlike no other country except Switzerland the American colonies possessed popular armed forces—the militias—and few men understood their quirks and shortcomings better than Washington. He admired professionalism, studied European organization and tactics, and embodied a quasi-aristocratic culture. But like Patrick Henry, Washington knew Americans could be mobilized only through a process of *mutual* deference. Their peculiarities must be tolerated, their obedience won, and their orders explained. Above all, they must be reminded incessantly they were fighting for *themselves* and their posterity, not for some abstraction and certainly not for some master. Washington had in effect to make amateur soldiers fight like professionals without ceasing to be good citizens of a republic. Only then might he fulfill his mission from Congress, which was "the maintenance and preservation of American liberties." Still, he took up his commission with little confidence. All he could answer for, he wrote his brother-in-law, was "a firm belief in the justice of our cause, close attention to the prosecution of it, and the strictest integrity." If those did not make up for deficient skill and experience, then "the cause will suffer, and more than probable my character along with it."[20]

The first principle Washington observed from the moment he took command on May 2, 1775, to the end of the war a hundred months later was that he and the army served at the pleasure of Congress. To be sure, he was highly solicitous of state and local officials upon whom he relied to feed and clothe his soldiers, but neither would he take orders from them. His was a national army. The second principle was discipline, the "soul of an army." What he found outside Boston was a purposeless mob of fourteen thousand living in squalor. No two seemed dressed or equipped in like fashion, few knew how to maneuver in ranks or fire a disciplined volley, and all were desperately short of powder. Adding to his troubles were the first companies of "Continentals" recruited by Congress. Mostly Scots-Irish frontiersmen, they had even less discipline and loved to pick fights with the locals. So Washington stooped to perform the duties of drill sergeants by teaching privates and officers alike how to police mess kitchens, latrines, and barracks, preside over a parade ground, flog miscreants as a deterrent to others, and drum out of the ranks all who refused to shape up. Such measures might have provoked mutiny but for the respect he won from officers and the support he received from clergy. The latter shared Washington's concern over vice in the ranks and seconded his request to Congress for chaplains. He also won over worried civilians by locating camps well outside of towns and responding to every petty complaint, be it a matter of soldiers bathing naked, stripping outbuildings for firewood, or carousing in taverns.

Washington set another example by serving without pay or furlough. But he was under no illusion that a people in arms would be virtuous. On the contrary, he confessed to having acquired "a small knowledge of human nature" in his earlier campaigns and privately rued "the dearth of public spirit" among soldiers and civilians. But he had at least to portray the Continental Army as a righteous remnant of the spirit of '75, a secular priesthood to whom some civilians, at least, might be moved to contribute, if only to expiate their own guilt.[21] Most of all, Washington scrupulously respected civilian supremacy. It must have exhausted him to write hundreds of letters every month to Congress, state governors, and other officials requesting authorizations and pleading for recruits and supplies. But he had constantly to reassure Congress and the people this army was not a law unto itself or a plague on the land. Washington even deferred to Congress on matters of strategy and personnel, though it rankled him to do so.[22]

Still the army suffered from constant suspicion and neglect, because the public resentment and apathy foreseen by Washington set in as early as 1776. When the British abandoned Boston, Washington refrained from marching through its streets like a Caesar (he went to church instead). But the Massachusetts militia and residents who swarmed back into Boston behaved as if the war was over and returned to business as usual. John Adams, so recently buoyant, reported "such selfishness and littleness" as to make him doubt whether the people could maintain a republic. Even farmers and artisans were corrupted by the "spirit of commerce."[23] But where Adams saw things in moral terms, Washington was pragmatic. War profiteering was to be expected and even encouraged if it helped to equip the army. Unfortunately, much of the corruption attending the war did nothing but harm. Governors promised recruits and supplies that never arrived. Farmers hid crops and animals from commissary officials to drive prices higher or refused to take inflated Continental money in payment. The slang of the time told of "smart money" (a recruiter's cut), "customhouse oaths" (a smuggler's lies), "mushroom gentlemen" (war profiteers), "jockeys" (speculators in currency), and "horse beef" (meat of uncertain provenance sold to the army). Washington's staffer Tench Tilghman summed up: "We Americans are a sharp people." Draft evasion and desertion were rife, and mothers initially proud to send sons to war (for six months) now begged them to remain on the farm. Recruiting officers pocketed or gambled away funds meant for enlistment bonuses. Towns double-counted enlistments and soldiers already in service, or rounded up prisoners, deserters, and the halt and lame in order to meet their manpower quotas. Some states permitted men to duck service by paying for a substitute, but that only created a market for hucksters who would pay a volunteer's bounty then "sell" him for a higher price to someone in need of a substitute. In 1775 and again in 1776, Washington had to make personal appeals to soldiers whose terms were expiring not to depart in the midst of campaigns. Throughout the war he had to train new recruits in the midst of operations. Thus did Tom Paine write in December 1776 of the times that try men's souls, when "the summer soldier and the sunshine patriot" shirk the service of their country. During the first flush of enthusiasm Congress authorized a permanent army of seventy-five thousand. As late as October 1777, a mere twenty-one thousand Continentals were fit for line duty, and many of them were unshod and hungry.[24]

In sum, Congress may have pledged its lives, fortunes, and honor to freedom, but many Americans hunkered down in hopes the war would pass them by, or packed up and moved to Kentucky, or figured they had done their part after one stint in the militia or gift of provisions. Some war governors, such as Connecticut's Jonathan Trumbull, were tireless in their efforts to organize citizens and provide the army with food and shot—Washington would not forget them.[25] But many were either lax or lacked the power to act under restrictive state constitutions. As for Congress, it never seemed to act until faced with a crisis: a bad habit it has never broken. Washington even had to "retrain" Congress continually because its president and members changed every year, usually for the worse as leading personalities obtained governorships or military and diplomatic assignments. General Charles Lee complained that field commanders had to play the diplomat, politician, and lawyer with their own government. Horatio Gates simply groused, "A general of an American Army must be everything; and that is being more than one man can long sustain."[26]

A free republic must rest on virtue—everyone mouthed that. In the absence of public virtue, the army must play the role of unspotted lamb—Washington accepted that. But so, too, must the army survive or the republican cause would be lost altogether. So whenever its foragers had no choice but to requisition foodstuffs, horses, and hardware, they worked on the principle that "as long as officers called their deeds sins and regretted that their sins had been forced upon them, sin could help save America."[27] Moreover, the army's sins were picayune compared to the ones some congressmen feared. Even during the worst days of the southern campaign, Continental soldiers did not engage in rapine and pillaging or impose widespread martial law. Nor did army commanders ransack the treasury, bully the states, or force soldiers to stay beyond their enlistments. Nor did Washington consider a military dictatorship even when some *civilian* officials urged him to do so.

Washington's own defensive strategy did nothing to boost the flagging morale of Patriots because it ensured the war would be long and offer few victories.[28]

But it was the only prudent one to adopt in the face of superior British forces in command of the sea. As he patiently explained to Congress, the new nation could triumph only by wearing down Britain's will to persist. But politics and public opinion obliged the army to try, at least, to defend America's largest cities. Hence the Continentals marched south in spring 1776 in anticipation of a British assault on New York. Washington's eye for terrain told him batteries on Brooklyn Heights might overawe lower Manhattan, but he was blind to the possibility his forces might be easily trapped on Long Island. That almost happened when Howe landed ten thousand redcoats, kilted Highlanders, and German jaegers on the island and made a crushing attack on August 22. Eschewing frontal assaults such as that on Breed's Hill, the British destroyed the American left flank commanded incompetently by the New Hampshire Irishman John Sullivan. On the American right sturdy Delaware and Maryland regiments fought fiercely—they would soon be the backbone of the army—but that only encouraged Washington to shift more troops to Long Island. A week later he realized the danger and ordered a withdrawal. Luckily, a storm prevented the British fleet from interdicting the East River, and John Glover's regiment of skilled Marblehead boatmen were on hand to ferry the army to Harlem. But once out of danger, some two thousand New England militiamen lit out for home. The frustrated Howe attacked north from Manhattan in a series of confused actions culminating at White Plains near the end of October. Thanks to its rearguard of Delawares, Marylanders, and McDougall's Yorkers, the Continental Army escaped across the Hudson. New York City, however, remained under occupation until the end of the war.

Howe and Charles, the marquis of Cornwallis were never hasty, but they eventually moved armies across New Jersey, nearly capturing Washington and forcing the Continentals across the Delaware River. The British settled into winter quarters, confident the whipped Yankees could do them no harm. Washington, with a spare three thousand men, again had to beg men whose enlistments were up to remain. They all did, and Washington bet them all in what may have been the greatest gamble of the conflict. Was it instinct telling him the Continental cause needed a triumph lest it dissolve, or fear that Philadelphia might fall if the enemy kept the initiative, or distress over the speed with which Jerseyites turned coat? Whatever the mix of motives, Washington called on Glover's boatmen to row his army back across the Delaware on Christmas night. The pitiful German mercenaries in Trenton were sleeping off their *Weihnachten* revelry when the Americans slipped into town, fired their muskets, and fixed bayonets. The butcher's bill was small—just twenty-two enemy killed—but more than a thousand surrendered. Cornwallis, enraged, advanced on Trenton only to find Washington had slipped around him and captured a garrison of proud South Lancashire redcoats at Princeton. That so alarmed Howe he pulled back his advanced Jersey garrisons, which allowed Washington to winter at Morristown, smack in the heart of northern New Jersey.

Appearances to the contrary, the British chiefs had a strategy, indeed several of them. When the fighting erupted, Lord North's secretary at war argued the cheapest and surest way to end the rebellion was by naval blockade. But that could take years, and the king wanted this business over in a hurry. He imagined armies of Irish Catholics could be easily recruited, while Lord George Germain, secretary for the colonies, and sybaritic Lord Sandwich of the Admiralty were beguiled by the prospect of arming American Loyalists. So in 1777 the cabinet determined to exploit the bases they had won the previous year to cut the thirteen colonies in half. One army under "Gentleman Johnny" Burgoyne was to push south from Canada and link up with Howe's on the Hudson. That would isolate rebellious New England and permit the British to arm the Six Nations Iroquois and New York Tories. But thanks to a blunder in London, Howe never received clear instructions. To him it appeared the best plan was to attack the rebels' capital of Philadelphia since Washington would be bound to defend it. As a result, British forces divided and were assured of decisive success in neither theater.[29]

They were also characteristically slow off the mark. Not until June 20 was Burgoyne satisfied his eighty-three hundred soldiers with 138 cannon were ready to move against Ticonderoga; not until late August did Howe's flotilla arrive in Chesapeake Bay. The two campaigns then played out simultaneously with results very bad for the British and Washington alike.

In spring 1777 the Continental Army crossed the Delaware River for the fifth time and stationed itself in Bucks County near the Tennants' revivalist college at Neshaminy. When the threat to Philadelphia became palpable, Washington marched his few veterans and half-trained recruits through the city's cobblestone streets and south to Chester County. Congressmen held their breath and kept their bags packed. The first collision at Brandywine Creek was Brooklyn Heights all over again. The British struck at the American flank commanded by Sullivan and might have rolled up the whole line but for the swift maneuvers of a Virginia regiment, fighting under Rhode Island's Nathanael Greene, and Jersey men under Pennsylvania's "Mad Anthony"

Wayne. Washington himself was fortunate not to be shot when he rode unawares into an enemy command post.[30] To their credit, the Continentals retreated in fairly good order, but a torrential storm soaked their powder supply, and the enemy captured a cache of irreplaceable stores at a place called Valley Forge. When the swift British advance surprised Wayne's men at Paoli, the whole American force retreated north over the Schuylkill River. Cornwallis and Howe paraded into Philadelphia, forcing the fugitive Congress to make York, Pennsylvania, the interim capital of the United States of America.[31]

Having lost another campaign and another big city, Washington tried to repeat his morale-boosting triumph at Trenton. On October 3 he attacked the main British position on Germantown Heights. But the plan was too complicated. Some units had to march forty miles and fight hungry, thirsty, and tired. Others did not appear at all. Still, the Continentals fought hard until their ammunition ran low and they were forced to retreat. Happily, Howe did not pursue: he wanted to clear out the rebel forts on the Delaware River so British ships could reach Philadelphia. Washington's spent regiments repaired to Valley Forge in December.

Contrast that with the extraordinary events unfolding over the same months on the Hudson. Burgoyne took Ticonderoga on July 6, which opened an easy water route (especially important for transporting heavy guns) to the Hudson. In a week or less the invaders might fall upon Albany, where an inferior force of New England militia was scarcely ready to meet them. But Burgoyne hurled away his advantages. First, he issued a pompous decree to the effect "Messengers of Justice and of Wrath" awaited any who dared name himself rebel, and allowing as how only his Christian mercy and gentleman's honor restrained Indians eager for scalps. To make matters worse, a band of Indians got drunk and took a scalp anyway from the lovely head of Jane McCrea, the fiancée of a prominent local Tory! As a result, Burgoyne found American soldiers and settlers united and angry, not divided and defeatist. Second, he gave the Continentals time to prepare by stupidly rejecting the water route and marching his army through twenty miles of dense forest. They emerged, tired and sore, at the end of July, and made camp a few miles upriver from Saratoga.

By the time Burgoyne resumed his advance Horatio Gates was in charge of the American defenses. But the decisive preparations were made by a German farmer, a sly Connecticut Yankee, a Polish engineer, and a weathered Virginia teamster. The farmer was Tryon County militia commander Nicholas Herkimer, who rallied eight hundred neighbors to help save Fort Stanwix.

British general Barry St. Leger and a sizable Iroquois war party threatened the fort. Herkimer realized that if the fort fell St. Leger would join up with Burgoyne while the Indians terrorized the frontier. Herkimer lost his life in the vicious melee, but his militia inflicted so many casualties the Indians ran off. Next, the Yankee, Benedict Arnold, duped St. Leger into retreating by spreading false reports of a powerful Patriot force on the march. Meanwhile, back on the Hudson, engineer Thaddeus Kosciuszko chose excellent ground for the army on Bemis Heights, then taught Gates' men how to dig proper breastworks. Finally, the "Old Wagon Master" Daniel Morgan ordered his corps of snipers and skirmishers to hide in the woods on the British right flank and await the uncanny turkey-gobbles Morgan used to send signals. Burgoyne, the would-be trapper, was trapped. But he realized it only after two violent assaults on Bemis Heights sapped his army's strength and he tried to retreat. Out of the woods came Morgan's marksmen to wither his flank and cover the road stretching north. When John Stark's Vermont militia then appeared in his rear Burgoyne asked for terms. On October 17 the British stacked their arms at Saratoga and marched into captivity. One thing more: many of the muskets and guns and almost all the powder Americans used in the campaign had arrived courtesy of Hortalez & Cie.

Saratoga was a disaster prompting many resignations and a Parliamentary inquiry. But the futility of British strategy was more clearly exposed by their *success* on the Delaware. Washington's forces were whipped, but they remained in the field. The rebels' capital was occupied, but their government simply moved. Nor did hordes of Loyalists rush to the king's colors: rather they fled to Canada by the tens of thousands or were disarmed and repressed by Patriot committees of safety. So Lord North's cabinet spent the winter of 1777–78 trading "I told you so's." The British also fretted over intelligence reports from Paris suggesting they might already have blown their chance to crush the rebellion in isolation from world politics.

Washington was just as discomfited that winter by rumors of a cabal aiming to sack him and make Gates commander in chief. Gates' pride and ambition gave it verisimilitude: he was quick to send reports of his glorious victory to Congress and the states, but not to his superior, Washington. Worse still, hearsay evidence circulated about a letter written by General Thomas Conway to Gates disparaging Washington's talents. Since Congress, bristling in exile at York, had just named Conway inspector general of the army, while John Adams and Benjamin Rush were warning of military dictatorships, it is not surprising

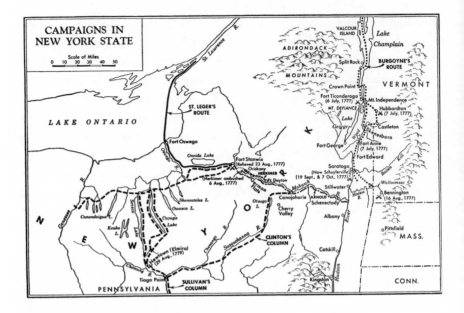

Valley Forge took such rumors seriously. Greene, Knox, Tilghman, and Alexander Hamilton urged Washington to defend himself, which he did in a series of testy letters to Gates meant to elicit clarifications, apologies, and assurances. It was not Washington's most seemly performance. But another man might have confronted Congress with threats of resignation or worse, or else responded to the "Conway Cabal" with a cabal of his own. Washington did none of that, and was gratified when "no whisper was ever heard in Congress" about his dismissal.[32]

Valley Forge lies eighteen miles up the Schuylkill from Philadelphia and is today a beautiful park in all seasons. The cannons and cabins on display look like props for toy soldiers. But the historically minded tourist must block out the joggers and picnickers, convention centers and shopping malls, to imagine what conditions were like there in December 1777. The army arrived from Germantown depleted by casualties, desertion, and the usual end of enlistments. With naught to eat but a few barrels of flour soldiers felt mocked by the croaking frogs and ubiquitous crows, Pennsylvania's airborne constabulary. The army lacked winter clothes, blankets, and boots. It had no shelter until men fashioned tiny huts in which they shared their bodily warmth (no room for a fireplace). Many were sick or injured; many did not survive. It was a "starving time" of the sort few Americans had experienced since the first colonies were planted in the 1600s. Contrary to legend, Washington did not "share the men's suffering"—officers repaired to nearby farmhouses and inns and socialized to the degree their purses and scrounging permitted. But they were responsible for the men, which is mental anguish enough. Washington sent foraging parties in every direction, but local farmers hid their flocks, sold their harvests for higher prices elsewhere, or, what was worse, took the ready cash offered by the British in Philadelphia. Even when crops were located, foragers lacked wagons and horses to carry them back to camp. To add insult to injury, Congress repeatedly questioned the accounts of Washington's commissary, replacing its chief four times over the winter. Such prominent generals as Greene, Wayne, and Lee were sent on veritable raiding parties through the snow to New Jersey and Delaware where, they surmised, most of the farmers were probably Tories anyway.[33]

The two greatest threats to military discipline are not hard work and danger, but boredom and privation. When those conditions exist, drilling and "spit and polish" are all the more necessary, which is why the bogus "Baron von Steuben" deserved the acclaim he received. One of the foreign volunteers sent over from Paris by Silas Deane, Steuben was really named Steube, acquired his noble title by fraud not by birth, and held none of the exalted posts he claimed to have occupied in the army of Frederick the Great. But that was precisely the point: America attracted hustlers precisely because it offered opportunity regardless of one's birth, education, or integrity, and if reinventing oneself required reinventing one's past, so be it. Congress was impressed by Steuben's false résumé and willingness to serve without pay. Washington was impressed by his knowledge of Prussian drill. He put him in charge of a company that might serve as a model for the rest of the army. Steuben succeeded beyond all expectations, but contrary to his ramrod, foul-mouthed image he proved neither brutal nor haughty. The Prussian grasped at once these curious free men in uniform required deviations from Old World practice. So he explained, as best his rudimentary English allowed, why marching and musket drill saved lives and won battles. Perhaps most of all, Steuben persuaded the otherwise miserable Continentals that he loved them and insisted they love one another. He rose every morning before sun-up, inspected the soldiers' huts, weapons, and rations, visited the sick, and punished only willful misconduct, never incompetence. Any soldier who has experienced basic training knows the strange *esprit de corps* and sense of invincibility a good drill instructor conjures in his men. By the time winter was over, Steuben was inspector general of the army.

Washington ordered his manual translated into passable English for distribution to all Continentals.[34]

The greatest boost to morale at Valley Forge, however, was a report received Sunday, March 29, 1777, from a "Gentleman of veracity." A ship had put in at New Haven, he said, bearing certain accounts of a treaty concluded by Dr. Franklin and the French, "upon which the good Doctor was received and acknowledged at that Court as Ambassador from the Free and Independent States of America."[35]

The primary purpose of the Declaration of Independence had been to secure foreign alliances, and even before it was voted Congress began work on a "model treaty" to be offered abroad. John Adams, its principal author, shared Tom Paine's assumption that France and other powers would recognize and support the new American nation in return for trading privileges alone. Congress also took seriously the danger of the United States becoming a pawn of the more powerful French, so it instructed commissioners Franklin, Jefferson, and Deane to offer commercial ties to all foreign states but political ties to none. Franklin was seventy years old, afflicted with gout, kidney stones, and psoriasis, and liable to be hanged if captured by the British. Nevertheless, he agreed to go. Jefferson begged off—his frail and pregnant wife was ill. So Congress appointed Arthur Lee, still spying in London, to join the others.

Franklin arrived in Paris on December 21, 1776, and for two months took the measure of his compatriots. Lee, a fanatic for the American cause, was a useful source of intelligence, but saw plots and treason everywhere—he even suspected Franklin. Deane worked well with Beaumarchais in the shipment of arms and outfitting of American privateers, but was a sucker for every adventurer seeking high rank or salary in the New World. He showed especially poor judgment by attempting to hire incendiaries to torch British shipyards. Above all, Deane's coterie was so compromised by British spies that the French government refused to share secrets with the Americans. Accordingly, the U.S. delegation's residence in a wing of a nobleman's house in suburban Passy was a snake pit in which the only "snakes" who trusted each other were Ben and his grandson William Temple Franklin.[36] Resuming his pose as the witty, naughty frontier philosopher in the bearskin hat, old Ben was fawned over by Parisian society. But he got nowhere with foreign minister Vergennes, who shunned a merely commercial treaty, claimed to fear provoking hostilities with Britain, and voiced expectations the Continentals would either settle with Britain or be beaten.[37]

Then the stunning news of Saratoga arrived, which some historians credit for allaying French doubts about an alliance. But that explanation makes sense only if one takes the devious Vergennes at his word. Historical evidence has since revealed the hawkish French ministry only meant to postpone war with Britain until its naval preparations were complete, while Vergennes purposely exaggerated chances of an Anglo-American rapprochement in order to frighten King Louis into alliance with the United States. Franklin ably supported that ploy by leaking, not concealing, the clandestine visits paid him by British agents. Most telling of all, the French government made secret plans well before Saratoga to enter the war by February 1778. Still, the American victory doubtless weakened the French peace party's position by suggesting to the king the price of glory might not be so high after all. In January 1778, Louis authorized his foreign ministry to draft a military as well as commercial treaty with the Americans. They were signed on February 6. For France, the purpose of the war was to disrupt the British empire, recover valuable fisheries off the Grand Banks, and possibly conquer some West Indian islands. For Spain, which joined the alliance in 1779, the war held out hope of recovering Florida and Gibraltar from Britain. For the United States, the alliance vastly increased the chances of securing independence before the American people grew sick of the war. Conscious of their divergent aims, the signatories promised they would make no separate peace, negotiate the peace treaty together, and remain allies after the war. The American Congress sitting at York toasted Dr. Franklin with gusto and ratified the treaties at once. By mid-June France was at war to assist what appeared to be a colonial rebellion against empire. It never occurred to Louis XVI that this was also a people's rebellion against monarchy, potentially as threatening to him as to George III.

By 1778 state conventions and committees of safety, backed by militias, had largely disarmed, disenfranchised, and in many cases dispossessed all Americans refusing to confess their republican faith. These days it is easy to condemn the Patriots for denying Loyalists the natural rights they invoked, just as it used to be easy to condemn Tories for their "treasonous" refusal to fight for Americans' rights. Far more rewarding, if more difficult, is to appreciate the quandary the Declaration of Independence created for Americans of all persuasions. A terrible war had begun in which the Patriots were the clear underdogs. Yet even as they struggled to field armies and raise supplies vast numbers of their neighbors openly or secretly prayed "God save the king." Gouverneur Morris thought half of New Yorkers were Loyalist. Some thirty thousand Americans took up arms for the king at various times. Perhaps one hundred thousand Tories fled the thirteen states during or after the war. The best estimates suggest roughly half a million, or about 20 percent of all white Americans, were of firm Tory sympathies. What were Patriots to do about these potential fifth columnists? To be sure, most opponents of independence just kept their heads down. But even they might do damage as informants, defeatists, or voters if permitted to exercise civil rights. Looked at from the other side, what were Tories to do, trapped in the middle of an insurrection of which they wanted no part? Play along with the rebellion while secretly rooting for the redcoats? Or show the courage of their convictions and place their own lives, fortunes, and honor on the line? All souls were tried in this conflict. But the nascent self-government the Patriots were trying to invent faced the most formidable test. That test was not whether it would *protect* the rights of dissidents who gave aid and comfort to the enemy at a time of grave emergency. Rather, the test was whether Congress and the states could *selectively* repress the rights of dissidents without undermining the rule of law for all.[38]

After July 4, 1776, Patriot elites in the states convened to set up new governments specifically designed to gut executive power so the malfeasances of the British crown would not be replicated. Pennsylvania's first constitution abolished the post of governor altogether, substituting a twelve-man executive council. Most states provided for governors to be elected by the legislature and to serve for only one year. All sharply curtailed executive power over administrative or judicial appointments—no patronage! All condemned the British notion of "virtual representation" against which they had rebelled. But what did real representation imply? Should each county or township have equal weight, as the states did in Congress? Or should the representation of states and communities within states be weighted according to population or, as John Adams proposed, relative *wealth*, since property was the bedrock of liberty? Hardly anyone believed in "one man, one vote" democracy. Political theory dating back to the Greeks predicted that would lead to the plundering of the rich by the poor. Indeed, the weaker the executive and judiciary, the more necessary it seemed to restrict the electorate through loyalty oaths and property qualifications or otherwise rein in its passions.[39] Congress went even further in the

Articles of Confederation adopted at York in November 1777 and quickly ratified by all states save Maryland. Drafted largely by John Dickinson, the Articles bestowed on the United States government no executive branch at all and even prohibited Congress from imposing taxes or assessments upon states. Moreover, since each state had one vote and major acts and amendments had to pass unanimously, even the smallest state could block initiatives (which churlish Rhode Island repeatedly did).[40]

Still, power exists and somebody has to have it, especially during a life-or-death conflict. So behind each state's façade of weak and popular government, a Patriot party or junto imposed its will, usually with majority support. Thus the constitutional convention in Pennsylvania, on paper the most democratic of states, was named by self-appointed committees. The Declaration of Right and Frame of Government it produced were in the best spirit of William Penn, but required all citizens to take an oath of allegiance before they could vote or enjoy rights of citizenship. Since Quakers and pietists believed oath-taking a sin, and most Loyalists refused to perjure themselves, that guaranteed sweeping electoral victories for the mostly Presbyterian Patriots. Persecution of the "disloyal" began as early as August 1777, when General Sullivan informed Congress that a certain Friends Meeting (which did not exist) was giving intelligence to the British. John Hancock then recommended to Pennsylvania's executive council the arrest of anyone who displayed "a disposition inimical to the cause of America." John Adams personally fingered Israel Pemberton, Jr., so-called "king of the Quakers." In all, forty-one people were arrested in defiance of a writ of *habeas corpus* and exiled to Winchester, Virginia.[41] In March 1778 the state assembly followed up with a law ordering all Loyalists to turn themselves in for trial. In the likely event they declined, their property would be deemed forfeit. At least four hundred estates were seized under the statute.[42]

That sounds awful, but consider, too, this initial panic about Quaker collaboration occurred during Howe's invasion of Pennsylvania and occupation of Philadelphia, where Tories spent the winter staging sumptuous galas for British officers while Washington's men starved outside of town and the Pennsylvania assembly was exiled to Lancaster. No less a figure than Jacob Duché, former chaplain of the Continental Congress, turned coat while Howe was in town. He wrote Washington urging him to step down on the grounds that Patriots were stupid, obscure, and violent men beneath the dignity of a gentleman such as himself. That was mild compared to the Tory propaganda that spewed forth from Philadelphia, New York, and wherever else British soldiers gave cover.

Broadsides described Congress as a den of "cruel and relentless tyrants" whose "bloody, dark, and deep plots" inspired "obdurate rebels" to rape, rob, torture, and kill the king's subjects at will and impose "a system so abhorredly infamous, as not to be equalled in any age or nation under heaven."[43]

Given some Americans did inform for the redcoats, take up arms, or incite Indians to terrorize the frontier, Patriot propaganda was equally vicious. Indeed, never was the old "paranoid style" of Anglo-American politics so in fashion as during this war. As early as spring 1776, Washington called for punishment of all the "abominable pests of Society" who spoke against the American cause. Congress responded after a plot to assassinate Washington was unearthed in June.[44] All states were instructed to define and punish acts of treason and all thirteen did, some going so far as to include trade with the enemy. States also proscribed expressions of fealty to the king, opposition to state governments, and the spreading of rumors or falsehoods. Loyalty oaths became universal. Neighbors informed on each other. Local committees of safety jailed any suspects they chose. Militias disarmed suspected Tories. Townspeople seized their property and banished them. Local judges such as Virginia's Charles Lynch (whence the term "lynch laws") looked the other way or positively encouraged mob rule. A Loyalist newspaper summed up: "The Cry was for Liberty—Lord, what a fuss! But pray, how much Liberty left they for us?"[45]

Most Loyalists lived in the middle colonies, but Georgia had the highest percentage, and significant pockets of Tories inhabited South Carolina and the Appalachian foothills. They consisted of a variety of people who either preferred the old arrangements under the crown or else feared or despised the scoundrels busy seizing control in the name of patriotism. Tories might be farmers on the old estates of the Hudson, Germans to whom King George's yoke seemed light, urban dwellers with official or business ties to the British establishment, Highland Scots, Quakers pleading for reconciliation, or pious Anglicans (not always a contradiction in terms). In all the colonies recent immigrants were far more prone to be loyal. But their very disparateness precluded coordination. Violent confrontations were rare except in the Carolina back country. Most Tories were just at the mercy of the people around them unless British troops happened to be there to shelter them. But the presence of redcoats was harmful if temporary, because anyone content under occupation was exposed to reprisal as soon as the British departed. Finally, state governments were not above harrying Tories just to sequester their land, which they awarded to military officers or sold off to reduce their war debt.

That Americans suspended their commitment to human rights under conditions of civil war is hardly surprising. Moreover, there were no reigns of terror, large-scale pogroms, or forced deportations: the Tories left on their own. Americans also ceased the harassment as soon as the war was over and reacted with disgust in the following decade when far milder measures were imposed under the Alien and Sedition Acts. Americans thus passed the test: they did not permit emergency acts of repression to ruin the larger cause. But the fact remains the thirteen states were effectively cleansed of all whites who opposed the hustling republic they meant to establish. If Tories who had to start over in Canada, the Bahamas, or England took any solace, it was likely the bitter one voiced by Harvard graduate and Anglican rector John Wiswall. He tried to cool passions in his hometown of Falmouth, Massachusetts, in 1775, but Patriot mobs forced his family to take refuge on a British ship where his wife and daughter died of food poisoning. In January 1776, Wiswall took ship for England. God alone, he reflected, could still this "madness" because the American people was altogether "too free and happy [ever] to be *contented* with its happiness."[46]

The entry of France and Spain into the war, combined with a series of upheavals in Britain itself between 1779 and 1781, made it appear the entire imperial project was on the verge of collapse. The Royal Navy now needed to patrol the Mediterranean, the West Indies, North America, and especially the English Channel lest the French invade Sussex or Ireland. Mindful that British force was spread thin, the Irish under Henry Grattan took the occasion to challenge Parliament's authority, Scottish and English dissenters under Lord George Gordon rioted against a 1780 act of toleration for Catholics, and the Wilkesite Yorkshire Association agitated for electoral reform. Wilkes himself railed against the conduct of the war while the Rockingham Whigs argued for the withdrawal of British forces from America. Lord North—exhausted, ill, and despondent—begged to resign, but George III's nerve held steady. He firmly believed if America broke free, the West Indies and Ireland would do so as well and England become "a poor island indeed."[47]

Still, the widening of the war required a more economical strategy. In March 1778 the king approved one. Sir Henry Clinton, who replaced Howe in command, was ordered to evacuate Philadelphia, transfer soldiers and ships to the West Indies, and launch modest amphibious invasions of Georgia and the

Carolinas on the assumption that southern Loyalists were itching to flock to the Union Jack. The first move got under way in June when ten thousand redcoats and Hessians, three thousand Tories, and an immense supply train floated across the Delaware into New Jersey. The retreat was risky. Washington rousted his army out of Valley Forge in hopes of attacking the vulnerable enemy. He was thwarted by the inexcusable paralysis of General Charles Lee, who held back and even ordered retreats, causing Lafayette, Wayne, and Knox to fume. When Washington arrived at the front, he sacked Lee, rallied the Continentals, and deployed before Monmouth Courthouse. The fierce, confused battle that followed ended in a draw. Clinton and Cornwallis resumed their retreat to New York unmolested. But so impressed were they by the Continentals' new discipline (Steuben had done his work well), the redcoats never ventured out of Manhattan again. Washington then tried to keep up momentum by ordering Continentals in New England to coordinate with a French fleet and recapture Newport, Rhode Island. But John Sullivan was on hand again to foul that up. He quarreled with the French admiral such that the latter (citing storm damage to his ships) sailed away without landing his four thousand troops. When five thousand Yankee militia promptly deserted Sullivan, only the "desperate valor" of an all-Negro Rhode Island regiment saved his command.

The war in the north was thus stalemated by 1779 while the southern campaigns were only beginning. But during the transition between them a flurry of combat on the frontier ensured that whoever emerged victorious in this war it would *not* be the Native Americans. In the beginning all the tribes from the Six Nations in the north to the Cherokees in the south were confused by the fratricide of the English and tried to stay out of it. But Indians were pressured to take sides and their reliance on trade with the whites made neutrality impossible. Most tribes gravitated toward the British because the Americans both coveted their land and failed to supply promised provisions. One tribe that did side with Congress, the Delawares, were betrayed by militia commander Edward Hand, whose "squaw campaigns" consisted of attacking Delaware camps when only women and children were present. The Iroquois Nations split down the middle and fell to killing each other. But American Tories John and Walter Butler teamed up with Thayendanega, an educated chief of the Mohawks, to do real damage to the Patriot cause. In 1777 and 1778, Butler's Rangers terrorized the Wyoming Valley, scalping, burning crops, and carrying off women and children while Washington seethed helplessly just 150 miles to the south.[48] Out at Detroit, British Colonel Henry Hamilton, "the hair buyer," paid Indians handsomely for American scalps while pioneers cried to Congress in vain.[49]

So George Rogers Clark, a twenty-five-year-old surveyor in wild Kentucky, took it upon himself to save his—and Virginia's—dreams of western empire. He won hearty approval from Governor Patrick Henry. Setting out from Pittsburgh with a mere 175 frontiersmen on flatboats, the six-foot-tall red-head descended the Ohio River to Illinois and within a month "liberated" the astonished French *habitants* in Kaskaskia, Cahokia, and Vincennes from their British garrisons. Hamilton recaptured Vincennes, but Clark led his men back there on a punishing march across flood plains neck-deep in water. They arrived frigid, starving, and weak. But Clark tricked Hamilton into surrender by lighting fires, raising banners, and making his force appear four times its size. He also had Indian prisoners tomahawked in view of the fort to demonstrate the price of resistance.

Clark said the only way to gain a name among Indians was to "excel them in barbarity." John Sullivan took that to heart when Washington asked him to dispose of the Indian threat, secure the Wyoming Valley's harvest, and strengthen postwar American claims to the frontier. Fearful of adding another flop to his war record, Sullivan refused to move up the Susquehanna River into New York until he gathered four thousand men, artillery, and a huge store of equipment. Butler's Rangers and Iroquois had to withdraw before such a force, but did capture two scouts whose severed heads, limbs, and genitals they left on the trail as a warning. Sullivan was undeterred: his army marched methodically up and down the Finger Lakes region, paused to admire the Six Nations' long-houses, neatly arrayed fields of beans, corn, and squash, and well-tended orchards, then set all aflame. "I flatter myself," Sullivan informed Congress, "that the orders with which I was entrusted are fully executed." He burned forty towns and 160,000 bushels of crops, forcing the survivors to flee to the British at Fort Niagara. Hundreds more Iroquois perished that winter when blizzards covered western New York with five feet of snow. But since Sullivan never even tried to capture Niagara as Washington hoped, Iroquois raiders returned in the spring more bloodthirsty than ever. Sullivan laid waste the greatest Indian civilization in eastern America to no strategic purpose at all.[50]

Britain's southern offensive began in November 1778, when thirty-five hundred redcoats shipped out from New York and joined with a column of Florida rangers under Augustin Prevost to conquer Savannah. The following year a bold, but futile Franco-American counterattack there cost eight hundred lives, including that of the dashing Polish volunteer Casimir Pulaski. In the meantime, Prevost left off sacking plantations and laid siege to Charleston where General Benjamin Lincoln's Continentals dug earthworks in a heat wave surpassing 100 degrees. But a second British amphibious force, this time under Clinton himself, slowly but surely invested the forts while British warships slipped past Fort Moultrie and trained their guns on the strand. In May 1780 Lincoln surrendered the port, a great cache of supplies, and five thousand soldiers. William Moultrie openly wept.[51]

Clinton exulted. Having forced the gate to the southern colonies, he figured just a few thousand redcoats could pacify the south, raise an infantry among Loyalists, and march unimpeded to the Chesapeake. "There are few men in South Carolina," boasted Clinton, "who are not either our prisoners or in arms with us." Indeed, he was so cocky about the campaign he withdrew forty-five hundred redcoats from Charleston, turned the theater over to Cornwallis and Colonel Banastre "Bloody" Tarleton, and sailed back to New York in June. In fact, Britain's "southern strategy" had three glaring flaws. The French fleet in the West Indies posed a constant threat to communications and supply. The British were still obliged to maintain an army in New York to prevent Washington from reinforcing the south. Most telling, their reliance on Tories was fanciful. Lukewarm Loyalists were loath to declare at all, while fiery Loyalists waged partisan war with such savagery they aroused even more Patriot partisans to enter the fray.[52]

The flaws in British strategy were not apparent at first thanks to the blunders of Horatio Gates. Widely popular since Saratoga, he was picked by Congress to march south with a ragged militia force leavened by the crack Maryland and Delaware lines. Crossing three states on foot was trying enough for his men, but Gates made matters worse by insisting on a direct route across counties already picked clean by foragers. His army was thus nearly prostrate when it bumped into Cornwallis near Camden, South Carolina, on a sweltering day in mid-August. Against the advice of his staff Gates ordered a night march and immediate attack. The raw militia broke and ran at the first exchange—as Gates himself did—leaving Baron de Kalb and his veterans to die covering their retreat. When the army reassembled in North Carolina, just seven hundred soldiers remained.[53]

Cornwallis had every reason to think the road to Virginia wide open. But unforeseen events revealed to the able European general how little he understood this war. The first surprise happened just after Camden when a mere seventeen horsemen in buckskin burst from the swamps at first light to capture a British column escorting prisoners to Charleston. Thus did Francis "The Swamp Fox" Marion introduce redcoats to the hit-and-run warfare that cut their supply lines and made pacification a farce. Marion was a small, violent man of Huguenot extraction, a slave owner and intense hater of Indians. But however unsympathetic today, he and other Patriot partisans, such as Thomas "The Gamecock" Sumter, earned their totemic nicknames with tactical brilliance, crazy courage, and charisma. They made life hellish for British and Tories.[54] Another surprise confounded Cornwallis in October when he ordered eleven hundred Loyalists under Major Patrick Ferguson into the Carolina hill country. His idea was to make the "over-mountain men" submit to royal authority, thereby securing his army's flank on its triumphant march north. But Ferguson stupidly sent before him a warning to the mountaineers that if they resisted he would burn their cabins and kill them like Indians. He thus achieved something Congress itself never could: he raised the highlands for the Patriot cause. Like Scottish clans the mountaineers mustered from far and wide, every man armed, horsed, and victualed on cracked corn and game. They soon cornered Ferguson at King's Mountain, South Carolina, charged up the slopes, and killed or captured his Tories—*all* of them. Needless to say, British recruitment tailed off rather sharply thereafter.

The third setback Cornwallis suffered was a decision by Congress to set aside politics for a change and permit Washington to select his own replacement for Gates. So it was Nathanael Greene arrived in Charlotte to command the southern front on December 2, 1780.

Greene was a fifth generation Rhode Island Quaker whose strict father expected him to replicate his own life of piety and management of the family's foundry and mills. But three rival attractions lured Nathanael away: books on mathematics and history, some of which he obtained from Knox's shop up in Boston; girls and dancing, which his father deplored; and the Patriot cause, especially after his neighbors burned the British revenue cutter *Gaspée* in 1772. Two years later Greene committed the unpardonable Quaker sins of admiring some drilling militia and "marrying out." His meeting expelled him. So Greene had no scruples about volunteering to fight after Lexington and Concord. But to his genuine surprise the Rhode Island assembly asked him to serve, not as a private, but as brigadier general. Why not? Greene was thirty-two, educated, and socially prominent. His stature, square face, and honest, determined gaze certainly made him look the part. His administrative skills were well known. In any case the assembly's first two nominees turned down the job. Greene, "The Fighting Quaker," thus won his spurs by just showing up. In the first of what soon was a ream of passionate love letters he wrote to his bride: "My bosom is knitted to yours by all the gentle feelings that inspire the softest sentiments of conjugal love. It had been happy for me if I could have lived a private life in peace and plenty. . . . But the injury done my country, and the chains of slavery forging for posterity, call me forth to defend our common rights, and repel the bold invaders of the sons of freedom. I hope the righteous God that rules the world will bless the armies of America. . . . Your loving husband, N. GREENE."[55]

During the siege of Boston, Washington noticed the relative smartness of the Rhode Island camp and named Greene to his personal staff. Over the course of four years he became Washington's confidante, fought in all the major campaigns, and learned combined arms operations by observing Knox's artillery, Kosciuszko's engineers, and Steuben's infantry. After Valley Forge, Greene also assumed the thankless job of quartermaster general and thus learned how to supply armies in the field. Even though Washington was loath to lose him, Greene was his obvious choice to redeem the southern campaign.

What of the girl he left behind? Well, he did not exactly leave her behind because officers' wives often joined their husbands, especially in winter quarters. But the irrepressible Catherine ("Caty" or "Kitty") Greene would not have stayed home on any excuse. She lacked the education and piercing intelligence of Abigail Adams, and had little of Martha Washington's benign dignity. But all the more becoming to an American "first lady" were qualities Caty displayed in abundance, including gaiety, charm, cheek, guile, and the nerve of a jewelry thief. She was at once devoted wife, mother, party girl, speculator, promoter, and—for her outrageous flirtations—the toast of two armies.

Born on misty Block Island, twelve miles out to sea from Newport, Catherine Littlefield might have seemed doomed to an isolated, monotonous life. But after her mother died she was sent to live with her aunt in East Greenwich just one block from the Boston Post Road. She was named for that aunt, resembled the aunt, and obviously emulated her, too. For Aunt Catherine reveled in entertainments and balls, preferred the company of men, loved to tease suitors (not least Benjamin Franklin), showed no interest in religion, and ended up wedding a

Greene.[56] A "small brunette with high color, a vivacious expression, and a snapping pair of dark eyes," Caty was twenty-one when she carried Nathanael back to the house on Block Island where they could drink and dance at far remove from his Quaker family. They were married within months. In 1775 Caty joined her husband with the army at Boston and immediately won almost parental affection from George and Martha Washington. She also entranced every officer in the camp, delighted when they danced and "took liberties" with her. She also got pregnant, presumably by Nathanael. The next year Caty left her firstborn (named George Washington Greene) with family, and followed the troops to Brooklyn. There she was fascinated to observe Tories being tarred and feathered and soldiers being reeled in by prostitutes. The British invasion chased her back to Rhode Island, where she gave birth to her second child, Martha Washington Greene. Then she rejoined the army at Morristown.

Caty probably did her greatest service to the American cause at Valley Forge. She nursed the sick and wounded. She insisted on music and mirth every evening in officers' quarters: even Washington danced with her once for three hours non-stop. Europeans especially adored her because she spoke *un peu de français* and swooned over aristocrats. Needless to say, rumors and scandals orbited Caty like planets around a sun, but they were rendered irrelevant by the unfailing trust Nathanael displayed. Even after he was sent south and received her letter warning of the consequences of a long separation, he never showed jealousy or questioned the paternity of her war babies (there would be five in all). Caty was Caty, and he adored her.[57]

Could anyone salvage the war in the south? Greene was dubious, and his stopover in Richmond made him even more pessimistic. He expected reinforcements and supplies from the largest and so far unmolested state of Virginia. But thanks to the indigence of its new governor, Thomas Jefferson, Virginia mustered only a third of the men, wagons, and provisions requested by Congress.[58] Hence the "army" Greene reviewed in Charlotte had just eight hundred men fit for duty, three days of rations, and no money. But after one night of briefings, a staff officer marveled, Greene understood the army's logistical problems "better than Gates had done in the whole period of his command." Greene inherited or attracted an array of outstanding officers, including "Old Wagoner" Morgan, Henry "Light Horse Harry" Lee (father of Robert E. Lee), and cavalry Colonel William Washington, a cousin of George. Greene also valued his precious core of Delaware and Maryland regulars, knew how to get the most from untrained militia, and sent envoys to keep peace with the Cherokees. Finally, he sent a courier into the swamps of the Great Pee Dee River where Francis Marion read with approval his proposal for coordinated action between partisans and the army. Then Greene huddled, ticked off his handicaps, and judged that the only way to defeat Cornwallis was to hustle him.

Less than three weeks after his arrival, Greene ordered Morgan and Washington to maneuver far to the west beyond King's Mountain while he drifted eastward to the Pee Dee with his remaining companies. Cornwallis received word of Morgan's maneuver—he was meant to—and could not make sense of it. No sane commander divided his force in the face of a superior enemy! Either this was a feint or else Greene had been reinforced. Whichever it was, Cornwallis dared not move his main army west lest he expose his supply line and bases all the way back to Charleston. So he played the sucker just as Greene intended and sent west only a strong reconnaissance force under the hated cavalryman Tarleton. Morgan, awaiting him quietly in a pasture known as The Cowpens, prepared a ruse of his own. When the British attacked, the Patriot militia he placed at the center feigned a collapse. The British, thinking this was Camden all over again, stormed up the hill only to find themselves enfiladed by disciplined Continentals raking their own front and flanks. After one hundred were killed, seven hundred more redcoats threw down their muskets.[59]

Cornwallis then realized his error, but by the time his main army arrived in pursuit, Morgan had reunited with Greene and begun a leisurely pullback to Virginia. Again Cornwallis took the bait, allowing himself to be lured far from his bases while Lee's and Marion's raiders played hob with his supply trains. On March 15, 1781, he at last forced battle on Greene, or so he thought. In fact, the Continentals had finally received reinforcements from Virginia and chose to make a stand at Guilford Courthouse (now Greensboro, North Carolina). The Americans again tried the "panicked militia" trick, but this time the trap failed to close. A furious free-for-all ensued until Cornwallis drove both armies off the field with indiscriminate cannonades. Having lost a fourth of his army Cornwallis drew off to Wilmington, North Carolina, to lick wounds and link up with the navy. That allowed Greene, after a respite, to tiptoe back into South Carolina and renew contact with Marion. At Hobkirk's Hill, Ninety-Six, Monck's Corner, Eutaw Springs, and a dozen lesser actions the Continentals struck at the British network of posts. Never did Greene try to take them by storm because he knew costly victories meant long-term defeat. But he and the Patriot partisans gradually took command of the countryside until the British abandoned their outposts as untenable. By summer 1781 nothing remained to them but Savannah and Charleston. Cornwallis concluded the campaign might be redeemed only if he invaded Virginia and cut Greene's army off from its source of men and supplies: the exact *opposite* train of events from that envisioned in Clinton's original plan.

Greene's alchemical maneuvers were the turning point of the war. But for Washington 1780 was the most nervous year yet. It began in the icy winter when mutinies broke in some ranks. They were led for the most part by soldiers tired of going unpaid while their families at home were in poverty. Congress had issued $241 million dollars in paper money and the states millions more, but by 1780 "Continentals" had lost 95 percent of their value. Inflation was so bad even those with hard currency were clobbered. The wholesale price of a ton of iron, for instance, rose from £29 in 1775 to £202 in 1778 and £2,601 in 1780. Congress spent huge sums just in anticipation of new foreign loans that Franklin and Deane might or might not procure. Superintendent of Finance Robert Morris did his best for the cause, but was not above exploiting his inside intelligence to buy up precious supplies, sell them to the army at inflated prices, then patriotically lend part of his profits to Congress. Many Continental and state representatives were corrupt or self-interested, speculating in land, bonds, war contracts, and Tory estates. So tawdry did the whole business become, General McDougall testified before Congress in August, the war for liberty had degenerated into a grab for empire and property. Soldiers had a right to expect "some of that property which the citizen seeks and which the army protects for him."[60] But niggling efforts by Congress to examine the books of quartermasters only magnified the frustration of field officers. One thus angered was Benedict Arnold, who succumbed to the blandishments of his beautiful Tory wife and turned traitor in September 1780. By the end of the year he commanded a British force in the heart of Virginia.[61]

Thankfully, some financial respite arrived in 1780 when a Polish Jew, Haym Solomon, escaped from a British jail in New York. He was twice arrested for espionage, but now was free to resume his brilliant mercantile career in Philadelphia. Solomon gladly invested all the profits he made in the Patriot cause and served as conduit for new subsidies from the French and Dutch because he was the only American they were willing to trust. The most hopeful event of the year, however, was the arrival of Donatien, comte de Rochambeau, with six thousand French soldiers at Newport, which the British had left.

Concerned about their seaborne communications, however, the elegant French commanders did not budge except to dance with a very pleased Caty Greene in her hometown.

Washington was at a loss. He neither dared to attack heavily fortified New York nor leave the vicinity lest Clinton's army break out for points unknown. But he had to do something in May 1781, when Cornwallis emerged from his winter quarters and linked up with Arnold in Washington's native Virginia. Tarleton's Legion pillaged inland at will and missed by ten minutes capturing Governor Jefferson, who thought himself safe in Charlottesville. Happily, Washington did persuade Rochambeau to march his white-coated infantry overland and join up with the Continentals at Dobbs Ferry, New York. That allowed Washington to release a token force under Mad Anthony Wayne to help Lafayette and Steuben duel with Tarleton. But Washington's real coup was to flummox Clinton with strategic deception. The Continentals' intelligence service, ably led by Benjamin Tallmadge, repeatedly fed false reports to the British about Washington's preparations to assault New York City.[62] Clinton grew needlessly insecure and as a result sent Cornwallis a series of confusing dispatches. Stay in Virginia and force battle. No, reoccupy Philadelphia if you think it wise. No, prepare to ship three thousand men to strengthen New York. Poor Cornwallis decided to repair to Yorktown on the coast and wait for Clinton to make up his mind.

Washington and Rochambeau put their heads together, but they too lacked a plan until a courier arrived with news of a stunning opportunity. A French fleet under Admiral François, comte de Grasse, was under sail for the Chesapeake with twenty-eight ships of the line and three thousand more troops. But he could only remain on station until mid-October when he must return to the West Indies. Rochambeau was hot to march south, rendezvous with de Grasse, and endeavor to capture Cornwallis' army. Washington wondered whether their armies could possibly march from New York to Virginia in time, whether sufficient supplies could be scrounged on the way, whether Congress could afford such an elaborate campaign, whether Cornwallis would still be there when they arrived, and above all whether the Royal Navy would interdict de Grasse and render the whole campaign futile. When Rochambeau generously turned over half his own war chest to the Americans, Washington, to his great credit, accepted the gamble.

The two armies crossed the Hudson in the third week of August and marched south through Philadelphia to the north end of Chesapeake Bay.

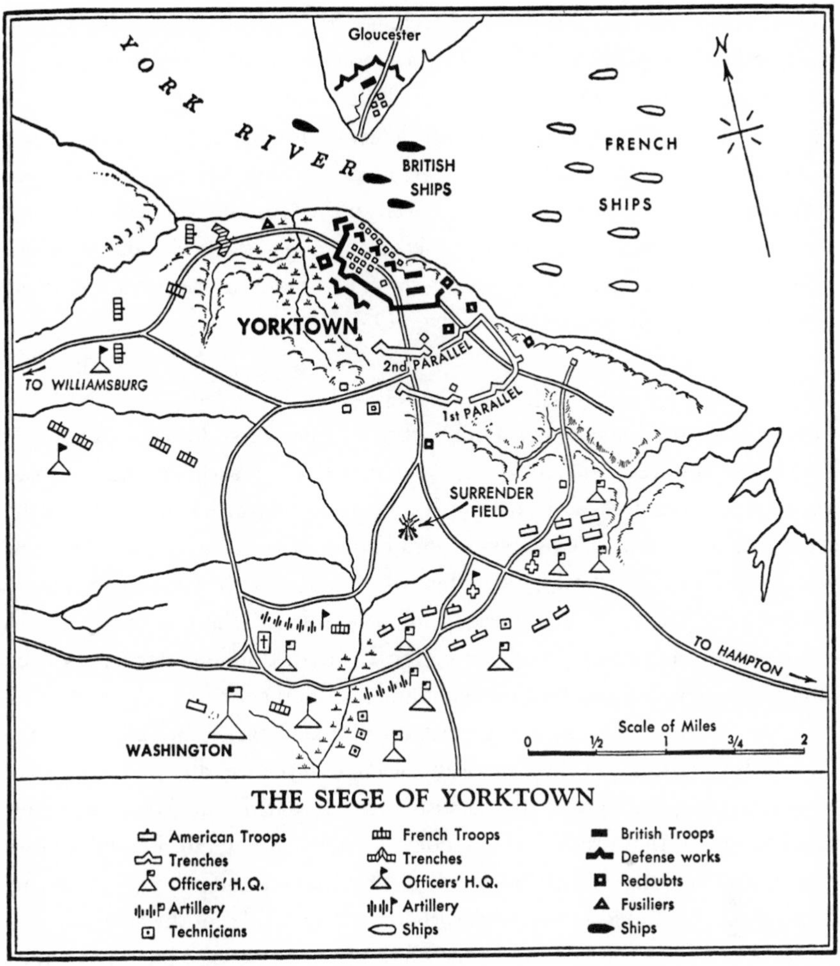
Gloucester
YORK RIVER
BRITISH SHIPS
FRENCH SHIPS
N
YORKTOWN
2nd PARALLEL
1st PARALLEL
TO WILLIAMSBURG
SURRENDER FIELD
TO HAMPTON
WASHINGTON
Scale of Miles
0 ½ 1 3/4 2
American Troops
Trenches
Officers' H.Q.
Artillery
Technicians
French Troops
Trenches
Officers' H.Q.
Artillery
Ships
British Troops
Defense works
Redoubts
Fusiliers
Ships
THE SIEGE OF YORKTOWN

Marbleheaders and doughty Maryland boatmen ferried most of the host, boat by boat, to the mouth of the James River. There they were greeted by the greatly relieved Lafayette and Wayne, who had kept watch on Cornwallis more by bluff than coercion. Washington paid a brief visit to Mount Vernon after an absence of more than five years, then took command of the siege outside Yorktown. But the whole campaign would be wasted if the Royal Navy came to its army's rescue. "What news from the sea?" became a daily refrain, but there was no news until, on September 15, magnificent news. The British fleet had indeed challenged de Grasse, but too late: the French had won the race to the

Chesapeake capes and after a brief exchange the British ships showed them their heels. Cornwallis was trapped by a French navy, two French armies, and one American army led in part by Frenchmen and trained in good part by a Prussian and a Pole. Even many of Knox's cannons and mortars, which pounded Yorktown incessantly, were cast in France. But when Cornwallis sued for terms Rochambeau generously deferred to the Continentals, whose fight it was and whose refusal to quit over six trying years made the day possible. Accordingly, the instrument of surrender read: "Done in the trenches before Yorktown, in Virginia, October 19, 1781—G. Washington."[63]

The British continued to fight for Gibraltar and West Indian islands, but Parliament resolved in February 1782 to make peace with the Americans.[64] Lord North resigned the next month and in April Lord Shelburne sent an agent to Paris to parley. Congress in turn appointed a peace commission composed of Franklin, Adams, Jay, Jefferson, and South Carolinian Henry Laurens. But Jefferson again pleaded his wife's illness (she was in fact dying) and Laurens was awaiting release from the Tower of London after having been captured at sea. So the task of negotiating with the British fell to Adams, Franklin, and Jay, all of whom distrusted or rankled each other as well as the French. But wait: hadn't the Americans pledged in their treaty with France not to negotiate separately with the British? Yes, they had, but Adams was prepared to ignore that promise if London was ready to bargain. Franklin, however, knew that the French alliance was America's principal *leverage* in any negotiation with London. So he cleverly played both sides of the channel.[65]

Problems arose because the French indulged ambitions of their own which the British were loath to grant, and because Vergennes was plotting to keep the United States weak and dependent by fixing their western frontier at the Appalachians. Moreover, the French promised Spain they would not conclude peace until Gibraltar was captured. Finally, the Americans had good reason to suspect Vergennes was negotiating with all parties behind their backs, even as they themselves did so behind his back. At length, Franklin and Jay informed Lord Shelburne's agent they were willing to negotiate secretly but only on condition London concede *a priori* the colonies' independence. Shelburne resisted, but finally agreed late in July in the hope of eroding the bargaining positions of France and Spain. Even then progress was plodding due to a kidney stone that sidelined Franklin and to Jay's distrust of all parties. On November 30, 1782, however, the British and Americans finally agreed on a draft, the French being "informed" one day before. The terms of this Anglo-American truce were so generous Shelburne was forced to resign. But the new cabinet acquiesced in the pact in order to focus on negotiations with France, Spain, and the Netherlands. Hence, the final Peace of Paris signed September 3, 1783, contained the birth certificate of the United States. The new nation was endowed with all the lands east of the Mississippi River south of Canada and north of Florida, which reverted to Spain. The British also granted New Englanders the valuable right to fish the Grand Banks, receiving in return the unlikely promise that British creditors and Tories would find relief in American courts.

The fires of war, except for hot embers that continued to flare in the southern back country, were extinguished by 1783. Washington's officers and soldiers wanted to go home, but not before they received the back pay, pensions, bounties, or land grants they had been promised. Unfortunately, Congress had no hard cash and no source of revenue despite Robert Morris' best efforts. In 1781 he won a charter to open the Bank of North America to handle public accounts, issue notes, and make loans to the government. (Of course, Morris and his partners stood to make paper fortunes if a solvent bank redeemed the Continental bonds they gobbled up for pennies on the dollar.) Unfortunately, the revenue scheme approved by Congress—a 5 percent duty on foreign imports—required the states' unanimous approval. Little Rhode Island blocked it. At that point, in January 1783, nationalists such as Morris and Alexander Hamilton joined with angry generals including Gates, McDougall, and Lincoln to warn the army might *not* disband until it got satisfaction. Soon rumors of a conspiracy in the Continental camp at Newburgh, New York, lent verisimilitude to talk of a coup. One last time everything depended on Washington. He confronted the alleged plotters in March 1783, perished the thought of his army betraying the cause it had bled for, and reduced some old comrades to tears by asking their pardon while he put on his spectacles: "I have grown gray in the service of my country and now feel myself growing blind." The mutinous mood dispelled. But all Morris managed to come up with was a month's pay for enlisted men and three months' pay in promissory notes for officers. Begging and borrowing just to get home, the weary Continentals disbanded.[66]

Washington, too, reckoned what Congress owed him. He asked for no salary, but totted his wartime expenses, after some soul-searching included Martha's as well, and submitted them on the first of July: £8,422, 22 shillings, and 4 pence. Then he took a vacation, his first in eight years, to explore New York state by horse, canoe, and on foot. He surveyed Saratoga, imagined a canal linking the Hudson River to Lake Erie, and added some land on the Mohawk to his speculative portfolio. He pined for Mount Vernon, but also confessed in a letter, "I shall not rest contented till I have explored the western country, and traversed those lines (or a great part of them) which have given bounds to a New Empire."[67]

A new empire, or thirteen anemic and squabbling republics bereft of a government, revenue, and now an army? Due to the zeal and will of a small minority of the former colonists, the United States had fulfilled Paine's mission of wresting the power to make laws away from the tyrants in London. But what laws, if any, could they manage to make for themselves? Washington had reason to ponder when he rode to Annapolis in December to receive the thanks of Congress and resign his commission. Annapolis: because some militiamen and regulars had refused to be fobbed off by funny money and pledges and marched on Independence Hall. Pennsylvania's executive council talked them out of a violent "Pride's Purge" (when Cromwell's soldiers invaded Parliament). Yet Congress was frightened enough to flee Philadelphia for Princeton, then Annapolis, Trenton, and finally New York, often unable to muster a quorum. Washington predicted "the worst consequences from a half-starved, limping government, always moving on crutches and tottering at every step."[68] But the whole point of the rebellion was to free the colonies from distant authority so they might get to work realizing their American dreams. If the states refused to grant any power to a central authority in wartime, what were the chances they would do so in peacetime? If the people spurned communal sacrifice while their liberty was in peril, what were the chances they would recover the "spirit of '75" now that private opportunity was secure?

The chances were slim unless the states and people could be scared, bribed, bullied, duped—or persuaded—into believing their *local* liberties and *private* pursuits of happiness required a national government. But that was only the prelude to two harder tasks. The first was to design a national government that did not repress and indeed harnessed the raw human nature of a free people. The second was to wrap that naked statue of wrestling interests in such resplendent rhetorical raiment that Americans could feel good about doing well, indeed make their nationhood a sort of religion. The British and French could not imagine such a thing. To them raw human nature was the solvent of order. That is why they concluded from America's sloppy war effort these

"United States" could not long survive. If instead they had asked how Americans managed to win *despite* their untidy behavior, the truth of Burke's lesson to Parliament might have sunk in. A people so loving of liberty, steeped in religion, rife with smart lawyers, and "full of chicane" would figure out how to make even vice the servant of virtue.

# FEDERALISTS, ANTIS, VESTALS, AND VICTIMS

## *The Brilliant Coups That Begat the Constitution, 1783–1790*

*F*ive feet six inches did not make a man small in the eighteenth century, but his frail frame, girlish features, and treble voice made James Madison, Jr., seem so. He also suffered from epileptoid hysteria. Hence the lad spent his youth at Montpelier, the family's Piedmont plantation near the Blue Ridge, reading books rather than riding, hunting, and dancing. When time came for college James, Sr., nixed William and Mary. He thought steamy Williamsburg too unhealthy for his son's constitution and its faculty far too Anglican. The Presbyterian College of New Jersey, however, boasted a dynamic new president, John Witherspoon, welcomed students from all the colonies (arguably making it the first American institution), and even charged the lowest tuition. So "Jemmy," in 1769, headed for Princeton.

The future president of the United States, needless to say, became Witherspoon's most famous ex-student. But during his tenure, from 1768 to 1794, Witherspoon also educated a future vice president, three Supreme Court justices, forty-nine congressmen, twenty-eight senators, and scores of governors and state legislators. How ironic then that Princeton's trustees' decision to hire him was based on a misconception. They thought he was an evangelical in the tradition of Jonathan Edwards. Only after they paid his way over from Scotland did they learn Witherspoon was not a (by now) old-fashioned product of the

"Great Awakening," but a novel exponent of the Scottish Enlightenment. For young minds such as Madison's that made all the difference.

There was no such thing as *the* Enlightenment. Rather, that term and its continental counterparts *éclaircissement* and *Aufklärung* bore witness to the diverse efforts made to uncover through reason the natural laws governing human behavior just as Newton revealed the laws of the physical world. Since eighteenth-century rationalists operated across political, religious, and linguistic divides they advanced radically different conclusions about epistemology, human nature, morality, and politics. Was mankind fundamentally selfish and brutal or benign and peaceful? Were society, property, and government the remedies for human corruption or the causes of it? Did human beings find freedom in order, or order in freedom? Could a reasonable morality to which men of all faiths might adhere be deduced from first principles or induced from experience? Or was reason itself a fallible tool or human beings in fact creatures of passion? Depending on the answers to those questions and more, one might arrive at diametrically opposed programs for the improvement of the human condition.

Scots intellectuals were uniquely placed to absorb all the strains of Enlightenment thought. Their country was linked to England, but retained its old ties to France and (via Calvinism) the Netherlands. Their country was poor, stripped of ancient traditions, and in desperate need of new ideas. Above all, Scottish savants learned how contingent, how fragile, was civilization itself when the Highland clans erupted in the Jacobite revolt of 1745. Francis Hutcheson, who first brought enlightened ideas over from Dublin, died during "the '45." Ian MacLaurin, who taught the Scots calculus, worked himself to death readying Edinburgh for a siege. Adam Smith, David Hume, Thomas Reid, Adam Ferguson, and Witherspoon—all philosophers in their twenties and thirties—admitted the revolt shaped their intellectual growth. But whatever the causes of their "sudden burst of genius," as Dugald Stewart named it, the Scottish savants arrived at truths eluding most of their peers in Europe. They saw human beings as a volatile mixture of reason and passion. They observed how men and women both made history and were made by it. They learned to temper dreams of what humanity might become with an appreciation of the immutability of human nature. They looked at themselves and wild Highlanders alike, admitting even the most erudite scholar could err and even an ignorant herdsman grasp truth. They became, in short, consummate realists who imagined no stylized states of nature or utopias crafted by man. They believed instead in what Reid called *common sense:* the innate power common to *all* human beings to apprehend reality through the senses, mind, intuition, and conscience and then exploit that grip on reality to advance what Hutcheson called the *pursuit of happiness.* A perfect society was impossible, but common sense taught that the least bad society was one that freed each person's passion for improvement and so made possible a measure of freedom and progress for all.[1]

Witherspoon saw no contradiction between "common sense philosophy" and Christian doctrine. That human beings were sinners was an empirical fact: ever met anyone perfect? But sin just as obviously co-existed in man with a moral sense and discernment. Witherspoon thus had no use for revivalists who spurned science and rationalism or for skeptics like Hume who considered heresy a mark of "vast learning and uncommon worth." God's handiwork made no sense unless faith and reason were partners, while civil and religious liberty were two sides of the same coin. That such liberty was said to prevail in New Jersey intrigued Witherspoon. But he did not answer Princeton's call until Dr. Benjamin Rush, completing his studies at Edinburgh, persuaded Mrs. Witherspoon to leave the bonnie brae and cross an ocean.[2]

Like Whitefield and Wilkes, Witherspoon was both "intolerably homely" and radiant with charisma. Before resistance could gather, he transformed Princeton by sweeping away the New Light Edwardsian faculty, inserting rhetoric and science into the curriculum, and requiring all students to take his critical seminar in moral philosophy. He reorganized the Presbyterian Church in the colonies and infused it with American patriotism. He attracted students of the caliber of Madison, John Dickinson, and Hugh Henry Brackenridge and Philip Freneau, the co-authors of a prophetic poem "The Rising Glory of America" (1771). Witherspoon helped organize New Jersey's Committee of Correspondence, served in the Continental Congress, and was the only clergyman to sign the Declaration of Independence. In his 1776 sermon, "The Dominion of Providence over the Passions of Men," he resisted British pretensions to rule simply "because they are men, and therefore liable to all the selfish bias inseparable from human nature." Americans' aspirations toward self-government, by contrast, allowed Witherspoon to imagine a new and great nation based on a "science of politics" and "that enlarged system called the balance of power."[3]

Madison relished Princeton's regimen. He rose at 5 A.M., prayed at 6, attended classes all day, and studied well into the night. What is more, he was proud of his reputation as a grind to judge by his ribald verse meant to tease a "lecherous rascal" in a rival club: "May whore & pimp & drink & swear, no more the garb of Christian wear." But mostly Madison drank in common sense philosophy and its emphasis on balance. Perhaps that was due to his own imbalance, not only from illness but eyes so out of focus he could not shave in a mirror without nicking his face. But no psychology is needed to explain Madison's glee over another simulacrum of balance that appeared in Nassau Hall in 1771. It was an orrery, a curious mechanical model of the solar system crafted by Philadelphia astronomer David Rittenhouse and purchased by Witherspoon. There, in a stately cabinet of polished wood and brass clockwork, the sun, moon, and planets appeared against the background of fixed stars. A handle rotated the planets while a chronometer recorded the passage of time. Madison was enthralled by the weights and gears simulating the gravitational forces driving the universe. That orrery became Madison's metaphor of a science of politics, and he left Princeton persuaded "the great law of proportion" governed all things in heaven and earth.[4]

Back home, Madison studied law and wrote in favor of independence. But more important, he served in Virginia's state convention and governor's council, which alerted him to something Jefferson, his political mentor, could not see. Virginia and the other states were so eager to undo the executive tyranny of the king they weighted the scales too heavily in favor of legislatures. In 1780, when Madison joined the Continental Congress, he spied another imbalance: the scales were also weighted too heavily on the side of the states vis-à-vis the national government. He pressed for ratification of the Articles of Confederation, but by war's end despaired of them. It was then he befriended a brilliant man several years younger but far more experienced and as loud and dynamic as Madison was reticent. In fact, this friend shared nothing in common with Madison save Scottish philosophy and the vision of a true national government.

Alexander Hamilton, in John Adams' uncharitable words, was the bastard son of a Scotch peddler. Hamilton liked to retort, inasmuch as that peddler was the son of a laird, he was of nobler birth than any other American founder. But that was irrelevant. What made Hamilton a great American, and America to a great degree Hamiltonian, was his determination to transcend humble origins and craft institutions allowing other poor men to do likewise. To him, true nobility attached to a nation that allowed *all* citizens to make the most of their God-given talents and chase riches. Sound crass? Not really, because money alone knows no social class, pedigree, race, or religion, while the creative pursuit of wealth fosters industry and commerce, expanding opportunity for all. But curiously Hamilton himself had little desire to amass wealth, choosing instead for his role model the Swiss financial wizard Jacques Necker. In 1783 Hamilton read his memoirs and zeroed in on Necker's moving appeal to men who were aware of their genius, but cramped in ordinary careers, to make the public good their private calling. Hamilton knew Necker was speaking to him. The source of happiness he pursued was not fortune, but the fame that would attach to the man who made America a land of opportunity for millions of homegrown and immigrant strivers far into the future. No wonder his biographers employ words such as odd, paradoxical, and romantic to describe his career. But most of Hamilton's contemporaries either suspected or misconstrued his intentions. They could not believe he had no ulterior motives.[5]

Rachel Faucett Lavien was sharp, gorgeous, and wayward, but a poor judge of men. Her first husband, John Michael Lavien (or Lavine), a merchant in the Danish West Indies, did not appreciate her "indecent and very suspicious" behavior and sued for divorce. Her second husband, James Hamilton, abandoned her and their two sons after learning that her estate reverted to Lavien upon her remarriage. Rachel herself then died of a fever in 1768, leaving the boys "beached" on the island of Nevis. So Alexander, born either in 1755 or 1757, apprenticed in the countinghouse of a New York firm and became one of those (once common, now unthinkable) teenaged prodigies who wheeled and dealed for cargoes with grizzled sea captains. The Reverend Hugh Knox, an Ulsterman educated at Princeton, discovered the boy in 1772 and taught him Presbyterian doctrine, Scottish philosophy, the blessings of work, the dangers of liquor, and the evils of slavery. He also sent him to school in New Jersey and encouraged his application to Princeton. Witherspoon turned him down. Myles Cooper of King's College did not, which is why Alexander Hamilton became a New Yorker. Within a year, the teenager was advocating the colonies' cause in lengthy essays worthy of the mature Dickinson, Adams, or Jefferson. When war broke out Hamilton enlisted and, thanks to Washington's keen eye for talent, landed on the commander's staff. In 1780 he won the hand of a general's daughter, Elizabeth Schuyler, and *entrée* into New York society. In 1781 he won glory as well by leading an assault on a British rampart that hastened Cornwallis' surrender. Hamilton even found time to send Robert Morris long letters suggesting ways to fix the United States' monetary woes. He then moved to Albany, obtained a license to practice law in just seven months, and was elected to the Continental Congress in November 1782. All that before his twenty-eighth (or was it his twenty-sixth) birthday.[6]

"What a country!" one might expect the West Indian orphan to cry. But Hamilton felt shame in his nation more keenly than pride in himself. As Washington's amanuensis he observed how the venality and inertia of profiteers and politicians kept the army in rags. To his friend Henry Laurens he privately declaimed the "epidemical spirit of extortion," wrote "I hate money making men," and again, "I hate Congress—I hate the army—I hate the world—I hate myself. The whole is a mass of fools and knaves. . . ." Upon studying law Hamilton also learned to despise the "cavilling petulance of an attorney," grousing that law was all about manipulating procedures, not administering justice. Given such disillusionment one might have expected the well-married war hero to retreat into domesticity. But again Hamilton spurned private pursuits of happiness to devote his outsized talents to the common weal. In a series of 1781 articles written under the *nom de plume* "The Continentalist," Hamilton seized on Hume's notion of "divided sovereignty." Before 1776 the British crown and Parliament had mocked the colonies' protests on the grounds that divided sovereignty was a contradiction in terms. But Hamilton saw what the colonists wanted *then*—local representative government within an empire led by a strong executive—was exactly what the thirteen states needed *now* if they were to survive. Yes, the states were sovereign in a sense, but would soon lose their freedom unless a strong "common sovereign" acted on behalf of them all. Nor was there any contradiction in that because Congress and the states alike derived their authority from *the people*. Finally, Hamilton found in Hume and his critics the clue to effective government: do not pretend human nature to be something it's not (that is, forget "republican virtue") and do not attempt to suppress human nature. Rather, fashion government so as to *encourage* individual greed for money, power, and prestige under sturdy legal procedures that do not dictate *what* people should strive for, but only *how* they must play the game. Thus did he devise a political counterpart to Adam Smith's "invisible hand." Thus did he seek to make corruption creative and—insofar as a reputation for honesty is an asset in business and politics—perhaps gnaw away at corruption over time.[7]


Given Americans had been at war for twenty-five of the previous forty-four years we may forgive them for taking a breather after the peace of 1783. But the remarkable fact about the era of the Articles of Confederation is not the sloth, but the exceptional speed with which Madison, Hamilton, and like-minded Federalists diagnosed the flaws in their government, drafted a new constitution, and rammed it through the reluctant states. To appreciate the magnitude of their achievement one need only recall that the colonists rebelled against Parliament in the name of local self-government, then turned their attention to local concerns even before the fighting ended. The so-called union formed in 1776 was a mere wartime alliance, did not function well even in war, and spawned only two national institutions one of which (the army) had disbanded and the other (Congress) proved impotent. So states had no choice but to rely on themselves to repair the war damage and restore their economies.

The damage was vast. Much of New York City was consumed by fire soon after the British occupation, making proud Broadway a noisome "canvas town" filled with rats, refugees, thieves, and prostitutes. Charleston was bombarded and burned. All ports lost population as Patriots and/or Tories fled enemy occupiers. Interior counties in New York, Pennsylvania, and the Carolinas were plundered and torched, reducing thousands of farmhouses and barns to black outlines in the mud. Luckier regions such as the Connecticut Valley, Lancaster County, and much of Virginia still suffered from shortages, especially of livestock. The Hessians brought with them a fly that blighted crops from New Hampshire to New Jersey. Iron production soared during the war, but that only caused widespread deforestation and erosion. Even fishing suffered as new dams and mills interfered with spawning salmon and alewives. Peace brought a sharp commercial depression as the British dumped huge quantities of goods on American docks to exploit pent-up demand and closed off their lucrative West Indian ports to now alien Yankee traders. Madison was especially angered by the earl of Sheffield's "Observations on the Commerce of the American States" (1783) predicting Britain's control over trade would reduce the United States to near-colonial status. From 1783 to 1785 the new nation ran a large deficit. New England's fishing, whaling, and shipbuilding industries languished. South Carolina's exports of rice and indigo temporarily collapsed, and tobacco planters went begging for markets.[8]

The passage was rough but, thanks to local initiative, brief. Since Congress lacked authority to regulate commerce, levy taxes, or issue currency to stimulate growth, states imposed their own tariffs and duties against goods from other nations and states. In larger, more self-sufficient ones such as Massachusetts, Pennsylvania, and Virginia, creditors formed coalitions to restore hard money and pay down public debt through taxes, partial repudiation, or elaborate

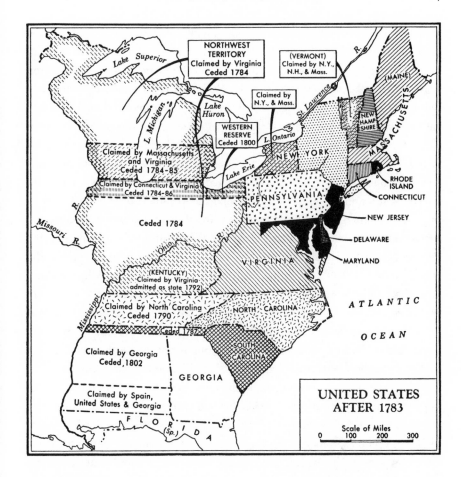

schemes to pay off bondholders with western land.[9] In smaller states, such as Rhode Island and Maryland, indebted small farmers and speculators obliged their assemblies to print more paper money and require creditors to accept it at face value. Bitter quarrels and pockets of poverty persisted. Somebody's ox was gored everywhere. But by the mid-1780s the depression was over, and by 1790 the nation's exports and internal commerce surpassed prewar levels. The trouble was, the states achieved recovery by declaring *de facto* independence from Congress. Hence their behavior inhibited the far more impressive growth that might follow if Americans could unite to fashion a national market and make favorable trade treaties with Europe.[10]

Demographic recovery was equally swift and problematical. During the war U.S. population declined from 2.6 to 2.4 million, but America's mothers made up that loss in about *thirty months*. Thanks also to new Scots, Irish, and German immigrants the nation approached 4 million by 1790. About nineteen of twenty Americans still lived on the land, but Philadelphia nevertheless grew from 30,000 to 42,000 over the decade, New York from 22,000 to 33,000, and Baltimore from 12,500 to 25,000. Then there was the frontier, which had been a haven from war for some and the principal prize in the war for many. In the Kentucky territory, nine new counties were established between 1776 and 1790, in the Tennessee territory six, in the uplands of Georgia, the Carolinas, and Virginia no less than eighty-six. The rugged men and women who cleared the forests within and beyond the Appalachians as yet made little contribution to the larger economic life of the nation. With the exception of occasional pig drives and flatboats of corn mash or whiskey poled upriver to Pittsburgh, they had no access to wider markets and little to sell at competitive prices. But nobody doubted America's future was on the frontier, which is why two hundred thousand Westerners and speculators eager to increase their numbers wielded leverage in the politics of the new nation. If Congress failed to protect the pioneers' interests against the British in the north, the Spaniards in the south, and Indians everywhere, Westerners might just secede and cut their own deals with foreign powers. In every case, therefore, be it finance, commerce, or western expansion, the crisis of nationhood in the 1780s was born not of prolonged depression, but of rapid *growth* beyond Congress' power to manage.[11]

Had Americans been a sated people content to bequeath their progeny such land and commerce as their forebears developed, the Articles of Confederation might, with a few amendments, have sufficed. But Americans were ambitious and increasing at a frenetic pace. So where Hamilton might imagine the United States an empire of commerce and industry, and Jefferson an empire of yeomen, everyone thought in terms of territorial growth. Without it a burgeoning people would be hemmed in, social conflicts would multiply, liberty would erode, and states would turn on each other. That is why the existential crisis of the 1780s had less to do with immediate, particular, economic interests than long-range, national, political interests.

Nothing illustrates the crisis more than the measures usually described as the one great *achievement* of Congress under the Articles of Confederation: the Northwest Ordinances designed to open the Ohio Country to settlement. To be sure, Americans gloated at first that Britain ceded all the land out to the Mississippi without so much as mentioning the original inhabitants of the region. That wrecked British prestige among Indians (shaming the crown, in

William Franklin's opinion) and seemed to acknowledge the American "Long Knives' " right of conquest. James Duane, mayor of New York and chairman of the Committee on Indian Affairs, even insisted that unless Congress made Indians into abject dependents "this Revolution in my Eyes will have lost more than half its Value." In the event, demoralized Iroquois, Delawares, and Shawnees relinquished western New York and Pennsylvania in powwows at Forts Stanwix (1784), McIntosh (1785), and Finney (1786).[12]

The Ohio Country, however, was another matter entirely. With the U.S. army reduced to a few hundred men, Congress had no hope of imposing similar treaties on the northwestern tribes. Yet the states and grandiose land companies with names like Vandalia, Indiana, and Illinois-Wabash behaved as if sovereignty were already assured. As early as 1784 Jefferson helped to draft an initial Northwest Ordinance. It promised Ohio settlers immediate self-government and statehood as soon as their population reached that of the smallest existing state. In 1785 a land ordinance envisioned the survey and sale of 640-acre townships, each divided into thirty-six sections, with land set aside for schools, veterans, and Congress itself. It was all fantasy. The lands in question were in Indian hands and the impecunious Congress lacked funds to survey and market, much less defend, thousands of square miles of forest. Not surprisingly, therefore, members of Congress jumped when a new company led by New England chaplain Manasseh Cutler offered to purchase for $1 million nearly 1.8 million Ohio acres around what became Marietta. Since Cutler expected to pay in veterans' land certificates redeemed at par (even though purchased at a 90 percent discount by his partners), it amounted to legal theft of a sort. But it was an easy matter for Cutler to bribe key congressmen by making them partners in a second land company and offering the president of Congress, Arthur St. Clair, the governorship of Ohio. All he need do to claim his wooded empire was arrange for repeal of the "self-government" clause in the 1784 ordinance. Congress obliged. The resulting Northwest Ordinance of 1787 made territories subject to appointed governors and postponed statehood until their population reached sixty thousand. A second great consequence of the ordinance derived from its permanent exclusion of slavery. Though high-minded on the surface, its limited application to the northwest strongly implied slavery would *not* be excluded from new territories and states south of the Ohio River. Indeed, southern congressmen approved the bill on that understanding.[13]

The incompetence of Congress as revealed in these acts was not, however, just a matter of its manipulation by states and speculators. The real indictment of the U.S. government under the Articles lay in the fact that while congressmen pored over maps and traded votes for a piece of the action, a Miami war chief named Little Turtle united the irate western tribes and enforced, through terror, a *ban* on white settlements north of the Ohio River. What is more, the tribes were encouraged by British agents and redcoats who refused to withdraw after 1783 from seven forts stretching from Lake Champlain to Detroit and Michilimakinac, even though these now lay on the U.S. side of the border. Their excuse for retaining the forts was the refusal of American states and courts, in defiance of the treaty of peace, to compensate dispossessed Tories or honor debts owed to Britons. But the British also exploited their footholds to keep control of the Indian trade and sow sedition among angry Vermonters seeking independence from their neighbors, New York and New Hampshire. Congress tried to parley, but King George sent no embassy to his ex-colonies, while his cabinet snubbed U.S. envoy John Adams.

South of the Ohio River the situation on the frontier was chaos. Pioneers, Indians, speculators, and expansionist states either ignored Congress or made it their plaything. Virginia retained title to the Kentucky territory, but could do no more than Congress to protect Boonesboro, Harrodsburg, and other settlements against Indians protecting their hunting grounds. North Carolina temporarily relinquished its hold over Tennessee's over-mountain men who promptly formed a new "state" called Franklin. But it fell into anarchy as rival factions and clans, allied to one or another land company, fought for control. Further south, congressional agents pressured the decimated Cherokees, Choctaws, and Chickasaws into making large cessions of land at Fort Hopewell in 1785. But inasmuch as the agreements guaranteed tribal rights to land further west, the Carolina and Georgia state governments repudiated them. Worse still, an educated chief of the Creeks named Alexander McGillivray rejected the American "right of conquest" altogether, obtained firearms from the Spanish governor in Florida, and made war on Georgia in 1786. Indeed, Spain's position was that *all* the land west of the Appalachians "belongs to the free and independent nations of Indians, and you [Americans] have no right to it." Spaniards concluded that grasping Americans had replaced the British as the principal threat to their largely vacant colonies of Florida and Louisiana. They hoped to maintain the Indian nations as buffers.[14] Americans, in turn, imagined wicked Spain meant to choke the growth of the United States by stirring up Indians and disgruntled pioneers. Each side gathered ample evidence for its fears after 1784, when the Spanish governor in New

Orleans closed the lower Mississippi River to American boats and rafts. Pioneers cried in real pain: to seal off New Orleans was to isolate the American interior from the rest of the world. But calling on Congress was a waste of energy. So Westerners spoke of making war themselves on Spaniards and Indians or else seceding from the United States and making their own bargain with Spain. General James Wilkinson, a Kentucky speculator, did both at once by placing himself at the head of frontier militias while pocketing Spanish gold.[15]

All Congress could do, as in the case of the British forts, was negotiate. Madrid obliged by sending a plenipotentiary, Don Diego de Gardoqui, with instructions to flummox the Yankees. He did it with gifts (including a breeding ass, Royal Gift, presented to George Washington), flattery (aimed especially at the wife of John Jay, secretary for foreign affairs), and a ploy to disrupt the American union. Gardoqui offered liberal commercial rights in the Spanish empire in exchange for U.S. acquiescence in the closure of the Mississippi. Jay initialed a treaty on that basis and the seven northern state delegations in Congress applauded. But southern states damned the treaty for a sellout and blocked ratification. The frustrated Jay asked for new instructions, but St. Clair informed him Congress was deadlocked. Meanwhile, news of Jay's "treason" provoked more talk of western secession and murmurs in northern and southern states about parting ways to form two or more unions of states.[16]

Financial insolvency, military impotence, commercial and monetary disunity, corrupt state governments, sectional rivalries, foreign and Indian resistance to U.S. growth and sovereignty, and a feckless committee called Congress presiding over it all like King Log: the United States clearly existed only in name and soon might cease to exist even in name. That was the origin of the "crisis" mentality gripping the men soon to be known as Federalists.

Who were they and what did they want? Aside from the difficulties of generalizing about any broad movement, those questions are obscured by two historical myths. Nationalist historians of the nineteenth century depicted the Federalists as wise, disinterested patriots bent on designing "a more perfect union." Progressive historians in the twentieth century imagined them rich reactionaries bent on rolling back democracy and making a killing in Continental bonds. But the first myth says nothing about why *some* prominent Americans wanted a new constitution whereas others from similar backgrounds were content with the Articles or at most wanted to tinker with them. The second myth is just false. Meticulous research has proven that thirty-one of the thirty-four major political and economic factions discernible in the states were represented at the Constitutional Convention and that delegates who had served in state governments divided equally over such issues as debtor relief, paper money, tariffs and commerce, the slave trade, and land speculation. That they were almost all men of distinction goes without saying: semi-literate farmers and mechanics were not likely to represent their states in a grand congress. That they feared direct democracy also goes without saying: Anti-Federalists were just as afraid of "mob rule." But to suggest Federalists were an elite cabal is to ignore their own differences and the support they received from humble mechanics, merchants, and farmers who hoped to enrich themselves in a growing national marketplace. What distinguished Federalists was their devotion to union, optimism about America's destiny, faith that a strong central government could shelter rather than endanger republican liberties, and contempt for venal and petty state governments.[17]

Another characteristic of Federalists was relative youth. They were on average ten to twelve years younger than their opponents and almost half the Federalists' leaders made their careers after 1775. Others, such as Washington, Jay, Morris, and James Wilson, reached new career pinnacles through national service. By contrast, the careers of most Antis, including Patrick Henry, George Mason, George Clinton, and Sam Adams, were made before the war and within their own colonies. Federalists considered the United States a work in progress. Antis saw 1776 as the climax of the American play and spied in the Federalist movement an effort to reimpose "monarchy." Finally, few Antis played major roles in the War of Independence, whereas war veterans numbered no less than twenty-one of the delegates at the Constitutional Convention. They supported a strong central government almost unanimously.[18]

One prominent veteran could not, alas, join them. Following the British evacuation of Charleston, General Nathanael Greene and wife, Caty, returned to Newport and their children to find their affairs in ruin. Greene's investments had lost 95 percent of their value, the family's businesses collapsed, Newport itself was half empty, and the economy choked on worthless Rhode Island scrip. With Congress unable to cover its war debts, all Greene could do to support his family was take possession of Mulberry Grove, a ruined Tory plantation the Georgia assembly awarded him in thanks for his war service. Greene abominated slavery, but intended to rent out the land and build a dream house for Caty on a sea island near Savannah. Best of all, the Greenes' closest friend, Mad Anthony Wayne, was granted another plantation nearby. Of course, whenever Nathanael was absent Wayne all but moved in with Caty, causing Savannah ladies to cluck. Nathanael ignored them. Instead, he rejoiced in the company of his wife and friend, explored bridle paths with them, and boasted in letters home about his garden's green peas and lettuce, succulent strawberries, and orchards of apple, peach, apricot, nectarine, and plum trees decorated with mocking birds. The Yankee loved Georgia until, one torrid June day in 1786, it killed him. Nathanael toured a neighbor's rice plantation on foot and bereft of a hat. He returned home with a splitting headache, then fell into a stupor. Doctors diagnosed severe sunstroke, but their continuous leeching further weakened the patient. Greene expired a week later at age forty-four.

"I have just seen a great and good man die," wrote Wayne in a shaky hand. "How hard is the fate of the United States to lose such a man in the middle of life," wrote Washington when the news reached Mount Vernon. He immediately offered to see to the education of the Greenes' eldest son, his namesake. Otherwise, Caty was left to raise five children alone, fight off creditors, and lobby Congress for the money an ungrateful nation owed her husband's estate. She returned to Newport, leaped into a hot affair with Jeremiah Wadsworth, an executor of the will, then did the same with Phineas Miller, a New York financier. But so long as the Articles of Confederation were in force even a war hero's widow got no satisfaction from Congress. Thus did private lives, thousands of them, come to rely on the Federalist movement.[19]

One by one, for disparate reasons, people lost confidence in the Articles. Hamilton wrote Duane as early as 1780 of the need for a constitutional convention in light of the army's woes. Morris made up his mind in 1784 after his plan for a national tariff was quashed. Charles Pinckney of South Carolina gave up on the Articles when half-empty sessions of Congress ignored his alarms over the threat posed by Indians and Spaniards. Jay joined the movement when Congress pleaded *non possumus* in the matter of his diplomatic instructions. John Adams perceived in 1786 that Congress was "not a legislative assembly, not a representative assembly, but only a diplomatic assembly." Arthur Lee realized endowing Congress with real fiscal power would place "the purse" in the same hand as "the sword," hence he saw the need for a separate executive branch. Leaders of small states came around when they realized their trade was at the mercy of larger neighbors and out-of-state ports. New Jersey was likened to "a cask tapped at both ends"; North Carolina to a "patient bleeding at both arms."[20]

Madison converted to Federalism while observing his incompetent state assembly. Jefferson might boast of Virginia's abolition of entails on land and of the established church, but those laws only made *de facto* practice *de jure*.[21] Far more in evidence were the "vices of the system." Congress could not act without approval from the states, state constitutions made their assemblies almighty, and most assemblymen were so fickle, short-sighted, capricious, and greedy Madison feared all respect for law and justice must dissolve. Finally, he thought the quality of representation was poor because voters were easily suckered by demagogues (Patrick Henry?) who played on their passions and local resentments. Madison thought officials elected on a statewide or national basis more likely to display a devotion to the general welfare, balance each other's interests, and check local abuses as well.[22] But whatever path Federalists traveled they all encountered the hurdle that amendments to the Articles of Confederation could not be made without the support of the very state governments they meant to tame or reform. Overcoming that hurdle required not only audacity, energy, and will, but guile, subterfuge, and a dose of extortion as well.

That it might just prove possible first occurred to Madison on the veranda at Mount Vernon overlooking the placid Potomac. There, in March 1785, commissioners from Maryland and Virginia met to resolve disputes over navigation and trade. Washington was interested because the Potomac stretched north and west, close to the headwaters of the Ohio River. Stimulating the river traffic was bound to increase the value of his western landholdings. The meeting proved an unprecedented example of interstate amity. The commissioners declared the river "a common High Way" and arranged common duties on goods, monetary equivalence between Virginia and Maryland, fishing rights, and joint investment in buoys, lighthouses, and law enforcement. So beneficial were the results Pennsylvania and Delaware soon sought for similar agreements in their waters. But potentially the most important features of the Mount Vernon conference were Washington's sponsorship and the commissioners' willingness to exceed by far the instructions of their own state assemblies.

Madison lodged those features in the back of his mind, then traveled to Richmond to propose Virginia ask her sister states to grant Congress authority to regulate trade. He got something much better when the assembly called for a *convention* to discuss a uniform system of commerce. The Virginians mistakenly thought that would better protect states' rights against Congress. In truth, a convention would take reform out of the hands of the weak Congress and give it to an extra-constitutional body far *more* likely to shuck off state tutelage.

The invitations went out and nine states accepted. When time came to convene, at Annapolis in September 1786, however, only five delegations were present. They might have discussed bilateral issues on the Mount Vernon model or else waited for the tardy four to arrive. But Hamilton slyly used the poor attendance as a pretext to draft a new resolution calling for a national convention to meet in Philadelphia in 1787 and "cement the union." Madison, realizing that phrase might be a red flag, shrewdly muddled its purpose to rendering "the constitution of the Federal Government adequate to the exigencies of the Union."[23] The next steps were: get Congress to endorse the proposal; get Washington to preside; and get the delegates in Philadelphia to "exceed their instructions."

The lever employed to nudge Congress was a stunning missive from war secretary Knox in the autumn of 1786: militiamen, perhaps fifteen thousand, were drilling in western Massachusetts for the purpose of overthrowing the government! For good measure Knox added to their host hundreds of Indians eager for scalps. In reality, the rebels never exceeded two thousand and no Indians had troubled the Berkshires for twenty-five years. But insurrection on any scale exposed Congress' helplessness and invited copycat revolts by the disgruntled (or enslaved) throughout the states. That is why Shays' Rebellion helped create the U.S. Constitution.

Samuel Ely, an angry preacher less concerned with theology than social justice, started it all in 1782 when he moved to the Connecticut Valley to preach rebellion against Boston. Jailed, then freed by a crowd of "peasants with pitchforks," he fled to heterodox Vermont. But as life got worse for the farmers of Hampshire County, the truth of Ely's message sank in. To pay off its war debts the Massachusetts General Court imposed high taxes that collectors insisted citizens pay in hard money even though falling commodity prices drained farmers of cash. Speculators and state officials grew rich, while honest folk, including war veterans, lost their farms or went to debtor's prison. In 1786 a demagogue named Luke Day called for resistance, but since Daniel Shays, who had fought on Breed's Hill, was his most famous disciple, the rebellion was named after him. By January 1787 New England farmers were sufficiently angry to march two thousand strong, in sub-zero temperatures, behind Day and Shays against the federal arsenal at Springfield. Militia armed with cannons scattered the mob and a Boston contingent under Benjamin Lincoln ran the fugitives to ground. But fears of anarchy were still peaking when Congress, on February 21, agreed it was "expedient" to convene a convention, albeit "for the sole and express purpose of *revising* the Articles of Confederation."[24]

The second task was to bring Washington to Philadelphia: nothing else would so elevate the convention's prestige and imbue it with a national spirit. He was reluctant to attend, had nothing to contribute in the legal or philosophical line, and wondered how association with the convention might affect his own image, especially if it should fail. But Washington understood also the damage his *absence* would do if taken to mean he disapproved. He really had no choice but to accept the invitation to join Virginia's blue-ribbon delegation, including Madison, Edmund Randolph, and George Mason. Washington's arrival on May 13, 1787, was sensational: the Father of His Country come north again to win the peace as he won the war. Taking care to wash up, change clothes, and powder his wig, as he always did before public appearances, Washington stepped from the boat at Gray's Ferry on the Schuylkill to be escorted through town by the Philadelphia City Troop in its spanking white breeches. Churchbells and cannons saluted the procession as it moved first to Benjamin Franklin's house and then to the mansion of Robert Morris, Washington's host. In another respect the day was anti-climactic: since the only other delegation in town was Pennsylvania's, twelve days passed before a quorum convened in Independence Hall. The delegates gave special honor to the eighty-one-year-old Franklin, literally borne to the scene in a Parisian sedan chair muscled by four convicts from Walnut Street jail. But everyone knew the only man to chair this convention, to serve as its president, was Washington.

That left the third task, which was to persuade delegates to ignore their instructions and design an entirely new government. Madison had in his pocket a plan based on a stunning new insight inspired by his reading of Hume. Contrary to inherited theory, he argued, republics were more likely to prosper the *larger* they were, not smaller. The origins of faction and strife lay in the nature of man, Madison would write in *The Federalist* No. 10, but "Extend the sphere, and you take in a greater variety of parties and interests," thus preventing any one faction or coalition from seizing dominant power. He imagined what he called a "middle way" and even a *feudal system* in which the federal, state, and local governments enjoyed overlapping sovereignties and reciprocal rights and responsibilities. In like manner, checks and balances among the executive, legislative, and judicial branches would prevent abuses of power at each layer.[25] Governmental bodies might thus revolve about each other according to the same "law of proportion" celestial bodies obeyed. Dickinson, another Princetonian, understood instantly: "Let our central government be like the sun and the states like the planets, repelled yet attracted. . . ." So did

Charles Pinckney, who called for federal power sufficient to "control the centrifugal tendency of the States; which, without it, will continually fly out of their proper orbits, and destroy the order and harmony of the political system." Astronomy may have held less sway over other early arrivals such as Robert Morris, the peg-legged patrician Gouverneur Morris, Pennsylvania's brilliant Scottish-born lawyer James Wilson, his house guest John Rutledge of South Carolina, and Connecticut's cadaverous Roger Sherman and stiff-necked Oliver Ellsworth.[26] But all shared Madison's goals and plotted strategy prior to the opening gavel.[27]

What was later dubbed the Constitutional Convention (no one dared call it that at the time) met over four months, beginning May 28, 1787. Its first chore, making the ground rules, took only one day. But it was extremely important because without a consensus on procedure the convention might have exploded on numerous occasions. What is more, the rules biased the enterprise toward success by providing for secret deliberations without minutes (Madison took his own detailed ones), approval of motions by a simple majority, a "one state, one vote" formula, and the revisiting of issues in light of subsequent developments. Finally, the convention agreed to sit as a committee of the whole, a House of Commons technique that encouraged informal, open debate. These rules were flexible, expeditious, and fair. They also isolated the convention from external pressures and politics.

The next day Randolph read the Virginia Plan. Its fifteen resolutions proposed to establish a bicameral Congress whose lower house would elect the upper house, the executive, and the judiciary, and have power to nullify state laws and admit new states into the union. This almighty lower house would itself be elected by the states proportional to their populations. That, of course, favored the large states and Madison expected small states to oppose it. But the politics of the convention were more complex than he imagined. Southern states combined, regardless of size, to defend the institution of slavery; New England states did likewise to promote commerce. States that possessed no western land claims opposed those that did. Tiny states wanted a strong central government but feared being dominated, while some delegates from large states were not interested in a central government *unless* they dominated it. Several delegations split down the middle. New York, for instance, raked in so much cash from its customs duties it was loath to yield control over commerce to Congress. So Governor George Clinton arranged for two Anti-Federalists, Judge Robert Yates and Albany Mayor John Lansing, Jr., to outvote Hamilton in New York's delegation and otherwise confound the proceedings. Maryland's delegation embodied a feud between the Carrolls' hard money faction and Samuel Chase's debtor relief faction, while the state's would-be spokesman Luther Martin proved a loquacious inebriate. Even Virginians turned unreliable when issues did not break their way. So Madison launched the convention on a federalist course, but soon relinquished its management to men more astute at brokering deals.[28]

After two weeks of debate William Paterson of New Jersey countered with the small states' proposal. It, too, loaded Congress with new powers, but envisioned a unicameral chamber in which the "sovereign" states would each have one vote as under the Articles. Madison objected the states were not really sovereign, Washington declared himself sick of the "monster" word sovereignty, and Hamilton fired a broadside against both the Virginia and New Jersey plans. To grant powers to Congress instead of an executive branch "would eventuate in a bad government or no government." Instead, Hamilton brashly proposed a British system comprised of an elected lower house, an aristocratic Senate serving for life, and a national governor-for-life to administer the executive branch and even appoint state governors! Nobody cheered and many were shocked— but not by the monarchical cast of the plan. Federalists had discussed for years what sort of executive America needed: "Emperors, Kings, Stadtholders, Governors General, with a Senate, or House or Lords, & House of Commons, are frequently the Topics of Conversation." Rather, Hamilton raised eyebrows by declaring the aspect of the British system he most liked was the one his colleagues most hated: to wit, its royal patronage, which in his view was the crown's only weapon against an all-powerful Parliament. "We must take man as we find him, and if we expect him to serve, the public must interest his passions in doing so." Even hard-boiled realists fled from such candor, while republican-minded delegates decided this dangerous man bore watching. Hamilton, having said his piece, contributed little more in Philadelphia.[29]

When it came to a vote, the convention agreed, six states to four, to proceed on the basis of the Virginia Plan, but it left unresolved Paterson's fear that Congress would be the plaything of the most populous states. Dickinson suggested a solution based on equal state representation in the Senate and proportional representation in the House, but the big states were not ready to make that concession while southern delegates objected to any formula likely to put slaveholding states in a minority. Charles Pinckney therefore demanded that enslaved persons be counted in a state's population, while fellow South

Carolinian Rutledge wanted wealth to be factored into the representation of states. The relatively poor and dependent North Carolinians objected strongly to wealth as a measure of clout. So their leader Dr. Hugh Williamson, a transplanted Pennsylvanian, fashioned a compromise with James Wilson to count slaves as three-fifths of a person for the purpose of apportioning seats in Congress. The convention agreed. But the July 2 vote on two houses with equal state representation in the Senate ended in a 5 to 5 tie. The Federalist movement seemed to reach a "full stop."[30]

Benjamin Franklin, fearing the Republic was melting like wax in the summer heat, rose at that moment to bewail "the melancholy proof of the imperfection of the human understanding." For over a month delegates had batted about trial balloons, groped for some compromise, and hoped someone would change his mind and swing a state's vote. The convention sought wisdom in history, parsed Montesquieu, Aristotle, Hume, and Locke, and invoked the Rittenhouse orrery, all in vain. So Franklin asked, "How has it happened, Sir, that we have not hitherto once thought of humbly applying to the Father of lights to illuminate our understandings?" He asked the convention to open each day's session with prayer.[31] The motion died on the absurd grounds no budget existed for chaplains. But delegates did swallow their pride by agreeing to appoint an *ad hoc* committee with one member from each state to recommend ways of breaking the stalemate. At Franklin's behest, the committee endorsed a proposal by Sherman, hence the "Connecticut Plan," under which states would have equal representation in the Senate, but power to introduce money bills would rest in a House of Representatives elected proportionally on the basis of one per forty thousand (later reduced to thirty thousand) with slaves counted as three-fifths of a person. Elbridge Gerry of Massachusetts mocked this provision. Given that "blacks are property and are used to the southward as horses and cattle to the northward," he sneered, why not count animals as three-fifths of a person in New England? But Lansing and Yates, the saboteurs in New York's delegation, were sufficiently worried this Connecticut Plan might be approved that they theatrically stormed out of the convention. Their thinking was, if a state or two switched sides and the plan were either passed or rejected, the losing delegations would follow their example and *bolt*. If, on the other hand, no state switched sides, the deadlocked convention would simply *dissolve*.

Accordingly, American unity hung by a thread when Washington called the roll of states on July 16. New Hampshire and Rhode Island were absent, New York now lacked a quorum, and Massachusetts' four delegates divided. So

Connecticut and New Jersey began the count with aye votes. Pennsylvania, to Franklin's and Wilson's dismay, voted nay, but Delaware and Maryland (thanks to the arrival of Daniel Carroll) voted aye. There remained the southern states, all of which were expected to reject the compromise out of large-state chauvinism, republican fear of central authority, or deference to Virginia, which cast a powerful nay. Then Washington spoke the words "North Carolina" and whatever prayers might have been silently offered were answered in majesty. The Tarheels divided three to one *in favor.* So even though South Carolina and Georgia said nay, the compromise passed 5 to 4. Of course, it might have been overturned later or else just repudiated. One of the most stubborn opponents of the Connecticut Plan was Madison himself, who believed it breached the principle of popular government and was prepared to resist even if that caused the small states to walk out! But when a caucus of big states failed to concert on any alternative, they acquiesced in the result as the best deal they were likely to get.[32]

What happened? Strange to say, nobody knows for sure why North Carolina flip-flopped to vote with the small states and quite possibly save the United States from death in the cradle. Was it significant that William Blount, erstwhile head of the North Carolinians, left the convention for New York to take up his seat in Congress? Did it matter if North Carolinians knew Rutledge was plotting to support Connecticut's western land claims in exchange for Sherman's support of the slave trade? Did North Carolinians resent the tendency of Virginians and South Carolinians to assume leadership of the south? Did North Carolina in fact imagine itself a "small state" even though it was sure to grow rapidly as its frontier filled up? Almost any private understandings are possible, given the fact so many of the key players slept just down the hall from each other in the Indian Queen Tavern on Third Street. But in the absence of evidence pointing to vote-trading, the most likely explanation is that vision and character carried the day.[33]

Hugh Williamson was born in 1735 in Chester County, Pennsylvania, to middle class Scots-Irish Presbyterians.[34] He was among the first class to graduate from the College of Philadelphia and remained there to take a master's degree in 1760 and teach mathematics. He intended to enter the ministry, but the tiresome disputes between Old and New Light clergy caused him to follow his second calling, medicine. Williamson studied in Edinburgh, London, and Utrecht, then returned to Philadelphia in 1768 to join the American Philosophical Society and publish research on such varied topics as climate, disease, comets, and electricity. While en route to London, he happened to witness the Boston Tea Party and testified to the Privy Council about the colonists' mood. While in London he wrote a tract making the colonists' case to the opposition Whigs, and—as noted above—may have been the man who purloined the infamous Hutchinson letters and gave them to Benjamin Franklin. In 1776, Williamson returned to join his brother in a Charleston merchant house, but the British assault on that port caused him to relocate to Edenton on North Carolina's Albemarle Sound. During the war he became surgeon general of North Carolina, the pre-eminent physician in the Continental Army, and a promoter of hygiene. His surgical heroics saved lives in both armies at the Battle of Camden. After the war he served in North Carolina's assembly, delegations to Congress and the Annapolis convention, and state college board of trustees. He was personally opposed to slavery, but also a fierce advocate of his adopted state's interests. In short, Williamson could not have been more unlike a provincial planter. The sturdy physician with a great head of white hair was a Pennsylvanian by birth and education, a scientist and reformer, a cosmopolitan protégé of Benjamin Franklin, and a nationalist sympathetic to the aspirations and fears of all American regions. To be sure, he took care to ensure North Carolina would be fairly represented and proportionally taxed under the Constitution. But once that was accomplished, one need not conjure self-seeking cabals to imagine Dr. Williamson persuading the Tarheels to vote for the Union, not least because it was Franklin's compromise plan they put over the top. As for Blount, Williamson's letters to him prove they were of one mind. As for North Carolina's governor, Williamson wrote him of "how difficult a part has fallen to the share of our State in the course of this business and I flatter myself greatly if we have not sustained it with a Principle & firmness that will entitle us to what we will never ask for, the thanks of the public. It will be sufficient for us if we have the satisfaction of believing that we have contributed to the happiness of Millions."[35] Hugh Williamson never has been properly thanked.

Following passage of the Grand Compromise, the convention's new working majority quickly endorsed an executive branch led by a single president endowed with all manner of "monarchical" powers. A Committee of Detail pulled all the resolves made so far into a draft constitution, and if any deals had been made they now became evident. The committee included Rutledge, Sherman's colleague Ellsworth, and Pennsylvania's Wilson, the skilled broker of northern and southern interests. Their articles included the ban on export taxes and protection of the slave trade desired by South Carolina and the senatorial control over western land desired by Connecticut. As it transpired, those clauses did *not* find their way into the final Constitution because circumstances suddenly changed. First, Congress sprang from its deathbed long enough to sell the Reverend Cutler's Ohio Company a tract one-third the size of Connecticut itself. Suddenly Sherman no longer needed *adjudication* of dubious future claims, but only *protection* of legal existing claims. He dropped his demand that land issues be hashed out in the Senate and asked they be settled in court.

Second, Maryland's Luther Martin suspected a devil in the Committee of Detail. Styling himself a people's tribune and opponent of slavery, he made a ruckus about the "high toned" federal government the convention seemed bent on creating. In August, Martin hosted a series of boozy evenings for malcontents who spread so many rumors about corrupt bargains the convention came close to reconsidering the whole constitution. Rutledge fiercely denied the allegations, but was obliged to climb down from his amoral perch to the effect that "Interest alone is the governing principle among nations" and not "Religion and humanity." The slave trade, he now agreed, might cease after *a grace period of twenty years.* Abolitionists such as Gerry and George Mason refused the sop, but enough Yankees (whose shippers, after all, engaged in the trade) accepted the concession so that the Federalist majority held.[36]

That cleared the way, finally, for decisions about the executive branch and its relation to Congress. The president was to be commander in chief of the American armed forces, but Congress alone had the right to declare war and raise armies. The president was chief magistrate for foreign affairs and administration of justice, but his ambassadors, treaties, and judicial appointments were subject to the advice and consent of the Senate. The president could veto bills, but two-thirds of Congress—down from three-fourths, thanks to Williamson—could override him. Thanks also to Williamson, Congress could, *in extremis,* impeach the executive. The method of the president's election, however, was still up in the air. Everyone trusted Washington to serve as first chief executive and not abuse his powers. But no one knew how to design an electoral system to ensure subsequent presidents would be independent, yet under control. If Congress picked the president the executive would not really be a separate branch. If state legislatures picked the president, the federal government might become as feeble as Congress under the Articles. If the people picked the president directly the door would fly open for demagogues. Finally, in late September, a committee on "miscellany" advanced an idea illogically brilliant: the electoral college. All states would choose, in ways their legislatures determined, a slate of electors equal in number to their House and Senate representation. The electors would meet in their states on the same day and cast votes for two persons, at least one of whom must hail from a different state. Whoever received the most votes nationwide would become president, and whoever came in second vice president. That way small states enjoyed a slightly exaggerated influence, no demagogue could stampede the masses, and the executive would be truly independent of Congress.

Its work done, the convention turned over all its resolutions and formulae to a Committee on Style. Hamilton and Madison were members, but they happily gave the task of writing the U.S. Constitution to the renowned wordsmith Gouverneur Morris. The wealthy financier with social pretensions was an excellent choice. He shared Jefferson's flair for stirring collects (hence "We, the People of the United States, in order to form a more perfect Union. . . .") but eschewed Jefferson's tiresome litanies. Rather, Morris adhered to the maxim of Edmund Randolph, who said the keys to drafting fundamental laws were to "insert essential principles only" and "use simple and precise language."[37] But neither was Morris above substituting a semi-colon for a comma in order to turn a sentence *restricting* the powers of Congress into one granting it *indiscriminate* powers to promote "the general welfare." (Sherman, the crabbed clerk of the Founding Fathers, caught the "error" and changed it back.)

It was no insignificant matter, because the battle for ratification of the Constitution was bound to be fought in large part over the question of whether the federal government's powers were dangerously broad or in fact sharply constrained. The leading Anti-Federalists still in town, Mason and Gerry, anticipated that when they insisted at the end of the convention on appending a Bill of Rights. The convention briefly considered the motion, than rejected it ten states to zero. Why? Sherman's answer was simple. The whole point of the Constitution was to *delimit* the powers of the federal government and uphold state constitutions eight of which already had bills of rights. Hamilton believed bills of rights were needed only in monarchies where the people were *not* sovereign. Wilson argued the Constitution was positive not natural law, and any attempt to "enumerate all the rights of man" would be to enter an ethereal maze. Charles Cotesworth Pinckney spoke for slaveholders when he noted the danger of naming "liberty" a fundamental right. But at bottom, the convention's thinking was this: to append a bill of rights would be to admit *a priori* that the federal government was something Americans needed protection *against*—and that was the worst impression to give on the eve of the fight for ratification.[38]


Shenanigans, log-rolling, and personalities aside, how was it fifty-five men representing a plethora of interests in a convention of dubious provenance succeeded in drafting a constitution thirty-nine of them were willing to sign on September 17, 1787? First, it was a primarily a meeting of lawyers. No less than thirty-four (62 percent) of the delegates boasted legal training and twenty-one were practitioners. Of course, lawyers can drag disputes on forever when it serves their clients and pocketbooks, but they also know how to reconcile contending parties and verbal contradictions when obstruction serves nobody's interest. Second, obstruction served few of the delegates' interests because they were on the whole a striving, self-selected group already convinced of the need for thorough reform. Third, 75 percent of them had served in the dysfunctional Congress or state legislatures and agreed on the need for checks and balances among separate branches of government. Fourth, whether Christians, skeptics, or "common sense" philosophers (by no means exclusive categories) all Federalists believed human nature was flawed. They envisioned no utopias, put little trust in republican virtue, and believed the only government liable to endure was one taking mankind as it was and making allowance for passion and greed.

Fifth, the delegates occupied a narrow ideological spectrum. None but Hamilton spoke publicly in favor of monarchy, while even the most republican delegates shared the high Federalists' suspicions about democracy. It was "the worst of all political evils," said Gerry (remembering Shays' Rebellion). The nation's evils were traceable to "the turbulence and follies of democracy," said Randolph. No one worth less than $100,000 should be eligible for president, said Pinckney.[39] Almost all believed in the wisdom of mixed government: it was just a matter of getting the right mix of powers between the states and the nation, and among the executive, legislative, and judicial branches. How well they succeeded remained to be seen. But the Constitution amalgamated to a remarkable degree the understandings of liberty brought to America by the four British cultures. It combined Cavaliers' hierarchical, even feudal notions of liberty, Puritans' notions of covenant and community, and Quakers' tolerance and broad representation, while making maximum space for the Scots-Irish Bordermen's libertarianism.

Sixth, the delegates (in true English style) turned their political task into a game, respecting its rules even in defeat, and settling for half a loaf when they could not have the whole. Indeed, none of the Federalists—not Madison, Hamilton, Franklin, Wilson, or anyone else—*liked* the final result. But they agreed with Gouverneur Morris that "With all its faults, the moment this plan goes forth all other considerations will be laid aside, and the great question will be, shall there be a national Government or not?"[40] Seventh, the physical setting probably helped. The convention met in a room just forty feet square, its windows shut against eavesdroppers and pestiferous flies. By noon it was stifling, especially for Yankees in woolen suits (southerners knew to wear linen or camlet). That made for hot tempers, but also *esprit de corps* and impatience to get on with business, if not in the Statehouse then in private quarters, taverns, along the quay or amidst the Wednesday and Saturday Market Street fairs. Wherever two or three delegates were gathered together, the convention was in session.[41]

Finally, there was the matter of who *wasn't* in Philadelphia. Patrick ("I smelt a rat") Henry, Sam Adams, John Hancock, and many other partisans of state sovereignty stayed home. Those from New York left in the middle, betting a rump convention would be barren. Rhode Island boycotted altogether because the populist party in charge of its legislature feared a federal hard money system. As Washington remarked from the chair, Rhode Island "still perseveres in that impolitic—unjust—and one might add without much impropriety scandalous conduct. . . . Consequently no representation is yet here from thence."[42] Finally, though it is only a guess, the fact that Jefferson and John Adams were on diplomatic missions in Paris and London may have been a stroke of luck for the Federalists. They were, in their different ways, idealists, and might have been formidable foes of the Constitution inasmuch as its "implicit endorsement of evil as the proper moving force of government ran counter to their very fiber."[43] Of course, that was the genius of the document. It embraced human nature in all its sordidness and, in potential at least, transformed private egos into public goods.

The cynical quip defining the Golden Rule as "whoever has the gold makes the rules" is not always true, but it is usually true that "Whoever makes the rules wins the game"—at least the first time. Federalists thus began work on the rules for ratification even before the convention's success was assured. Did they dare place such a subtle document before the people at large, or the jealous state legislatures? At length, Wilson and Rufus King carried the day with a novel proposal to maximize chances of ratification. Voting would indeed be by states, but in special conventions, not legislatures. Moreover, the Constitution would be deemed in force after just nine of the thirteen states ratified. That was wonderfully clever because it gave Federalists two shots to win in each state (in the selection of delegates and again in the conventions' debates) and because the rapid ratifications expected from small states would create a momentum reluctant large states would find hard to resist. The fact that only five members of the old Congress answered the call to order in November 1787 helped as well. The U.S. government had ceased to exist, so ratification became a take-it-or-leave-it referendum on American union.[44]

Nevertheless, Federalists left little to chance. They campaigned, propagandized, dispatched private couriers to speed information, and plotted joint strategy. Before their opponents had got up to speed, Delaware ("The First State"), New Jersey, and Georgia ratified unanimously and Connecticut by a wide margin. But most shocking was the speed with which rancorous Pennsylvania and Massachusetts voted in favor, leaving the Federalists in need of just three more states as early as February 1788. How did they pull it off? Pennsylvania was won by a veritable *coup d'état*. On September 18, 1787, just a day after the signing of the Constitution, Federalists in the state assembly called for a convention to meet in just two months. But the assembly lacked a quorum, so sergeants-at-arms were ordered to drag two western assemblymen (who happened also to be Anti-Federalists) from their rooms to the Statehouse, permitting the guffawing majority to pass the bill. Wilson then orchestrated a whirlwind campaign and assembled a war chest to bribe newspapers into printing pro-Federalist essays. The result was a 2 to 1 sweep: the Pennsylvania convention ratified the Constitution 46 to 23 on December 12.

In Massachusetts, Federalists could not readily influence the town meetings that selected delegates and had to contend with rural backlash against the *suppression* of Shays' Rebellion.[45] So they borrowed a tactic from New England's popular game of ninepins: they bowled over one potential adversary whose fall then toppled the next. Thus, Paul Revere was quietly hired to stage a mass meeting of mechanics and artisans and present "their" pro-Constitution petition to Sam Adams. Adams felt obliged to hearken to the voice of "his" people. That in turn made Governor John Hancock teeter. The Federalists closed the deal by promising to support a bill of rights after ratification and hinting to Hancock he might be just the man to serve as Washington's vice president. The vote was perilously close, but Massachusetts ratified 187–168.[46]

Maryland and South Carolina ratified in spring 1788, bringing the total one shy of the number needed for the Constitution to take effect. But the nation would not amount to much without Virginia and New York, whose strong Anti-Federalist factions were led by the formidable Patrick Henry and George Clinton. They might, at this late date, have scuttled the American ship of state if their Anti-Federalist followers had not been so disparate, disorganized, and profoundly negative. Some prominent Antis protested the Constitution for what it did not do, for instance abolish the slave trade. Some were soft-money men who thought the Constitution a plot to enrich an elite and squeeze the smallholder. (Federalists in turn accused Antis of seeking only "to defraud their creditors" and "establish iniquity by law.") Some Antis were state loyalists who feared subjection to distant, authoritarian power. As an anonymous "Essay of an Old Whig" put it, the people dare not submit to "some heaven-sent PHAETONS amongst us, who, like the son of Apollo, think themselves entitled to guide the chariot of the sun." Some Antis were people who happened to profit, whether from land speculation, tariffs, or government posts, from existing state laws. But rank and file Antis consisted mostly of republican-minded farmers and planters who had no use for "high-toned" city folk, albeit they lacked the money and media access to compete with them.[47] In sum, Anti-Federalists were sort of like Tories during the war: they opposed the national project, but for such various reasons they had no alternative to propose. They were numerous, but scattered and out of touch with each other. They accused their opponents of self-interest, but were vulnerable to the same charge, all the more so because their interests were glaringly local. Above all, Anti-Federalists were compelled to rely on scare tactics, conjuring *hypothetical* disasters that *might* happen at *some* point in the future *if* some aspect of the Constitution went awry. Federalists, by contrast, marketed hope based on a manifest program to forge a great empire, and all they needed to do was reassure.

To reassure delegates, New York's above all, was the purpose of *The Federalist* series of essays, authored by Madison and Hamilton with an assist from John Jay, in 1787–88. There is no point in trying to adumbrate this greatest of all political treatises except to say Hamilton played the pragmatist and Madison the theorist, Hamilton the salesman for vigorous government, Madison for limited, balanced government, Hamilton the exponent of unified sovereignty to defend liberty against foreign enemies, Madison of divided sovereignty to defend liberty against domestic enemies. *The Federalist* papers addressed everyone's pet wants and concerns and might have proved a master-piece of political spin if wavering citizens bothered to study them. But there is no evidence the essays affected the outcome in New York or anywhere else. Sad to say, therefore, *The Federalist* papers are best understood as a sublime but ano-dyne transitional genre between the long, closely reasoned essays, sermons, and pamphlets that decorated Anglo-American culture for the previous two cen-turies and the short, polemical editorials that have degraded public dialogue over the subsequent two centuries.

What did determine the outcome in the final battleground states was time, or rather delaying tactics that in the fullness of time wore out the Antis. Virginians sweated in Richmond for three weeks in June 1788 while Patrick Henry staged a dazzling exhibition of oratorical fireworks, on one occasion holding his audience for seven hours. He warned of the danger of tyranny: "If a wrong step be now made, the republic may be lost forever." He asked why the Constitution began "We, the People" instead of "We, the States"? He implored Virginians to consider how well off they were and not to risk the fruits of the Revolution.[48] But most of all he hoped for news that New York had rejected the Constitution, or at least ratified it subject to stringent prior conditions, where-upon Henry might deliver one final stemwinder and carry the day. But that did not happen because up in Poughkeepsie, Hamilton, Jay, and Robert Livingston also dragged things out, insisting the convention debate every clause of the Constitution. So when Richmond did get news from up north it told of New Hampshire's ratification as the ninth state. Henry then made a motion to ratify on condition a bill of rights be added prior to the Constitution's taking effect. It narrowly lost, and ratification passed 89 to 79. The New York convention dragged on until July 17, when Hamilton cracked the Clintonites with a veiled threat that New York City was prepared to secede from the state. Nine days later the convention voted to ratify, on the understanding a bill of rights would be later attached, 30 to 27, with 7 abstentions. Just as in 1776, New York was dragged, protesting and almost inert, into the United States.[49]

Only fifty-five men worked on the Constitution and only sixty thousand or so (about one and one-half percent of the U.S. population) voted in favor of it.[50] But those numbers do not mean the majority's will was thwarted. To be sure, mobs in Albany ceremoniously burned copies of the document, but most Antis were more apprehensive than hostile and went back to their plows with a "wait and see" attitude. Almost all urbanites, from blacksmiths to merchant princes, celebrated madly. In New York City a horse-drawn float carrying a

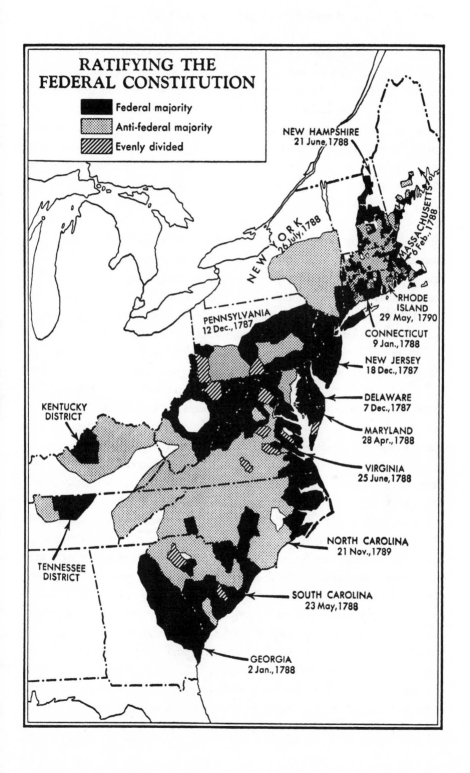

RATIFYING THE
FEDERAL CONSTITUTION

- Federal majority
- Anti-federal majority
- Evenly divided

NEW HAMPSHIRE
21 June, 1788

NEW YORK
26 July, 1788

MASSACHUSETTS
6 Feb., 1788

RHODE
ISLAND
29 May, 1790

PENNSYLVANIA
12 Dec., 1787

CONNECTICUT
9 Jan., 1788

NEW JERSEY
18 Dec., 1787

KENTUCKY
DISTRICT

DELAWARE
7 Dec., 1787

MARYLAND
28 Apr., 1788

VIRGINIA
25 June, 1788

TENNESSEE
DISTRICT

NORTH CAROLINA
21 Nov., 1789

SOUTH CAROLINA
23 May, 1788

GEORGIA
2 Jan., 1788

scale model thirty-two-gun frigate christened "Hamilton" led the raucous parade. Philadelphia turned out to cheer the "Grand Foederal Edifice" with thirteen Corinthian columns pulled by ten horses. The procession, estimated at seventeen thousand, included floats and displays for every state, profession, and trade. When the citizens reached Union Park, they heard a few words from James Wilson then dove into casks of hard cider, porter, and beer to raise toasts to the People and Constitution of America. Benjamin Rush recorded its meaning in just seven words: " 'Tis done. We have become a nation."[51]

Some readers may have noticed that the words "revolution" and "modern" have scarcely appeared in this book. That is because people of the sixteenth through the eighteenth centuries defined them so differently than we do today, their casual use might confuse more than clarify. In their parlance the word revolution implied an orbit, a revolving back to some prior position. Hence political revolution involved (at least in propaganda) a return to some happy past state of affairs, not invention of something strikingly novel. As for "modern," its original meaning was simply "current"—what is (or is fashionable) today. In historical terms the eighteenth-century opposite of modern was not feudal, but ancient. To impose twenty-first-century usages on earlier eras is even more problematical because "revolutionary" is likely to conjure images of Robespierres and Lenins, violent class conflicts and utopian ideologies anachronistic in a pre-1792 setting. Even the word "radical" can befuddle because to be radical meant to return to the roots of something (if only to yank them out "root and branch"), perhaps even be backward rather than forward looking.[52]

Nevertheless, colonists called their rebellion a revolution and their nation a *Novus Ordo Seclorum*, new order for the ages. So linguistic problems notwithstanding, historians are compelled to ask how much those events really changed political, social, economic, or other relationships among people, whether that change was unprecedented, and whether the institutions and attitudes born in the years 1776–89 foreshadowed even more striking change in the future. Granted, "change" is a pretty bland word; it would be far more zesty to ask how "revolutionary" or "radical" was the American founding. But change it is: everyone knows what it means.[53]

One may begin by disposing of the contemptuous argument that the American founding was conservative and the Constitution reactionary because the most *outré* political activists of the time did not get their way. In other words, just because real democracy, social leveling, and female emancipation did not triumph after 1776, the Founding Fathers were hypocrites to speak of the rights of man.[54] But if the refusal of a people at large to embrace the agenda of its most extreme members makes them conservative, then every society is conservative all of the time. Likewise, if the failure of one generation of reformers to achieve all their progeny accomplished a century or two later makes them reactionary, then every society has been so. The only accurate method to judge the magnitude of historical change is to examine the context in which it occurred without reference to what one *wishes* had happened or what *did* happen later. That method reveals the American Revolution changed plenty.

Consider the mid-eighteenth-century colonists. They lived in a monarchy, empire, and matrix of hierarchies in which everyone bowed to his betters and even wives addressed their husbands as Mister. Privileges, not freedoms, determined one's prospects, and privileges were obtained either by birth or patronage. Social equality was not just restricted, it did not exist. The republican revolution born of the English, Scottish, and American critiques of monarchy changed all that. People in a republic were citizens, not subjects, individual human beings endowed with rights and responsibilities, not minions, dependents, or petitioners. And the change was pervasive. John Adams surmised that the revolutionary spirit was born of "a systematical dissolution of the true family authority" inasmuch as American sons and daughters increasingly left their homes and hometowns, married whom they pleased, changed churches, and chose their own trades. Americans as a whole rebelled against the metaphor of a "mother country" nurturing her colonial children. The men of 1776 were in most cases the first of their families to obtain a college education, wealth, or social prestige. They imagined something Europeans considered outrageous and, in their settings, impossible: that *every* man might aspire to education, wealth, prestige, and power. Just as shocking was the founding Americans' conception of virtue. To be sure, their views of human nature were derivative, but they carried into practice the astounding proposition that what others damned as sin or vice might "have the virtue" of enriching lives, expanding liberty, and fostering the pursuit of happiness. Commerce was "next to religion in humanizing mankind," thought Dr. Rush, and if Jefferson and Adams dissented, it was because they missed part of what their countrymen were about. Americans craved equal opportunity, equal rights, and a broadly expanded franchise. To be sure, no leading Founder endorsed raw democracy, but all rebelled against "slavery" in the sense of abject dependence on lords, masters, or the state, and translated equality of souls before God into equality before the law.[55]

An argument has been made and supported by a mountain of evidence that the American Revolution was not the cause of these great changes so much as the product of them. That is, the colonists gradually became republican, egalitarian, and socially mobile over the course of the eighteenth century, which explains why they shucked off the old order at the moment they did.[56] No doubt there is much truth in that. But the run-up to the rebellion, the war, and the political soul-searching that followed just as surely completed that process by expelling dissenters, inviting Patriots to think of themselves as citizens, and making them aware of the "new men" they had become. Americans ceased to *behave* and self-consciously started to *act*.

Most telling, once Americans started to "make laws for themselves," as Tom Paine had urged, they produced three astounding innovations in the ways people related to each other, their government, and the human race. The first was religious liberty, the second federalism, the third free immigration.

Do not be misled by the failure of the Federalists to say much about religion or even make a polite reference to the Almighty in the Constitution. The reason was *not* that they were enlightened secularists who thought faith unimportant. On the contrary, a large majority of the Framers were confessing Christians and church officers, while even skeptics repeatedly named faith and morals indispensable props for self-government. But Americans were a people of many denominations; to favor or punish one or another was sure to imperil the Union. So the Framers said nothing about religion because it was just *too* important; the only solution lay in forbidding federal restrictions on free exercise of religion and leaving it up to states to decide whether to have local religious establishments. Madison even endorsed religious liberty as the best means to *promote* sincere faith in people, and of course almost all the Framers agreed with Witherspoon that civil and religious liberty leaned on each other.[57]

Federalism based on overlapping sovereignties was a stunning innovation that defied Old World logic and appeared cumbersome, if not self-destructive. It remains a novel and fragile experiment even today. But the Federalists meant somehow to reconcile both order and liberty and *empire* and liberty in a way Rome and Great Britain had not. They attempted it not only because they were eager to gobble up North America, but because they realized an America "too free" to defend itself in an imperialist world would soon cease to be free at all.[58]

It goes without saying the prospects of the new nation relied on immigration as much as the original colonies had. If the United States were to make good its claim to half a continent or more and develop its riches, it needed lots and lots more people than it contained in 1789. Over the life of the colonies, from 1607 to 1776, they had finessed British law with regard to immigrants by treating naturalization as a contract. Thus, colonies did not "adopt" aliens into the king's family and make them subjects, but asked only that they swear local allegiance and behave themselves. After 1776 all the states legislated lenient procedures for naturalization, some requiring as little as a year or two of residency. But no uniform standard existed and confusion reigned as to what made one an American citizen. The Constitutional Convention drafted a comity clause requiring states to recognize each other's citizens, but could not agree on whether to make naturalization easy or hard. What if Turks began sailing over or Loyalists flooded American shores, some delegates cried. The periodic fight over whether to exclude "undesirables" thus dates from the nation's birth. But Americans' initial bias was strongly in favor of immigration. The first law Congress passed in 1790 required of naturalized citizens only two years of residency, good character, and an oath to uphold the Constitution. No literacy test, no religious test, no property requirement. It was, as John Adams might have put it, an *epocha* in history.[59]

The most powerful argument *against* the hypothesis that the American founding brought stunning change would seem to be that women gained nothing while Indians and Negroes were outright losers. Or rather, that *would* be a powerful argument if significant changes in the status of those groups were occurring anywhere else in the world at that time. With one exception—a judicial decree abolishing slavery in Britain itself in 1772—such changes occurred nowhere, so Americans can scarcely be branded as retrograde. A contrary argument can be made, however, that the roles scripted for women and imposed upon Indians and blacks during the founding were necessary supports for the advances in civil liberty Americans *did* achieve.[60] Once that subtle, ironic insight sinks in, much of nineteenth-century American history begins to make sense as well.

It is the fate of eighteenth-century women to be described in the collective. Few sources have been unearthed concerning the lives of individual women, and those that are known are necessarily special. Consider, for instance, the remarkable Eliza Lucas Pinckney, born in 1722 to a British army officer in the West Indies. The family moved to South Carolina when the Spanish war of 1739 loomed, and since her father was often absent and her mother bedridden, young Eliza took on the management of their *three* large plantations. But she did more than raise and sell crops and oversee slaves. She conducted diligent experiments with vines, fruit parings, silkworms and mulberries, and most of all, indigo, which thanks to her became a Low Country staple. She taught herself French and the harpsichord, wrote, did expert needlework, and after marriage to Charles Pinckney raised three famous children as well. How did she find the time? By rising each day at 5 A.M.: it made life longer, she quipped. When her sons became Patriots after 1776, Eliza was torn: her father was by then British governor of Antigua. But she embraced the American cause and not only persevered when the enemy sacked her plantations and scattered her slaves, she even pronounced herself rich beyond measure to have fine sons and "contentment in mediocrity." Eliza died of cancer in 1793, but not before Washington offered her the nation's praise and thanksgiving.[61]

It is tempting to make Eliza Pinckney, Catherine Littlefield Greene, Mercy Otis Warren, who published a history of the American Revolution in 1805, or her friend Abigail Adams, who famously asked her husband, John, to "remember the ladies," into prefigures of the feminist movement of the subsequent century. But they were not. Pinckney and Greene were dutiful daughters and wives and taught their children to embrace traditional sex roles according to nature, virtue, reason, and piety. Abigail did not seriously expect Congress to legislate household equality, and John replied teasingly that "our Masculine systems" of law were the only defense men had against their total control by women! In the event, no mention of women was made in the Constitutional Convention, the only reference to women in *The Federalist* was Hamilton's warning in Number 6 against the intrigues of courtesans, and the only state to experiment with women's suffrage, Quaker-influenced New Jersey, repealed it in 1807. The legal status of wives remained what is was under Common Law, which is to say *feme covert*. That meant a wife was "covered" by her husband just as a daughter was a legal extension of her father. Accordingly, adult white women in 1774 owned on average about half the property men did, with the ratios most extreme in New England and least extreme in the South (thanks to their respective male death rates).[62] But few voices were raised against a system set up ages before for the *protection* of women during their virginity, childbearing years, and widowhood. So long as society remained agricultural and a woman's main calling in life was procreation, female emancipation as understood 50 or 150 years later was unthinkable. Thus, Jefferson meant and gave no offense when he hoped ladies would be "contented to soothe and calm the minds of their husbands returning ruffled from political debate" and observed, "Appointment of a woman to office is an innovation for which the public is not prepared, nor am I."[63]

In terms of cultural roles, by contrast, the American founding worked a decided change in the status of women. In the eighteenth century, once widely regarded as a "golden age" for colonial women by contrast to their sisters in Europe, women possessed no cultural space outside the household and their status was a function of their relation to men. They might "rule the roost" and regard the house, furniture, and servants as "theirs," but the household was all that they had, and daily life on the farm was an eternal cycle of tedious chores. Thus do women's diaries speak of spinning and weaving, weaving and spinning, in the interstices of time between other duties. If one's marriage was happy and children healthy, that was great solace. If not, life was awful. Then the War of Independence broke out. Women could not help but get caught up in it, whether by hearing men argue over the table, taking over men's functions as bookkeepers, tillers, merchants, and purchasers, or defending their barns and larders against raids. British plunder and rapine turned many apolitical women into hot Patriots. A Ladies' Association arose under Esther DeBerdt Reed for the relief of the army. Spinning clubs donated clothes. Washington pronounced himself vexed by the long train of camp followers trailing his army, but appreciated the service they performed as nurses, washerwomen, cooks, and sources of comfort. Abigail Adams even considered patriotism in a woman a higher virtue than in a man since women served without hope of honor, glory, or office.[64]

Among the effects of the rebellion and war was a new appreciation of women as partners and supports in the otherwise male American enterprise. The erosion of rigid patriarchy observed by John Adams sped up. Old notions of women as mentally dim (if not daft) and morally weak gave way among many men to a notion of women as gritty, alert, self-reliant, and above all keepers of virtue. This might have been, at least partly, a reaction *against* the freedom a growing proportion of eighteenth-century women claimed to engage in pre- and extra-marital sex. The New England practice of allowing sweethearts to share a bed (bundling), the increase in illegitimate births, the spread of venereal disease, and the importation from Britain of didactic tracts impressing on girls the wages of sin all testify to sexual indiscipline and the anxiety it invoked.[65] But if the founding fathers and mothers of republican culture wanted young women to guard their petticoats and thereby discipline young *male* behavior as well, they had to accord women a new moral independence and social status. To be sure, the change was uneven and gradual, more in evidence in towns than on farms. But a new "rhetoric of self-worth" was emerging whereby women were expected to assert themselves rather than remain silent and obedient. Author Judith Sargent Murray celebrated "the excellency of our sex." Dr. Benjamin Rush preached: "Let the ladies of a country be educated properly and they will form its manner and character." A Connecticut academy accorded mothers the highest national calling, because they alone "plant the seeds of vice or virtue in their offspring." If the American founding proved anything, it was the thinness of most men's devotion to country, each other, or God. But women, it was decided, were another matter entirely. Women ought and in fact *must* be the keepers of the flame, the repositories of ethical precept and heroic myth, the vestals guarding the household gods, the transmitters of true religion and virtue, the tamers of men. After the American Revolution, and especially after 1800, many women exploited their new status as republican vestals to sally forth from the household and invade two other mighty bastions of culture: churches and schools.[66]

Native Americans, by contrast, were orphaned by the creation of the United States. In the 1780s the lingering presence of redcoats and the weakness of the Articles of Confederation did permit northern tribes to stage a brief rally. As late as 1791, Little Turtle's confederation inflicted the worst defeats ever suffered by American forces in Indian wars. President Washington tried conciliation, offering to purchase Ohio for $50,000 and sending the message: "We should be gratified with the opportunity of imparting to you all the blessings of civilized life, of teaching you to cultivate the earth, and raise corn; to raise oxen, sheep, and other domestic animals; to build comfortable houses, and to educate your children, so as ever to dwell upon the land." The tribal council replied, "Money, to us, is of no value," and continued to ambush intruders. But then the new Constitution came into play. Congress voted to double the size of the regular army, and Washington, testing his powers as commander-in-chief, called Mad Anthony Wayne out of retirement to conquer Ohio. In August 1794, when Wayne burned the Indian towns around Fallen Timbers and the British based in Detroit refused Indian cries for help, Little Turtle's alliance dissolved. The Treaty of Grenville opened up most of the present state of Ohio to land speculation and settlement.[67]

McGillivray, chief of the alliance of southern tribes, did not try to resist. He was savvy to the white man's politics and knew the Constitution meant he could no longer fight Georgia in isolation. So he led a delegation of Creeks to New York in 1790 and concluded a treaty with War Secretary Knox confirming the southern tribes' title to lands to the west. Of course, that was contingent on the federal government somehow forcing state governments and wild pioneers to honor treaties with Indians. But the Creeks had no other choice besides glorious extinction in war.

Enslaved Negroes, likewise orphaned, lacked even that choice. Why was chattel slavery never discussed at the Constitutional Convention? For the same reason religion was not: it was a deal-breaker. Of course, abolitionist sentiment made some headway in the years of the United States' founding. Northern states' constitutions or statutes provided for the more or less gradual extinction of slavery. (New York held out until Governor John Jay shamed it into grandfathering slavery in 1799.) Washington integrated the army as early as 1775, enabling some five thousand black soldiers and sailors to fight for the Patriot cause. Prominent Virginians such as Mason, Henry, and Washington groped for means of purging their state of an institution they imagined a curse. Jefferson affected agreement, but in fact opposed a bill in the state legislature for gradual emancipation because it did not provide for deportation of blacks beyond Virginia's borders. He thought white prejudice, black resentment, and "the distinctions that nature had made" were bound in the end to spark "convulsions which will probably never end but in the extermination of the one or the other race."[68] That fear was more pronounced in the Carolinas and Georgia, where blacks were a majority in numerous counties.

Accordingly, the Constitutional Convention dared not notice the Banquo's Ghost haunting its every debate, while the thirteen state ratifying conventions mentioned slavery *not once* in some 150 suggested amendments. Abolitionists later claimed that since the word *slavery* did not appear in the Constitution there was no explicit sanction of it. But that was hogwash. The Constitutional compromise sheltered slavery in numerous ways, as Charles Cotesworth Pinckney told South Carolinians: "Considering all circumstances, we have made the best terms for the security of this species of property it was in our power to make."[69] The notorious three-fifths clause gave whites in slaveholding states extra representation in Congress and the electoral college. The prohibition on the taxing of exports was a disguised subsidy for plantation commodities. The compromise over the slave trade gave the South a twenty-year grace period before other arrangements needed to be made. The obligation of the federal government to suppress domestic violence meant even northern states would have to help quell slave revolts. The cumbersome procedures needed to amend the Constitution gave the South veto power over efforts to legislate abolition. Northerners went along with it all because in return they got a nation united for commerce and defense and the right to *suppress* slavery in their own neighborhoods.[70]

The mightiest reason to ignore the one-seventh of Americans who were in shackles was that slaveholders and the laws of their states held them to be a species of *property*. What was at stake was thus more than national unity, but the right to private property that all Americans, north and south, understood to be the bedrock of liberty. Imagine a government with the power to condemn tens of millions of dollars worth of private property at the stroke of a pen or the barrels of guns! Such a government would be a tyranny beyond the imagining of King George and Lord North. Even northern states did not really "free" any slaves, they merely banned creation of new slaves by import or natural birth. The only means to abolish the institution while maintaining a rule of law, therefore, was for slaveholders voluntarily to relinquish their property under some suitable formula, or gratuitously exit the Union.

Apologists for the Framers often claim they postponed the divisive issue of slavery in the belief the problem would solve itself over time. Abolitionist sentiment was spreading throughout the upper and backwoods South, thanks largely to Methodists. Growing numbers of planters lamented their own thralldom to the institution and manumitted their slaves. Washington did an experiment at Mount Vernon, claiming to find hired labor more economical than caring for slaves. The soil of the Tidewater was wearing out. The clock was ticking on the slave trade. It seemed reasonable to conclude slavery was slowly dying . . . until, in late 1792, Caty Greene hired a young college man to tutor her children in Georgia.

The thirty-eight-year-old mother of five was frisky as ever and, for a change, feeling flush. Thanks to the Constitution, her friends Washington and Hamilton now presided over a solvent national government. Thanks to her friends, Congress finally voted in 1792 to indemnify the estate of Nathanael Greene.[71] So Caty asked Yale president Ezra Stiles to recommend someone to school her brood. Stiles mentioned a promising graduate with a gift for mechanics: Eli Whitney. He was twelve years younger than Mrs. Greene and fell entirely under her spell, especially when she offered to set up a laboratory for him at Mulberry Grove and bankroll his experiments with machines. Georgia planters had dabbled in cotton, but the labor required to gin raw cotton, that is separate the seeds from the fiber, made the process slow and expensive. Whitney heard "a number of respectable Gentlemen at Mrs. Greene's who all agreed that if a machine could be invented which could clean the cotton with expedition, it would be a great thing both to the Country and to the inventor." He promptly designed a wooden cylinder with teeth that combed the cotton when turned by a crank. It had only one glitch: the sticky cotton clung to the teeth, clogging the machine after just a few turns. Caty watched, considered, and stepped away for a moment. She returned with a brush (whether a hearth broom or clothing brush is disputed) and held it against the cylinder to clean away stubborn fibers. "Thank you for the hint," said Whitney. "I have it now."[72]

A full-size prototype driven by a horse walking in circles was soon in operation at Mulberry Grove. Whitney went north to apply for a patent from Secretary of State Jefferson and set up a factory. Caty pledged her plantation as collateral to other lenders and endeavored to raise more cash for Whitney by plunging into a scam that was the talk of all Georgia: the Yazoo Company. Its scheme was to buy up land Georgia claimed way out on the Mississippi and sell it to the planters bound to pour in once cotton gins were available. Then everything fell apart in quintessential American fashion. Mad Anthony Wayne's hated political rival was elected governor of Georgia, and his first act was to revoke the Yazoo Company's privileges and call down "fire from heaven" (through a magnifying glass) to burn all its deeds and accounts. Then Whitney reported their business was ruined. "Surreptitious gins are erected in every part of the country; and the jurymen at Augusta have come to an understanding among themselves that they will never give a verdict in our favor, let the merits of the case be as they may." At length Whitney quit to take up an offer to mass produce firearms for the U.S. army. Poor Caty was ruined again, her beloved Mulberry Grove sold at auction for a mere $15,000.[73]

In 1791 the United States produced just 9,000 bales of cotton, of which less than 10 percent was for export. Nine years later, America harvested 156,000 bales, over half of which was for export. A few decades more and Whitney's invention made fortunes for thousands of planters from Georgia to Texas, who demanded slaves in such numbers that Virginians, far from freeing their bondspeople, began to *breed* them for sale in the Gulf states. That was hardly the future Gouverneur Morris imagined when, after writing the Constitution, he mused: "This generation will die away and give place to a race of Americans."[74]

So the orrery, a magnificent meld of science and art, began turning. Thanks to the inspiration of Madison and Hamilton, the wisdom of Franklin, the mediation of Wilson, the clerking of Sherman, the eloquence of Gouverneur Morris, the blessing of Washington, and not least Hugh Williamson's virtue, the U.S. Constitution was drafted and ratified. It made the nation an elegant solar system in which the federal government attracted and glowed life into the states without consuming them in its central fire. The states in turn gave the sun glory precisely because they were free to spin in their own orbits. Checks and balances kept the spheres in proportion, their celestial music in harmony. But the orrery was only a "more perfect union," not perfect; it was not astronomical, not God's creation, but a legal creation of men. The real solar system moved of itself by the mysterious force of gravity. The Rittenhouse orrery was turned by a crank, moved by the hand of man. That meant the United States government could function "like clockwork" only so long as willing hands turned its crank, turned it forward not backward, and agreed to take turns at the handle. The orrery in fact demanded so great a self-discipline and *respect for the law* from the American people, odds were they would wreck the machine in short order. That is why Franklin, asked if the Convention had formed a republic or a monarchy, told the inquiring woman, "a republic—if you can keep it."

# MASTER BUILDERS, PARTY MEN, AND A ROGUE
## Freemasonry, Republicanism, and America's Future, 1791–1800

"The revolutionary wars of Europe, commencing precisely at the moment when the Government of the United States first went into operation under this Constitution, excited a collision of sentiments and of sympathies which kindled all the passions and imbittered the conflict of parties till the nation was involved in war and the Union was shaken to its center. This time of trial embraced a period of five and twenty years, during which the policy of the Union in its relations with Europe constituted the principal basis of our political divisions and the most arduous part of the action of our Federal Government. With . . . the wars of the French Revolution terminated, and our own subsequent peace with Great Britain, this baneful weed of party strife was uprooted."

Thus did John Quincy Adams, at his presidential inaugural in March 1825, adumbrate America's first quarter century under Constitutional government. No sooner did "this experiment upon the theory of human rights" begin in 1789 than the French Revolution erupted. Soon Europe and the Atlantic became theaters of ideological war. No one knew whether America's republican sapling could ride out the storm or how the twig might be bent. The name "United States" was more wish than reality before the 1790s, while during that decade the passions noted by Adams verged on paranoia. Did Federalists like Hamilton tilt toward Britain because they really meant to impose corrupt oligarchy, perhaps even monarchy, on the United States? Did Republicans like Jefferson tilt toward France because they really meant to impose mob democracy, perhaps even terror, on the United States? Such dissension threatened "all our earthly hopes," but in retrospect Adams felt "exultation and cheering hope" because both parties displayed talent, patriotism, sacrifice, and "a liberal indulgence for a portion of human infirmity and error." Both helped to forge a disparate people into a mighty *nation.*

No sources reveal the American mind more pithily than presidential inaugural speeches. They are the epistles in the bible of civic religion, which is why new presidents (or their speechwriters) are careful to echo past orthodoxies even if they mean to reinterpret them in light of new circumstances. So it was, said John Quincy Adams, Americans embraced a "political *creed,* without a dissenting voice": that the will of the people is the source, and the happiness of people the end, of all legitimate government; that popular elections and divided sovereignties are the best guards against abuse of power; that a suitably strong military under civil control is the best defense; that freedoms of the press and religion are inviolate; that "the policy of our country is peace, and the ark of our salvation union, are articles of *faith* upon which we are all now agreed." Then Adams quoted Psalm 127—"Except the Lord keep the city the watchman but waketh in vain"—and like his five predecessors committed the nation to "His overruling Providence."[1]

How *did* the nation survive the trials of 1789–1815? Obviously the Framers drafted wise rules for a game in which citizens hustled for happiness, however defined. But why did citizens and states choose to obey those rules? Why didn't they evade them, rebel, or secede from the Union when votes went against them, or they suspected the worst of their internal opponents, or shuddered over external threats? Why did all faithfully continue to turn the crank on their Constitutional orrery? One reason was that attempts by Britain or France to bully and divide Americans tended instead to unite a people jealous of their liberty and continental destiny. In short, courage (or pride) and hope (or cupidity) required they hang together. But Americans also exercised self-restraint because many believed their Union an "ark of salvation" watched over by a God both universal and tribal. Already, in the eighteenth century, evangelicals imagined America the agency for the Second Coming and Millennium (or vice versa).[2] But Methodists, Old Light Calvinists, Deists, and Unitarians likewise believed God smiled on America. Even Anglicans, Catholics, and Jews were free to worship in their ways so long as they conformed or subordinated their creeds to America's calling. Continental Army chaplain John Hurt preached love of *country* should be "the governing principle of your soul" and called for sacrifice of sins "on the altar of *liberty*." Chaplain Israel Evans rewrote the beatitudes: "Blessed be that man who is possessed of the true love of liberty; and let all the people say, *Amen*. Blessed be that man who is a friend to the common rights of mankind; and let all the people say, *Amen*. Blessed be that man who is a friend to the United States of America; and let all the people say, *Amen*."[3]

It is commonplace to explain the absence of religion in the Constitution by an accident of timing. Enlightenment rationalism peaked in the 1780s, while the Revolution's upheaval and frontier expansion unchurched many Americans. Had the Constitution been drafted twenty years later, after the miscarriage of the French Revolution, the rise of Romanticism, and the revivals known as the Second Great Awakening, American law might have been grounded literally on Biblical faith.[4] We cannot know. But this supposition obscures a deeper truth: people are never secular in the sense of having no supreme loyalty. *Something* ranks first in their hierarchy of values, and if it is nation then nationalism is their religion. What the U.S. experiment in religious liberty meant was not indifference—on the contrary, all the Framers considered religion broadly conceived the source of the self-control republics required. But they did insist sectarian loyalties never trump loyalty to the nation itself. Preachers sensed this at once, which is why all denominations scrambled quickly and adroitly to pledge allegiance to the United States of America.

Francis Asbury was born in 1745 on a prosperous farm in Staffordshire, England, and raised by his parents on the Bible and prayer. His one stint of schooling was ended by the taunts of classmates and the master's switch. But his intellectual engagement with Scripture was intense and then rendered emotional when "God sent a pious man, not a Methodist, into our neighbourhood and my mother invited him to our house; by his conversation and prayers, I was awakened before I was fourteen years of age." The "not a Methodist" mattered because Francis was soon attracted to followers of John Wesley, the Anglican pastor who founded the Methodist movement to teach piety, charity, literacy, and self-help to England's poor. Bishops were not pleased, so Wesley's clergy took to "riding the circuit" like country lawyers and preaching in fields like George Whitefield. Asbury observed them, judged by their fruits, and concluded: "The people God owns in England, are the Methodists." At age twenty-five he answered Wesley's call for missionaries to go to America.[5]

"Whither am I going?" he wrote aboard ship. "To the New World. What to do? To gain honour? No, if I know my own heart. To get money? No: I am going to live to God, and to bring others so to do. . . . If God does not acknowledge me in America, I will soon return to England." Asbury was instead so warmly acknowledged that the "circuit" he rode took him to every colony, then every state, almost *every year* for forty-two years. His journal includes thousands of place names from the ports to the trans-Appalachian frontier. He wore out dozens of horses in the course of preaching some seventeen thousand sermons. "In traveling thus I suffer much from hunger and cold." In 1798 a doctor found Asbury suffered "from boils, fevers, rheumatism, sore throat, weak eyes, bronchitis, asthma, toothache, ulcers, neuralgia, intestinal disorders, swollen glands . . . and galloping consumption." His portraits depict a benign, weather-beaten face framed by flowing white hair, but the most famous image shows only a weary horse and bundled-up rider leaning into a cruel storm.[6]

As he labored to make Americans Methodist, Asbury contrived to make Methodism *American*. He remained a British subject after 1776 and was banned from Maryland for refusing its loyalty oath. John Wesley made matters worse with pamphlets condemning the rebellion, hence Methodists were taken for Tories. "I . . . am truly sorry," Asbury wrote, "that the venerable man ever dipped into the politics of America." So he petitioned Wesley for permission to set up on his own and, after the Treaty of Paris, Wesley said yes. In 1784 American Methodists convened in Baltimore, a strategic location from which Methodism could reach north, south, and west. Oxford's Dr. Thomas Coke ordained Asbury superintendent and his pastors elected him bishop. A new Sunday Service purged the Prayer Book of all references to the English church and crown, and added an article blessing the U.S. government. Asbury's message was also peculiarly tailored to American needs. No matter what the text for the day he invited sinners to repent and promised sanctification *in this life* as well as salvation in the next. He inveighed against alcohol, gambling, promiscuity, and other vices that ruined promising careers, promoting instead temperance, marriage, and thrift. He founded Sunday Schools to spread literacy and published scores of tracts. He insisted Methodist chapels be built "plain and decent" lest the church be indebted to wealthy patrons. He inveighed against slavery and ordained such path-breaking African American clergy as "Black Harry" Hosier and Richard Allen, founder of the African Methodist Episcopal (A.M.E.) Church.

Above all, Asbury and his cohorts combined disciplined top-down administration with local flexibility. Neighbors gathered in private homes to sing, pray, and hear sermons whenever a circuit rider passed through. Women especially were encouraged to witness to husbands and sons and lead Bible study. Methodists required no pedantic training from ministers or complicated catechism from converts. Theirs was a populist religion for humble women and men, personal, emotive, and joyful. If Whitefield pioneered advertising techniques in evangelism, Methodists pioneered marketing techniques, their circuit riders serving as traveling salesmen who "knew the territory." Finally, Methodists became natural leaders of the frenzied revivals that began on the frontier in the mid-1790s. By the time Asbury died amidst a circle of hymn-singing friends at Spotsylvania Courthouse, Virginia, in 1816, he had traversed 275,000 miles and built a denomination numbering 2,500 pastors and 150,000 parishioners stretching from New England to beyond the Mississippi. More than that, he bequeathed spiritual and organizational methods that would, a generation later, make Methodism the largest and most self-consciously American denomination in the land.[7]

Father John Carroll, by contrast, was not only a native (born in Maryland in 1736) but a cousin of a signer of the Declaration of Independence and brother of a signer of the Constitution. Yet Carroll knew his church was the most suspect of all. Catholics, the old enemies of freeborn Englishmen, swore fealty to a monarch and court composed of Machiavellian cardinals in distant, decadent Rome. What is more, John expatriated to Europe and dreamed of serving at the Vatican until the pope broke his heart by disbanding his Jesuit order. Only then did he come back to Maryland to rue the "ignorance, indolence, delusion, and irresolution" of American priests in the turmoil after 1776. If the Catholic church was to survive in the new republic, it needed firm leadership soon. So Carroll wrote the pope requesting an American bishop: "You are not ignorant that in these United States our Religious system has undergone a revolution, if possible, more extraordinary than our political one." But the papacy *was* ignorant; it planned to appoint a vicar apostolic from its office of Propaganda. No! replied Carroll in "his strongest animadversion." If Catholics were to be tolerated in America, they must be led by a bishop of their own nationality and choosing. He won his point after the Vatican petitioned Congress for the right to send over a legate and received this reply: "being purely spiritual, [the proposal] is without the jurisdiction and the powers of the Congress, who have no authority to permit or refuse it." Perplexed by this strange new doctrine, the papacy simply made Carroll shepherd of America's twenty-four priests and twenty-three thousand communicants pending resolution of their status.[8]

Carroll seized the chance to domesticate Catholicism. When his kinsman Charles Henry Wharton turned Anglican and attacked the Roman church as alien and hostile to liberty, Carroll rebutted his charges with controlled passion. When Catholic laymen asked for guidance, he encouraged them to incorporate under local state laws. But when Catholics in New York and Philadelphia insisted on choosing their own pastors, Carroll saw how democracy might compromise "unity and Catholicity." In 1788 he asked once again for an American bishop and praised God when this time Pius VI granted his wish. Catholics, like Methodists, chose Baltimore, the burgeoning brick city on the Chesapeake, for their base. Carroll was their unanimous choice to establish the see. Consecrated in England in 1790 he returned with a commitment from the Society of St. Sulpice to found a seminary. He charged his priests to build "as it were, from the foundation" a great church, but always to cultivate "a warm charity and forbearance towards every other denomination." But the defining crisis of his ministry was provoked by Rome, not by Protestants. In 1797 Carroll disciplined a schismatic German Franciscan, only to be rebuked by the Vatican. He protested it was "entirely out of place" for Rome to intercede without due process. He warned such undermining of episcopal authority might cause the American church to fly apart. He again won his point.[9]

Thanks to Carroll's sensitivity to American opinion, compliance with civil law, and respect for lay vestries, the Catholic Church quietly flourished, not least in the nation's capital. A friendly Protestant donated the plot in Georgetown on which the first Catholic college arose. Catholic planters ceded most of the land on which the federal buildings arose. The first mayor of Washington City (as the new town was initially dubbed), was Catholic and the Baltimore cathedral was designed by Benjamin Latrobe, architect of the U.S. Capitol. The priesthood grew rapidly, thanks to an influx of clerics fleeing the French Revolution. Holy orders were founded, most famously by the great educator Mother (now Saint) Elizabeth Seton.[10] In 1808 the church spun off new dioceses in Philadelphia, New York, and Boston, making Carroll an archbishop. By 1829 the American province would boast six seminaries, six colleges, three universities, thirty-three monasteries, and a laity of two hundred thousand. When Carroll died on the Feast of St. Francis Xavier (December 3), 1815, Baltimore newspapers were trimmed in black, an honor previously given only to Washington. *The Telegraph* called him a patriot endeared among Protestants, and a man whose charities "fell around him like the dews of heaven, gentle and unseen." In sermons Carroll lauded Providence for so directing human affairs that Catholics, "agreeably to the dictates of our own consciences, may sing canticles of praise to the Lord, in a country now become our own, & taking us into her protection."[11]

Scarcely less problematical was the future of the Church of England. Most of its priests had fled, many adherents were tarred (sometimes literally, often justly) with Toryism, and its established status was lost. To survive, it needed to cease being the "Church of England," but the fourteen priests who gathered at Woodbury, Connecticut, in 1784 did that cause more harm than good. They elected as American bishop-designate Samuel Seabury, a "High Churchman" of Tory leanings. That was anathema to the state's Congregationalists and indeed to most American Anglicans. Seabury then made himself anathema to the English church, too, by accepting consecration from "non-juring" (pro-Stuart) Scottish bishops! Happily, down in Philadelphia the Patriot rector William White proposed to reorganize the church on a federal basis, provide for election of bishops, and draft a republican Book of Common Prayer. When at last Parliament approved an American province, White and Samuel Provoost of New York were made bishops and in 1789 called a convention in Philadelphia to found the Protestant Episcopal Church of the United States. Seabury insisted its General Convention include a House of Bishops, but otherwise the Episcopal Church was governed by lay vestries and diocesan standing commit-tees. It was no less than a "quiet revolution" in the most royalist denomination.[12]

America's 420 Presbyterian congregations were already organized thanks to John Witherspoon. But a synod in 1788 reconciled their Scottish and English wings, designed a democratic Plan of Government, and adopted an American version of the Confession of Westminster. Most Dutch Reformed had declared independence from the Netherlands in 1755 and founded Queen's College (Rutgers) in 1770. In 1794 the last Dutch holdouts agreed to join a Reformed church in America. Lutheran pastors convened in 1781 to establish national norms, permit lay voting, and prepare a more evangelical liturgy. Lutherans also merged with German Reformed and in 1787 founded Franklin (later Franklin and Marshall) College in Lancaster. Baptists had no need to Americanize and were among the fiercest of patriots. Nor had their growth ever slowed. The 25 Baptist houses of worship in New England in 1740 grew to 266 by 1790, with 218 more in Virginia. To the extent Baptists reorganized it was mostly to lobby for disestablishment of the Congregational church in New England and promote the revivals of the Second Great Awakening. Almost every denomination purged hymnals of monarchical lyrics and added patriotic psalmody.[13]

So the great revivals that began in the 1790s did not, as some say, "Christianize" Americans who, though scattered and ignorant, had never been pagan. Nor did the revivals "Americanize" Christianity. The churches themselves did that soon after independence when smart clergymen saw the way to succeed in this market was to embrace the civic religion, whereas the sure way to fail was to suggest the American dream was mundane, hypocritical, or idolatrous. But what was the *content* of this civic religion to which all knees must bow? Certainly it evolved over time, as John Quincy Adams' speech stated. But the original tenets of American civic religion derived in good part—dare one confess?—from Freemasonry.

According to its *Constitutions* of 1738, the modern Masonic movement began with a meeting of four London lodges at the Apple Tree Tavern in 1717. Three of them traced their origins to the medieval fraternities of stonemasons and other artisans who erected the great cathedrals. The fourth was made up of gentleman-scholars such as Sir Isaac Newton, and when one of their number was chosen Grand Master, the order fell permanently under their sway. These intellectual Freemasons were seekers after ultimate truth. While they extolled science and reason they by no means rejected numerology, astrology, alchemy, revelation, indeed anything deemed truly ancient. We know English Whigs made hoary precedent the measure of rectitude in politics, law, and religion, and were prepared to concoct versions of history in accord with their views. Thus did country-party critics of Walpole invoke the Anglo-Saxon utopia they presumed had existed before 1066. But Freemasons delved deeper and had grander ambitions. They meditated on the pyramids, Diana's temple in Ephesus, Stonehenge of the Druids, and above all Solomon's Temple. How were these built, and what truths had they expressed? Freemasons craved the lost skill, virtue, and wisdom evidently possessed in antiquity, and imagined a mystical kinship between themselves and those ancient builders.[14]

Accordingly, the *Constitutions* traced the roots of Freemasonry to the descendants of Adam and Eve who first learned husbandry, metallurgy, geometry, and construction (Genesis 4 and 5). After Noah's Flood human beings grew in wisdom under the watchful Eye of the Creator until they achieved the apotheosis of "Divinely inspired Architecture and Masonry" considered by Newton a reflection of the heavenly Jerusalem. That was Solomon's Temple, the construction of which was overseen by the Lebanese master Hiram Abiff

(1 Kings 5–7). The Babylonians razed the edifice after the conquest of Judah, but just as devastating, in Masonic lore, was the premature death of the Master Builder himself. According to legend Hiram was accosted at noon by three workers who demanded to know the Master's Word. When he would not divulge it, they murdered him. Solomon sent out a search party that discovered his grave but, finding no hint of The Word on the corpse, reburied it with a sprig of acacia. Solomon then ordered Hiram dug up again and carried by masons in white gloves and aprons to the temple's Holy of Holies. This death and "resurrection" of the Master and loss of his Word were re-enacted in rituals promoting apprentices to the Master's degree.

The elaborate rites celebrating advance in one's Craft to the second, third, and higher degrees involved secret liturgies, tests and confessions, handshakes, passwords, and symbols such as the all-seeing Eye, the builder's compass, rule, and angle, the zodiac, and the letter "G" for the god whose name is Geometry.[15] Some eighteenth-century Londoners considered all this sophomoric silliness. But the order's strict secrecy also caused outsiders to accuse Freemasons of conspiracy, even conjuring. Jesuits imagined the cult a *faux* Christianity based on gnostic, necromantic, and Jewish cabalistic traditions. Freemasons placed great store in Old Testament history, but seemed to ignore the New Testament save for the prologue to the gospel of John ("In the beginning was the Word"). What is more, their philosophy seemed to deny original sin and affirm human progress through science, enlightenment, and obedience to a Supreme Architect of the Universe calling men to their destiny. The destiny to be made manifest was the building of a more perfect earthly union represented as a glorious pyramid reaching toward heaven.

Freemasonry materialized the Judeo-Christian quest for salvation. Consider what those aspiring to the degree of Royal Arch Mason experienced. They dedicated themselves to illuminating the darkness with the Way, the Truth, and the Life. They passed under a "living arch" of companions who lowered their weight upon them until they were crawling, because "he that humbleth himself shall be exalted." They gazed up to a Royal Arch supported by the two pillars of Solomon's Temple and crowned by a zodiac revealing mysteries from heaven. Beneath were seven stars for the seven degrees passed to achieve this point, the morning star rising on peace and salvation, and a coat of arms depicting the soul's evolution from lion (wild beast) to ox (tamed servant), to man (rational being), and finally to eagle (soaring to heaven). There was also a coffin, Hiram's acacia sprig, the chest bearing the Ark of the Covenant, a snake for secret wisdom, a cornucopia, the letter G, and a checkered floor expressing the light and darkness co-existing on earth. Then the Word was revealed to be—not Jesus or Hiram—but Osiris, the Egyptian demiurge who created the world at the behest of the Supreme Being.[16]

Who is the Supreme Being, the Divine Architect? The ultimate mystery is not that Freemasonry claims to replace Christianity, Judaism, or other religions, but that it transcends them. The Divine Architect is the ultimate God, "ineffable and inconceivable, whose religion includes in itself Christianity as its highest humanly achievable stage, but is not, itself, Christian." Freemasonry was a sort of metaphysics superimposed on human religions, rooted in history but aimed at the future, and offering truth beyond truths, an ecumenical truth all men might accept. How much lodge members believed the mystical teachings cannot be guessed. Benjamin Franklin, one of the first colonial initiates, quipped as early as 1730, "Their Grand Secret is, That they have no Secret at all." But Freemasons did promote the enlightened ideals of science, useful knowledge, toleration and brotherhood, personal virtue, and progress. The order grew rapidly in Britain, France, Italy, and across Europe to Russia. It appealed to Deists, but also to men seeking a middle ground between lax Anglicanism and fierce Puritanism. Finally, it welcomed Jews into the highest social and intellectual circles without asking them to convert. Indeed, Freemasons never proselytized because men must already be enlightened to qualify, the proof of it being simply their desire to join. The presence of Jews, however, had momentous consequences. Because many of them were outspoken on matters spiritual and moral, the London Masters began in 1741 to restrict *all* sectarian disputation in lodge meetings, thereby anticipating by fifty years the secularization of American political discourse.[17]

Colonial elites fell in love with Freemasonry, not least because it gave them a chance to rub shoulders with high-born Englishmen of advanced views. But they took the fellowship home and by 1776 planted over a hundred lodges. The combined membership of about fifteen hundred seems small, but it included many of America's most prominent merchants, professionals, and civic leaders, including at least sixteen signers of the Declaration of Independence (some put the count much higher). The war posed a crisis because some lodges were torn between Tory and Patriot sentiments. What is more, Puritans suspected Freemasons of heresy, Deists scorned its mysticism, and both despised its almost Catholic love of ritual. But Freemasonry not only survived, it flourished as a semi-official cult. First, American Freemasons downplayed the "ancient mysteries," stressing instead the science, brotherhood, and vision of progress uniquely suited to the founding of a virtuous republic. Second, they were instrumental in importing the ideas of Europe's enlightened philosophers, most of whom were Masons themselves. Third, American lodges did not hide their lamps under bushels, but proudly radiated their public benevolence. (The Masonic Hall in Philadelphia opened in 1755 with a grand procession through the streets.) Fourth, Freemasonry all but captured the Continental Army's officer corps thanks to the patronage of Washington, Greene, Knox, Sullivan, and other generals. Their watchwords were honor and brotherhood. They imagined themselves a sacrificial vanguard. After the war they founded the Society of the Cincinnati to preserve that martial fraternity. Fifth, Freemasonry adjusted to independence as quickly as churches. One by one lodges swore off obedience to London's Grand Lodge and became in effect congregational with each choosing its Master. Finally, patriotic Freemasons forgave brothers of Tory sympathies and encouraged all Americans to do likewise.[18]

In the army and Congress, Freemasons helped design the symbols of the republic. The first American flag depicted the snake of secret wisdom hissing "Don't Tread on Me." The second battle flag borrowed the Union Jack's red, white, and blue, but replaced the crosses of St. George and St. Andrew with thirteen stars implying a heavenly destiny and thirteen stripes suggesting the blood and bandages (or body and blood?) of the army. In the gloved hands of soldiers the flag soon became holy: an icon handled with priestly care and disposed of when necessary by ritual burning in the same manner as blessed palms and vestments. The Great Seal of the United States, adopted in 1782, was a Masonic amulet with the now sacred number thirteen. The obverse depicted thirteen stars, the thirteen letters of *E pluribus unum,* and an eagle (highest stage of the soul) with a thirteen-striped shield. The arrows and olive branch in its talons invoked a fighting faith, but one whose purpose was brotherhood. The reverse depicted the all-seeing Eye, the thirteen-letter motto *Annuit Coeptis* (He favors these undertakings), and the unfinished pyramid of the *Novus Ordo Seclorum* (New order of the ages). Both Latin expressions were lifted from Virgil, shortened to the right number of letters, and subtly changed so that what Virgil meant as a prayer ("please favor") and a prophecy ("a new order of ages begins") became declarative statements of fact.[19]

"As Men from Brutes distinguish'd are, a Mason other Men excels." Freemasons considered themselves the Master Builders of the nation, the priesthood of its civic religion, the natural aristocracy touted by Jefferson, the agents of Benjamin Rush's dream of turning Americans into "republican machines." The Boston, New York, Philadelphia, and Charleston lodges included most of their states' leaders. At least thirty Freemasons attended the Constitutional Convention. No less than ten of Virginia's thirteen governors and some 50 percent of its assemblymen between 1786 and 1819 were Freemasons. In cities and across the nation ambitious men joined or formed lodges if only to "network" with men who could make their careers. By 1820, New York had over 500 lodges, Virginia 114, and national membership was estimated at eighty thousand. Such growth could not have occurred without the blessing of clergymen, and indeed they joined in large numbers or lauded the order. Freemasons founded more voluntary associations to assist widows and orphans than did churches over these decades. Yale's Nathan Strong, head of Connecticut's missionary society, was a Mason. So was Presbyterian John Taylor, first president of Union College. So was Congregational pastor William Bentley, who believed anyone "unable to separate the social character from the religious opinion" could never exercise a "rational and universal benevolence." So was Bentley's friend Prince Hall, an ex-slave who became a leader of the free Negroes in Boston and Grand Master of the first African lodges. So was Philadelphian Absalom Jones, first African American Episcopal priest.[20]

Nothing confirmed the Freemasons' function as republican priests like their ground-breaking ceremonies. It was customary to bless government buildings, schools, canals, bridges, war memorials, even churches in rituals celebrating the Supreme Being's favor on America. The only known public address by Paul Revere occurred when his lodge laid the cornerstone of the new Massachusetts Statehouse on the Fourth of July, 1795. America, he said, was the land where science and the arts flourished in liberty, and he admonished his brothers to live within the "compass" of good citizenship so they might enter that "Temple where Reigns Silence and Peace." Revere was only saying out loud what the mystical portrait of a Freemason's Heart revealed with pen and ink. Its superscription read SUPPORTERS OF GOVERNMENT, the heart nourished all virtues, and its core declared: "The Bible rules our faith without Factions / The Square and Compass our Lives and our Actions."[21]

Where is this leading? To a sinister revelation of the gnostic origins of the United States, or some conspiracy theory?[22] Not at all. First, recall Freemasons believed a man must *already possess* love of wisdom to join a lodge in the first place. Hence, one cannot attribute the political behavior of Freemasons to some sort of indoctrination. Second, Masonic fellowship, far from encouraging faction, demanded *suppression of partisanship*, at least inside the temple. But however inchoate, Masonic influence can hardly be denied when almost the entire elite in states such as Virginia, North Carolina, and Kentucky were suckled in universities run by Freemasons. What the fraternal order did between 1790 and 1830 was offer Americans in leadership and those aspiring to it a republicanism above faction, region, and sect, a civic religion enjoining unity and restraint so citizens might get on with the sacred task of completing that pyramid beneath the Eye and before the eyes of the world. No man embodied that cause more than the Master from the Alexandria lodge who marched at the rear (like the celebrant at the start of a mass) of a procession of officials, soldiers, and bedecked Freemasons to the groundbreaking ceremony for the United States Capitol. When the two columns arrived they turned toward each other, forming a corridor through which strode the Master. His white apron and gloves in place, he lowered a silver plate into a niche in the foundation, eyed the plumb line to ensure the cornerstone was laid with precision, and strewed sacramental elements of corn, oil, and wine. The assembly made an "awful [awe-filled]" invocation to the Supreme Architect, the Masons "chanted honors," and the soldiers fired a salute. Finally, a short address declared the unity of Freemasonry with the republic as symbolized by the silver plate whose inscription read: "in the thirteenth year of American independence . . . and the year of Masonry, 5793."[23] By the Christian calendar, the ceremony on Capitol Hill occurred September 18, 1793. The Master in apron was George Washington.

## *The Fourteenth State: Vermont, 1791*\*

**The Green Mountains quilted with firs, maples, beeches, and birches, remained a "no-man's-land" during the French and Indian wars. But as early as 1749, New Hampshire governor Benning Wentworth began chartering towns between the Connecticut River and Lake Champlain, taking care to grant himself the choice parcels. Yorkers across the Hudson River sued on the grounds that these "New Hampshire Grants" lay within their own charter. When the king in council upheld their claim in 1764, New York created its own Green**

---

\*One of my goals in this new American history is to ensure that every region and state receives the attention it deserves. Hence, each state admitted to the Union beyond the original thirteen is presented in this format within the text. Readers eager to press on with the main narrative may skip them or return to them at leisure. But these "historical travelogues" of new states do illustrate the general themes of the narrative in addition to providing rich, sometimes humorous, local color.

Mountain grants and courts to enforce them. But by 1775 some sixteen thousand farmers, mostly from western Massachusetts and
Connecticut, squatted in the Grants and habitually broke up legal
proceedings with riots. Then the American Revolution erupted.
Feisty "Green Mountain Boys" took up arms to secure independence, not only from Britain but from their neighboring states.

The brothers Allen (Ethan, Heman, Ira, Levi, and Zimri) were
chieftains of that frontier militia, and chief among them was
Ethan. The family traced its lineage to a companion of Thomas
Hooker, the founder of Connecticut, but had not done well in the
century prior to Ethan's birth in 1738. All they had was a middling
farm in Cornwall, a rustic town chided by Hartford wit Timothy
Dwight: "The God of Nature, from his boundless store/threw
Cornwall into heaps, and did no more." The God of Nature
obsessed Ethan when his father died suddenly in 1755. A skeptic
disgusted by the New Light/Old Light debates among Calvinists,
he had denied original sin and conversion and believed divine justice required the salvation of all. Was his father in hell, Ethan wondered, and what of his own soul? At length, a friend of advanced
Enlightenment views, Dr. Thomas Young, helped Ethan adopt his
father's philosophy and focus on bettering himself and his seven
siblings in worldly ways. But a decade of farming and iron monger-
ing got him nowhere. In 1765 Ethan sold the forge only to decide
he had been cheated. Not one to delay satisfaction, he stripped
himself naked like a Celtic warrior, beat up the purchaser, then
ignored a restraining order and did it again! Ethan decamped for
Northampton, only to be expelled in 1767 for *defending* Jonathan
Edwards' disciples when the town tried to silence them. Finally he
noticed where lay fortune and fame: in those New Hampshire
Grants whose value was so depressed by the English court judgment that vast tracts could be had for nearly nothing. The Allens
lit out for the north to establish themselves as "the most enterprising, if not the most scrupulous" speculators.[24]

They were shrewd to choose Lake Champlain's eastern shore
as a base. The soil was fertile and the water route north ensured
an outlet for timber, potash, grain, and skins. It was also defensible. By 1772 Ethan and "twelve or fifteen of the most Blackguard

Fellows" (in the words of an absentee landlord) formed the nucleus of a vigilante band hot to punish Yorkers bent on stealing homesteads with pieces of paper. They set up their own courts and assembly and their decisions stuck because the Green Mountain Boys enforced them. Styling himself Colonel Commandant, Ethan won national fame with his victory at Fort Ticonderoga, but then joined the abortive invasion of Canada. Captured in September 1775, Ethan spent two years in harsh British confinement. Back in the "Grants" his brothers consolidated the family's almost feudal authority. In June 1777, town selectmen gathered to frame a republican constitution for what was now called Vermont ("New Connecticut" being quickly rejected). It provided for universal manhood suffrage, making it the most democratic of all state constitutions, and was the first to prohibit slavery. But so long as New York challenged Vermont's right to exist the Allens refused to join the U.S.A. On the contrary, they entertained petitions from sixteen New Hampshire towns eager to join their republic and even imagined annexing Berkshire County, Massachusetts, to form "Greater Vermont." New York governor George Clinton had had enough. In 1779 he ordered Vermonters to submit or face an invasion (this while redcoats occupied New York City). Ethan's answer was to arrest all Yorker officials and seize their gunpowder. Green Mountaineers sang: "Come York or come Hampshire—come traitors or knaves, if ye rule o'er our land, ye shall rule o'er our graves; our vow is recorded—our banner unfurled; in the name of Vermont we defy *all the world!*"[25]

After Saratoga the northern frontier fell quiet. From 1780 to 1784, Ethan wrote his apologia, *Reason the Only Oracle of Man,* perhaps to comfort himself anew upon the death of his wife. It was the first openly Deist tract published in America, and while its ideas were derivative they were nonetheless shocking. Original sin was a "pious fraud" and all established churches from Moses onward were instruments of oppression. Christ was a worthy moralist, but no one honored his precepts less than Christians themselves. The truest religion was a natural one that invited men to rely on their own reason and conscience and live in equality.

That was where happiness, the "glorious purpose" of creation, might be found. Allen had to pay for the book's publication and it met with little acclaim. But neither did it arouse indignation, which says much about the peculiar culture of Vermont.[26]

What would become of the Green Mountain republic? That question became acute after 1783, when Britain ceded the land to the United States, but Ethan remained a law unto himself. He could get no satisfaction from the impotent Congress, was not keen on statehood if it meant sharing in the national debt, and realized his republic's economic channels ran north. So Vermont sought a treaty with Canada and even considered returning to British rule. London was interested, but loath to provoke new hostilities in America. So Vermonters imagined their land a "New World Switzerland." That was where matters stood in 1789, when Ethan died at fifty-one, the victim (his brothers thought) of the harm done him as a prisoner of war. The family mourned, took counsel, and decided Levi should sail for London and make one last bid for a British alliance.

In his absence, everything fell apart. Vermont's population approached eight-five thousand, most of the new residents farming the southwestern region around Bennington. They looked to the United States for their markets, resented the Champlain junto and its "treasonous" British demarches, and were vexed by the same indebtedness that provoked Shays' Rebellion. When the Allens' front man, Governor Thomas Chittenden, proposed to fund debtor relief through a tax on lawsuits (a Stamp Act), the electorate was irate; when he proposed a state bank, his opponents cried fraud. Then a scandal confirmed their suspicions: Chittenden confessed to granting a lucrative charter to Ira Allen on the sly. The October 1789 election swept out the regime, and the new assembly moved to settle New York's claims and petition for statehood. The groundwork was done by Alexander Hamilton. He quietly talked terms with Vermont Federalists, persuaded Yorkers to quit their claims for $30,000, and courted Allen supporters with talk of a canal linking Lake Champlain to the Hudson. In October 1790, a convention at Bennington ratified the Constitution, and Congress made Vermont the first fruit of its magnificent federal provisions on March 4, 1791.[27]

The Allen brothers' influence faded, but their legacy did not. Smallholders and debtors, the Champlain district, and the state's various exiles from orthodoxy regained control of the state, raising up such volatile Anti-Federalists as "Spittin' Matt" Lyon.

On the map Vermont is New Hampshire turned upside-down. Its farms, towns, churches, and mills look the same, and the people of both were of solid New England stock. But whereas New Hampshire was settled from eastern Massachusetts in Puritan days, Vermont was peopled later by non-conformists from western New England. Both states love liberty (the New Hampshire motto is "Live Free or Die"), but the Hampshireman claims freedom to *resist* change, especially if that nettles Bostonians. The Vermonter claims freedom to *embrace* the heterodox, especially if it nettles New Yorkers.

Did Washington ever glance skyward and ask the Divine Author, "Why must it always be me?" He wanted only to improve Mount Vernon and some of his lands in the west. He had served his country beyond the call of duty. He cherished his reputation and knew politics could only besmirch it. Yet he also knew the Constitutional Convention designed the presidency for him, and by late 1788 he worried lest Anti-Federalists promote a candidate such as New York's Governor Clinton, opposed to a strong federal executive. Hence Washington's stipulation to the effect he would serve only if elected unanimously was statesmanship rather than vanity: he was already protecting the office. For his part, Hamilton was learning to manipulate the rules of American politics and realizing the rules were flawed. Under the Constitution each member of the electoral college was to cast two votes *for president*, with the second place finisher becoming vice president. So Hamilton had to promote a second candidate, preferably a northerner, strong enough to defeat other opponents but not so strong as to rival Washington! His choice was John Adams, but his work that winter was to conspire with some Federalist electors *not* to cast their second votes for him. Hamilton succeeded too well. When the Senate tallied the vote in April 1789, Washington was named on all ballots, but only Massachusetts and New Hampshire were solid for Adams. He won the vice presidency with a mere thirty-four of the remaining sixty-nine votes. Adams was livid when he learned of the ploy, a fact pregnant with mischief should he and Hamilton ever need to unite in a party.

Washington's purpose was to prevent the emergence of parties. So he made his journey to the erstwhile capital city of New York a leisurely procession in which he displayed his dignity and republican humility to the people of the middle states. Later he toured New England and in 1791 journeyed south so Americans might see and respect, but not fear, their president. In churches, Masonic temples, and synagogues he denounced bigotry and exhorted good citizenship. At the inauguration he added the pledge "So help me God" to the presidential oath, noted how Providence had guided Americans to liberty and "unparalleled unanimity," and concluded by invoking the benign Parent of the Human Race.[28]

The fifty-seven-year-old Virginia gentleman then mustered his characteristic stage presence and placed it at the service of his new office and country. "Characteristic" is the right word, because Washington knew any effective leader must be an actor sufficiently self-possessed not to step "out of character." The least lapse into haughty, capricious, or otherwise regal behavior, even if born of honest frustration, would be seized upon by Cassandras who believed with Patrick Henry that the presidency "squinted toward monarchy." Washington's unique position also required deliberation. He confided to Madison that as everything he would do "will serve to establish a precedent, it is devoutly wished on my part that these precedents be fixed on firm principles."[29] He must resist being hasty or frivolous, however trivial the issue at hand, lest he plant seeds of discord to sprout in the future. Thus, while many Americans and most Europeans doubted this Constitution could survive a few years, Washington asked what it would take to make it an order for *ages*. Accordingly, he appeared at his inauguration in a modest brown suit sewn in Connecticut and was pleased when the House of Representatives rejected titles for him such as His Excellency. He kept open house for citizens and courted members of Congress. He applied no litmus test for officials save support for the Constitution, appointed men of all regions, and shunned using patronage to reward friends or build personal power.[30] He even refrained from exercising his veto power lest he appear to thwart the will of the people.

On the other hand, Washington spent his generous salary of $25,000 on entertainments, a coach-and-four attended by liveried footmen, and other displays befitting a head of state. He brooked no indignity and used symbols and ceremony to elevate his office. But if restraint was needed to make an elected monarch acceptable to the American people, energy was needed if the executive were to fulfill his role sketched in the Constitution. So Washington protected his prerogative whenever national interests were engaged and established the president's right to name and dismiss cabinet members. He stormed out of the Senate rather than await its "advice and consent" *in advance* of a diplomatic mission and asserted what is now called "executive privilege" regarding sensitive information. Most subtle, but of surpassing importance, was Washington's elevation of the federal executive above those of states, as symbolized by his refusal in Boston to call on John Hancock. It was up to the governor to pay court to the President.[31]

The legislative branch took some months to get organized. The last session of the laughingstock Congress under the Articles degenerated into a shouting match over where to house the new federal government. At length Congress temporized, making New York "the place for *commencing*" the new regime. But Yorkers were, as always, so divided they never managed to stage an election in 1789, with the result that only ten states (Rhode Island and North Carolina not yet having ratified) elected the first president and Congress. How to choose senators and representatives? State kingpins had to learn that part of the political game, but it came to them naturally. Where one faction comfortably dominated a state the legislature opted for at-large elections so its candidates could win a clean sweep. States with competitive politics resorted to district elections, but that only inspired what was later dubbed gerrymandering. Bostonians proved masters at this, but down in Virginia, James Madison nearly lost his campaign for Congress in a mostly Anti-Federalist district cobbled together by Patrick Henry.[32]

Federalists rode the wave of ratification to a majority of seats in both houses, but the First Congress embarrassed itself by not showing up on March 4, 1790. News of a flu epidemic was partly responsible—one member later died of it. Thanks to a well-run *executive* agency (the post office), the House and Senate did meet quorum calls on April 1 and went to work with an energy the old Congress never displayed. But then, the old Congress had no executive branch in need of a watchdog. The populism of the House was evident in its choice of the German (and high-degree Freemason) Frederick Augustus Muhlenberg as first Speaker and its decision to open the doors to the public and press. The House also insisted on its equality, but senators, thinking theirs was an upper house, did not reciprocate. They kept their gallery closed and informed the president they owed him no explanation for decisions that did not go his way (this over a rejected appointment).[33]

Besides approving departments of the executive branch and setting up a federal judiciary, the most pressing task of the First Congress was to pass that Bill of Rights sought by several states at the moment of ratification. Madison himself endorsed the idea in his tough congressional race and was persuaded of its utility by Jefferson. Perhaps an enumeration of rights was only a "parchment barrier" against executive abuse, wrote Jefferson, but "the legal check which it puts in the hands of the judiciary" would empower courts to strike down oppressive acts by a *legislative* majority. (Thus did he endorse judicial review, to his later regret.) To be sure, no bill of rights could be exhaustive or unambiguous, but the damage of having none might be "permanent, afflicting, and irreparable." Politics also militated in favor of a Bill of Rights. If Anti-Federalists were still hoping to abort the Constitution by peddling fear, it was up to Federalists to provide reassurance. Thus, Madison determined to pass the very Bill of Rights his Federalists at the Convention rejected, while *Anti*-Federalists determined to block what they previously (but disingenuously) demanded! On June 8, 1789, Madison delivered a great speech arguing that all power is prone to abuse, not least by the people themselves. That was the gap in the British system: it provided a bill of rights against the king, but placed no restraints on the caprice of Parliament. The American system must fix that by checking the Congress and states as well, and making the courts "peculiar guardians of those rights."[34]

Did Anti-Federalist skeptics cheer? On the contrary, they made noises about there being more pressing business, while stupid High Federalists aided their obstruction by continuing to oppose a Bill of Rights and then, six weeks later, referring the matter to a committee. But Madison was on the committee. Under his whip the 210 amendments proposed by state conventions were distilled down to a manageable list. The House tabled the report for ten days, but finally took it up on August 13 when enough Federalists awoke to the fact the Antis *wanted* to block a Bill of Rights, pin the blame on them, and persuade their states to bolt the Union. With the air thus cleared, the Federalist majority quickly debated and passed seventeen amendments, twelve of which survived conference with the Senate. Two more fine touches completed the masterpiece Americans revere. First, Madison's nutty notion of inserting amendments into the Constitution itself was nixed by Connecticut's owlish Roger Sherman. Patching new clauses into the body of the text would invalidate the signatures on the original document. Second, the states in their wisdom failed to pass exactly two of the amendments, hence America's civic religion was blessed with its own Ten Commandments: the Bill of Rights.

The first eight amendments were guarantees of individual rights lifted mostly from George Mason's Virginia list: free exercise of religion, freedom to bear arms, freedom from the quartering of soldiers and unreasonable search and seizure, the right to due process and speedy trial by jury, and protection against excessive bail, fines, or cruel and unusual punishment. The ninth amendment stated the enumerated rights did not deny by implication additional rights, and the tenth, borrowed from the Articles of Confederation, reserved to the states all powers not delegated to the federal government. Over two centuries Supreme Courts would interpret these rights in ways some Americans hated and others thought long overdue. But their immediate purpose was political and that purpose was met. As Anti-Federalist Richard Henry Lee complained, their hope of exploiting Federalist resistance to a Bill of Rights to sink the Constitution after its launch was "little better than putting oneself to death first, in expectation that the doctor, who wished our destruction, would afterwards restore us to life."[35] Virginia, still in denial, delayed ratification of the Bill of Rights until December 1791. But Anti-Federalism at the national level soon disappeared and busily reinvented itself as a more or less loyal opposition to the party of government.

The issue that ignited opposition was public finance. Everything else Federalists desired, including a strong foreign policy and uniform tariffs and laws to promote trade, depended on "raising a revenue" and establishing credit. But no sooner did Treasury Secretary Alexander Hamilton deliver his Report on the Public Credit to Congress in January 1790 than everyone realized the modalities chosen to finance government were not just a matter of who paid how much, but what sort of society the United States would become. Indeed, one might ask how the nation might have fared if Robert Morris, Washington's first choice for the Treasury, had accepted the post. No one doubted his brilliance. But Morris' speculative empire was always on the verge of collapse. He had no time for daily administration and would have been sorely tempted to dip into the till. By contrast, Hamilton was a scrupulous manager eager to spend his energies on public service. He was also too candid and trusting, qualities that rendered him tragic, but not before he made America safe for all hard-driving people, whether honest or not.

First, Hamilton's handful of clerks performed a statistical feat just to learn how deeply in debt the nation had fallen. Congress had amassed some $11 million in foreign loans and $40 million in domestic debt, while states still owed about $25 million. The secretary's bold plan called on the federal government to

(1) refinance the foreign debt at a lower interest rate, now possible thanks to Congress's power to tax; (2) fund the domestic debt *at par* with an interest rate lowered from 6 to 4 percent; and (3) assume all state debts. Nothing less would liquidate the monetary confusion left by the war, establish the good faith and credit of the United States, and supply the money and credit needed by a growing economy. If these plans were rejected, Hamilton warned, the nation would soon be bankrupt and impotent. "In the affairs of nations, there will be a necessity for borrowing. Loans in times of public danger, especially from foreign war, are found an indispensable resource, even to the wealthiest of them." He granted the apparent injustice of paying full value to speculators who had purchased bonds at a discount. But to discriminate in favor of their original holders—to pick and choose which citizens to reward or punish on the basis of some *moral* scale—would destroy public credit, kill the market for a floating government debt, and be a contractual breach "inconsistent with justice."[36]

Think how that message went down in some circles of Congress. Justice demanded government make speculators rich while stiffing penurious war veterans! Justice required people in states that paid off their debts to assume those of irresponsible states! Justice required a floating national debt for insiders to juggle while honest citizens were taxed to pay interest! Within days there emerged a "states rights" faction led by a thirty-three-year-old hothead from Georgia, James Jackson. A rice and cotton planter and slaveholder, he had fought for six years in the militia and helped found the state university. Now he emerged as the Patrick Henry of Congress, shooting fiery oratorical darts at everything northern. Delighted reporters soon spread his message: Morris alone stood to clear $18 million from Hamilton's plan and Jeremiah Wadsworth $9 million. If republican virtue was the soul of the nation, it was being killed in the cradle.[37]

Hamilton assumed his collaborator on *The Federalist* papers would manage his bills in Congress. But the debate over assumption revealed how much he and Madison misunderstood each other. They both believed in a federal government, but differed over what it should do. Hamilton envisioned a vigorous executive endowed with the credit needed to mobilize national strength and promote trade. His model was Britain and his hero was Walpole. Madison envisioned a government checked and balanced with minimal debt and low taxes so a largely agricultural people could look to their own parochial needs. His *foil* was Britain and his *demon* was Walpole. The sad end to their friendship can be explained by their backgrounds. One was a true nationalist raised in the Indies, trained in commerce, and indifferent (if not hostile) to the states. The other was a true Virginian raised on a plantation, hostile to foreign merchants, and suspicious of central authority. They had been allies because both were disciples of the Scottish Enlightenment, students of British politics, and Whigs. They became rivals now because Hamilton filtered all that through the "court party" lens and Madison that of the "country party."[38] Once the government they both desired was a going concern, with Hamilton leading the executive branch and Madison the legislative, it was apparent that their perspectives had always differed. Both understood the symbiosis between freedom and order. But Hamilton feared too little order while Madison feared too much. Both conceded the ubiquity of corruption. But Hamilton sought to harness it while Madison sought to repress it.

Accordingly, Madison moved to amend the funding bill so speculators were paid only the market price for their government bonds and original holders were compensated. Hamilton lobbied hard against this because it would defeat the greater good, which was to make federal obligations fully negotiable and thus, for all practical purposes, *money*. In any case, sorting out original holders (many of whom were long dead) would be costly, if not impossible, and unfair to investors who bet on the good faith of the United States. But Madison spurned all efforts toward compromise until his motion to gut the Treasury plan failed by 13 to 36 on February 22, 1790: a nice birthday present for Washington. Pennsylvania's shrewd Senator William Maclay attributed it to "the obstinacy of this man." So the chastened Madison changed tactics in the next fray over assumption of state debts, which all southern states save South Carolina opposed. He dickered over so many compromise plans that action was postponed until the chance came on June 19 to make the first and perhaps grandest "log-rolling" deal in the history of Congress. Jefferson recounted: "Going to the President's one day, I met Hamilton as I approached the door. His look was sombre, haggard, and dejected beyond description. . . . He opened the subject of the assumption of state debts, the necessity of it in the general fiscal arrangements and it's [*sic*] indispensible necessity towards a preservation of the union. . . ." The next day, over dinner, Jefferson and Hamilton urged Madison to move the issue in the House. But "it was observed, I forget by which of them, that as the pill would be a bitter one to the Southern states, something should be done to sooth them; that the removal of the seat of government to the Patowmac [Potomac] was a just measure, and would probably be a popular one with them, and would be a proper one to follow the assumption." Hamilton agreed to court Pennsylvania votes for this *quid*

*pro quo* by moving the capital to Philadelphia on an interim basis while
Madison won over wavering Virginia votes for the federalization of debts.
"This," Jefferson punctuated, "is the real history of the assumption."

The tale is a little too simple. Debate over the permanent capital was
ongoing, with Pennsylvanians touting Philadelphia or a new city on the
Delaware River (Morris, Justice James Wilson, and others wagered heavily
on that outcome) and Southerners calling for a truly "central" location (thereby
lodging the capital in rural, slaveholding country). Prior to Jefferson's dinner
the compromise was sketched out. But the fact Jefferson, Hamilton, Madison,
and above all President Washington were on board for the deal ensured the
votes would be there to pass both measures. In August Congress voted to
assume state debts and move the capital to Philadelphia until 1800, when
the federal government would take up permanent residence in a new city
upriver from Mount Vernon. New Englanders whose debts disappeared,
Pennsylvanians, and Southerners all sang *Hallelujah!* New Yorkers were the only
ones scowling.[39]

Hamilton pressed on with reports asking for an excise tax, a national bank,
and a national mint. He was happy to have Congress oversee the bank, but
expected 80 percent of its capital to be private since the government, at current
revenue levels, could never come up with the necessary $10 million itself.
Rather, the bank would be the vehicle whereby a cash-strapped but potentially
rich nation might mobilize the capital needed to provide liquidity for investment in manufacturing and trade. It would also give the executive branch a
safe, central place to deposit its revenues, keep its books, and draw funds in
emergencies. It all made excellent sense and passed both houses comfortably.
But Madison objected to a monopolistic bank sure to favor the rich and those
in proximity to its offices. He thought putting all the nation's financial eggs in
one basket courted disaster. He also objected on constitutional grounds, thus
framing the first "strict constructionist" argument. The federal government had
no power to charter a corporation. If permitted to breach its Constitutional
limits, it might "take possession of a boundless field of power, no longer susceptible to any definition." Madison had a point, a big point, and President
Washington, Secretary of State Jefferson, and Attorney General Randolph—
three more suspicious Virginians—shared his doubts. But Hamilton fought
back with a *tour de force* making the case for "implied powers." Article 1,
Section 8 of the Constitution authorized Congress to make all laws "necessary
and proper for carrying into execution the foregoing Powers." If a bank was a

necessary means to a Constitutional end, then this elastic clause authorized it. Washington deferred to his treasurer and signed the bill. On July 4, 1791, the first United States Bank opened its Philadelphia headquarters and branch offices in Boston, New York, Baltimore, and Charleston.

Madison's institutional fears proved groundless. The Bank worked, and thanks to Hamilton's probity no scandals tarnished the Treasury. But Madison's moral concerns were confirmed within days. The plan was to attract $8 million in public subscriptions by asking investors to pay a mere one-sixteenth of the cost of each share, in exchange for which they received scrip entitling them to pay the remainder on installment and receive options on additional shares. Since everyone expected the U.S. Bank to be trustworthy and profitable, investors mobbed the agencies on July 4, bought up the whole subscription in one hour, then took to the streets to hawk scrip for quick profit. Even artisans and shop-keepers sold off their inventories to get in on the "scrippomania." The priggish Jefferson despised it. Of course, he finagled his own finances by using his slaves as collateral, but this bank fostered British-style corruption, city corruption. He called it public plunder and was not surprised when Scottish and English mer-chants appeared in New York "to dabble in federal filth." The inevitable crisis arrived in August, when $25 scrip peaked at $325, and crashed. The Treasury promptly intervened to buy bonds and stabilize the market. For the first time Americans had a responsible central banker, and so great was their confidence that even once despised Continental bonds now hovered around par.

Thanks also to Hamilton, the U.S. Mint opened the following spring to confirm the dollar as the nation's currency. The word came from *thaler,* a Bohemian coin first struck in 1517, the year Luther launched the Reformation. Via the Habsburgs it came to Spain, whose peso was similar in size and silver. Since the peso was equal to eight *reals,* known in English as bits, Spanish dol-lars were called pieces of eight. Congress wisely dispensed with these "bits" in favor of a decimal system based on "cents" two years before the copycat French revolutionaries. When it came to designing paper money and coins, the Mint made good use of Masonic heraldry.[40]

Accounts of Hamilton's achievements usually conclude with his Report on Manufactures of December 1791. It seems to illustrate neatly how his economic vision differed from those of philosophical agrarians like Jefferson and alleged free-traders like Adam Smith. The report discussed the merits of protective tariffs, bounties for manufactures, constraints on exports of raw materials, pro-motion of inventions, and public works (internal improvements). Yet it was not

Hamilton's initiative, it was Washington's, because the President feared the United States would never know security until it was self-sufficient in the tools of war. Hamilton agreed, though his zeal to protect infant industries was tempered by the Treasury's dependence for revenue on duties from British imports. That he was not in favor of total free trade was obvious, but then neither was Smith, who exempted many goods and required reciprocity from foreign nations. Nor did Hamilton lack sympathy for the agrarian South, believing "the aggregate prosperity of manufactures, and the aggregate prosperity of Agriculture are intimately connected." Still, the report was construed by opponents as a design to favor northern interests and lobbyists able to bribe Congress into giving them subsidies. "Establish the doctrine of bounties," cried Hugh Williamson, and "people of every trade and occupation may enter at the breach, until they have eaten up the bread of our children." The Report on Manufactures inspired only a modest revenue tariff in 1792.

Hamilton's novel proposals for "research and development" and "industrial espionage" were also stillborn. The Society for Establishing Useful Manufactures organized by his assistant secretary Tench Coxe quickly raised $500,000 and a generous New Jersey charter for a town named for Governor William Paterson. Alas, society president William Duer and several directors unloaded their shares at a profit and abandoned the project. The same fate befell Hamilton's scheme for bribing skilled English mechanics to bring their employers' secrets to America. Congress would not fund such a plan, and Hamilton himself shrank from openly alienating the English . . . especially when the wars of the French Revolution erupted in 1792.[41]

## The Fifteenth State: Kentucky, 1792

"A richer and more beautiful country than this, I believe has never been seen in America yet," wrote George Rogers Clark the day he gazed upon the region soon known as the Bluegrass. "What is heaven like?" asked a preacher stumbling for words. "Why it is a mere Kentucke of a place." That colony of Virginia did appear to dispense all the needs of mankind, including lush pasturage, rich soil, woods dense with game, and precious salt abounding in licks. Over two hundred streams begged for mills. The Ohio, Cumberland, and Tennessee Rivers offered avenues to the interior and, via the Mississippi, the world. To be sure, the eastern Mountain District was ragged with gorges and pinnacles, the

Knobs a waste of steep hills and soggy canebreaks, the Pennyrile region pocked with sinkholes and caverns, and the Barrens burned over by Indians during buffalo hunts. But even Kentucky's wastelands were gorgeous habitats for birds, trees, flowers, and beasts native to all points of the compass. The land just south of the Ohio River seemed the heart of the continent.[42]

First in, of course, were the speculators. But rather than sort out their enormous claims, Virginia's burgesses just threw the frontier open to squatters in 1779. They arrived in the first of the "fevers" characterizing westward expansion. Long Hunters, those wilderness-loving leatherstockings, showed them the way. One was James Harrod, a black-bearded bear of a man who learned French and Indian tongues and made the first permanent settlement in the Kentuck. Fellow Pennsylvanian Daniel Boone was another. In 1775, Judge Richard Henderson's Transylvania Company hired Boone's party of thirty men and two women (his second wife and a slave girl) to widen the old Warriors Path for wagons and mark a trail through the Cumberland Gap. The going was as rough as legend decrees. When no Indian or buffalo trails were handy, the men hacked through forests and cane to make room for pack horses. Indians ambushed their hunters and scouts, and the late winter weather was cruel. But they arrived in March 1776 and threw up a rude fort. Henderson followed a month later, ecstatic with visions of Kentucky's future. He named the place Boonesboro and rewarded its founder with five thousand acres.[43]

Some twelve thousand pioneers followed Boone's trail during the war and another sixty-two thousand arrived overland or by keel- and flatboat from Pittsburgh in the seven years following 1783. All they learned was how hard it is to get into "heaven." For instead of settling rich farmland, the men, women, and children were forced to huddle in "stations" or build tiny log cabins on their perimeter. Cherokee chief Dragging Canoe's prophecy that whites would find Kentucky a dark, bloody land was borne out for nearly two decades, making daily life a choice between claustrophobia and terror. "The spring at this place," wrote an official at Harrodsburg, "is . . . fed by ponds above the Fort so that the whole dirt and filth of the Fort, putrified flesh, dead dogs, horse, cow, hog excrements and human odour all wash into the spring with the Ashes and sweepings of filthy Cabbins." Clearing land and planting a crop invited Indian raids, so pioneers lived mostly on salted venison, buffalo, bear fat, and "turkey pot pie." Even tools were scarce, but every man was obliged to turn out with a musket, powder, cartridges, bayonet, and canteen. Every convoy in the mountains was an armed force, every station a fortress, and women, too, were expected to work and perhaps fight. Only after Fallen Timbers in 1794 did the Indian threat fade.[44]

Most heartbreaking, the pioneers were just too numerous for most to obtain farms, and since Virginia's land laws permitted claims to be lodged prior to surveying, every farm's boundary was challenged. It was said Kentucky townships were too small to support one lawyer, but two or three could flourish, and "Whoever buys land there buys a lawsuit." The state of Virginia set up a commission in 1779 that found incompetent surveyors habitually recorded deeds with such reference points as "three oak trees" or "sharp bend in the creek." Commissioners still managed to settle 1,328 claims covering 1.3 million acres, but for every winner there were multiple losers. Boone was among them. He lost all his acres to frontier lawyers and fled in search of "elbow room" to Missouri (only to lose his land there after the Louisiana Purchase). By 1792 two-thirds of Kentucky's white males were landless.[45]

That helps explain the confusion attending Kentucky's movement for statehood. It began in 1784, when "Kentucky Colonel" Benjamin Logan called a meeting in Danville to organize government, but so bitter were the counties' politics that eight conventions over five years failed to produce a consensus. An elite faction was formed by Virginia planters who procured large estates through money, influence, or legal finagling. (Their flavorful Kentucky burley helped reinvigorate tobacco exports.) These planters, led by the father of future Chief Justice John Marshall, expected statehood to secure their land and slaves. Next, a "court party" united judges and lawyers who craved the high offices and business statehood would bring them. A "partisan" faction united the luckless men who cared less about statehood than land distribution. There was even a joker in the pack: the popular General

Wilkinson, who hinted at independence and a bargain with Spain to open the Mississippi. Finally, in 1788, a ninth convention accepted the Virginia assembly's terms for separation and the U.S. Congress offered statehood effective June 1, 1792, pending ratification of a state constitution.

Few believed the brawling factions could do it until fat, bald George Nicholas ("a plum pudding with legs") arrived to broker the tenth Kentucky convention. A friend of Madison, Nicholas meant to replicate Virginia's aristocratic republic, which meant siding with planters, bribing the lawyers, and stiffing the partisans. When Presbyterian minister David Rice pleaded for an antislavery provision, Nicholas argued the Virginia Compact forbade interference with property and in good Jeffersonian fashion warned emancipation would cause miscegenation and violence. When a motion to abolish slavery lost 16 to 26, the convention not only established the precedent for slavery south of the Ohio River, it added a clause forbidding clergy to serve in the state legislature! The planter/court coalition also provided for a strong governor chosen by an electoral college and a supreme court with *original* jurisdiction in land disputes. The populist faction did win a broad suffrage and secret ballot. But that only inspired such stuffing of ballot boxes the state became notorious for "the damndest politics."[46]

Thanks to the phosphate-rich loam feeding its grass Kentucky was always about horses. Early on, laws were passed "to preserve the breed" (being the get of Bulle Rock and other thoroughbreds Virginians had imported from England), fix the quality and price for stabling to protect the animals, and set aside commons for racing. In 1793 the French consul noted that "horses and lawsuits comprise the usual topics of conversation." Then, around 1800, the first kegs of *poa pratensis* (bluegrass) seed were shipped to Louisville by Mennonites in the Conestoga Valley.[47] A second Kentucky gift was whiskey, especially the nectar named after the county of Bourbon. Yet a third was frontier education. Precocious Transylvania College, founded twelve years before statehood, became alma mater to 2 vice presidents, 50 U.S. senators, 101 congressmen, and 36 governors. But most "all American" were the people. Quakers and Germans, French *habitants,* migrating Yankees such as Abraham Lincoln's forebears, Virginians, their African servants, and Scots-Irish bordermen mingled to make Kentucky the quintessential "border state," not only in terms of topography, but politics, culture, and eventually war.

One day in April 1791 a pantheon gathered in Philadelphia to dine and trade *aperçus* over the wine. Vice President Adams opined the British government would be "the most perfect constitution ever devised" if Parliamentary elections were more democratic and statecraft leeched of corruption. Jefferson blanched at such toleration of monarchy. So imagine his reaction when Hamilton retorted the British government "*as it stands at present,* with all its supposed defects" was the most perfect and would only be neutered by the reforms Adams proposed! To Hamilton, aristocracy kept the hands of the people ("a great beast") off the machinery of government, while corruption greased its gears. Jefferson, far from examining his own illusions about human nature, left disillusioned with Hamilton, convinced he meant to subvert the republic.[48]

Hamilton had indeed sinned, but his sin was truth-telling about the way all governments work. Jefferson was no less a hustler for power, but he scorned such straight talk and told people what they wanted to hear. He also hated Hamilton as much as he feared him. Jefferson, after all, was twelve years older, author of the great Declaration, and secretary of State. Yet Hamilton functioned as Washington's prime minister, oversaw the largest department, controlled the purse, and even trespassed in foreign affairs. Jefferson was a fellow Virginian, yet Washington seemed to prefer the New Yorker who had served by his side in the war (while Jefferson had skulked in the Piedmont). Lastly, where Hamilton was a dynamo the secretary of State was lazy. Six months to a year sometimes passed without a U.S. envoy overseas receiving a missive from Jefferson. He had plenty of time as well as resentment to pour into politics.[49]

In 1791–92, Jefferson and Madison moved to oppose what they imagined was Hamilton's "court party." They hired poet Philip Freneau to edit the *National Gazette* and savage the pro-administration *Gazette of the United States.* They encouraged other dissident journals, such Benjamin Franklin Bache's *Pennsylvania Daily Advertiser,* to expose Hamilton's alleged plots. They made a "botanical expedition" to New York where the Livingstons, Clintons, and the promising Aaron Burr might prove mighty allies. They called themselves

Republicans, implying their opponents were royalists. They encouraged Republican slates in the 1792 elections. And while none yet attacked Washington, Jefferson tried to get the President's ear and undermine the Treasury secretary. Hamilton and his allies fought back in their own newspapers and began to call themselves Federalists, implying their opponents meant to neuter the Union. Poor Washington attempted to mediate. "I regret, deeply regret," he wrote Jefferson, "the difference in opinions which have arisen, and divided you and another principal Officer of the Government; and wish, devoutly, there could be an accommodation of them by mutual yieldings." The breach could "introduce confusion, and serious mischiefs, and for what? Because mankind cannot think alike, but would adopt different means to attain the same end. For I will frankly, and solemnly declare that, I believe the views of both of you."[50]

"Believe the views of both": Washington was a Hamiltonian *and* a Jeffersonian! He saw the need for national strength and mobilization of men's baser instincts, but for the purpose of increasing the liberty that made republican virtue possible. Most Americans had a foot in both camps, although decades of paranoia and strife had to pass before they realized it. That was because the idea of a party system—a loyal opposition differing only over the "means to attain the same end"—was repugnant to American political philosophers, including Washington. Hence, the only purpose of strife could be to restore consensus through the *extirpation* of one faction by the other. Jefferson cloaked his intentions, only later confessing his purpose was to sink Federalism into an abyss beyond resurrection. Hamilton named the opposition "the first symptom of a spirit which must either be killed, or will kill the Constitution of the United States." The mortal duel was postponed in 1792 when Washington reluctantly agreed to serve another term. But Jefferson observed how this time all New York's and Virginia's second votes went to Clinton, and expected "a decided majority in favor of the republican interest" in Congress. Partisan flames were kindled, and gales off the Atlantic fanned them at once.[51]

From 1785 to 1789 Jefferson had served as U.S. minister in Paris. There he witnessed, through the eyes of his informant Lafayette, the first months of the French Revolution. He showed little interest in its exciting events until they turned violent, whereupon he had an epiphany. Was not the French Declaration of the Rights of Man and the Citizen an echo of his own Declaration? Were not the ugly accounts of "mobs and murders" with which

English newspapers obscured the great happenings "like the rags in which religion robes the true god"? He docked in Norfolk to find almost all his countrymen of the same mind. Washington was moved when Lafayette sent him the key to the Bastille. When Benjamin Franklin died in 1790, the French National Assembly declared three days of mourning. After September 1792, when news reached America the French had declared a republic, Federalists and Republicans alike staged "civic feasts." John Adams, one of the first Americans to adore his revolution but despise all those abroad, had early doubts. Jefferson, the first to *link* his revolution to those abroad, had early fears. In 1791 he shared with George Mason his view that if the French cause should falter, America herself would likely fall back into "that kind of Half-way house, the English constitution." In January 1793 he wrote William Short, his former secretary in Paris, that rather than the French Revolution fail, "I would have seen half the earth desolated. Were there but an Adam and Eve left in every country, and left free, it would be better than as it now is."[52]

No Cromwellian ever spit hotter fire than that. Did Jefferson mean to enlist Americans in a global war against all the monarchs of Europe? No, he did not. When the French Republic sent Louis XVI to the guillotine and Britain declared war, Jefferson recommended only that the United States maintain its tacit alliance with France (as leverage against Britain). Nor did he object when Washington declared the United States would remain "friendly and impartial" toward the belligerents. So Jefferson's letter to Short was really an invitation to Americans to enlist with *him* in a fight against "monarchism" at home. What is more, Jefferson's claim that ninety-nine out of a hundred Americans shared his sentiments seemed only somewhat exaggerated. The fever of ideological war and the example of French Jacobin clubs inspired the founding of thirty-five Democratic Republican Societies in the United States over two years. The German Republican Society was the first, but the movement's true "mother" (as Federalist muckraker William Cobbett damned it) was the Democratic Society of Pennsylvania, founded by David Rittenhouse, Charles Biddle, and other worthies. If Europe's monarchies stamped out the French Revolution, its charter explicitly stated, "this country, the only remaining depository of liberty, will not long be permitted to enjoy . . . the happiness of a republican government." These clubs were not officially partisan, but in practice they served as auxiliaries to the Republican party. Federalists were appalled when the clubs displayed seeming insouciance toward Robespierre's bureaucratized Reign of Terror. Did Jefferson's followers hope to exploit sympathy for the French Republic to attack life, liberty, and property at home in the name of defending those rights?[53]

Federalists feared the answer was yes; the war party in Paris *hoped* the answer was yes. It dispatched Edmund Charles "Citizen" Genêt to America with explicit instructions to incite an American attack on Spanish New Orleans (and make it a French naval base), conclude an alliance making the United States a veritable junior partner in the French "empire of liberty," and cajole the U.S. Treasury into paying the $5.6 million it still owed to France. The ecstasy with which Charleston welcomed Genêt in April 1793 raised his hopes. Crowds serenaded him in the streets; dignitaries and ladies toasted his mission. Governor William Moultrie brazenly offered his port to outfit French privateers and spoke of recruiting freebooters for an invasion of Florida. A triumphant eighteen-day procession north brought more of the same, climaxing in Philadelphia. So Genêt merrily outfitted privateers, offered George Rogers Clark command of an Army of the Mississippi, and violated U.S. sovereignty in so many ways even Jefferson was abashed. In August, Washington demanded the French government recall Genêt.[54]

That contretemps was embarrassing to Republicans. But what occurred down in Saint-Domingue (Haiti) was a nightmare from hell. When news of the revolution in Paris reached that French sugar colony in the West Indies, rich planters pressed for home rule, poor whites for equality with the rich, and free mulattoes for equality with the whites. None of them wondered how the Revolution's slogan "Liberty, Equality, Fraternity" might be interpreted by the island's slave gangs. Not, that is, until summer 1791 when the Africans ceased cutting cane and applied their machetes instead to the necks of planters and all who defended them. Savage civil war drove hundreds of white and black refugees into American ports, where terrified planters feared their own slaves might get ideas. Jefferson was paralyzed, because both possible means of restoring order in Saint-Domingue—a British invasion or a free black republic—sickened him. To make matters worse, the British cracked down on Yankee smugglers in the Indies, seizing 250 ships and causing New England to cry for relief. Nothing good could come from any of this so far as Jefferson was concerned. So he resigned from the State Department on December 31, 1793. Madison begged him to stay if only to check Hamilton. But the nimble Jefferson quit precisely to avoid being implicated in Hamilton's policies and to benefit if they proved ruinous. So he went home to redesign Monticello all over again and trade politics for the bucolic. Perhaps he even believed it; as John

Adams wrote after bidding Jefferson "good riddance," ambition is "wonderfully adroit in concealing itself from its owner."[55]

With Hamilton's help Washington laid the cornerstone of a temple of prosperity. But its foundation could not be extended until Spain opened the Mississippi to American trade and Britain evacuated those western forts on U.S. soil. To accomplish the latter (and head off a Republican campaign to boycott British goods), Washington dispatched John Jay to London. He returned with a treaty that caused Republicans to burn him in effigy. Given his lack of bargaining power, Jay did not do badly. The United States had no navy and a smaller army than a rich English boy's toy soldier collection. Hamilton openly confessed the nation was impotent to defend neutral rights. Meanwhile, over in Paris, U.S. minister James Monroe was fawning all over the French Revolution. So the British, in their anger and strength, demanded Americans swallow a long list of restrictions on their trade with the French, grant most-favored-nation status to Britain, pay their pre-Revolutionary debts, and drop counter-claims for slaves freed by redcoats during the war. Although not trivial concessions, they were well worth making in exchange for a British withdrawal from the whole Great Lakes region. Republicans railed nonetheless, hating especially the "pay your debts but no slave compensation" provisions. Then they leaked Jay's treaty to Bache's new screed, the *Aurora*. Senate ratification seemed a pipe dream.[56]

Some 240 miles west of Philadelphia, however, avid Republican constituents inadvertently spoiled their own cause. Ever since 1791, Scots-Irish frontiersmen fumed over the excise tax Hamilton imposed on whiskey distillers. Of course, large producers of mash could pass the cost on to consumers, while small producers simply evaded the tax in classic American (and Scottish) style. But the *principle* of the thing was irksome. Wicked Federalists were trying to fund their hifalutin bank through a "sin tax" imposed on the little man. Mobs gathered to tar and feather revenue agents and distillers who paid the tax. Posters signed "Tom the Tinker" promised worse violence. When General John Neville, Allegheny County's excise official, dared serve writs on unregistered stills, the local Democratic Society formed a militia and attacked Neville's house in July 1794. Two weeks later six thousand of these "Whiskey Rebels" formed up on Braddock's Field, threatening to sack Pittsburgh.

Was this just a tax revolt or, as Hamilton believed, a revolutionary plot hatched by Jacobins? Washington did not wait for an answer: if armed resistance to U.S. authority were even once tolerated or appeased, the federal government might as well close up shop. But it was equally important to observe due process. So the President asked Justice James Wilson to certify the existence of "combinations too powerful" for local law enforcement, which in turn authorized Secretary of War Knox to request governors to call out their militias. Washington himself promised Pennsylvania governor Thomas Mifflin he would respect his state's sovereignty and proceed with moderation. Finally, in September 1794, Washington donned his old uniform and led thirteen thousand soldiers west along roads familiar to him since the 1750s. The rebels dispersed and were gratified when the President pardoned the two "leaders" convicted. The events that cooled tempers for good were Wayne's victory at Fallen Timbers and the British offer to evacuate the Northwest. The way west was open! Land prices around Pittsburgh boomed. Suddenly nobody cared about a few pennies tax on a jug of hard stuff.[57]

The President had called out soldiers against American citizens—just the sort of executive tyranny fevered Republicans had predicted. Yet Madison approved of Washington's firmness, and even Jefferson lay low when the President thunderously pronounced the Whiskey Rebellion "the first *ripe fruit* of the Democratic Societies." Almost at once the societies began to disintegrate. So did resistance to Jay's Treaty, ratified by the Senate 20 to 10 in June 1795, and signed by Washington after captured papers suggested his (Republican) Secretary of State Edmund Randolph was in the pay of the French! Later in the year the rout of the party men seemed complete when Thomas Pinckney reported from Spain. The Spaniards, hard pressed to enter the war on the French side, agreed with unusual dispatch to settle accounts with the United States. The 1795 Treaty of San Lorenzo fixed the boundary of Florida, liquidated reciprocal claims, ended Spanish collusion with Indians, and opened New Orleans to U.S. shipping and deposit of goods. There was nothing here to which Republicans might object. The treaty breezed through the Senate.[58]

Was the game up? Were Republicans to go the way of Tories and Anti-Federalists? The answer seemed both yes and no, as the nation's first contested presidential election approached in 1796. Yes, because the Washington administration could point to heady accomplishments at home and abroad. Trade, production, and real wages steadily rose, the West was open, and the rule of law secure.[59] That seemed to make the Federalists a lock, causing Jefferson to bark about Washington: "Curse on his virtues, they've undone his country." But the answer was also no, because Washington's Farewell Address of September 1796 declared his intention not to stand for a third term. That great state paper, drafted mostly by Hamilton, deplored the scourges of sectionalism, party spirit, and foreign intrigue. It admonished Americans to seek peace, harmony, and commerce with all nations, but permanent alliances with none. Washington posed a clear choice: "slavery" to foreign powers seeking to manipulate and disrupt the Union, or a moral and prudent neutrality permitting Americans to *exploit* Europe's wars and realize their destiny.[60] The Republican and Federalist managers had no time to ponder sermons: Washington's farewell meant they had just a few months to maneuver a new president into power.

All Federalist candidates were bound to seem puny next to Washington. The natural choice was John Adams, but how much support could he garner outside New England? In any event, what did Federalists know about organization, grassroots campaigns, and appeals to the masses? Master Builders did not believe in such things, whereas Republican party men were stirred by their recent defeats to frenetic activity on the state and local levels. They included men weaned on the dirty factional strife of New York and Pennsylvania, the gentry-led rabble-rousing politics of Virginia, and the wild democracy of the frontier. Their state leaders were learning to build coalitions and exploit local resentments. Their editors, learning the power of the negative campaign, smeared Adams and, for the first time, Washington. Above all they were learning to get the greatest number of voters to blame their ills on the smallest number of vague, distant malefactors. Lofty Federalist rhetoric played right into their hands.

But Republicans were just *learning* those things. Nor could populist politics as yet be decisive since a competitive "winner take all" popular vote for president was staged only in Pennsylvania (where Republicans grabbed fifteen of sixteen electors on a dubious plurality of two hundred votes). Instead, what proved truly decisive in 1796 was the frustrating aloofness of the Republican candidate. Jefferson holed up in Monticello throughout the campaign. He told Madison he hoped only for a second or third place finish. He even offered, in case of a tie with Adams, to defer to the senior statesman. Jefferson was not being coy: he knew the timing was wrong. Washington was an impossible act to follow, Federalists were liable to retake the Congress, and the Jay and Pinckney treaties guaranteed the next president's chief antagonist would be his beloved *France*. Let Adams do that dirty work . . . and let Jefferson reap the harvest of Adams' misfortunes.[61]

Meanwhile, Hamilton groped for a strategy. Pinckney was chosen the Federalists' second candidate for president under the Constitution's weird rules, but this time Hamilton refrained from asking electors to withhold a few votes from the second man. He wanted to maximize chances one or the other would beat Jefferson. The results were chaotic. South Carolinians were such southern partisans they cast all their votes in the electoral college for Jefferson and Pinckney—a perfectly split ticket. In the end Jefferson got his precise wish: he finished just three votes behind Adams, while Adams' seventy-one was an embarrassing one more than the minimum needed.

A strange outcome, though no revolution, which is why histories tend to skip ahead to 1800 when the government really changed hands. But stop and think how critical was the election of 1796. It was hotly contested and very close; indeed more votes than Adams' margin of victory might have been thrown out due to glaring irregularities in the choice of electors. Yet none of the losers reached for their muskets; no state legislature debated secession. Moreover, the head of one party became president while his bitter opponent became vice president, just "a heartbeat away." Were this Mexico, Macbeth's Scotland, the late Roman Republic, or the scurrilous French Directory of the late 1790s, John Adams might have suffered a "tragic accident" or been shot walking out his front door. But even the nuttiest "democrats" never considered assassination. Jefferson knew the power of the presidency, when and if he were to wield it, would be greater and more secure if Republicans just spent the next four years crying "Foul!" If that is republican virtue then Americans on both sides displayed it, and it is not to be taken for granted.

## *The Sixteenth State: Tennessee, 1796*

In 1768 Gilbert Christian crossed the Great Smokies into the Watauga valley and found nothing but "howling wilderness." He returned a year later to see cabins "on every spot where the range was good." This sudden influx was composed mostly of angry "regulators" pushed out of North Carolina. One of the fiercest was John Sevier. His portrait shows a benign, bewigged gentleman in uniform. As first governor of Tennessee, that was evidently how he wished to go down in history. But his character was forged taking vengeance on Cherokees who scalped and burned women and children. Once in 1776 he spied twelve milk-maids fleeing toward his frontier station with Indians in pursuit.

Eleven made it to safety, and Sevier rescued the last, Catherine Sherrill, by heaving her over the wall with one arm while he fought off the "redskin" with the other. When his wife later died, Catherine not only cared for his ten children, she married Sevier and bore him eight more. That's how the West was won.

North Carolina's western claim stretched 432 miles beyond the Smokies to the Mississippi River. It might well have become three states if not for the Tennessee River that bends like a sine curve across it. The first regions settled were the Great Valley of East Tennessee and the rolling Cumberland basin where Nashborough (Nashville) rose in 1780. Further west lay the Tennessee River's other great valley and the Gulf Coastal Plain on the Mississippi. It seemed highly unlikely that North Carolina could effectively govern it all. It seemed just as unlikely Tennesseans could unite to govern themselves.[62]

For one glorious moment in 1780 they did unite when Sevier and the other border chieftains annihilated the Tories at King's Mountain. But their postwar effort to organize a new state called Franklin was a farce. Sevier and rival John Tipton feuded, Franklin disintegrated, and Carolina authorities arrested Sevier in 1788. But with the aid of his sons he jumped bail and won forgiveness by helping Hugh Williamson win North Carolina's belated ratification of the Constitution. Then in 1790 North Carolina ceded its western lands to the federal government, and President Washington named William Blount territorial governor. The Northwest Ordinance would prevail with one mighty exception: slavery was expressly permitted.

Blount, of Craven County's Blount Hall, was a direct descendant of a "distressed cavalier" who fought with Charles I, then fled to Virginia. Over time the family moved into Carolina and gave up tobacco for business. William himself made a killing in war contracts after 1776 (to his credit he also served in the army) and sat on the state committee awarding Tennessee land to veterans. The hustling Blount knew what to do in that plum assignment. He purchased warrants from soldiers and gave himself title to a million acres of rich bottom land. But unlike other western empire-builders Blount wanted a strong federal government that could pacify Indians, pressure Spaniards, and enforce legal deeds. So Blount attended the Constitutional Convention and befriended Washington, which earned him that appointment as governor. Blount made it a principle "never to stand between a friend and a benefice," and one of those he favored with patronage was a hyperkinetic young lawyer named Andrew Jackson. Blount also persuaded Secretary of War Knox to authorize annual gifts of $1,000 per year to the Cherokees (hence the naming of Knoxville). He also considered it "in the interest of the United States" to be as liberal with whiskey as the Indians were thirsty. Still, massacres of settlers continued until Sevier's enraged mountain men ran the Cherokees down at Etowah, Georgia, in 1793. The quintupling of gifts to the Indians, a U.S. Army presence, and Spain's abandonment of the tribes in Pinckney's Treaty sufficed to secure the territory.[63]

Blount thought the time ripe for statehood, but that required sixty thousand residents. At last count (1790) the Cumberland counties numbered but seven thousand and East Tennessee twenty-eight thousand. Blount was undeterred. Having first flattered the feds by naming counties after Jefferson, Washington, and Hamilton, he staged an election, census, and referendum. Lo and behold! The tally reported a surprising (and surprisingly exact) 77,262 persons in Tennessee; the referendum a three to one majority for statehood. Middle Tennesseeans smelled a skunk and a rebellious Watauga Valley faction emerged as well. Led by the aptly named Alexander Outlaw, it demanded a weak executive, a democratic unicameral legislature, and an oath requiring officials to affirm "the divine authority of the old and new testament." But Blount simply packed the convention, wrote a state constitution himself, and asked Congress to ratify his *fait accompli.*

He got away with it, barely. Republicans were happy to overlook his chicanery because they craved two more senators and (thanks to the bogus census) two more congressmen, hence four more electoral votes. Federalist William Loughton Smith challenged Blount's coup, hoping to postpone Tennessee statehood until after the 1796 election. Madison chided Smith for "spinning a finer thread" of legalism than was called for. At length the House approved statehood but the Federalist Senate did not, whereupon

Blount simply showed up in Philadelphia, demanding his seat as a Tennessee senator! In May 1796, Republicans proposed a compromise awarding Tennessee statehood but only one congressman. A conference committee chaired by Aaron Burr warmly endorsed it, the Senate relented, and Washington signed the statehood bill on June 1.[64]

Whatever the state's population in 1796, it surpassed two hundred thousand within fifteen years. Treaties with Cherokees and Chickasaws opened the rest of the state, culminating in the Jackson Purchase of 1818 and the founding of Memphis. Prosperity grew on the strength of bountiful corn and tobacco, iron foundries, cattle, hogs, and cotton. Blount College in Knoxville planted the seed that would grow into the University of Tennessee. But the over-mountain men (and women) still loved a good fight, as proven by their violent internal feuds and the Tennessee volunteers who swarmed to the 1812, Texas, and Mexican wars. House- and barn-raisings and corn-husking parties were communal occasions fueled by kegs of "white lightning" or "moonshine" and "chaws" of tobacco in the mouths of both sexes. "Hoe-downs" (put that hoe down and dance!), horse racing, cockfighting, wrestling, hunting, shooting, and gambling were ubiquitous, and even revivals a time to "kick up your heels." Davy Crockett spun a yarn about a wedding where the bride and groom "rassled" before tying the knot and delighted the crowd when the buxom lass "th'owed" her intended three times.[65]

One man who did not see the great state mature was its godfather. When the French pressured Spain into their war against Britain, fears of a British attack on New Orleans caused western land prices to plummet. Blount was illiquid and threatened with ruin. So he gambled for still higher stakes in a conspiracy to get British support for an unofficial American invasion of Louisiana. One of his co-conspirators ignored his instructions to "read three times and burn" a secret letter. It found its way into the hands of Vice President Adams. Blount was obliged to resign from the Senate, but expected a long reign in Tennessee politics. Then, in 1800, he caught a chill. For four days the doctors blistered and purged. Blount weakened, then evidently gave up when he lost the power of speech. At the last, the proud cavalier turned his face to his wall lest onlookers notice "two large tears" descending his cheeks. He died at age fifty-one. Tennessee's future now lay with the old East Tennessee chieftain Sevier, but Nashville's young chieftain Andy Jackson defied him until, in 1815, Sevier's death and the Battle of New Orleans propelled Jackson and Nashville to leadership.[66]

John Adams believed liberty could not survive without virtue, yet liberty bred wealth and the luxury, sloth, envy, and greed that swallowed up virtue. Mixed government and the ordered liberty of his Puritan fathers might arrest the decay for a time, but deep down Adams feared the American experiment was ephemeral. As a politician he never had a chance. Nor was the party he did not want to lead (not believing in parties) any help to him. Hamilton, whom Adams despised, had left the Treasury but still influenced it, while other High Federalists confirmed Republican suspicions by stomping for war against France. Adams' response was to pack his administration with loyal New Englanders, further reducing his appeal outside the Northeast. Finally he displayed the same flaw as Hamilton: truth-telling. Adams warned voters of the dangers inherent in liberty; Jefferson preached the only real danger was loss of liberty. Adams feared success might spoil his countrymen's character; Jefferson named his countrymen's character the guarantee of success. As one eminent historian tartly put it, "The glass was always half-full at Monticello and half-empty at Quincy, even though it was the same glass."[67]

After ratification of Jay's Treaty the French declared open season on American ships and captured three hundred before Adams even took office. He might have exploited the anger sweeping the coast from Boston to Charleston. Instead he sent to Paris a delegation so distinguished that the snub it received was humiliating. John Marshall, Charles C. Pinckney, and Elbridge Gerry never got to see foreign minister Talleyrand and were fobbed off on three minor agents demanding tribute and bribes. Adams dubbed the *messieurs* "X, Y, and Z," and sent the delegation's reports to Congress for secret deliberation. The reports did not stay secret long. Republicans, mistakenly thinking they reflected badly on Adams, demanded publication. The result was a national outcry and the famous toast "Millions for defense but not one cent for tribute."

Philadelphia was rapidly emptying in that summer of 1797, as hundreds died and thousands fled a virulent outbreak of yellow fever. Congress succumbed to an equally virulent war fever. A naval construction program begun under Washington was increased from six to thirty-three ships led by heavy frigates named *United States, Constellation,* and *Constitution.* A separate Navy Department emerged under the able Maryland merchant Benjamin Stoddert. The small frontier army was expanded by twelve thousand men and Congress authorized ten thousand more in the event of hostilities. Direct taxes on land, slaves, and buildings were to pay for it all. A Federalist faction led by Secretary of State Timothy Pickering even considered asking for a declaration of war. Hamilton was shrewder. He understood the only way to unite the American people for war was to goad the *enemy* into firing the first shot. But he, too, dreamed of military glory and perhaps the conquest of Louisiana and Florida. Worst of all, in Adams' view, Washington agreed to command the army only on condition Hamilton be made its ranking field general. Not just the French, but his own administration seemed beyond Adams' control.[68]

Finally, Congress enacted a series of laws to crack down on potential fifth columnists. These Alien and Sedition Acts included a Naturalization Act increasing the residency requirement for citizenship to fourteen years, an Alien Act permitting deportation in peacetime of any foreigner deemed "dangerous to the peace and safety of the United States," an Alien Enemies Act permitting the same in time of war, and a Sedition Act outlawing opposition by deed or by "false, scandalous, or malicious writing" to legal acts of the federal government. Given the malicious mendacity of certain Republican organs, John and Abigail Adams might have considered that last law richly deserved. But contrary to myth, Adams sponsored none of the bills, many other Federalists were uncomfortable with them, and one of them (the Alien Enemies Act) was mostly a Republican initiative. The bills all passed by tiny margins, and the President construed them so strictly they were virtually dead letters. In one sense it is too bad no "wild Irishman" or "French Jacobin" was incarcerated under the Alien Act, because it would be interesting to know how the courts would have ruled. But the Sedition Act did lead to convictions of nine acerbic journalists and a sitting congressman, Matthew Lyon. A wild Irishman indeed, he arrived from Dublin in 1764, aged fifteen, with one guinea in his pocket. He worked off his passage in Connecticut where he learned to hate Congregationalists, then followed the Allens to Vermont where he learned to hate Federalists. Following statehood, he founded a newspaper that earned him the sobriquet "Democratic Lion" and a seat in Congress in 1797. There Lyon targeted Connecticut Federalist Roger Griswold, spitting in his face and twice exchanging blows on the floor of the House. Lyon was just the type to test this Sedition Act. Of course, persecution only increased "Spittin' Matt's" popularity. Like Charles Wilkes, he was re-elected from jail.[69]

Still, Federalists rode the war scare of 1798 to victory in 63 of 106 congressional races in the midterm elections, breaking the Republicans' hold on a score of districts in the south and west. But since the war scare did *not* end in war, the Federalists' military buildup, taxes, and restrictions on free speech played into Republicans' hands. One palimpsest of the reaction was Fries' Rebellion, or the Hot Water War (so called for the scalding pots women dumped on soldiers and tax collectors). This second rural Pennsylvania uprising was born in Bethlehem when a German auctioneer refused to pay the new taxes, then gathered a mob to spring two tax resisters from prison. Again federal troops were dispatched. Again the President pardoned the ringleaders. But it made taxes a hot Republican issue. Jefferson and Madison made the Alien and Sedition Acts another "wedge" issue by secretly distributing briefs arguing that states had the right to nullify them since they exceeded the authority of Congress. It is often assumed Jefferson was striking a blow for freedom of the press. In fact, he consistently advocated strict laws against slander and libel. What he despised about the Sedition Act was its imposition of *federal* standards of dangerous speech. That threatened the power of his own "Richmond Junto" to manage the press in Virginia.[70] Jefferson was also trying to score political points, which he did when the Virginia and Kentucky legislatures passed his "anonymous" resolutions late in 1798. He correctly predicted resistance to taxes masquerading as a campaign for civil liberties would bring the Federalists down in two years' time. Assuming no war broke out, the timing would be just right.[71]

Thanks to President Adams, it was. He never thought war in the national interest, never considered stirring one up for his political interest, and fretted that Hamilton and Pickering might provoke the French into formal hostilities. So Adams did a *volte-face*. In February 1799, he told a stunned Congress of his intention to send a new peace commission to Paris. Hamilton did his best to delay the mission. Pickering insisted on waiting for the French to promise no repetition of the XYZ nonsense. Then yellow fever forced the whole government to relocate to Trenton. But it turned out the delay was a boon. By November, when the full U.S. commission arrived in France, the undeclared naval war had shifted in America's favor. Thanks to Stoddert's leadership in the Navy Department, the swift, sturdy, and heavily gunned frigates designed by Philadelphia Quaker Joshua Humphreys, and a cadre of intrepid captains, the American ships were now seizing more prizes than the French. The U.S.S.

*Constellation* (Thomas Truxtun commanding) captured the swiftest frigate in the French navy, while the U.S.S. *General Greene* (Raymond Perry commanding) helped Toussaint L'Ouverture establish his ex-slave republic in Haiti. Another reason delay turned out well was a change of regime in Paris. The undirected French Directory that even Talleyrand could not budge was overthrown on 18 Brumaire (November 6, 1799) by young General Bonaparte. Facing a full roster of enemies in Europe, he considered the Quasi War with America a nuisance. It also made sense to pull the wool over Americans' eyes given his secret plans to reclaim Louisiana from Spain. So Napoleon instructed the French foreign ministry to receive the Americans graciously. When news arrived of George Washington's death at Mount Vernon on December 14, Napoleon pulled out all the stops in a Masonic celebration of his life at the Temple of Mars.[72]

Still, the negotiations involved money (mutual indemnities for all the ships seized and the American debts dating from 1776), so they dragged on for a year while the United States entered another electoral cycle. Some Federalists were so angry with Adams they wanted to run a different candidate for president in 1800. After their caucus decided in May to stick with Adams, Hamilton circulated a pamphlet naming him unfit. It was supposed to be confidential, but a copy fell into the sticky hands of Republican Aaron Burr, who gleefully made it public. Thus did Hamilton's backroom maneuvers, apparently so clever in previous presidential elections, undo the Federalist cause at the hour of its greatest need. The party, not wishing to be a party, went up against their worst enemy defensive and divided.

What was this fearsome Republican party about, what sorts of people did it attract, and who was this Aaron Burr? The easy answer to the first question is a disparate coalition of "outs" determined to oust the "ins." The easy answer to the second is frustrated, ambitious men who wanted to open up the frontier, open up trades and professions, open up banks for the little man, and open up government jobs. To the third question there is no easy answer. But to elaborate, the national vision of rank-and-file Republicans in the 1790s overlapped only a little with Jefferson's stylized vision of a nation of yeomen led by a natural aristocracy oozing republican virtue. On the contrary, Republicans imagined a "new social order" without closed elites where every man willing to hustle might get on in life, be it in agriculture, trade, or finance.[73]

Nor did Republicans want to hear disquisitions on human nature. They preferred to think themselves good, and if they did not then preachers and wives, not laws, were the antidotes. Republicans were scarcely "individualist," a word that did not even exist until 1840. Rather, they took for granted one's obligations to family, neighbors, community, and nation for reasons of faith, loyalty, self-interest, and simple pursuit of happiness.[74] But Republicans rejected the notion that an immutable human nature meant America must, at bottom, be like other countries. America, to them, was something new under the sun. For the first time in history a society had emerged in which famine was almost unknown, farm surpluses freed young men for other careers, and an urban emporium or even rude country store provided all one wanted or needed . . . so long as there was money to be had. For the first time in history a society existed in which each family's private pursuit of happiness helped everyone to prosper. For the first time in history work itself ceased to be God's curse on Adam and became enterprise, a joyous fulfillment of ambition. The freedom to work and either *consume or invest* the fruits of one's work was holy. Hence, any power, foreign or domestic, that dared interfere with Americans' progress was evil. Republican tracts and newspapers did not damn enterprise or even speculation of the sort attending Hamilton's bank. They only damned markets people could not *participate* in for lack of sufficient money or status, or just for living too far afield. No wonder states' rights advocates, back-country people, urban mechanics and storekeepers, social climbers, and immigrants voted Republican. So did people in the fastest-growing parts of the nation where new fortunes beckoned. So did pioneers, planters, and frontier lawyers who were by no means opposed to getting rich quick, but rejected the idea that such aspirations were corrupt (Hamilton) or corrupting (Adams) *so long as* they were not restricted to exclusive elites.

The United States "is a country in flux," wrote a French duke on tour in the late 1790s. "That which is true today as regards its population, its establishments, its principles, its commerce will not be true six months from now."[75] Republicans reveled in flux and called it progress precisely because it was *not* tending to make the nation a larger and richer version of Britain. Delicious proof of that was the sudden collapse in 1798 ("how are the mighty fallen!") of the speculative empires of Robert Morris, John Nicholson, James Wilson, and other High Federalists, whose privilege and influence could not save them from debtor's prison and early death.[76] One of the most influential tracts Republicans circulated was Thomas Cooper's *Political Arithmetic* (1800), which predicted America would be the breadbasket of the world and might dispense with navies and floating debts. Jefferson's official platform echoed these themes by calling for states' rights, reduction of the national debt, a small military, peace with all nations, and no federal constraints on religion or the press. But Republican tracts and newspapers carried in coaches and saddlebags along hundreds of miles of new post roads promised something far less abstract: a society of equals in which everyone had a fair shot to get rich in an ever expanding economy. By "equals" they meant, of course, only white males and their mates. The solicitude toward Indians and opposition to slavery displayed by many Federalists, not to mention Adams' pro-Haiti policies, would be absent in a Jefferson administration. But for white males, Republicanism meant a chance to do well and feel good about it—and only white males could vote.

Finally, what of the religious revivals beginning to burn in upstate New York, Kentucky, and Tennessee? Did Jefferson bless holy-rolling evangelicals? Heavens no: he imagined a day when all Americans might embrace a reasonable Unitarian or Deist ethic. But Republican party managers did not care what voters did on Sunday. It happened their social message dovetailed with that of egalitarian, self-reliant Baptists and Methodists. Anyway, Americans learned in good Freemason style to separate religion and politics or else subordinate their sects to the civic religion. All this drove Federalists nuts. They cried "Where's the outrage?" as they branded Jefferson an atheist, fornicator, and vivisectionist (Monticello was nicknamed Dogs' Misery). But out in the sticks folks praised the Lord, passed the bottle, and jostled on down to vote for Long Tom. Jefferson probably didn't even know why.

Finally, what about Aaron Burr?[77] To begin with, his father was an honored Presbyterian clergyman and second president of the College of New Jersey, while his mother was the third daughter of Jonathan Edwards. But yellow fever took them both soon after Aaron's birth in 1756. So he and sister Sally were raised in Massachusetts by Uncle Timothy Edwards, who spoiled them, and tutored by Tapping Reeve, who indulged Aaron and married Sally. There was no question of Aaron's precocious brilliance: accepted to Princeton at age thirteen he persuaded Witherspoon to let him matriculate as a sophomore. His classmates, including Madison and Freneau, marveled at Burr's easy mastery of ancient and modern languages, not to mention girls. He was glib, gorgeous, and rich, having inherited £10,000 on his sixteenth birthday. But Burr evidently believed in nothing. Theology bored him (even Joseph Bellamy's Philadelphia seminary for "free thinkers" was not apostate enough), and he showed no interest in the colonies' dispute with the crown. So he enrolled in Reeve's Litchfield law school where, for the first time, he encountered frustration. Burr fixed on no less a prize than Dolly Quincy, John Hancock's lovely fiancée, but could not persuade her to break the engagement. It was probably to rid himself of this rake that Hancock agreed to write Burr a letter of introduction to General Washington in 1775.

In the army Burr learned more things about himself: he was impervious to danger, a natural leader, and a crack shot. He helped Benedict Arnold drag his frozen command to Québec, then rode to Montréal disguised as a priest to get a message to General Montgomery. In the climactic battle Burr rallied the troops mere yards away from the enemy's guns, then bore off Montgomery's corpse while redcoats held their fire in stunned tribute. Later, as a member of Washington's staff, Colonel Burr endured Valley Forge, quelled a mutiny, and served without leave despite exhaustion and illness. But he never made general and blamed it on Hamilton, Washington's favorite. In 1779, while based at White Plains, Burr resigned from the army to marry a widow ten years his senior and get richer. His law firm on Wall Street soon rivaled Hamilton's in the courts and politics of the city. Still, Burr felt nothing for the United States, predicting in 1789 the Constitution would give way to a monarchy within fifty years. In search of power and prestige, he arranged in 1791 for the legislature to elect him (in Hamilton's absence) to the Senate. He served six years, proposing no bills, ducking contentious votes, and taking a seat in the exact middle of the chamber.

What Burr really wanted to do was wrest the governorship of New York from the perennial Clinton. In 1797 he recruited a club likely to help. The Tammany Society was envisioned by founder William Mooney to be a neighborhood fraternity of artisans, mechanics, sailors, construction and dock workers. But Burr saw its potential as a political machine. In just one year the organization attracted so many new members Burr helped them move to a larger "wigwam" on Nassau Street.[78] Presumably this network of ward heelers would turn out a bloc vote for Republicans, but Burr still played both sides. The army buildup of 1798 revived his lust for glory, so he made oily appeals to President Adams, seeking a general's command. Only after Hamilton thwarted him again did Burr declare his politics, win election to the state legislature, and style himself the paladin of the "little man." Up in Albany he called for abolition of debtors' prisons and obtained a charter of dubious legality for a Manhattan Company. Its alleged purpose was to build a waterworks as a public health measure. However, under its umbrella Burr founded the Manhattan Bank (now Chase Manhattan) to serve as a political war chest and make loans to Republican friends. When Hamilton irately denounced the scam, Burr branded him a monopolist. He silenced other critics with threats of duels.[79]

In 1799 Pennsylvania's Thomas McKean added to newspapers, local organizations, and banks yet another powerful tool of party politics: the spoils system. After winning the governorship he fired all state officials of Federalist persuasion and replaced them with "every scoundrel who could read and write." Jefferson gushed, "With Pennsylvania, we can defy the universe." But to win the presidency he also needed New York, whose electors were chosen by the state legislature. So it all came down to the streets of Manhattan, where Federalists usually fared well. On May 3, 1800, however, they were shocked to learn they had lost all twelve New York City districts, hence their majority in the legislature, hence New York's presidential electoral votes. Jefferson, who previously dismissed Burr as "a crooked gun," now dispatched Madison to promise him "high office" in return for support. Burr wanted the vice presidency; the Republican caucus granted his wish.[80]

Given all the Democratic Republicans' advantages in 1800 and the fact they dominated politics for the next forty years, it is sometimes forgotten how close the vote was. Adams received just six fewer electoral votes than in 1796. Jefferson won just five more. So Burr, Tammany, and New York were the difference. But, as is *never* forgotten, the result was a tie. Republican electors were so desperate to defeat their diabolical opponents and so distrustful of their own northern or southern brethren that no "throw away vote" deals proved possible. Accordingly, all seventy-three Republican electors cast ballots for both Jefferson and Burr, which threw the election into the House of Representatives. The fluky outcome gave Burr a golden opportunity to serve himself and his country, render his corruption creative, and become a secular saint. He needed only to bow out in favor of his party's genuine first choice, accept the lauds of a grateful nation, and wait his turn just as Jefferson had. Instead, he sat silent in Albany and refused to answer his mail.

So the lame duck Congress assembled in a half-completed wing of the new Capitol on a snowy February 11, 1801, to ballot, one vote per state as the Constitution provided. Since Federalist members hated Jefferson and thought Burr more "malleable," six state delegations voted for Burr and two split, leaving Jefferson eight states and one short of a majority. The House called more ballots, now secret, and sat up half the night. Always a deadlock. At length thirty-five ballots over six days proved fruitless until, in an echo of July 2, 1776, one man from Delaware carried the day. Federalist James A. Bayard was that state's sole representative, and Federalists in two split delegations (Maryland and Vermont) agreed to follow his lead. That is why Hamilton, who alone feared the rogue Burr more than party man Jefferson, wrote Bayard a "Pauline epistle" interpreting the civic religion:

> "I admit that [Jefferson's] politics are tinctured with fanaticism, that he is too much in earnest in his democracy, that he has been a mischevous [*sic*] enemy to the principle [*sic*] measures of our past administration, that he is crafty & persevering in his objects, that he is not scrupulous about the means of success, not very mindful of truth, and that he is a contemptible hypocrite. But it is not true as is alleged that he is an enemy of the power of the Executive. . . . Nor is it true that Jefferson is zealot enough to do anything in pursuance of his principles which will contravene his popularity or his interest. . . ."

The probable result of a Jefferson win, he concluded, would be "the preservation of systems," whereas Burr's brand of corruption might tear up the Union's foundations. Jefferson was a sinner; Burr a heretic. Did Bayard bow to Hamilton's judgment, or seize on a veiled promise by Jefferson not to purge Federalist officials, or just wilt under pressure? Whatever the case, blank ballots cast by several Federalists on the thirty-sixth poll removed Delaware from Burr's column and added to Jefferson's Maryland and Vermont. Spittin' Matt Lyon himself joyously cast the last vote.[81]

Clearly, the voting for president and vice president had to be separated before the next quadrennium. The Twelfth Amendment was duly ratified by 1804. But the 1800 campaign also revealed how American politics worked. The Federalists, observed Noah Webster, "attempted to resist the force of current public opinion, instead of falling into the current with a view to direct it." John Marshall was blunter. He named Federalists "those few real patriots who love the people well enough to tell them the truth." There was some talk of secession in New England; a few militiamen drilled. But the official Federalist press only complained of "bells ringing, guns firing, dogs barking, cats mewling, children crying, and Jacobins getting drunk."[82]

John Adams did not stick around. Citing Abigail's health, he boarded a carriage for home before the inauguration. But he left behind the best present imaginable. Those negotiations he started in Paris concluded with the Convention of Mortefontaine, signed at Joseph Bonaparte's chateau in October

1800. It terminated both the Quasi War at sea and the Franco-American alliance. It thereby relieved Jefferson of the burden of French militancy and the burden of ideological affinity he himself had promoted. Adams did his nation a signal service. He wrecked his presidency and his party in the process.

For his part, Jefferson urged reconciliation and unity, adding to the scripture of the civic religion a Washingtonian phrase: "We are all republicans—we are all federalists." Of course, he really meant "you must *all* become republicans now." But the words expressed a deeper truth Jefferson did not suspect when he emerged from the Freemasons' temple known as the Capitol and gazed over muddy triangular boulevards toward the construction site at the president's house. Master Builders were hard at work. But now he, the party man, was their leader.[83]

# RELUCTANT
# NATIONALISTS, EAGER
# IMPERIALISTS

*Having Fashioned a State, Americans*
*Turn into a Nation, 1801–1815*

*H*enry Adams, whose name must kick off any chapter of U.S. history beginning in 1800, described the city of Washington as the "symbol of American
nationality." Yet he observed:

> The contrast between the immensity of the task and the paucity of the
> means seemed to challenge suspicion that the nation itself was a mag-
> nificent scheme like the federal city, which could show only a few log-
> cabins and negro quarters where the plan provided for the traffic of
> London and the elegance of Versailles. . . . A government capable of
> sketching a magnificent plan, and willing to give only a half-hearted
> pledge for its fulfillment; a people eager to advertise a vast undertaking
> beyond their present powers, which when completed would become an
> object of jealousy and fear,—this was the impression made upon the
> traveller who visited Washington in 1800, and mused among the
> unraised columns of the Capitol upon the destiny of the United States.

Adams called his nine-volume, thirty-six-hundred-page history an "historical
mud pie," but its themes were ripe lemons: fat, juicy, pleasantly sour, and ready

to flavor the rest of nineteenth-century history. The above passage near the beginning reveals them barely in flower. Americans were eager to *advertise* their destiny, but reluctant to *grasp* it because they were not as yet a nation.[1] To put it another way, the Federalists were masterful at building a state, but only the Republicans could build a nation and reconcile it to the state. It took them fifteen years to get it right, by which time Jefferson's Capitol was a smoldering shell. But so deep were the people's resources and so mighty their civic religion, the hustling and fighting of a small number of citizens earned the whole country what Madison called "the smiles of heaven."

George Washington chose the ten-mile-square Potomac site for the federal city and laid the cornerstone of its central edifice. But Jefferson brokered the Compromise of 1790, persuaded his fellow commissioners to name the city "Washington," the district "Columbia," and the house of Congress the "Capitol." The designer of Monticello, Virginia's new capital at Richmond, and later the state's university, loved the chance to build national symbols from scratch. Then another of Washington's war buddies, French Major Pierre Charles L'Enfant, intervened. A fervent Freemason, he transformed Jefferson's 1791 street grid by superimposing upon it 160-foot-wide diagonal boulevards to be named after the states. William Thornton, Étienne-Sulpice Hallet, and Benjamin Latrobe, the architects of the Capitol, were also Freemasons. So was Irishman James Hoban, who designed the President's House. Accordingly, the federal buildings' interiors, architecture, relationships to each other and the boulevards, even the orientation of the whole city to the heavenly zodiac described Masonic geometries "as readable as any book" to those with unclouded eyes. Jefferson tinkered with the plans—he could not help himself—and L'Enfant protested at such dreary length in such poor English that the commission in charge of construction dropped him within a year. But his essential blueprint survived to display the states and branches of government (originally laid out in a triangle) as building blocks of a republican pyramid with a continent for its base. Washington and Jefferson approved.[2]

Unfortunately, they dared not ask Congress to pay for it all lest debate resume over the wisdom of the whole enterprise. They were, after all, conjuring a city on the scale of St. Petersburg without a tsar's power to command taxes and labor, not to mention compel people to come and live in the place. So the commissioners tried to do it the American way: they hawked the city's potential in hopes of inflating a real estate bubble. In 1791, Washington, Jefferson, and Madison presided over an auction of ten thousand town lots; thirty-five sold. Two more auctions proved just as embarrassing, while agents hoping to entice European investors were thwarted by the financial chaos attending the French Revolution. If not for Daniel Carroll of Duddington, who donated Capitol Hill and the grand avenue strips gratis; Washington's friend Colonel John Fitzgerald, who chaired the Potomac Company; and the Morris-Greenleaf-Nicholson partnership, which purchased a large block of lots, work on the capital might never have started. Finally, in 1796, Washington stooped to ask Congress for leave to sell bonds. Alas, only the governments of Maryland and Virginia showed interest. That explains the sneers of the visiting duc de la Rochefoucauld. The way to plant cities, he wrote, is "to erect taverns, shops, to open billiard tables, and to create lotteries; in a word, to furnish the means of dissipation and pleasure. . . . Without them, cities will never be extensive." Future American boomtowns took his advice. But the District of Columbia's potential was severely limited because it was put in a swamp (Foggy Bottom) remote from everywhere save Mount Vernon, with no provision made for industry, shipping, or even a military base. The only way to make a living was to house and feed officials, but the federal branch was too small to support more than a village and one business, a brewery. The only people to flock to the district were itinerants, mostly Irish, hoping for jobs in construction. Many survived off the charity of the Catholic community in the little tobacco port of Georgetown.[3]

The Washington City to which the federal government repaired in 1800 thus consisted of 372 structures, mostly "small miserable huts." Even twenty years later the population numbered less than ten thousand whites, many of them swindlers, vagabonds, and "swaggering sycophants" in search of a sinecure. There was no business, no cultural life besides a racetrack and a theater stinking of tobacco and whiskey, and no access to the outside save one bridge over the river. Hamilton would have scoffed. "A government continually at a distance and out of sight can hardly be expected to interest the sensations of the people," he wrote in *Federalist* No. 27. But a rural, remote, and southern locale facing not the Atlantic but the western interior was just what appealed to Jefferson. In 1789, the *Gazette of the United States* advocated a rustic location for the Federal City because in "seaport towns, we know, the floods of horrid vice o'erflow. There business, noise, and dissipation distract the rulers of the nation . . . till on the rocks of tempting beauty, they shipwreck honor, truth, and duty. No, let us to the woods repair, for peace and innocence dwell there. . . ." Jefferson imagined the capital a new Rome on a new Tiber, symbolizing an "empire of liberty" in the safe hands of virtuous men working the soil.[4]

He got his wish, but rusticity proved no inducement to virtue. Rather, congressmen slept, drank, went to the privy, and plotted in a few cramped boardinghouses where there was nothing to do *except* engage in "a thousand corrupt cabals." Still, the stakes were low given the minuscule federal budget. Wives hated the place. Almost one-fifth of the Senate voluntarily resigned every two years to return to state politics where the real action was. It is hard to imagine today, but in 1802 the entire federal headquarters numbered 291 people, of whom 138 comprised Congress itself. The executive branch totaled 132. The State Department had ten employees, the war and navy departments thirty, and the attorney general's office one: the attorney general. The government played *no* part in law enforcement, justice, agriculture, business, transportation, health, education, and welfare. Aside from 6,500 military personnel, the federal bureaucracy nationwide amounted to 2,875 people, and the only way it affected the lives of the vast majority of Americans was by delivering mail.[5]

That suited Jefferson, too, and he took office determined to cut the budget further. So even though momentous decisions would be made in Washington, let us for now turn away from the "unraised columns" of the toy government in the wilderness and tour the empire Henry Adams thought the Federal City symbolized.

In 1800 the U.S. population reached 5.3 million, of whom 900,000 were enslaved and 109,000 free persons of color. That staggering increase of 31 percent in a decade prompted states, too, to relocate their capitals in more central locations.[6] But less than 2 million adult white males were a small force to defend and develop a country roughly four times the size of France. Since the European wars depressed immigration to less than ten thousand per year, most of the increase was due to fertile American women. In the Connecticut Valley they still averaged almost seven live births apiece. The number of Americans residing in towns over 2,500 also rose from about 5 to 7 percent due mostly to explosions in four cities. From 1790 to 1800 Philadelphia grew from 33,482 to 61,559, Boston from 16,000 to 24,937, booming Baltimore from 6,734 to 26,514, and soon to be largest New York from 22,000 to 60,515. Since their horizontal spread was still sluggish, however, the cities became more congested than before or since, cesspools of human and animal waste, clouded in dust or mired in mud, vermin-ridden, and feverish. In exchange for the risk of living in ports, the poor knew a measure of variety and the chance to learn a trade or go to sea.

The rich knew a measure of culture and a choice of careers. By contrast, the rural 93 percent of Americans lived in relative health, but had few choices other than improve their farms or go west in search of one.

Many who went west left New England, where even marginal farmland was densely populated. Moreover, those who stayed put shed the vestiges of communal Puritanism and became rural capitalists, while Connecticut breeders not only supplied western demand for horses and mules but exported four thousand to five thousand per year. New England also took the first tentative steps toward building an American industrial base when Samuel Slater of Providence opened the first "Arkwright spindle" textile works in 1790 and Eli Whitney returned to New Haven in 1798 to manufacture firearms. Finally, Boston shippers got a new lease on life thanks to Hamilton's reforms and the reduction, by war, of European competition. The share of U.S. commerce carried in American bottoms rose from 60 to 90 percent between 1790 and 1802; net earnings on the carrying trade rose from $5 to $30 million. Exports soared from $20 to $90 million; re-exports from zero to $50 million as West Indian firms sought a neutral flag under which to ship sugar, coffee, cocoa, and pepper. To be sure, any given year might be calamitous if the British or French chose to seize ships having truck with their enemies. But that only made business for the forty marine insurance firms founded in Boston and Hartford by 1804. So prosperous was Boston the old city was virtually rebuilt in these years in the neo-classical Federal style, providing high wages to skilled and unskilled labor alike.[7]

The middle states prospered even more because New York, Philadelphia, and Baltimore not only traded in Europe, South America, and China, they were entrepôts for their populous hinterlands and hubs for an interstate commerce that doubled over the decade. Pittsburgh was still a frontier town, but the jumping-off point for the settlers streaming to the Ohio Valley after Pinckney's Treaty with Spain reopened the Mississippi River. Even the South knew better days than in anyone's memory. Tobacco prices rose, slaves were sold to new plantations in the Deep South, and cotton exports tripled from 20 to 60 million pounds between 1802 and 1807.[8]

The U.S. economy fed in part off Europe's wars, but those wars also shrank foreign investment in the "emerging market" that was the United States. How did Americans come up with capital in these years? One method was corporations, 219 of which were chartered by state governments from 1783 to 1800. This was novel, given that Parliament forbade incorporation in the Bubble Act of 1720 and American colonists had not complained: corporations seemed to create privileged and "immortal" monopolies that outlived their founders. After 1776, however, entrepreneurs in league with politicians, first in Massachusetts, then other northern states, incorporated factories, bridge, road, and canal companies, waterworks, and port facilities, religious, educational, and charitable organizations. Corporations might bring great wealth to a few, but were arguably in the interest of all, hence any corruption used to charter them was creative. Americans embraced this seemingly undemocratic tool simply because they were short of cash. Even the rich few could not have raised the capital needed to develop the continent if deprived of the right to sell stocks and bonds to the many. "The corporation, therefore, became, and remains, a child of the American Revolution."[9]

The second method was banking. Once Hamilton established the national credit and currency, entrepreneurs persuaded political friends to charter banks (which in turn did favors for politicians). But the twenty-nine banks opened before 1801 were almost all Federalist and northern, and only seven were capitalized at more than $1 million. Burr's Manhattan Bank changed everything. Once in office Jefferson declared, "I am decidedly in favor of making all the banks Republican by sharing deposits among them in proportion to the dispositions they show." He could not do that so long as the first U.S. Bank was the government's sole depository. But Republican clout in the states was sufficient to charter sixty-one new banks by 1811. Three trends resulted: increasing leadership over the U.S. economy by financiers rather than merchants; democratization of investment as Republican inventors, farmers, and mechanics gained access to loans; and the gradual shift of the nation's financial leadership from Philadelphia to New York.[10]

A booming economy was powerful national glue, but only *so long as* regions and sectors did not view each other as competitors and the federal government did not seem to favor one over the other. Republicans accused Hamilton of attempting to do just that. But if Republicans in turn did nothing to assist *any* sector of the economy, what was the relevance of the federal government?[11] It delivered the mail, and that is not to be scoffed at. The number of post offices across states and territories rose from sixty-six in 1783 to more than nine hundred by Jefferson's inaugural; the miles of post roads from 1,875 to 21,000. Along those roads moved newspapers brimming with paid advertisements, allowing the American press to grow from thirty-eight journals with 53,700 subscribers to two hundred journals with over 1 million subscribers by 1800. A great boon for business, they also made possible something like a national culture.

Almanacs had long been marketed beyond the environs of their publication. Now they were joined by Noah Webster's *American Spelling Book* (1783) and later dictionaries and grammars, Nicholas Pike's *Arithmetic* (1788), Jedidiah Morse's *American Geography* (1789), Daniel Fenning's *American Youth's Instructor* (1795), John M'Culloch's American history text (1795), Mercy Otis Warren's *History of the American Revolution* (1805), and the sophisticated doggerel of the "Hartford wits" and "New York knickerbockers." Morse imagined every American child a geographer, as befit an infant empire. Webster believed every American "as soon as he opens his lips, should rehearse the history of his own country." Self-help books were a perennial favorite, especially "useful knowledge" for the farmer, husbandmen, carpenter, and sailor. Scientific and medical societies arose in most states, sharing information by post.[12]

But a national culture was still in gestation. Americans faced more immediate material tasks. It should not surprise that the nation's first great artists were either architects such as Latrobe, Jefferson, and Boston's Charles Bulfinch, or painters such as Charles Willson Peale, Benjamin West, and Gilbert Stuart. Otherwise, local and regional loyalties outweighed national ties. Most of Philadelphia composer Francis Hopkinson's musical oeuvre was not even published. Histories of individual states remained more numerous and popular than national ones. Educated Americans showed far more interest in the latest European ideas than indigenous ones. Families such as the Hancocks and Saltonstalls, Schuylers and Livingstons, Whartons and Pembertons, Byrds and Fairfaxes, Pinckneys and Rutledges set the cultural tone for their locales. Even New Englanders, who invariably authored the texts and founded the schools Americans elsewhere would learn from, believed a national culture unlikely. Fisher Ames was a sourpuss, but echoed the opinion of many Harvard and Yale snobs when he deemed America "too big for union, too sordid for patriotism, and too democratic for liberty."[13]

Nothing conveys better the image of an American culture still in the womb than the life, legend, and literature of Hugh Henry Brackenridge. His original middle name was Montgomery and his last name spelled with an "e" not an "a," but like so many Americans he reinvented himself. His father, another poor Scottish farmer, and mother, a woman of keen intelligence, brought five-year-old Hugh to Pennsylvania's York County "barrens" in 1753. Like Hamilton in the Indies the boy was taught well by a Presbyterian talent scout; so well he was tutoring others in Gunpowder Falls, Maryland, at the tender age of fifteen. At Princeton Brackenridge collaborated with Freneau on *The Rising Glory of*

*America* and *Satires Against the Tories,* and penned America's first short story, *Father Bombo's Pilgrimage to Mecca.* He served in the Continental Army as yet another chaplain preaching liberty first and God second, then left the ministry in 1778 to study law under future Justice Samuel Chase. Back in Philadelphia, Brackenridge tried to launch a national magazine. When even local highbrows ignored it, he rode to Pittsburgh in 1781 "to advance the country and thereby myself." He instead found himself tending the crucible in which eastern gentility and frontier crudity melded into the American character.

Who was Brackenridge? Whatever people didn't want him to be. He started out a keen supporter of the Constitution and founded the Federalist Pittsburgh *Gazette.* But hard knocks taught him the Scots-Irish laddies hated anything smacking of high-toned authority. So he turned Republican and founded another paper, *Tree of Liberty,* to rival his first one. He even hired a Jewish editor, completing his ostracism back in Philadelphia. As a lawyer Brackenridge upheld property rights, yet defended squatters against no less a landlord than George Washington. He hated Indians, having fled massacres as a boy, yet bravely defended an Indian on trial for murder. He honored the rule of law, yet pleaded for sympathy toward Whiskey Rebels. He was proud of his appointment as state circuit judge, yet was known to preside with bare feet on the bench and rye on his breath. Legend holds he once rode to court naked in a rainstorm so as not to get his only suit wet. In 1799, Governor McKean named Brackenridge to the state supreme court where he served until death in 1816. But there, too, his quest to reconcile freedom with order and republicanism with Common Law rendered his judgments erratic.

What made him famous, for a while, was his fiction. Brackenridge's picaresque *Modern Chivalry* was an updated *Don Quixote* set west of the Alleghenies where (Emerson was to say) America begins. His anti-heroes were gentleman John Farrago, a font of half-understood philosophy and pretended idealism, and his bog-trotting sidekick Teague O'Regan, who is elated to learn that in America even simpletons can become mighty and rich. As one character puts it upon hearing the county's gauger (tax collector) is a respected figure but its congressman a mere weaver: "I dinna ken how it is, but I see they hae everything tail foremost in this kintra to what they hae in Scotland, a gauger a gentleman and weavers in the legislature!" The author finds occasion while recounting his characters' travels to mock the superstitions of ignorant and learned alike, the ways rich and poor dupe themselves and each other, and the pomposity of professors, lawyers, politicians, and doctors. But never does

Brackenridge veil the drunkenness, violence, and feral cupidity of the frontier or deny it *needs* the law and knowledge of the conceited east. Finally, it was no cynic who asked his countrymen, "What use is in fighting, and gouging, and biting?" and invited them to share America's bountiful table: "Come see if you cannot produce, a barbecued pig, a nice mutton leg, or turkey, or bit of a goose. We have store of good liquor, so bring something quicker, and club your potatoes and yams. We'll make a great feast, and turn all to jest, so away with your frowns and your damns." Brackenridge said *Modern Chivalry* graced every parlor in Pennsylvania and made publishers rich, if not himself. But his serrating satire had no echo in American letters until Artemus Ward and A. B. Longstreet, the western humorists who influenced Melville and Twain. Perhaps Brackenridge was too American for people still smitten by European tastes. Or perhaps Americans were not ready to peer into the mirror he held.[14]

Only one book held the power to bind or loose the whole nation. That, of course, was the Bible. However awkward the chronology for historians eager to focus on Jefferson, the greatest of all American revivals exploded during his first year in office. At the center of it were more Scots, whose Presbyterian church practiced a form of joint communion unique in Protestant practice. Once or twice a year crofters and townfolk would gather by the hundreds and thousands for Holy Fair services lasting three to five days. The faithful fasted and prayed, sang hymns, and heard round-the-clock sermons exhorting them to examine their souls lest they partake unworthily. By Saturday night old and new converts, stripped of pretense and masks, wept or shouted in joy or pain. On Sunday a bevy of pastors prepared long tables draped in linens scrubbed white by fullers, blessed the elements, and invited the throng to dine—not a wafer and sip, but a full meal. With thousands to serve in shifts, the sacrament lasted all day.[15]

America's first "Great Awakening" had been dominated by the English field preaching of Whitefield and the church preaching of Edwards. But tens of thousands of Scots-Irish immigrants who retained a folk memory of Holy Fair provided kindling for a second blaze. By 1787, when pastors and students at Hampden-Sydney Academy in Virginia prayed for revival, two Scots-Irish clergymen struck the spark. Ulster-born William Graham studied at Princeton and founded Liberty Hall (later Washington College, after George made a donation). Though orthodox, Graham broke with Presbyterian norms by preaching fervently and extemporaneously, rather than from a didactic text, and by hiring a choral master to lead hearty hymns. Graham journeyed to Hampden-Sydney with students who caught fire and spread the revival through the Piedmont and Shenandoah. James McGready, a child of Ulster-born parents, was schooled by Presbyterians near Pittsburgh. On his way home to Guilford County, North Carolina, he, too, visited Hampden-Sydney and took flame. Then, in 1796, he accepted a call to tame the wild pioneers of Logan County, Kentucky.

McGready was just what pioneers wanted. He was long, lanky, loud, stern, and uncompromising. His sermons were erudite, but delivered like stump speeches. He preached hellfire to leatherstockings who refused to mend their ways, but never failed to offer the mercy of a forgiving God through the atonement of His son. So eloquent was McGready that Francis Asbury himself would read one of his letters when he was stuck for a sermon. Most of all, McGready brought the Holy Fair joint communion to a flock scattered among rugged glens many miles apart. Such gatherings were exciting social as well as spiritual events; they made a welcome contrast to the land quarrels, feuds, and Indian and war scares that plagued the frontier for a decade. Year by year the gatherings grew until, in summer 1800, more than a thousand people from Logan County and Tennessee attended two great communions. For the first time ecstatic converts began "falling"; for the first time Methodist and Baptist ministers joined; for the first time whites and blacks gathered by the river to praise their Lord.

The climax came in August 1801 at an ecumenical communion in Cane Ridge, Kentucky.[16] The local pastor, Barton Stone, added another novelty by advertising far and wide and inviting all clergy to participate. So McGready, like Whitefield, learned the uses of an advance man. Rough roads came alive with men, women, and children, horses and wagons, all converging on Cane Ridge until possibly twenty thousand people appeared at some point during the week. How they fed themselves, fashioned latrines, or kept dry (it rained all weekend) is a mystery. Equally imponderable is how many people could hear or participate since the meeting house measured just thirty by fifty feet. But thirteen Presbyterian ministers, at least four Methodists, and several other clergy held outdoor services so that simultaneous sermons, hymns, and prayers reverberated all day and, by the light of great bonfires, night. One astonished witness likened the roar to Niagara Falls. To skeptics it seemed people went mad. Rough-and-tumble frontiersmen writhed in the mud trying to vomit their sins.

Women swooned or jerked their limbs and torsos. Children, Negroes, and illiterate rubes made spontaneous, eloquent exhortations. None of this was unfamiliar to veterans of Scottish revivals such as James Campbell:

> Sinners dropping down on every hand, shrieking, groaning, crying for mercy, convoluted, . . . praying, agonizing, fainting, falling down in distress, for sinners, or for raptures of joy! Some singing, some shouting, clapping their hands, hugging and even kissing, laughing. . . . And with what is doing, the darkness of the night, the solemnity of the place, and of the occasion, and conscious guilt, all conspire to make terror thrill through every power of the soul, and rouse it to awful attention.

Even after the grand communion many people did not want to leave. Newcomers arrived, and the phenomenon ended only when the exhausted pastors slipped away near the end of the week. But Cane Ridge inspired a series of ingatherings in 1801 that attracted more than a hundred thousand people as enthusiasm spread to Tennessee, the Carolinas, Virginia, New York, and New England.

To a believer no explanation is necessary; to a non-believer no explanation is possible. So runs the old Christian adage. Whether one treats "born again" experience as psychological in the manner of William James or spiritual in the manner of Campbell, above, there is no point denying it happens. People who undergo the experience, whether alone, with a pastor or friend, or in a crowded revival, may recall falling down because the legs go limp in the awful presence of God: that's something mortals "can't stand." But the crisis begins when the conscious mind, call it the ego, first admits to itself the Holy Spirit, not just the Devil, is present and fighting to claim it. The Holy Spirit is the enemy of the "old man," the natural sinful will. If the new birth of conversion results, it is not because the human will *defeats* Satan, but because the will *surrenders* to God. Sometimes it gives up quickly, quietly, with a few tears and a heart "strangely warmed" as in John Wesley's case. But the "old man" may instead "fight like the Devil" against extinction. His death throes are what cause the mind to rave and the body to jerk. His death is what causes the legs, limp no longer, to "jump for joy."

On the other hand, there is no point denying Cane Ridge and the nineteenth-century revivals that followed on the frontier and urban rookeries alike owed much to social pathologies, artful promotion, and crowd psychology. As in the first "Great Awakening," staid clergymen doubted such conversions were genuine and even thought unholy spirits at work. Did the Lord sanction "jerks" that sometimes bared women's bodies and resembled lewd dancing? Did not some young people take advantage of the confusion to sneak off and "do what comes naturally"? Was it healthy to countenance commingling and preaching by women and Negroes? Such queries so divided Presbyterians that even though they began the revivals they derived the least reward from them. Rather, Baptists and Methodists, who had no doctrinal doubts about a democratic, personal, and liberating spirituality, perfected McGready's style and domesticated it in three critical ways. First, they downplayed or eliminated the joint communion in order to zero in on the task of converting sinners. Second, they put effort and ingenuity into logistics, including the choice of sites, provision of services, and handbooks listing what to bring. In short, they invented the "camp meeting." Third, they followed up with efforts to sanctify converts, inveighing especially against alcohol, philandering, gambling, and (in the Methodist case) slavery. Rural Americans responded with such zeal that by 1820 in Kentucky alone Methodists and Baptists numbered about forty-two thousand and Presbyterians but twenty-seven hundred.

Several features of the Cane Ridge revival became permanent fixtures of American evangelism. They included the "altar call" or appeal to the "anxious bench" of waverers, the generous use of hymns both sentimental and joyous, a certain ecumenism among Protestants, millenarian expectations hitherto rare outside New England, and the presentation of Christ as a personal savior who touches each man and woman directly. "In that awful day," preached McGready, "when the universe, assembled, must appear before the judge of the quick and the dead, the question, brethren, will not be, Were you a Presbyterian—a Seceder—a Covenanter—a Baptist—or a Methodist; but, Did you experience the new birth? Did you accept of Christ and his salvation as set forth in the gospel?"[17]

Evangelists called themselves "spiritual republicans" and counterparts to the Jeffersonians in the political sphere. They interpreted revivals as new evidence of America's special dispensation, believing the day not far off when there would be "but *one soul in the nation*."[18] They were wrong. New England Congregationalists and their Unitarian offspring, conservative Presbyterians, and Episcopalians rejected revivalism and rued the multiplication of sects. So in religious as in secular culture the building blocks of a national temple seemed not to fit with each other. The so-called United States contained such a riot of accents, ethnicities, faiths, material interests, and hopes and fears that their unity was by no means assured. The only place their representatives met to arbitrate differences was in the ramshackle wings of the un-domed Capitol. Even there they could hardly converse. The acoustics were simply awful.

## *The Seventeenth State: Ohio, 1803*

On New Year's Day, 1788, General Rufus Putnam and twenty-six surveyors and artisans of the Ohio Associates left for what their Hartford neighbors derided as "Putnam's Paradise." Three snowy weeks later they stopped in Pittsburgh to construct roofed vessels known as "Kentucky boats," and christened one *Mayflower* in honor of two descendants of Pilgrims in their company. On April 1, 1789, they set out down the Ohio River to occupy the first northwestern land grant awarded by Congress. A curtain of drooping willows rendered their preferred landing invisible, so they just put in opposite the army's Fort Harmar and went to work on a stockade and town. They called it Marietta to honor Marie Antoinette. That took on ironic significance five years later when the queen lost her head in the revolution so admired by Jefferson.

Ohio was a major stake in all the colonial wars, but none of them resolved the issue because Little Turtle's confederacy made the Northwest a death trap. Marietta began as a fragile armed camp. Every male mustered to arms on Sunday, turning the Sabbath into a day of drill. The company directors, or "Board of Police," issued stern regulations to conserve food and suppress drunkenness against the day when Indians attacked. The other enemy was the forest. Ohio was low-lying and well watered, but covered with woods only occasionally broken by prairie. Since New England folk wisdom held any land *not* covered by trees must be infertile, pioneer farmers invariably chose the least hospitable tracts to clear by girdling and ax. Still, the company platted elaborate towns under Northwest Ordinance guidelines, setting aside plots for churches, schools, and courthouses. It seemed seventeenth-century Massachusetts had sprung back to life. Governor Arthur St. Clair hoped that was the case. A strict Calvinist patriarch whose arrival an aide thought "the birthday of the western world," St. Clair extolled "good government, well administered" and "the beautiful fabric of civilized life." At once he created courts, codes, officials, counties, and in 1790 a new capital nearby Fort Washington on the Little Miami River. But he was not pleased when, instead, the "extremely debauched" town of Cincinnati spawned more litigation than civilization. Cincinnati's first newspaper quipped: "Three Kentucky boats have lately arrived with a fresh assortment of attorneys." But the first Ohioans had to do backbreaking work just to survive. Thomas Ewing, a future senator, told of meeting a pretty girl on a flatboat after a hard day at the mill. He was so ashamed of his black calloused hands "I hardly dared to offer them to help her out of the boat."[19]

What breathed life into St. Clair's paper plans was Anthony Wayne's victory at Fallen Timbers in 1794. The Indians ceded all but Ohio's northwestern quadrant and settlers streamed in. Alas, most were not to the governor's liking. First, the Scioto Company obtained congressional grants halfway between Marietta and Cincinnati, hoping to resell the wilderness to gullible Europeans. They failed, save for a miserable five hundred French men and women whose presence created headaches for St. Clair, not to say Catholic Bishop John Carroll. Next, numerous squatters from Virginia and Kentucky moved into the Scioto Valley to found Chillicothe. They resisted St. Clair's "ordered liberty" with the ferocity of a Patrick Henry. Yet another wave of newcomers came courtesy of Ebenezer Zane, who in 1796 offered Congress a deal. He would build at his own expense a road from his land around Wheeling, (West) Virginia, to Cincinnati in exchange for a concession to run river ferries and land grants around them. That, of course, ensured him title to the valuable spots where towns would spring up. But thanks to Zane's Trace, wagons, packhorses, cattle, and settlers streamed into Ohio. Zane met their needs by deeding land to blacksmiths, tanners, and other artisans if they pledged to stay four years. His entrepreneurship filled Zanesville, St. Clairsville, and Chillicothe with New Englanders, Scots-Irish, Germans, and Welsh.

Finally, Ohio's northeast was born in 1796 when General Moses Cleaveland led fifty men and two women from the Hudson River to the "good and promised land" of Connecticut's Western Reserve. Cleaveland, who sank $32,600 into the company, was so intent on a profit he refused to make the usual gifts to local Indians. His own people, he lectured the miserable Massasagas, "lived by industry, and to give away their property lavishly, to those who live in indolence and by begging, would be no deed of charity." For his own colonists Cleaveland popped kegs of punch, toasting their procreation in hopes their children would multiply "sixteen times fifty." The company's cartographer mistakenly recorded the site on the Cuyahoga River as "Cleveland." The company's marketing was no better. It asked an outrageous $50 per lot in a locale so boggy and buggy few buyers stayed. Some farmers trickled in to found villages such as Youngstown in the Western Reserve, but not until the War of 1812 did Cleveland begin its career as Cincinnati's cross-state rival.[20]

Ohio's population reached forty-five thousand in 1800, so statehood was just a matter of years. St. Clair was not pleased. "A multitude of indigent and ignorant people are but ill qualified to form a constitution and government for themselves," he insisted. As for political principles, "they have none." Worse still, the original river counties were eclipsed by the interior ones where Jeffersonians dominated. Federalists conceived a last-ditch defense: dividing the territory in twain at the Scioto River would delay statehood for both portions. That plan so enraged Republican "Bloodhounds" that they burned the governor in effigy on Christmas Eve, 1801, threatening to kill anyone promoting partition. More respectable men, led by land baron Thomas Worthington, journeyed to Washington where they denounced St. Clair as "an enemy of the republican form of government." Since statehood meant three more electoral votes for their party Republicans in Congress invited Ohio in 1802 to draft a constitution. They even promised to build a National (or Cumberland) Road linking Ohio to the Atlantic seaboard.[21]

St. Clair, now desperate, damned the statehood movement as a plot to extend slavery north of the Ohio River. Worthington wasted no time informing Jefferson of those remarks. The President sacked St. Clair and Congress approved Ohio statehood on February 19, 1803. Worthington became a U.S. senator; his partner Edward Tifflin the governor. Ohio Republicans proved highly partisan and especially adept at what they called "log rolling." But otherwise St. Clair misjudged his wards. Ohio politics were clean by comparison to Kentucky. Elections turned less on issues than character. Land speculation passed from the hands of distant companies into those of creative developers. Nor were Ohioans "ignorant": they founded Ohio University (1804), Miami University (1809), the University of Cincinnati (1819), and Oberlin (1833), America's first co-educational and racially integrated college. Nor did Ohioans want slavery. Indeed, their legislature even tried to ban the entry of free blacks and induce resident blacks to depart! In that, Ohio became a template for the whole Middle West.[22]

Already by 1810 Ohio counted 230,760 residents. In 1816 the capital moved to Columbus. The state's central location and varied population also made it a bellwether state and birthplace or home to eight presidents.[23] Finally, Ohio merged quickly into the nation's economy. Beginning in 1806 Joseph Hough transported "fresh eastern goods" such as pots and pans, nails, dishes, guns, and ammunition by flatboat down the Ohio, thence to storekeepers who traded for pork, corn, and whiskey. The commodities piled up in Hough's Cincinnati warehouse until early autumn when his boats raced down to sell them on New Orleans' wharves. Hough or his agents then sailed to Philadelphia with a satchel full of bills of exchange to begin the cycle anew. Pork, corn, whiskey ... and apples, because after 1800 another Ohio feature became a Middle West legend. John Chapman, a nurseryman from Massachusetts, gathered great bags of apple seeds from Pennsylvania German cider presses and headed west to sell or strew them in Ohio and beyond. He also planted twelve hundred acres of orchards. But "Johnny Appleseed" preferred roaming until, in 1845, he died of exposure near Fort Wayne, Indiana. If there is such a thing as the all-American meal, it surely consists of pork chops, corn on the cob, and apple pie.

Near the end of his two terms as president Thomas Jefferson did serious harm to the Union. Prior to that blunder he saved the Union by what he did *not* do. He did not take up executive power in order to abolish it, nor did he wield it so vindictively as to provoke schism. How much credit he deserves is a matter of warm dispute, but the fact that his "Revolution of 1800" proved so unrevolutionary gave the federal Constitution a sixty-year lease on life.

The red-headed, long-legged polymath was the anti-Washington: a man of, not above, the people, and more the symbol of the nation than chief of state. He dispensed with the ornate president's coach, staged no lavish receptions, and refused to address Congress in the manner of King-in-Parliament. He dressed like a gentleman-farmer, sometimes greeting visitors in soiled clothes or a dressing gown. In the sticky summer months he left town entirely. His leadership derived not from prerogative, but persuasion and public opinion. The first president to head a political party, he governed through that party in Congress so it seemed that the will of the people moved the president, not the president's will them. At social events he insisted no one give way: he was just Mr. Jefferson and his only rule of etiquette was "ladies first." This was studied playacting, homage to an equality in which he did not believe. But in part it was personality. Now fifty-seven, Jefferson was still the shy introvert who despised contradiction and fled from debate, leaving polemics to his factotums. When he "presided," it was over small groups, especially his famous dinner parties for a dozen (rarely more) congressmen or foreign dignitaries. The French wines and cuisine were exquisite, but the air was informal, the table round to discourage side conversations, and no eavesdropping servants stood behind chairs (Jefferson dished out the portions himself). In this manner he petted every member of Congress, taking their measure during free-flowing banter about policy, philosophy, or just gossip. The cost of these meals exceeded his salary. The dividend was a compliant House led by a loyal Speaker, floor manager or "whip," and clerk John Beckley, who doubled as the first national party chairman.[24]

Jefferson's Inaugural Address was a masterpiece. He redefined the fierce election campaign of 1800 as a mere "contest of opinion," celebrated its resolution "according to the rules of the Constitution," and expressed assurance the people would unite behind the rule of law and common good. He declared it a "sacred principle" that to be rightful, the will of the majority must also be "reasonable" and the law protect minority rights. "Let us, then, fellow citizens, unite with one heart and one mind. Let us restore to social intercourse that harmony and affection without which liberty and even life itself are but dreary things.... Let us, then, with courage and confidence pursue our own Federal and Republican principles, our attachment to union and representative government." He pledged equal justice for all, peace and commerce with all nations but "entangling alliances with none," respect for states' rights but "preservation of the General Government in its whole constitutional vigor," public economy, and support for agriculture, commerce, and the Bill of Rights. All these principles "should be the creed of our political faith, the text of civil instruction. . . ." Thus did Jefferson reaffirm the civic religion and place Republicanism at its orthodox heart. All that remained was the benediction: "And may the Infinite Power which rules the destinies of the universe lead our councils to what is best, and give them a favorable issue for your peace and prosperity."[25]

In practice, restoring "harmony and affection" meant returning to Washington's precedent of appointing cabinet officials from all sections of the country,[26] while only gradually replacing Federalist officials with Republican appointees. Protecting minority rights meant reducing the residency requirement for citizenship to just three years, allowing the Alien and Sedition Acts to lapse, and reimbursing with interest the fines paid by convicted journalists. Public economy meant repeal of the excise taxes to the delight of frontier distillers and topers. All that Congress did speedily. But the third branch of government was a vexation. The outgoing Congress's Judiciary Act of 1801 created sixteen circuit courts for Adams to fill. It also shrank the Supreme Court by one so Jefferson could not fill its first vacancy. Worst of all, Adams appointed John Marshall chief justice. A remote Virginia cousin of Jefferson, Marshall combined George Washington's vision of Federalism with George Wythe's devotion to Common Law, and Patrick Henry's swashbuckling style. He and Jefferson matched wits and wills at once. The President considered Adams' "midnight appointments" unethical if not illegal, telling Secretary of State Madison to ignore those who had not yet received their commissions. One such, William Marbury, sued, but before the case was heard Congress considered a bill to repeal the Judiciary Act of 1801. At first it failed in the Senate, when Vice President Burr cast a tie-breaking vote *against* it, thereby cementing Jefferson's hatred of him. In 1802, however, Republicans not only passed a new Judiciary Act, they postponed the next Supreme Court session for a year. Marshall stewed, thought matters through, and exercised his own persuasive powers on his associate justices. The Court convened to deliver two thundering judgments. First, in *Stuart versus Laird,* the Court arrogated to itself the right to review laws, in this case affirming the constitutionality of the Republicans' Judiciary Act! Second, in *Marbury versus Madison,* the Court ruled it did *not* have the power to compel the officer's commission because a section of the original 1789 Judiciary Act was *not* constitutional. Thus did Marshall accept a minor defeat (sacrificing Marbury) in order to win a major constitutional victory (establishing judicial review). Jefferson's defeat was ironic given his prior advocacy of a Bill of Rights to empower judges to restrain legislatures.[27]

The administration's top priority, however, was public finance. That made Albert Gallatin Jefferson's most important adviser. A forty-year-old native of Geneva, Switzerland, Gallatin came to America to get rich because he hated being dependent, even on family. He did not get very rich, but found his calling as the sole Republican congressman with enough financial acumen to chop logic with Hamilton. Jefferson named him Treasury secretary with instructions to liquidate the national debt. Gallatin figured that was possible in just sixteen years if federal expenditures were sharply reduced. But there was no fat in the budget and the only muscle was in the military's 40 percent share. So Jefferson and Gallatin reached for their scalpels and sliced defense estimates from $3.5 to $1 million per year . . . *in the midst of a world at war.* What were they thinking?[28]

To their credit, they *were* thinking, but wishfully. The point was to kill two birds—a corrupting national debt and a threatening military—with one stone. The army could hardly be abolished so long as Indian frontiers needed policing. Jefferson was also enough of a scientist to realize the need for a cadre trained in artillery and engineering. Accordingly, his military bill of 1802 created both the U.S. Military Academy at West Point, New York, and the Army Corps of Engineers, measures Republicans would doubtless have opposed if a Federalist tried to take them. But the same bill restricted the standing army to a mere 3,350 men scattered out west where no ambitious generals could make mischief. In the event of war, Jefferson believed, state militias drilled by the small professional corps would suffice to repel invasion. But since Congress was not willing to impose rigorous standards on the militias, the U.S. military was incapable of doing much more than skirmishing with Indians.[29] Jefferson's ideas about the navy were riskier still. He hated its expense and association with mercantilism. So he stopped naval construction and meant to dry dock the powerful frigates that proved so effective during the Quasi War against France. He believed coastal defense required no more than a fleet of gunboats armed with a cannon or two and propelled by sail or oar. What was more, twenty-five gunboats could be built for the cost of one $250,000 frigate. The President's enthusiasm for them waxed greater still when he absorbed the apparent lessons of the nation's first foreign conflict.

It began in 1801 when the pasha of Tripoli on the North African coast ordered the Stars and Stripes chopped down from the American consulate. Like the king of Morocco, the dey of Algiers, and the bey of Tunis, the pasha lived off piracy, tribute, and selling captives into slavery. The Washington administration, lacking a navy, suffered the Barbary Pirates' protection racket, while Adams' navy was absorbed with the French. But Jefferson had idle ships, a hatred for these barbarians, and a Virginian's honor to uphold. To Gallatin's chagrin he ordered a fleet to blockade Tripoli: blockade, but take no offensive action, and blockade duty in the Mediterranean sun soon ruined sailors' morale. Then, in August 1803, the forty-four-gun frigate *Constitution*, Commodore Edward Preble commanding, passed through the Straits of Gibraltar. Preble, a down-east skipper and veteran of the Revolution, suffered painful ulcers but not grandees or fools. When a British captain, bluffing that his own ship (hidden by fog) mounted eighty-four guns, insisted Preble heave-to, the Yank damned his eyes and prepared for action. The arrogant Brit backed down; American sailors felt a pride unknown since the days of John Paul Jones. Preble proceeded to purge the squadron of slackers and sea lawyers, put officers and men through gunnery drills, and promise to drub any Arab daring to cross the bar.[30]

Thanks to Preble's leadership even a potentially crippling disaster became an occasion for glory. The frigate *Philadelphia* ran aground pursuing corsairs. The delighted pasha seized the ship for ransom and amused himself by torturing the captive crewmen. But a twenty-two-year-old lieutenant not only kept up their spirits during nineteen months of captivity, he turned the Tripolitan prison into a school teaching trigonometry, navigation, and tactics. Meanwhile, Preble calculated the odds of retaking and refloating the frigate, deciding at length to destroy it. On a dark night in February 1804, Lieutenant Stephen Decatur and sixty men sneaked toward shore in an Arab galley, routed the defenders, and put *Philadelphia* to the torch. Not a single American was lost in what Admiral Horatio Nelson called "the most bold and daring act of the age." The following year irascible U.S. consul William Eaton complemented Preble's assaults by sea with an unlikely ground campaign. Just fifteen U.S. Marines led some forty Greek soldiers and a band of Arabs across the desert from Egypt to Libya. That sufficed to frighten the pasha into ransoming the *Philadelphia*'s crew and dropping his demands for $300,000 in tribute.[31]

This first clash with the Barbary Pirates conjured three portents. First, the British Admiralty noted most of the ransomed crew were in fact British subjects who signed on with the Yanks to evade the war with Napoleon. So it authorized the Royal Navy to board American ships and impress "draft-dodgers," a practice sure to enrage U.S. opinion. Second, American officers on the Barbary Coast received invaluable training. Proudly calling themselves "Preble's Boys," they would provide twenty-four of the twenty-six captains and masters commanding ships in the War of 1812. Third, Preble himself raved about how effective the little galleys and gunboats were in the harbors of Tripoli, encouraging the administration to freeze capital ship construction and build 176 gunboats that proved almost useless in 1812. Indeed, when a hurricane washed two of the boats inland and deposited them in a Georgia field, mirthful Federalists suggested they might take root in the fertile soil and *grow* into frigates.

Jefferson's penury can be easily derided as an ostrich maneuver. But from his novel and very American point of view, to prepare for war was the worst of blunders, first because it invited war, and second because every dollar invested in economic growth added more to the nation's strength than a thousand dollars spent on armies and ships. Many American statesmen of all parties have since said the same. What is more, Jefferson thought, the British and French (not being pirates) had every incentive to *court* the lucrative free trade of America rather than inhibit it. His early dealings with Europe seemed to vindicate him in spectacular fashion.

The strategic stage in 1801 can be briefly described as follows. Bonaparte had seized power as First Consul in the *coup d'état* of 18 Brumaire; his armies were masters of Western Europe. But the fleet he took to Egypt in 1798 lay at the bottom of Aboukir Bay courtesy of Admiral Nelson, so he had no way to get at the British. They, in turn, had no way to get at the French, while the naval war strained the Admiralty and Exchequer alike. In consequence, the French and British inched toward the Peace of Amiens, the only interruption in twenty-three years of warfare. Napoleon meant to exploit it to revive French fortunes in the Americas, crushing *en passant* the imperial destiny of the United States. Thus, during the same weeks in 1800 when one French delegation worked with John Adams' envoys in Paris to terminate the Franco-American alliance, another was in Madrid demanding retrocession of Louisiana. It was a terrible blow to Spain's pride and New Spain's security. But the expense of defending the Mississippi basin from New Orleans to St. Louis was beyond Spanish means. When Napoleon sweetened the deal with a dubious promise to bestow an Italian kingdom on the Spanish king's son-in-law, Madrid approved the Treaty of San Ildefonso.

Napoleon's next step was to fool the Americans. His *chargé d'affaires* in Washington approached Secretary of State Madison in 1801 asking what stance the United States would assume should France reimpose colonial rule over the rebellious Haitian republic on Saint Domingue? Jefferson, terrified of slave revolts, cannily saw a way to achieve three goals at once. He promised to collaborate with a French blockade to "starve" Toussaint's army on condition that France conclude peace with Britain and open French Caribbean ports to American merchants.[32] But since rumors circulated about some secret deal involving Louisiana, Jefferson sent Robert R. Livingston to Paris with orders to spy out the truth. Bonaparte duly made the Peace of Amiens with the British in 1802 while hastily outfitting a Caribbean expedition under his brother-in-law, Charles Leclerc. When Leclerc's fleet arrived off Cap St. François, however, he discovered twenty American ships, not blockading, but merrily trading with the rebellious ex-slave regime! Leclerc corralled them and protested to Washington City. Jefferson, having now put two and two together, responded with a tremendous bluff. He asked his friend Pierre Du Pont de Nemours to bear a letter to Livingston "secretly" warning that the United States would make war and even ally with Great Britain should French forces land on the North American mainland. "There is on the globe one single spot," he wrote, "the possessor of which is our natural and habitual enemy. It is New Orleans, through which the produce of three eighths of our territory must pass to market." In fact, U.S. minister Rufus King reported from London the British intended Louisiana either to remain in Spanish hands or fall into their own. But Jefferson hoped the mere specter of Anglo-American unity would scare Bonaparte off like some voodoo spell.[33]

Imagine now the quandary of poor Juan Morales, Spanish intendant at New Orleans. Was a French fleet even now approaching to oust him? Was a British fleet en route to pre-empt the French? Was an American frontier militia mustering upriver? Fearing a "yes" to any of the above, Morales summarily sealed off New Orleans to all foreigners in October 1802. Westerners screamed and Congress protested. Worst of all, Leclerc began shipping some of his Haitian captives to American ports by way of protesting Jefferson's failure to help him as promised. "The infernal French," a South Carolinian wrote, "at this moment are vomiting their wretched blacks upon our coast."[34] Jefferson desperately hoped something would turn up, and thanks to a grand miscalculation by Du Pont he was ready the moment it did. Du Pont reported Napoleon and Talleyrand really intended to *sell* New Orleans and West Florida to the

United States for just $6 million. Since France owed $4 million in compensation for the Quasi War, it meant the port could be had for just $2 million in cash. Jefferson named James Monroe plenipotentiary while the obedient Congress authorized the money. Du Pont's information was wrong, but by the time Monroe's ship made French waters, it was close to the truth. Leclerc's campaign, after initial successes and wanton cruelty, had aborted. Guerrilla attacks and yellow fever killed more than half the thirty thousand French troops, including Leclerc himself. Moreover, the Peace of Amiens was unraveling due in large part to Napoleon's violations of its terms. So the First Consul, in a spasm of pique, ordered Talleyrand to dispose of the New World empire like a scorned mistress while he fell back in the arms of his first and true love, war in Europe. Talleyrand took a wry pleasure in watching the Americans' jaws drop when he offered to sell *all* of Louisiana—a territory nearly equal in size to the existing United States—for cash and debt relief totaling $15 million.

Britain and Spain were quick to call the United States a receiver of stolen goods and deny the legality of the sale. The French, Spanish, and Native American inhabitants of Louisiana asked how they could be "purchased" without so much as a *s'il vous plaît*. Federalists in Congress, rightly expecting this boded a host of future Republican states, suddenly saw the merits of strict construction and called the purchase unconstitutional. For their part, Jefferson and Gallatin had to swallow their principles and increase the national debt by 20 percent. But Alexander Hamilton, scorning party politics for the national interest, heartily approved of Jefferson's coup. The Senate ratified the treaty 26 to 6, the House approved the additional debt, and Jefferson gloated he had done it all peacefully whereas the "federal maniacs" would have rushed into a ruinous war. He named the Louisiana Purchase "one of the most fortunate events which have taken place since the establishment of our independence," since it "secures to an incalculable distance of time the tranquillity, security & prosperity of all the Western country."[35]

That last claim was, for the moment, silly. Having made the greatest real estate acquisition in history, Jefferson thought it meant he could now *reduce* western army garrisons. General Wilkinson, who took possession of New Orleans in December 1803, thus pestered the secretary of War with complaints: "When I estimate the number and force of the Indian nations, who inhabit the Country watered by the Missouri and the Mississippi . . . When I cast my eyes over the expanse of Territory to be occupied or controuled, and glance at futurity, I hope you will pardon me Sir for observing . . . that we are not in sufficient strength, of men or means, to meet the occasion and profit by the favorable circumstances of the moment." Wilkinson was right—but since he was secretly on Spain's payroll, too, he hinted to officials in Mexico they might send out patrols to capture Jefferson's scouts Lewis and Clark![36]

Even before the Louisiana treaty was inked, Congress gave Jefferson money to reconnoiter the West. He dispatched a series of expeditions of which the Corps of Discovery was only the most famous. From 1804 to 1806, two Freemasons named Meriwether Lewis and William Clark paddled and trekked from St. Louis to the Pacific and back via the Missouri, Jefferson, Salmon, Snake, and Columbia Rivers. The Shoshone woman Canoe Launcher (Sacajawea), the wife of a French trapper, was an indispensable guide and interpreter. Most gratifying to Jefferson was the expedition's faithful record of the geography, flora, fauna, and tribes of the American Northwest. But its success also lured American trappers and mountain men into the Rockies before any Hudson's Bay Company competitors arrived, and bolstered the State Department's flimsy claim to the Oregon Territory. That in turn kindled the imperial imagination of a great American hustler, John Jacob Astor. Born in Germany in 1763, he arrived in New York at age twenty with nothing but a consignment of flutes. A merchant told him the fur business was the way to get rich in America, so Astor began hiring trappers in the Great Lakes. By 1800 he had amassed a fortune. When news of Lewis and Clark reached Astor in 1807, he boasted to New York's mayor, De Witt Clinton, he meant to monopolize the whole North American fur trade by planting a colony on the Columbia River and outflanking the British in Canada. Jefferson approved, although his principles prevented him from granting a government charter or protection. Astor's first party of colonists took ship around Cape Horn and after a series of adventures built a fort at Astoria in 1811. A second, overland, party straggled into the fort in 1812, just in time to surrender to the Royal Navy when the war of that year was declared.[37]

Jefferson ordered two other expeditions to proceed from Natchez up the Red and Arkansas Rivers. But they were undermanned, underfunded, and under orders to avoid conflict with Spaniards and Indians. They did not get very far. By contrast, Lieutenant Zebulon Pike's two missions, inspired by Wilkinson, got very far and made a deeper impression than Lewis and Clark because Pike published first. Between 1805 and 1807 his party of twenty soldiers explored the Mississippi from St. Louis to Minnesota, informing the great Sioux nations on the way they were now subject to U.S. authority. Pike carefully located the best sites to build forts. Wilkinson then ordered him west across the Great Plains to befriend the Osages, Comanches, and Pawnees. Instead Pike discovered Indians loyal to Spain, indeed eager to "renew the chains of ancient amity, which was said to have existed between their father, his most Catholic majesty, and his children the red people." Worse still, Pike's troop spent a brutal winter astride the Colorado Rockies only to be arrested by Spaniards and marched south to Mexico before being released. His briefings were a bonanza of military intelligence, but his published journals discouraged southwestern settlement for decades. He likened the Great Plains to a rolling ocean of sand "on which not a speck of vegetable matter existed," suitable only for "uncivilized aborigines." Bad public relations for land speculators, but excellent disinformation from the *Indian* point of view.[38]

In the 1790s the danger to American unity was frontier rebellion or even secession should Federalists press their programs to extremes. By 1804 the United States confronted the opposite danger of a New England rebellion or secession should Republicans go to extremes. Jefferson's popularity and his party's power seemed unassailable, and why not? Jefferson had cut spending, preserved peace, and doubled the size of the country. Agriculture and commerce boomed as U.S. carriers exploited the resumption of war in Europe. Then there was the Republican party machinery, which Federalists belatedly copied with indifferent results.[39] Was the American Union the Federalists had fought for, designed, and preserved from 1775 to 1800 to become the plaything of "atheists" and democrats? If so, would it not be better to dissolve the Union and at least keep liberty's flame burning in holy New England? Senator Timothy Pickering took it upon himself to promote a secessionist movement and spied a chance for success when the disgraced Vice President Burr agreed to accept the *Federalist* nomination for governor of New York. The grand plan was for Burr to merge New York with New England and form a separate country. What the rudderless Burr might really have done is anyone's guess. But his candidacy alarmed Hamilton. With a fury both personal and patriotic he urged Federalists to vote for Morgan Lewis, the Republican nonentity fronting for the Livingston faction. More damaging to Burr, perhaps, was the confusion his party switch caused among Tammany loyalists. The mud slinging on both sides was intense. When in April 1804 Burr gleaned just 40 percent of the tally, he invoked the *code duello* and called Hamilton to pistols on the green at Weehawken, New

Jersey. Hamilton's son had been killed in such an affair just a year before and he was well aware of Burr's marksmanship. But Hamilton consented in July 1804 to perform one last service for his country. He killed Burr's career by permitting Burr to kill him.[40]

Jefferson cleverly mended Republican fences in New York by asking George Clinton to be the first "running mate" in a U.S. presidential campaign. In 1804 the two of them buried Federalists Charles C. Pinckney and Rufus King, 162 electoral votes to 14. Only Connecticut and Delaware remained firmly Federalist. Pickering's secession schemes evaporated. Burr's schemes, however, condensed. In his last days as vice president he chaired the Senate trial of impeached Supreme Court justice Samuel Chase. It was a landmark case, probably more important to the survival of an independent federal judiciary than *Marbury versus Madison*. For if Jeffersonians, drunk with victory, succeeded in ousting Chase, they might clear the whole court, John Marshall included. Chase was a righteous High Federalist who made no secret of his bias. So the House tested its powers by arguing his political improprieties amounted to "high crimes and misdemeanors." Burr controlled no votes, but he put members on the spot by staring them in the eye and intoning *272 times* (there were eight counts and thirty-four senators), not "How do you vote?" or "Guilty or not guilty?" but rather: "Senator _____! How say you? Is Samuel Chase, the respondent, guilty of high crimes and misdemeanors as charged in the article just read?" Five articles of impeachment failed of a simple majority, and thanks to nine Republican defectors none got a two-thirds majority.[41]

Having flummoxed Jefferson again, Burr bade a shameless farewell to the Senate. "This house is a sanctuary; a citadel of law, of order, and of liberty; it is here—it is here in this exalted refuge—here, if anywhere, will be resistance made to the storms of political frenzy and the silent arts of corruption. And if the Constitution be destined ever to perish by the sacrilegious hands of the demagogue or the usurper, which God avert, its expiring agonies will be witnessed on this floor. . . . I, of a certainty, shall always remember, with respect and affection, the years I spent here." Senators stood and applauded as Burr left the chamber. But since he was under indictment in two states for the "murder" of Hamilton and no longer enjoyed immunity, Burr changed horses, disguised himself, and hired a closed coach to spirit him away. He had already made secret contact with certain Spanish officials.[42]

Burr never plotted to become president by disposing of Jefferson. But once quit of the vice presidency he played the very demagogue and usurper against which he warned the Senate. He chose the West for his stage because federal authority, such as it was, lay in the hands of another conspirator, Wilkinson, while western state and territorial leaders already evinced secessionist tendencies. They might be easily enlisted in a crusade to plunder the mines of Mexico. Even the British minister gave Burr veiled encouragement in hopes of splitting the United States. Whether he in fact conjured any plot substantial enough to deserve the name is unknown. Andrew Jackson, Henry Clay, Senator John Smith of Ohio, and others Burr tried to enlist kept their distance. But Harman Blennerhassett, an eccentric Irish lord and savant who lived on a woody isle in the Ohio River, opened his mansion and pockets to Burr. So did New Orleans merchant Daniel Clark. So, paradoxically, did Spanish minister Carlos Yrujo, because to him Burr hinted at independence for the American West and an alliance with Spain. Wilkinson must have known both these schemes were absurd and had nothing to offer *him:* he was already a proconsul by grace of the U.S. government and rich by grace of the Spanish government. But Wilkinson exchanged enciphered messages with Burr, introduced him around New Orleans, and whispered with him over dinner at the Philadelphia home of their mutual friend Charles Biddle. In Washington, Burr traced out secret maps and even met with Jefferson several times early in 1806. Meanwhile, Burr's agents made western recruits with gold coins and promises, instructing them to assemble on Blennerhasset's island.

Of all the calculations and deceptions in train, Burr's were probably the *least* important. What logic can be imposed on the evidence suggests he was played for a puppet by Yrujo, Wilkinson, and Jefferson during years when Spain and the United States were engaged in a war dance. Potential flash points included the boundaries of Louisiana and American designs on the Floridas. With tense negotiations in progress Jefferson might well have tolerated and even encouraged Burr's harmless plots as a sort of veiled threat against Spain. They were harmless because he really had no chance of winning British support for mad schemes, while Jefferson seems not to have worried about western secession. After all, those were his people out there. It is known the President received eight warnings about "armed conspiracies." He never lifted a finger.

By summer 1806, when sixty adventurers boarded flatboats and drifted downriver to rendezvous with Burr near New Orleans, the geopolitical context was transformed. The war crisis with Spain had passed and chilling new twists in the European war risked embroiling the United States with France, Britain, or both. As a result, Burr's utility vanished. That made it Wilkinson's moment to act lest his letters and clouds of witnesses surface to link him to Burr's plots. The devious general, who might at any time have provoked war with Spain, now made a joint peace-keeping pact with the Spanish commander across the Sabine River in Texas. Then Wilkinson hurried back to New Orleans to jail all Burr's accomplices and rush letters to Washington City exposing a "wicked and wide-spread conspiracy." That made it Jefferson's moment to act. He blessed Wilkinson's summary violations of *habeas corpus* and ordered Marines to New Orleans. The President called for Burr's arrest *even though* he had as yet done nothing illegal. Burr cried betrayal *even though* Wilkinson had made no promises to betray. Then Burr lit out toward Pensacola *even though* it was one of the Spanish towns he presumably hoped to conquer. All the while Wilkinson paraded himself as a patriot *even though* he surreptitiously sent the Spaniards a hefty bill for services rendered.

The penultimate act in the farce occurred in April 1807, when Burr was arraigned for high treason in Richmond. Presiding judge John Marshall, prosecutor Edmund Randolph, and defense counsel Luther Martin, for various reasons, all hated Burr less than they hated Jefferson. A young journalist named Washington Irving was pleased to embellish their courtroom theatrics. Jefferson behaved no better: he issued pronunciamentos affirming Burr's guilt, leaked documents to the press, and offered co-conspirators immunity. But Marshall, who at one point in the trial broke bread with Martin and Burr, construed treason so narrowly the jury had no choice but to acquit. All Jefferson gained from the affair, besides a migraine, was a President's right to ignore a subpoena. In 1808, the ultimate act in the farce began. Burr, still under an Ohio indictment, jumped bail, borrowed $2,000 from his son-in-law, and sailed to Europe. There he made and lost fortunes at gaming tables, offered his services to both Napoleon and George III, and wooed wealthy women. In 1812 he returned on cat's feet to New York, resumed his law practice, and married a rich widow whose fortune he squandered. Later she sued for divorce on grounds of adultery: he was eighty years old at the time. In 1836, when Burr was at death's door, a pastor asked if he had prepared his soul for heaven. "On that subject," Burr replied, "I am coy."[43]

Aaron Burr insisted to the end he was misunderstood or mistreated by vindictive rivals. Perhaps he was. As a soldier he helped win American independence. As a politician he helped to invent the urban machine and banks serving the masses. As vice president he helped to blunt Jefferson's assaults on an independent judiciary. But his inner demons were such that everything he did was to promote Aaron Burr, not America, until he made himself a pariah to Jeffersonians and Hamiltonians alike. It was not his corruption that earned him the nation's scorn, but the fact that his corruption was never seen as *creative*, never devoted to the service of the nation at large.

For two years after Europe plunged back into war American producers and merchants profited. But in 1805 Lord Nelson confirmed Britain's maritime hegemony at Trafalgar while the same year the Emperor of the French (as Napoleon now styled himself) confirmed his continental hegemony by whipping the Austrians and Russians at Austerlitz, then the Prussians in 1806. Unable to coerce their enemies with arms, both sides resorted to economic war. A British Order in Council of May 1806 imposed a blockade on northern Europe. Napoleon's Berlin Decree in November declared all ships trading with Britain fair game and banned British exports from the continent. Two more Orders in Council in 1807 prohibited neutrals from trading in European waters without paying duties in Britain. Napoleon lashed back with the Milan Decree outlawing any neutral ship submitting to Britain's terms, then the Bayonne Decree presuming *any* American ship to be in violation. Neutral rights ceased to exist; Americans had no way of appeasing one power without courting seizure by the other.

Now, the British were fighting for the freedom of the world; Napoleon was a tyrant. But Yankee skippers happily took their chances with French privateers, while Jefferson sought to appease their emperor by slapping an embargo on the republic of Haiti.[44] By contrast, the Royal Navy could mount an effective blockade all the more obnoxious for its impressment of sailors. Of course, every American port did a lively business in counterfeit papers for British draft dodgers, but seafaring Yankees cried foul anyway. In June 1807 they cried for war when H.M.S. *Leopard* intercepted the U.S.S. *Chesapeake* off Norfolk, Virginia. Commodore James Barron was defiant, but due to Gallatin's strapped naval budget the *Chesapeake* was nowhere near fighting trim. She struck her colors when the British opened fire, losing twenty-one sailors to wounds and four to impressment. Congress was in a mood to declare war, but Jefferson dared not. The three U.S. frigates on the Barbary station would be sitting ducks and otherwise the nation was toothless. His whole fiscal and military strategy since 1801 lay exposed, and he did not know what to do.

Months passed, Jefferson suffered more headaches, and Britain and France kept tightening the screws. Then Secretary of State Madison came to the rescue, or so the President thought. Another lifelong Anglophobe who imagined commercial interests ignoble, Madison recalled how effective *and* edifying the thirteen colonies' non-importation movement had been. Now he took economic sanctions a giant step further in the belief a cessation of American *exports* would bring the belligerents to their knees. Gallatin hated the idea because no trade meant no customs revenues. Jefferson was skeptical, too, but agreed on "the absolute necessity of a radical cure." The latest Orders and Decrees from Europe made up his mind. He would call on the American people to display supreme republican virtue and salvage their pride without war. On December 18, 1807, he proposed a *total ban* on foreign trade. Within four days the Embargo Act passed both houses of Congress and was signed into law.[45]

Thus began exactly what Federalists had always feared: a Republican reign of terror, if not against persons then against rights and property. Imagine yourself a wheat farmer, horse breeder, cattle rancher, tobacco, rice, or cotton planter, timber cutter, fisherman, not to mention merchant, sailor, chandler, or anyone providing goods and services to all the above. Suddenly your high-profit foreign markets no longer existed even as the resulting oversupply of goods and services drove domestic prices to the floor. Henry Adams judged the embargo "an experiment in politics well worth making," then proceeded to savage it. New Englanders' livelihoods disappeared. Mid-Atlantic farmers watched the price of grain fall from $2 to 75 cents a bushel. But the hardest blow fell on Jefferson's fellow southerners. Tobacco became almost worthless and cotton piled up on wharves, but the four hundred thousand slaves who produced them still had to be fed. Adams thought it "touching" how passively Virginia "drained the poison which her President held obstinately to her lips." Other Americans, however, invoked their time-honored tradition when faced with restrictive laws. They cheated in every way possible. New England and upstate New York smuggled great wagons and barges of corn, beef, and timber across their long, rugged borders with Canada. The Carolinas and Georgia were suddenly glad Florida was still foreign soil. Hundreds of Yankee and middle state captains slipped out of port clandestinely or else claimed to engage in coastal trade only to tack for the open sea. Astor tricked out a Chinese sailor washed up in New York as a great mandarin merchant and won approval for him to sail "home"—with $200,000 of Astor's wares in the hold. Thus, to the extent the ban was enforced or obeyed, "liberties and rights of property were more directly curtailed in the United States by the embargo than in Great Britain by centuries of almost continuous foreign war." To the extent the embargo was *not* enforced or obeyed, it "opened the sluice-gates of social corruption."[46]

Jefferson fumed at such treason. He rammed through Congress additional acts requiring coastal shippers, river boatmen, even fishermen to deposit huge bonds before leaving port. Next came a ban on overland exports subject to a fine of $10,000 and loss of cargo. Next, the President was granted authority to enforce the embargo by any means necessary. He instructed customs agents to assume guilty motives, sequester cargoes without warrant, and close down internal trade in all commodities except food: "Where you are doubtful, consider me as voting for detention." Such steps went far beyond the hated writs of assistance granted royal officials before 1776. Finally, to suppress smuggling to Canada, Jefferson declared northern New York and Vermont in a state of "insurrection" and ordered soldiers and militia to police them. Skirmishes were fought, people were killed: Americans fleeing a foreign war made war on each other.

Over and over again these federal acts were challenged in court, and judges and juries invariably upheld the scofflaws. Even Republican justice William Johnson, though he granted the Constitution gave Congress power to regulate commerce, ruled the President had exceeded his authority. Evasion increased as 1808 dragged on, Federalists became popular again in ports south of New York, and New Englanders talked of nullification in language echoing Jefferson's Kentucky and Virginia Resolutions. The British and French chortled at the prospect of the United States cutting off its nose to spite its face. Napoleon joked he was only helping enforce the embargo by seizing American ships! Indeed, the foreigners most harmed were West Indians, especially slaves, who went hungry for lack of American grain, and British millworkers laid off due to the shortage of cotton. Jefferson never relented; he stiffened enforcement until the day he left office. But the disaster revived Madison's long-dormant epilepsy, and when the fits subsided he and Gallatin admitted "peaceable coercion" was a contradiction in terms. Their new plan was to extend the embargo for just six more months to buy time for rearmament, but northern Republicans in Congress found their voice. In late February 1809, they voted with the Federalists to repeal the Embargo Act effective the day Jefferson left office.[47]

He left office, needless to say, under the blackest of clouds. In the 1808 elections the Federalists doubled their seats in Congress. But so well oiled were the national and local Republican machines, they not only held their majority but delivered 122 electoral votes for Madison against just 47 for Pinckney. In his inaugural address Madison did not apologize for the "Dambargo" and instead put all the blame for the recent unpleasantness on "the injustice and violence of the belligerent powers." Even John Quincy Adams, son of a Federalist president, attended the Republican caucus in 1808 and joined the party the following year. The Republican party was bullet-proof. That is why Thomas Jefferson, though eager to escape the presidency's "splendid misery," must also have smiled as he cantered through snow toward Monticello in March 1809. He had made good his vow to bury the Federalists.

What else did he achieve? Does Jefferson deserve the sobriquet "father of liberty"? Not where Africans, Indians, or political opponents were concerned. To be sure, Congress duly abolished the slave trade in 1808 when the Constitution's twenty-year grace period ended (easy to do with an embargo in progress). But Jefferson did not free his own slaves and was loath to free anyone else's unless they could be deported to Haiti or Africa. Likewise his outwardly beneficent schemes to help Indians really amounted to a choice between total assimilation and deportation to the Louisiana Territory.[48] What about white citizens? Did Jefferson promote independence and virtue by resisting Britain and rolling back Federalist fiscal and military programs? For a while, but the embargo exposed a treasury dangerously *de*pendent on foreign trade, a military denuded, and a people demoralized. In his defense, he played a weak hand well in foreign affairs until 1807, while his willingness to postpone insoluble problems of race was a trait all southerners and most northerners shared. What is more, let no one forget, *everything* Jefferson did was cheered by a large majority in the Congress and public, and the Virginia-led Republican dynasty he founded would last twenty-four years. Jefferson was simply the best politician of the early republic. That, by definition, made him a model American.

## *The Eighteenth State: Louisiana, 1812*

On December 20, 1803, a sullen crowd gathered in the plaza of New Orleans' Old Spanish Statehouse as a French color guard, a regiment of U.S. Army bluecoats, and a hundred mounted Mississippi militia formed up. At high noon French prefect Pierre Laussat strode out to meet commissioners William C. C. Claiborne and General James Wilkinson. Laussat was still hoping Napoleon might contrive somehow to regain France's New World birthright, but his mission this day was to surrender it and release French citizens from their allegiance. Muskets and cannons barked. The French tricolor descended. But the Stars and Stripes seemed to pause, as if hesitant, before soldiers pulled the flag smartly to the peak. A claque of Kaintucks cut loose with their "Hip, hip, hoorays" and the crowd dispersed, fearing the worst. Louisiana had changed hands again.[49]

Le Sieur de Bienville, first commandant of the 1698 colony on the Mississippi, fancied building a capital on a crescent-shaped bank (hence Crescent City) some fifty miles up from the delta. In 1720, Adrien de Pauger realized his dream, laying out the grid of *rues* and *grandes places* of the *Vieux Carré* (Old Quarter). The chartered company in charge of the colony shipped out convicts, two thousand Palatines (hence the "German coast" north of New Orleans), and enslaved Africans, while advertising its gaudy potential. But French investors bid up shares to such outrageous prices during the financial reign of John Law that Louisiana became a *mot sale* (dirty word) when the bubble burst. In 1731 the crown took control. Jesuits, Capuchins, and Ursuline sisters arrived to found a hospital and school. They also lobbied for a *Code Noir* (Black Code) requiring slaves be granted all church sacraments including marriage, thereby establishing their humanity. In the 1740s the "Grand Marquis" de Vaudreuil and his wife presided over a modest commercial boom and the exhibitionist *joie de vivre* for which the town became famous (legend makes Vaudreuil first patron of Mardi Gras). But clashes with Indians, a lack of labor and money, and war with the British stifled its growth. When the Spaniards took over in 1763 they moved energetically to make Louisiana a buffer zone blocking English expansion. Alejandro O'Reilly crushed a Creole revolt in 1769, then reconciled French *habitants* by granting them political rights. When Spain and France allied with the thirteen colonies in 1779, Governor Bernardo de Gálvez earned thanks from the Continental Congress by capturing British garrisons at Baton Rouge, Natchez, Mobile, and Pensacola. Governor Estaban Miró attracted new blood, including Canary Islanders (the *isleños*), Haitian planters and slaves fleeing the revolt, and Americans to whom Miró gave land on condition they swear fealty to Spain and become Catholic.

Of course, those "Kaintucks" faked it—assimilation was for *other* people—but so long as Wilkinson was on the governor's payroll there was hope of keeping the United States at arm's length.[50]

The fourth and most important group of new settlers were Acadians scattered during their *grand dérangement* from Nova Scotia (and despised, until Longfellow's *Evangeline* romanticized them in 1847).[51] Miró invited them to settle the bayous west and south of New Orleans where the "Cajuns" crafted a culture based on hunting and fishing, subsistence farming, and community values. Anglos ridiculed their language and customs, while Creole merchants and planters considered them bumpkins. They were in fact a modest people content to see to their families' needs, gather with neighbors for *ramasserie* (harvest) and *boucherie* (slaughter), and share surpluses rather than sell on the market. Most bayou Cajuns had one-room houses, one hand-sewn dress or trousers, and one pair of shoes worn only to church and *bals de maison* advertised every Saturday by messengers crying, "*Bal ce soir chez _____!*" These dances were tame by frontier standards. Only strong coffee was served, gamblers were exiled to the barn, and mothers kept watch over the girls. Old men regaled children with tales of ghosts, gators, and *feux-follets* (will-o'-the-wisps, probably swamp gas). *Traiteurs* dispensed folk medicine, sorcery, and Catholic amulets. At midnight zesty gumbo and rice were served and guests danced until tired fiddlers, banjo pickers, and squeeze-box players announced "*Le bal est fini.*" Between 1790 and 1810 a growing number of Cajun youth moved out to found sugar plantations, buy slaves, and marry Creoles. But most remained *petits habitants,* indifferent to the Vanity Fair in New Orleans and suspicious of all authority.[52]

Thanks to Spanish policies Louisiana's population was diverse and growing in 1803. Some eight thousand people lived in New Orleans, about thirty-five hundred in the alluvial soil below the city or in the bayous, and three thousand more around northwestern villages such as Natchitoches and Washita. Given the large percentage of "foreigners," Jefferson fretted over his choice of governor until settling on twenty-eight-year-old Claiborne, a loyal Republican (and friend of John Sevier) with experience in the

Mississippi territory. But Claiborne felt himself "a stranger in the country" and wisely decided to move slowly to Americanize it. Congress simplified his task by dividing the vast purchase in two, leaving Claiborne responsible only for the Territory of Orleans (the future state). Wilkinson performed another service when he agreed with the Spaniards to honor a "neutral strip" from the Sabine River to the Arroyo Hondo. This no-man's-land attracted rustlers and desperadoes which soldiers periodically had to sweep out, but it minimized the danger of war.

Still, Claiborne learned the French were not pleased with American rule. The tariff, the Kaintucks, the Common Law, even jury duty were sources of vexation. The governor concluded Creoles were "uninformed, indolent, luxurious" and unfit to be citizens. They tended to resign from office whenever a decision went against them. Their territorial assembly vested local power in the traditional parishes and restored the Napoleonic Code for all civil cases. Creole planters patronized smugglers, the most colorful of whom was a blacksmith turned pirate named Jean Lafitte. He gathered a formidable band on the lawless islands of Barataria Bay and preyed on Spanish shipping. Creoles adored him because he sold goods and slaves (with the aid of Jim Bowie) at much lower prices than tariff-paying merchants. When Claiborne advertised a $500 reward for Lafitte's capture, the pirates offered a $15,000 reward for the capture of Claiborne! In one respect only did Louisianans prefer American ways: they replaced the *Code Noir* with a harsher slave code. In 1811 the largest slave revolt in U.S. history erupted just west of New Orleans. Little is known about it except the names of two leaders, the mulatto Charles Deslonde and one Jupiter, and the fact that about five hundred rebels armed mostly with farm tools marched on New Orleans. Local armed whites intercepted them, killed sixty-six, and displayed the severed heads of the leaders to serve as a warning.[53]

In 1809 the legislature passed a petition for statehood, which Claiborne submitted with misgivings. He believed Louisiana far from ready to govern itself and doubted it met the population requirement. Indeed, the 1810 census counted just 34,311 whites, only 18 percent of whom were of U.S. origin. But Republicans sniffed three more electoral votes so they counted Louisiana's enslaved population, while Henry Clay stilled worries about admitting "foreigners" by requiring Louisiana's official business to be conducted in English. That drove Josiah Quincy out of his chair. "You have no authority," he cried, "to throw the rights and liberties, and property of [the American] people, into a 'hotch-pot' with the wild men of the Missouri, nor with the mixed, though more respectable race of Anglo-Hispano-Gallo-Americans, who bask on the sands, in the mouth of the Mississippi." But his nativist (and anti-slavery) cause was weakened when Congress annexed to the territory the four thousand Anglos and seven thousand slaves in West Florida. After the statehood bill passed in February 1811, a convention at Tremolet's New Orleans coffeehouse made short work by copying Kentucky's constitution. But since twenty-six of the forty-three delegates had French surnames, ratification required a temporary alliance between Anglo and Creole elites. It helped that many leaders in both were Freemasons. The state constitution gave the governor broad powers, restricted high office to the wealthy, and disenfranchised two-thirds of adult males. Congress cheerfully approved it on April 30, 1812. Even Claiborne was reconciled when the legislature retained him as governor.[54]

Six weeks later the War of 1812 was declared. In the Battle of New Orleans, militia, free black volunteers, and the merry men of the pirate Lafitte rallied behind Andrew Jackson.[55] But that spirit disappeared rapidly as Louisiana politics degenerated into running fights of Anglo against Creole, north against south, urban against rural, Catholic against Protestant, slaveholder against smallholder. Congress stirred the pot by amending the laws governing Spanish land grants so often no one felt secure in his property. Negative campaigns were the norm. Half the small electorate ceased to vote at all, while Africans, Cajuns, Creoles, and hardscrabble Anglos learned to assert their freedom and purge their sorrow in music. Not until 1845 and 1852 did the lower white social orders organize to compel a broad franchise, direct election of the governor, and public schools. They also moved the capital to Baton Rouge, where a *faux* castle with Moorish battlements was erected. Mark Twain called it "bastard gothic," yet somehow the architecture fit the Mediterranean, feudal character of the Bayou State.[56]

Jefferson left office with the United States disarmed and depressed. Yet he assured his successor the nation must soon absorb Florida, Cuba, and Canada as it had Louisiana, and become "such an empire for liberty as [the world] has never surveyed since the creation; and I am persuaded no constitution was ever before so well calculated as ours for extensive empire and self-government." Madison was not so buoyant, but Canada was very much on the mind of the gentle Princeton alumnus. Ever since reading the earl of Sheffield's 1783 prediction that America would revert to economic dependence on Britain, Madison had groped for ways to declare, in effect, independence all over again. But he was successively foiled by Jay's Treaty, the commercial boom of the early 1800s, and the equal and opposite predations of France. After the *Chesapeake* affair he finally got an embargo, but that was foiled in good part by "odious" smuggling along the Canadian border. What followed was worse. Congress replaced the embargo in 1809 with a Non-Intercourse Act that still forbade trade with Britain and France so long as their Orders in Council and Decrees remained in effect, but otherwise threw American ships onto the seas to venture wherever they dared. That all but invited illicit trade with the enemy. So in 1810 Nathaniel Bacon's "Bill Number 2" *legalized* trade with belligerents while threatening to reimpose the embargo against one if the other lifted restrictions. That all but invited the belligerents to cheat, which Napoleon did by lifting his decrees, then stipulating so many conditions nothing really changed. Meanwhile, Gallatin and John Jacob Astor amassed evidence showing not only an increase in trade on the Canadian border, but a flood of Canadian exports (re-exports of smuggled U.S. commodities) to the West Indies. Finally, the British found time during the world war to strengthen Canada by promoting immigration, fortifications, agriculture, and the fur trade. They especially needed Canada's ship stores (masts, tar, pitch, and hemp) since Bonaparte had closed their Baltic Sea sources. In sum, no U.S. sanctions against Britain could be effective unless *the Canadian loophole was closed.* Madison understood that, which is why his administration's mouthpiece, the *National Intelligencer,* published a series of alarms in 1811 about Canada's value to Britain and threat to the United States.[57]

Frontier Republicans concurred for a different reason: Indian unrest that they blamed on the British. For a decade after Fallen Timbers the northwestern tribes seemed resigned to their fate. Jefferson took advantage by authorizing officials such as William Henry Harrison in the Indiana Territory to negotiate eight more land cessions opening the Wabash River valley to settlement. But during these years the Great Spirit sent the Shawnee a prophet said to steer the moon and bless harvests. Tenskawatawa ("The Open Door") was an alcoholic and flop as a brave (he put out his own eye with an arrow), but once turned medicine man he had visions. Soon Indians were coming from hundreds of miles to hear his oracles at Prophet's Town near the confluence of the Wabash and Tippecanoe Rivers. The Prophet demanded Indians reject the white man's alcohol, clothing, farming, herding, and land ownership—everything except firearms. The Prophet's brother, a chief named Tecumseh, assumed the role of missionary to other tribes in what seemed an attempt to create a grand alliance.

The reality proved otherwise. Since Tecumseh called for the murder of chiefs who signed treaties with whites, his appeal caused several tribes to fracture. Moreover, he positively forbade the Prophet's followers to start wars, at least not until he returned from a mission to southern tribes. Nor were the British encouraging hostilities when they sharply increased their "gifts" in the Great Lakes. They were only trying to befriend Indians in the event Canada was attacked. But it all looked sinister to Harrison as he pondered Tecumseh's words: "How can we have confidence in the white people; when Jesus Christ came upon the earth you killed him and nailed him on a cross, you thought he was dead but you were mistaken." Eager to forestall an Indian "resurrection" Harrison begged federal support. Madison reluctantly obliged him with a regiment to which Harrison added militia from Indiana and Kentucky. He marched from Vincennes to Prophet's Town with 1,290 men in November 1811, spurning the Prophet's plea for a parley. The Indians struck first before dawn. Both sides took heavy casualties in the Battle of Tippecanoe, but Harrison burned the town and reported a great victory that pacified the frontier. Madison chose to believe him. All the battle ensured was the tribes would indeed align with Britain if the whites again went to war.[58]

That very month Congress assembled with Republicans in a mood to make a decision. Too many aggravations had been tolerated for too long at too high a cost to American honor—all on the Republicans' watch. So a caucus of freshmen, many of them Scots-Irish frontiersmen born after 1776, beat the tom-tom. One War Hawk was South Carolina's John C. Calhoun. He damned the British for the depressed cotton trade, but struck a higher tone in his rhetoric: "This is the second struggle for our liberty." Another War Hawk was Speaker of the House Henry Clay, the thirty-four-year-old "Cock of Kentucky." Americans were once again being told "to bow the neck to royal insolence"; it was time to "come home to our own history; it is not by submission that our fathers achieved our independence." A few old Jeffersonians such as John Randolph of Roanoke still feared the power a war might deliver to the executive branch. He distilled the War Hawks' speeches down to "one eternal monotonous tone—Canada, Canada, Canada!" But Clay confidently told Madison the votes for war were there for the asking. When the latest ship arriving from London reported no change in the Orders in Council, Madison asked. His war message, like the Declaration of Independence, recited British outrages to show a state of war already existed. Calhoun, however, went far beyond Madison's defensive posture in a report justifying a war. He named this a "to be or not to be" turning point in America's history, imagined not a dangerous "standing" army, but a "moving, fighting, conquering" one opening a new epoch of national growth and prosperity. This was not just a war *against* the Old World, but *for* a bolder vision of the New World, a patriotic war uniting "*the whole American Nation*" behind one sentiment, "confidently trusting that the Lord of Hosts will go with us to Battle in a righteous cause. . . ." Federalists and Republicans had indeed been on the *defensive*—against each other, against anarchy, monarchy, and foreign antagonists. Calhoun told Americans to quit being afraid and *attack* past ghosts, present tormentors, and doubts clouding their future. In June 1812 the House voted 79 to 49 in favor of war, and the Senate concurred 19 to 13. Weirdly, the British cabinet had just resolved to lift the Orders in Council. But the war was waged anyway, and Calhoun's speech helps explain why.[59]

Why war in 1812? Britain's contempt for neutral rights was obviously a pretext, not the cause, because every Federalist plus fourteen northern Republicans voted against war, whereas all but two western and southern Republicans voted in favor. Yankees and Yorkers knew that war, like the embargo, would ruin commerce altogether. But War Hawks, representing producers, figured they had little more to lose from a saltwater struggle and much to win if they cleansed the continent of Indians and redcoats. How else to explain passage, in January 1812, of a bill to expand the regular army to ten thousand men, but *rejection* the same month of a bill to build ten new frigates? The War Hawks were an internal Republican coalition forged to repair their splintering party, boost Madison's re-election chances, force New England to get on board the national bandwagon, and invade Canada for any of four motives: to seal the gaping hole that spoiled the embargo, open vast lands to American settlers, stop British assistance to Indians, or just take vengeance on Britain by the only route possible. But even this list does not get to the beating, cultural heart of the matter.

Did American citizens display much republican virtue? Not so you'd notice. Rather, perceptive observers saw their hustling countrymen turn selfish and devious in their prosperity and lie to themselves about it. Virginian John Taylor of Caroline decried a "finance capitalism" that injected "avarice and ambition" into the national character, spread distrust and fraud, and turned the world "into a scene of ambuscade, man against man." Puritan John Adams rued how Americans squandered their riches while coveting the riches of others. "Our country is in masquerade! No party, no man, dares to avow his real sentiments. All is disguise, visard, cloak." His fellow Yankee, Lyman Beecher, likewise embraced the War of 1812 as a chastisement: "This nation must be purified in the furnace of affliction." Borderman Hugh Henry Brackenridge was scolding the nation when his fictional gentleman chided Republicans in fact "destitute of republican virtue, the basis of which I take to be *humility* and *self-denial.*" His fellow Pennsylvania Republican Benjamin Rush agreed that a "nation debased by the love of money . . . is a spectacle far more awful" than bloodshed. "War has its evils," but so does a long peace."[60]

All these positions were voiced by the War Hawks. Clay came east convinced the nation must fight for its soul. Americans had grown soft; their resort to a flaccid embargo they were too selfish to honor proved it. "The source of alarm is in ourselves," he said. "A new race of heroes" must replace the Founding Fathers. Whichever way the war went, "we shall at least gain the approbation of our own hearts." War was the tonic and truth serum to cause Americans to spring from their counting rooms, tear off their masks, and feel good again about doing well. If, as Washington Irving smirked, "our great men are those who are most expert at crawling on all fours," then war would make them stand up and fight. From war the nation would emerge purer, much stronger, and self-reliant. In 1810 Clay recommended an "American System" of political economy based on the lessons of the embargo. Agriculture was the "greatest source of our wealth and happiness," but the United States could never be independent without a manufacturing base to supply its needs in peace and especially in war. Nothing would stimulate those manufactures better than war itself. This "Jeffersonian Nationalism" resurrected much of Hamilton's program, but for the purpose of defying, not replicating, Great Britain. Who in

American culture stood foursquare against war? Quakers, pietist Germans, and most Congregationalists. But if New England's "black regiment" sat this one out, a new one sprang up among evangelical clergy.[61]

Whether or not republics periodically need "blood sacrifices" to rededicate their young, the United States has gone to war on a generational calendar. By 1812 a new crop of ambitious men meant to seize their nation's destiny from tired men who took counsel of their fears. But 1812 was also a one-shot phenomenon in the life of a people who were always imperial minded, yet hesitant to build either the nation or state that an imperial mission required. Nor did Madison's cabinet, the leaders in Congress, and the military officer corps know quite how to balance a Hamiltonian state atop a Jeffersonian nation. But all of those leadership groups were heavily Freemason in 1812. They meant to build and unite, not tear down and divide.[62]

At least, that was the spirit extolled. The real spirit of 1812 could be grotesque, as Revolutionary War hero "Light Horse" Harry Lee quickly learned. A heavy investor in Potomac land, he had been dragged down by the collapse of Robert Morris. His defaults earned the proud Virginian a reputation for swindling. He blamed Republicans, but in 1808 was desperate enough to beg Madison for a diplomatic post in hopes of escaping creditors. Instead, he spent two years in jail. So by 1812 Lee was a bitter old lion eager to roar, if not claw, at the people he thought had ruined himself and his country. A theatrical chance came when a Baltimore mob drove Federalist editor Alexander C. Hanson out of town for daring to question the war. Defending freedom of the press, Hanson reoccupied his newspaper office with a "Spartan Band" of supporters. Lee was among them. Word spread quickly and by evening on July 27 a gang of every sort of Republican—sailors and boys, upscale merchants, workers, and immigrants—roiled through the streets, beat up some Negroes for sport, then converged on Hanson's office to denounce the "traitors" and "tory general" within. The mayor persuaded the Federalists to spend the night in jail for their safety and promised to police the streets. He reneged. The next evening the mob stormed the jail, crying, "We'll feather and tar every damned British tory; this is the way to American glory!" Self-righteous war fever and booze moved them instead to break down the door and maim. One Federalist was murdered while he vainly displayed his scars from the Revolution. Others had their eyes stabbed with knives or filled with hot wax. Lee flailed madly against blades meant to carve off his nose. When at length the Federalists fell unconscious, impervious to torture, the attackers formed a circle, cheered Tom Jefferson and Jemmy Madison, and dispersed. The unabashed Republican press called Lee a notorious scoundrel, hinted Hanson was in the pay of the British, and concluded the mob was provoked. Up in Federalist New Haven an enterprising Yankee also knew what to do with the incident. He set up a wax museum exhibit depicting "Cruelties of the Baltimore Mob" and charged 25 cents admission.[63]

If the war's spirit was sometimes less than pristine, its conduct was often ridiculous. Thanks to the embargo, customs receipts fell from $16 to $6.5 million, barely enough to cover ordinary government expenses, much less a war. Thanks to Republican principles, Congress still opposed excise taxes and blithely allowed the charter of the U.S. Bank to expire in 1811. So Gallatin had no option but to float loans on the open (high interest) market and trust "monied men" would display patriotism. When the first $11 million in bonds were offered, almost half went unsold and the "monied men" were notably absent. In any event, the federal government's Lilliputian bureaucracy could not scare up supplies for the invasion of Canada. The War Department hired two private contractors whose agents scoured the Connecticut Valley in vain. Farmers had already sold their cattle and crops, in many cases to Canadian buyers! Philadelphia's purveyor, the illustrious Tench Coxe, went begging for arms and even gunpowder, since Jefferson's military cutbacks had forced Irénée Du Pont to cut capacity sharply at his Eleutherian Mills. Coxe suggested arming the people with pikes. He was also told to buy cloth, no matter what color or texture, sufficient for twenty thousand uniforms, but reported the army's "summer" coats would not be ready until October. That did not matter much because only 9,823 men volunteered for the new army of 25,000. As Ohio senator Thomas Worthington explained, a promise of 160 acres of land was not enough to induce a man to "get himself killed." By late summer the War Department promised local officers a bonus of $2 per head to drum up recruits, and the means they employed included patriotic orations and posters, martial music, and copious liquor. Deserted wives protested, but the army refused to bar use of alcohol on the grounds "such an instruction would prevent half the enlistments." The recruits who did come forward were underfed, underclothed, unshod, and untrained. Crammed into hot makeshift barracks, they were also unhealthy. In August a surgeon declared one entire regiment unfit to campaign. They marched off to Canada anyway. Finally, the scraggly units lacked leaders because the Republican party was short of experienced veterans yet resisted appointing Federalists.[64]

The war began at an optimal moment. After Napoleon deposed the King of Spain in favor of his own brother, Spaniards rebelled and the Duke of Wellington sailed with a British army to assist their "Peninsular War." By 1812 there were few redcoats to spare for Canada. Had the Americans managed to assemble just one doughty army at Lake Champlain, they might have occupied Montréal and mopped up the Great Lakes at their leisure. Instead, the War Department deployed three tremulous armies. Out in Ohio a column under the drugged and besotted stroke victim William Hull marched to Detroit only to be cut off by British and Indians. He spent days drooling and mumbling in a fetal position, then surrendered in August when the British threatened to unleash Indians on settlers. All the western tribes flocked to the Union Jack. At Niagara, New York's General Stephen Van Rensselaer seized the high ground on the Canadian side with six hundred men and was poised for a victory when his main body of troops went on strike. Being militiamen they were not obligated to serve outside the state. They leaned on their muskets while the advance guard was defeated. The furious Van Rensselaer resigned, but his successor also wished he could trade the "degenerated" Yorkers for Seneca braves. In fact, New York all but sat out the war. Speculators feared it would kill land prices, farmers feared it would kill wheat prices (by closing the Canadian trade), and De Witt Clinton feared it would kill his chances to unseat Madison. But none of that was unique. Half the Pennsylvania militia deserted and General Henry Dearborn's attack from Lake Champlain aborted when Vermonters refused to cross into Canada.[65]

By the end of 1812 the United States was more in danger of invasion than Canada was. At least as embarrassing to War Hawks, the only U.S. victories were won by regular naval officers, almost all Federalists. It was astonishing news in August when the U.S.S. *Constitution,* Captain Isaac Hull, outsailed and outgunned H.M.S. *Guerrière.* Astonishment melted into confident pride as those heavy frigates designed by Joshua Humphreys won a series of single-ship actions.[66] But the Royal Navy could scarcely be beaten. Its ships on the "North American station" blockaded the coast save for some Federalist ports where they openly *traded* and spread antiwar propaganda. The effects showed in the 1812 election. Federalists joined with many northern Republicans to support New York mayor De Witt Clinton. He received more than 40 percent of the electoral college, a shocking vote of no confidence in a war president.

No wonder Madison was excited to learn from diplomat John Quincy Adams that Tsar Alexander I offered to mediate peace between Britain and the

United States. Gallatin, struggling to cobble together a budget for 1813, used the prospect of an imminent peace to pry loans out of the "monied men," especially Philadelphia merchant and banker Stephen Girard. Born in France in 1750, Girard traded with Haiti, came to America almost by accident in 1773, and grew rich through an uncanny skill in assessing risk and a rare reputation for honesty. He was depressed for years when his wife went inexplicably mad, but consoled himself with hard work, a mistress, and patriotic service. He promised to subscribe $8 million of Gallatin's war paper in exchange for a promise the Treasury would do some business in Girard's bank. That may sound self-serving, but bear in mind Girard did not take the occasion to mention the U.S. government was at that moment *suing him* for $1 million over a cargo that by accident became illegal in 1812. Girard's generosity—and some timely personnel changes by Madison—made possible the rescue of the American Northwest.[67]

First, the new secretary of War John Armstrong ran his eye over a map and saw that mastery of Lake Erie would render untenable the British strongholds at Detroit and Niagara. Next, the new secretary of the Navy William Jones ran his eye down the service list and picked Commodore Oliver Hazard Perry for the job. The handsome twenty-eight-year-old Perry was another of Preble's boys, expert at close-in sea fighting. He jumped when Jones ordered him to pick his best 150 men and repair to Presque Isle (the future Erie, Pennsylvania) to build an inland fleet from scratch. The expedition chopped down cedar, oak, chestnut, and pine, scrounged army cannon in Pittsburgh, and sent Jones what seemed outrageous bills for everything from flour to lead for ballast. By September, Perry's mostly Rhode Island crews fashioned *ex nihilo* a brig, a sloop, and five schooners. When soldiers and oxen pulled two additional brigs from the foaming Niagara River into Lake Erie, the American fleet counted nine ships mounting fifty-four guns with a broadside weight of 896 pounds. The British deployed just six craft on the lake with a broadside weight of 459 pounds. In September, Perry located the enemy near the mouth of the Sandusky River and captured the "weather gauge," meaning his ships were upwind and free to give battle on their own terms. The British concentrated furious fire on Perry's flagship until, after three hours, only 19 of its 142 men remained in action. So Perry boarded a gig, shot swarming like mosquitoes about him, and resumed command in another ship. The American weight of metal finally told, and one by one British ships struck their colors. Perry did not exaggerate when he wrote William Henry Harrison, "We have met the enemy and they are ours."[68] The British realized

Detroit and Niagara were now indefensible, but Tecumseh insisted they make a stand. That allowed Harrison to bring them to battle at Malden on Ontario's river Thames. In just minutes, two hundred U.S. regulars and twenty-five hundred Kentucky rifles under Governor Isaac Shelby pierced the redcoats' line to inflict a withering fire from rear and front. The British surrendered, Tecumseh was killed, and the Indians fled.[69]

Way down south another frontier chieftain exploited the war to crush Indians. Back in 1811 Tecumseh preached resistance to the Cherokees, Choctaws, Chickasaws, Seminoles, and Creeks, whose young braves, known as "Red Sticks" (*batons rouges*), won bloody victories at Burnt Corn and Fort Mims north of Mobile. The territorial governors of sparsely populated Alabama and Mississippi appealed to Tennessee, two thousand of whose militiamen rallied behind Andrew Jackson. He had recently taken a bullet in the shoulder during a feud with Thomas Hart Benton and his brother Jesse. But Jackson marched south from Fayetteville to wage a vigorous campaign that climaxed in March 1814. At Horseshoe Bend, where the Tallapoosa River meets the Alabama, his volunteers killed twenty-five hundred of the Creeks' four thousand warriors and garrisoned Fort Jackson to overawe the survivors. Secretary of War Armstrong commissioned Jackson a major-general in command of the Southwestern Military District. That was another excellent personnel move by an administration learning to wage war.[70]

It came just in time because the American theater, previously a sideshow to the British, took center stage the very month of Jackson's triumph. Napoleon had made desperate efforts to recoup from his calamitous 1812 invasion of Russia, but could not prevent a coalition of Russian, Prussian, Austrian, and British armies from crossing the French border in 1814. The emperor abdicated in March. That released Britain's sea and land forces to deal with the upstart Yankees, and Lord Castlereagh's cabinet devised a grand strategy. Militarily, it would contain U.S. expansion by restoring the Louisiana Purchase to Spain and annexing Maine and northern New York to secure Canada. Politically, it would stoke New Englanders' antiwar sentiment by invading Vermont and quench westerners' martial ardor by seizing New Orleans. Attacks in the Chesapeake would serve as diversions.[71]

Curiously, the diversions did not succeed in drawing American strength from the frontiers because no one except Madison thought the British would be so rude as to violate Washington City. But since he instructed Armstrong to strengthen the defenses of all seaboard cities, the War Department paid little attention to the economically trivial capital. When General Robert Ross put ashore he had only to brush aside some Maryland militiamen posted at Bladensburg. The U.S. government scattered. Armstrong resigned in undeserved disgrace. On August 24 the British took leisurely possession of L'Enfant's city and proceeded to torch the Capitol, President's House, and other structures. Evidently, that atrocity angered the Divine Architect. Tornadoes, lightning, and downpours soon caused the redcoats to trudge through the muck out of town. Now it was Baltimore's turn. But thanks to the preparations of Senator Samuel Smith that fierce Republican city was braced for a fight. The invaders marched four thousand strong into withering fire from militia well protected by ramparts; Ross was killed. The British then rained eighteen hundred rockets and bombs on Fort McHenry through the night of September 13–14. But the Americans, whose guns lacked the range to menace the enemy anyway, hunkered down and took only thirty-odd casualties. The new secretary of War, James Monroe, claimed credit, buttressing his claim to be Madison's successor, while Francis Scott Key bestowed on the civic religion a hymn to its Star-Spangled Banner.[72]

The Duke of Wellington was offered command either in Canada or New Orleans. Luckily for the Yanks he preferred the diplomacy and society of the peace congress convened in Vienna. So the governor-general of Canada, George Prevost, commanded the crack regiments invading the United States at the same time Baltimore was besieged. He might have swept away the Vermont and New York militia blocking his path at Plattsburgh, but Prevost believed (probably rightly) his supply line needed control of Lake Champlain. Unfortunately for him, U.S. Commodore Thomas Macdonough and shipwright Noah Brown deployed on the lake four craft whose cannons again outweighed their opponents'. When the flotillas clashed on September 11, the British pummeled the American flagship *Saratoga*, silencing its starboard guns. With shot hot about them, Macdonough's crew pulled off a risky coup called "winding ship." They secured spring lines to capstans anchored at opposite ends of the ship and hauled it about through sheer muscle power. That brought the port guns into play on the already wounded British flagship, tipping the scales of the battle. Prevost, cursing this second lacustrine defeat, dared not face a winter campaign with his supply line in danger. He marched back to Montréal minus numerous deserters and precious supplies. Macdonough's triumph may well have saved Maine and the Adirondacks for the United States.[73]

It may also have saved the Union by sucking wind from the sails of New

THE WAR OF 1812

- → American routes
- ⇨ British routes
- ━·━ Hull's route, 1812
- ······ Dearborn's route, 1812 –13
- ▼▼▼ Harrison's route, 1813
- ━¡━ Wilkinson's route, 1813
- ━ ━ British advance against Washington, 1814

Scale of Miles
0    50    100    150

England secessionists. Suffering the Royal Navy off Boston Harbor and red-coats at Maine's Penobscot River was enough to cause Massachusetts and neighboring states to stage an emergency meeting at Hartford. Had Prevost been marching down the Hudson when it met, extremists might have persuaded New Englanders to sue for a separate peace. Instead, the threat of invasion was postponed at least until spring. So the Hartford Convention contented itself with seven proposed Constitutional amendments meant to weaken the Republicans' grip on the federal government.[74] By the time the proposals were voiced in January 1815, however, the nation was awash with relief and pride over peace and battlefield victory. Federalist secessionism thus went the same way as Anti-Federalist secessionism. The second defeat of Napoleon, at Waterloo in June 1815, then buried the Federalist party altogether. Its selling points had always been the danger of revolutionary France and the need for a strong federal establishment. With the French threat a memory after 1815 and

Republicans implementing much of the Federalist program, the party had no appeal whatsoever.[75]

What of the third British offensive that aimed at the conquest of New Orleans? Thanks to Wellington's disinterest that enterprise fell to his brother-in-law Edward Pakenham. Just thirty-seven years old, inexperienced, and doubtless fearing humiliation more than he craved glory, Pakenham dallied so long in Jamaica his armada did not arrive in Louisiana's Lake Bourne until mid-December 1814. Andy Jackson was grateful. He had ridden in haste with two thousand men from Pensacola and arrived in New Orleans with two weeks to spare. Governor Claiborne warmly greeted his fellow Freemason and together they assured residents they could deliver the city if everyone pitched in. Old Hickory, worn out by a year of non-stop campaigning, looked gaunt and older than his forty-five years. But the enemy might arrive any day. So he imposed martial law, made summary arrests in Wilkinson's high-handed fashion, and disciplined by lash and leadership a parti-colored army of regulars, Kentucky rifles, Creole militia (fully 40 percent of the force), free Negroes, a few Indians, and Jean Lafitte's pirates. Jackson also issued stirring calls to arms and unity addressed to "Fellow Citizens of Every Description," "Natives of the United States," "Citizens of Louisiana," and especially "Soldiers." Finally, while American gunboats slowed the cautious Pakenham's advance, Jackson consulted with his engineers on where to place barricades and batteries on both sides of the river. The British could not go around them—cypress swamps guarded both flanks—but neither did Pakenham call up his navy to bombard the defenses. Instead, on January 8, 1815, he marched his veteran columns straight into Jackson's lines, throwing away more than two thousand lives, including his own. Only twenty-one defenders were killed. Legend holds that sharpshooting Kaintucks "hiding behind cotton bails" and holding fire "til we looked 'em in the eyes" won the battle. In fact, the largely Creole-attended artillery did most of the damage by enfilading the attackers with ball and grapeshot. But Jackson took care to congratulate every unit on the line accompanied by an army band playing Francis Hopkinson's "Hail, Columbia!" over and over again.[76]

Two weeks before, on Christmas Eve 1814, British and American delegations meeting in Belgium signed the Treaty of Ghent. Tsar Alexander's offer to mediate did not bring it about; the British preferred bilateral negotiations with the weaker Americans. But Madison was inspired to assemble a truly national team of envoys so the United States might speak with one voice. John Quincy Adams, Albert Gallatin, and Federalist James Bayard—all unhappy with the war for various reasons—joined War Hawk Henry Clay and Rhode Island's Jonathan Russell, who as minister to Britain had delivered the declaration of war in 1812. Not surprisingly, the delegates nettled each other, but they conducted the first bipartisan, trans-sectional U.S. diplomacy since 1783. Thus, when the British demanded land cessions, Indian buffer states, and a ban on American fishing off the Grand Banks, the Americans overcame their regional interests to reject them. So, too, they agreed to drop their regional demands in the national interest of peace. The result was that the Treaty of Ghent did little but restore the *status quo ante bellum.* Was the Battle of New Orleans, which happened after the treaty was signed, thus "sound and fury signifying nothing"? Or did it, as some historians say, save the whole Louisiana Territory since Parliament could have refused to ratify the treaty in the event Pakenham had won? There is no telling what might have happened had war resumed. But even if the United States were coerced into disgorging the West, would not American settlers flooding the Mississippi have recovered it sooner or later? Perhaps what Jackson did on the levees was spare the United States another war down the road or else a much larger invoice than the one Jefferson paid in 1803.

Every political earthquake inflicts aftershocks that confirm its effects or hint at the fault lines that will trigger the next. In 1815 two such shocks involved Africa. No sooner was Madison free of the war than he dispatched a fleet under Stephen Decatur to tour the Barbary Coast and compel deys and beys to renounce tribute and piracy, release all American prisoners, and pay indemnities. Simultaneously, the Congress of Vienna declared the African slave trade an affront to mankind and commissioned the British and French navies to suppress it. Of course, the United States now banned slave imports as well. But Congress voted no funds for enforcement and its silence on the future of slavery was thunderous.

Peace broke out. For the first time since 1765 (that's *fifty years*) Americans knew both unity and security. For the first time since 1776 they enjoyed peace, a strong national government, full sovereignty in the family of nations, and freedom to pursue their happiness across their continent and the oceans. Such boons were not normalcy, but a novelty swelling the nation's pride and pocketbook almost beyond reckoning. In just eight months after the Treaty of Ghent, U.S. merchants sold $50 million in exports. Southern planters hurled tobacco, rice, and especially cotton onto world markets, thereby making or remaking fortunes. Manufactures, as Clay predicted, took off during the war as entrepreneurs hustled to supply the domestic market and military with goods previously imported. Over 320 new factories (especially for metallurgy, chemicals, and textiles) were founded from 1812 to 1814 as compared to 114 over the decade preceding. The war's stimulus induced the government to invest $1.8 million on roads and canals during the 1810s as compared to just $120,000 in the 1800s. New England did suffer a wrenching depression after 1815 when the British dumped $40 million of manufactures on the market. Many of the new cotton and woolen mills went out of business, throwing thousands of Yankees out of work. But Henry Adams exaggerated when he wrote of Massachusetts' "ruin." Rather, the temporary slump just accelerated a "Yankee Exodus" destined to fix an indelible New England stamp on the Midwest.[77] For that infant region the war and its aftermath were a weaning. To be sure, for a brief moment in 1812 it seemed the British and Algonquians had united again "on the middle ground" and might wrench the whole *pays d'en haut* from the Americans as they had from the French. But Harrison's victory at Malden dealt their alliance a mortal wound; Ghent laid it to rest. The Ohio Valley and Great Lakes lay wide open to U.S. development. So, too, thanks to Jackson, did the southwest. Finally, Indian removal (and the expansion of slavery) were sure to continue under the hegemony of Jefferson's party.[78]

The War of 1812 shaped the nation's self-image like no other experience. It taught Republicans their notion of a tiny executive branch was inadequate to the task of administering war and empire. Yet the war also proved Americans could mobilize a mere fraction of their potential and still fight the greatest world power to a draw. The navy deserved most of the credit, but Harrison, Jackson, young Winfield Scott, some early West Point graduates, and even some state militias proved U.S. soldiers could match tactics with European veterans and best them in gunnery. Indeed, *every* U.S. battlefield success was a matter of superior firepower: more cannon, bigger cannon, faster and more accurate service of cannon. Abundant humiliations there were, and Canadians spun their own "brave underdog" myths out of them. But after 1815 Americans preferred to remember the victories won by so few and claim them somehow as their own. They forgot militiamen balking or fleeing, state governments spurning pleas from the War Department, taxpayers cheating, merchants trading with the enemy, and politicians talking secession. Madison assured them they were "a brave, a free, a virtuous, and an intelligent people," and Francis Scott

Key sang of "the land of the free and the home of the brave." Now that land's future was boundless, its flag saluted by all, and its citizens free to choose from a bountiful platter of evangelical faiths, society churches, and secular fraternities—whatever made them feel best about doing well. No wonder they called it an "era of good feeling."

Finally, the "passions" that threatened the American experiment were leeched without enfeebling the body politic. For twelve years Federalists governed. But their tenure did *not* usher in monarchy, aristocracy, or a permanent, corrupt plutocracy. Instead, they surrendered power through acts of statesmanship such as Adams' 1800 convention with France and Hamilton's opposition to Burr. Then for sixteen years Republicans governed. But their tenure did *not* usher in Jacobin tyranny, atheism, or dissolution. If anything, Republicans erred too much on the side of liberty until their fiscal, military, and foreign policies were discredited, whereupon they adopted much of the Federalist program. At the end of the war Gallatin, his successor as treasurer Alexander J. Dallas, financiers Girard and Astor, and War Hawks Calhoun and Clay moved energetically to charter a second United States Bank. Congress passed the bank bill in March 1816 and Madison signed it without a peep uttered about its constitutionality.[79] The President and young Republican lions also granted the need for an elite professional army and navy, federal support for transportation, and tariffs to protect infant industries. Had the Republicans thereby been "Federalized"? Not really: they still favored states' rights and congressional powers to a degree Hamilton would have abhorred. But the Republicans' nationalism was no longer reluctant. Events proved federal institutions could serve and respond to *all* Americans who confessed the civic religion and played the political game under Republican rules. Almost all white Americans did so confess and so play.

That is why Virginia Freemason James Monroe boasted, in his inaugural address of March 1817, that "discord does not belong to our system." For that he gave serial thanks to the Divine Author, gracious Providence, the Almighty. Monroe also found occasion in his brief text to employ variations on the word "happy" *eight times.*[80]

# ENGINEERS, PIONEERS, PEDDLERS, AND DEMOCRATS
## *The Rise of the West, 1816–1828*

*I*n 1819, four years after the Congress of Vienna restored legitimate monarchy and a balance of power to Europe, the continent was still far from tranquil. Tsar Alexander I claimed the right to suppress revolution wherever it recurred. The Carlsbad Decrees empowered Austrian and Prussian police to repress free speech and assembly throughout the German Confederation. The French aristocracy returned from exile "more royalist than the king," vowing to imprison or exile anyone still devoted to liberty, equality, and fraternity. Spain's mad Bourbon king imagined his army and fleet reimposing imperial rule from Argentina to Mexico. In 1819 even Britain knew a spasm of reaction when redcoats killed or wounded more than four hundred Manchester workers demonstrating for electoral and social reform. Parliament hastily passed the Six Acts restricting free speech and association.

In 1819 the U.S. population of 9 million was still less than Spain's and was dwarfed by Britain's 21 million and France's 30 million. But Americans' numbers were growing by one-third *every decade*, while the events they witnessed in 1819 contrasted starkly with those of Europe. Alabama, the fourth new state in as many years, embraced universal male suffrage as a matter of course. The Supreme Court created a free national marketplace through verdicts protecting property, contracts, and corporations. The new president of the second Bank of the United States pledged to cleanse the nation of funny money and wild speculation. The secretary of State signed and the Senate ratified a treaty annexing Florida and claiming the whole Oregon Territory. The National Road reached over the mountains to Wheeling, Virginia. Canal mania swept the country. A new national magazine, *Niles' Weekly Register,* heralded the "almost universal ambition to get forward." A robust federal republic was spreading, in Chief Justice John Marshall's words, "from the St. Croix to the Gulph of Mexico, from the Atlantic to the Pacific." Europeans might mock the U.S. experiment or else flee, full of hope, to America. But current events in 1819 offered proof in abundance the Old and New Worlds stood worlds apart.[1]

The War of 1812 settled the matter. Britain held Canada, but failed to arrest the growth of the United States. Spain gripped her empire with no more than one legal finger. All Indians within reach were vanquished. Americans, by contrast, tasted power. For two generations their struggles had been over *whether* their Union would be. Now they were free to ask *what* unity was for. But that question spawned others, some of which they dared not answer lest they reopen the question of *whether.* So white male Americans and their help-mates addressed the safe questions while ducking the hard ones until, by 1828, they increased enormously their short-term prospects and narrowed danger-ously their long-term ones. Such is the penchant of free people.

The first theme defining American life after 1816 was a nearly universal faith in the national destiny. It seemed a brilliant sun pierced the clouds and flooded the land with heavenly light. But sectional and sectarian lenses refracted that confident beam into a veritable "interference pattern" of congru-ent and contrasting images. Was the Union a contract among sovereign states, in which case excessive localism might frustrate its destiny? Or had "We the People" fashioned a strong federal Union, in which case excessive consolidation might tempt a majority to *impose* its version of national destiny, trampling the rights of the states?

The second theme was explosive territorial and material growth. But Americans' lust for opportunity and sudden prosperity begged questions about how to promote them. Could the government design legal, financial, and eco-nomic institutions permitting all regions and sectors to grow larger and richer together? Or did free movement of people, goods, and capital inevitably enrich some people and regions at the expense of others?

The third theme was the stunning triumph of white man's democracy on the frontier and back east. Americans demanded self-government. But mass party politics *ipso facto* divided the nation and presented the keepers of legal, moral, and economic authority with an existential dilemma. Either politicians, lawyers, clergy, and businessmen must discard genteel notions of ordered liberty and *surrender* to popular passions, or else they must somehow *indulge* populist democratic yearnings while in fact governing through dispassionate compromise.

Nationalism, growth, and democracy: all three were at bottom about power. How to expand it *now,* how to distribute it *now,* how to employ it *now.* That impatience also explains why Americans rushed to judgment on many complex matters in a mere dozen years and postponed judgment on the rest. There was too much power to grab, too much land to develop, too much money to make, too many souls to save to waste time worrying. The future is now; today is the day of salvation.

Robert Fulton did not invent the steamboat, at least not alone. He did not name his prototype *Clermont.* He did not even think steam navigation his true calling in life. But he believed in perfection, wanted it now, and thought mechanics the key to universal peace and prosperity. Born to Scots-Irish parents in Lancaster County, Pennsylvania, in 1765, Fulton lost his father when he was six. But his mother and a Quaker schoolmaster fostered the genius they spied in the boy. He did experiments, invented things, and read science and philosophy texts in the library. He even displayed talent for painting, earning himself an apprenticeship with a Philadelphia silversmith. Then, in 1786, a bout of pneumonia removed him to the spas at Bath, Virginia, where James Rumsey, a carpenter and friend of George Washington, was secretly building a steam-powered boat.[2]

Whether Fulton was privy to Rumsey's project is unknown, but steam navigation teased many visionary Americans. Down such great watery thoroughfares as the Connecticut, Hudson, Delaware, Susquehanna, Potomac, James, Ashley and Santee, Savannah, Alabama, Tombigbee, and Mississippi/Ohio, the bulk commodities of half a continent flowed easily to port and market. The problem was how to get *up* them. On broad lower waters a sailboat might tack against the current, but only when conditions were right and only as far as a river's fall line. Keelboats and barges struggled against even mild currents and were subject to all manner of mishap. Boatmen might try to row upriver, or else pole if the river was shallow and the bed firm. But those were backbreaking methods. Boatmen might even wrap a rope around trees and laboriously "warp" or "bushwhack" upstream. None of those means worked with a boat heavy with cargo; all were painfully slow. Thus, the downriver trip from Pittsburgh to New Orleans took four to six weeks; the reverse trip four to six months. No wonder keelboats were torn up for firewood when they reached port. Rumsey knew the answer lay with James Watt's newfangled steam engines. So did John Fitch, a Connecticut clockmaker who launched a working steamboat on the Delaware River in 1787. But as yet no engines of sufficient horsepower or reliability existed in America. Rumsey sailed to England in quest of one, only to die there in 1792. Then Fitch went bankrupt, damning Secretary of State Jefferson for refusing his patent, and killed himself in 1798.[3]

Fulton, meanwhile, decided to pursue an artistic career in London after someone (possibly Franklin) gave him a letter of introduction to famed painter Benjamin West. He arrived in 1787, remained in Europe for twenty years, and might have become the second American painter to win acclaim overseas. West thought him gifted; Mrs. West practically adopted the tall youth with tousled brown hair. But Fulton's life changed around 1793 when he met the Duke of Bridgewater, Lord Stanhope, and utopian industrialist Robert Owen, all avid promoters of applied science. In their company Fulton observed how canals carrying coal to steam-powered textile mills were making Britain the world's workshop. In 1794 he was awarded a patent for a machine to lift barges on railed inclines and thus dispense with canal locks. Two years later, styling himself an "engineer," he published a treatise on canals.

Fulton migrated to Paris in 1797 just as the French Republic tumbled into the Quasi War with the United States. Thanks to American poet and diplomat Joel Barlow, however, Fulton ascended to France's loftiest scientific and political circles, where he grew dizzy with ambition for republicanism, freedom of the seas, free trade, and himself. His essays "To the Friends of Mankind" and "Republican Creed" named free thought, education, and industry the cardinal virtues. Above all, Fulton fixated on the idea of a machine to end war. A "Mechanical Nautulus" [*sic*] or submarine, he promised the French, would "annihilate the British" and render all navies obsolete. Napoleon displayed keen interest. In 1800 Fulton tested the first cigar-shaped submersible, complete with periscope, propeller, candles for light, lime jars for oxygen, and undersea bombs with a trigger of his own devising. Alas, his dreams of prize money were dashed by spies who warned off British ships around Cherbourg whenever the submarine put to sea. So Fulton disassembled the boat in 1801 and offered to sell its design for a hefty fee. But the Peace of Amiens intervened, Napoleon lost interest, and Fulton went in search of new patrons.[4]

The first one he found was U.S. minister to France Robert Livingston. The Hudson River squire already owned a New York state steamboat monopoly; he just needed a steamboat! So he teamed up with Fulton, promising to spend whatever it took. By 1803 Fulton had a small paddlewheel craft chugging along the Seine. But knowing he needed powerful engines available only from the firm of Boulton & Watt, Fulton slipped back to England. There he found a second new patron in the Royal Navy, which put him on the payroll just to deny Bonaparte his services. Fulton did win permission, however, to export a custom-made steam engine to America. In 1806 Fulton finally went home, still hoping to peddle undersea bombs. President Jefferson loved the notion of making navies obsolete, but the U.S. Navy did not. So it was almost by default that Fulton turned his mind to Livingston's project.

In less than a year the American Da Vinci constructed around his coal-fired low-pressure engine a lovely 146-foot, narrow-stemmed, sidewheeler christened the *North River Steamboat*. (His first biographer erroneously renamed it *Clermont* after Livingston's manor overlooking the Catskills.) On August 9, 1807, Fulton ran it a mile upriver at four miles per hour. Newspapers deriding "Fulton's Folly" had no appreciation of his technical triumph or his detailed business prospectus. Fulton imagined fleets of steamboats on the Hudson and Mississippi turning profits of $40,000 to $50,000 per year on each river. He then made his famous voyage to Albany and back, August 17–21. Crowds gawked, expecting the boat to explode. Only the West Point cadets cheered without reserve when the *North River* slapped along below them. Safely back on Manhattan after four days of round-the-clock worry and ceremony, Fulton realized the contribution he had just made to mankind. Even so, he could not help adding: "I will not admit that [the steamboat] is half so important as the torpedo system of defense and attack; for out of this will grow the liberty of the seas."[5]

In 1808 Fulton married his partner's second cousin, Harriet Livingston, who bore him four children. He built more and better boats, taking special pride in their perfect safety record, not to mention the company profits. During the War of 1812, Fulton also won the big government contract he craved, designing the world's first steam-assisted frigate. In February 1815, Fulton was in Jersey City to check on the 167-foot, 120-horsepower *Fulton 1* when an Arctic air mass froze the Hudson River. Since ferries were not running, Fulton and his companions decided to row out to the ice and *walk* to New York! A stout fellow broke through the ice. Fulton saved him, but the chill revived his pneumonia. He tried to work through it. He died within weeks at age forty-nine. Eulogist De Witt Clinton said Fulton was "destroyed by the fire of his own genius." He might added "and love of his fellow man."[6]

The *North River* was often called simply "The Steamboat" during the year and a half it was the only one in the world. But its Hudson River service netted Livingston $16,000 in 1808. That conjured competitors. John Stevens, the first steamboat man on the Delaware River (not counting poor Fitch), failed to crack Livingston's Hudson monopoly and moved on instead to the Connecticut River. Aaron Ogden, by contrast, used his influence in New Jersey politics to obtain a rival Hudson monopoly that Livingston reluctantly honored. Then Ogden was challenged by his erstwhile partner Thomas Gibbons. A rich southern planter, Ogden bankrolled a third company, hiring for his skipper a true American hustler. Cornelius Vanderbilt, just twenty-four years old, made fortunes for himself and Gibbons "smuggling" passengers and cargo across New York's waterways in defiance of all monopolies. In 1824 the fracas reached the Supreme Court, where Chief Justice Marshall ruled in *Gibbons versus Ogden* that states might regulate commerce within their borders, but interstate commerce was a federal affair. The monopolies were illegal. When New York's legislature abolished internal monopolies as well in 1825, the United States became the largest wholly competitive, unified market on earth.[7]

Eastern steamboats grew larger, lavish, safe, reliable, and capable of churning up to twenty miles per hour. A canal at Enfield, Connecticut, permitted upriver service from Hartford to Springfield. In 1818, *Walk-on-the-Water* was launched on Lake Erie. But Fulton's belief that the best venue for steamboats was the Mississippi/Ohio proved out after two hurdles were surmounted. It seemed Fulton's *New Orleans*, which steamed up to Pittsburgh in 1811–12, and indeed all boats of eastern design, were ill suited to wild western rivers. Their "sharp" (pointed) bows and sterns designed to reduce water resistance in fact caused boats to be whipped around by turbulent currents. Western boats needed flatter, shallower hulls. But that in turn required more powerful engines for upstream navigation. Oliver Evans of Louisiana already had the solution in high-pressure steam engines used in his lumber and grist mills. In 1811 Evans built a factory in Pittsburgh to make high-pressure engines, his success spawning competition in Cincinnati and Louisville. By the 1820s, two-thirds of all U.S. steam engines were made on the Ohio River, while the number of steamboats on western waters rose from twenty in 1818 to more than two hundred by 1830.

With a fine steamboat costing the manageable sum of $20,000 (thanks mostly to the cheapness of wood), and the most elegant $50,000, entrepreneurs quickly introduced service on the Arkansas, Wabash, Missouri, Tennessee, and Cumberland Rivers. Boats carried settlers, manufactures, furnishings, and fripperies upstream at five miles per hour; cotton, livestock, foodstuffs, and whiskey downstream at double that speed. The *George Washington,* designed by Henry M. Shreve in 1823, was triple-decked, its two tall smokestacks piercing the sky and its boilers placed above the water line for safety. It seemed so top-heavy scoffers said it would capsize. But Shreve's mathematics proved out. The exterior design and splendid saloons within became the beau ideal of Mississippi steamboats for decades to come. To be sure, service was not always reliable. Winter ice, spring floods, and summer droughts might interrupt transport. Dreaded snags (submerged trees from eroding banks) caused 40 percent of all steamboat damage. When multiple snags congealed into "rafts" an entire channel might choke. The U.S. government appointed Shreve head of a commission to build the *Heliopolis,* a double-hulled steam barge equipped with a giant windlass. After 1829 that craft, too, silenced skeptics by clearing the rafts blocking the Red River. Still, snags, high-pressure engine explosions, collisions, and other disasters ended the careers of one in three western steamboats, while killing some fourteen hundred people over the decades. But Americans loved steamboats, risk notwithstanding. They were humanity's first triumph over gravity. They integrated the Middle West and Deep South into the nation.[8]

What about roads? Did not Americans, like ancient Romans, build an empire of roads to connect farms with mill, market, church, and village, villages with neighboring villages, plantations with river docks, colonies with each other; roads to speed postmen, soldiers, and settlers into the heart of the continent? The answer depends on how much a footpath must be improved before earning the title of road. Overland routes were terrible for the most part, yet most Americans did not mind. The labor, especially to "grub" out tree stumps, was intense, and labor, not to say money, was in short supply. Settlers only grudgingly worked on community projects. In the colonial era only New England and southeast Pennsylvania aspired to roads better than muddy ruts or back-wrenching "corduroy roads" made of logs splayed over the mud.

Then in 1794 Pennsylvania's Lancaster Turnpike (present-day U.S. 30) matched Caesar's notion of a proper road. Privately capitalized at the unprecedented sum of $4.1 million, it boasted a rock foundation and fine surface gravel, peaked and shouldered to facilitate drainage. Using air-bubble levels, precise surveys, and a great deal of spade work, the builders also eliminated grades of more than 5 percent (462 vertical feet per mile), the most a horse-drawn loaded wagon could manage. Most impressive, the corporation paid stockholders 2 to 3 percent annual dividends from the tolls. Expecting similar returns, New York state chartered 4,000 miles of turnpikes between 1815 and 1830, Pennsylvania 2,400, New Jersey 550, and Maryland 300. The work required to survey such distances, fell thousands of trees, remove stumps, grade, drain, haul and lay stones, bridge creeks, and finally gravel boggles the mind. Yet merchants and land speculators both invested and lobbied states to invest in improved transportation.[9]

The greatest turnpike was a federal initiative. In 1806 Congress made good on its promise to Ohio by authorizing funds for a Cumberland or National Road (present-day U.S. 40). The route at once became a political issue. Marylanders and Virginians imagined this American "Appian Way" running along the Mason-Dixon Line so their western counties would benefit. But building the road that far south meant crossing much higher mountains at much higher cost. In 1811 the route was shifted north through Pennsylvania and Wheeling into central Ohio. A foreigner marveled at the energy Americans poured into the road, but was appalled by their waste: "Many thousands of trees, that were cut for making the turnpike lay rotten by the side of it. I believe I have seen more timber in their wasting state, than all the growing timber I ever saw in my life in England." After 1818 work ceased while arduous surveys were made as far afield as Illinois. Finally, on July 4, 1825, dignitaries at a star-spangled ceremony turned their spades on a road they declared would someday reach the Rocky Mountains.[10]

It would, a *century* later, but road-building mania ended that year. Lancaster Pike notwithstanding, few companies even made enough money to keep their roads in repair. Animal-powered land transport of bulky goods was still too slow and expensive to attract much traffic. The wages (and theft) of toll collectors ate up revenue. Teamsters learned quickly to sneak by tollhouses at night or evade them via "shun pikes" tramped out by their oxen.[11] Long distance roads were destined to become a rich and romantic part of American history, but not until the invention of internal combustion. Indeed, the National Road ceremony was eclipsed just three months later by another one, up at Buffalo, heralding completion of the Erie Canal.

# The Nineteenth State: Indiana, 1816

"In the beginning was the word, and the word was Hoosier." But nobody knows what it meant. No proof can be found for the flattering theory about a contractor named Hoosier (or Hoosher), whose Indiana work crews were renowned for their productivity. Nor is it likely the word derived from "Who's 'ere?" shouted by pioneers after a knock on the door, or (as humorist James Whitcomb Riley quipped) "Who's ear?" shouted after a brawl fought with knives. The most likely source is the word "hoozer" connoting "high hills" in England's Cumberland dialect. Most of the early settlers in Indiana emerged from the uplands of Kentucky and Virginia: they were "hoozers" or "hillbillies." But the origins don't really matter, because proud Hoosiers have redefined their nickname to mean people of horse sense, homespun wit, and small-town values.[12]

The territory named generically after the Indians originally consisted of all the Northwest Territory left over when Ohio prepared for statehood. Indiana, destined to be the smallest state west of the Alleghenies, was carved out by Congress in 1809. Like Ohio and Illinois, all but the southernmost fraction of Indiana was honed by glaciers in the last Ice Age. They left behind rich soil, gravel deposits, and moraines defining the north-south Continental Divide. Thus, the waters of the Wabash and White Rivers eventually find their way to the Gulf of Mexico, while the St. Joseph and Maumee Rivers run to the Great Lakes. The midwestern climate has four distinct seasons, but the Ohio River country is far muggier in summer while the plains and dunes in the north verge on the Michigan snow belt. As George Ade, another local humorist, wrote, "Indiana is not Out-West or way Down-East or Up-North or south in Dixie." A Hoosier is "the happy average."[13]

That was not always the case. Unlike Ohio, Indiana received no initial leavening of Yankees, so Kentucks and Virginians dominated the territory from its inception. To this day, Indiana is by far the most "southern" of midwestern states. As late as 1850 just 8.8 percent of its population originated in New England and the Middle Atlantic as compared to 17 percent for Illinois, 19 percent for Ohio, 35 percent for Wisconsin, and 45 percent for Michigan. Southern culture was reinforced during the long tenure of territorial governor William Henry Harrison. His father was a planter, signer of the Declaration of Independence, and governor of Virginia. But he died poor, leaving his son with no way to realize his Cavalier expectations except through war and politics. He went to Ohio, married Judge John Symmes' resourceful daughter Anna, and proved his adroitness by getting both John Adams *and* Jefferson to approve his appointment as Indiana's governor in the overheated political year of 1800.

But there were two sorts of southerner, both in their ways Jeffersonian. Harrison considered himself a natural aristocrat, expected deference from the settlers and squatters along the Ohio River and at Vincennes on the Wabash, and endeavored to transplant Virginia's hierarchical system. He cemented his authority through a patronage system and sought federal assistance to speed Indiana's development by, among other things, suspending Article VI of the Northwest Ordinance and permitting slavery! The reason was simple: a desperate shortage of labor. Whites would not work for other whites, and why should they, with plenty of $2 per acre land to buy or just squat on. When Congress tabled his proposals Harrison prevailed on the territorial legislature to legalize a disguised form of slavery it called "voluntary indentured servitude" of blacks and mulattoes. None of this prevented Jefferson and Madison from reappointing him governor in 1806, 1809, and 1811. Indeed, Jefferson relied on Harrison to be his "eyes and ears" in the West. Madison loaned him the soldiers to burn Prophet's Town. Had Harrison's "court party" remained unchallenged he might well have petitioned Congress to admit Indiana as a slave state. But Harrison's plans aborted thanks to another sort of Jeffersonian eager to get ahead via politics.[14]

Jonathan Jennings was born, somewhere, sometime around 1784. It is known his father was a Presbyterian minister and lived in New Jersey before moving on to western Virginia and Pennsylvania, where Jonathan was educated. In 1806 he moved to Steubenville, Ohio, to study law with his older brother, then pushed on to remote Vincennes, assuming a twenty-three-year-old with learning must rise quickly. Instead, he ran afoul of a Harrison protégé and left within a year, damning the "Virginia aristocrats" for so many "rascals," and the land office where he lost all his money. He could not even afford to pay last respects when tuberculosis carried off his brother. But down on the Ohio River, in Clark County, Indiana, Jennings found his voice. It seemed folks in that rapidly growing region also resented Harrison's regime. They were refugees from Kentucky mostly, not would-be plantation owners. Their economic outlet was Louisville, not distant Vincennes. And they loved a handsome, lettered chap who told them "no proud nabob" dared look upon them with contempt. When Congress in 1809 mandated popular election of Indiana's territorial delegate, Jennings discovered how good he was at campaigning. Anticipating a future midwestern politician, Jennings split rails, helped raise log cabins, and traded jests over hard cider with the common folk. When he won, his Harrison-party opponent cried fraud. But Congress seated Jennings even as President Madison reappointed Harrison. Such were the accommodations made under Republican one-party rule.[15]

Within a year Jennings' populists won control of the legislature, repealed the law permitting "indentured servitude," and moved the capital to Corydon in their own neck of the woods. By 1813 Harrison resigned to win glory in war. By 1815 the statehood movement began in earnest. The new governor was skeptical, arguing Indiana's tiny tax base precluded government without federal subsidies. He was right, but the territory nonetheless won permission to hold a convention in April 1816. Of the forty-three men who met in Corydon, thirty-four had roots in the South. Following Ohio's example, they banned slavery, but also discouraged free black residency. The constitution likewise empowered the legislature at the expense of the governor. When Indiana achieved statehood in December 1816 and elected Jennings its governor, his victory was sweet and complete. But so tiny was the state budget he could do nothing more even if he had not taken to drinking. Indiana's founding father retired in 1831, died in debt three years later, and was placed in an unmarked grave.[16]

The new state grew in just two decades from 147,000 to 685,000 as migrants arrived via the Ohio River and National Road. Otherwise, as a traveler's graffito read, "The Roads are impassable—hardly jackassable; I think those that travel 'em should turn out and gravel 'em." One such track led to Indianapolis, the first state capital planned entirely from scratch. Its location in the dead center of the state also bespoke boosters' optimism because northern Indiana was still nearly vacant in 1825. But as a keen observer of the Ohio Valley wrote the following year, no people was so artful at "trumpeting, and lauding the conveniences and future prospects, of the town to be sold." Thanks to such advertising Terre Haute, Bloomington, Indianapolis, and a score of boomtowns shifted the demographic fulcrum. In 1826, the Wabash River carried no less than 152 flatboats loaded with 250,000 bushels of corn, 100,000 barrels of pork, 7,000 barrels of salt, 2,500 cattle, and 5 tons of beeswax. By 1836 the ebullient state, bankrupt no longer, launched a $10 million program of internal improvements to make Indiana "crossroads of the nation." Instead, graft, embezzlement, and the Panic of 1837 threw the state back into default. "Neither a borrower nor a lender be" became a proverb beloved by Hoosiers. In 1851, they amended their constitution to make imbalanced budgets illegal.[17]

Private, especially religious donations, however, attested to the value Indiana placed on education. Presbyterians founded secondary schools for boys and girls alike, as well as Hanover College in 1829 and Wabash College in 1834. Methodists, the dominant sect thanks to their circuit-riders, began Indiana Asbury (later DePauw University) in 1837 and the Baptists planted Franklin College in 1834. Finally, Jesuit missionaries arrived to minister to the Indians in lands first explored by the French. Benjamin Marie Petit was ordained a priest at Vincennes, Indiana, in 1837 and founded a mission to the Potawatomi near the South Bend of the St. Joseph River. Petit defended the tribe before white authorities, but in vain. When the Potawatomi were forcibly removed to the west, the priest trudged with them until weakness and hunger killed him, at age twenty-eight, in St. Louis. "Father Black Robe" was not forgotten, however. In 1856 his body was shipped back to the site of his old mission, known, since 1842, as the University of Notre Dame.

Meditating on the greatness of ancient Egypt, China, France, and England, Fulton wrote in 1796 it is "worthy of observation that in these countries where canals were most in use, they never encouraged foreign commerce, but seem to have arrived at their great opulence by a home trade, circulated through their extensive and numerous navigations." His inspiration was the Duke of Bridgewater, whose Manchester canal earned him "immortality and £130,000 a year." Fulton sent a copy of his treatise to George Washington, who needed no convincing. The American canal mania had already begun.[18]

Massachusetts, ever precocious in economic development, chartered a company in 1793 for the purpose of linking the Charles and Merrimack Rivers.[19] It seemed modest enough, less than twenty-seven miles across low terrain. But company president James Sullivan and construction chief Laommi Baldwin had no idea how to begin. Secretary of War Henry Knox said not to worry. Canals were "more a matter of accurate perceptions and judgment than of science." Still, accuracy is hard to achieve without science, as one of Baldwin's surveyors discovered after making a forty-one-foot vertical error. Nor did his pick-and-shovel men know what to do with the dirt they removed, how to cut rock, design locks, or prevent the canal from "weeping" (leaking). So Sullivan and Baldwin looked around for a knowledgeable foreigner and located William Weston. An early drop in the continuous nourishing brain drain to America, Weston was in Philadelphia working for Robert Morris when the call came from Boston. His "shocking" fee of $2,000 proved a bargain, because Weston not only brought a state-of-the-art English level, his head contained all the secrets of the Duke of Bridgewater's legendary foreman James Brindley. The only illiterate millwright ever to be voted the thanks of Parliament, Brindley learned by mother wit and experience how to build bridges, lay turnpikes, and dig watertight canals. His "rules of thumb" were to use stone, not brick or wood, to secure locks, build beside rivers to draw their water while avoiding their currents, and secure canal sides (the "prism" or "trough") by puddling rich clay until it becomes as impermeable as a potter's fine crockery. Brindley was said to have died with "Puddle it again!" on his lips. The Middlesex novices never did puddle enough. But Sullivan and Baldwin went on to found engineering dynasties in New England. Weston stayed in America until 1801 working on other canals, the Lancaster Pike, Philadelphia's Market Street Bridge, and New York City's water system. He left behind a cadre of apprentices needing only to be assembled on some great project for an American engineering profession to arise.[20]

New York in those years was at last becoming the republic's center of gravity. Between 1790 and 1820 the state grew fourfold to 1.37 million people, and in ranking from fifth to first. New York City doubled to 124,000 on the strength of its port, location, aggressive business houses, and the opening of its hinterland. Indeed, that hinterland, from Albany west to the Finger Lakes and Lake Erie, filled up so rapidly that by 1820 upstate New York contained most of the state's population. Should New York's leading citizens realize their main chance lay in domestic development, not just foreign trade, they might live up to the boast "Empire State."

Elkanah Watson did. He rose from indentured servitude in the household of the Browns of Providence to become a trusted agent of the Continental Congress over in Europe. There Watson wondered at the elaborate Dutch canal system and the Canal du Midi built by Louis XIV. After 1783 he moved to Albany, where he imagined a grand canal connecting the Hudson River to the Great Lakes. Was it possible? In 1806, when the National Road was approved, Watson led a delegation of New York notables to Washington City and presented his plan. President Jefferson's answer was this: "It is a splendid project . . . and may be executed a century hence. . . . You talk of making a canal three hundred and fifty miles long through a wilderness! It is little short of madness." So Watson, fearing New York would lose out in western development, proselytized instead on the Mohawk, enlisting Judge James Geddes of Onondaga (Syracuse) and Judge Benjamin Wright of Rome. After the War of 1812, upstate New Yorkers flexed their political muscles, attracting in turn the attention of De Witt Clinton.[21]

Nephew of long-serving Governor George Clinton, the aristocratic De Witt grew up expecting popular deference. He graduated in the first class of Columbia College (formerly King's College), where scientist David Hosack, Hugh Williamson's friend, was one of his mentors. He continued to read science, the classics, law, and philosophy even after entering politics. In all those ways Clinton was a northern Jefferson. But where Tom was timid and thin, De Witt was overbearing and strong (sarcastic scribblers called him "Magnus Apollo"). Above all, he was a Masonic Grand Master devoted to building his career, state, and country. As the long-standing mayor of New York he promoted full rights for Catholics, debtor relief, abolition of slavery, and internal improvements. Many Manhattan town fathers liked none of those things, singling out the "Great Western Canal" as a harebrained scheme from upstate. Some old Federalists supported the canal, but close association with them was politically crippling. Finally, the minions of Tammany Hall rallied behind

Republican Martin Van Buren of Kinderhook, who opposed anything Clinton favored. In 1815, they even managed to oust him from City Hall.

Geddes and Wright refused to give up, taking heart from President Madison's speech trumpeting "roads and canals which can best be executed under the national authority." Indeed, the charter for the second U.S. Bank devoted part of the "bonus" it paid the federal government to internal improvements. So the canal party approached Congress where no less an advocate than John C. Calhoun cried, "Let us then . . . bind the Republic together with a perfect system of roads and canals. Let us *conquer space*." Of course, every congressman wanted to dip in this pork barrel while brushing away hands from other states. But a Bonus Bill including funds for an Erie canal narrowly passed. Madison, on his last day in office, vetoed it! It seemed nobody noticed a quiet caveat in Madison's 1815 message regarding a "defect of constitutional authority." He believed an amendment necessary to empower the federal government to spend money on projects favoring only certain states.[22]

Van Buren chuckled, then gagged. First, a special gubernatorial election (to replace Daniel Tompkins, Monroe's vice president) swept Clinton into the statehouse on the strength of upstate votes. Next, an angel appeared in the person of Federalist patroon and amateur scientist Jacob Rutson Van Rensselaer. Impressed by the surveys of Geddes and Wright, he offered to finance the canal himself. Van Buren was at a crossroads. He now had to get his faction on board the popular canal project, but still somehow oppose Clinton. His solution was to support a bill to dig an Erie canal through state-issued bonds. That way it would belong to "the people" instead of "aristocrats" like Van Rensselaer. With the votes of Van Buren's Bucktails (so-called for their furry Tammany hats), the bill breezed through the legislature. Still the project hung fire, because the state's Council of Revision, a relic of the colonial Governor's Council, was empowered to veto legislation. Vice President Tompkins himself argued forcefully that if the state meant to spend huge sums of money, better it build fortifications in case of another war. But James Kent, a protégé of Alexander Hamilton and New York's greatest jurist, replied, "If we must have war, or have a canal, I am in favor of the canal." Kent carried the council.[23]

On the Fourth of July, 1817, Clinton presided over a Freemasons' field day, turning the first spade in the name of "the vast destinies of these United States." Whether the last spade would ever be turned was dubious. Clinton was no monarch but an elected official attempting to pull off an imperial enterprise at public expense. To sustain funding he thought it best to build the canal in stages, promising to complete the first stage from Utica to the rich salt ponds at Salina in just two years. Tolls from it might then pay for successive stages. He was also wise to pick Wright to oversee the central portion, Geddes the western, and Charles C. Broadhead the eastern. All excellent administrators, they hired hustling contractors willing to pay top dollar to veterans of Weston's canals. Even common laborers, or "canawlers," received the enticing wage of 80 cents a day, a shot of whiskey every two hours, and all the eggs, pork, potatoes, and bread they could eat. British and German immigrants, some Irish, and thousands of New Englanders ("Yankee Yorkers") signed up.[24]

Surveyors led, staking an avenue sixty feet wide. Next came lumberjacks to confront old growth up to seventy feet tall. They were aided by the invention of a giant screw rotating a drum. It slowly reeled in a great chain that enabled a single man to "snap" large trees at the turn of a crank. Next came the grubbers to pry out tree stumps and roots. They were aided by the invention of a root-ripping plow and mammoth winch that enabled one team of horses to extract forty stumps per day. Next came the diggers to move earth. They were aided, especially when rock was encountered, by the infant American chemical industry. Irénée Du Pont, a student of the great chemist Antoine Lavoisier, knew more about mixing charcoal, sulfur, and saltpeter than anyone outside of China. He did not invent a new mixture—gunpowder is gunpowder—but in 1802 he pioneered what is now called quality control at his Delaware mill on the Brandywine. The New York State Canal Commission, needless to say, became the biggest customer for Du Pont's predictable, pre-packaged charges. Next came the patient puddlers and finally the masons. The eighty-three locks required to allow for the 568-foot rise from the Hudson to Lake Erie seemed to be budget busters since expensive hydraulic cement had to be imported from Europe. But Clinton appointee Canvass White discovered a novel deposit of limestone in central New York that hardened rather than softened in contact with water! His find not only saved the commission a great deal of money but created another lucrative industry dependent on canal transport.

The ninety-six-mile stretch from Utica to Syracuse opened on schedule in 1819, just 10 percent over estimates. So, too, did the Lake Champlain connection. As tolls began to replenish the Canal Fund foreign and local investors eagerly advanced the rest of the once "impossible" sum of $7.5 million. Predictably, Van Buren ceased to maneuver against "Clinton's Big Ditch" and tried instead to take credit for it. His Bucktails proudly "guaranteed" the Canal Fund in a new 1821 state constitution. The following year their opposition caused Clinton to step down as governor to devote all his time to the canal. Finally, in 1824, Van Buren's "Albany Regency" even ousted Clinton from the Canal Commission. That humiliating injustice at last moved Clinton to fight fire with fire. He organized a People's party—the very name a cuff to the Bucktails' pretensions—and garnered enough sympathy votes to win back the statehouse.

Over those years so many marvels occurred upstate that none got the acclaim it deserved. Romanesque aqueducts, eighteen in all, spanned the Mohawk, Genesee, and lesser rivers. Culverts and bridges recalled Roman roads. Greek temple façades gave a sacral air to great locks with novel gates and sluices allowing one man at a lever to bind and loose waters. The climactic achievement was made at the western end. Nathan S. Roberts, chief engineer, hated the route surveyed across the Niagara escarpment raised up ages before by the same ancient earthquake that created Niagara Falls. Then he noticed a cleft some miles to the north that allowed for a lower altitude cut. It still meant blasting 1.5 million cubic yards of limestone and pasting five tiers of locks to the cliffs through ingenious melding of stone, cement, and iron. For four years redoubled gangs drilled holes for "powder monkeys" to fill with Du Pont charges, hauled away endless tons of stone, and fashioned the most ambitious locks ever conceived. Foreign observers such as Lafayette gaped at what free people proved willing and able to do. Meanwhile, the people of Buffalo laboriously dredged a harbor from Lake Erie's sandbars to secure their city's future as terminus for the canal and entrepôt for the entire Great Lakes.[25]

Philip Freneau wrote, "By hearts of oak and hands of toil / The spade inverts the rugged soil / A work that may remain secure / While suns exist and moons endure." On October 26, 1825, Governor Clinton honored New York's oaken hearts and toiling hands with a parade through Buffalo to a boat draped in red, white, and blue bunting. At 10 A.M. he signaled a cannon to fire. Miles to the east, within earshot, a second cannon saluted, then a third, and so on along the whole stretch to the Hudson and south to Manhattan. The last cannon began an answering echo that reached Buffalo at 1:20 P.M. Clinton then declared the wedding of waters done "by the authority and by the enterprise of the people of the State of New York," and set off on the canal. On November 4 the barge reached New York City, where hundreds of ships and boats were anchored in welcome. Clinton solemnly praised the "Holy cause of Republican Government," poured two kegs of Lake Erie into the harbor, and wept.[26]

The Erie Canal cut freight rates to the West by 75 to 90 percent, made bustling cities of the classically named Rome, Utica, and Syracuse, as well as

Rochester and Buffalo. It accelerated the influx of Yankees inventing new industries such as mass milling of Genesee flour, new religions such as Mormonism, and new amusements such as baseball. It sharply accelerated the growth of the upper Midwest and filled it with abolitionist northerners. It created the nation's first post-Revolutionary folklore. Its financial success inspired Pennsylvania's "Main Line" canal to Pittsburgh, the Chesapeake and Ohio Canal, the Chesapeake and Delaware Canal, and the Santee Canal at Charleston. Within fifteen years of the Erie's completion, 3,326 miles of canals were in operation, almost all paid for by a mix of state and private investment.[27]

The Erie Canal suckled the engineering profession. Scores of men who learned "on the job" freed their nation from European expertise. They applied their knowledge to North American topography, learning to trust their own innovations. They acquired confidence to think big, mobilize labor and capital on a huge scale, and hitch public and private enterprise to the same wagon. They validated once and for all a national ethic of progress bound up in the personal, self-made career. John B. Jervis is a case in point. Born in 1795 to a strict Calvinist carpenter, he showed up in the cedar groves near Rome in 1817 with nothing to offer the canawlers but his axe. The first day he learned to chop trees so they fell along a pre-arranged line. Within weeks he was begging surveyors to initiate him into their mysteries. When the snow blew, he had the temerity to ask Benjamin Wright if he might graduate in the spring to a survey team. Wright gave the lad two mathematics texts while Nathan Roberts taught him to level and plot. Jervis was soon promoted to rodman, then tallyman, surveyor, assistant engineer, and superintendent of maintenance on a completed stretch of canal. When the Erie was done, Jervis was hired to survey a Delaware and Hudson Canal to float Pennsylvania's anthracite coal to New York. Tramping the high bluffs near the Delaware Water Gap in a snowstorm, he sensed as keenly as the most romantic Hudson River painter a "grandeur in this lonely, purposeful labor in the wilderness."

Jervis made numerous contributions to dams, bridges, railroads, aqueducts, and canals, displaying in most cases as deft a touch with his paymasters as with earth, water, iron, and stone. Hundreds of similar careers were made in the canal boom, belatedly confirming Joseph Ellicott's early advice to Robert Morris: "I would recommend employing Americans solely, and avoiding foreigners; they know very little about the management and conducting of business economically in this country." By the 1830s West Point, Rensselaer Polytechnic, and Vermonter Alden Partridge's Academy supplemented the engineering talent of the New York State Canal System. But "on the job" training continued to be a ladder up for youngsters willing to hustle in one industry after another. Jervis himself helped train three generations of master builders before dying at age ninety in 1885.[28]

De Witt Clinton died young, in 1828, but not before showing his countrymen how to accomplish great things by dint—or in spite—of their politics.

## The Twentieth State: Mississippi 1817

George Strother Gaines, number eleven of thirteen children, was far down the list of his parents' priorities. But their family trees were rooted deep in colonial Virginia (Edward Randolph was an uncle) and North Carolina (the Blounts had been partners) and had recently branched out in Tennessee (Andrew Jackson and William C. C. Claibourne were friends). Thanks to that patronage George was named at age twenty-one an assistant factor of the federal government's Indian post on the Tombigbee River. Arriving in June 1805 he discovered to his "surprise and admiration" the Choctaw chiefs were "not such savages as I had imagined." He recalled especially how aged Chief Mingo-Homa-stubbee pulled the leg of an American lieutenant who asked about his tribe's greatest warrior. Mingo replied *he* used to be so considered, but discovered otherwise after a visit to the white Father Washington. The President arranged for them to go home by sea, and when a storm blew up waves that "kissed the clouds," Mingo admitted to fear. So he went below decks to see how a fellow warrior, Puckshennubbee, was faring. The American lieutenant leaned forward and asked, "What was he doing?" Mingo, gravely but with "a humorous twinkle" replied, "Why, he was making love to an old squaw we took along as a cook for us, and he seemed to be as unconcerned about the danger as if he was at home in his own cabin sitting by the fire and listening to the songs of the winds."[29]

Thus did Gaines begin thirty years of intimate contact with the Choctaw and sixty-five years with the history of what was then the Mississippi Territory. At the start little besides piney woods, varmints, and Indians might be seen along the three-hundred-mile path linking Natchez on the Mississippi and the rustic settlements near Mobile Bay. Greedy Georgians had touted the Yazoo Land

Company, but that fraud did little except wreck reputations and fortunes. The Louisiana Purchase did not remove the danger posed by Creeks, Spaniards, British, and traitors. Indeed, Gaines' brother was the officer who captured Aaron Burr during his flight in 1807. But the Gulf Coast was a salubrious climate and political "planters" already strewed seeds of what became Mississippi and Alabama.

The first was a Yankee lawgiver. Winthrop Sargent, son of a Gloucester merchant, Harvard graduate, veteran of Knox's artillery, and later assistant to puritanical Ohio governor Arthur St. Clair, was the last person one would expect to make an impression on the Deep South. But President Adams appointed him governor when Congress set up the Mississippi Territory in 1798. In just two years Sargent imposed ordered liberty on the wilderness by drafting an elaborate Common Law code, setting up courts, and appointing like-minded judges. Given the distances involved he also gave local justices of the peace *carte blanche* to suppress discord, mete out harsh punishments, seize people's land to discharge debts, and expel non-residents. In effect, Sargent's peace officer was the antecedent of the latter-day southern sheriff. The Natchez elite applauded his enforcement of commercial law, tolerated his excise taxes to build public works, and cheered his defense of property rights and slavery. But pioneers and squatters raged against Sargent to the point that Jefferson sacked him. Still, Sargent's legal system survived more or less intact while he himself wedded a planter's belle, embraced the languid plantation life, and even died aboard a New Orleans steamboat.[30]

The second seed of statehood was sown by another northerner, Treasury secretary Gallatin. Southwestern surveys had barely begun, but in 1809 he threw open a broad swath of the territory stretching east from Natchez across the Pearl River to the Tombigbee. Why? asked President Madison. "For the purpose both of quieting the people & of encouraging population," said the secretary. Indeed, planters, speculators, and pioneers had gathered at Natchez in anticipation of Mississippi bottom land being thrown on the market. But in truth, Jefferson's embargo so drained Gallatin's coffers he hoped to raise cash by selling off federal land.

The Land Office did not clear much because buyers colluded, but the southern third of the territory began filling up rapidly.[31]

Mississippi's third godfather was, of course, Andrew Jackson. During and after the War of 1812, he broke the power of the Creeks and Seminoles and extracted extensive concessions of Indian land. Another wave of immigration resulted, this time concentrated in the eastern half of the territory (Alabama). That, in turn, prepared the pitch for a pack of Georgia bulldogs to chew up the Deep South to their advantage.

They included William H. Crawford, secretary of war and the treasury under Monroe, and Senators William W. Bibb and Charles Tait. All three came from the Broad River region of Georgia and had family and friends among the first big landlords around Huntsville, Alabama. With population growing rapidly in the Southwest they determined to break the Mississippi Territory into two states in order to secure their own interests in Alabama as well as create four southern Senate seats to balance those of Indiana and Illinois. After some grumbling, Natchez planters saw the wisdom in this, and cheered as Bibb and Tait shepherded bills through Congress to invite the western half of the territory to petition for statehood. Indeed, the only vigorous debate at the constitutional convention was over what to call the new state. The word Mississippi ("Big River") was coined by Indians far to the north and neither the river's source nor mouth was within their boundaries. "Washington" was proposed instead and lost by a narrow vote of 17 to 23. So it was that Mississippi crept quietly into the union in December 1817.[32]

It was ideal cotton country. After the Peace of Ghent in 1815 no quantity of cotton seemed to satiate British mills, the spot price in New Orleans doubled within a year and continued to rise until the Panic of 1819. Mississippi's alluvial soil was unusually deep thanks to the prime midwestern topsoil carried downriver. The climate was sultry and damp, the growing season almost year-round, and the only enemies were the rivers themselves. The Yazoo and Mississippi formed an elliptical-shaped flood plain in the state's northwestern "Delta" too risky to invest in for decades until levees were raised. The rest of the northern part of the state, mostly loess hills and pine forests, was still Choctaw hunting ground. The soil of the Coastal Meadows or Terrace was too sandy to farm. Biloxi was a mere fishing port. But in between lay the eastern Black Belt, where corn and cattle thrived, and the Central Prairie from the Pearl River to the Mississippi, simply the best cotton patch on the continent. There the state capital of Jackson arose in 1820. There wooden dwellings scarcely more impressive than slave shacks grew into plantation manors. Docks and piers punctuated rivers at every landing, and steamboats offered scheduled service. Like the Jamestown colonists with their tobacco, Mississippi planters got a cotton crop in the ground their second, or even first year. But unlike the first Virginians they did not lack for food because hundreds of small farmers migrated in from Georgia or Tennessee. Their principal crops, one migrant quipped, were corn and children. And unlike Virginians, Mississippi settlers deferred to no one. Thomas Dabney learned that, after uprooting his family from an old Virginia plantation and moving to Hinds County, Mississippi, in 1835. He wanted to ingratiate himself with his neighbors and readily lent slave gangs to assist homesteaders in building or clearing fields. But he always appeared on a great steed, gloved in white, and the little people scorned the haughty pose. Dabney's daughter recorded: "The plainer classes in Virginia, like those in England, from whom they were descended, recognized the difference between themselves and the higher classes, and did not aspire to social equality. But in Mississippi the tone was different. They resented anything like superiority in breeding." Clearly these folks were no longer Jeffersonian, but Jacksonian.[33]

Amidst the pines, live oak, fruit trees, and palms swarming with migratory birds, people made themselves Mississippians. A mere 31,306 in 1810, they numbered 75,448 by 1820, and 130,621 by 1830. But as many were enslaved blacks as were white, and soon there were scarcely any Indians at all. When in 1829 their removal was ordered, the Choctaws threatened to resist. Who did the War Department call upon to appease them and help them scout out their exile in Arkansas? Who else but the Choctaws' best friend for almost three decades, George Strother Gaines. Now a big banker in Mobile, he pleaded to be excused from the shameful chore and accepted only to ensure his Indian friends were shown some mercy. All it earned him was a legal imbroglio when the government claimed he spent too much money helping the tribes. The Choctaws' land, he bitterly noted, was already put up for sale.[34]

Mississippi whites were peculiarly homogeneous in that the vast majority were of British stock and either Baptists or Methodists. Only around Natchez did New Orleans spillover create much diversity. But in antebellum times the cultural divide was more between rich and poor than between black and white. Poor whites and slaves both worked the soil with their hands and made their own yokes, furniture, spinning wheels, and musical instruments. They shared folk tales, tall tales, ballads, and spirituals, creating that mix of English, Scots-Irish, and African moods and rhythms that in time produced Muddy Waters and Elvis Presley alike, not to mention William Faulkner, Eudora Welty, and Tennessee Williams. But as foreign as the Deep South seemed to many northerners, Mississippi displayed a curious power to seduce Yankees who went there. One was John Anthony Quitman of Rhinebeck, New York, who studied theology and law, but migrated penniless to Natchez in 1821. He rose quickly in the Mississippi bar, married well, and achieved a general's rank in the Mexican War. Quitman then became governor, a champion of slavery, and Grand Master of Mississippi Freemasons. Another transplant was Sheffield, Massachusetts, native and Yale graduate Frederick Augustus Porter Barnard, to whom Mississippians were pleased to entrust their new university at Oxford (Ole Miss) in 1854. Alas, the Civil War intervened. Barnard returned north to head Columbia University from 1864 to 1887, lending his name to its women's college. Consider it the Magnolia State's gift to the Upper West Side.[35]

The Cotton Kingdom later stretched from Georgia to east Texas, but Mississippi's soil and water transport made it the crown land. Prior to 1815, Gallatin's liberal land sales, relatively low prices for slaves, and an excellent strain of Siamese seed cotton attracted investors, especially Tidewater planters whose soil was exhausted. After 1815, when the cotton price soared, the pioneers plowed back their profits into more land and slaves even as they built mansions, turned out carriages, and bought thoroughbreds for themselves and luxuries for their ladies. Then three technical breakthroughs made Mississippi cotton truly "white gold." First, Eleazar Carter and William Dunbar fixed the main flaws in Whitney's gin with devices that reduced damage to fiber as it was combed and cleaned it as well. Second, Natchez planters slashed their shipping costs with a prodigious press. It smashed raw cotton into bales so dense four hundred pounds took up no more space in a ship's hold than two hundred pounds stuffed in bags. Third, planters discovered the finest of all cotton strains after a fungus killed half the 1811 crop. They imported a Mexican strain that cross-pollinated with Siamese and Georgian plants to make a species resistant to blight and profuse with puffier bolls. Slaves previously able to pick seventy-five pounds per day might now surpass two hundred or three hundred, permitting planters to double or triple their acreage without expanding their workforce. When news spread of thousand-acre plantations clearing $50,000 per crop, the southwestern migration accelerated.[36]

Without expanding their workforce? That seems impossible when one recalls how laborious tobacco cultivation was back in the Chesapeake. But unlike tobacco, cotton seedlings did not need to be nursed and transplanted. Unlike tobacco, cotton plants did not need to be topped and pruned. Unlike tobacco, cotton bolls needed no curing before being pressed and shipped. Unlike tobacco, cotton ran little risk of spoilage on lengthy voyages. Some similarities remained. Both crops required a gang system in which slaves were "herded" by "drivers" (usually slaves themselves). The work was drudgery, but not physically demanding, so women and men worked in the fields in roughly equal numbers. Mixing of sexes, in turn, both increased fertility and reduced the likelihood of revolts. On West Indies sugar plantations, where gangs were comprised of young males, violence was frequent. What is more, four features combined to ameliorate treatment of slaves in the cotton South. First, the rapid spread of plantations made slaves more valuable. Second, the shutdown of the overseas slave trade in 1808 cut the supply of new labor, causing planters to encourage mating in the slave quarters. Third, that new strain of cotton was so bountiful a planter's production limit was fixed by the sheer ability of his slaves to pick the stuff. Knowing that, slaves engaged in "collective bargaining" through slowdowns: not enough to bring on the lash, but enough to discredit a hated overseer or win carrots instead of sticks. Fourth, the cotton boom coincided with the religious revivals spreading throughout the frontier. Almost all newcomers on the lower Mississippi were Methodist, Presbyterian, or Baptist.

Obviously they rejected the abolitionism preached by some of their northern brethren, but they knew the Pauline injunction about the mercy due servants. Southern magazines and how-to books even instructed planters what work regimen, diet, rewards, and punishments sowed tranquillity and productivity in the fields. That is not to suggest slaves were loved (though some household ones surely were), much less that they loved their lot. It is simply to say whites and blacks both understood a slave's economic value and exploited it to their best advantage.[37]

Migration forged another link between colonial slavery and that of the Deep South. Most plantations in Alabama, Mississippi, and Louisiana were founded by families established in Virginia, the Carolinas, and Georgia. Thus, 84 percent of the Cotton Belt's slaves had to march, manacled together in tethered coffles, with their master's livestock and wagons along primitive roads to Mobile or Natchez. The other sixth were the internal "exports" of slavemongers who purchased their cargoes in the Tidewater and Piedmont, assembled them at Baltimore, Alexandria, Norfolk, or Charleston, and shipped them around Key West to New Orleans. The firm of Franklin & Armfield owned a fleet of ships sufficient to transfer two hundred bondsmen per month over a winter. By whichever route, an estimated seventy-eight thousand blacks were relocated in the 1810s alone, reducing the Chesapeake's share of the national slave force from 56 to just 35 percent. Cotton production rose from 178,000 bales in 1810 to 732,000 in 1830.[38]

Finally, the new cotton culture, like the old tobacco one, was a transoceanic industry run by factors, resident middlemen or brokers. Some planters pored over reports of price fluctuations from Natchez and New Orleans to New York and London, making their own decisions about where to offer a crop. Most relied on American factors or "commission merchants" to serve as financial advisers, purchasing agents, and creditors. A factor might advance a portion of the proceeds to be gleaned from the sale of next year's crop. He might cover the costs of marketing a crop, including shipment, insurance, storage, and repairs, later deducting expenses plus commission from proceeds. If high prices were anticipated, the factor might extend a hefty loan to a planter eager to purchase more land and slaves. The only service a factor rarely provided was the long-term mortgage. That is why southern planters, even more than northern farmers, cried out for banks. Treasury Secretary William H. Crawford lamented in 1820: "Banks have been incorporated, not because there was capital seeking investment . . . but because men without active capital wanted the means of obtaining loans." Such was planters' political clout the cotton states chartered sixty-five banks by the 1830s. Highly sensitive to cotton prices, they were a major cause of the "panics" that jarred the U.S. economy. That in itself bespeaks the importance of plantation wealth to the nation. If southerners sometimes resented their dependence on the north, so northern merchants, shippers, bankers, and manufacturers were uncomfortably dependent on the slaveholding Cotton Kingdom.[39]

Did the rise of cotton create a wealthy oligarchy dominating the politics and society, markets and mores, of slave states? Yes and no. Large-scale planters invariably assumed leadership roles, but slaveholding also grew more democratic as it spread. By 1830 some 36 percent of southern white families owned one or more slaves; in some counties over 50 percent. Immigrants considered purchase of a slave the sign of "making it" in America. The average number of bondsmen in a slaveholding household was consistently between four and six. Nor was slavery a whites-only privilege. By 1830 more than two hundred Cherokees owned slaves. So did 3,775 free blacks. Finally, Louisiana mulattoes with French or Spanish names might acquire plantations hoping for acceptance as "whites." At least a tenth of all masters were women who inherited slaves from husbands or fathers. Women also managed domestic servants while presiding over the care of blacks sick or in childbirth. In sum, "the typical master did not really exist." Slavery was an American, not just a white male institution.[40]

Economic history and econometrics have proven beyond serious doubt that southern slavery was a profitable capitalist expression of Americans' development ethic. However, northern and southern apologists, before and after the Civil War, did not want to believe that. They stressed the paternalism, hierarchy, and rural character of an undifferentiated South, judging it either an honorable arcadia or an immoral atavism. They imagined slaves either as beloved retainers whom planters cared for *despite* the expense, or else as dehumanized chattel. Bereft of economic or emotional motivation, they became lazy, stupid (or feigned stupidity), preyed upon by sadistic overseers and lascivious masters, and either rebellious or pathetically passive. Raw statistics and common sense belie such stereotypes.[41] The fact planters invested heavily in slave property for two hundred years hardly suggests the institution was bankrupting them. The fact they employed strategies to coax and goad the most work out of slaves shows they understood the blacks' human impulses. The fact many encouraged child-rearing, rewarded fertile women, and bestowed "title" to cabins and gardens on their mates demonstrates an appreciation of the placating power of family. The fact slaves were anguished when kinfolk were sold proves in turn their love of family. The fact agriculture in the South, by one calculation, was 35 percent more efficient than in the North—with slave-worked farms 28 percent more productive than white southern ones—belies the myth of the lazy African.⁴² The infrequency of violent crime and revolt among slaves hardly suggests innate rebelliousness. As for the contrary charge of passivity, it seems evident slaves did what they could to assert themselves given their plight. The lash and gun did not keep them down. What kept them down was the *law of the land*, attachment to kin and companions, and entrapment in a slaveholding realm stretching hundreds of miles in every direction. Later in the century a shifting balance of risks and rewards encouraged numerous slaves (mostly young men) to attempt escape. In the early decades of the Cotton Kingdom there was nowhere to run. Federal courts made sure of that. Anyway, the north did not want them.

In 1774 a Connecticut correspondent signing him- or herself "A Negro" ridiculed the colonies' cries for freedom while perpetuating bondage themselves. "O mighty God! let conscience seize the mind / Of inconsistent men, who wish to find / A partial god to vindicate their cause, / And plead their freedom, while they break its laws." After 1776 northern states did move more or less swiftly, more or less thoroughly, toward extinction of slavery. Whether Quakers, Anglicans, Congregationalists, or evangelicals, a large majority in the Northeast and a bare majority in the Northwest agreed with John Jay that "prayers to Heaven for liberty will be impious" without abolition. Nor did the northern economy need slaves. Thanks to immigration and overpopulated New England cheap labor was usually available to northern employers who, in any case, enjoyed their freedom to fire or lay off workers at will. Finally, white farmers and workers hated slave labor in the belief it caused unemployment and lower wages and prices. But abolition was nonetheless gradual and not at all liberating. Respect for property rights necessitated slavery be "grandfathered," hence 36,505 northern African Americans were still enslaved in 1800; 3,568 as late as 1830. New York's emancipation provision invited hucksters to purchase local slaves cheaply for resale down south, while its law permitting non-residents to enter the state with slaves remained on the books until 1841. What is more, few northern whites believed Negroes capable of citizenship. Their right to vote was restricted or denied everywhere except in upper New England. They could not serve on juries, attend white churches and schools, or reside in white neighborhoods. Hence, free blacks huddled in notorious slums such as Boston's Nigger Hill, Cincinnati's Little Africa, and New York's Five

Points district. Most were confined to menial jobs and trades. Ohio, Indiana, and Illinois tried to purge free blacks altogether. The federal government restricted naturalization to whites, expelled blacks from militias and the post office, and blessed state restrictions on free blacks' mobility.[43]

Dissenting Federalists reasoned that if blacks were not subject to bondage they could not be denied full citizenship. But northern Republican leaders not only agreed with Jefferson about the natural inferiority of Africans, they stoked white fears for political advantage ("Federalists with *blacks* unite" was an 1808 Tammany slogan). The result of all this was the peculiarly northern conundrum about assimilation. If blacks ought to be free, but can never be equal, what must become of them?[44]

The American Convention of Delegates from Abolition Societies, founded in 1794, was dominated by Quakers and Federalists from Pennsylvania and New York. They understood successful assimilation of free blacks, hence emancipation generally, depended on changing *whites'* perceptions. But the burden of doing so fell upon blacks. The convention's tracts urged free black communities to encourage churchgoing, sobriety, fidelity, education, and hard work. Whether its preachments (which only echoed those of black churches and Masonic lodges) had any effect on black behavior is moot. They had no effect on white attitudes. An 1826 study showing Negroes, just 2 or 3 percent of the northern population, accounted for one-sixth of all prison inmates in Massachusetts, one-fourth in New York, and one-third in Pennsylvania, seemed to prove free Negroes were lawless. Northerners also judged many retarded. In census data the ratio of blacks deemed "insane and idiots" exactly *decreased* as one moved from north to south. Thus, Maine reported 1 black in 14 to be mad, New Hampshire 1 in 18, Massachusetts 1 in 43, New York 1 in 257, Virginia 1 in 1,229, South Carolina 1 in 2,477, and Louisiana (where everyone, thus no one, is mad) just 1 in 4,310. Southerners often cited northern discrimination as proof of hypocrisy. Now they could argue "free" life in the north drove Negroes crazy. The Abolitionist Convention, its strategy of uplift in tatters, would disband in 1838.[45]

Long before that most northerners came around to Jefferson's opinion. To set black people loose in the midst of a dynamic white society would be disastrous for both races. Accordingly, deportation was the platform of the American Colonization Society, founded in Washington City in 1816. That assimilation was impossible, it asserted, "is not the fault of the coloured man, nor of the white man, nor of Christianity, but an ordination of Providence, and no more to be changed than the laws of nature." The movement seared New England like a revival. All the states save Rhode Island (where the percentage of blacks was *highest*) had chapters; clergy enlisted their congregations; money was raised every Fourth of July, as if America would not be fully independent until cleansed of Africans. Daniel Dana of New Hampshire believed African resettlement the only humane solution, since "This is not their country. . . . O let them breathe the air of the land of their fathers. . . . Send them home." Since it was hardly conceivable the federal and state governments would cough up millions to purchase slaves' freedom and ship them to Africa, the effect of colonizationist propaganda was to worsen the image of free blacks. They seemed criminal, licentious, either a threat or a burden. In 1821, the American Colonization Society did found a West African colony for "repatriates" (as if any by that date were African-born). A Methodist minister christened it Liberia. But southern blacks remained in fetters while few northern blacks wanted to emigrate, hence colonizationists became as risible as assimilationists. That cleared the stage for a new generation of crusaders determined to abolish slavery whatever the consequences for American society. For the time being, though, most northerners preferred to ignore the conundrum or else shrug with Ralph Waldo Emerson, "It will happen by & by, that the black man will only be destined for museums like the Dodo."[46]

## *The Twenty-first State: Illinois, 1818*

*Ilini*, in the language of that tribe, meant simply "the men" as if all other bipeds were something less. The French pluralized it with an "s," gallicized it with an "o," and doubled the "l." They also bequeathed to *le pays des Illinois* its first river towns, a thousand black slaves, and the word *prairie* for its flat grasslands. The prairie's black topsoil, the five hundred watercourses carved out by glaciers, and the temptation of slavery later combined to turn a seemingly typical Ohio Valley region into a fractious *northern* state fashioned by *southerners* posing as *westerners*. Illinoisans would thus never achieve the strong identity of their neighbors in Indiana, Iowa, or Wisconsin. Illinoisans, like Missourians, were too often at odds with each other.[47]

Prominent among the first U.S. speculators were John Edgar and William Morrison who bought large tracts from the demoralized French, forged bills of sale for vacated lands, or else bribed *habitants* to attest to "improvements" that strengthened a claim. Edgar and Morrison also lobbied to escape Indiana, and Congress obliged by spinning off an Illinois Territory in 1809. The following year a federal commission sorted out existing claims and opened land offices at Shawneetown on the Wabash River and Kaskaskia on the Mississippi. As elsewhere, the Treaty of Ghent in 1815 fired the opening gun for a land rush, inspiring a British colonel to prophesy doom for the Ilini, Sauk, and Fox. The Americans will deny them guns and powder and poison them with raw whiskey, he ventured, until "in fifty years time, there perhaps will not be an Indian left between this and the Rocky Mountains." For the time being the U.S. Army was content to build stockades at Peoria, Rock Island, and Chikagou, persuade the disheartened tribes to cede most of southern and central Illinois, and set aside a Military Tract for veterans between the Illinois and Mississippi Rivers. The white population, less than thirteen thousand in 1812, tripled in three years, with 75 percent of the newcomers arriving from Kentucky, Tennessee, Virginia, and the Carolinas. Six of the future state's first seven governors were among them.[48]

Pioneers from the South, however, came in two varieties: old Jeffersonians espousing republican virtue and aristocratic patronage; and frontier democrats assailing all privilege and authority. Most Illinois settlers were the latter sort, most of its early leaders the former. Thus, Nathaniel Pope became the territory's secretary and delegate to the U.S. Congress while his brother John, a senator from Kentucky, advised President Madison to appoint Ninian Edwards governor. A Maryland native and Dickinson College graduate, Edwards was Kentucky's chief justice. Edwards in turn named the Popes' nephew, Daniel Pope Cook, territorial accountant and clerk of the assembly. Cook also edited and partly owned the Kaskaskia *Western Intelligencer*, Illinois's first newspaper. Within eighteen months Cook was thundering against federal "tyranny" and demanding immediate statehood. Thanks to his uncle's influence, Congress obligingly lowered the population requirement to forty thousand and granted Governor Edwards the privilege of conducting the census! Cook would not wait: he just assumed the numbers were there and pushed a statehood petition through the assembly. Nathaniel Pope presented the petition in Congress and got himself chosen chair of the committee reviewing it. It is not recorded how much cronyism, back scratching, and bribery was required, but Pope pulled off coup after coup. First, Congress allowed Illinois to enter the Union with a record low population (probably about thirty-six thousand). Next, it granted the state a generous share of land office receipts and all the revenue from its rich salt licks. Finally, Congress agreed to extend the state's northern boundary from the tip of Lake Michigan up to the latitude of 42 degrees 30 minutes. That bestowed on Illinois an additional eight thousand square miles, sixty-three miles of lake frontage, and the future site of Chicago in the County of Cook.[49]

The state constitutional convention might have thrown all that away if the pro-slavery majority had pressed its advantage. Instead, delegates realized legalization of slavery north of the Ohio might set off a firestorm in the Congress. So Illinois's constitution banned involuntary servitude, but permitted temporary "indentured servitude" while forbidding importation of slaves for the purpose of manumitting them. Congress winked, Illinois joined the Union on December 3, 1818, and land speculators bribed the first General Assembly to move the capital to Vandalia up the Sangamon River.[50]

Having won statehood by stealth, Illinoisans nearly fell into premature civil war when another well-connected newcomer was elected governor in 1822. Edward Coles was a scion of the first families of Virginia. His older brother served as Jefferson's private secretary, and Edward held the same post under Madison. Then Monroe named Coles registrar of a new land office at Edwardsville, Illinois, where he already owned six thousand acres. Upon arrival Coles made a grand public display of freeing his slaves and settling them on his land. Even though 60 percent of the young state's voters were pro-slavery, Coles ran for governor and squeaked by in a four-man race with a mere third of the vote. Enraged "white folks," as small farmers called themselves, promptly founded a movement calling for a second constitutional convention, presumably to legalize slavery. Did they aspire to own big plantations worked by gang labor? Not at all, because to

Illinois farmers "white folks" was a *social* category distinguishing them from high-toned southern or Yankee "big folks" as much as from Negroes and Indians. ("I am getting skeery about them 'ere yankees," said one frontier wife. "There is such a power of them coming that they and the Injuns will squatch out all the *white folk*.") Farmers also hated banks and the "rag money" they issued. In the hard times following 1819, two Illinois banks failed, while land offices, eastern merchants, and Ohio River shippers sucked what cash there was in the west back east. A pioneer's only income was from commodity sales downriver, but the second U.S. Bank refused to set off bills of credit earned in New Orleans against debts owed to Philadelphia or New York. These hardships gave birth to the first prairie rebellion aiming to break local oligarchies, defy the federal government, and deny rights to the black and red man.[51]

Illinoisans were tempted by slavery—just one or two bondsmen could be a big help on a pioneer farm. They especially resented being denied choice in the matter by an old national fiat. They also feared losing new immigration to Missouri where slavery was legal. Assemblymen "Honest Irish" John McFerron and Conrad Will even argued republican equality among whites *required* the right to own slaves. Now that Illinois was a sovereign state, its people were free to legalize slavery if they wished. That "popular sovereignty" doctrine was later made famous by Illinois senator Stephen Douglas.[52]

Passions flared. Mysterious fires consumed the bank, land office, and statehouse in Vandalia in 1823; Governor Coles' farm was attacked. Convention advocates founded a committee, newspapers, and clubs. When the assembly fell just one vote shy of the number needed to hold a referendum, the majority summarily expelled a member in favor of a pro-slavery man. Religion entered the fray when "whole hog" Presbyterians damned "milk-and-cider" Methodists. Their circuit-riders were stoned; to be "yankee'd" meant to be cheated.[53] Coles and the other "big folks" opposing a new state convention lost ground until they wisely conceded "white folks" did have the right to remake their laws. That shifted debate to the issue of slavery itself, whereupon anti-conventioneers spread rumors of rich planters hoping to "sucker" Illinoisans into legalizing slavery so they could flood the state with Negroes. Amidst this tornado of accusations people went to the polls in 1824. The *fact* of the referendum attested to popular rebellion against abolitionist elites. Its *result*–defeat of a new convention 6,640 votes to 4,972–attested to popular rejection of slave-owning elites. Illinoisans thus declared themselves not northern or southern but westerners, insisting on white equality while opposing Africans, Indians, outsiders, and local "big folks." Coles, seemingly vindicated, became a lame duck and was later trounced in a race for Congress.[54]

Illinois sod, once "busted" by ox-drawn iron-tipped plows, was rich and well watered by moist winds from the Gulf. Visitors remarked on the fertile if monotonous frontier. In 1819 a German naturalist gaped to see how Indian hunting grounds on Vandalia's Sugar Creek turned in a single year into oceans of corn: "No region in all this broad America will be so quickly populated as this." He was right–the population tripled again by 1830 to surpass 150,000. But what made Illinois an economic giant was transport. Great Lakes shipping spawned by the Erie Canal mocked the judgment of a University of Pennsylvania professor who dismissed Chicago's commercial prospects. The Black Hawk War of 1832 (in which young Abe Lincoln captained militia) opened northern Illinois, sparking new migration from New York and New England. In 1836 the state proposed internal improvements capped by the Illinois and Michigan Canal. The assembly approved when Lincoln's "Long Nine" faction (they were all six feet or taller) brokered a deal linking the bill with one that moved the capital to Springfield. As in Indiana, the Panic of 1837 bankrupted the state. But reform governor Thomas Ford pushed the projects to completion by paying off contractors with land and a share of future tolls. In 1848 the canal linked the Great Lakes to the Mississippi, Chicago's first railroad began chugging, Cyrus McCormick opened his reaper factory there, and John Deere located his farm implement business in Moline.[55]

Alas, the state's destiny was also division. The explosive growth of the northern tier soon made "downstate" an abstraction to Chicagoans whose economic ties were national and who were mostly of Yankee or foreign extraction. Almost four hundred miles south, the folks of "Little Egypt" near Cairo felt closer to Dixie than Springfield, much less Chicago. The southwestern counties became part of Greater St. Louis, those carved from the old Military Tract shared life on the Mississippi with Missouri and Iowa, while the southeastern counties retained Hoosier characteristics. But almost all Illinoisans acquired an accent as flat as the land and the middle class, middlebrow, white-bread demeanor displayed by the voters in 1824. That helps explain why to this day even Chicago's movers and shakers tend not to put on airs lest they be mistaken for "big folks."[56]

The eyes of James Monroe revealed in Gilbert Stuart's portrait do not gleam with passion or wit. They just stare out over a long nose and pursed mouth as if to say, here I am at my desk, doing my duty. Monroe's equally modest Albemarle County estate seemed to bow, as if in obeisance, to grandiose Monticello up the hill. Inaugurated at age fifty-seven, the diffident Monroe was also a relic of sorts: the last president to have served in the Revolution, the last to wear eighteenth-century breeches, wigs, and cocked hats, the last of the Virginia dynasty, the last presiding "above party." His loyalty to agrarian virtue seemed, by 1816, almost wistful. Suffice it to say, the race to succeed him began the moment he took office. Jefferson foresaw it: "When the republicans should have put all things under their feet, they would schismatize among themselves." So Monroe's two terms were like a long pregnancy. No one knew what sort of new leaders and parties were struggling to be born, only that the mother, the Jeffersonian one-party system, would surely die in delivery.[57]

Monroe himself was so sure the nation would not tolerate another Virginian as heir apparent he selected as secretary of state the Yankee convert John Quincy Adams. William H. Crawford remained as Treasury secretary. A native Virginian who clawed his way to the top of Georgia's political brawls, Crawford had the temerity to challenge Monroe for the nomination and was miffed not to become secretary of State. Another presidential aspirant, South Carolina's Calhoun, became secretary of War. But the *dramatis personae* were still not complete. Kentuckian Henry Clay refused a cabinet post in order to campaign for president as Speaker of the House. Finally, out in Nashville lurked General Jackson, "Napoleon of the New World."

All were Republicans and all, for the time being, nationalists. In 1816 the second U.S. Bank and a tariff to protect infant industries passed Congress comfortably under the guidance of southerner Calhoun, westerner Clay, and northerner Daniel Webster. But the use of federal funds for internal improvements remained a hot button because Monroe shared Madison's doubts of its constitutionality. The new Congress appointed a committee that found the federal government did have authority to fund roads and canals; indeed it had already used it in the service of the military, post office, and interstate commerce. Clay intoned in March 1818 that anyone (that is, Monroe) who could not "elevate his views to the height which this nation is destined to reach" lacked "the character of an American statesman." In Monroe's own cabinet, Calhoun likewise urged "a judicious system of roads and canals." They were posturing, to be sure. But they also pricked the body politic in a sensitive spot. If the federal government lacked power to develop existing land, what was the point of further expansion? If the federal government *did* have the power to bestow largesse on selected regions, how else might it discriminate against states, for instance in matters regarding Indians and slaves?[58]

Happily for Monroe, these divisive questions were pushed in the background for a few years by some permanent diplomatic successes and transient economic ones. John Quincy Adams and Richard Rush provided the former. Believing America's continental destiny could not be thwarted except by the British, they hastened to liquidate possible causes of war between the two Anglo-Saxon empires. Lord Castlereagh, obsessed with European affairs, was a fit partner. The 1817 Rush-Bagot Accord demilitarized the long boundary between the United States and British North America by restricting armed vessels on the Great Lakes to a few revenue cutters. Of course, this was also a gross abnegation: a promise the United States would never again invade Canada. Fearing a treaty might run into trouble on that account, Monroe forgot his constitutional scruples. He simply asked the Senate if there were any objections to Rush's accord, thereby establishing a precedent for presidential "executive agreements" with foreign powers. The Convention of 1818 then fixed the U.S.-Canadian boundary at 49 degrees North Latitude from Lake of the Woods to the Continental Divide, opened the Oregon Territory to settlers from both countries, and granted American fishing rights in the Grand Banks. But Americans had scarcely begun to appreciate these boons before they were literally "swamped" by a furious course of events in the South. Andrew Jackson, who more than anyone wanted whatever he wanted *right now,* took it upon himself to invade Florida.[59]

Jackson, so gigantic, misunderstood by contemporaries, and variously construed by historians, is himself a battleground. For how one parses the meaning of Jackson goes far to reveal what one wants to believe about the American character. In his time he was "honored above all living men," his influence "towering", his career proof of America's "unparalleled success."[60] His spirit and will were "fierce, intractable"; his energy "that of a magnet, which defies gravity." His was a "passionate idiosyncrasy, a conviction that he was always right." He was "feral in his enmities, conservative in his politics, absorbed in the pursuit of wealth." He was calculating but not opportunistic, cruel yet romantic, rational though an "intemperate rebel."[61] Whence came the man's inner blaze that both illuminated and blinded all other men?

The proud and desperate Jackson clan that settled in western Carolina's Waxhaws Valley seemed to live under a curse. The father had not even finished a ramshackle homestead before he died in an accident. His pregnant widow gave his name, Andrew, to the boy she bore on the Ides of March, 1767, and went to live as a ward and servant on the farm of her sister's husband. A devout woman, she intended Andrew for the ministry, but despite or because of his mother's entreaties, he had no patience for church. Nor would he sit still for schooling, whether out of restlessness, resentment of authority, or his "big itch," a skin ailment that irritated an already tense personality. Andy picked fights, took offense, defended his turf, got into trouble. Finally, as if some *daemon* with the skill of a Dante were crafting an image in purgatory, the War of Independence devoured Andy's already truncated family. One brother died in battle; the other of smallpox after imprisonment. Two Jackson cousins were captured. Andy's mother, hoping to parole them, journeyed to Charleston where she, too, caught the fever and died. His grandfather's death in 1783 completed the rout. Andy inherited £400. The confused, angry orphan squandered it on a horse, watch, pistols, and gambling. He decided he was a loser. Then he decided he wasn't. He spent the rest of his life proving he *deserved* to live though his whole clan had died. He imagined his father a hero, his mother a saint, and himself destined to live out the Highland Scot motto "Conquer, or die."[62]

Hard drinking, skirt chasing, gambling, and feuding were Jackson's preoccupations in youth. Between times he noticed, as did James Wilson, Hugh Brackenridge, and other Scottish Americans, the ladder of success was the law.

Though rudely lettered, Jackson studied with an attorney who liked whiskey as much as he did, proved a ferocious advocate, and broke into politics and land speculation in William Blount's service. Appointed district attorney for the Cumberland region in 1788, he found a permanent home in Nashville. He also found a wife, the beautiful black-haired Rachel Donelson, whose scandalous divorce and remarriage to Jackson allied him with one of Tennessee's first families. He served briefly in Congress on two occasions until, in 1802, he found his true calling as commander of the militia. From then until 1812, like a true Scottish laird, he hankered for war against England, Spain, or Indians, fighting rivals at home in the meantime. Every conflict was personal to the wiry dynamo, as if enemies were placed on the earth for the sole purpose of testing his will.[63]

Following his famous victories of 1813–15 Jackson turned his southern military commands over to colonels and rode back to his wife, land, and slaves at the Hermitage. The ambitious Calhoun would have done well to leave him alone. Instead, the War secretary called Jackson back to center stage in December 1817 with orders to "punish" the Seminole Indians. Jackson knew, as Calhoun should have, the Creek renegades (which is what "Seminole" means) would never be pacified until U.S. forces occupied and policed their Florida sanctuary. He had no authority to do so, but claimed unofficial sanction via a coded letter (later destroyed) from a Tennessee congressman. Whatever the administration's intentions, Jackson's speed rendered them nugatory.

Florida thrust from the mainland like an elongated sore thumb, its small Spanish garrisons at St. Augustine, St. Marks, and Pensacola neither willing nor able to police the swampy dunes of the panhandle and peninsula. Hence Florida offered Indians, Africans, and pirates a haven from American power and law. As recently as 1816, no less than eight hundred escaped blacks occupied an old British fort on the Apalachicola River. They overreached that year by attacking a convoy and killing five American sailors. The ships returned fire, a lucky cannonball struck the fort's powder room, and 344 people perished in the explosion. Seminoles, however, carried what weapons survived into the woods for use against white Georgians who, they said, stole their land. The "eye for an eye" code of the frontier ensured a spiral of violence unless order was imposed on a province Spanish only in name.

In March 1818, Jackson rode down the Apalachicola with two thousand mounted militia, a few regulars, and some friendly Indians. Over eleven weeks he galloped five hundred miles to Fort Gadsden, east to St. Marks and the

Suwanee River, back to Gadsden, and west to Pensacola. He captured the Seminoles' strongholds, hanged their prophet and chief, took the Spaniards' surrenders, and for good measure tried and executed two British subjects for alleged gunrunning. When reports reached Washington City, Monroe and Calhoun turned red with embarrassment and Spanish minister Don Luís de Onís red with fury. American forces were withdrawn, but Florida stayed "won." In Congress, two resolutions to censure Old Hickory failed to get a majority. In the State Department, John Quincy Adams displayed Jacksonian haste and bravado by penning a lengthy diatribe against *Spanish* malfeasance and *British* incitement of "creeping and insidious war." In London, Castlereagh contented himself with a protest, having no desire to stick his neck out for decrepit Spain. In Madrid, the royal government acknowledged Jackson's *fait accompli* by instructing Onís to settle for the best terms he could get. Leaning over a map of North America that was really half-guesswork, Adams and Onís proceeded to partition the continent. By degrees, Adams withdrew U.S. claims to portions of Texas, while Onís dropped Spanish claims in the north. At length they agreed, in the Transcontinental Treaty of February 1819, that Spain would cede Florida, the United States would drop $5 million in damage claims, and both would accept a division of their empires along a line running north and west along the Sabine and Red Rivers, west along the Arkansas River to its source in the Rockies, due north to the 42nd parallel, then west to the Pacific Ocean (the future northern boundaries of Utah, Nevada, and California). Revolutions in Spain and Mexico delayed ratification, but by 1821 it was official: the United States was master of the Atlantic and Gulf coasts and potential master of the Pacific Northwest.[64]

While the army and State Department were busy expanding the country, the second U.S. Bank and Land Office were busy developing it. At least, after a fashion. Bank president William Jones, a bankrupt Philadelphia merchant whose private incompetence somehow qualified him for high public office, realized Jefferson's worst fears. It seems a junto of Bank directors conspired to elect Jones *expecting* corruption and speculation to flourish under his blinkered eyes. In 1817 Stephen Girard resigned from the board in protest. Limited to $6 million in outstanding loans, the Bank directors issued twice that amount. Expected to accumulate silver and gold by selling bank shares either for specie or government bonds, the Bank accepted state and local bank drafts of dubious worth. Obligated to function conservatively and under central direction, the Bank hastily opened eighteen branches, including six west of the Alleghenies, whose shenanigans sullied the faith and credit of the whole institution. So the second U.S. Bank achieved the opposite of the Treasury's intentions: many crooked tails wagged the dog. George Williams of Baltimore purchased 1,172 shares in the Bank under 1,172 different names, assigning himself power of attorney. Two Baltimore tellers issued themselves unsecured loans for $50,000 and $84,000. Their boss, James A. Buchanan, jobbed $4.5 million worth of bank stock on his own account.[65]

The central directors in Philadelphia were faithful in one matter only: paying fat dividends to drive up the price of their shares. To that end they eagerly subsidized a speculative frenzy in which the federal Land Office was an inadvertent accomplice. Gallatin's liberal interpretation of the 1800 Land Law allowed purchasers to acquire 160 or more acres for $1.64 apiece, putting just 25 percent down and paying the rest over four years. He also opened fourteen new land offices in the Ohio Valley and Southwest before awaiting full surveys. After 1815, Treasury Secretary Crawford founded more land office "hives" for swarming settlers and speculators from Illinois to Alabama. To avoid competitive auctions speculators naturally rigged every deal in advance, offering no more than the minimum price even for choice property. Having acquired title to vast tracts on credit, brokers then sold land by prior arrangement to planters and farmers. The former made immediate profits while the latter still got good land at low prices. In Illinois pioneers even formed up to bully anyone so anti-social as to bid up the price of acreage. Jared Marshall thought the frontier to blame for the failure of yeomen to display Jeffersonian virtue: "Landed speculation, Survey jobbing, Pettyfogging, Fakery, Electioneering for public places, & everything except labour & industry are the means in operation." But *all* America was a frontier inviting "get rich quick" schemes as the mischief in eastern banks richly proved. Nor were land agents above playing the game. They bought choice parcels themselves or took kickbacks for sharing intelligence. To be sure, a land agent's life in frontier exile was rough, hectic, and tense. He might confront riots and threats. His paperwork backed up for months or years. But his was a lucrative, powerful post, to which only the well-connected won appointment.[66]

Even "dirt cheap," millions of acres of government land would not have been sold if credit were not widely available. State-chartered banks met the demand whether they had any assets or not. The U.S. Bank not only encouraged this by accepting their dubious paper, its branch managers joined the party. The results were a land bubble and grossly imbalanced books from the littlest farmhouse in Indiana to the marbled hall of the Bank's Philadelphia headquarters. By summer 1818 the Bank's liabilities surpassed $22 million against hard money reserves of just $2.3 million. It papered over the gap with local notes backed mostly by mortgages issued to people who themselves had no cash. In 1818 the bubble trembled. The U.S. Treasury routinely requested $2 million only to learn the Bank could not raise it. In 1819 the bubble burst. Congress investigated; the Baltimore frauds were exposed; William Jones resigned. His replacement, South Carolinian Langdon Cheves, immediately suspended dividends, vetoed new loans, and husbanded specie. He then hurled the nation into its first "business cycle" recession by calling on state banks to redeem their notes in hard currency. State banks foreclosed on the public and everyone went broke together. "The Bank was saved and the people were ruined," said an observer. But nobody blamed the Monroe administration or Congress for this Panic of 1819. Instead, they blamed the U.S. Bank during the very years Cheves and his 1823 successor Nicholas Biddle made it a genuine central bank protecting the currency and financial structure. A national bank still seemed "royalist" to Republicans, above all strapped westerners starting to look to Jackson for succor.[67]

An old Federalist wielding a gavel remembered why Hamilton had wanted a bank in the first place: to ensure the nation's growth was orderly and centripetal, not spasmodic and centrifugal. In January 1819, even as Adams drafted blue-prints for a nation spanning the continent, John Marshall handed down blue-prints for an economy spanning the nation. Sadly, law and history texts have turned Marshall into the stoniest of the Founding Fathers. He was the great chief justice who presided for thirty-five years and wrote more than five hundred opinions himself. He was father of the judicial branch who made the Supreme Court a respected arbiter among the other branches and levels of government. He was the oracle whose arguments seem somehow more real than the mind that made them. The truth is, no statue or sibyl interpreted the Constitution for the generations, but a thinking, drinking, laughing, slovenly country lawyer.

Marshall was the eldest of fifteen children sired by a Piedmont and Blue Ridge planter. Born in 1755, he got just a smattering of formal education before enlisting in the Continental Army in 1776. After three years' service that included the Valley Forge winter, Marshall went home to hear a few lectures from legal scholar George Wythe. That was enough to earn him a license and election to the House of Burgesses. In 1783 he wed sweet Mary Ambler, whom he called Polly. They raised up six children, but Polly was evidently thrown into lifelong depression by her loss of four others to miscarriage and infant death. Jefferson coldly dismissed her as mad, but Marshall remained doting and faithful to Polly for forty-eight years. A staunch Federalist like so many veterans, Marshall battled Patrick Henry over ratification of the Constitution. Despite Washington's pleas he resisted high office until finally agreeing to serve on President Adams' commission to Paris (the XYZ Affair). He then won election to Congress, where he *opposed* the Alien and Sedition Acts. Admiring Marshall's devotion to principle, raw intelligence, and humility, Adams named him secretary of State, then chief justice in 1801.

What sort of man was he? Besides being a loving husband and father, Marshall played as hard as he worked. His wine cellar was open to all; when not entertaining at home he could be found tippling and gaming at Richmond's Tavern, Jockey, and Quoit clubs. When court was in session he respectfully wore breeches and silk stockings, but otherwise rousted about in a farmer's trousers and socks. One anecdote tells of an out-of-town gentleman asking a rudely dressed fellow to deliver a chicken, never suspecting the favor was done by Mr. Chief Justice. Another tells of his habitually popping a bottle of wine for the justices whenever they met on rainy days. When Joseph Story once objected that the sky was blue, Marshall rendered his judgment: "Such is the broad extent of our jurisdiction that by the doctrine of chances it must be raining somewhere." A third tells of Marshall as septuagenarian getting down on his knees to adjudicate quoit tosses. Most telling, he was magnanimous. When pressed, Marshall even had generous things to say about Jefferson, though the latter never reciprocated.[68]

Marshall's powers of persuasion were legendary. New appointees on the court invariably came around to his way of thinking, vexing Republican presidents and members of Congress. In their view, the Marshall Court was dangerously "discretionary" and "consolidationist" insofar as it arrogated to itself power to interpret the Constitution and overrule state legislatures and courts. But Marshall's purpose was to defend a Constitution whose *raison d'être* was national unity. He remembered what the ebullient post-1815 generation tended to forget: republics had a way of degenerating and dying. How might law be interpreted, even adjusted, to enhance the American republic's chances of survival? Invoking memory and the Framers' original intent, the Marshall Court adopted four strategies. First, the justices pored over the Constitution like theologians or literary critics, teasing from words such as "contract" and "commerce" legal principles of universal and timeless validity. Second, the Court rendered decisions in non-Constitutional cases with an eye to their implications for Constitutional ones. That way new social or economic disputes might be adjudicated so as to reinforce first principles. Third, Marshall established prerogatives and procedures the Supreme Court has employed ever since, including secret, collective deliberations, the quest for consensus, and opinions expressed in non-partisan language.[69] Fourth, Marshall drew on eighteenth-century precedents to establish the novel American doctrine of judicial review. Where overlapping legislative jurisdictions resulted in contradictory laws, whether among the thirteen colonies or between the states and the federal government, only the courts could decide which laws violated the Common Law and/or Constitution.[70] In all things the Marshall Court's calling was to resist demagoguery, to tame the wild horses of social change with bridles of principle. In the early nineteenth century the wild horses were state governments, hence Marshall lectured Americans (fellow southerners most of all) that their federal polity was a compact of the *people*, not the states.

In practice that meant the states lacked power to nullify laws or restrict the federal government's exercise of its lawful powers. It also meant states had no power to override or restrict citizens' exercise of their lawful rights. For if states *did* have such powers then each state or region would choose, as if from a smorgasbord, which laws to obey, quickly dissolving the Union. Likewise, if states *did* have such powers they would adopt jealous mercantilist policies, as under the Articles of Confederation, quickly dissolving the Union. Marshall doubtless meditated on those dangers for years, but he could not confront them until the right litigation popped up. In 1818 a perfect case arrived when Maryland levied a stamp tax on U.S. Bank notes and a Baltimore clerk ignored it. Did Marshall himself encourage the plaintiff to challenge the state just to get the issue before the Supreme Court? He surely thought about the case in advance because he delivered a lengthy, closely reasoned opinion just a week after closing arguments in March 1819. The Bank, declared the Court in *McCulloch versus Maryland*, was created by the federal government in the proper discharge of its duties. The federal government, in turn, "is emphatically, and truly, a government of the people." Hence, no state had power to tax the Bank for "the power to tax involves the power to destroy." Marshall adumbrated Hamilton's defense of the "necessary and proper" clause of the Constitution, declaring it a principle "that the constitution and the laws made in pursuance thereof are supreme: that they control the constitution and laws of the several states, and cannot be controlled by them." Maryland's law was unconstitutional.[71]

Next, Marshall ruled on states' rights with regard to private contracts, corporations, and individuals. New Hampshire's legislature was the culprit this time. Its Republican majority hated the fact Dartmouth College, chartered in 1769 by George III, was governed by a Federalist board of trustees. It wanted to purge the board in the name of political correctness. Daniel Webster cemented his reputation as a stemwinder in tearful defense of the college: "Sir, you may destroy this little Institution; it is weak; it is in your hands. . . . But if you do so, you must carry through your work! You must extinguish, one after another, all those great lights of science which, for more than a century, have thrown their radiance over our land! It is, Sir, as I have said, a small College. And yet, *there are those who love it.*" Marshall, himself a former attorney for the College of William and Mary, again prepared his opinion well in advance. In *Dartmouth versus Woodward* the Court found the college charter to be a legal contract immune from political tampering. At a blow, the Marshall Court sheltered private corporations and contracts nationwide. That, plus its decisions limiting state power to impair contracts through debtor relief (*Sturges versus Crowninshield,* 1819) and striking down steamboat monopolies (*Gibbons versus Ogden,* 1824), completed the legal foundation for a national marketplace.[72]

Was Marshall a laissez-faire visionary eager to make America the industrial capitalist giant it became by the 1890s? On the contrary, his America was the one imagined by Federalists in the 1790s. Suffice it to say he was attacked by states' rights Republicans for being too *backward*-looking, too eager to buck the "will of the people." Indeed he was. After 1815, the people were in full forward flight like panic buyers on Wall Street. They demanded immediate destruction of all barriers real or imagined to their accumulation of power and wealth. Marshall reminded them theirs was a nation of laws, property, and reciprocal obligations. He meant to dampen passion in the name of the Union and the security of each citizen's private pursuit of happiness. The last Master Builder, he defended the edifice the Federalists raised with sturdy ramparts of logic.

## The Twenty-second State: Alabama, 1819

The Georgia senators who drew a vertical line through the Mississippi Territory first considered a horizontal line. That would have created two more "Tennessees" stretching all the way to the Mississippi River. Their reasoning was that the first settlements in what became Alabama could not be further apart or more different. But since they instead split the territory into eastern and western halves they condemned Alabama to a sectional feud that survives to this day.

Spaniards were first to the Gulf Coast, planting Fort San Esteban de Tombecbé (hence Tombigbee River) and rendering the local tribe's name Mauvila (hence Mobile). In 1699 Frenchmen paddled up the other great river, naming it after Indian "thicket-clearers" called Alibamons (hence Alabama). In 1763 Mobile fell to the British. When the thirteen colonies rebelled, it served as a haven for southern Tories until 1779, when Gálvez recovered it for Spain. Then in 1803 Jefferson claimed that Mobile lay within the Louisiana Purchase, justifying an American filibuster and annexation in 1810. The following year a land office opened at the extreme *northern* end of the territory. There, on the Tennessee River's "big bend" to the south, Huntsville sprang up. During the War of 1812, soldiers and pioneers hacked out a road from Huntsville to the Tombigbee, while Jackson's victory at Horseshoe Bend in March 1814 broke the Red Sticks' resistance. The Treaty of Fort Jackson in August turned half the future state over to whites.

"Alabama Feaver rages here with great violence," wrote a North Carolinian, "and has carried off vast numbers of our citizens." Tennesseeans and Georgians also arrived to swell Alabama's population to 128,000 in just five years. Men and women on horseback, ox-drawn wagons, or their own two feet cursed the broken hills and rattlesnakes on Bear Meat Cabin Road, Three Notch Road, or the Federal Road in from Georgia. Others came by sea to Mobile and poled up the rivers. By and large they were yeomen with at most one or two slaves. They survived on corn cakes, cornpone, cornbread, corn fritters, corn grits, and wild game, and wore skins or clothing home spun from cotton or flax. Their titles to land were tenuous; whatever law and order they knew were made by their own muskets. Yet a mere forty-eight months after Alabama Fever began, the pioneers found themselves citizens of a new state run by an altogether different cast of characters.[73]

These were lands once claimed by Georgia under its colonial charter, and Georgia's "Broad River Men," including Senator Charles Tait and his son James, Senator William W. Bibb and his brother Thomas, John William Walker, and Leroy Pope, meant to make it their own. They pushed a bill through Congress creating the Alabama Territory. They named the land office agents. They bought up the best land around Huntsville. They governed through William Bibb. When he called for a territorial assembly, Huntsville men led by Walker controlled it. In 1818 Walker judged Alabama ready for statehood. Tait won approval from Congress, and President Monroe himself honored Huntsville with a visit in June 1819. The following month the town hosted the state convention, and by December Alabama was a state. Who says politicians can't get anything done?

The little people and rival land speculators knew how to organize, too. In 1816-17 promoters founded Selma, Montgomery (after a general who died at Horseshoe Bend), and Marion (after the Swamp Fox) in the Black Belt of south-central Alabama. Settlers planted cotton in its rich limestone and marl soil and shipped it down the rivers to Mobile. They had no intention of bowing toward Huntsville. Hardscrabble farmers in the Cumberland plateau and tough Wiregrass region in the southeast likewise resisted a clique they scorned as the Georgia Faction or Royal Party. So did Mobile's proud residents. Finally, smallholders in Huntsville's own Madison County, mostly Tennesseeans, resented the Georgians' money, slave gangs, and friends in high places. As early as January 1818, the touring chronicler Anne Newport Royall reported 260 brick houses in Huntsville, some three stories tall, of better construction than Philadelphia's or Baltimore's. Such wealth was sudden, amazing, enviable. Accordingly, delegates at the state convention rebelled against the constitution drafted by the elite. Southern counties demanded one of the state's two U.S. senators as well as the capital (it was placed at Cahaba just south of Selma). Northern counties demanded the legislature be apportioned according to white population with no "two-thirds" provision favoring slaveholders. All opposing factions called for a weak governor elected directly by universal white male suffrage, a powerful legislature that appointed judges, and a bill of rights. The constitution even required suitable food and clothing for slaves, while criminalizing their maiming or killing.

The constitution also restricted private banks. When in fact Pope's Planters and Merchants Bank failed in 1820, a new rival to the Royal Party placed an indelible stamp on Alabama. Israel Pickens was a former North Carolina congressman put in charge of the land office at St. Stephens near Mobile. Already wealthy, he founded the Tombeckbe Bank and managed it so well it did not suspend payments during the Panic of 1819. He also bought two cotton plantations and moved to the Black Belt. But Pickens *posed* as the champion of the little man, promising cheap credit at low risk, and twice defeated the Georgians' candidate for governor. While in office Pickens plundered land set aside for a state college in order to fund a state bank, reapportioned the legislature, and relocated the capital in Tuscaloosa (it moved to Montgomery in 1847). Pickens died young in 1827, but his hand-picked successor for governor ran twice unopposed, while a new generation of lawyer-politicians made Alabama a bastion of populism and states' rights. Clement C. Clay, his son C. C., Jr., John McKinley, and the 350-pound Dixon Hall Lewis opposed the U.S. Bank branch at Mobile, opposed federal spending for internal improvements, and opposed federal Indian policies as unconscionable meddling.[74]

Few today affect sympathy with Alabama opinions. But in 1832 the state got an early taste of what the federal government might cook up. Recent treaties offered Choctaw and Creek families the choice of removing themselves to the west or assimilating on federal homesteads. The Indians were promised a grace period pending their harvest of crops and the completion of land surveys. The Alabama legislature would have none of that. It pronounced eminent domain over lands reserved for Indians in the state's southeastern corner and carved out new counties. Farmers and speculators took that as their cue either to push the Creeks out or else "purchase" large tracts with a few coins and bottles of liquor. So much violence ensued even federal soldiers could not maintain order. Their patience exhausted, the bluecoats burned down a squatters' town in Barbour County and moved to evict state commissioner Hardeman Owens in Russell County. Owens was by all accounts a murderous bully; Indians said his house was an arsenal. When soldiers came to beat down the door Owens lit a fuse and blew up the place as he fled out the back. He was soon cornered and shot in the woods. An Alabama grand jury, far from bowing to *force majeure,* indicted the U.S. soldiers for murder, only to have the process-server turned away at gunpoint. Clement Clay and the state's congressmen warned of "incalculable distress and injury" should federal impositions continue. An icon of patriotism, Francis Scott Key, was dispatched as mediator and the crisis subsided. But white Alabamans never forgot how the U.S. Army burned and killed on behalf of mere Indians. They wondered whether it might do the same someday for Negroes.[75]

Human beings get along with themselves and each other by conveniently ducking truth. Truth hurts. It may even kill by spoiling the conspiracies of silence people forge to transcend irreconcilable differences. American politicians made such a conspiracy in the matter of slavery. Someday it was supposed to wither away. Someday all blacks would be magically wafted to Africa. Someday the Lord would descend with angelic hosts and lions lie down with lambs. In the meantime, to protest aloud the expansion of slavery was taboo. To revisit the compromises made at the Constitutional Convention was to assault the civic religion and possibly risk the Union.[76] In the watershed month of February 1819, the taboo was broken, whereupon awful truths leaped from mouths like the plagues of Pandora.

The heretic was James Tallmadge, Jr., a peripatetic congressman from Poughkeepsie, New York. An ally of De Witt Clinton, he later ran with Van Buren's Bucktails, became lieutenant governor, and helped to found New York University. But in 1819, for reasons still obscure, Tallmadge decided to "redeem our beloved country from Disgrace & Danger" by halting the spread of slavery. The venue was the semi-circular Hall of Representatives refurbished after the fire of 1814 with marble columns, blood-red drapery, and brass spittoons. The issue was an enabling act inviting the Missouri Territory to petition for statehood. Settled mostly by southerners, Missouri already contained ten thousand enslaved blacks. To try to roll back slavery there would be to assault popular sovereignty and property rights. Yet Tallmadge moved an amendment to prohibit new transportation of slaves into Missouri and to grant freedom at age twenty-five to people born into servitude there. Fellow Yorker John Taylor seconded the motion, warning if slavery were permitted in Missouri "its baleful consequences would surely conquer the West." Did not southerners themselves speak of slavery as an "original sin" of which they must someday repent? Now was the moment of truth; Missouri the place chosen by destiny.[77]

Admission of new states was routine. Everyone granted Congress' power to regulate territories and stipulate conditions for statehood. But southerners were shocked by the Tallmadge amendment, then terrified when it passed on a sectional vote by 79 to 67. Georgia's Thomas W. Cobb accused Tallmadge of kindling a fire only "seas of blood" could extinguish. Tallmadge replied if blood sacrifice was required he would contribute his mite. Southerners argued the diffusion of slaves into the West would ameliorate their condition and hasten the institution's demise. Tallmadge retorted some fourteen thousand slaves were illegally smuggled into the United States in the past year alone just to supply new western plantations. Look outside, he cried: "A slave driver, a trafficker in human flesh, as if sent by Providence, has passed the door of your Capitol, on his way to the West, driving before him about fifteen of these wretched victims." The bill for Missouri statehood with the restrictive amendment passed the House 87 to 76; just ten northerners voted against it, not one southerner for it. The Senate, divided equally between slave states and free, was another matter. Thanks to northern defections Tallmadge's "no new slaves" clause was struck 22 to 16; the "freedom at 25" clause 31 to 7. Twice the House refused to reconsider, placing Missouri statehood in limbo.[78]

When Congress reconvened in December Henry Clay shuddered to hear senators mutter of sparks, explosions, prairie fires, the "hottest paroxysm," disunion, civil war. Northerners spied plots to extend slavery everywhere. Southerners spied abolitionist plots. Most congressmen danced around these fears by arguing the constitutionality of this or that bill, Missouri's demographics and economics, the original intent of the Framers. But restrictionists escalated debate with moral condemnations of slavery that southern gentlemen regarded as insults to their honor and manhood, not to say threats to property and states' rights. Then Senator Jonathan Roberts of Pennsylvania fired the ultimate weapon. Without restrictions on slavery, he cried, Missouri would enter the union "with her features marred as if the *finger of Lucifer* had been drawn across them!" That was too much for Nathaniel Macon of North Carolina. He bade northern men accompany him home to observe "the glad faces and the hearty shaking of hands" when a master returned to his beloved servants. No northern employer ever engaged his "hirelings" in the easy, human conversation that occurred daily between whites and blacks in the South. But Macon was tame compared to South Carolinian William Smith. On January

26, 1820, he trumpeted slavery as a positive good mandated by the God of Abraham, Isaac, and Jacob, Moses, Jesus, and the Apostles. "Christ came to fulfill the law not to destroy it," Smith intoned. "Mr. President, the Scriptures teach us that slavery was universally practiced among the holy fathers."[79]

Truth: Slavery was not fading away; it was *spreading*. Truth: Northerners had little love for their own white, much less black, lower classes, but were prepared to *smash the Union* rather than see slavery in the West. Truth: Southerners mouthed regrets over slavery, but in their hearts believed it a God-given right worth a *fight* to preserve.

Where was President Monroe during all this? Writing anguished letters, fretting some northerner might run against him on an anti-slavery ticket, and hinting he would veto any Missouri bill containing restrictions on slavery. He was, in other words, at a loss.[80] Happily for the Union, Speaker Clay knew how to get colleagues to holster their lethal truths. He professed to hate slavery. He even gave the keynote address at the founding of the American Colonization Society and later served as its president. To be sure, he owned slaves on his Ashland estate—they were better off under his care, he said, and anyway he could not compete in Kentucky without them. But he believed slavery doomed by Malthusian law. America's white population was bound to grow geometrically, driving down wages until simple balance-sheet calculations impelled southerners to transport their blacks and hire free labor. That was fantasy, but Clay's vision of greatness was not. The Freemason and promoter of the American System for national growth shuddered at the thought sectional feuds might cheat the United States (and himself) of glorious destinies. So Clay pleaded with eloquence for moderation, buttonholed waverers from Ohio Valley free states, and hammered out deals.[81]

What made compromise possible was the lucky chance that Maine also petitioned for statehood in 1819. Admitting Maine and Missouri in tandem would preserve equality in the Senate and perhaps mollify pro- and anti-slave members alike. Clay also noticed how northern congressmen accepted slavery in the Arkansas Territory even as they resisted it in Missouri. That suggested the possibility of a geographical compromise banning slavery in most, but not all, of the trans-Mississippi frontier. Illinois Senator Jesse B. Thomas put it in writing: admit Missouri with slavery, but otherwise ban slavery north of 36 degrees 30 minutes. The Senate bought this package, but the House majority still resisted. So Clay used his power as speaker to appoint pliable members to a House-Senate conference, then he called for *separate* votes on the three parts of

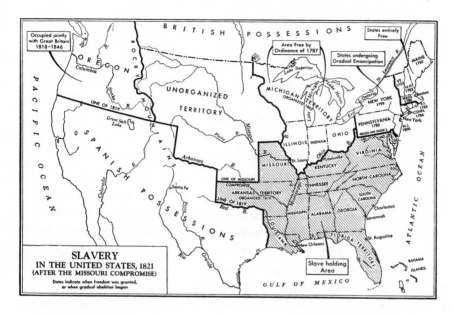

the deal. That prevented southern "ultras" angry over the Thomas amendment from joining with northern restrictionists to defeat the package. Maine statehood breezed through. Missouri statehood with slavery squeaked through on the votes or abstentions of nineteen northern "dough faces." The Thomas amendment passed 134 to 42. On the evening of March 2, 1820, Clay secretly ratified the votes and rushed them to the Senate to pre-empt motions to reconsider. Monroe, much relieved, signed off.[82]

The Missouri Compromise was not much of one. All southerners relinquished was the right to extend slavery into lands no one thought arable anyway. The losers in tangible terms were northern restrictionists. The only real "compromisers" were the nineteen "dough faces." The other 102 northern members voted against the Missouri bill while southern members voted 98 to 0 in favor! The "Compromise" nevertheless altered American politics in two fateful ways. Having tasted northern bile over extension of slavery southern leaders found it almost impossible to countenance any enhancement of federal power lest in the future it be trained against them. Having heard slavery condemned as evil southern leaders felt compelled to portray it as a genuine boon while damning northern "wage slavery" as evil.[83]

Jefferson called the affair a fire bell in the night, its settlement just a reprieve. John Quincy Adams wondered if the *North* ought to have seceded in

1820, but welcomed the fact that sectional strife was put back to sleep. Which was it? Did Clay save the Union or condemn it to civil war? He did neither. The events of 1820 made inevitable none of the decisions or flights from decision made by Americans later. It can be said, however, Clay purchased valuable time during which the North industrialized and the Middle West matured. That meant, should civil war come, the North was far more likely to win.

## The Twenty-third State: Maine, 1820

A jagged coastline facing a cold, foamy ocean; rugged mountains, dense forests, and glaciated valleys ruled by moose and bear; a climate chilly and damp by the sea and icily Canadian in the interior; a very short growing season and an extractive economy: in all these ways Maine was an Atlantic Alaska. Beginning in 1607, Sir Ferdinando Gorges tried without success to plant paying colonies on the coast he called Maine (meaning great, as in Spanish Main). In 1677 Gorges' heirs sold out their claim to Massachusetts Bay Colony, beginning Maine's 143 years as a sub-colony ruled from Boston. Why is no mystery. The Maine District was sparsely peopled, legally subject, and dependent on outside protection from the French and Abenaki Indians. Then, after the Battle of Québec made all secure, investors Thomas Hancock, William Bowdoin, and James Pitts won generous grants of Maine land. Being commercial property it was also lightly taxed, whereas their tenants, no matter how poor, were subject to poll taxes. Maine farmers hated their absentee landlords, but had no way to resist, while Maine's merchants and lawyers were allies of Boston interests and rivals of each other.[84]

After American independence Maine townships convened to gripe about taxes, underrepresentation, and price controls on their timber. But their separatist sentiment ebbed as trade recovered. Then Shays' Rebellion frightened the port towns and its repression the farmers. Then the Constitutional movement distracted attention. So only by 1791 did Maine begin to display the territorial pattern of elite juntos vying for leadership of the statehood movement while existing authorities resisted and rural settlers hoped someday the meek would inherit. The movement began when Maine Federalists caucused to discuss separation and their Massachusetts colleagues pooh-poohed them. Daniel Davis, a young Portland lawyer with a grudge (he had been denied admission to Harvard), wrote a fifty-seven-page tract explaining why the union of Maine with Massachusetts was "thwarting the designs of nature." Statehood would put government "in the midst of the people," improve the "melancholy state of religion and learning," and hasten development. But a referendum in 1792 proved skeptics right. Only 4,598 people bothered to vote in a district nearing 100,000, and they split 50–50. A 1797 referendum was also embarrassing. Evidently, Maine's farmers and loggers did not care whether cocked hats in Boston or Portland reigned over them. They made clear what they did care about when a self-styled tribe of white "Indians" went on the warpath.[85]

The proximate cause was the Kennebec proprietors' determination to collect rents, fees, and high prices from tens of thousands of tenants wedged into Maine's few arable valleys. War hero Henry Knox was one: an affable man, but a high-toned Federalist behaving in the fashion of a Lord Proprietor. Philadelphian William Bingham owned properties in Maine half the size of lower Massachusetts. Charles Vaughan styled himself a Unitarian friend of mankind, but his family fortune rested on Jamaican sugar and slaves; he meant to profit from Maine as well. Congregational church pillar Josiah Little of Massachusetts was struck dumb by a stroke, but the octogenarian miser still badgered tenants and squatters. Meanwhile, Maine farmers lived on the edge of famine. A summer a bit wetter than normal ruined the hay; a winter a bit colder killed livestock. Fat flies and mosquitoes tortured the plowman. Rocky ground resisted the plow. Selectmen filed pathetic petitions describing weeks without bread, naked children, frigid huts. The Duc de la Rochefoucauld attested "the condition of human life in that place is exceedingly wretched." Nor did Maine farmers have much incentive to change their primitive methods so long as they were liable to eviction.[86]

In the year of Jefferson the farmers struck back. When Knox sent a team of surveyors to divide up the Sheepscot district, men in painted faces and Indian garb came running suddenly out of the trees. Their muskets wounded three surveyors and forced all to flee. In 1800, episodic resistance became epidemic and violent. The rebels called themselves Liberty Men as if they were fighting the Revolution all over again. They took a page from the Boston Tea Party by donning Indian disguises, a page from Ethan Allen by terrorizing the agents of landlords, and yet another from Whiskey Rebel "Tom the Tinker" by posting obscene threats against all who *failed* to resist the proprietors. That they also held their cause to be holy is suggested by the religious upheaval in Kennebec County. While Congregational churches increased from 12 to 30 between 1790 and 1820, Baptist and Methodist ones grew from 14 to 175. "For religion and freedom, of old 'twas decided, springs both from one root, and can't be divided": the Liberty Man who wrote that named proprietors servants of Satan.[87]

The farmers deserted the Federalist party along with the Puritan faith. *Eastern Argus,* the first Jeffersonian newspaper, appeared in Portland in 1803. Two years later a native of Maine became Massachusetts' first Republican governor. Surely now the state would legislate tax and debtor relief. Instead, Maine's Republican junto revived the statehood movement they had opposed so long as Federalists led it. William King, half brother to Rufus King, was the kingpin. A school dropout, he went into the West Indies trade, owned the first Maine vessel to ship New Orleans cotton to Liverpool, and tried banking, insurance, and real estate. When he failed to win Federalist backing for a minor office he jumped to the Republican party ostensibly out of sympathy for the poor. He in fact meant to ride Maine statehood to power. King badly misjudged. Maine voted Republican by a wide margin, but *rejected* separation 3,370 to 9,404! Perhaps back-country farmers reckoned only the Massachusetts government could alter the terms of Massachusetts land grants. As for the Republican ascendancy, all that gave them was the hated embargo that ruined maritime trade. Maine's proprietors, themselves strapped for cash, squeezed tenants harder, goading the white Indians into another rampage. Finally, King clued in. He persuaded General Court to pass a Betterment Act obliging owners to sell tenants land at the low, unimproved price or else pay them full value for improvements they made. That splintered the Liberty Men. The poorest farmers still could not afford to purchase their land, but middling ones could, or else received enough cash to emigrate to Ohio.[88]

The social reform and 1812 war finally focused attention on Maine's status. The British imposed martial law on the coast northeast of Penobscot while Massachusetts did nothing except return Federalists to power and sponsor the Hartford Convention. King's junto demanded another referendum in May 1816 and this time won 60 percent of the vote. However, less than half the eligible voters turned out so the result was invalid. Bay State Federalists were vexed: by now they *wanted* Maine to secede since its population, now 250,000, was heavily Republican. So they permitted yet another vote in 1816, asking only a 50 percent turnout and a 5 to 4 vote in favor. The Down Easters—curmudgeonly, confused, and conflicted—came up 2½ percentage points short. At that point William Pitt Preble said, "Let's cheat." A former mathematics tutor at Harvard, he totted votes from each town on a "winner take all" basis and nudged the result over the 5 to 4 benchmark. General Court would have none of it. Again, King belatedly clued in. Since some opponents of statehood feared separation would disadvantage Maine's shipping, he lobbied Congress for a new "coasting trade" law assuring all Atlantic states equal treatment. Since other opponents of statehood feared a Republican monopoly of offices, he lied about granting Federalists a proportional share. Lastly, King inundated the district with cheery propaganda. In 1819 separation won handily.[89]

The Republican junto of lawyers and merchants dominated the state constitutional convention, but gave farmers a solid Jeffersonian document. It began with a bill of rights, stipulated almost universal male suffrage, waived religious or property qualifications, and enjoined every town to support free public schools. Mindful of the Supreme Court decision upholding the trustees of Dartmouth, Maine Republicans granted their legislature power to regulate Bowdoin College (that is, purge it of Federalists). They even let voters approve the constitution, a courtesy few other territorial bosses extended. Maine petitioned Congress for statehood, only to suffer more scares and delay in the run-up to the Missouri Compromise. Rather than sanction extension of slavery, all seven Massachusetts congressmen hailing from Maine chose "Martyrdom in the cause of liberty" and voted nay! But thanks to Clay's compromise Maine was not martyred; it emerged at last as a sovereign state in March 1820.[90]

"Acutely self-conscious" is the way one historian has characterized the people of Maine. Earnest to a fault might be another. Thinking to spur development Governor King proposed the state buy timberland tracts to which Massachusetts retained title and use tax incentives to stimulate industry. The legislature, suspecting special interests at work, refused, causing King to resign in disgust. Maine voters also opposed federal internal improvements, relying on their own rugged selves to build lumber, granite, fishing, and ice cutting industries.[91] Down East folk were less reticent when it came to telling outsiders how to live. The Maine Peace Society decried ambition, greed, and vengeance. The Maine Temperance Union taught bluenoses how to lobby for prohibition. Elizabeth Oakes Smith was one of America's first female orators (and the first woman to climb Mount Katahdin), while Bangor boasted a female academy as early as 1816. Reformers founded Colby and Bates Colleges. Bowdoin graduated such cultural critics as Nathaniel Hawthorne and Henry Wadsworth Longfellow. The Maine Anti-Slavery Society was a model of political activism. But when abolitionism helped spark civil war, Maine's pacifists faced a hard choice. In 1862 one gentle Bowdoin professor applied for a foreign sabbatical to escape. Then Joshua L. Chamberlain changed his mind, joined the 20th Maine Regiment, and turned the tide at Gettysburg.

"In our whole system, national and State, we have shunned all the defects which unceasingly preyed on the vitals and destroyed the ancient Republics." So said Monroe at his second inaugural in March 1821. Not once in his long speech did he allude to the Missouri Compromise. He hoped, and might have believed, the matter of slavery settled. No abolitionist rose to challenge his re-election in 1820. The defunct Federalists nominated no one at all. The campaign was a study in apathy. The electoral college chose Monroe 231 to 1, the rogue being a New Hampshire man who thought John Quincy Adams more qualified. Yet, even as Monroe prepared his address Congress provided ample proof his optimism was misplaced. Northerners objected to a clause in the proposed Missouri constitution banning the entry of free blacks and mulattoes. That was in technical violation of the Constitution's reciprocity clause ("The Citizens of each State shall be entitled to Privileges and Immunities of Citizens in the Several States"). Again the two camps argued states' rights. Again southerners reminded Yankees of their own discriminatory laws. Again, no one dared ask whether Negroes were capable of being free, equal citizens. Instead, the Great Pacificator Clay marshaled a majority in favor of obfuscation. Missouri statehood was approved on condition its legislature solemnly declare it would never deny citizens of other states their Constitutional rights. In effect, Missourians were told they might have their race code so long as they didn't enforce it. They responded in kind by mouthing assent while denying Congress' right to request it.[92]

Monroe's point about ancient republics was a half-truth. The American federal system, with its checks and balances and Bill of Rights, did cure some of the defects of Athens and Rome. But in their day slavery and paganism were universal. The United States, by contrast, was only half-slave and decidedly Christian. These "defects" became shockingly evident soon after the Missouri dispute. Panicky white authorities in Charleston, South Carolina, claimed a diabolical conspiracy had been hatched to arm thousands of slaves, burn down the city, and kill all its white people. City officials led by intendant (mayor) James Hamilton, Jr., subjected some 130 blacks to secret interrogations throughout the sweltering summer of 1822. On the strength of the evidence the tribunal condemned thirty-five men to the gallows and forty more to exile. The alleged ringleader, fifty-five-year-old Denmark Vesey, was a free black carpenter of long residency. More to the point he was a literate, well-to-do pillar of the local African Methodist church with a special interest in the story of Exodus. It all added up, or was made to add up in the court's *Official Report*, as follows: Vesey, believing the Lord meant to deliver his people from bondage and no doubt taking heart from the abolitionist sentiment expressed in the Congress, conspired to lead a slave insurrection. It was smoked out just before the June 1822 date he had fixed.

Abolitionists and northern historians wanted to believe it was true. As late as 1999 three new books appeared more or less depicting Vesey a latter-day Spartacus.[93] An obviously intelligent man, born to slavery in the Danish West Indies and owned by a Captain Vesey, he purchased his freedom after winning a lottery and set up shop in Charleston. But like his fellow carpenter Jesus of Nazareth, Vesey's life is then a great blank until he emerges decades later as a slain savior. However, it struck one reviewer as fishy that all the data concerning the Vesey conspiracy emerged from secret hearings conducted by white authorities anxious to root out any blacks with seditious ideas; that witnesses faced death if they did not collaborate; that three-fourths of the damning evidence came from just three squealers; that much of the testimony was contradictory; that no proper trials with counsel or cross-examination were held; that Vesey himself worked quietly at his bench until—after three weeks of mounting hysteria—he was arrested. That hardly seemed credible behavior for a bloodthirsty rebel whose plot had aborted. It seemed more likely the only conspiracy afoot was that of white planters eager to suppress Charleston's free black community and church, purge any slaves spreading dangerous rumors, and (not incidentally) propel the career of James Hamilton, Jr., who won election to Congress and eventually became the state governor.[94]

Whether or not Vesey conspired to launch a revolt, the panic resulting in the greatest mass executions in American history magnified southern white fears of educated blacks, abolitionist agitation, and not least Christian millennialism. So much for President Monroe's cheerful prognosis. More to the point was South Carolina essayist Edwin C. Holland, whose "refutation of the calumnies" made against slavery urged southerners never to forget "that our NEGROES are truely the *Jacobins* of the country; that they are the *anarchists* and the *domestic enemy; the common enemy of civilized society,* and the barbarians who would, IF THEY COULD, become the DESTROYERS *of our race.*"[95]

## The Twenty-fourth State: Missouri 1821

*Pekitanoui* was the real Indian word for the "Big Muddy" river that flushed silt from as far away as Montana. But the one that stuck was Père Marquette's rendering of the Indian word *Missouris,* or "people with big canoes." Soon *coureurs de bois* in big canoes of their own came to trap beaver, otter, and mink, trade with Indians, boil salt off the licks, and prospect in cave-pocked red clay. They found rich deposits of lead and put African and Indian slaves to work digging and smelting. The first European settlement arose at Ste. Geneviève around 1750; New Madrid, Cape Girardeau, and St. Charles rose later under the Spaniards. But St. Louis, founded by Pierre de Laclède Liguest in 1763, owned the future by dint of its flood-proof location on a promontory a few miles south of the Missouri-Mississippi confluence. During and after the War of

Independence, American leatherstockings came in numbers that frightened Governor Carondelet. But his conspiracies with Citizen Genêt, George Rogers Clark, and General Wilkinson availed nothing. Then his own government undercut him when Pinckney's Treaty opened the river to American flatboats. "You cannot lock up an open field," sighed Spanish foreign minister Godoy. All Spain could do was offer Americans land grants and no taxes in hopes of winning their loyalty. Daniel and Rebecca Boone arrived at this time to scout out Boon's Lick, two hundred miles up the Missouri. So did Moses Austin, master of the lead fields fifty miles southwest of St. Louis. "Nature has undoubtedly intended this Country," wrote Austin, "to be not onely the most agreeable and pleaseing in the World, but the Richest also." By the time of the Louisiana Purchase over 60 percent of Missouri's ten thousand people were of U.S. origin, prompting French official Charles Delassus to close his journal: "The devil take all."[96]

The ceremony marking Missouri's transfer to U.S. sovereignty was rococo. When Wilkinson and Claiborne down in New Orleans delegated Captain Amos Stoddard to stand in for them at St. Louis, the French commissioner empowered him to do the same on behalf of his government. So Stoddard staged two ceremonies in March 1804 during which he first transferred title to Upper Louisiana from Spain to France, then transferred it to himself in the name of the United States! Back in Washington City, Jefferson briefly entertained the idea of prohibiting white settlement west of the Mississippi and filling it with Indians removed from the east. But Rufus King gently persuaded him: "Nothing but a cordon of troops will restrain our people from going over the River." Indeed, William Henry Harrison took temporary charge intending to make Missouri hospitable for no one *except* white Americans. The Catholic Black Code, with its guarantee of limited rights for slaves, was abolished, while the Sac and Fox tribes ceded 15 million acres in exchange for the White Father's protection against the fierce Osages. A year later Wilkinson arrived in St. Louis to curse the humidity, bugs, and charivari of fortune hunters even he damned as "pettifoggers, renegadoes, and impatient natives." Speculators scarfed Spanish land grants, Creoles protested, squatters squatted, and no one went outdoors without pistols and knives on display. Rowdy boatmen such as Mike Fink brawled in the streets. Gentlemen dueled on St. Louis's "Bloody Island." Frontier lawyers made saints of any land shark or killer who could come up with their fee.[97]

Most notorious was John Smith T, whose slight frame, effeminate features, education, and breeding masked the soul of a wolf. He was born around 1770 to a fifth generation Virginia planter and a mother related to Wilkinson. After independence the family hooked up with William Blount and plunged into western land speculation. Young John founded Smithland on the Cumberland River, but Indians, the Mason and Harpe bandits, and Wilkinson himself drove him out. That was when he added the T for Tennessee to his pedestrian name and lit out for Missouri. He purchased a Spanish "floating concession" entitling him to claim ten thousand acres wherever he wished and used it to muscle into Austin's lead-mining realm. For two years their hired gunmen and lawyers did battle until Wilkinson blessed Smith T's claims and named him justice of the peace. In 1805, a federal land commission arrived, but since one of its members was Wilkinson's nephew and another a friend, Smith T's private empire grew. The Burr conspiracy was a setback. Jefferson replaced Wilkinson with a new governor ordered to root out Burrism in Missouri. So Smith T put stewards in charge of his properties and rode off to filibuster in Texas. There is evidence he may even have fought with Jackson in the Battle of New Orleans.[98]

Meanwhile, sanity came to Missouri by grace of Lewis and Clark, whom Jefferson appointed governor and Indian agent respectively. They spurned the Austin and Smith T factions alike, summoned the first territorial assemblies, and made a treaty with the Osages opening land between the Missouri and Arkansas Rivers. Lewis' mysterious death in 1809 was a blow. So was the thundering New Madrid earthquake of 1811. It flattened towns and forests, parted rivers like the Red Sea, and rattled furniture as far away as Virginia. The next year war loomed with the British and their Indian allies. But Missouri was spared thanks to the preparations of Clark and Daniel's son, Nathan Boone, "a remarkable woodsman who could climb like a bear and swim like a duck." The end of the war and congressional validation of Spanish claims acquired by 1804 kicked off a Missouri land rush. One of the newcomers was Tennessee's Thomas Hart Benton. After nearly killing Andrew Jackson in a gunfight in 1813 he, like Smith T, went looking for a place where power was still up for grabs. Between 1814 and 1820 Missouri's population grew from 25,000 to 66,586 as the central river counties known as Little Dixie filled up with plantations. In 1817 St. Louis cheered the *Zebulon M. Pike*, first steamboat to ply the Mississippi above the Ohio. Land prices soared and construction pushed wages for skilled labor above $3 per day. The Panic of 1819 punctured the bubble. But by then a St. Louis junto defending their pre-1804 grants, an anti-junto challenging their oligopoly, and the mass of plain "white folks" clamored for statehood.[99]

It began and ended in violence. The St. Louis junto's candidate for territorial delegate, John Scott, won a razor-thin victory in 1816 thanks to ballots he himself carried to Governor Clark in his saddlebags. The loser appealed, resulting in a second election scarred by riots and fraud. A St. Louis worker murdered a prominent merchant only to be acquitted by a friendly jury. Thomas Hart Benton killed the son of Judge John Lucas on Bloody Island. But the victorious Scott assured Congress Missouri was tame and ready for statehood. (He also lobbied, on behalf of a New Madrid planter eager to get out of Arkansas, to affix to Missouri the curious "boot heel" in its southeastern corner.)

By the time Scott returned, Missourians of all stripes were livid over attempts made in Congress to restrict slavery. Not only planters, but land speculators, lawyers, politicians, farmers, mechanics, and miners believed their prosperity hinged on the influx of southern settlers. Baptists and Methodists who spoke up were driven out, beaten, and in one instance killed. Smith T, upon learning an abolitionist was agitating in the mines, found him "playing cards with the niggers by torchlight" and shot him. He claimed self-defense and went free: slaves could not legally testify even if they dared do so.[100]

Missouri voters chose a constitutional convention unanimous in favor of laws sheltering slavery and keeping free blacks and mulattoes out of the state. The two juntos also joined forces to protect property rights through a judiciary appointed for life by the governor. But St. Louis delegates thought to appease the frontiersmen with a centrally located capital, Jefferson City, and universal male suffrage. They were not so easily appeased. When the illustrious Clark threw his hat in the ring for governor, voters identified him with the St. Louis junto. A Scots-Irish populist, Alexander McNair, buried Clark 70 to 30 percent. Judge Barton, a leader of the anti-junto, did win a U.S. Senate seat and scared up just enough votes in the legislature to help Benton defeat his blood-rival Judge Lucas. But Benton saw right away that mass popularity, not juntos or patronage, was the key to winning frontier elections, and that popularity was earned by touting cheap land, hard money, and Andy Jackson. So Benton broke with his patron, made peace with Jackson, and took the "people's" side on every issue.[101]

Senator Thomas Hart Benton represented the Gateway to the West for thirty years, both reflecting and shaping its politics. He protected slavery where it existed to mollify southerners, but opposed its extension to mollify northerners. He favored low taxes, hard currency, and internal improvements. He trumpeted Manifest Destiny and imagined frontier democracy spreading to the Pacific and beyond. He helped open the Sante Fe Trail, which brought over $100,000 in bullion each year to Independence and the City of Kansas near Fort Osage. The Mexican trade in turn stimulated Missouri mule-breeding and production of wagons, the great prairie schooners. Benton personified a border state whose western, populist, nationalist glue helped hold the Union together.[102]

Contrast that with the other Tennessee nomad, Smith T. After Austin went bankrupt in 1820, Smith T's lead empire yielded 1,350 tons per year. He branched out into lumber, iron, salt, and cattle, becoming possibly the richest man in the West. He might have become a civic leader as well if his corruption had been the least bit creative. Instead, Smith T turned to drink after his wife and brother died, suffered business reverses, and sued or dueled competitors. Thinking to capitalize on his legend, he ran for governor in 1832 and got just 314 votes statewide. He was laughed at, then scorned after another killing (his twentieth, said those keeping score). Sensing Missouri was no longer a wild place to plunder, he chose to retire to a southern plantation. Instead, he died of fever near Hale's Point, Tennessee, in 1836. The loyal slave Dave carried Smith T's corpse back to Missouri, but his death was unmourned and his grave site forgotten.[103] A few months before, in a tiny village upriver, a true son of Missouri was born to Jane Lampton and John Marshall Clemens. They named him Samuel, but as Missouri's ambassador to the world he was better known as Mark Twain.

"Damn this sectional strife. There's a *continent* out there for the taking, the Pacific Ocean beyond it, the riches of Asia beyond that. We can sort out slavery later, after our empire's won." In fact, no American booster seems to have said that in so many words, yet Americans acted as if that were the plan all along. One of Robert Morris' ships sailed to Canton in 1784 to trade ginseng for a fortune in tea, silks, and porcelain. The whaler *American Hero* returned from the Pacific in 1789 with a record two thousand barrels of sperm oil. Nantucket's whaling fleet began rounding Cape Horn, earning 200 to 300 percent profit per voyage. The remote North Pacific explored by Captains Cook and Vancouver was plied by Yankee merchants seeking Hawaiian sandalwood and Alaskan otter and seal pelts to peddle in China. In 1805 Lewis and Clark reached the Pacific, inspiring Astor to challenge the Hudson's Bay Company on the Columbia River. In 1818, Opukahaia, a runaway from the Kona Coast, died in Connecticut praying the gospel might be brought to his people. Within a year the first team of Congregational missionaries was en route to Hawaii. The U.S. government never decided to grasp for the Pacific because Americans began doing it from the birth of the nation.[104]

How would western North America be parceled out? As of 1821 the new republic of Mexico inherited Texas, California, and the deserts between. The United States claimed the Great Plains east of the Rockies and south of Canada. Russians thinly occupied the Alaskan coast. In the midst of these empires lay Oregon to which the United States, Britain, and Russia all laid claim. The Russian presence dated from the courageous voyages of Vitus Bering, who built two sturdy brigs in remote Kamchatka and sailed into the icy Pacific. In 1741 his was the first European expedition to spy the Alaskan coast. Fur-hunters, the ferocious *promyshlenniki,* followed in boats and seagoing canoes, slaughtering seals and otters and virtually enslaving the native Aleuts. In 1799 Tsar Alexander I tried to impose order by chartering the Russian-American Company and dispatching Orthodox priests. But Russia's navy and merchant marine were not up to the job of victualing the colony. Its manager, the gentle Alexander Baranov, thus had no choice but to welcome British and American merchants to his castle at Sitka and exchange pelts for food and supplies.

A Russian admiral warned that Britain or the upstart United States might someday seize Alaska. So the tsar issued a bellowing ukase in 1821 that declared North Pacific waters as far south as Vancouver Island a *mare clausum* forbidden to all foreign vessels. It was a colossal bluff. Russia could scarcely patrol a thousand miles of subarctic coastline. But a foreign policy crisis, an assault on freedom of the seas no less, was exactly what the U.S. Congress needed to get over the Missouri affair. Virginia's John Floyd, a friend of William Clark, demanded Secretary of State Adams *do something* to secure a region whose potential exceeded "the hopes even of avarice itself." Thomas Hart Benton drafted a bill authorizing fortification of Oregon. China trader William Sturgis denounced the ukase as "little short of a declaration of war."[105]

Adams needed no prodding. He long imagined a United States someday coterminous with the continent. But the U.S. military was as yet too weak—and the stakes too remote—to permit him to do more than meet bluff with bluff. First Adams warned Britain not to use the Russian decree as an excuse to conquer Alaska. What, and do you mean to annex Canada as well? asked the British minister. "Keep what is yours, replied Adams coldly, "but leave the rest of the continent to us." Next, he rejected the tsar's pretensions, asking what right Russia had to *any* footing on American soil. "And is it not time," he told a congressman, "for the American Nations to inform the sovereigns of Europe, that the American continents are no longer open to the settlement of new European colonies?" That was the first formulation of what later became known as the Monroe Doctrine, although the idea of an exclusive, republican American system of states dated back to Tom Paine.[106]

Adams instructed the U.S. minister in St. Petersburg to engage the Russians in bilateral talks, hoping to freeze out the more powerful British. There matters stood in August 1823 when the U.S. minister in London, Richard Rush, reported astounding news. George Canning, the belligerent Liberal who took over the Foreign Office following Castlereagh's suicide, asked if the U.S. government might consider joining with Britain in a declaration forbidding attempts by Spain and/or France to suppress the emerging Latin American republics! That fear arose when the Bourbon army of Louis XVIII crossed the Pyrenees in 1823 to crush a liberal revolution in Spain and restore its Bourbon monarch. Canning's offer amazed, but even more amazing were the reactions of American statesmen. Jefferson, the old Anglophobe, urged Monroe to leap at the bait since a United States allied to Britain "need not fear the whole world." Calhoun, the old War Hawk, likewise approved. Only John Quincy Adams, the supposed Anglophile, dissented. The foxy, wizened diplomat thought it no more likely the "Holy Allies will restore the Spanish domination on the American continent than that the Chimborazo [a great Andean mountain] will sink beneath the ocean." He wondered why Canning asked for help the Royal Navy did not need. He sniffed perfidy in Canning's suggestion the United States and Britain benignly declare: "We aim not at the possession of any portion of [the Spanish colonies] ourselves." Did the United States wish to renounce for all time ambitions in the Hispanic New World? Did the United States wish to violate Washington's rule against permanent alliances, coming in "like a cock boat in the wake of the British man-of-war"? Did the United States wish to risk war by pledging to fight the Bourbons on behalf of volatile juntos in Buenos Aires, Lima, and Bogotá? When Clay had cried for just such a crusade in 1821, Adams insisted America "is the well-wisher to the freedom and independence of all. She is the champion only of her own."[107]

In heated cabinet sessions Adams persuaded Monroe to make a declaration along Canning's lines, but to do so *unilaterally*. Monroe missed the point. His draft declaration condemning European intervention in the Americas included rebukes of the French intervention in Spain and Ottoman Turkish resistance to a violent independence movement in Greece. Adams patiently explained the United States might persuade European courts not to interfere in the *New* World only by assuring them the United States would not interfere in the *Old* World. Any American crusade against monarchy and imperialism, even if confined to rhetoric, would place U.S. national interests in gratuitous peril. His purpose was solely to advise Spain, France, Russia, and not least Britain that: (1) new colonization in the Americas, (2) transfer of existing colonies, or (3) attempts to reconquer ex-colonies would manifest "an unfriendly disposition to the United States." When Monroe made Adams' text the highlight of his December 2, 1823, message to Congress, Americans cheered as one. European courts, by contrast, either ignored or scoffed at such spread-eagle arrogance. But the very next year the Monroe Doctrine's principles paid their first dividend when the Russian government granted U.S. ships free use of Alaskan waters for ten years and relinquished territorial claims south of the latitude 54 degrees 40 minutes. Now only Britain remained to contest the United States for title to the great Oregon Territory.

"The poor little political bird of ominous note and plumage, denominated a CAUCUS, was hatched at Washington on Saturday last," announced a Baltimore newspaper in February 1824. "It is now running around like a pullet. . . . The sickly thing is to be fed, cherished, pampered for a week, when it is fondly hoped it will be enabled to cry the name of Crawford, Crawford, Crawford." For two decades the key to becoming president had been to win the nomination of the Republican congressional caucus dominated in turn by the Virginia machine. The scorn shown the caucus this time signaled a seismic shift in American politics. Monroe was right. Northerners and westerners were tired of deferring to a self-perpetuating Jeffersonian dynasty. A new word—*democracy*—was heard in the land. A new party known simply as "Jackson men" challenged Monroe's four other would-be successors. The first to drop out was Calhoun. Though an avid nationalist he had little appeal in the North and was in any case everyone's first choice for vice president. Crawford, though pleased to hear Caucus squawk his name, lay half-paralyzed from a stroke. The Tennessee and Kentucky legislatures, in a burst of frontier assertion, nominated Jackson and Clay respectively *two years* in advance of the election. Massachusetts offered Adams. Since no candidate could prevail without making inroads into the others' geographical bases, national organizations, brokered coalitions, and mud-slinging became campaign committees' weapons of choice. They have remained so ever since.

As for issues, there were none. The positions of Adams, Clay, and Crawford on internal improvements, the bank, and tariffs were not far apart, while Jackson seemed to espouse no positions at all. So Clay men portrayed Jackson as an adulterous murderer. Jackson men hawked the first presidential "campaign biography" lauding their chief, while denouncing Clay as a drunken gambler. Adams men said Crawford pilfered the Treasury. Crawford men hinted Adams was a Federalist in disguise. If just half the attacks were warranted, one participant scoffed, "our Presidents, Secretaries, Senators, and Representatives, are all traitors and pirates." Why national politics degenerated in 1824 is no mystery. As more states entered the Union, more legislatures mandated popular voting for president, and more people moved west, the political cultures of the original thirteen states lost their leverage. Did the Puritans' ordered liberty, Quakers' quiet pacifism, or Cavaliers' hierarchical virtue spread west to civilize the frontier? Quite the contrary, the Scots-Irish Bordermen's brawls spilled back to roil the east.[108]

Jackson won 43 percent of the national vote, carrying most of the South in addition to Pennsylvania, Maryland, and New Jersey. Crawford's 13 percent share won him Virginia and Georgia, but also Delaware and support in New York. Clay's 13 percent carried Kentucky, Ohio, and Missouri, and included some eastern votes. Only Adams, whose 31 percent won him all of New England, failed to appeal outside his base. Smart poll-watchers like Van Buren grasped the new political rules and re-hitched their wagons accordingly. For the moment, however, the electoral college divided among Jackson (99), Adams (84), Crawford (41), and Clay (37), throwing the election into the House. Over the winter their supporters haggled incessantly to secure a majority of state delegations. Jackson remained aloof. Adams decried the whole sordid process. Clay, determined to avoid a stalemate as in 1801, threw his support to Adams and lobbied hard. By the time Congress convened in February 1825, Clay had lined up twelve states for Adams but needed one more: New York. Its delegation was split down the middle between Adams men and Van Buren's pro-Crawford clique. Van Buren intended to block Adams on the first ballot, knowing defections would follow. But he feared the weak-willed Representative Stephen Van Rensselaer, who tended to agree with whoever spoke to him last, might break ranks. So what in fact happened? Did Clay and Webster persuade him to spare the nation a protracted crisis? Or did Van Rensselaer open his eyes after prayer to see a ballot marked "Adams" lying providentially at his feet? Whichever testimony is true, his vote put Adams over the top.[109]

A glowering toad who joked only about his own lack of humor, John Quincy Adams charmed none but the subtle. He thought he deserved the presidency after three decades of service, but also berated himself for ambition. He rose every day before dawn to study his Bible in the belief it taught all the principles needed to conduct republican diplomacy. He prayed for the chance to "do good to the utmost of my power." Yet he feared slavery, an "outrage upon the goodness of God," disqualified the United States for true greatness. It was unlikely he could do much about that even in the White House.[110] Told he was President-elect, Adams took the news like a curse. Nothing had happened in "a manner satisfactory to pride or to just desire . . . with perhaps two-thirds of the whole people adverse to the actual result." Worse still, he named Clay secretary of State, inviting irate Jackson men to accuse the Yankee and the "Judas of the West" of making a corrupt bargain. Worst of all, Adams' own rhetoric confirmed suspicions he was as "royalist" as his father. The purpose of his December 1825 message to Congress was to propose bold federal initiatives on behalf of agriculture, manufacturing, commerce, science, and education. Alas, his approach was to *scold* countrymen hostile to federal power, praise *European monarchies* as worthy of emulation, *insult* his audience, and predict the *loss of God's favor* should the nation not heed his advice! Adams lectured: "While foreign nations less blessed with that freedom which is power than ourselves are advancing with gigantic strides in the career of public improvement, were we to slumber in indolence or fold up our arms and proclaim to the world that we are palsied by the will of our constituents, would it not be to cast away the bounties of Providence and doom ourselves to perpetual inferiority?"

Who did the man think he was, Louis XIV? Crawford thought Adams' imperious program unconstitutional. Calhoun spied a flank attack on states' rights. Van Buren heard a one-term president talking. All three defected to Jackson. The 1828 campaign was already on.[111]

Adams was right about sectional jealousies, penury, and prejudice retarding national growth. Adams was wrong about Americans dooming themselves to inferiority. For even as he stewed in the role of spurned philosopher-king, hustlers were abroad in the land, building, inventing, selling. Thanks to the army and Supreme Court decisions they even had some federal support.

Eli Whitney invented the cotton gin, for which he earned lawsuits and poverty. Whitney did *not* invent interchangeable parts, for which he earned a sizable fortune. His luck changed in 1798 when fellow Yale graduate, War Secretary Oliver Wolcott, paid Whitney up front to make four thousand muskets. The government arsenals at Springfield, Massachusetts, and Harper's Ferry, Virginia, relied on artisans turning out weapons one at a time. Whitney's idea was to replace craftsmen with cheap unskilled workers using water-powered machines to mass-produce firearms. Only it wasn't his idea. General Jean-Baptiste de Gribeauval began chasing that dream in 1765. Twenty years later, Jefferson learned of *le système Gribeauval.* But no one claimed to realize the dream until 1801, when Whitney duped Jefferson by screwing ten random gunlocks into the same musket. (The intricate locks themselves he did not dare disassemble.) The president pronounced Whitney a genius, resulting in more government subsidies. Whitney was a decade late fulfilling the musket contract, but just in time for the War of 1812 to enrich him.[112]

Meanwhile, a Connecticut scythe maker named Simeon North made real progress toward what became known as the American System of Manufactures. Awarded a government contract for small arms, North learned "by confining a workman to one particular limb of the pistol until he has made two thousand, I save at least one quarter of his labor. . . ." Thus did he apply Adam Smith's theory of the division of labor. In 1813 the War Department was so impressed it asked North to make twenty thousand pistols with each part "to correspond so exactly that any limb or part of one pistol may be fitted to any other. . . ." North figured it might be achieved by fitting each part to one standard gunlock. So in 1816 he invented a milling machine able to grind molds to exact specifications. By then federal armories joined in the hunt thanks to Major Louis de Tousard, who popularized interchangeable parts through the West Point curriculum and his 1809 treatise, *American Artillerist's Companion.* Tousard's disciples, Chief of Ordnance Colonel Decius Wadsworth and Springfield superintendent Colonel Roswell Lee, assembled military and civilian talent to experiment with milling parts in conformity with standardized gauges. In 1818, a third piece fell into place when a stammering Massachusetts tinker named Thomas Blanchard invented a lathe to turn wooden blocks into identical musket barrels. The ingenious Blanchard went on to invent thirteen more machines to mass-produce barrel stocks, shoe lasts, ax handles, and saddle molds.

John H. Hall, a Maine cooper and cabinetmaker, combined all these techniques in one place. In 1811 he applied for a patent on a breech-loading rifle, only to be cheated of half his royalties by the patent commissioner himself (who claimed to have made the same invention years before). But the War Department made recompense in 1819 by awarding Hall a rifle contract, a salary, royalties, and *free use of Harper's Ferry* where the colonels had mustered so much talent. By 1824 Hall could boast, "I have succeeded in establishing methods for fabricating arms exactly alike, & with economy, by the hands of common workmen." He also taught the government about economies of scale, asking why it ordered one thousand rifles when three thousand could be made for the same fixed cost. Thanks to North, Wadsworth, Lee, Blanchard, and Hall, the "armory practice" inspired many New England manufacturers, including one Samuel Colt.[113]

Many Americans needed a gun. Few needed a clock. Farmers got along fine obeying the rhythms of sun and season. Mechanics and shopkeepers were their own bosses. Bells summoned people to church. Yet by the late 1820s every farm and townhouse from New England to Illinois seemed to have a Connecticut clock on the mantle. It was the first mass-produced product peddled as a symbol of status that consumers decided they could not do without. Eli Terry of Plymouth, Connecticut, started the fad when he learned to mass-produce wooden clockworks. Brass was far better, but fashioning every part save the pendulum bob and weights out of wood allowed him to sell clocks for half their usual price. By 1820, standardized lathes and the division of labor enabled Terry to make twenty-five hundred clocks per year. But his partnership's real breakthrough was door-to-door marketing. The Yankee peddler's wagon was a familiar sight and sound, clattering farm to farm with tools, utensils, fabric, needles, and thread. Now Terry and copycat entrepreneurs in Bristol, Burlington, Waterbury, and Torrington, placed tens of thousands of clocks in the hands of peddlers. If a farmer resisted the sales pitch, they appealed to his wife. If both resisted, they might offer a free trial, collecting payment on their next visit. By the 1830s, when new stamping machines and gauges made even brass clocks economical, artificial synchronization of Americans' daily lives had become the norm throughout the north.[114]

Nothing made northerners slaves to the clock more than the industrial mills springing up. America's wooden age blossomed after 1795 when Jacob Perkins invented a machine able to cut and head two hundred thousand nails per day. That made possible "balloon frame" houses any carpenter's apprentice could bang together. But mass production of "two by four" studs and joints remained a challenge until Poughkeepsie's William Wordsworth patented a planing machine with rolls and belts that fed timber and rotary cylinders that cut to specification. By 1829 Americans were consuming 850 million board-feet per year, three and a half times the *per capita* wood usage in Britain. A hundred new ironworks arose in the 1820s to meet an annual demand for nails, horseshoes, plows, cartwheels, shovels, crowbars, ax-heads, harrow teeth, and scythes surpassing a hundred thousand tons. Leather production soared after 1809 when Gideon Lee centralized the leaching, currying, and cutting processes in a single mechanized plant. That made possible mass manufacture of shoes.[115]

By far the largest industrial sector was textiles. John Goulding's patent condenser revolutionized wool carding in 1826. Good thing, too, because imports of Spanish merino sheep in the 1810s so improved American herds their average shear more than doubled. But fully mechanized, waterwheel-driven factories to spin, card, draw, rove, and weave cotton cloth were what really brought an end to the "age of homespun." Nathan Appleton's Boston Manufacturing Company opened its Waltham mills in 1814. Ugly, noisy, and filthy we would think his brick sweatshop today. But Appleton wrote of "the state of admiration and satisfaction with which we sat by the hour, watching the beautiful movement of this new wonderful machine, destined as it evidently was, to change the character of all textile industry." The company's annual dividends averaged 24 percent from 1820–25. By then Francis Cabot's Merrimack Manufacturing Company, capitalized with $600,000, set a new standard at Lowell, Massachusetts. The instant city on "the hardest working river in the world" soon numbered twenty thousand people employed by twenty-five mills producing 30 million yards of cloth per year. At first mills applied English technology, but Yankee technicians were quick to innovate. Cyrus W. Baldwin's double-threaded loom mass-produced strong, seamless sacks for the shipment of America's bountiful harvests. Erasmus Bigelow's powered carpet looms put "a Bigelow on the floor" of American drawing rooms.[116]

Everyday life changed at a frenetic pace in these years, at least for the wealthy and middling sort living in towns. Lengthy experimentation with Pennsylvania's clean, hot-burning anthracite coal culminated in the 1818 Bethlehem stove, making coal grates and heaters the must-have appliances of the late 1820s. Boston and New York introduced gas lighting. Swank Philadelphia and New York hotels advertised their toilets and indoor plumbing. Groceries displayed hermetically "canned" fish, pickles, jellies, and other perishable foods based on a French process. Daniel Treadwell's powered printing press and Robert Hoe's cylinder press allowed American editors to produce thousands of cheap impressions at the cry "Roll the presses!" By 1830 the United States was awash with 863 newspapers. That created insatiable demand for Massachusetts' Berkshire County inventors Thomas Gilpin, and John and David Ames. Their assembly-line paper making machine turned wet rag pulp into "cut and dried" paper in one continuous process: twenty-four miles worth per day. A "miracle of inscrutable intricacy" to Herman Melville, it made the youthful United States the largest paper consuming country in the world. Much of that consumption came in the form of manuals teaching everyone who could read how to improve their family's diet, hygiene, furnishings, clothing, and manners. Reinforced by the dicta of preachers and social reformers, the ambience of material culture made drunkenness, lewdness, spitting, cursing, and fighting less acceptable if not always less prevalent. Gradually, from the coastal towns inland, travelers remarked on the "advance in civilization."[117]

Nor need John Quincy Adams have feared for the nation's knowledge base. Harvard created its first chair in science and the useful arts in 1814. Disciples of Benjamin Rush made the University of Pennsylvania a center of chemistry, engineering, and mineralogy. Benjamin Stillman carried Yale's scientific tradition to Princeton, founding the American Journal of Science in 1818. Williams College alumnus Amos Eaton oversaw the Rensselaer Polytechnic Institute (1824) and New York State Agricultural Society. Thomas Law, the English husband of George Washington's ward Anne Custis, inspired the Federal City's Columbian Institute where, in 1827, Samuel L. Stoddard cried, "let us found An Empire—An Empire of Science!" Philadelphia's influential Franklin Institute (1824) offered a national journal and regular instruction in agronomy, architecture, chemistry, geology, mineralogy, and mechanics.[118]

Doubtless American technology, business, and agriculture could have benefited from the programs imagined by Adams. But protection of patents and contracts, a national market, and modest tariff protection were all American investors, inventors, and peddlers required to launch an industrial revolution. Did this concatenation of legal, technical, and commercial creations also comprise a "market revolution," as some historians suggest? Was American society before 1815 not only pre-industrial, but pre-capitalist as well? If so, was the generation of 1815–30 victimized by a Hamiltonian power elite scheming to ruin a Jeffersonian idyll? All one need do is recall the capitalist, expansionist, Common Law-based "improvement ethic" that inspired English colonization in the first place to realize the answers are no, no, and no.[119]

Opponents of internal improvements, the U.S. Bank, the tariff, or federal support of manufactures were in just as big a hurry to develop America as the proponents. The opponents simply feared centralization of economic power might create a closed aristocracy of wealth denying opportunity to the "little man." No American party, region, faction, or interest was anti-development or anti-market. Southern planters were keen capitalists. Western farmers demanded transportation to provide access to markets and boost real estate values. Eastern farmers had long sold their surpluses to urban and foreign customers. Mechanics and artisans celebrated their freedom from guilds, masters, and fixed prices, while the more ambitious dreamed of becoming proprietors through ingenuity or marketing skill. That merchants from Boston to New

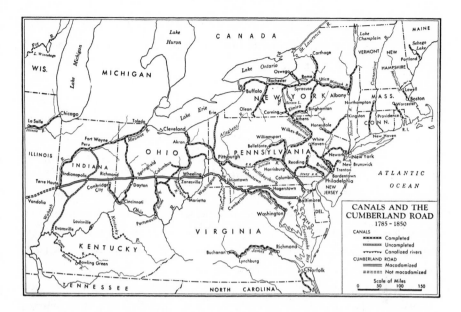

CANALS AND THE CUMBERLAND ROAD
1785 - 1850

Orleans were market-oriented goes without saying. Protestant Americans of British extraction and most German and French immigrants, too, arrived in the New World ready to hustle. They did not need to learn market behavior or have it thrust upon them.

Andy Jackson himself was a capitalist in whom "wanna-be" capitalists placed their trust. When his supporters expressed an opinion they said "I reckon" or "calculate" as often as "think." Their preachers urged charity, but not poverty or communalism. Rather, Methodist circuit-rider Peter Cartwright scolded the frontier husband who lived like a troglodyte: "Now, brother, do fill up this hole in the hearth, and go to town and get you a set of chairs, knives and forks, cups and saucers, and get you a couple of plain bedstead and bed-cords. . . . *Give your wife and daughters a chance.*" In America, reported an Englishman, "there is no clinging to old ways; the moment an American hears the word 'invention,' he pricks up his ears." Alexis de Tocqueville famously wrote, "I know of no country, indeed, where the love of money has taken a stronger hold on the affections of men."[120] Only a smattering of Catholics and pietists such as the Amish fled Vanity Fair. Otherwise, Americans believed accepting God's blessings with thanks, on behalf of one's self, family, and neighbors, was itself a devotion. Commercial expansion after 1815 was simply the latest expression of a cult of material progress bred in Americans' bones; its breadth and rapidity simply a result of population growth and the removal of external and internal barriers.


Government is also technology of a kind, and a republic a market in power. In 1828 Americans learned how their politics worked, indeed *must* work if their federal system was to function. The *way* it worked was corrupt, of course—ethically if not legally. But the creative *result* was a two-party system in which victory required the building of coalitions across potentially hostile regions and social groups. The men who tutored Americans in their politics included Van Buren, Benton, Calhoun, John Eaton of Tennessee, and the rest of Andrew Jackson's brain trust. Their campaign, kicked off in the first year of Adams' presidency by the legislature in Nashville, was in full swing by the spring of 1827. On the national level, congressmen combined to deny Adams' "government party" the smallest success. They even conspired to pass an exorbitant Tariff of Abominations in 1828 so Jacksonians might claim credit where high tariffs were popular and blame the administration where they were not. A committee in Washington City raised campaign funds, while congressmen used their franking privileges to distribute partisan speeches to a national pro-Jackson newspaper chain. On the state level, committee chairmen divvied up duties (and spoils) while planning work in the grassroots. On the local level, volunteer "Hurra Boys" planted hickory trees and passed out hickory sticks, brooms, and canes during rowdy political rallies. From top to bottom a "driving corps of politicians and newspapermen" devoted itself, above all, to winning. Van Buren demurely dubbed it "substantial reorganization." Virginian John Taylor of Caroline thought it a revolution.[121]

Jackson men called themselves Democratic Republicans as opposed to the National Republicans led by Adams and Clay. Later they would simply be Democrats or the Democracy. They promised voters victory over the "purse-proud" aristocrats in control of the executive branch. They alleged Adams lived in royal splendor, having turned the president's house into a "palace" of gaming tables and luxuries. They called him King John II to brand him with the stigma of his Federalist father. They even made hay out of Jackson's bad grammar, contrasting his common touch with Adams' eloquent speeches peppered with classical allusions. What did Adams mean by some highfalutin phrase? "It's Greek to me!" Jackson men targeted ethnic minorities, lying to Pennsylvanians about Adams' alleged habit of referring to Germans as "stupid Dutch," and lying in Boston about Jackson's alleged Irish ancestry. Most of all, the campaign frightened farmers with tales of how eastern bankers and merchants manipulated money and prices to cheat them. Had hard issues mattered, Adams' well-chiseled program for internal improvements pitched by the Kentuckian Clay might have won western support. Instead, Jackson men chanted how the Great Compromiser compromised western interests through his "corrupt bargain" with Adams.

What did Jacksonian Democracy mean? Even as Old Hickory managed his lieutenants like a general at war he never once hinted what the movement was meant to achieve. "I am not a politician," said Jackson, thereby writing a script for future American candidates. He promised unspecified "reform," even jibing, "My real friends want no information from me on the subject of internal improvement and manufactories, but what my public acts have afforded, and I never gratify my enemies." In sum, the 1828 Democratic campaign was all spin and most of the spin was false. Jackson was no humble Tennessee farmer reluctantly heeding his country's call, but a wealthy and powerful insider, lawyer, and slaveholding landowner. He was cunning, impatient, ambitious, having dedicated his life to soaring as far *above* the mass of suffering humanity as he possibly could. He supported democracy "primarily because it supported him." But who Jackson was did not matter so long as voters projected *their* illusions on him. Lest he disillusion the people, Jackson kept his mouth shut. National Republicans called these tactics by the name Federalists used for Jefferson's: demagoguery. They were defenseless against it.[122]

"Organization is the secret of victory," wrote a pro-Adams editor. "By the want of it we have been overthrown." That plus Jackson's deft ducking of issues left National Republicans no alternative to the character issue. So Clay's party flacks revived the old scandals and slurs, adding a few of their own. Jackson was named a bastard, mulatto child of a whore, member of the Burr conspiracy, fornicator and bigamist, murderer. A widely distributed "Coffin Handbill" accused him of wantonly executing militiamen in 1813 on spurious charges of mutiny. Jackson did not seek out his accusers and shoot them—a testimony to his growing self-discipline—but he never forgave Adams and Clay for insulting his wife, Rachel, especially after she weakened and died in December 1828. One more accusation naming Jackson a heathen bequeathed a third trope to American politics. Van Buren ordered a New York journalist to portray Old Hickory, in suitably humble fashion, as a prayerful man. Soon Jacksonian newspapers nationwide were reporting his family's daily devotions at the Hermitage and Sunday attendance at the Presbyterian church. That hooey may have fooled a few Old Lights back east, but was not even needed out west. Evangelicals lined up behind Jackson as eagerly as their parents had rallied to Jefferson. They never doubted their Protestant God was a Democrat.[123]

Jackson's well-known Freemasonry, however, gave Van Buren a scare in New York's electoral battleground. The lodges lining the Erie Canal attracted many genuine stonemasons who did not always mix well with their upper-crust brethren in the craft. In 1826 the drunken, disorderly William Morgan bolted his Batavia lodge threatening to publish its secrets. He was arrested, then mysteriously abducted. The scandal spawned a virulent Anti-Masonic Party that declared secret societies "subversive to true democracy." Two rising politicians in upstate New York, Thurlow Weed and William Henry Seward, hoped fusion between Anti-Masons and National Republicans might defeat the Albany Regency and deliver New York for Adams. Their bold stroke went awry. Van Buren's journals publicized how many leaders in Adams' camp were also Freemasons, not least Henry Clay, while Anti-Masons chose not to dilute their message by involvement in national politics. They ran their own slate, split the opposition, and allowed Jackson to win most New York electors.[124]

Adams foresaw the debacle. On polling days the Democrats turned out their base and then some. (One Irishman crowed he had voted for Jackson twice in every ward in New York City, celebrating each one with a beer.) The turnout was thrice that of 1824. Jackson took 56 percent, winning 178 electoral votes to Adams' 83. He swept the South and West, adding Pennsylvania, 5 of Maryland's 11 votes, and 20 of New York's 36. Democracy triumphed, which is to say whatever triumphs in a democracy is by definition democratic. In Jackson's case perhaps it was. Van Buren, thinking back to the candidate's orphaned youth, mused Jackson's "blood relations—the only blood relations he ever had" were the American people.[125]

John Quincy Adams left town as his father had done before the inauguration of a hated successor. Washington City teemed with Hurra Boys, jobseekers, panhandlers, honest workers, and immigrants—plain "white folks" all. Justice Story called them King Mob. The irreverent Anne Newport Royall wrote the only thing "mild and serene" on March 4, 1829, was the weather. By some "hard squeezing" she forced her way in the inaugural pavilion only to find "the earth was literally covered with people, who maintained neither order nor regularity. If ever I am caught in such another crowd, it will be an accident."

That she could not hear a word of Jackson's address was no loss. He just spoke briefly about "reform" before entrusting the nation to "the goodness of that Power whose providence mercifully protected our national infancy." Hoping for a better view, Royall entered the Capitol. "I ran upstairs to look out some upper windows, and here I found a colored man in a violent passion." Someone had locked him inside. The man cried, "I was always for Jackson, but if this is his way, I wish Adams was President again." Royall mingled with congressmen, remarked on their wives' gaudy dress, then joined the throng careening toward the White House. She was relieved to discover the East Room was not the alabaster salon of Jacksonian propaganda, because revelers soiled the sofas and carpets and made "disgraceful scenes in the parlors, in which even women got bloody noses." At last someone put tubs of punch on the lawn "to lure the new 'democracy' out of the house."

There Royall bumped into the Reverend Ezra Stiles Ely, a Presbyterian political crusader. How was it a man so hostile "to the firm republican principles of General Jackson" got invited to the inaugural fête? It turned out Ely was a close friend of Emily Donelson, who served as Jackson's hostess in lieu of her deceased Aunt Rachel. The pious Emily thought Ely "a very fine man." Royall, her suspicions aroused, observed in ensuing days how evangelicals were "thickening in the city, particularly around the person of the President." She trusted Old Hickory to resist their sermons, but wondered at the affection they showed him.[126]

Wondrous it was, and to the genteel a nightmare. Washington, Franklin, Madison, Hamilton, Adams, and Jefferson had imagined the American experiment coming to all sorts of bad ends. They *never* imagined the Federal City overrun by frontiersmen who cared nothing for history and loved only cheap land and credit, whiskey, tobacco, guns, fast women, fast horses, and Jesus. Not necessarily in that order.

# TRAVELERS

## *Apotheosis and Apocalypse in American Culture, c. 1830*

*W*hat became of those four original spirits of English colonization dating from the late sixteenth century? The initial capitalist drive to enclose and improve common lands within a commercial market triumphed in the United States more thoroughly than in its island of origin. The thirteen colonies rebelled in part because crown and Parliament began to restrict Americans' freedom to expand their agrarian frontier, commerce, and industry. Having won independence, the states crafted a Constitution in part to forge a national market. Having achieved unity, they then made and interpreted laws, and embraced secular and religious values, promoting the swiftest possible development of their nation. Likewise, the "God is English" Protestant spirit damning Roman Catholicism's dogma, hierarchy, and universality triumphed in the United States. To be sure, Americans embraced religious liberty as an indispensable adjunct of civil liberty. But in so doing they created a vast spiritual marketplace in which evangelical Protestants proved the sharpest competitors. Americans' anti-Catholicism was never far from the surface, nor their belief the United States was a Promised Land destined to usher in the Millennium. Third, England's geopolitical challenge to Spanish and French imperialism reached its acme in U.S. war and diplomacy. Americans claimed the right, indeed believed it their destiny, to rid the New World of European possessions and add as many as possible to their own empire of liberty. Finally, the English notion of a racial hierarchy justifying expulsion or enslavement of lesser breeds who got in the way of expansion characterized American behavior even more than it did the British. "White man's democracy," tolerant or else fiercely supportive of slavery and Indian removal, triumphed with Andrew Jackson in 1828. Americans also invented much that was new under the sun, even glorious, thanks to the influence of Reformed Christianity, English Whig thought, the Scottish Enlightenment, Freemasonry, and the power of their own founding myths. Rarely did Americans go into battle with conscience tying one hand behind them. Nevertheless, the roads they traveled from Jamestown and Plymouth to Jacksonian Democracy were surveyed, plotted, and paved in Tudor, Stuart, and Hanoverian Britain.

A brooding coterie of self-consciously American artists, all born between 1783 and 1794, knew that. William Cullen Bryant, Washington Irving, James K. Paulding, James Fenimore Cooper, and others bristled at British jibes to the effect that what passed for American culture was either derivative or vacuous. Nathaniel Hawthorne later explained why that was, asking how one could write romances "about a country where there is no shadow, no antiquity, no mystery, no picturesque and gloomy wrong. . . . Romance and poetry, ivy, lichens, and wall-flowers, need ruin to make them grow."[1] Americans loved building not ruin, the future not the past, while sin, death, and tragedy were unnatural, even embarrassing in a New Jerusalem. Traditional, orthodox Christians thought death a passage from the Church Militant to the Church Expectant. But Americans were *already* expectant, believing heaven on earth just a matter of time and deeming moral progress, like material progress, a matter of will. Where, then, was the stuff of tragedy, epic, heroism, broken dreams, sacrificial love?

In 1817 Paulding came up with an answer. Development *is* the American epic, its hero the "active, hardy, vigilant, enterprising, fearless" pioneer selflessly taming the frontier for travelers to follow. Irving had a second answer. America's lack of ancient history and ruins constituted its glory. Its "wild magnificence" was the ideal stage for drama, its whippoorwills, fireflies, honeysuckle, storms and torrents the perfect props, its physical greatness the natural setting for political greatness. Cooper's third answer completed the loop. Yes, development was the epic, wilderness the backdrop, and the pioneer the hero. But in development there is ruin and death: for the Indian, the pioneer, every frontier village overrun by newcomers hot to exploit what others had built. Americans *did* have a history, often tragic, of their own making.[2]

Cooper witnessed it personally. His father William was a visionary New York developer (not just a speculator) who scouted lands once roamed by Iroquois, laid out towns, and invested heavily. Closest to his heart was the masterwork he named after himself at the point where Lake Otsego empties into the Susquehanna River. There, in Cooperstown, he platted village lots and farms around three cultural centers: a library, an academy, and a Freemason lodge. As settlers poured in he also helped erect a courthouse, tavern, brewery, newspaper, waterworks, and, last of all, churches. Cooper, a Mason, belonged to no denomination, but affiliated with the Episcopalians to boost his sons' social status. For a decade life was joyous. Cooper served his constituents and they honored him. Running as a Federalist he won election to Congress with 84 percent of the vote. Then life turned sour. Tenants defaulted, cheated, pilfered, challenged his titles. They turned Jeffersonian and swept him from office. In 1809 Cooper died.[3]

Son James (he added his mother's maiden name Fenimore in 1826) went to sea after being ousted from Yale. But expecting to live off his inheritance, he married Susan DeLancey in 1811 and resigned from the Navy. Instead, his father's estate got tied up in probate—his land grants proved dubious after all—leaving James and his brothers with no property and a mountain of legal fees. James was distraught until, one evening, he jeered at a novel he was reading aloud. Susan's cousin said, Write one yourself if you think you can do better! Cooper's first effort was a mediocre English novel of manners. Then he found his American voice in *The Spy, A Tale of Neutral Ground* (1821). Some later critics (notably Mark Twain) thought it and Cooper's subsequent bestsellers stilted and contrived, laced as they are with derring-do, stock female characters, and outrageous coincidences. But reading them with the mood of the 1820s in mind one can well understand their success. Cooper gave his country a history free of Europe, free of its own lingering feuds, free above all of guilt. *The Spy* was a fictional account of the genuine Revolutionary War intrigues in Westchester County, a dangerous no-man's-land between the redcoats in Manhattan and the Continental Army to the north. It depicted Patriots and Tories alike as honorable men and women caught in a terrible family feud. Washington's character haunts the book, but he is never named and remains offstage until the denouement. The unforgettable double agent Harvey Birch is an ordinary American who risks his life, property, reputation, and very identity for the liberty of his compatriots. He will not even take pay for his service. He is a master of disguise and ruses. He is, in brief, a hustler, his every deception and apparent corruption a flourish of bold creativity. In *The Pilot* (1824) and *Lionel Lincoln* (1825), two more tales of the Revolution, Cooper again lets humble American patriots save the day.[4]

*The Pioneers* (1823) told Cooper's own story. The village of Templeton is Cooperstown, Judge Marmaduke Temple his father. The Judge has his flaws, make no mistake, but the wreck of his model community results in good part from his own misplaced trust in human nature. The grandeur of his American dream certainly contrasts with the pettiness of his tenants. But even Temple's best aspirations prove ruinous to the real pioneer who made the town possible in the first place. Temple, impatient for "towns, manufactories, bridges, canals, mines" to spring up in the wilderness, cannot understand frontier scout Natty Bumppo, who once roamed the forest in freedom only to be jailed by the Judge for shooting a deer out of season. "Talk not to me of law," says the leatherstocking. "I've travelled these mountains when you was no judge, but an infant in your mother's arms." One man's freedom eclipses that of another. Bumppo, who "keened elegiacally over the despoiling march of civilization through the beauty of the American landscape," must flee beyond the Mississippi to escape landlords and lawyers. So popular was Bumppo with readers Cooper resurrected him in *The Last of the Mohicans* (1826), adding his Indian companion Chingachgook (Twain quipped, "I think it's pronounced Chicago"), and again in *The Pathfinder, The Prairie,* and *The Deerslayer.* Did Cooper romanticize crude frontiersmen and noble savages in a way Brackenridge, for instance, would have pilloried? Of course, but in sentimentalizing the past he melted the hearts of his readers. Bitter conflict with Tories, British, High Federalists, "lawless" leatherstockings and Indians was *over,* was *history,* was in any case *necessary* to propel America on its foreordained path to glory. Cooper invited Americans to remember and honor the sacrifices of those who blazed trails long ago so they might, in all honesty, feel good about doing well. He also celebrated democracy by elevating ordinary people to heroism. He also identified the American spirit with the West, where the future was pregnant with the past. He also made a comfortable living, the first U.S. novelist to do so.[5]

Cooper said his purpose was to make "American manners and American scenes interesting to an American reader." Beyond that he meant to effect the "conservative consolidation of the revolutionary frontier" by legitimating the violence of the national founding, then laying that violence to rest. "Books are, in great measure," he wrote, "the instruments of controlling the opinions of a nation like ours. They are an engine alike powerful to save or destroy." He also hoped to control European opinions. In 1828 James Fenimore Cooper was in London promoting American letters along with Washington Irving and Samuel F. B. Morse (who, like fellow inventor Fulton, began life as an artist). Cooper complained to the Marquis de Lafayette that travelers from Europe misunderstood the United States. Then set them straight, urged Lafayette. At once Cooper penned a two-volume apologia called *Notions of the Americans: Picked up by a Travelling Bachelor.* Anticipating Tocqueville by a few years Cooper named five sources of American dynamism: boisterous population growth; rapid development of internal transportation; a unified national market stimulating commerce, which in turn stimulated manufactures and agriculture; a political theory that "leaves every man . . . on grounds of perfect equality"; and the success of "confederated government" in holding together a continental polity. He noted especially the progress of education ("this is emphatically an age of reading"), which encouraged him to think his books might indeed shape public opinion.[6]

Leaving aside chattel slavery, Cooper was right about the five characteristics of the United States. He was also right about the power of letters. He neglected to mention, his own popularity notwithstanding, Americans were being moved even more deeply by literature of decidedly different sorts: mendacious partisan newspapers, salacious novelettes with ostensibly moral messages, and above all evangelical tracts. Anne Newport Royall, who traveled to places like Muscle Shoals and Racoon Creek rather than New York and London, knew better what dangerous truths and lies moved hearts far removed from the parlors of the urbane.

An unabashed American original, Royall is as discomfiting today as she was in her time, which may explain why histories usually omit her. But no one since Bishop Asbury was so well acquainted with all sections and strata of U.S. society. She traveled in coaches, on steamboats, on horseback, on foot, in blizzards and heat, flush and in poverty, healthy and sick. She visited every state, every town of any size. She published nine volumes describing her journeys, wrote pen-portraits of more than two thousand notable citizens, and interviewed every President from John Adams to Franklin Pierce. She was an accomplished journalist and acerbic critic. But mostly she was a pushy itinerant book peddler scratching for next week's rent while searching, usually in vain, for honest men and women.[7]

Anne came into the world near Baltimore in 1769, the daughter of William Newport and an unknown woman named Mary. When she was three, the family moved to Hanna's Town near Pittsburgh where Anne learned to read on her father's lap. He died, her mother remarried, then that man died, possibly in the Indian attack that took many scalps and wiped out Hanna's Town in 1782. So

DISTRIBUTION
OF
POPULATION
1830

Under 6 Inhabitants
to the sq. mile
6 to 45 Inhabitants
to the sq. mile
45 and over

her mother removed to Staunton, Virginia, where they worked on a farm as domestics. Anne hated the drudgery, the company of illiterate servants, and sitting alone and ignored all day Sunday at the Presbyterian church. She also resented being taken for an up-country "Cohee" (from the Scots-Irish "quoth he" or "quo' he") whom Tidewater "Tuckahoes" held in contempt. Finally, in 1787, her mother was employed by William Royall at his mountain estate near Sweet Springs, (West) Virginia. Mr. Royall was a wealthy tobacco planter who traced his Virginia lineage back to 1622. He was an avid student of Enlightenment philosophy. He was a veteran of seven and a half years in the Continental Army, having fought in all of Nathanael Greene's battles. He was also a bachelor. In him young Anne found a father, teacher, friend, hero, moral exemplar . . . and lover.

Royall noticed Anne's sparkle and gave her the run of his library. "Heathen stuff" the Cohees called it, but she devoured Voltaire and Tom Paine. As for religion, Royall gave her one that lasted a lifetime: Freemasonry. Whereas preachers imposed dogma and took up collections, he said, Masons *lived* Christian principles and were self-confident enough to extend toleration to others. Soon master and maid were sharing a bed; in 1797 they were married, Cinderella at age twenty-eight, Prince Charming about fifty-five. Anne assumed management of the estate while William dreamed Jeffersonian dreams of founding a larger enlightened community over the mountains. But it was William Cooper's fate all over again. Behind his back Royall's tenants laughed at his theories and chivalries, scorned his offers of help, demanded free land, aspired to become planters themselves while cursing those already rich. Royall took solace in madeira and brandy—so much so that three loyal slaves began following him out of doors lest he harm himself or others. In 1812 the old gentleman died leaving everything to his bride.

Since Anne was itching to travel she sold off most of the property and lit out for Alabama. But Royall's relatives sued, claiming Anne had lived in sin, mistreated the old drunk, and forged his will. They won on appeal in 1819, leaving Anne penniless and in debt. There was nothing for it, she wrote her lawyer, but to duck her creditors and try to make money: "Don't laugh. I have the notion of turning author."[8] Like Parson Weems, she hoped to get rich peddling books on the road. Like J. F. Cooper, she produced one ugly flop before finding her voice as "A Traveler" commenting on American mores. By 1830 her *Sketches of History, Life, and Manners in the United States, The Black Book, Mrs. Royall's Pennsylvania,* and *Mrs. Royall's Southern Tour* would make her one of the most infamous scribblers loose in the land. But every mile down the road was a struggle, sometimes of her own making.

Now a veteran's widow, she headed first for the Federal City in search of a pension. On a cold December eve in 1823 she arrived in "the worst carriage I ever was in" at Alexandria's famed City Tavern. The proprietor, a Mason, stood her a week's rent and the boat fare over the Potomac. In Georgetown she admired the brick townhouses starting to line the streets, but found Washington City either ugly and poor or rich and exclusive. Many a time Negroes at servants' entrances slammed doors in her face. She lived off the charity of Freemasons, a priest, Irish workers who passed the hat, and a nephew of Catholic landowner Daniel Carroll. "How much have I heard said about these Roman Catholics!" she wrote. "I have heard them accounted little

better than heretics. But I must confess, I never was amongst people more liberal." She often observed the only Americans who practiced real charity
seemed to be Masons or Catholics. Yet on Capitol Hill (where Anne counted
more prostitutes than congressmen) she persuaded Daniel Webster to plead for
her pension. Secretary of State Adams also received her. When she mentioned
her plans to tour New England, Mr. Adams urged, "Stop at Quincy and see my
father," while Mrs. Adams made her the gift of a shawl against winter.[9]

In Baltimore Anne heard *The Star-Spangled Banner* performed, but
thought the town's ladies quite poorly turned out. In Philadelphia she walked
door to door until her feet bled without making a single sale. (A Quaker philanthropist later said he "loved thy book" and "loved thee," but did not buy "thy
book," borrowing a copy instead.) She was relieved when a price war between
steamboat companies enabled her to buy a ticket to New Jersey for only $2,
then collapsed in tears when told she had boarded the wrong boat. Escaping
Philly at last, she recorded "I never left a place with less regret." In New York,
by contrast, she was encouraged by Cooper's publisher Charles Wiley and the
witty Tammany editor Mordecai Noah, who advertised her as "the new literary
comet" and "Mrs. Walter Scott of America." New York's Masons came through
as well, purchasing $180 worth of subscriptions. In Albany she interviewed
De Witt Clinton, whom she called "a canal himself" whose mind "flows
steadily on." In Springfield, Massachusetts, she marveled at the ingenious
machinery and workers at the government arsenal and paper plants. In Boston
she paid her respects to John Adams and saw eighteen-year-old Charles
Francis Adams perform at Harvard. Turning west Anne was bemused by the
lacy New York socialites "dying with ennui" at Saratoga Springs as if there were
nowhere else in the world to go (one dame asked her what state "Alabama" was
in). Royall rode on the Erie Canal, made a less than sentimental journey
through Pennsylvania, and embraced her mother in Cincinnati where she had
moved with her third husband. Royall saw the future in Illinois, gasped at the
Mississippi, and toured Jackson's New Orleans battleground. She hunted alli-
gators outside Savannah beneath great stands of sycamore, cypress, and holly.
She thought Charleston's gentlemen "another species"—elegant, but seemingly
unmanned by their preachers and women. Mobile she found a "rendezvous of
renegades, outlaws, pirates, and obnoxious characters." Everywhere she peddled her books while accumulating material for the next.[10]

Then in 1827, the fifty-eight-year-old widow discovered a less mercenary purpose in life. The revivals known as the Second Great Awakening swept over New York, New England, and Pennsylvania. A new generation of emotional preachers carried frontier religion to cities. Presbyterians and Congregationalists merged to pursue political power. Worst of all, from her standpoint, the Anti-Masonic Party took off. As a vocal friend of Masons and critic of evangelicals, she was verbally assaulted and physically threatened, usually (she wrote) after dark when "the out-pouring of divine goodness" was strongest. Anne retaliated in print: "Under the name of *foreign* missions, *home* missions, *Bible* societies, *children's* societies, *rag-bag* societies, and *Sunday School* societies, the missionaries have laid the whole country under tribute. . . . The gospel has nothing to do with it. The true gospel of Christ could not be bought and sold for a price." When in Philadelphia she heard Ezra Stiles Ely call for "a Christian party in politics," Anne wrote, "The missionaries have thrown off the mask." She called them Holy Rollers, Holy Willies, Blackcoats, and Blueskins engaged in "vile speculations to amass money." Up in Vermont it was suggested she might make more money herself if she wrote about religion. Anne hissed, "But I *am* writing about religion," and in any event worked "for my country, not money." In Burlington, Vermont, a hostile Congregationalist pushed her down his front stoop, then left her in the slush with a broken leg. In Pittsburgh an Anti-Mason took a horsewhip to her. In Virginia Presbyterian college students rode her out of town on a rail.[11]

After 1830 age and infirmity limited Anne's peregrinations. She settled down in Washington City to savage the intolerant, hypocritical, and corrupt in periodicals she scrimped to publish herself. Politicians fled at her approach; clergymen scorned her; those not in her line of fire chuckled at the "silly old hag." She was even hauled into court and fined $10 for the ancient offense of being a "common scold" (the judge thought dunking, the Common Law punishment, beneath the court's dignity). Of course, the hilarious trial boosted book sales while giving Anne a platform to rail about religious conspiracies. But as Anne lived on, watching the national scene like an old rook on a bough, she realized the danger was not what it seemed. Evangelicals did wound Freemasonry, but they were not about to suppress free speech or undo the Revolution. On the contrary, they meant to invoke free speech and the Revolution's ideals to condemn slavery, thereby endangering the prosperous, enlightened Union fashioned by Master Builders both northern and southern. So worried did America's virago become she concluded her 1854 journal *The Huntress* (after a long encomium to Dr. Morse's Invigorating Elixir) with a prayer "that the Union of the States may be eternal." The prayer did not avail. Neither did the elixir. Anne Newport Royall died ten weeks later.[12]

The outburst of rural revivals in the first year of the Deist Jefferson's presidency was no more a coincidence than the outburst of urban revivals in the first year of the Freemason Jackson's presidency. For the Second Great Awakening is best understood as the spiritual component of the same egalitarian wave that washed over the nation's politics. All observant religious leaders recognized from the moment of independence they must adjust their doctrine, ecclesiastical governance, and evangelical style to Americans' civic religion and rollicking freedom of movement and choice. Orthodox or Antinomian theology stressing original sin could scarcely compete with Arminian theology stressing human benevolence. Theology stressing the soul's helplessness (not to say predestination) before the stern judgment of God had no chance beside theology stressing the soul's free access to grace and God's loving forgiveness. Theology preaching delayed gratification for the suffering of this present life was a poor product compared to theology promising instant gratification and heaven on earth.

Although Royall thought it strange Jackson attracted the "black coats," they were to religion what Democratic campaign managers were to mass politics. Baptist John Leland, Presbyterian Lyman Beecher, Methodist Peter Cartwright, African Methodist Richard Allen, Barton Stone of the ecumenical Christian sect, Alexander Campbell of the Disciples of Christ, and the "Napoleon among his marshals," heterodox Presbyterian Charles Grandison Finney, organized grassroots movements *as if* they were political parties. They used newspaper chains and the post office like the Jacksonians. They scorned lofty seminarian disquisitions in the same way Jacksonians teased Adams' "Greek" orations. They cried from the pulpit or stump in the idioms of the people, addressing their real-life concerns and appealing to emotion rather than reason. They were wildly inclusive, reaching out to all social and geographical categories, the educated and illiterate, women and children. Their message, like Jackson's, was vague but universal *reform*. To old-fashioned rationalists they seemed like hucksters hawking tracts and trolling for money. To old-fashioned Puritans they seemed like politicians trolling for votes: "They measure the progress of religion by the numbers who flock to their standards, not by the prevalence of faith and piety, justice and charity and the public virtues of society in general."[13]

Looking back, some social historians surmised the Second Awakening was an auxiliary of the "market revolution," a conservative movement to transform rowdy frontiersmen and farmers into passive industrial workers.[14] Aside from the fact no evidence of such motives can be found among revivalist leaders, the effect of their new dispensation was exactly the opposite. They preached popular sovereignty, democracy, community, liberty, opportunity. They did so, in fact, to a degree heretical in traditional Christian terms but thoroughly orthodox in terms of the American civic religion. Far from exhorting the virtues of poverty and submission, they taught that God poured out his blessings on reformed individuals: "Seek ye first the kingdom of God and all this shall be added unto you." But the ultimate goal of personal reform was social perfection. All denominations founded academies, colleges, and Sunday schools to promote literacy. All supported Beecher's American Temperance Society, founded in 1826 to help free men become *more* than wage slaves. What is more, most revivalists raced far ahead of their Jacksonian counterparts by challenging the social order on the touchiest subject of all: race. Jedidiah Morse urged his Andover students to educate and protect Indians. Theodore Weld and his wife Angelina Grimké carried abolitionism into the political arena. William Lloyd Garrison's followers even drew parallels between the enslavement of Negroes and the subjection of women.[15]

Nor were evangelists' methods conservative. They were on the cutting edge of technological and cultural change. Cooper and Royall might hope to sell a few thousand books. The American Bible Society (founded 1816) took advantage of mass-produced paper and steam-powered presses to print three hundred thousand copies of Scripture *per year* in the late 1820s. The American Tract Society (founded 1825) boasted of 5 million items in circulation by 1830. But Bible study is hard, time-consuming work. A busy, commercial, consumer culture needed quicker, more entertaining spiritual sustenance, something Parson Weems was first to discover. Since 1794 he had peddled books on the road for Mathew Carey, the Philadelphia printer who learned his trade working for Franklin in Paris. But Carey loaded Weems down with so many "puritanical" books that the marketing genius rebelled. "Let the moral and religious be as dulcified as possible," he urged. "Divinity for this climate should be natural and liberal, adorned with the graces of style, and clothed in splendid binding." He had in mind a hot seller called *Onania* that titillated readers with stories of masturbation while of course warning against "the sin of self-pollution." Weems and his copycats churned out scores of "penny godlies" such as *Hymen's Recruiting Sergeant* and *The Bad Wife's Looking Glass.* Methodist minister

George Lippard wrote a whole series called *The Quaker City, or Monks of Monk Hall* to impress on readers the wages of sin. Other authors capitalized on Cooper's success with frontier potboilers in which white maidens, captured and stripped by Indians, defended their virtue until rescued by their gallant menfolk.[16] Thus did salesmen of the Second Awakening stumble on the ideal American genre: pornography tricked out as moral uplift.

Sexuality was surely a weapon in the cultural battles of the early nineteenth century. The task before Americans, as Cooper said, was to render conservative (predictable, civilized) a potentially anarchic frontier nation. On the already civilized Atlantic seaboard, where the wars and turmoil of national birth were over, Unitarian, Anglican, and Old Light clergymen fell into a tacit alliance with women in hopes of taming the unruly male sex. They campaigned against dueling, brawling, boozing, whoring, and indigence by imposing a romantic and mawkish brand of religion. Their tracts and sermons stressed a parental, almost motherly God, a sweet, suffering Savior, and a church called to nurture, sacrifice, turn the other cheek. No more were young Calvinists charged with shirking a holy duty if they failed to enlist in the militia. No more were ungodly men told their souls dangled over hellfire like Jonathan Edwards' spider. Instead they were hit with something more real and immediate: shame. Henry James, Sr., lamented the trend: "Religion in the old virile sense has disappeared, and been replaced by a feeble Unitarian sentimentality." Harriet Beecher Stowe called the trend a veritable "Pink and White Tyranny." Harriet Martineau wrote of effeminate, over-educated clergy as "halfway between men and women." For centuries patriarchs reinforced by biology had defined what womanhood meant. Now matriarchs reinforced by theology defined what manhood meant in an urban, middle-class, consumer society. Meekness now befitted husbands and fathers. Children became tender sprouts to be carefully "raised," not little adults to be broken to work. Church cemeteries, once a grim reminder of death and judgment, began in 1831 to be moved out of town and made into gardens of peace. Domesticity was becoming the cardinal virtue.[17]

Revivalists, by contrast, embraced the opposite tactic. The way to tame men was not to make religion feminine, but to make masculinity religious! Beecher told ministers in training to eschew a pedantic "professional manner" and instead recall they were *men* before they were clergymen. The evangelist must "thrust" and "lunge" and "pour his manhood out" on the assembled throng. Finney likened missionary work to fighting a war. It had nothing in

common with the flaccid Sunday services staged by eastern theological graduates. Revivalists should look sinners in the eye, grab their arms, challenge them
"man to man," and ask if they had *the guts* to confess the truth about themselves
and society. Did not Jesus exhort, "Be ye perfect"?[18]

Perfect? Way back in 1783 David Tappan tossed a wet blanket over
Americans' celebration of independence by asking: "Is human nature essentially
different in this new world, from what it ever has been and still is in the old?
Or are we more strongly fortified against the insinuating, bewitching charms of
a prosperous condition? Are we a people of more established virtue than all
others that have lived before us? Alas, Sirs, such self-flattering ideas are equally
false and vain—our national character . . . is perhaps as degenerate as that of
any people in the world." Evangelical preachers went even further. They compared American society, not to France, Russia, or seventeenth-century Boston,
but to the Bible's standard of perfection. Yet, at the same time, they insisted as
loudly as their colonial forebears that America was destined to prepare a place
for the Second Coming and host the thousand-year reign of the saints. How
could the damnable *failings* of Americans be squared with the heavenly *expectations* placed in America? There was only one way: reform, reform, reform until
Americans, purged with hyssop as in Psalm 51, emerged whiter than snow.[19]

The Second Great Awakening: outburst of bizarre mysticism, mass psy-
chosis, gigantic flim-flam, capitalist plot, or ultimate expression of "anti-
intellectualism" in America? Charles Grandison Finney, no dummy, knew it
was none of those things. Born in Connecticut in 1792, he was launched on a
legal career when, in 1821, he grappled violently with the Scriptures. He felt his
heart and mind struggle to master his will. He saw a vision of Christ on the
main street of Adams, New York. "I could feel the impression," he testified,
"like a wave of electricity going through and through me." Finney surrendered,
gave up his practice, and took up a commission as traveler for God. Though
licensed to preach by the Presbyterians, he had no use for Calvinist formulas.
When asked if he adhered to the Westminster Confession, Finney said he had
never read it. What had Geneva, Leyden, or Westminster to do with America?
He spurned Yale and Princeton theology, boasting instead of "coming out of
the woods" like Natty Bumppo. He argued, with keen intellect, the inadequacy
of intellect. Such was the state of America, he wrote, "to expect to promote
religion without excitements is unphilosophical and absurd. The great political,
and other worldly excitements that agitate Christendom, are all unfriendly to

religion, and divert the mind from the interests of the soul. Now these excitements can only be counteracted by religious excitements."[20]

Thanks to his eerily luminescent, hypnotic blue eyes and a voice to match, Finney went on the road stirring excitement. Did he convert the unchurched or high-brow skeptics? At times, but mostly Finney re-energized hundreds of thousands of existing church members starved for that "wave of electricity," that almost orgasmic thrill Finney could generate. He did not call down the Spirit on sinners, but instead kindled the embers *within* farmers, mechanics, lawyers, merchants, canal workers, and their communities. He asked how might the country be saved, what needed reforming, what do YOU need to change? Finney's modestly named "new measures" forced people to ask questions all the more frightening because they already knew the answers. But his watchword was community, not individualism. Personal sin was not only a blight on one's soul, it was a curse on one's family, neighbors, and nation. Finney defined sin as selfishness pure and simple, challenging men and women to be "useful in the highest degree possible" and "make the world a fit place for the imminent return of Christ."[21] In effect, what Finney called Perfectionism or Religious Ultraism *reversed* John Winthrop's "Citee on a Hill" sermon. Winthrop told Puritans that falling back into sin once in America would be an offense against God. Finney told disciples that wallowing in sin once a Christian would be an offense against *America,* an offense that risked its Providential destiny.

Here was religion of the sort most Americans craved, a religion of the heart promising instant improvement in every household and community, the blessings of heaven in this life, in America, perhaps even "the complete moral renovation of the world," as William Sprague gushed in his 1833 *Lectures on the Revivals of Religion.* Like Beecher, Finney summoned the "animal spirits" in preachers and congregations. Like McGready, Finney extended his camp and town meetings long into the night and day after day. Like King David, Finney slew his ten thousands, first in rural New York, then Rochester in 1830, then in Boston, Philadelphia, and New York City, where he presided over a non-stop revival at the grand Broadway Tabernacle. Tirelessly Finney worked the "anxious bench," grabbing men by their lapels, calling them to the gospel by name, staring into their hearts. Scoffers called him a heretic, ignoramus, showman who stirred up emotion at the expense of instruction. Finney replied with precocious psychology that that was precisely the point. Everyone, he wrote, might follow logic to similar philosophical conclusions. "We have reason to believe that holy angels and devils apprehend and embrace intellectually the same truths, and yet how differently are they affected by them!" The difference was some people grasped truth with their heads alone. The *heart* must be won over, the heart where all pleasure and pain, sanctity and sin resided and wrestled. The Old Lights, even some Methodists and Baptists, taught tired dogma powerless to change hearts while offering "false comforts for sinners." They claimed men could not save themselves, but must wait upon God, persevere, and pray. Waiting, persevering, and praying, they remained forever inert. Finney insisted preachers yank Christians out of their seats with direct, simple language whose truth people could feel and whose appeal was "directly for action." The only thing holding Americans back, holding *America* back, was a weakness of will. Thus, where other divines told people to believe in this doctrine or await that feeling, Finney cried: "Don't wait for feeling, DO IT!"[22]

In these years upstate New York was still considered "the West." But beyond the Erie Canal and National Road the next and greater West loomed. Evangelists seemed drawn there in person or the mind's eye. It was in Cincinnati in 1829 that one of the great debates of American history occurred between Robert Owen, the Welsh industrialist and utopian socialist, and Alexander Campbell, the fiery Scottish American preacher. They agreed mankind's destiny was heaven on earth, but where Owen argued (after Rousseau) a wicked *society* caused all human ills, Campbell blamed a fallen *human nature* for the ills of society. Europeans would mostly travel down Owen's path in the company of Rousseau, Karl Marx, and their successors, seeking personal fulfillment through some social rebirth. Americans would mostly travel down Campbell's path in the belief social rebirth required "radical changes in the human spirit." Expecting the religion of Christ to "melt the hearts of men into pure philanthropy," Campbell founded *The Millennial Harbinger* in 1830 to promote "the ultimate amelioration of society."[23]

Two years later Lyman Beecher arrived in Cincinnati to become head of an evangelical seminary. He knew at once he had come to the decisive theater in the war for America's soul, writing in a *Plea for the West* (1835): "The West is a young empire of mind, and power, and wealth, and free institutions, rushing up to a giant manhood with a rapidity and a power never witnessed below the sun. And if she carries with her the elements of her preservation, the experiment will be glorious." In 1837, Finney left Broadway for a parish in Oberlin, Ohio, next to America's first co-educational, bi-racial college. He agreed with William Cogswell's 1833 tract warning the "Great Valley of the Mississippi . . . may be said, in general terms, to be little better than one immense field of moral desolations." It was enough to "break any heart unless harder than adamant, and to rouse it into holy action." America's future, hence God's whole plan for history, depended on winning the West for Christ and Perfection by, among other things, slaying that old serpent called slavery.[24]

James Fenimore Cooper never followed his fictional Leatherstocking into the West. After returning from Europe in 1833, he lived out his life in New York City and Cooperstown. But his heart told him the American West would *not* host the millennium whatever the future of slavery there. Rather, his father's dashed dreams, the heartbreak of Bumppo, the dispossession of Indians, the greed of the mob, and the sly maneuvers of lawyers would play themselves out, over and over, until all frontiers were despoiled. His testament was *The Crater* (1847) in which American shipwrecks marshal their political and technical savvy to construct an idyllic society on a Pacific isle. Alas, they are not satisfied with the best human nature can do, craving even more freedom and power. Litigation, sectarian strife, vicious journalism, and hedonism wreck everything. Cooper, as if weary of the farrago, conjures an earthquake to sink the island's "whole squabbling cargo into the sea."[25]

Freedom, just around the corner, but with truth so far off, what good would it do? On the Fourth of July, 1826, John Adams and Thomas Jefferson gave up the ghost. On the Fourth of July, 1828, John Quincy Adams and Charles Carroll of Carrollton, the last surviving signer of the Declaration of Independence, broke ground for the B&O Railroad. Americans were spinning through time and space at what seemed then preternatural speed. They traveled in faith theirs was the climactic pilgrimage of the whole human race. But Americans didn't know whether it would end in apotheosis or an apocalypse. So they contented themselves, in the meantime, with the advice of Johnson Hooper's satirical Captain Suggs: "It is good to be shifty in a new country."[26]

# NOTES

AMERICAN ARCHETYPES

1. Herman Melville, *The Confidence-Man: His Masquerade* (San Francisco: Chandler, 1968 [1857], introduction by John Seelye (quotes in first paragraph from pp. 1–5; review quoted on p. xxxvii).

2. Ibid., p. 10.

3. Jonathan A. Cook, *Satirical Apocalypse: An Anatomy of Melville's* The Confidence-Man (Westport, Conn.: Greenwood Press, 1996), pp. 1–2.

4. Mark W. Summers, *The Plundering Generation: Corruption and the Crisis of the Union, 1849–1861* (New York: Oxford University, 1987), p. 283. Melville's was not a voice in the wilderness. The national anxiety about a marketplace of deceit is the subject of Karen Halttunen, *Confidence Men and Painted Women: A Study of Middle-Class Culture in America, 1830–1870* (New Haven, Conn.: Yale University, 1982).

5. Melville, *Confidence-Man*, chapter VI (quote from p. 52).

6. Ibid., chapter VII (quote from p. 62). The "methodization" of benevolence is a dig at Methodism. Melville's bitter reference to the "Wall street spirit" doubtless stemmed from his father's ruin through speculation.

7. Ibid., chapter XLIII (quotes from pp. 359, 361, 363, 371).

8. Carolyn L. Karcher, *Shadow over the Promised Land: Slavery, Race, and Violence in Melville's America* (Baton Rouge: Louisiana State University, 1980), p. 192.

9. Ibid., p. 181. See also John P. McWilliams, Jr., *Hawthorne, Melville, and the American Character: A Looking-Glass Business* (Cambridge, U.K.: Cambridge University, 1984).

10. Cited by Carl N. Degler, *Out of Our Past: The Forces That Shaped Modern America*, 3d ed. (New York: Harper Perennial, 1984), pp. 48–49.

11. See Paul Radin, *The Trickster: A Study in American Indian Mythology* (New York: Greenwood Press, 1956), quote from p. ix.

12. "We're All Dodgin'," The Classics Record Library, text © 1961 Loom Music Publishers.

13. One scholar supposes that Melville was inspired by a "new, very limited conception of humanity" as *Homo economicus*, the same materialist conception that inspired Marx and Engels over the same years: Helen P. Trimpi, "Daumier's Robert Macaire and Melville's Confidence Man," in *Savage Eye: Melville and the Visual Arts* (Kent, Ohio: Kent State University, 1991), p. 196.

14. Mark Twain (Samuel Langhorne Clemens), *A Connecticut Yankee in King Arthur's Court* (New York: Penguin Signet, 1988), quotes in previous paragraph from pp. 11, 14–15.

15. Ibid., quotes from pp. 16, 24.

16. Ibid., quotes from pp. 112, 85, 218. Yes, Franklin D. Roosevelt borrowed the phrase "New Deal" from Twain.

17. Ibid., p. 318.

18. Edmund Reiss, "Afterword," in ibid., p. 331.

19. Historic Winchester served as George Washington's headquarters in the French and Indian War and Stonewall Jackson's headquarters in the Civil War. It was also the hometown of Senator Harry Byrd and the polar explorer Admiral Richard Byrd, in addition to Cather.

20. For sensitive accounts of this shock, see Walter Prescott Webb, *The Great Plains* (Boston: Ginn and Company, 1931), any number of pioneer journals kept by women, or just the "Little House on the Prairie" books by Laura Ingalls Wilder.

21. Willa Cather in the appendix to *O Pioneers!* (New York: Oxford University, 1999), p. 172. Quotes in previous paragraph from p. 9.

22. Ibid., quotes from pp. 17, 20.

23. Ibid., pp. 39–41.

24. Ibid., pp. 63, 68–69.

25. Ibid., pp. 89–93.

26. Ibid., p. 169.

27. Coincidentally, Kristofferson is of Scandinavian stock and Dylan grew up in Minnesota. Certain ghostly tropes seem to haunt the Great Plains, and violence, injustice, and loneliness are never far away.

28. Introduction by Marilee Lindemann in ibid., p. xvii. Cather had several long-term relationships with women, but was not a feminist in any ideological or political sense. See also Lindemann's *Willa Cather: Queering America* (New York: Columbia University, 1999), Sharon O'Brien, *Willa Cather: The Emerging Voice* (New York: Oxford University, 1987), and James Woodress, *Willa Cather: A Literary Life* (Lincoln: University of Nebraska, 1987).

29. William Safire, *Scandalmonger: A Novel* (New York: Simon & Schuster, 2000), quotes in previous paragraphs from pp. 37, 43.

30. Alexis de Tocqueville, *Democracy in America*, vol. 1 (New York: Vintage Books, 1945), p. 235.

31. Samuel P. Huntington, *Political Order in Changing Societies* (New Haven, Conn.: Yale University, 1968), pp. 59–71.

32. The term is mine, coined in *Let the Sea Make a Noise. . . . A History of the North Pacific From Magellan to MacArthur* (New York: Basic Books, 1994). The inspiration came from my research on the finances and construction of the first transcontinental railroad. That the Central Pacific's Big Four (Leland Stanford, Collis P. Huntington, Charles Crocker, and Mark Hopkins) swindled American taxpayers out of fortunes in loans and lands has become conventional wisdom. But as I followed their extraordinary exertions and imagined the risks that they took, I concluded the railroad would not have been built so quickly, if at all, save for the "grease" of corruption. See also my essay on comparative corruption in *Orbis: A Journal of World Affairs* 43:4 (Fall 1999): 525–30.

33. Samuel P. Huntington, *American Politics: The Promise of Disharmony* (Cambridge, Mass.: Harvard University, 1981), especially pp. 61–75 (quote, p. 262).

## SAINT GEORGE AND THE DRAGON

1. A pithy summary of the flaws in major theories about the roots of capitalism is renegade Marxist Ellen Meiksins Wood's *The Origin of Capitalism* (New York: Monthly Review, 1999). She in turn praises the insights of Karl Polanyi's classic *The Great Transformation* (Boston:

Beacon, 1957). China under the Song Dynasty (960–1279) may be considered a precursor, albeit an ephemeral one, to England's commercial agriculture. See J. R. McNeill and William H. McNeill, *The Human Web: A Bird's Eye View of Human History* (New York: W.W. Norton, 2003), pp. 121–27.

2. For a brief introduction to the Common Law tradition see the entry in the *Oxford Companion to British History* or *Encyclopaedia Britannica*. For extensive expositions of Common Law development see Frederic W. Maitland, *The Constitutional History of England* and *The History of English Law Before the Time of Edward I* (London: Cambridge University, 1968 [1903]), or J. G. A. Pocock, *The Ancient Constitution and the Feudal Law* (New York: Cambridge University, 1957)

3. There is a huge literature on the rise of agrarian capitalism in England, but a good summary of contesting views is in T. H. Aston and C. H. E. Philpin, *The Brenner Debate: Agrarian Class Structure and Economic Development in Pre-Industrial Europe* (Cambridge, U.K.: Cambridge University, 1985). See especially Robert Brenner, "The Agrarian Roots of European Capitalism," pp. 213–327.

4. J. A. Yelling, *Common Field and Enclosure in England 1450–1850* (Hamden, Conn.: Archon Books, 1977), p. 7.

5. H. P. R. Finberg, ed., *The Agrarian History of England and Wales* (Cambridge, U.K.: Cambridge University, 1967), pp. 161–63, 198–99.

6. Carl Bridenbaugh, *Vexed and Troubled Englishmen 1590–1642* (New York: Oxford University, 1968), pp. 210–12.

7. See Allan Kulikoff, *From British Peasants to Colonial American Farmers* (Chapel Hill: University of North Carolina, 2000), pp. 16–27.

8. Eric Kerridge, *Agrarian Problems in the Sixteenth Century and After* (London: Allen and Unwin, 1969), p. 132

9. On the grand trends in English society see E. A. Wrigley and R. S. Schofield, *The Population History of England, 1541–1871: A Reconstruction* (Cambridge, Mass.: Harvard University, 1981); Peter Laslett, *The World We Have Lost* (London: Methuen, 1965); Keith Wrightson, *English Society, 1580–1680* (New Brunswick, N.J.: Rutgers University, 1982); Joan Thirsk, *Economic Policy and Prospects: The Development of a Consumer Society in Early Modern England* (Oxford: Oxford University, 1978); A. L. Beier, *Masterless Men: The Vagrancy Problem in England 1560–1640* (London: Methuen, 1985); Buchanan Sharp, *In Contempt of All Authority: Rural Artisans and Riot in the West of England, 1580–1660* (Berkeley: University of California, 1980); Paul Slack, *Poverty and Policy in Tudor and Stuart England* (New York: Longman, 1988). Quote from Kulikoff, *From British Peasants*, p. 17.

10. T. S. Willan, *The Inland Trade: Studies in English Internal Trade in the Sixteenth and Seventeenth Centuries* (Totowa, N.J.: Rowman & Littlefield, 1976), pp. 1–3, 78–79. A bill to tax peddlers finally did pass in the 1690s, dunning them 4 pounds sterling per year plus an additional four for every horse, mule, or ass they employed.

11. Richard Grassby, *Kinship and Capitalism: Marriage, Family, and Business in the English-Speaking World, 1580–1740* (Cambridge, U.K.: Cambridge University, 2001), p. 417.

12. Richard L. Greaves, *Society and Religion in Elizabethan England* (Minneapolis: University of Minnesota, 1981), pp. 214–33.

13. Bridenbaugh, *Vexed and Troubled Englishmen*, pp. 361–93 (quotes pp. 361, 362, 387). Figures on trials and lawyers from Donald R. Kelley, "Elizabethan Political Thought," in J. G. A. Pocock, ed., *The Varieties of British Political Thought, 1500–1800* (Cambridge, U.K.: Cambridge University, 1993), p. 66.

14. Louis Hartz probably did the most to make this a standard interpretation in *The Liberal Tradition in America: An Interpretation of American Political Thought Since the Revolution* (New York: Harcourt, Brace, 1955). Marxist historians were quick to agree, albeit in order to damn rather than praise (viz. Douglas F. Dowd, *The Twisted Dream: Capitalist Development in the United States Since 1776* [Cambridge, Mass.: Winthrop, 1974]). For a general discussion of the historiography see Christopher Clark, *The Roots of Rural Capitalism: Western Massachusetts, 1780–1860* (Ithaca, N.Y.: Cornell University, 1990), pp. 8–17.

15. Joyce Oldham Appleby, *Economic Thought and Ideology in Seventeenth-Century England* (Princeton: Princeton University, 1978), p. 242.

16. See "The Inflationary Spiral, c. 1300–c. 1520" in R. W. Southern, *Western Society and the Church in the Middle Ages* (New York: Penguin, 1970), pp. 133–69.

17. John Guy, *Tudor England* (New York: Oxford University, 1988).

18. R. B. Smith, *Land and Politics in the England of Henry VIII* (Oxford: Clarendon: 1970), pp. 254–55. The standard price for church lands was twenty times their annual income compared to the $2 or $3 per acre the U.S. Land Office would realize.

19. A. G. Dickens, *The English Reformation* (New York: Schocken, 1964), pp. 139–66.

20. On anti-clericalism see G. R. Elton, *England Under the Tudors* (London: Methuen, 1962), pp. 102–16.

21. See Diarmaid MacCulloch, *Thomas Cranmer* (New Haven: Yale University, 1996), Dom Gregory Dix, *The Shape of the Liturgy* (London: A & C Black, 1960), and R. T. Beckwith, "The Anglican Eucharist: From the Reformation to the Restoration," in Cheslyn Jones, Geoffrey Wainwright, and Edward Yarnold, eds., *The Study of Liturgy* (New York: Oxford University, 1978), pp. 263–71.

22. Bridenbaugh, *Vexed and Troubled Englishmen*, p. 13.

23. Lacey Baldwin Smith, *Treason in Tudor England: Politics and Paranoia* (Princeton: Princeton University, 1986), p. 142. Two famous epigrams of courtier Sir John Harington summed up the mood: "He that thriveth in a court must put half his honesty under a bonnet" and "Treason doth never prosper, what's the reason? For if it prosper, none dare call it treason."

24. Francis I cited in Max Savelle and Robert Middlekauff, *A History of Colonial America*, rev. ed. (New York: Holt, Rinehart, and Winston, 1966), p. 42.

25. Carlo M. Cipolla, *Guns, Sails and Empires: Technological Innovation and the Early Phases of European Expansion 1400–1700* (New York: Pantheon, 1965), pp. 36–41.

26. D. W. Waters (RN), *The Art of Navigation in England in Elizabethan and Early Stuart Times* (New Haven: Yale University, 1958), p. 104.

27. John W. Shirley, "Improvement in Techniques of Navigation in Elizabethan England," in Per Sörborn, ed., *Transport Technology and Social Change* (Stockholm: Tekniska Museet, 1980), pp. 117–28 (rhyme p. 128).

28. Cipolla, *Guns, Sails and Empires*, pp. 86–89.

29. A. L. Rowse, *The Elizabethans and America* (New York: Harper & Brothers, 1959), pp. 24–25.

30. Ibid., pp. 31–32.

31. E. G. R. Taylor, ed., *The Original Writings and Correspondence of the Two Richard Hakluyts* (London: Hakluyt Society, 1935), 2 vols.: II: 211ff. See also David B. Quinn, ed., *The Hakluyt Handbook* (London: Hakluyt Society, 1974) and George Bruner Parks, *Richard Hakluyt and the English Voyages* (New York: American Geographical Society, 1930 [1900]). The infamous "Black Legend" of the Spaniards' unspeakable greed and brutality in the New World was

already current in England. See William S. Maltby, *The Black Legend in England: The Development of Anti-Spanish Sentiment, 1558–1660* (Durham, N.C.: Duke University, 1971).

32. Rowse, *Elizabethans and America*, p. 34.

33. See David B. Quinn, *The Voyages and Colonizing Enterprises of Sir Humphrey Gilbert*, 2 vols. (London: Hakluyt Society, 1940); patent described, I: 35.

34. Louis B. Wright, *The Dream of Prosperity in Colonial America* (New York: New York University, 1965), pp. 13–15, 42–43.

35. Paul Johnson, *A History of the American People* (New York: HarperCollins, 1998), p. 12.

36. By the way, Virginia Dare of Roanoke Island was not the first white child born in what is now U.S. territory: a Frenchwoman gave birth at Fort Caroline in 1565. On Ralegh's colonial promotions see David B. Quinn, *Set Fair for Roanoke: Voyages and Colonies, 1584–1606* (Chapel Hill: University of North Carolina, 1985), which summarizes his lifetime of research and inclines at the end toward the theory that the lost colony went native. The most recent work is Lee Miller, *Roanoke: Solving the Mystery of the Lost Colony* (New York: Arcade, 2001), but see also Karen Ordahl Kupperman, *Roanoke: A Colony Abandoned* (Totowa, N.J.: Rowman and Allanheld, 1984); David Stick, *Roanoke Island: The Beginnings of English America* (Chapel Hill: University of North Carolina, 1983); David B. Durant, *Raleigh's Lost Colony: The Story of the First English Settlements in America* (New York: Atheneum, 1981).

37. Rowse, *Elizabethans and America*, p. 71.

38. According to legend the Irish defeated themselves thanks to their fondness of whiskey. While stoking his courage for the final assault one of Tyrone's lieutenants ran out of drink and brazenly sent a messenger to the English lines to beg a bottle and give away the game by gratuitously boasting of the great victory the Irish anticipated that very night: A. L. Rowse, *The Expansion of Elizabethan England* (New York: Harper & Row, 1955), pp. 415–38. Whatever his intelligence source, however, Mountjoy was almost certainly tipped off about the planned Irish attack. See the account of the Battle of Kinsale in G. A. Hayes-McCoy, *Irish Battles: A Military History of Ireland* (Belfast: Appletree, 1989), pp. 144–73. For an in-depth account see R. F. Foster, ed., *The Oxford Illustrated History of Ireland* (New York: Oxford University, 1989).

39. Nicholas P. Canny, *The Elizabethan Conquest of Ireland: A Pattern Established 1565–1576* (London: Harvester, 1976), pp. 160–63. See also Jane H. Ohlmeyer, "Colonization Within Britain and Ireland," in Nicholas Canny, ed., *The Oxford History of the British Empire*, vol. 1: *The Origins of Empire: British Overseas Enterprise to the Close of the Seventeenth Century* (Oxford: Oxford University, 1998), pp. 134–46.

40. John Locke, *Two Treatises of Government*, ed. Peter Laslett, 2 ed. (Cambridge, U.K.: Cambridge University, 1967), p. 306.

41. Oscar and Lilian Handlin, *Liberty and Power 1600–1760* (New York: Harper & Row, 1986), p. xix.

PLANTERS, PATROONS, AND PURITANS

1. The draft of this chapter was already complete when Alan Taylor, *American Colonies* (New York: Viking, 2001) appeared. It is a grand comparative synthesis of the colonization of North America that covers much of the same ground as my early chapters, albeit in a more analytical, less narrative voice. For the planting of the Jamestown colony, see his pp. 117–37.

2. M. L. Brown, *Firearms in Colonial America* (Washington, D.C.: Smithsonian Institution, 1980), pp. 151–58.

3. Thomas L. Purvis, *Colonial America to 1763* (New York: Facts on File, 1999), pp. 34–36.

Quote is from Plymouth Colony Governor Bradford, cited by Howard N. Simpson, *Invisible Armies: The Impact of Disease on American History* (Indianapolis: Bobbs-Merrill, 1980), pp. 7–8. See also William H. McNeill, *Plagues and Peoples* (Garden City, N.Y.: Anchor, 1976).

4. An authoritative summary is Neal Salisbury, "Native People and European Settlers in Eastern North America, 1600–1783," in *The Cambridge History of the Native Peoples of the Americas*, Bruce D. Trigger and Wilcomb E. Washburn, eds. (Cambridge, U.K.: Cambridge University, 1996), pp. 399–460.

5. Until the 1960s American historiography was influenced by the old "Black Legend" according to which the English colonists enjoyed relatively benign relations with friendly (as opposed to hostile) Indians in contrast to the cruel Spanish conquistadors. But since then Americans' consciousnesses have been raised by a new orthodoxy stressing English perfidy and racism toward peoples they deemed "savage." See especially Francis Jennings, *The Invasion of America: Indians, Colonialism, and the Cant of Conquest* (Chapel Hill: University of North Carolina, 1975). A less fevered way of putting the matter, however, is that "The Indian, it was understood, had little to contribute to the goals of English colonization and was therefore regarded merely as an obstacle": Gary B. Nash, *Red, White, and Black: The Peoples of Early America* (Englewood Cliffs, N.J.: Prentice-Hall, 1974), p. 67.

6. Roughly 200,000 of the mostly young, mostly male emigration of the seventeenth century made for Barbados and the other sugar islands of the Caribbean, 120,000 to the Chesapeake, 80,000 to New England and later the Middle Colonies, and 100,000 to Ireland: James Horn, "Tobacco Colonies: The Shaping of English Society in the Seventeenth-Century Chesapeake," in Nicholas Canny, ed., *The Oxford History of the British Empire*, vol. 1: *The Origins of Empire: British Overseas Enterprise to the Close of the Seventeenth Century* (Oxford: Oxford University, 1998), pp. 176–77. Alison Games, *Migration and the Origins of the English Atlantic World* (Cambridge, Mass.: Harvard University, 1999), examined embarkation records in London for the year 1635 that support the generalization first suggested by Bernard Bailyn, *The Peopling of British North America: An Introduction* (New York: Knopf, 1986).

7. James Horn, *Adapting to a New World: English Society in the Seventeenth-Century Chesapeake* (Chapel Hill: University of North Carolina, 1994), p. 126.

8. Wesley Frank Craven, *The Southern Colonies in the Seventeenth Century, 1607–1689* (Baton Rouge: Louisiana State University, 1949), p. 37.

9. Ibid., p. 73. See Edward Arber and Arthur G. Bradley, eds., *Travels and Works of Captain John Smith*, 2 vols. (New York: B. Franklin, 1967 [1884]).

10. Why the "starving time" at Jamestown was so severe and lasted for several years is a mystery. The most outlandish (but thoroughly American) explanation is that the Spaniards planted in the company one or more saboteurs who somehow poisoned the food supply. However, analysis of skeletons excavated on the site reveals no evidence of that. Another theory is that the colony was unluckily planted in the midst of a regional drought, and analyses of the rings of ancient trees in the Tidewater do seem to indicate that the years around 1610 were unusually dry. If so, that might explain why the Indians were chary of sharing more corn than they did with the newcomers. In any event, the company quite obviously failed to provide the colony with sufficient reserves from the start, and the colonists themselves did little to help matters.

11. Carl Bridenbaugh, *Vexed and Troubled Englishmen 1590–1642* (New York: Oxford University, 1968), pp. 400–22; Craven, *Southern Colonies in the Seventeenth Century*, pp. 82–84, 102–3. The centerpiece of the promotion was the official company tract, "A True Declaration of the estate of the Colonie in Virginia, With a confutation of such scandalous reports as have

tended to the disgrace of so worthy an enterprise." Theodore K. Raab, *Jacobean Gentleman: Sir Edwin Sandys, 1561–1629* (Princeton, N.J.: Princeton University, 1998) is the definitive biography.

12. Games, *Migration and the Origins of the English Atlantic World*, pp. 101–6 ("macabre lunacy," p. 101); Horn, *Adapting to a New World*, pp. 8–11 ("grotesque parody," p. 8). See also Robert D. Mitchell, "The Formation of Early American Cultural Regions: An Interpretation," in James R. Gibson, ed., *European Settlement and Development in North America: Essays on Geographical Change* (Toronto: University of Toronto, 1978). He argues that self-selected immigration and the effects of the American environment made the early settlers "liberalist, individualistic, and capitalist . . . to a degree rarely encountered in Europe" (p. 69). The key word is "rarely": those qualities were already present in England and far better nourished in America.

13. On Maryland and the Chesapeake generally from 1650 to 1750, see Taylor, *American Colonies*, pp. 138–57.

14. All colonial land was the monarch's to dispose of through charters to companies or individuals. The latter, in turn, were free to distribute the land reserved to them in exchange for quit rents, regular cash payments that made tenants "quit and free" of all old-fashioned obligations to the landlord and permitted them, in turn, to sell the land to third parties. But quit rents were hard to collect in the New World, especially by absentee landlords, and the colonists were loath to pay, so for all practical purposes a free market in land grew quickly. Still, the quit rent system survives to this day in the real estate taxes Americans pay to their counties or townships: default on your taxes and the government seizes and auctions off your land. A clear and short summary of land tenure terminology is in Jonathan Hughes, *American Economic History* (Glenview, Ill.: Scott, Foresman, and Co., 1983), pp. 15–19.

15. Horn, *Adapting to a New World*, pp. 153–55.

16. Thomas J. Condon, *New York Beginnings: The Commercial Origins of New Netherland* (New York: New York University, 1968), pp. 3–35 (quote p. 24).

17. David De Vries, the merchant-adventurer who founded the first Staten Island settlement, cited by Ellis Lawrence Raesly, *Portrait of New Netherland* (New York: Columbia University, 1945), p. 33.

18. Kieft was a butcher, but it is a canard that whites invented scalping. See James Axtell and William C. Sturtevant, "The Unkindest Cut, or Who Invented Scalping?" *William and Mary Quarterly* 37 (1985): 451–72, and the old *Handbook of American Indians*, Frederick Webb Hodge, ed., 2 vols. (Washington, D.C.: Smithsonian Institution, 1912), II: 242.

19. Terry G. Jordan and Matti Kaups, *The American Backwoods Frontier: An Ethnic and Ecological Interpretation* (Baltimore: Johns Hopkins University, 1989), quotes from p. 55.

20. Sigmund Diamond, "From Organization to Society: Virginia in the Seventeenth Century," *American Journal of Sociology* 63 (1958): 475.

21. David B. Quinn, ed., *North American Discovery circa 1000–1612* (Columbia: University of South Carolina, 1971), pp. 246–47.

22. William Bradford, *Of Plymouth Plantation, 1620–1647* (New York: Knopf, 1952), pp. 120–21.

23. The absurdly wide-muzzled blunderbuss with which cartoon Pilgrims blast away at wild turkeys is a myth. The real blunderbuss (*Donderbus,* or thunder gun) was of Flemish or Dutch origin, had only a slightly flaired muzzle, and was an effective fowling piece in the manner of today's shotgun. But whereas the Pilgrims might have encountered the blunderbuss while at Leyden, there is no evidence any were included in the otherwise carefully recorded arsenal they brought with them to America: Brown, *Firearms in Colonial America*, p. 143.

24. An exquisite portrait of the most influential humanist scholar searching for certitude is William J. Bouwsma, *John Calvin: A Sixteenth-Century Portrait* (New York: Oxford University, 1988).

25. See for instance Carl Degler, *Out of Our Past: The Forces That Shaped Modern America*, 3 ed. (New York: HarperCollins, 1984), pp. 9–22.

26. Rowse, *The Elizabethans and America*, pp. 156–57 ("at war" a quote from literary historian Moses Coit Tyler; "a foul sink" a quote from Puritan divine Rev. Thomas Shepard).

27. "Reasons For Forsaking England," in Alden T. Vaughan, ed., *The Puritan Tradition in America*, rev ed. (Hanover, N.H.: University Press of New England, 1997), pp. 25–33. On Winthrop's errand, see Perry Miller, *Errand into the Wilderness* (Cambridge, Mass.: Harvard University, 1956).

28. Allyn B. Forbes, ed., *Winthrop Papers*, 5 vols. (Boston: Massachusetts Historical Society, 1929–47), II:118.

29. Alden T. Vaughan, *New England Frontier: Puritans and Indians 1620–1675*, 3 ed. (Norman: University of Oklahoma, 1995), pp. 104–9 (quote from Roger Williams, p. 105).

30. Richard S. Dunn, *Puritans and Yankees: The Winthrop Dynasty of New England, 1630–1717* (New York: W. W. Norton, 1971 [1962]), p. 9.

31. John Winthrop, *The History of New England from 1630 to 1649*, 2 vols., James Savage ed. (Boston: Little, Brown, 1853), II: 271–82.

32. "Zion in the wilderness" from Benjamin W. Labaree, *Colonial Massachusetts: A History* (Millwood, N.Y.: KTO, 1979), pp. 66–83; "Peaceable kingdoms" from Michael Zuckerman, *Peaceable Kingdoms: New England Towns in the Eighteenth Century* (New York: Knopf, 1970). See also Sumner C. Powell, *Puritan Village* (Middletown, Conn.: Wesleyan University, 1963).

33. Bradstreet is celebrated less for her poetry than her sincerity in writing of her husband Simon: "If ever two were one, than surely we. If ever man were lov'd by wife, then thee. . . .": "To My Dear and Loving Husband," in Kenneth Silverman, ed., *Literature in America: The Founding of a Nation* (New York: Free Press, 1971). Statistics on Andover in Labaree, *Colonial Massachusetts*, p. 86.

34. Nathaniel Ward, *The Simple Cobbler of Aggawam in America* (1647) cited by Murray N. Rothbard, *Conceived in Liberty*, 2 vols. (New Rochelle, N.Y.: Arlington House, 1975), I: 176.

35. Ray Ginger, *People on the Move: A United States History* (Boston: Allyn and Bacon, 1975), p. 43.

36. Miller, *Errand into the Wilderness*, pp. 12–15.

37. T. H. Breen, *Puritans and Adventurers: Change and Persistence in Early America* (New York: Oxford University, 1980), p. 51.

38. Brooke Hindle, ed., *America's Wooden Age: Aspects of Its Early Technology* (Tarrytown, N.Y.: Sleepy Hollow, 1975), pp. 16–36.

39. Vaughan, *New England Frontier*, pp. 220–22.

40. Joseph A. Goldenberg, *Shipbuilding in Colonial America* (Charlottesville: University of Virginia, 1976), pp. 3–23.

41. Carl Bridenbaugh, *Fat Mutton and Liberty of Conscience: Society in Rhode Island, 1636–1690* (Providence: Brown University, 1974), pp. 9–26; Sydney V. James, *Colonial Rhode Island* (New York: Charles Scribner's Sons, 1975).

42. Bridenbaugh, *Fat Mutton*, p. 15.

43. Albert E. Van Dusen, *Puritans Against the Wilderness: Connecticut History to 1763* (Chester, Conn.: Pequot Press, 1975), p. 11.

44. Robert West Howard, *The Horse in America* (Chicago: Follett, 1965), pp. 31–44. Few

piers existed, however, for the debarkation of livestock, so most animals shipped to America in the early colonial period had to be pushed overboard in the hope they could safely swim ashore.

45. Dunn, *Puritans and Yankees*, pp. 59–72.

46. Most recently, Taylor, *American Colonies*, pp. 185–86, simply calls declension a myth.

47. Williams cited in Ginger, *People on the Move*, p. 47; Sir William Alexander, "An Encouragement to Colonies," cited in Phillip H. Round, *By Nature and By Custom Cursed: Transatlantic Civil Discourse and New England Cultural Production, 1620–1660* (Hanover, N.H.: University Press of New England, 1999), p. 9.

48. In this final engagement the old men, women, and children were spared thanks to Thomas Stanton, who courageously entered the camp to negotiate their release. The 180 Pequot warriors, however, persisted in trying to break out until all were taken or killed. See Charles Orr, ed., *The History of the Pequot War: The Contemporary Accounts of Mason, Underhill, Vincent and Gardner* (Cleveland, Ohio: Helman-Taylor, 1897); Vaughan, *New England Frontier*, pp. 122–54; Nash, *Red, White, and Black*, pp. 84–86; Salisbury, "Native People and European Settlers," pp. 406–7; Taylor, *American Colonies*, pp. 188–203.

49. Max Savelle and Robert Middlekauff, *A History of Colonial America*, rev. ed. (New York: Holt Rinehart, and Winston, 1966), p. 177.

### BARBADIANS, YORKERS, AND QUAKERS

1. See the fascinating analysis by John Adamson, "England Without Cromwell: What if Charles I Had Avoided the Civil War?" in Niall Ferguson, ed., *Virtual History: Alternatives and Counterfactuals* (New York: Basic Books, 1999), pp. 91–124.

2. Thus Bishop Aylmer could boast in Elizabeth's time, "the regiment of England is not a mere monarchie, as some for lacke of consideration thinke, nor a meere oligarchie, nor democracie, but a rule mixte of all these . . . to be sene in the parliament house": Patrick Collinson, "The Monarchical Republic of Elizabeth I," in John Guy, ed., *The Tudor Monarchy* (London: Arnold, 1997): 110–34 (quote p. 115).

3. See J. G. A. Pocock and Gordon J. Schochet, "Interregnum and Restoration" in Pocock, ed., *The Varieties of British Political Thought, 1500–1800* (New York: Cambridge University, 1983), pp. 146–79.

4. Mark Kishlansky, *A Monarchy Transformed: Britain 1603–1714* (London: Allen Lane, 1996), pp. 250–57.

5. Thomas C. Barrow, *Trade and Empire: The British Customs Service in America, 1660–1775* (Cambridge, Mass.: Harvard University, 1967) and Michael Kammen, *Empire and Interest: The American Colonies and the Politics of Mercantilism* (Philadelphia: Lippincott, 1970).

6. Richard S. Dunn, *Sugar and Slaves: The Rise of the Planter Class in the English West Indies, 1624–1713* (Chapel Hill: University of North Carolina, 1972). Population figures from pp. 54–56, 311–13, except for the 150,000 figure, which is from Michael J. Braddick, "The English Government, War, Trade, and Settlement, 1625–1688," in Nicholas Canny, ed., *The Oxford History of the British Empire*, vol. 1: *The Origins of Empire: British Overseas Enterprise to the Close of the Seventeenth Century* (Oxford: Oxford University, 1998), pp. 30–31. On the British West Indies generally see Alan Taylor, *American Colonies* (New York: Viking, 2001), pp. 204–21.

7. See inter alia Winthrop D. Jordan, *White over Black: American Attitudes Toward the Negro, 1550–1812* (Chapel Hill: University of North Carolina, 1968); David Brion Davis, *The Problem of Slavery in Western Culture* (Ithaca, NY: Cornell University, 1966); Edmund S. Morgan, *American Slavery, American Freedom: The Ordeal of Colonial Virginia* (New York: W. W. Norton, 1975).

8. It is worth adding Dunn's observation that true happiness eluded the rich on Barbados as well. They recorded at length their contempt for the climate, claustrophobia, boredom, disease, irregular food supplies, and constant danger mounted by Spaniards, French, Dutch, and their own gangs of African captives: *Sugar and Slaves*, p. 116.

9. Robert M. Weir, *Colonial South Carolina: A History* (Columbia: University of South Carolina, 1983), pp. 52–53. The replication of West Indian plantation in the Carolinas is most recently treated by Taylor, *American Colonies*, pp. 222–44.

10. Wesley Frank Craven, *The Southern Colonies in the Seventeenth Century 1607–1689* (Baton Rouge: Louisiana State University, 1949), pp. 333–59 ("Ayr gives a strong Appetite," p. 359). "Fertility of the Earth" in George Brown Tindall, *America: A Narrative History*, 2 ed. (New York: W. W. Norton, 1988), I: 73.

11. Sothel's avoidance of conflict and pursuit of personal fortune may be explained in part by the fact that his America-bound ship had been captured by Turks and he spent five years in an Algiers dungeon before making his escape: Hugh T. Lefler and William S. Powell, *Colonial North Carolina: A History* (New York: Charles Scribner's Sons, 1973), pp. 54–55. Weir presents a more favorable view of Sothel's administration, stressing the creative aspects of his corruption: *Colonial South Carolina*, pp. 67–68.

12. M. Eugene Sirmans, *Colonial South Carolina: A Political History 1663–1763* (Chapel Hill: University of North Carolina, 1966), pp. 19–54.

13. Braddick, "English Government, War, Trade, and Settlement, 1625–1688," p. 303.

14. See Stephen S. Webb, *The Governors-General: The English Army and the Definition of the Empire, 1569–1681* (Chapel Hill: University of North Carolina, 1979) on James Stuart's military expertise.

15. Patricia U. Bonomi, *A Factious People: Politics and Society in Colonial New York* (New York: Columbia University, 1971), p. 11.

16. Lawrence H. Leder, *Robert Livingston, 1654–1728, and the Politics of Colonial New York* (Chapel Hill: University of North Carolina, 1961); Robert Carse, *The River Men* (New York: Charles Scribner's Sons, 1969), pp. 45–57.

17. See Michael G. Kammen, *Colonial New York: A History* (New York: Scribner's, 1975), chapters 1–3.

18. See Wesley Frank Craven, *New Jersey and the English Colonization of America* (New York: Van Nostrand, 1964), Richard P. McCormick, *New Jersey from Colony to State, 1609–1789* (Newark: New Jersey Historical Society, 1981), John E. Pomfret, *The Province of West Jersey, 1609–1702* and *The Province of East Jersey, 1609–1702* (Princeton: Princeton University, 1956 and 1962).

19. For a stock nineteenth-century hagiography see Samuel Macpherson Janney, *The Life of William Penn* (Philadelphia: Hogan, Perkins, 1852). A good recent biography is Catherine Owens Peare, *William Penn* (Philadelphia: Lippincott, 1956). The best treatments of Penn's political convictions and maneuvers are Joseph E. Illick, *William Penn the Politician* (Ithaca, N.Y.: Cornell University, 1965), Mary Maples Dunn, *William Penn, Politics and Conscience* (Princeton: Princeton University, 1967), and Gary B. Nash, *Quakers and Politics: Pennsylvania, 1681–1726* (Princeton: Princeton University, 1968).

20. Illick analyzes the various theories in *Penn the Politician*, pp. 23–40. On the undoubted friendship between Penn and James Stuart see Vincent Buranelli, *The King and the Quaker: A Study of William Penn and James II* (Philadelphia: University of Pennsylvania, 1962).

21. Sally Schwartz, *"A Mixed Multitude": The Struggle for Toleration in Colonial Pennsylvania* (New York: New York University, 1987), pp. 12–35. See also Taylor, *American Colonies*, pp. 264–72.

22. Nash, *Quakers and Politics*, pp. 28–47 ("Governments, like clocks" on p. 46). For more

detail see Edward C. O. Beatty, *William Penn as a Social Philosopher* (New York: Columbia University, 1939).

23. Joseph E. Illick, *Colonial Pennsylvania: A History* (New York: Scribner, 1976).

24. Isaac Norris in 1710, quoted by Nash, *Quakers and Politics*, pp. 341–42.

25. Craven, *Southern Colonies in the Seventeenth Century*, pp. 372–79.

26. Edmund S. Morgan, *American Slavery, American Freedom: The Ordeal of Colonial Virginia* (New York: W. W. Norton, 1995), pp. 258–65.

27. Stephen S. Webb's title *1676, The End of American Independence* (New York: Knopf, 1984) rather exaggerates the extent of the new royal impositions on the colonies, but rightly emphasizes the extent of colonial home rule prior to the crises of 1675–76.

28. For a laudatory account of Bacon see Thomas J. Wertenbaker, *Torchbearer of the Revolution: The Story of Bacon's Rebellion and Its Leader* (Princeton: Princeton University, 1940). For contemporary accounts see Charles McLean Andrews, ed., *Narratives of the Insurrections, 1675–1690* (New York: Charles Scribner's Sons, 1915). For a balanced summation, see Wilcomb E. Washburn, *The Governor and the Rebel: A History of Bacon's Rebellion in Virginia* (Chapel Hill: University of North Carolina, 1957). As evidence of a general crisis of authority it should be noted that Maryland swam again in Virginia's wake. Resentment against the proprietorship there exploded in violence in 1676 and 1681 after Lord Baltimore cut the size of the elected assembly in half, having already limited the franchise to owners of fifty acres. The leaders of the former rebellion, William Davyes and John Pate, were hanged; the leader of the latter one, Josias Fendall, was exiled.

29. John Winthrop, Jr., thus proved himself an excellent diplomat as well as politician, pioneer, scientist, industrialist, soldier, town planner, and medical doctor: the Benjamin Franklin of the seventeenth century. He was also instrumental in helping John Clarke, Rhode Island's agent, obtain a charter for that colony. Finally, John Winthrop, Jr.'s sons, Fitz and Wait, were among the Puritans' most determined hustlers. They spent their entire careers speculating in real estate and suing their neighbors over disputed claims. See Richard S. Dunn, *Puritans and Yankees: The Winthrop Dynasty of New England, 1630–1717* (New York: W. W. Norton, 1971), pp. 117–42 (Connecticut charter), 191–211 (the sons), and Robert C. Black III, *The Younger John Winthrop* (New York: Columbia University, 1966).

30. Indians considered cattle as much of an enemy as the English settlers themselves. They performed ritual tortures on the beasts, including the carving out of their eyes and tongues, and slitting their throats and bellies. Some prominent Indians, including King Philip himself, possessed large herds of their own, but competed with the white colonists for pasturage. See Virginia DeJohn Anderson, "King Philip's Herds: Indians, Colonists, and the Problem of Livestock in Early New England," *William and Mary Quarterly* 51:4 (October 1994): 601–24.

31. The Swansea incident is related in Russell Bourne, *The Red King's Rebellion: Racial Politics in New England, 1675–1678* (New York: Atheneum, 1990), pp. 109–10 (Metacom quote, p. 107). On "King Philip's War" as it became known, contrast Alden T. Vaughan, *New England Frontier: Puritans and Indians 1620–1675*, 3 ed. (Norman: University of Oklahoma, 1995), who absolves Puritans of seizing land and impoverishing Indians (pp. 322–33), with Gary B. Nash, *Red, White, and Black: The Peoples of Early America* (Englewood Cliffs, N.J.: Prentice-Hall, 1974), who holds the Puritans responsible for their failure to pursue genuine assimilation with people of another race (pp. 123–27). The latest, most balanced account is James D. Drake, *King Philip's War: Civil War in New England, 1675–1676* (Amherst: University of Massachusetts, 1999).

32. See Patrick M. Malone, *The Skulking Way of War: Technology and Tactics Among the New England Indians* (Baltimore: Johns Hopkins University, 1993), who argues American colonists first

mastered in King Philip's War the hit-and-run tactics they subsequently used against the French and English. On the colonists' war effort see, in addition to Bourne and Drake, Harold E. Selesky, *War and Society in Colonial Connecticut* (New Haven: Yale University, 1990), p. 16–32.

33. See Michael Garibaldi Hall, *Edward Randolph and the American Colonies, 1676–1703* (Chapel Hill: University of North Carolina, 1960) for a detailed account of this diligent and prescient servant of the crown.

34. Benjamin W. Labaree, *Colonial Massachusetts: A History* (Millwood, N.Y.: KTO, 1979), pp. 106–15; Quaker persecutions described in Murray N. Rothbard, *Conceived in Liberty* (New Rochelle, N.Y.: Arlington House, 1975), pp. 237–50.

35. On Increase Mather, see Robert S. Middlekauff, *The Mathers: Three Generations of Puritan Intellectuals, 1596–1728* (New York: Oxford University, 1971) and Michael Garibaldi Hall, *The Last American Puritan: The Life of Increase Mather, 1639–1723* (Middletown, Conn.: Wesleyan University, 1988).

36. Viola F. Barnes, *The Dominion of New England: A Study in British Colonial Policy* (New Haven: Yale University, 1923) broke with the traditional American interpretation that was hostile to King James' grand design and argued for its logic, at least from Whitehall's point of view.

37. Wesley Frank Craven, *The Colonies in Transition 1660–1713* (New York: Harper & Row, 1968), pp. 212–25; Labaree, *Colonial Massachusetts*, pp. 115–20; Michael G. Hall, et al., *The Glorious Revolution in America* (Chapel Hill: University of North Carolina, 1964), pp. 9–79.

38. See Jerome R. Reich, *Leisler's Rebellion, A Study of Democracy in New York, 1664–1720* (Chicago: University of Chicago, 1953); Hall, et al., *Glorious Revolution in America*, pp. 81–140; Leder, *Robert Livingston*, pp. 57–64.

39. A good short summary of the post-1689 settlements is in Craven, *Colonies in Transition*, pp. 247–85. For provocative details, see Stephen S. Webb's chapter "The Coup in the Colonies," in *Lord Churchill's Coup: The Anglo-American Empire and the Glorious Revolution Reconsidered* (New York: Knopf, 1995), pp. 171–225. Richard R. Johnson concludes his study of the political pacification of New England after the Glorious Revolution by praising the "creative synthesis" achieved by British and colonial authorities. Far from anticipating 1776, it helps to explain why transatlantic relations remained stable as long as they did: Johnson, *Adjustment to Empire: The New England Colonies 1675–1715* (New Brunswick, N.J.: Rutgers University, 1981), p. 420.

40. See Richard S. Dunn, "The Glorious Revolution and America," in Canny, ed., *Oxford History of the British Empire*, I: 445–65, and J. C. D. Clark, *The Language of Liberty 1660–1832: Political Discourse and Social Dynamics in the Anglo-American World* (New York: Cambridge University, 1994), pp. 240–49. Contrary to what some textbooks relate, John Locke's philosophical treatises defending rebellion against unlawful authority were written in 1682, not 1689, and did not play a role in the Glorious Revolution. They would, of course, play a significant role in the American Revolution. See J. P. Kenyon, *Revolution Principles: The Politics of Party, 1689–1720* (Cambridge, U.K.: Cambridge University, 1977).

## PAPISTS, WITCHES, SCOFFLAWS, AND PREACHERS

1. J. M. Bumsted, *The Peoples of Canada: A Pre-Confederation History* (Toronto: Oxford University, 1992), p. 1. The most recent summary of the founding of *Nouvelle France* is Alan Taylor, *American Colonies* (New York: Viking, 2001), pp. 91–113, 363–95.

2. Samuel Eliot Morison, *Samuel de Champlain: Father of New France* (Boston: Little, Brown, 1972), pp. 145–46. For a translation of the original see Edna Kenton, ed., *The Jesuit Relations and Allied Documents*, abridged edition (New York: Albert and Charles Boni, 1925), pp. 118–21.

3. The politics and culture of the Iroquois nations have been a source of heated debate of late. They received, understandably, a very bad press from the Jesuits and later American triumphalists such as Francis Parkman. He emphasized their predations, merciless tactics, and exquisite techniques for torturing prisoners. Recent revisionists, by contrast, celebrate the sophistication of the Iroquois federation, its consensual decision-making, representation, and the prominent role accorded to women. In order to understand their place in the development of the European colonies, however, it is not enough to depict the Five Nations as savages or victims. They were important players in the complex geopolitics of northeastern America, terrified surrounding tribes as well as the French, and served as a valuable buffer for the English colonies until their War of Independence gave them the chance to crush the Iroquois nations themselves.

4. Robert Carse, *The River Men* (New York: Charles Scribner's Sons, 1969), p. 69.

5. The English intervened in the name of Protestant solidarity when Richelieu laid siege to the fortified Huguenot port of La Rochelle.

6. Since in most cases Iroquois raiders left captured pelts to rot instead of hauling them away for sale, W. J. Eccles concludes their motive was strategic, not economic. He assesses the various interpretations in *France in America* (East Lansing: Michigan State University, 1990), pp. 46–47.

7. Canada also lacked support during the 1650s because during that decade the French nobility made its last stand against "absolute" monarchy in the rebellion known as the *Fronde*. Meanwhile, France's war with Habsburg Spain also dragged on until the Peace of the Pyrenees in 1660.

8. Virginia planter William Byrd of Westover and a few other British Americans admired this French practice, ruing the "false delicacy" that inhibited British colonists from co-mingling with Indians. See Gary B. Nash, *Red, White, and Black: The Peoples of Early America* (Englewood Cliffs, N.J.: Prentice-Hall, 1974), pp. 99–108.

9. Bumsted, *Peoples of Canada*, pp. 44–47.

10. On Garacontié see Stephen S. Webb, *1676: The End of American Independence*, pp. 251–79. For an outstanding synthesis of Iroquois politics, economics, and society see Daniel K. Richter, *The Ordeal of the Longhouse: The Peoples of the Iroquois League in the Era of European Colonization* (Chapel Hill: University of North Carolina, 1992). For a brief summary of the diplomacy and war surrounding the Covenant Chain, see Neal Salisbury, "Native People and European Settlers in Eastern North America," in Bruce G. Trigger and Wilcomb E. Washburn, eds., *The Cambridge History of the Native Peoples of the Americas* (Cambridge, U.K.: Cambridge University, 1996), pp. 407–22. For the French point of view on the Iroquois campaigns in the West see W. J. Eccles, *Frontenac: The Courtier Governor* (Toronto: McClelland and Stewart, 1965), pp. 157–72.

11. Richard R. Johnson, "Growth and Mastery: British North America, 1690–1748," *Oxford History of the British Empire*, vol. 2: *The Eighteenth Century* (Oxford: Oxford University, 1998), pp. 276–91 (quote p. 291).

12. There is a huge literature on the Salem witch craze, but a rich sample of intellectual and theological, sociological, psychological, and gender-related interpretations includes Perry Miller, *The New England Mind: From Colony to Province* (Boston: Beacon Press, 1961), John Putnam Demos, *Entertaining Satan: Witchcraft and the Culture of Early New England* (New York: Oxford University, 1982), Paul Boyer and Stephen Nissenbaum, *Salem Possessed: The Social Origins of Witchcraft* (Cambridge, Mass.: Harvard University, 1974), Carol F. Karsten, *The Devil in the Shape of a Woman: Witchcraft in Colonial New England* (New York: W. W. Norton, 1987), Frances Hill, *A Delusion of Satan: The Full Story of the Salem Witch Trials* (New York: Da Capo,

1997), and Robert S. Middlekauff, *The Mathers: Three Generations of Puritan Intellectuals, 1596–1728* (New York: Oxford University, 1971), pp. 139–61.

13. Mary Beth Norton, *In the Devil's Snare: The Salem Witchcraft Crisis of 1692* (New York: Knopf, 2002) appeared while this book was in press. It supports my interpretation of the Salem phenomenon as, among other things, a war scare over fifth columnists in the colony's midst. My own inspiration was the suggestive passage in T. H. Breen, *Puritans and Adventurers: Change and Persistence in Early America* (New York: Oxford University, 1980), pp. 104–5. I do not mean to deny the findings and theories of other authors, but rather to suggest the craze might never have happened but for the military emergency.

14. Cotton Mather's eulogistic biography of Phips is singularly unhelpful. It states only the new governor wisely "did consult the neighboring Ministers of the Province" (chief among them Cotton himself) before authorizing the trials, then just as wisely judged it "safest for him to put a stop unto all future Prosecutions." The rest of the little biography is an unrelieved fret about the plots of satanic *Catholicks, Salvages* (sic), *Hereticks* and *Traitors* to murder "innocent New-Englanders" and impose the Romish church: Cotton Mather, *The Life of Sir William Phips* (1697), ed. Mark Van Doren (New York: Stratford Press, 1929), quotes from pp. 145, 151. In fact, Cotton may himself have helped prepare the ground for the craze with his *Remarkable Providences* of 1684 and subsequent tracts laying out evidence of witchcraft in their midst.

15. Middlekauff, "The Invisible World," in *The Mathers*, pp. 149ff.

16. Miller, *New England Mind*, p. 191.

17. The wife and two of the children of the pastor at Deerfield were killed in the attack. He and his five other children were marched to Montréal where, to add insult to injury, one of his daughters converted to Catholicism and married an Indian. See Benjamin W. Labaree, *Colonial Massachusetts: A History* (Milwood, N.Y.: KTO, 1979), p. 203–4.

18. On Graffenried and the Tuscarora War see Hugh T. Lefler and William S. Powell, *Colonial North Carolina: A History* (New York: Charles Scribner's Sons, 1973), pp. 56–80.

19. The thaler equal to eight Spanish "pieces" inspired the American ditty "two bits, four bits, six bits, a dollar."

20. When, for instance, Massachusetts was forbidden to issue any new bonds in 1733, its governor and General Court simply lay low until war broke out again in 1739, whereupon they increased the colony's volume of money *sevenfold*. See John J. McCusker, *Money and Exchange in Europe and America, 1600–1775: A Handbook* (Chapel Hill: University of North Carolina, 1978), pp. 313–17.

21. M. L. Brown, *Firearms in Colonial America* (Washington, D.C.: Smithsonian Institution, 1980), pp. 240–60; Joseph A. Goldenberg, *Shipbuilding in Colonial America* (Charlottesville: University of Virginia, 1976), pp. 31–51; Thomas L. Purvis, *Colonial America to 1763* (New York: Facts on File, 1999), p. 99.

22. The rise of the colonial assemblies is best studied through the histories of individual colonies, but a classic description of overall trends is Jack P. Greene, *The Quest for Power: The Lower Houses of Assembly in the Southern Royal Colonies, 1689–1776* (Chapel Hill: University of North Carolina, 1963).

23. Virginians continued to pay that old tobacco tax in support of their executive branch, but Massachusetts and South Carolina again led the revolt against permanent cash payments to officials, and other colonies rode their coattails. The previous colonial ploy had been to vote governors' salaries year by year, thereby obliging the executives to curry favor with their constituencies. Once the burden of paying those salaries was thrown back on Britain the colonists

maintained leverage over governors by periodically voting them "gifts" in exchange for their passivity. In 1702, the crown forbade the practice, succeeding only in making it surreptitious.

24. Edward Teach (or Thatch or some similar name) was born around 1685 in Bristol, enlisted on a British privateer in Queen Anne's War, then set up on his own to plunder British, French, Spanish, and American colonial shipping alike. "Blackbeard" was known for insane brutality. He reportedly strangled thirteen of the sixteen women he took to wife. But he and his crew spent their pieces of eight lavishly in the otherwise down-at-heels ports of Cape Hatteras so North Carolina's Governor Charles Eden made him welcome (no doubt for a cut). It was left to Governor Alexander Spotswood of Virginia to bankroll an expedition under Lt. Joseph Maynard of the Royal Navy to subdue the pirate. After a ferocious battle in which forty of Maynard's sixty sailors were killed, Blackbeard was finally dispatched in November 1718 by five gunshot and twenty sword wounds.

25. For the involved maneuvers leading to Pennsylvania's Charter of Privileges (or Frame of Government) of 1701, see Gary Nash, *Quakers and Politics: Pennsylvania, 1681–1726* (Princeton: Princeton University, 1968), pp. 224–40. For the abolition of the Carolina proprietorship, see Robert M. Weir, *Colonial South Carolina: A History* (Columbia: University of South Carolina, 1997), pp. 75–103.

26. The following examples are cited by Thomas C. Barrow, *Trade and Empire: The British Customs Service in Colonial America, 1660–1775* (Cambridge, Mass.: Harvard University, 1967), pp. 84–105 ("Reports from the Field").

27. Barrow, *Trade and Empire*, p. 97. See also Ian K. Steele, *The Politics of Colonial Policy: The Board of Trade in Colonial Administration, 1696–1720* (Oxford: Clarendon, 1968).

28. See J. H. Plumb, *The Origins of Political Stability: England, 1675–1725* (Boston: Houghton Mifflin, 1967) and *Sir Robert Walpole*, 2 vols. (London: Cresset, 1956–61); on the feeble opposition see Linda Colley, *In Defiance of Oligarchy: the Tory Party, 1714–60* (New York: Cambridge University, 1982).

29. Some British governors and officials were simply corrupt. Others farmed out their appointments to lieutenants of their own choosing. Still others were highly competent and popular for the very reason that they were willing to accommodate the colonists in return for certain emoluments. A governor or official both efficient and honest was not likely to remain long at his post. See Ian K. Steele, "The Anointed, the Appointed, and the Elected: Governance of the British Empire, 1689–1784," P.J. Marshall, ed., *The Oxford History of the British Empire*, vol. 2: *The Eighteenth Century* (Oxford: Oxford University, 1998), pp. 105–17.

30. See James A. Henretta, *"Salutary Neglect": Colonial Administration Under the Duke of Newcastle* (Princeton: Princeton University, 1972).

31. Barrow, *Trade and Empire*, p. 253.

32. Few censuses were conducted in the colonies although governors were often pestered to do so. But the numbers that were compiled may be supplemented by tax rolls and other data to arrive at fairly accurate estimates. Thus, the numbers in the detailed charts of Purvis, *Colonial America to 1763*, pp. 128ff, vary by only a few percentage points from those earlier arrived at by John J. McCusker and Russell R. Menard, *The Economy of British America, 1607–1789* (Chapel Hill: University of North Carolina, 1985), pp. 103, 136 172, 203.

33. Parke Rouse, Jr., *The Great Wagon Road from Philadelphia to the South* (New York: McGraw-Hill, 1973), pp. 11–17. Spotswood was born to a staunchly royalist Scottish peer, but chose allegiance to William and Mary rather than follow the Stuarts into exile. He made his career by fighting with Marlborough and was wounded in the Battle of Blenheim. The absentee

royal governor of Virginia appointed Spotswood his lieutenant in 1710, offering him half his £2,400 salary. He exploited his position to amass eighty-five thousand acres of land before losing his post in 1722 at the behest of the planter and Anglican elites in Virginia. His legacies, however, included the vision of endless western expansion, the elegant layout and much of the architecture of the new capital Williamsburg, measures to improve the quality of tobacco, and Virginia's first iron industry. Later appointed deputy postmaster for the colonies, Spotswood was the man who hired Benjamin Franklin in 1737. See Walter Havighurst, *Alexander Spotswood: Portrait of a Governor* (Williamsburg, Va.: Colonial Williamsburg, 1967).

34. These notes on agriculture are drawn *inter alia* from Edward J. Perkins, *The Economy of Colonial America* (New York: Columbia University, 1980), pp. 41–66, David Freeman Hawke, *Nuts and Bolts of the Past: A History of American Technology, 1776–1860* (New York: Harper & Row, 1988), pp. 11–19, Purvis, *Colonial America*, pp. 50–78, and John Schlebecker, *Whereby We Thrive: A History of American Farming, 1607–1972* (Ames: Iowa State University, 1975), chapters 1–2.

35. Precipitation in the British isles, while constant, tends to be light and misty, doing no damage to topsoil. Heavy American rains, by contrast, wash away furrows cut against the slope of the drainage.

36. Alan I. Marcus and Howard P. Segal, *Technology in America: A Brief History* (Orlando, Fla.: Harcourt Brace Jovanovich, 1989), pp. 16–21.

37. Ibid., pp. 21–25. Hopewell Furnace National Historical Site near Pottstown, Pennsylvania, is a remarkably well-preserved eighteenth-century iron "plantation."

38. John Bunyan, *The Pilgrim's Progress*, ed. Roger Sharrock (New York: Viking Penguin, 1987), pp. 136–48. *The Pilgrim's Progress* was published in 1678 (first part) and 1684 (second part). Bunyan was released from prison under the First Indulgence of Charles II and elected pastor of Bedford Church, where he lived and preached happily until his death in 1688.

39. *"Religio peperit Divitias, Filia devoravit Matrem": Magnalia Christi Americana* I: 59.

40. Linda Colley, *Britons: Forging the Nation 1707–1837* (New Haven: Yale University, 1992), p. 60. Jack Greene, "Empire and Identity," *Oxford History of the British Empire*, vol. 2: *The Eighteenth Century*, pp. 213–17, describes how Protestantism made "Great Britain" possible and fed the notion of England as an "elect nation."

41. The most important sources for this and later discussions of religion in the colonial and early national periods are Sydney E. Ahlstrom, *A Religious History of the American People* (New Haven: Yale University, 1973), Mark A. Noll, *A History of Christianity in the United States and Canada* (Grand Rapids, Mich.: Eerdmans, 1992), Jon Butler, *Awash in a Sea of Faith: Christianizing the American People* (Cambridge, Mass.: Harvard University, 1990), Patricia U. Bonomi, *Under the Cope of Heaven: Religion, Society, and Politics in Colonial America* (New York: Oxford University, 1986), Frank Lambert, *Inventing the "Great Awakening"* (Princeton: Princeton University, 1999), Ernest Lee Tuveson, *Redeemer Nation: The Idea of America's Millenial Role* (Chicago: University of Chicago, 1968), and the sources on New England Puritanism cited previously. A fine new corrective on the health of the church in Virginia is John K. Nelson, *A Blessed Company: Parishes, Parsons, and Parishioners in Anglican Virginia, 1690–1776* (Chapel Hill: University of North Carolina, 2001).

42. See Frederick B. Tolles, *Meeting House and Counting House: The Quaker Merchants of Colonial Philadelphia, 1682–1763* (Chapel Hill: University of North Carolina, 1948). In fairness to the Quakers, Keith was a zealot suspected of wanting to assume Fox's mantle and his blanket accusations could hardly be justified. In any case, it was thanks to the Quakers' (grudging) toleration that Pennsylvania rapidly became the "keystone state" of American religiosity as

Presbyterians, Anglicans, Lutherans, Pietists, Baptists, and even Catholics and the first African American church established themselves there (Ahlstrom, *A Religious History,* pp. 212–13).

43. Ralph J. Coffman, *Solomon Stoddard* (Boston: Twayne, 1978). Although born in Boston and educated at Harvard, Stoddard became a rebellious Connecticut valley spirit in all things. It was he who prepared the garden in which Jonathan Edwards took root and bloomed.

44. Mather's keen self-consciousness and precocious historical objectivity are celebrated by David Levin, *Cotton Mather: The Young Life of the Lord's Remembrancer, 1663–1703* (Cambridge, Mass.: Harvard University, 1978), and Sacvan Bercovitch, *The Puritan Origins of the American Self* (New Haven: Yale University, 1975). On Mather's views about slavery and children, see Kenneth Silverman, *The Life and Times of Cotton Mather* (New York: Harper & Row, 1984), pp. 261–75. On his millennialism see Middlkauff, *The Mathers,* pp. 324–49.

45. Boyd Stanley Schleuther, "Religious Faith and Commercial Empire," *Oxford History of the British Empire,* vol. 2: *Eighteenth Century,* pp. 128–145.

46. Milton J. Coalter, Jr., *Gilbert Tennent, Son of Thunder: A Case Study of Continental Pietism's Impact on the First Great Awakening in the Middle Colonies* (New York: Greenwood, 1986); Ahlstrom, *A Religious History,* pp. 269–7.

47. Bruce Kuklick, *Churchmen and Philosophers: From Jonathan Edwards to John Dewey* (New Haven: Yale University, 1985); quotes, pp. 22, 15.

48. See, above all, George M. Marsden, *Jonathan Edwards: A Life* (New Haven, Conn.: Yale University, 2003), a lengthy, scholarly, sympathetic biography, as well as: Ahlstrom, *A Religious History,* pp. 295–313 ("shall take the Kingdom" and "in America," p. 310); Kuklick, *Churchmen and Philosophers,* pp. 15–42; Perry Miller, *Jonathan Edwards* (New York: Sloane, 1949); Ola Elizabeth Winslow, *Jonathan Edwards, 1703–1758: A Biography* (New York: Macmillan, 1940); Patricia J. Tracy, *Jonathan Edwards, Pastor: Religion and Society in Eighteenth-Century Northampton* (New York: Hill and Wang, 1980); James Hoopes, "Jonathan Edwards' Religious Psychology," *Journal of American History* 69 (1983): 849–65.

49. Such things are a matter of taste, but the gem that is Savannah, Georgia, may be the most charming and tasteful American town south of Québec.

50. Kenneth Coleman, *Colonial Georgia: A History* (New York: Charles Scribner's Sons, 1976); Oglethorpe quotes pp. 34–35. On the origins and early politics of Georgia see also Harvey H. Jackson, "Parson and Squire: James Oglethorpe and the Role of the Anglican Church in Georgia, 1733–1736," and Phinizy Spalding, "Oglethorpe, William Stephens, and the Origin of Georgia Politics," in Spalding and Jackson, eds., *Oglethorpe in Perspective: Georgia's Founder After Two Hundred Years* (Tuscaloosa: University of Alabama, 1989), pp. 44–65, 80–98.

51. Harry S. Stout, *The Divine Dramatist: George Whitefield and the Rise of Modern Evangelicalism* (Grand Rapids, Mich.: Eerdmans, 1991); "I think God," p. 12.

52. There is a wide literature on the commercial and consumer revolutions of the eighteenth century. See, for instance, T. H. Breen, "An Empire of Goods: The Anglicization of Colonial America, 1690–1776," *Journal of British Studies* 25 (October 1986): 467–99; Neil McKendrick, John Brewer, and J. H. Plumb, eds., *The Birth of a Consumer Society: The Commercialization of Eighteenth-Century England* (Bloomington: Indiana University, 1982); Ian Steele, *The English Atlantic, 1675–1740: An Exploration of Communications and Community* (New York: Oxford University, 1986).

53. Stout, *Divine Dramatist,* pp. 49–65 (quote p. 61).

54. Frank Lambert, *"Pedlar in Divinity": George Whitefield and the Transatlantic Revivals, 1737–1770* (Princeton: Princeton University, 1994), pp. 220–33.

55. Whitefield and his promoters took full advantage of a network of revivalists every bit as extensive as the religious and commercial links among Quakers in Great Britain and America. That, too, was a feature of the commercialization of culture in the eighteenth century. See Susan O'Brien, "A Transatlantic Community of Saints: The Great Awakening and the First Evangelical Network, 1735–1755, *American Historical Review* 91 (December 1986): 811–32.

56. Lambert, *"Pedlar in Divinity,"* p. 93.

57. On the revival movements and their effects see Edwin S. Gaustad, *The Great Awakening in New England* (New York: Harper, 1957; Wesley Gewehr, *The Great Awakening in Virginia, 1740–1790* (Durham, N.C.: Duke University, 1930), J. M. Bumsted and John E. Van de Wetering, *What Must I Do to Be Saved? The Great Awakening in Colonial America* (Hinsdale, Ill.: Dryden, 1976); Bonomi, *Under the Cope of Heaven*, pp. 131–60; Butler, *Awash in a Sea of Faith*, pp. 164–93.

58. Among his other achievements in Philadelphia was Whitefield's outreach to slaves, the success of which he considered "a good omen that God intends the Salvation of the Negroes" (Stout, *Divine Dramatist*, p. 103). The emancipated Olaudah Equiano attended a Whitefield sermon and was amazed to see "this pious man exhorting the people with the greatest fervour and earnestness. . . . [He] worked as much as I ever did while in slavery on Montserrat beach" (Lambert, *"Pedlar in Divinity,"* p. 155). Gary B. Nash, *Forging Freedom: The Formation of Philadelphia's Black Community, 1720–1840* (Cambridge, Mass.: Harvard University, 1988), goes so far as to associate Whitefield's ministry with the founding of black Christianity in America.

59. See Lambert, *Inventing the "Great Awakening"* (quotes from Edwards, p. 256). It is rather amusing, but not surprising, that Lambert's books were published by Princeton. For an artful account of the historical debate over the scope and importance of the "Great Awakening" see Allen C. Guelzo, "God's Designs: The Literature of the Colonial Revivals in Religion, 1735–1760," in Harry S. Stout and D. G. Hart, eds., *New Directions in American Religious History* (New York: Oxford University, 1997).

GERMANS, FOUR SORTS OF BRITONS, AND AFRICANS

1. "Observations concerning the increase of Mankind, Peopling of Countries, &c, (1755)" in Leonard W. Labaree, ed. *The Papers of Benjamin Franklin*, 25 vols. (New Haven: Yale University, 1959-), IV: 227–34.

2. Lucy Forney Bittinger, *The Germans in Colonial Times* (New York: Russell & Russell, 1968 [1901]), p. 30.

3. German colonists began to get the attention they deserve in A. G. Roeber, *Palatines, Liberty, and Property: German Lutherans in Colonial America* (Baltimore: Johns Hopkins University, 1993), Eberhard Reichmann, et al., eds., *Emigration and Settlement Patterns of German Communities in North America* (Indianapolis: Max Kade Center, 1995), and Aaron Spencer Fogelman, *Hopeful Journeys: German Immigration, Settlement, and Political Culture in Colonial America, 1717–1775* (Philadelphia: University of Pennsylvania, 1996). Otherwise, see Joseph E. Illick, *Colonial Pennsylvania: A History* (New York: Scribner's, 1976), Sally Schwarz, *"A Mixed Multitude": The Struggle for Toleration in Colonial Pennsylvania* (New York: New York University, 1987), Alan Tully, *William Penn's Legacy: Politics and Social Structure in Provincial Pennsylvania 1726–1755* (Baltimore: Johns Hopkins University, 1977), and James H. Hutson, *Pennsylvania Politics 1746–1770: The Movement for Royal Government and Its Consequences* (Princeton: Princeton University, 1972). A rich primary source is Theodore G. Tappert and John W. Doberstein, eds. and trans., *The Journals of Henry Melchior Muhlenberg*, 3 vols. (Philadelphia: Lutheran Historical Society, 1982).

4. While most of the German refugees may have originated in the Pfalz (Palatinate), an

electoral principality of the Holy Roman Empire centered in Heidelberg, many came from neighboring realms, especially Württemberg. The Dutch, then English, then American colonists, however, referred to them all as Palatines.

5. Parliament's 1707 Act of Settlement ensured a Protestant succession to the throne after the death of William III. First in line was Princess Anne who reigned from 1702 to 1714. Second in line was Sophia of the Palatinate, a Protestant granddaughter of King James I. But she died in June 1714, just two months before Anne. So the throne passed to the third in line, Sophia's son Georg Ludwig. King George I spoke no English, conversed with his ministers in French, imported to England a host of German influences, and patronized composer Georg Friedrich Händel. He evidently had no knowledge or concern about the plight of his German subjects in the colonies.

6. Conrad Weiser, the German-English-Indian interpreter of later fame, was a son of the Weiser patriarch.

7. Schwartz, "*A Mixed Multitude*," pp. 85–103 ("these Colonies . . . ," p. 90).

8. Fogleman, *Hopeful Journeys*, pp. 127–48; Schwartz, "*A Mixed Multitude*," pp. 159–76 (quote, p. 175).

9. Bittinger, *Germans in Colonial Times*, pp. 215–24.

10. Conrad, the son of the patriarch Weiser whose Palatines were saved by the Indians, returned the favor during a lifetime of friendship and service to the tribes. See Paul A. W. Wallace, *Conrad Weiser, 1696–1760: Friend of Colonist and Mohawk* (Philadelphia: University of Pennsylvania, 1945). Matthias Zimmerman crafted the first American pipe organ in 1737. The Collegium Musicum, first large ensemble in the colonies, was founded by Moravian Brethren in Bethlehem, Pennsylvania, in 1748.

11. Zenger is often dubbed the godfather of America's freedom of the press. That is romantic, because restrictive British libel laws remained in effect long after his trial. Rather, he and his supporters displayed in the realm of censorship the same American zest for nullification of outside authority other colonists displayed in the commercial and political realms. See Patricia U. Bonomi, *A Factious People: Politics and Society in Colonial New York* (New York: Columbia University, 1971), pp. 112–20, and Stanley N. Katz, ed., *A Brief Narrative of the Case and Trial of John Peter Zenger* (Cambridge, Mass.: Harvard University, 1963), pp. 1–35.

12. The "Holzsteiner" barn, as the name implies, was a wooden construction on a stone (sometimes brick) foundation. See D. W. Meinig, *The Shaping of America: A Geographical Perspective on 500 Years of History* (2 vols.), vol. 1: *Atlantic America, 1492–1800* (New Haven: Yale University, 1986), p. 447–48; Robert West Howard, *The Horse in America* (Chicago: Follett, 1965), pp. 66–67 (quote, p. 66); and Robert F. Ensminger, *The Pennsylvania Barn: Its Origin, Evolution, and Distribution in North America*, 2 ed. (Baltimore: Johns Hopkins University, 1992).

13. James T. Lemon, *The Best Poor Man's Country: A Geographical Study of Early Southeastern Pennsylvania* (Baltimore: Johns Hopkins University 1972), pp. 67–69.

14. Howard, *Horse in America*, pp. 67–70 (quotes, pp. 67–68); Parke Rouse, Jr., *The Great Wagon Road from Philadelphia to the South* (New York: McGraw-Hill, 1973), pp. 21–28; Jerome H. Wood, Jr., *Conestoga Crossroads: Lancaster, Pennsylvania 1730–1790* (Harrisburg, Pa.: Pennsylvania Historical and Museum Commission, 1979).

15. M. L. Brown, *Firearms in Colonial America* (Washington, D.C.: Smithsonian Institution, 1980), pp. 264–66. The Mercer Museum in Doylestown, Pennsylvania, contains a fine specimen of an early American *jaeger*-type rifle. It supposedly belonged to Edward Marshall, one of the "walkers" who helped the Penns' agent James Logan cheat the Tulpehocken Lenape tribe out of most of Bucks County in 1737. The Indians agreed to sell only the land one day's walk distant (perhaps twenty miles) from Neshaminy Creek and the bend of the Delaware

River. Logan's three athletic walkers, working in shifts, covered seventy-five miles. The Indians protested this "Walking Purchase" but the governor judged a deal was a deal. See Frederick B. Tolles, *James Logan and the Culture of Provincial America* (Boston: Little, Brown, 1957), pp. 178–83.

16. The following comparative survey of the four major British cultures in the American colonies follows David Hackett Fischer, *Albion's Seed: Four British Folkways in America* (New York: Oxford University, 1989). The 946-page tome goes far toward realizing the author's ambition to write a "total history" describing the roots, trunk, and branches of America's family tree. Still, Fischer's brilliant, meticulous scholarship requires some disclaimers. First, no generalization however nuanced or qualified is always correct. Not all Puritans or Quakers shared all the same customs and attitudes. Second, characteristics a distinct group of colonists shared at the start clearly devolved, evolved, and diluted with the passage of time. Third, all colonies grew increasingly heterogeneous however mighty the impress of their dominant culture. Fourth, characterizations of the Yankee, Virginia gentleman, or frontier "leatherstocking" can descend into caricatures Fischer himself would be the first to denounce. But the rewards of leaning on Fischer far outweigh the dangers so long as it is remembered the people in every colony became over time a "mixed multitude."

17. Contemporary readers may wonder how modest Puritans found the privacy to copulate so frequently in small farmhouses already teeming with children. But most of their houses contained a small second story or loft in which youngsters were stowed, while a farm, in any season but winter, provides ample outdoor refuges.

18. The above material on the Puritans adumbrates Fischer, *Albion's Seed*, pp. 13–199 (baseball discussed, p. 148), but see also Virginia DeJohn Anderson, *New England's Generation: The Great Migration and the Formation of Society and Culture in the Seventeenth Century* (New York: Cambridge University, 1991) and the works on New England cited in previous chapters. The origins of baseball remain mysterious. All that is surely known is the official tale about General Alexander Cartwright inventing the game on a field in Cooperstown, New York, was itself invented out of whole cloth. Recently discovered newspaper references to "base-ball" push the game back to the 1820s, increasing the likelihood it evolved in New England from old English town ball and was transplanted to New York City. See Harold Seymour, *Baseball: The Early Years* (New York: Oxford University, 1980).

19. Fischer, *Albion's Seed*, pp. 199–205.

20. The above material on the Quakers adumbrates Fischer, *Albion's Seed*, pp. 419–595 ("our mob" on p. 462), but see also the works on Penn and Pennsylvania cited *seriatim* above.

21. Henry Adams, *The United States in 1800* (Ithaca, N.Y.: Cornell University, 1961), p. 54.

22. Digby Baltzell, *Puritan Boston and Quaker Philadelphia: Two Protestant Ethics and the Spirit of Class Authority and Leadership* (New York: Free Press, 1979), especially the charts on pp. 152–53, 481.

23. Fischer, *Albion's Seed*, pp. 595–603.

24. Michal J. Rozbicki, *The Complete Colonial Gentleman: Cultural Legitimacy in Plantation America* (Charlottesville: University of Virginia, 1998); Martin H. Quitt, "Immigrant Origins of the Virginia Gentry: A Study of Cultural Transmission and Innovation," *William and Mary Quarterly* 25 (1988): 631–54.

25. J. H. Breen, *Puritans and Adventurers: Change and Persistence in Early America* (New York: Oxford University, 1980), p. 152.

26. Louis B. Wright and Marion Tinling, eds., *The Great American Gentleman: William Byrd of Westover in Virginia, His Secret Diary for the Years 1709–1712* (New York: Putnam, 1963).

27. Breen, *Puritans and Adventurers*, p. 170.

28. See Richard Beale Davis, *Intellectual Life in the Colonial South 1585–1763*, 3 vols. (Knoxville: University of Tennessee, 1978).

29. The most notorious case was that of Jane Sparrow, who remarried in 1660 just five days after her husband succumbed to an illness he caught from her: Edmund S. Morgan, *American Slavery, American Freedom: The Ordeal of Colonial Virginia* (New York: W. W. Norton, 1995), pp. 164–65. On women in Virginia, see Kathleen M. Brown, *Good Wives, Nasty Wenches, and Anxious Patriarchs: Gender, Race, and Power in Colonial Virginia* (Chapel Hill: University of North Carolina, 1996); price of female indentures, pp. 81–82.

30. The above material on the Virginians adumbrates Fischer, *Albion's Seed*, pp. 207–410 ("I never beheld . . . ," p. 385; "I thank God . . . ," p. 347), but see also the works on Virginia cited in previous chapters.

31. Fischer, *Albion's Seed*, pp. 410–18.

32. Thomas L. Purvis, *Colonial America to 1763* (New York: Facts on File, 1999) relies on Aaron Fogelman, "Migrations to the Thirteen British North American Colonies, 1700–1755: New Estimates," *Journal of Interdisciplinary History* 22 (1992): 698, and comes in at the low end. Fischer relied on older estimates for the 250,000 total, which however includes emigration to Canada and the West Indies.

33. On Scotland's misery, waves of emigration, and bequest to America (and the world) see especially Arthur Herman, *How the Scots Invented the Modern World* (New York: Crown, 2001). H. Tyler Blethen and Curtis W. Wood, Jr., eds., *Ulster and North America: Transatlantic Perspectives on the Scotch-Irish* (Tuscaloosa: University of Alabama, 1997) challenges, as does Herman, the caricature of all "Scotch-Irish" as wild and ignorant, and rightly so. But by 1750 educated, commercial Scots were well assimilated into the British Empire and contributed little that was unique to the culture of the colonies. (Their great contribution to political philosophy and economics is another matter to be considered in due course.) The rough Bordermen, by contrast, contributed much that was not only unique, but destined to shape the character of the American West. See also Ian C. C. Graham, *Colonists from Scotland: Emigration to North America, 1707–1783* (Ithaca, N.Y.: Cornell University, 1956), R. J. Dickson, *Ulster Emigration to Colonial America, 1718–1775* (London: Routledge, 1966), and Maldwyn A. Jones, "The Scotch-Irish in British America," in Bernard Bailyn and Philip D. Morgan, eds., *Strangers Within the Realm: Cultural Margins of the First British Empire* (Chapel Hill: University of North Carolina, 1991), pp. 284–313.

34. Benjamin Franklin considered the leatherstocking "betwixt a man and a beast," even less civilized than Indians: Oscar and Lilian Handlin, *A Restless People: Americans in Rebellion 1770–1787* (Garden City, N.Y.: Doubleday, 1982), p. 116.

35. Richard J. Hooker, ed., *The Carolina Back Country on the Eve of the Revolution: The Journal and Other Writings of Charles Woodmason, Anglican Itinerant* (Chapel Hill: University of North Carolina, 1953).

36. The creeks once named Tickle Cunt, Shitbritches, and Fucking will not be found on a contemporary road map, but eighteenth-century upcountry Virginians knew them well. See Richard R. Beeman, *The Evolution of the Southern Backcountry: A Case Study of Lunenburg County, Virginia, 1746–1832* (Philadelphia: University of Pennsylvania, 1984), p. 18. The latest edition of George Rippey Stewart's classic *Names on the Land: A Historical Account of Place-Naming in the United States* (San Francisco: Harper & Row, 1982) contains more examples that were bowdlerized from the book's earlier editions.

37. Traditional scotch was a product of barley malt, but the Scots soon learned to make a palatable blend from the mash of American corn and rye. See Gerald Carson, *The Social History*

*of Bourbon: An Unhurried Account of Our Star-Spangled American Drink* (Lexington: University of Kentucky, 1963) and John Charles Campbell, *The Southern Highlander & His Homeland* (Lexington: University of Kentucky, 1921).

38. The above material on the back country settlers adumbrates Fischer, *Albion's Seed,* pp. 605–776. For a lively, faithful account of the centuries' old experiences of the Bordermen see George MacDonald Fraser, *The Steel Bonnets: The Story of the Anglo-Scottish Border Reivers* (London: Collins Harvill, 1986). Fraser is also the author of the erudite, satirical *Flashman* historical novels.

39. Fischer, *Albion's Seed,* pp. 777–82 ("shun everything . . . ," p. 777).

40. Boone is a bit anomalous inasmuch as he was born to Pennsylvania Quakers near Reading (itself named for the Penn manor in England). When the local meeting ostracized the Squire Boone on account of his love of guns and his daughters' penchant for "marrying out" to non-Quakers, the family headed for the hills of North Carolina. Daniel, a teenager at the time, took to the Bordermen's ways like a bear to honey.

41. This is the formulation of John W. Blassingame, *The Slave Community: Plantation Life in the Antebellum South,* rev. ed. (New York: Oxford University, 1979).

42. Philip D. Curtin, *The Rise and Fall of the Plantation Complex: Essays in Atlantic History,* 2 ed. (New York: Cambridge University, 1998).

43. See Philip D. Curtin, *The Atlantic Slave Trade: A Census* (Madison: University of Wisconsin, 1969) and the extraordinary survey of slave-trading voyages edited by David Eltis, Stephen D. Berendt, and Herbert S. Klein, *The Transatlantic Slave Trade: A Database on CD-ROM* (W. E. B. Du Bois Institute, 1999).

44. Analysis of the Du Bois Institute data by David Eltis, "The Volume and Structure of the Transatlantic Slave Trade: A Reassessment," *William and Mary Quarterly* 58 (2001): 17–46.

45. David Richardson, "Shipboard Revolts, African Authority, and the Atlantic Slave Trade," *William and Mary Quarterly* 58 (2001): 70–92, and Herbert S. Klein, Stanley L. Engerman, Robin Haines, and Ralph Shlomowitz, "Transoceanic Mortality: The Slave Trade in Comparative Perspective," in the same issue, pp. 93–117.

46. Blassingame, *Slave Community,* pp. 3–48. The examination was understandable given the high probability that Africans surviving the Middle Passage might be diseased or otherwise "blemished." Still, a visitor from New England pronounced himself shocked to observe a Virginia dame at an auction examine an enslaved man's genitalia with what he deemed excessive interest: Fischer, *Albion's Seed,* p. 305.

47. On the status of early African Americans compare Oscar and Mary Handlin, "The Origins of the Southern Labor System," *William and Mary Quarterly* 7 (1950): 199–222, Winthrop Jordan, *White over Black: American Attitudes Toward the Negro, 1550–1812* (Chapel Hill: University of North Carolina, 1968), and T. H. Breen and Stephen Innes, *"Myne Owne Ground": Race and Freedom on Virginia's Eastern Shore, 1640–1676* (New York: Oxford University, 1980). The latter concludes that while lifetime bondage was the norm, some slaves in the early years obtained freedom and property. On Anthony Longo see Morgan, *American Slavery, American Freedom,* pp. 156–57.

48. Thanks to these economic shifts, Maryland slaves came to be reckoned in probate 2 to 2½ times more valuable than indentured contracts: Russell R. Menard, "From Servants to Slaves: the Transformation of the Chesapeake Labor System," *Southern Studies* 16 (1977): 361–72. As for the much maligned Royal African Company, it was in fact diligently managed and somewhat more scrupulous about protecting its "cargoes." But the company could never prevent cost-conscious (read: ruthless) competitors from plying the African coast or hope to police

American ports year round. By 1730 the company ceased financing voyages; it 1752 it closed its books. See David W. Galenson, *Traders, Planters, and Slaves: Market Behavior in Early English America* (New York: Cambridge University, 1986), pp. 145–47; Stephen D. Berendt, "Markets, Transaction Cycles, and Profits: Merchant Decision Making in the British Slave Trade," *William and Mary Quarterly* 58 (2001), pp. 171–204.

49. See T. H. Breen, "A Changing Labor Force and Race Relations in Virginia, 1660–1710," *Journal of Social History* 7 (1973): 3–25.

50. Morgan, *American Slavery, American Freedom,* pp. 297–315 ("prepensed malice," p. 312).

51. Jack P. Greene, *Pursuits of Happiness: The Social Development of Early Modern British Colonies and the Formation of American Culture* (Chapel: University of North Carolina, 1988), pp. 87–88; Gerald W. Mullin, *Flight and Rebellion: Slave Resistance in Eighteenth-Century Virginia* (New York: Oxford University, 1972); Rhys Isaac, *The Transformation of Virginia 1740–1790* (Chapel Hill: University of North Carolina, 1982), pp. 305–10; Gloria L. Main, *Tobacco Colony: Life in Early Maryland 1650–1720* (Princeton: Princeton University, 1982), pp. 97–139.

52. T. H. Breen, *Tobacco Culture: The Mentality of the Great Tidewater Planters on the Eve of Revolution* (Princeton: Princeton University, 1982), pp. 44–70 ("greatest possibility..." from Whitefield's journals, cited on pp. 60–61). See also Main, *Tobacco Colony,* pp. 27–47. That "the relationship between masters and slaves involved something akin to negotiation" is argued by Robert M. Weir, *Colonial South Carolina: A History* (Columbia: University of South Carolina, 1997), p. 180.

53. The "separation" did not, however, extend to Charleston itself. There Africans worked as domestics, stevedores, or tradespeople, while a demimonde of African tavern keepers, prostitutes, and thieves both attracted and preyed on white sailors and raconteurs. See Ira Berlin, *Many Thousands Gone: The First Two Centuries of Slavery in North America* (Cambridge, Mass.: Harvard University, 1998), pp. 156–61. See also Peter H. Wood, *Black Majority: Negroes in Colonial South Carolina from 1670 Through the Stono Rebellion* (New York: Knopf, 1974); Greene, *Pursuits of Happiness,* pp. 146–50; Weir, *Colonial South Carolina,* pp. 173–88; and Philip D. Morgan, *Slave Counterpoint: Black Culture in the Eighteenth Century Chesapeake and Low Country* (Chapel Hill: University of North Carolina, 1998).

54. Gustavus Vassa, *The Interesting Narrative of the Life of Olaudah Equiano, or Gustavus Vassa,* was published in London in 1794, and Venture Smith, *A Narrative of the Life and Adventures of Venture, a Native of Africa,* was published in New London, Connecticut, in 1798. Quote from Olaudah in Weir, *Colonial South Carolina,* p. 178.

55. The new slave code also prohibited slaves from beating drum messages just as the English banned bagpipes, used to summon the Highland clans to war, after the revolt of 1745.

56. Jon Butler, *Awash in a Sea of Faith: Christianizing the American People* (Cambridge, Mass.: Harvard University, 1990), pp. 129–39 ("Gros Barbarity...," p. 133; "We are a People...," p. 138).

57. Robert William Fogel, *Without Consent or Contract: The Rise and Fall of American Slavery* (New York: W. W. Norton, 1989), pp. 29–34. In New York and New Jersey slaves numbered 14 or 15 percent of the population. The overall ratio of whites to blacks in 1760 was 35:1 in New England, 18:1 in the middle colonies, 1.7:1 in the Chesapeake, and 1.3:1 in the lower south. The ratio for all the colonies was 4:1. All the colonial codes defined slavery as lifetime and hereditary and slaves as a racial category equal to property: William M. Wiecek, "The Statutory Law of Slavery and Race in the Thirteen Mainland Colonies of British America," *William and Mary Quarterly* 34 (1977): 258–80.

58. Butler, *Awash in a Sea of Faith,* pp. 152–63, argues Africans suffered a "spiritual holocaust" between 1680 and 1760 during which their religious systems were shattered, leaving behind only a

congeries of folk practices. By the latter eighteenth century, however, slaves had restored family and community ties and invented a syncretic religious life combining English (especially Baptist) and African practices. See also Albert J. Raboteau, *Slave Religion: The "Invisible Institution" in the Antebellum South* (New York: Oxford University, 1978) and Mechal Sobel, *Trabelin' On: The Slave Journey to an Afro-Baptist Faith* (Westport, Conn.: Greenwood, 1979).

59. Blassingame, *The Slave Community*, p. 115.

60. No ordained rabbi lived in America during the colonial era, but Jews numbered about 3 percent of the white population of New York in the eighteenth century, comprised some 3 percent of the initial settlers in Georgia, and founded synagogues in Newport, Philadelphia, and Charleston as well. All contained a mix of Sephardim and Ashkenazim: Eli Faber, *A Time for Planting: The First Migration* (Baltimore: Johns Hopkins University), 1992.

61. The congestion is analyzed by Carole Shammas, "The Space Problem in Early United States Cities," *William and Mary Quarterly* 57 (2000): 505–42. As late as 1790, when Secretary of State Thomas Jefferson took up residence in the capital of Philadelphia, his real estate agent apologized for renting a townhouse at Chestnut and 9th Streets only to discover Chestnut was unpaved beyond 7th Street (p. 539). On eighteenth-century American towns see above all Carl Bridenbaugh, *Cities in the Wilderness: The First Century of Urban Life in America, 1625–1742* (New York: A. A. Knopf, 1955); "continually Dirty and Mire . . . ," p. 167.

62. Daniel J. Boorstin, *The Americans: The Colonial Experience* (New York: Random House, 1958), pp. 335–40. The Goddards scooped the "official" press in Maryland when their post riders were first to bring news of the Boston Tea Party. See also Louis B. Wright, *The Cultural Life of the American Colonies 1607–1763* (New York: Harper & Brothers, 1957), pp. 238–51. The first travelers' guide to the colones, *The Vade Mecum for America: or, A Companion for Traders and Travellers* (1732) included information on roads, distances, taverns, and stables.

63. Ian K. Steele, *The English Atlantic 1675–1740: An Exploration of Communication and Community* (New York: Oxford University, 1986); on coastal commerce, pp. 57–77, on newspapers, pp. 132–67; Tom Bell in Oscar and Lilian Handlin, *Liberty and Power 1600–1760* (New York: Harper & Row, 1986), p. 203.

## SOLDIERS, SPECULATORS, AND SAVAGES

1. Geoffrey Perret, *A Country Made by War: From the Revolution to Vietnam—The Story of America's Rise to Power* (New York: Random House, 1989).

2. Frank O'Gorman, *The Long Eighteenth Century: British Political and Social History 1688–1832* (London: Arnold, 1997); quote p. 84.

3. The continental war was sparked by the untimely deaths of the Austrian Habsburg Emperor Charles VI and the Prussian King Frederick William I. Under the Holy Roman Empire's Salic Law only males could inherit, but Charles had no male heir. So he invested considerable diplomatic capital to get all the other European monarchs to permit his daughter Maria Theresa to reign over his undivided possessions. But just prior to Charles' own death from food poisoning Frederick William also died. His son Frederick II (the Great) repudiated the bargain, demanding the rich Austrian province of Silesia. When the doughty Maria Theresa refused, Frederick invaded Silesia bidding to make the small but militant kingdom of Prussia a major power. Austria's traditional foe, Bourbon France, as well as Spain, Bavaria, and Saxony joined Prussia in hopes of seizing Habsburg lands in the Netherlands, Rhineland, Italy, or central Germany.

4. Douglas Edward Leach, *Arms for Empire: A Military History of the British Colonies in North America, 1607–1763* (New York: Macmillan, 1973); quote p. 217.

5. Kenneth Coleman, *Colonial Georgia: A History* (New York: Charles Scribner's Sons,

1976), pp. 63–76. Oglethorpe was acquitted of any wrong-doing and went on to pursue a colorful career as a British soldier and spy in Germany in the 1750s.

6. G. A. Rawlyk, *Yankees at Louisbourg* (Orono: University of Maine, 1967); origins of the expedition, pp. 27–40; Leach, *Arms for Empire*, pp. 229–43 ("my shop is filled," p. 237; "This Night," p. 238); Harry M. Ward, *"Unite or Die": Intercolony Relations 1690–1763* (Port Washington, N.Y.: Kennikat, 1971), pp. 244–54, on the "holy cause." See also John A. Schutz, *William Shirley: King's Governor in Massachusetts* (Chapel Hill: University of North Carolina, 1961) and for the long-term perspective on New England's expansion Douglas Edward Leach, *The Northern Colonial Frontier 1607–1763* (New York: Holt, Rinehart and Winston, 1966).

7. According to Franklin's *Pennsylvania Gazette* (July 18, 1745) the Philadelphia mob made "Bonfires, Illuminations, and other Demonstrations of Joy," but also "roamed the streets and broke the windows of houses that were unlit," presumably those of Quakers. The town's glaziers must have been doubly pleased. See Leonard W. Labaree, ed., *The Papers of Benjamin Franklin*, 10 vols. (New Haven: Yale University, 1959–66), III: 57.

8. In 1747 French privateers penetrated the Delaware River to pillage some farms, prompting Franklin to publish a not-so-anonymous pamphlet entitled *Plain Truth: or, Serious Considerations on the Present State of the City of Philadelphia, and Province of Pennsylvania*. He rudely attacked the Quakers, concluding "the Way to secure Peace is to be prepared for War." The New Light evangelist Gilbert Tennent called Franklin's militia "the best *Expedient* that could be concerted." Hundreds of back-country men volunteered. But the association disbanded the following year when peace was restored (Leach, *Arms for Empire*, p. 298).

9. Benjamin W. Labaree, *Colonial Massachusetts: A History* (Millwood, N.Y.: KTO, 1979), pp. 157–58.

10. Even revisionist biographers such as Rex Whitworth, *William Augustus, Duke of Cumberland: A Life* (London: Leo Cooper, 1992), must confess the cleansing of the Highlands was undertaken with "excessive zeal." They blame Cumberland's subordinates, but his name was on orders that mandated the killing, pillaging, raping, and burning out of hundreds of families, including some loyal to the Hanoverian cause. Wounded rebel soldiers were put to the sword and those taken in flight hanged by the heels as an example to others. Cumberland's nickname "The Butcher" was not just a consequence of "Jacobite lies."

11. Francis Jennings, *Empire of Fortune: Crowns, Colonies, and Tribes in the Seven Years War in America* (New York: W. W. Norton, 1988), pp. 109–38; James A. Henretta, *"Salutary Neglect": Colonial Administration Under the Duke of Newcastle* (Princeton: Princeton University, 1972), pp. 317–18.

12. Quoted in Hugh Cleland, *George Washington in the Ohio Valley* (Pittsburgh: University of Pittsburgh, 1955), pp. 225–26.

13. Jennings, *Empire of Fortune*, pp. 21–45 ("more conspiracies," p. 37); Neal Salisbury, "Native People and European Settlers in Eastern North America," in Bruce G. Trigger and Wilcomb E. Washburn, eds., *The Cambridge History of the Native Peoples of the Americas*, vol. 1: *North America, Part 1* (Cambridge, U.K.: Cambridge University, 1996), pp. 399–460 (western Indians during the 1740s, pp. 440–50); and Richard Aquila, *The Iroquois Restoration: Iroquois Diplomacy on the Colonial Frontier, 1701–1754* (Detroit: Wayne State University, 1983).

14. That lovely simile belongs to Thomas A. Lewis, *For King and Country: The Maturing of George Washington 1748–1760* (New York: HarperCollins, 1993), pp. 7–8. On Washington's lifelong interest in western land see Warren R. Hofstra, ed., *George Washington and the Virginia Backcountry* (Madison, Wis.: Madison House, 1998) and Charles H. Ambler, *George Washington and the West* (New York: Russell and Russell, 1971).

15. Washington did later write his brother, "I can find it worthwhile pushing my Fortune in the Military way": Bernard Knollenberg, *George Washington: The Virginia Period 1732–1775* (Durham, N.C.: Duke University, 1964), p. 31. See also John R. Alden, *Robert Dinwiddie, Servant of the Crown* (Williamsburg, Va.: Colonial Williamsburg Foundation, 1973). On Washington's early life see James T. Flexner, *George Washington: The Forge of Experience, 1732–1775* (Boston: Little, Brown, 1965) and Lewis, *For King and Country*, pp. 6–39.

16. Quotes from Washington's journal cited by Leach, *Arms for Empire*, pp. 329–30.

17. Washington's excuse was he did not know French and his interpreter, a Dutchman, mistranslated the words into English. But Knollenberg, *George Washington: The Virginia Period*, p. 23, considers that account lame. On the circumstances of Jumonville's death, see Jennings, *Empire of Fortune*, pp. 68–70, who suspects the French ensign "died under the hatchet, not by gunshot," and in the heat of battle, not by Washington's orders.

18. Leach, *Arms for Empire*, pp. 344–52 ("all possible Precaution," p. 344); Jennings, *Empire of Fortune*, pp. 116–38; William R. Nester, *The Great Frontier War: Britain, France, and the Imperial Struggle for North America, 1607–1755* (Westport, Conn.: Praeger, 2000), pp. 200–11 ("the war was contrived," p. 207). On Shirley see Fred Anderson, *A People's Army: Massachusetts Soldiers and Society in the Seven Years' War* (Chapel Hill: University of North Carolina, 1984), pp. 8–14 and Schutz, *Shirley: King's Governor of Massachusetts*. On the politics behind Britain's escalation of the frontier conflict see also T. R. Clayton, "The Duke of Newcastle, the Earl of Halifax, and the American Origins of the Seven Years' War," *The Historical Journal* 24 (1981): 571–603.

19. Max Savelle and Robert Middlekauff, *A History of Colonial America*, rev. ed. (New York: Holt, Rinehart, and Winston, 1966), p. 491.

20. The following account is based mostly on the excellent book by Timothy J. Shannon, *Indians and Colonists at the Crossroads of Empire: The Albany Congress of 1754* (Ithaca, N.Y.: Cornell University, 2000), but also Richard White, *The Middle Ground: Indians, Empires, and Republics in the Great Lakes Region, 1650–1815* (Cambridge, U.K.: Cambridge University, 1991), Francis J. Jennings, *The Ambiguous Iroquois Empire* (New York: W. W. Norton, 1984), and Georgiana C. Nammack, *Fraud, Politics, and the Dispossession of the Indians: The Iroquois Land Frontier in the Colonial Period* (Norman: University of Oklahoma, 1969).

21. Jennings, *Ambiguous Iroquois Empire*, pp. 325–75; Nammack, *Fraud, Politics, and Dispossession*, pp. 39–69.

22. Shannon, *Indians and Colonists*, pp. 161–73; Jennings, *Empire of Fortune*, pp. 101–8.

23. In recent decades much has been made of the influence the Iroquois confederation itself may have had on Franklin's blueprint for unity. Shannon discusses and dismisses (pp. 6–8) this "Iroquois influence thesis" to the effect that Native American models anticipated the Albany Plan, the Continental Congress, and even the Constitutional Convention. A forum on the debate was published in the *William and Mary Quarterly* 53 (1996): 587–636. Further support for the thesis may be found in José Barreiro, ed., *Indian Roots of American Democracy* (Ithaca, N.Y.: Cornell University, 1988) and Bruce E. Johansen, *Native America and the Evolution of Democracy: A Supplementary Bibliography* (Westport, Conn.: Greenwood, 1999). Major critics of the thesis include Laurence M. Hauptman, *Tribes and Tribulations: Misconceptions About American Indians and Their Histories* (Albuquerque: University of New Mexico, 1995) and William N. Fenton, *The Great Law and the Longhouse: A Political History of the Iroquois Confederacy* (Norman: University of Oklahoma, 1998). However fetching the notion of Native American contributions to federalism and democracy, there is little evidence Franklin studied the Iroquois. Evidence of British influence on his ideas abounds.

24. Shannon, *Indians and Colonists*, pp. 92–104 (quote, p. 195). The snake cartoons included sections abbreviated for New England, New York, New Jersey, Pennsylvania, Maryland, Virginia, North Carolina, and South Carolina, but curiously not Delaware or Georgia. On snake images in the late colonial period, culminating in the "Don't Tread On Me!" American flag, see Albert Matthews, "The Snake Devices, 1754–1776, and the Constitutional Courant, 1765," *Publications of the Colonial Society of Massachusetts* 11 (1910): 409–53.

25. Max Farrand, ed., *Benjamin Franklin's Memoirs* (Berkeley: University of California, 1949), pp. 326–28.

26. Paul Johnson, *A History of the American People* (New York: HarperCollins, 1998), quotes Voltaire and Horace Walpole as saying the young Virginian's volley in the woods "set Europe in a blaze" and "set the world on fire." But satirical phrase makers are not the best authorities for cause and effect. Nester, *Great Frontier War*, pp. 210–11, argues Washington's actions were not a sufficient cause or even pretext for war. They did, however, provide the war party with proof that a war, should it come, had to be fought with regular army regiments.

27. Leach, *Arms for Empire*, pp. 262–306; on assemblies' attempt to exploit the war effort, Alan Rogers, *Empire and Liberty: American Resistance to British Authority, 1755–1763* (Berkeley: University of California, 1974).

28. "I must be ingenuous enough," Washington wrote, "to confess that, in addition to a desire to serve King and Country, I am not a little biass'd by selfish and private views. To be plain, Sir, I wish for nothing more earnestly than to attain a small degree of knowledge in the Military Art; and believing a more favourable opportunity cannot be wished than serving under a Gentleman of his Excellencys known ability. . . .": Knollenberg, *Washington: The Virginia Period*, pp. 30–31.

29. On Braddock's relations with Indians see Salisbury, "Native People and European Settlers," p. 444.

30. Braddock's disaster is subject to an almost circular debate. He was trying to fight "by the book" in European style and ignored advice from Indians and colonials. No, he did listen to advice but lost the Indians by being too honest with them. He walked into an ambush by preventing his subordinates from taking the proper steps. No, he had flankers correctly posted to prevent being surprised, but his subordinates let him down, especially by failing to occupy hills above the trail. His soldiers were cowards as opposed to the brave colonial troops (Washington's own line). No, his soldiers held discipline until his own contrary orders and movements got them all tangled up with each other. And so on. It is even possible Braddock was handicapped by the one advantage he had: a map of Duquesne's defenses spirited out by one of the hostages the French took at Fort Necessity. The map might have encouraged the general to think he could take the fort without Indian assistance. But three observations that may withstand contradiction are these: Braddock did alienate Indians, some of whom went over to the French in disgust; Braddock prepared for a *siege* of Fort Duquesne, not a running fight in the forest, hence his army was bogged down by a long wagon train and heavy artillery; Braddock's soldiers themselves were second-rate, untrained for American conditions, and spooked by all they had heard about Indian savagery. For a recent summary of the debate see Jennings, *Empire of Fortune*, pp. 151–60.

31. Washington quote in W. W. Abbot, ed., *The Papers of George Washington, Colonial Series* (Charlottesville: University of Virginia, 1983–), III: 58–62. On his service with Braddock and defense of the Virginia frontier, see Cleland, *Washington in the Ohio Valley*, pp. 141–162. On class conflict in Virginia during the war see James Titus, *The Old Dominion at War: Society, Politics, and Warfare in Late Colonial Virginia* (Columbia: University of South Carolina, 1991); draft riots, pp. 63–64.

32. Nester, *Great Frontier War,* pp. 260–61; Kerry A. Trask, *In Pursuit of Shadows: Massachusetts Millennialism and the Seven Years War* (New York: Garland, 1989), pp. 235–47 (quote p. 236, from the *Boston Evening Post,* July 7, 1755).

33. Ward, *"Unite or Die,"* pp. 79–80.

34. As one courtier recorded, "The Duke of Newcastle hated Pitt as much as Pitt despised the Duke," but both recognized they could accomplish nothing without the other's skills and supporters in Parliament: Richard Middleton, *The Bells of Victory: The Pitt-Newcastle Ministry and the Conduct of the Seven Years War, 1757–1762* (Cambridge, U.K.: Cambridge University, 1985), p. 19. On the complex party and personal politics of this era and Cumberland's role as power behind the throne, see J. C. D. Clark, *The Dynamics of Change: The Crisis of the 1750s and English Party Systems* (Cambridge, U.K.: Cambridge University, 1982).

35. John Brewer, *The Sinews of Power: War, Money, and the English State, 1688–1783* (New York: Knopf, 1989), p. 174.

36. Middleton, *Bells of Victory,* pp. 1–21; O'Gorman, *The Long Eighteenth Century,* pp. 180–87. For a summary of historical debates on Pitt's role, see M. Peters, "The Myth of William Pitt, Earl of Chatham, Great Imperialist," *Journal of Imperial and Commonwealth History* 21 (1993): 31–74 and 22 (1994): 393–431.

37. Whitworth, *William Augustus, Duke of Cumberland,* p. 199.

38. On the role of Hanover in British foreign policy and the ongoing tension between continental and colonial commitments see Jeremy Black, *America or Europe? British Foreign Policy, 1739–1763* (London: UCL, 1998), especially pp. 144–63.

39. Leach, *Arms for Empire,* pp. 8–9, and more generally Fred Anderson, *A People's Army: Massachusetts Soldiers and Society in the Seven Years' War* (Chapel Hill: University of North Carolina, 1984).

40. Cleland, *Washington in the Ohio Valley,* pp. 163–67.

41. Ward, "Unite or Die," pp. 91–104.

42. In addition to Jennings' *Empire of Fortune* and Leach's *Arms for Empire,* see Fred Anderson, *Crucible of War: The Seven Years War and the Fate of North America* (New York: Knopf, 2000), the latest and most exhaustive one-volume history of the French and Indian War. But no one should snub the classics by Francis Parkman, *France and England in North America,* 9 vols. (Boston: Little, Brown, 1865–92) and *Montcalm and Wolfe* (Boston: Little, Brown, 1899), however faulty or fraught with Whig bias. For French and Canadian perspectives on the war, see William J. Eccles, *The Canadian Frontier 1534–1760* (Albuquerque: University of New Mexico, 1983) and Guy Frégault, *Canada: The War of the Conquest,* trans. Margaret M. Cameron (Toronto: Oxford University, 1969).

43. No one was more frustrated by the French abandonment of Duquesne than Colonel George Washington. Not only was he cheated of a glorious, vengeful battle, but his Virginians got confused in the one action he led and killed or wounded forty of their own people. Thus, the high points of Washington's military career to date included an "assassination," a humiliating surrender, a massive defeat, a bloodbath caused by friendly fire, and the unopposed capture of a mound of smoldering wood. As Lewis pithily puts it, "To Washington the victory clearly tasted of ashes, although he was too good a soldier to say so" (*For King and Country,* p. 271).

44. Middleton, *Bells of Victory,* pp. 97–129.

45. Anderson is persuaded by Wolfe's outrageous deeds and the testimony of his brigadiers that the man was psychotically determined to make for himself a glorious death, that much of his army was spared his fate only because Montcalm panicked, and that in any case the Battle of Québec was not as decisive as legend would have it (*Crucible of War,* pp. 344–68). He may well

be right, but his account is properly balanced with the hard battlefield analysis in C. P. Stacey, *Québec 1759: The Siege and the Battle* (New York: St. Martin's, 1959), W. J. Eccles, "The Battle of Québec: A Reappraisal," *Essays on New France* (Toronto: Oxford University, 1987), and John Keegan, *Fields of Battle: The Wars for North America* (New York: Knopf, 1996). They stress Montcalm's rigid adherence to European-style warfare, refusal to listen to advice from Vaudreuil, a native Canadian, and a chivalric pride that led him to throw away all his advantages, including a strong defensive posture, superior forces, and the weather. In any event, all recent authors agree the British conquest of Canada was far from inevitable.

46. One who tendered this judgment, albeit in jest, was Benjamin Franklin. He wrote in the *London Chronicle* (December 27, 1759) that permitting the French to conduct "a constant scalping war" would stint the American colonies' growth whereas if they were freed from that threat "the children might in time be as tall as their mother": Verner W. Crane, ed., *Benjamin Franklin's Letters to the Press, 1758–75* (Chapel Hill: University of North Carolina, 1950), pp. 13–14.

47. See O'Gorman, *The Long Eighteenth Century* and J. C. D. Clark's *English Society, 1688–1832: Ideology, Social Structure, and Political Practice During the Ancien Regime* (Cambridge, U.K.: Cambridge University, 1985) and *Revolution and Rebellion: State and Society in England in the Seventeenth and Eighteenth Centuries* (Cambridge, U.K.: Cambridge University, 1986).

48. Britain's precocious financial mechanisms are discussed most recently in Niall Ferguson, *The Cash Nexus: Money and Power in the Modern World, 1700–2000* (New York: Basic Books, 2001). But this discussion of the eighteenth century is based mostly on Brewer, *The Sinews of Power*, especially pp. xiii–xxii, 30–63, 221–51. The term "fiscal-military state" is Brewer's.

49. Mayhew quoted in Leach, *Arms for Empire*, p. 467; on the reasons New Englanders volunteered, see Anderson, *A People's Army: Massachusetts Soldiers and Society*, pp. 196–223, and Harold E. Selesky, *War and Society in Colonial Connecticut* (New Haven: Yale University, 1990), pp. 209–15.

50. Jennings, *Empire of Fortune*, pp. 426–37. For proof Washington did "tell a lie" on occasion see the assessment of evidence regarding his bounty land in Knollenberg, *Washington: The Virginia Period*, pp. 135–37. Washington claimed that he bore most of the expense regarding the land, but in fact paid only a fifth; that his land was chosen arbitrarily and was "jumbled" with others, but in fact it was based on four precise surveys; that he did not choose his own portions, but somehow got the best land; that if not for him the troops would have gotten nothing, but it is hard to imagine the governor stiffing the soldiers and risking a mutiny.

51. Gary B. Nash, *Red, White, and Black: The Peoples of Early America* (Englewood Cliffs, N.J.: Prentice-Hall, 1974), pp. 268–75; Salisbury, "Native People and European Settlers," pp. 440–50; Anderson, *Crucible of War*, pp. 457–75; and generally David H. Corkran, *The Cherokee Frontier: Conflict and Survival, 1740–1762* (Norman: University of Oklahoma, 1962); the Vision of Eloh quoted by James Wilson, *The Earth Shall Weep: A History of Native America* (New York: Atlantic Monthly, 1998), pp. 142–43.

52. On Pontiac's Rebellion and the ensuing Indian treaties, see Howard H. Peckham, *Pontiac and the Indian Uprising* (Princeton: Princeton University, 1947); Salisbury, "Native People and European Settlers"; White, *The Middle Ground;* Jennings, *Empire of Fortune* ("dogs clothed in red," p. 442); Ian K. Steele, *Warpaths: Invasions of North America* (New York: Oxford University, 1994), pp. 226–47.

53. Quoted by Thomas L. Purvis, *Colonial America to 1763* (New York: Facts on File, 1999), p. 49.

54. Trask, *Pursuit of Shadows, Massachusetts Millenialism*, pp. 287–340, argues the heavenly expectations raised in New England during the Seven Years War help to explain the intense bitterness toward Britain after the war. Jonathan Mayhew and other millenialist clergy had

expected defeat of the French would finally usher in the New Jerusalem, the City on a Hill, of John Winthrop's vision. Instead, London replaced Paris and Madrid as the bane of free and virtuous Calvinism.

55. Americans who won their spurs in the Seven Years War included eleven future generals in the Continental Army: Washington, Charles Lee, Horatio Gates, Daniel Morgan, Benedict Arnold, Philip Schuyler, Francis Marion, William Moultrie, John Stark, Israel Putnam, and Richard Montgomery, the first four of whom survived Braddock's rout. For many examples of ill will between the colonists and British army see John Shy, *Toward Lexington: The Role of the British Army in the Coming of the American Revolution* (Princeton: Princeton University, 1965) and Douglas Edward Leach, *Roots of Conflict: British Armed Forces and Colonial Americans 1677–1763* (Chapel Hill: University of North Carolina, 1986).

SONS OF LIBERTY AND "TWO-BOTTLE" TYRANTS

1. On Medmenham, see Donald McCormick, *The Hell-Fire Club* (London: Jarrolds, 1958), David Mannix, *The Hell Fire Club* (New York: Ballantine, 1959), and Betty Kemp, *Sir Francis Dashwood: An Eighteenth-Century Independent* (New York: St. Martin's, 1967). The contemporary sources on Medmenham, especially the *roman à clef* by Charles Johnstone, *Chrystal, or the Adventures of a Guinea* (London, 1760) are assessed in Marvin Olasky, *Fighting for Liberty and Virtue: Political and Cultural Wars in Eighteenth-Century America* (Washington, D.C.: Regnery, 1995), pp. 87–91.

2. Olasky, *Fighting for Liberty*, pp. 89–90. Franklin refers to Dashwood's "paradise" and their Prayer Book project in letters: Albert Henry Smyth, ed., *Writings of Benjamin Franklin* (New York: Macmillan, 1905–7), VI: 111 and IX: 358. On English sexual mores generally, see Jeremy Black, *An Illustrated History of Eighteenth-Century Britain, 1688–1793* (Manchester, U.K.: Manchester University, 1996), pp. 62–72 (quotes pp. 64, 67–68).

3. Quotes in Bernard Bailyn, *The Ideological Origins of the American Revolution* (Cambridge, Mass.: Harvard University, 1967), pp. 90–91.

4. Voltaire and Boswell quoted in Roy Porter, *English Society in the Eighteenth Century* (New York: Penguin, 1990 (1982)), pp. 172, 256. On manners and mores generally in eighteenth-century England see Paul Langford, *A Polite and Commercial People: England 1727–1783* (Oxford: Clarendon, 1989).

5. Porter, *English Society*, p. 21.

6. On colonists' embrace of the country-party ideology see Bernard Bailyn, "The American," and Gordon Wood, "The Logic of Revolution," in Bailyn, et al., *The Great Republic* (Boston: Little, Brown, 1977), pp. 216–25, 263–76 (Burgh quote p. 223). On the terms Tory and Toryism see Paul Langford, "Old Whigs, Old Tories, and the American Revolution," *Journal of Imperial and Commonwealth History* (1980): 106–30, and Ian R. Christie, "Was There a 'New Toryism' in the Earlier Part of George III's Reign?" in Christie, *Myth and Reality* (Berkeley: University of California, 1970), pp. 196–213.

7. Peter D. G. Thomas, *John Wilkes: A Friend to Liberty* (Oxford: Clarendon, 1996) is the latest biography. For analysis of the social movement behind Wilkes see George F. E. Rudé, *Wilkes and Liberty: A Social Study of 1763 to 1774* (Oxford: Oxford University, 1962). "Life can little else" quoted by Porter, *English Society*, p. 279.

8. Preface to *Analogy of Religion*, cited by Herbert Schlossberg, "How Great Awakenings Happen," *First Things* 106 (Oct. 2000): 47.

9. Edward J Perkins, *The Economy of Colonial America* (New York: Columbia University, 1980), pp. 145–70, assesses Americans' income and standards of living. He also notes (p. 141) that

American per capita tax rates were ten times *higher* after independence (1792–1811) than between 1765 and 1775. John J. McCusker and Russell R. Menard, *The Economy of British America, 1607–1789* (Chapel Hill: University of North Carolina, 1985), p. 354, conclude the cost imposed on the colonies by British restrictions was between 1 and 3 percent, and was far outweighed by the benefits the colonies received from membership in the empire.

10. Good summaries of the historiography of the American independence movement may be found in Jack P. Greene, *The Reinterpretation of the American Revolution 1763–1789* (New York: Harper and Row, 1968), pp. 2–74, and Marc Egnal, *A Mighty Empire: The Origins of the American Revolution* (Ithaca, N.Y.: Cornell University, 1988), pp. 1–15. See also the bibliographical note in Edmund S. Morgan, *The Birth of the Republic 1763–1789*, 3 ed. (Chicago: University of Chicago, 1992), pp. 185–92. The imperial school of the 1920s and 1930s was associated *inter alia* with the great names of George Louis Beer, Charles McLean Andrews, and Lawrence H. Gipson. The progressive school of the 1930s and 1940s was associated *inter alia* with Carl Becker, Arthur M. Schlesinger, and to a lesser extent Carl Bridenbaugh. The neo-Whig school dating from the 1960s cannot be imagined without the contributions of Bernard Bailyn and his students. Finally, contemporary scholars such as Gordon Wood, Jack P. Greene, Pauline Maier, Edmund S. Morgan, and Gary B. Nash combine the best aspects of several of these traditions in nuanced interpretations of the roles played by ideas, economic interests, and the colonists' sheer pragmatism and inventiveness. Those arguing for a prominent, perhaps predominant, place for evangelical religion include Alan Heimert, Patricia Bonomi, Robert S. Middlekauff, and Paul Johnson. The expansionist school is represented by Marc Egnal and Francis Jennings. The latter's brilliant research into colonists' relations with the Indians and British is marred only by his pose of being "shocked, shocked" to discover Americans exhibiting greed and chicanery. See Jennings, *The Creation of America: From Revolution to Empire* (Cambridge, U.K.: Cambridge University, 2000). Jon Butler, *Becoming America: The Revolution Before 1776* (Cambridge, Mass.: Harvard University, 2000), synthesizes a tremendous amount of recent research, but his conclusion to the effect that the colonists made the first "modern" revolution because they had built the first "modern" society strikes me as a word game. I don't know what "modern" means beyond "whatever is."

11. Letter of February 13, 1818, in *The Works of John Adams*, 10 vols. (New York: AMS, 1971), X: 283.

12. Richard R. Beeman, *Patrick Henry: A Biography* (New York: McGraw-Hill, 1974), pp. 1–32 (quotes pp. xii, 18, 19, 25).

13. Alan Heimert, *Religion and the American Mind from the Great Awakening to the Revolution* (Cambridge, Mass.: Harvard University, 1966), pp. 1–24, describes Mayhew's milieu including such rationalist and political theologians as Harvard's Ebenezer Gay, author of *Natural Religion* (1759). Adams quote from Carl Bridenbaugh, *Mitre and Sceptre: Transatlantic Faith, Ideas, Personalities, and Politics* (New York: Oxford University, 1962), p. 233. On the "spectre of bishops" in Virginia see Rhys Isaac, *Transformation of Virginia, 1740–1790* (Chapel Hill: University of North Carolina, 1999), pp. 181–205.

14. On the origins of the British imperial reform movement, see Peter D. G. Thomas, *British Politics and the Stamp Act Crisis* (Oxford: Oxford University, 1975) and John L. Bullion, *A Great and Necessary Measure: George Grenville and the Genesis of the Stamp Act 1763–1765* (Columbia: University of Missouri, 1982).

15. Edmund S. Morgan and Helen M. Morgan, *The Stamp Act Crisis: Prologue to Revolution* (Chapel Hill: University of North Carolina, 1963), pp. 21–52. Yorkers, as will be seen, were always among the last to contemplate a fracture with Britain, but they were fierce defend-

ers of their pocketbooks. Hence the New York assembly broke new ground in its October 1764 petition to Parliament: "An exemption from the burden of ungranted, involuntary taxes must be the grand principle of every free state. Without such a right vested in themselves, exclusive of all others, there can be no liberty, no happiness, no security; it is inseparable from the very idea of property." See Ian R. Christie and Benjamin W. Labaree, *Empire or Independence 1760–1776: A British-American Dialogue on the Coming of the American Revolution* (New York: W. W. Norton, 1976), p. 42.

16. On planters' economic distress see T. H. Breen, *Tobacco Culture: The Mentality of the Great Tidewater Planters on the Eve of Revolution* (Princeton: Princeton University, 1985), pp. 31–39. For statistics on the rapid rise of the Baptists, who would outnumber Episcopalians in Virginia by 1776, see Roger Finke and Rodney Stark, *The Churching of America, 1776–1990* (New Brunswick, N.J.: Rutgers University, 1992), p. 29. For the impact of dissenting sects generally, see Isaac, *Transformation of Virginia*, pp. 243–69. On the development of the new politics see Richard R. Beeman, "Deference, Republicanism, and the Emergence of Popular Politics in Eighteenth-Century America," *William and Mary Quarterly* 49 (1992): 401–30. Byrd cited in Richard R. Beeman, *The Evolution of the Southern Backcountry: A Case Study of Lunenburg County, Virginia, 1746–1832* (Philadelphia: University of Pennsylvania, 1984), p. 22. On Washington's views see Warren R. Hofstra, " 'A Parcel of Barbarians and an Uncouth Set of People': Settlers and Settlements of the Shenandoah Valley," in Hofstra, ed., *George Washington and the Virginia Backcountry* (Madison, Wis.: Madison House, 1998), pp. 87–114. The Landon quote is cited by Michael Kammen, *Sovereignty and Liberty: Constitutional Discourse in American Culture* (Madison: University of Wisconsin, 1988), p. 16. The popularization of Virginia politics and increased pandering to a mass electorate were lovingly satirized in Robert Munford's 1772 play *The Candidates.*

17. Colonial land speculators after 1763 thought they could ensure success by the simple expedient of awarding key British influence peddlers generous shares in their companies. But as relations between the colonies and the crown deteriorated even bribes could not overcome British resistance to the founding of new western colonies. See Daniel M. Friedenberg, *Life, Liberty, and the Pursuit of Land* (Buffalo, N.Y.: Prometheus, 1992), pp. 104–36, Helen Hill Miller, *George Mason, Gentleman Revolutionary* (Chapel Hill: University of North Carolina, 1975), pp. 66–69, and David T. Morgan, *The Devious Dr. Franklin, Colonial Agent* (Macon, Ga.: Mercer University, 1996).

18. On the John Robinson scandal, see Joseph Albert Ernst, *Money and Politics in America 1755–1775: A Study in the Currency Act of 1764 and the Political Economy of Revolution* (Chapel Hill: University of North Carolina, 1973), pp. 174–96; Breen, *Tobacco Culture*, pp. 103–6, and David John Mays, *Edmund Pendleton 1721–1803: A Biography* (Richmond: Virginia State Library, 1952), pp. 174–208. Jefferson quote from Julian P. Boyd, ed., *The Papers of Thomas Jefferson* (Princeton: Princeton University, 1950–), X: 27.

19. Statistics on population from Thomas L. Purvis, *Colonial America to 1763* (New York: Facts on File, 1999), pp. 128–33, 164. The best exposition of social turmoil in the ports is Gary B. Nash, *The Urban Crucible: The Northern Seaports and the Origins of the American Revolution* (Cambridge, Mass.: Harvard University, 1986).

20. Morgan, *Stamp Act Crisis*, pp. 67–68. They also inspired the name of the town settled by Connecticut's Susquehanna Company in northeast Pennsylvania: Wilkes-Barre.

21. McDougall was among the earliest colonial leaders to decide independence was the only way forward. He became a general much admired by Washington in the War of Independence. See Roger J. Champagne, *Alexander McDougall and the American Revolution in New York* (Schenectady, N.Y.: Union College, 1975).

22. On the Virginia resolves see Beeman, *Patrick Henry*, pp. 35–41.

23. On the Sons of Liberty see Pauline Maier, *From Resistance to Revolution: Colonial Radicals and the Development of American Opposition to Britain, 1765–1776* (New York: Vintage, 1974), pp. 77–112. On Dulany's *Considerations on the Propriety of Imposing Taxes in the British Colonies, for the Purpose of Raising a Revenue, by Act of Parliament* (Annapolis, 1765) see Morgan, *Stamp Act Crisis*, pp. 71–87. For a thorough analysis of the content and importance of political pamphlets during the run-up to 1776, see Bailyn, *Ideological Origins of the American Revolution*.

24. Excellent sketches of Sam Adams are in William Appleman Williams, *The Contours of American History* (New York: Franklin Watts, 1973), pp. 106–14, and Robert S. Middlekauff, *The Glorious Cause: The American Revolution 1763–1789* (New York: Oxford University, 1982), pp. 158–60. An old but full-length treatment is J. C. Miller, *Sam Adams, Pioneer in Propaganda* (Boston: Little, Brown, 1936). Stephen Johnson quoted in Heimert, *Religion and the American Mind*, pp. 460–61.

25. On Mayhew's conflation of religion and politics and possible role in provoking the riots, see H. Trevor Colbourn, *The Lamp of Experience: Whig History and the Intellectual Origins of the American Revolution* (Chapel Hill: University of North Carolina, 1965), pp. 63–65, and Martin E. Marty, *Pilgrims in Their Own Land: 500 Years of Religion in America* (Boston: Little, Brown, 1984), pp. 132–38 ("ye have been called," p. 136).

26. Bernard Bailyn, *The Ordeal of Thomas Hutchinson* (Cambridge, Mass.: Harvard University, 1974); "Authority is . . . ," pp. 73–74. As John Adams recalled, James Otis was one of the first to kindle the flames of liberty, but he began to lose his will during the Stamp Act crisis, then lost his mind in 1769 after an irate British customs official clubbed him on the head in a coffee house brawl.

27. Mayhew, *The Snare Broken* (1766), cited by Colbourn, *Lamp of Experience*, p. 64.

28. Townshend quote in Miller, *Sam Adams*, p. 115. Dickinson sketch and quotes in John Dickinson, *Letters from a Farmer in Pennsylvania*, reprinted as *Empire and Nation* with introduction by Forrest McDonald (Englewood Cliffs, N.J.: Prentice-Hall, 1962); quotes, pp. 3–4, 14, 44.

29. Jack Greene, *Peripheries and Center: Constitutional Development in the Extended Politics of the British Empire and the United States, 1607–1788* (Athens: University of Georgia, 1986); Franklin quote, p. 67. Greene acknowledges his debt to Andrew C. McLaughlin, *The Foundations of American Constitutionalism* (New York: New York University, 1932) and Charles H. McIlwain, *The American Revolution: A Constitutional Interpretation* (New York: Macmillan, 1923). See also Ian R. Christie and Benjamin W. Labaree, *Empire or Independence 1760–1776: A British-American Dialogue on the Coming of the American Revolution* (New York: W. W. Norton, 1976). On colonial notions of popular sovereignty, see Michael Kammen, *Sovereignty and Liberty: Constitutional Discourses in American Culture* (Madison: University of Wisconsin, 1988).

30. J. G. A. Pocock, "Political Thought in the English-speaking Atlantic, 1760–1790, Part I: The Imperial Crisis," in Pocock, ed., *The Varieties of British Political Thought, 1500–1800* (Cambridge, U.K.: Cambridge University, 1993), pp. 246–82; Kenneth R. Andrews, *Trade, Plunder, and Settlement: Maritime Enterprise and the Genesis of the British Empire, 1480–1630* (Cambridge, 1984); George Shelton, *Dean Tucker and Eighteenth-Century Economic and Political Thought* (New York: St. Martin's, 1981); Christie and Labaree, *Empire or Independence*, pp. 20–39; Buckinghamshire quote from Bernard Donoughue, *British Politics and the American Revolution: The Path to War, 1773–75* (London: Macmillan, 1964), p. 47. On early predictions of American independence see J. M. Bumsted, " 'Things in the Womb of Time': Ideas of American Independence, 1633 to 1763," *William and Mary Quarterly* 31 (1974): 533–64.

31. H. T. Dickinson, "Britain's Imperial Sovereignty: The Ideological Case Against the

American Colonists," in Dickinson, ed., *Britain and the American Revolution* (London: Longman, 1998), pp. 64–96.

32. In addition to Pocock, "Political Thought," see the outstanding summaries by Gordon Wood, "The Logic of Revolution," in Bailyn, et al., *The Great Republic*, pp. 263–76, and J. C. D. Clark, *The Language of Liberty 1660–1832: Political Discourse and Social Dynamics in the Anglo-American World* (Cambridge, U.K.: Cambridge University, 1994).

33. On the sources of colonial ideology see Colbourn, *The Lamp of Experience*, pp. 59–82 (Mayhew quote, pp. 61–62; Adams quote, p. 95) and Bailyn, *Ideological Origins*, pp. 22–54. Franklin quote of December 27, 1765, in Verner W. Crane, ed., *Benjamin Franklin's Letters to the Press, 1758–75* (Chapel Hill: University of North Carolina, 1950), p. 41. On the Anglo-Saxon myth see also Pocock, *The Ancient Constitution*, pp. 243–44.

34. Bailyn, *Ideological Origins*, pp. 158–59.

35. Quoted in David McCullough, *John Adams* (New York: Simon & Schuster, 2001), pp. 67–68. Thus did Adams exploit the death of Crispus Attucks, a mulatto who fled from slavery and found work on merchant ships sailing from Boston.

36. Frank Lambert, *"Pedlar in Divinity": George Whitefield and the Transatlantic Revivals, 1737–1770* (Princeton: Princeton University, 1994), pp. 220–21.

37. Franklin never dropped so much as a hint about the identity of the person or persons who leaked the Hutchinson letters and his latest biographer, Edmund S. Morgan, *Benjamin Franklin* (New Haven, Conn.: Yale University, 2002) found no new clues. Bernard Bailyn thinks Pownall, who collaborated with both Whately and Franklin, the most likely candidate. But the most fascinating nominee is Williamson. In 1764, while a young doctor in Philadelphia, he accused "B.F." of plotting to overthrow the Penns and, for good measure, stealing others' scientific ideas! Just a few years later, however, he became Franklin's close friend and protégé. Indeed, Williamson's support for the "Franklin compromise" later saved the 1787 Constitutional Convention (as described in due course). After Williamson's death in 1819, an eminent New York physician published the following revelation about the Hutchinson affair: "It is time that I should declare to you, that this third person from whom Dr. Franklin received these famous letters (and permit me to add this is the first time the fact has been publicly disclosed) was Dr. HUGH WILLIAMSON." The story, confided to him by an old, highly respectable, and still living friend of Williamson, went as follows. While in London on scientific business, Williamson learned the Hutchinson letters had been deposited in a minor Treasury office under casual security. So he simply affected an air of authority before the obsequious clerk, requested the packet, and walked out with it! See David Hosack, *A Biographical Memoir of Hugh Williamson, M.D. LL.D.* (New York: C. S. Van Winkle, 1820), pp. 50–51. Assuming the story is true, the questions remain as to who stored the letters in that vulnerable office and told Williamson (or Franklin) where they were. Pownall, perhaps. But the story cannot be confirmed because existing evidence about Williamson's travels suggests he did not sail to London until after Franklin sent the letters to Boston. See Burton Craige, *The Federal Convention of 1787: North Carolina in the Great Crisis* (privately published, 1987), pp. 134–35.

38. Bailyn, *Ordeal of Thomas Hutchinson*, pp. 224–73 (Adams quotes, pp. 240, 242). Franklin's motives can only be guessed at. Was he sincere when he sent the letters on condition they *not* be published? Did he really believe they would or could be suppressed? Was he merely forwarding intelligence in his capacity as Massachusetts' agent in London, or did he have designs of his own? If so, were they to stir up trouble or foster reconciliation? Most historians believe Franklin did not swing around to a pro-independence position until after his humiliation by the Board of Trade in January 1774. But who knows what passed through the mind of that subtle fox?

39. Ormond Seavery, *Becoming Benjamin Franklin: The Autobiography and the Life* (University Park: Pennsylvania State University, 1988), pp. 175–209.

40. See Jack P. Greene, "Pride, Prejudice, and Jealousy: Benjamin Franklin's Explanation for the American Revolution," in J. A. Leo Lemay, *Reappraising Benjamin Franklin: A Bicentennial Perspective* (Newark: University of Delaware, 1993), pp. 119–42, and Morgan, *The Devious Dr. Franklin.* Quote from Albert Henry Smyth, ed., *The Writings of Benjamin Franklin,* 10 vols. (New York: Macmillan, 1905–7), VI: 311–12.

41. Quote from Christie and Lebaree, *Empire or Independence,* pp. 199–200. Washington was unusually forthright in completing his thought to the effect that "Britain is to us as we are to the Africans." Colonial propaganda habitually left this implicit. See Patricia Bradley, *Slavery, Propaganda, and the American Revolution* (Jackson: University of Mississippi Press, 1998).

42. Middlekauff, *The Glorious Cause,* pp. 239–43, provides a brief, but elegant sketch of the impressions the delegates made on each other. Longer studies include Edward C. Burnett, *The Continental Congress* (New York: Macmillan, 1941) and Jack N. Rakove, *The Beginnings of National Politics: An Interpretive History of the Continental Congress* (New York: Knopf, 1979).

43. The Carrolls were an ancient family of Irish planters who over the generations became the largest holders of land and slaves in Baltimore's colony. But their faith always precluded them from public affairs until 1773 when the London-trained lawyer Charles took on Daniel Dulany in a celebrated suit over the payment of British officers' fees. Dulany tried to whip up prejudice while claiming Carroll's religion disqualified him from trying the case. But Carroll pleaded Maryland's cause and after a Patriot Party electoral landslide, the assembly named him First Citizen of Maryland. Carroll went on to become the only Catholic to sign the Declaration of Independence. "Most flaming Patriot" quote is from Ellen Hart Smith, *Charles Carroll of Carrollton* (New York: Russell & Russell, 1942), p. 109. An excellent new history of the family is Ronald Hoffman, *Princes of Ireland, Planters of Maryland: A Carroll Saga, 1500–1782* (Chapel Hill: University of North Carolina, 2000). For a quick summary of the status of Catholics in the colonies see Marty, *Pilgrims in Their Own Land,* pp. 141–44.

44. Williams, *Contours of American History,* p. 114.

45. Isaac, *Transformation of Virginia,* p. 247.

46. Speech in the Lords by Chatham (January 20, 1755), in R. C. Simmons and P. D. G. Thomas, eds., *Proceedings and Debates of the British Parliaments Respecting North America 1753–1783* (White Plains, N.Y.: Kraus International, 1982), pp. 268–82 (quote p. 278).

47. Speech in the Commons by Burke (March 22, 1775), in Ibid., pp. 595–631 (quotes pp. 600, 606–8, 610–11).

48. Michael Zuckerman, *Peaceable Kingdoms: New England Towns in the Eighteenth Century* (New York: Knopf, 1970), pp. 248–52, argues persuasively that towns formed the back-bone of Massachusetts' resistance after the provincial assembly was prorogued. That London should forbid Yankees even to hold their town meetings was more than arrogant, it was wicked, and towns resolved "to pay no regard to the late act of Parliament." Instead, town meetings became more frequent than ever in the summer and fall of 1774, and it was the towns that organized the Convention, the militia, and its supplies.

49. Beeman, *Patrick Henry,* pp. 64–68; Paul A. W. Wallace, *The Muhlenbergs of Pennsylvania* (Philadelphia: University of Pennsylvania, 1950), pp. 112–17 (quote p. 116). Peter Muhlenberg went on to become one of Washington's most trusted generals and, in the 1790s, a congressman.

50. David Hackett Fischer, *Paul Revere's Ride* (New York: Oxford University, 1994), is the book to read on Lexington and Concord.

51. Don Higginbotham, *The War of American Independence: Military Attitudes, Policies, and Practice 1763–1789* (Boston: Northeastern University, 1983), pp. 70–75.

52. On March 16, 1775, Franklin sat in the gallery of the House of Lords to hear Lord Camden speak on the American crisis. Once again critics rose one by one to denounce the colonists as knaves and deadbeats, none more viciously than Sandwich, the Medmenham "monk." Franklin was so infuriated he drafted a long rebuttal, but friends persuaded him not to release it. Had he done so, the British authorities might not have permitted him to sail, four days later, for America. But the very fact Franklin was allowed to leave England stoked suspicions in the colonies. Was he a British spy? Had he been bought? All Franklin could do was speak boldly for the American cause. That satisfied the public but alienated his own son William for whom he had obtained the post of royal governor in neighboring New Jersey. A staunch Tory, William was arrested in June 1776 and incarcerated in Connecticut until 1778 when he was released in a prisoner exchange. After an unhappy stint as a Tory leader in New York, he exiled himself to England in 1782.

53. Among the "black regiment" who upheld the American cause on Christian principles were Samuel Langdon, president of Harvard, John Witherspoon, president of the College of New Jersey (Princeton) and only clergyman to sign the Declaration of Independence, Nathaniel Niles, Connecticut's leading pastor, Levi Hart, author of "Liberty Described and Recommended" (1774), and Isaac Backus, who damned British acts as an effort to deprive the colonists "both of manhood and Christianity." The list could be expanded at will. See Perry Miller, "The Moral and Psychological Roots of American Resistance," in Greene, ed., *Reinterpretation of the American Revolution*, pp. 251–74 (quote pp. 251–52); Heimert, *Religion and the American Mind*, pp. 454–509; Bonomi, *Under the Cope of Heaven*, pp. 187–216; and Mark A. Noll, *A History of Christianity in the United States and Canada* (Grand Rapids, Mich.: Eerdmans, 1992), pp. 114–42.

54. The following observations are based on a brilliant article by Robert A. Ferguson, "The Commonalities of Common Sense," *William and Mary Quarterly* 57 (2000): 465–504.

55. For the skeptical view of the role of religion see Jon Butler, *Awash in a Sea of Faith: Christianizing the American People* (Cambridge, Mass.: Harvard University, 1990), pp. 195–224, and Henry F. May, *The Enlightenment in America* (New York: Oxford University, 1976), pp. 341–57. For an affirmative view of the role of religion, see Heimert, *Religion and the American Mind* and Bonomi, *Under the Cope of Heaven*. On religious millenarianism see Ernest Lee Tuveson, *Redeemer Nation: The Idea of America's Millennial Role* (Chicago: University of Chicago, 1968), especially pp. 20–25. On the American rebellion as the product of an alliance between the Awakened and the Enlightened, see Olasky, *Fighting for Liberty and Virtue*, pp. 115–69.

56. "It is unreasonable to suppose, that France or Spain will give us any kind of assistance, if we mean only to make use of that assistance for the purpose of repairing the breach, and strengthening the connection between Britain and America. . . . Under our present denominations as British subjects, we can neither be received nor heard abroad: the custom of all courts is against us, and will be so, until by an independence we take rank with other nations": Philip S. Foner, ed., *The Complete Writings of Thomas Paine*, 2 vols. (New York, Citadel, 1945), I: 39.

## PATRIOTS, TORIES, SLACKERS, AND SPIES

1. Durand Echeverria, *Mirage in the West: A History of the French Image of American Society to 1815* (Princeton: Princeton University, 1957), p. 21. See also Samuel Flagg Bemis, *The Diplomacy of the American Revolution* (Bloomington: Indiana University, 1957 [1935]), pp. 16–17.

2. Echeverria, *Mirage in the West*, pp. 3–21 (quotes, p. 7). Another excellent source on

European views of America is Franco Venturi, *The End of the Old Regime in Europe, 1776–1789*, vol. 1: *The Great States of the West* (Princeton: Princeton University, 1991), pp. 3–143.

3. French *philosophes* were much taken with a story Franklin wrote years before about one Polly Baker. This lusty New Englander was put on trial by the Puritans for serial pregnancies out of wedlock. She rose to deliver an eloquent self-defense and was spared being whipped and shunned by the community when the judge himself undertook to marry the woman. This tale of Puritan oppression and hypocrisy so deliciously confirmed French prejudices the Abbé Raynal told it in full in his 1772 history of European colonization. Franklin felt compelled to inform him it was a hoax—he had made the whole story up—whereupon Raynal replied he preferred "the telling of your tales to the truths of others." See Venturi, *End of the Old Regime*, vol. 1, p. 6, and Max Hill, *Benjamin Franklin and Polly Baker: The History of a Literary Deception* (Chapel Hill, University of North Carolina, 1960).

4. Echeverria, *Mirage in the West*, pp. 22–38 (quotes, pp. 36–37). The methods used by Franklin to seduce the French while appearing to be seduced are elegantly described by Claude-Anne Lopez, "Was Franklin Too French?" in J. A. Leo Lemay, ed., *Reappraising Benjamin Franklin: A Bicentennial Perspective* (Newark: University of Delaware, 1993), pp. 143–53. Other articles in the same volume provide additional clues: J. L. Heilbron, "Franklin as Enlightened Natural Philosopher," pp. 196–220; Ellen G. Miles, "The French Portraits of Benjamin Franklin," pp. 272–89; and Daniel Royot, "Benjamin Franklin as Founder of American Humor," pp. 388–95.

5. See Charles H. Metzger, *Catholics and the American Revolution* (Chicago: Loyola University, 1962). The mission, which also included Benjamin Franklin, failed to stir interest among Canadians in the thirteen colonies' revolt, but it helped to persuade many Americans that Catholics could be patriots, too. Later that year Charles Carroll became the only Catholic to sign the Declaration of Independence and in 1790 John Carroll (with Franklin's recommendation!) was consecrated the United States' first Catholic bishop.

6. Beaumarchais was the author of *The Barber of Seville* and *The Marriage of Figaro*, and his touring theater productions provided him with the best cover imaginable for a spy. On the secret negotiations with France, see Bemis, *Diplomacy*, pp. 23–28, Jonathan R. Dull, *A Diplomatic History of the American Revolution* (New Haven: Yale University, 1985), pp. 57–65, Edward S. Corwin, *French Policy and the American Alliance of 1778* (New York: Burt Franklin, 1970), pp. 54–79, and Lawrence Kaplan, *Colonies into Nation: American Diplomacy, 1763–1801* (New York: Macmillan, 1972). Some sources say the powder figure is closer to 90 percent. The French chemical industry was also the most advanced in the world, so Americans had the best masters possible when they began to increase domestic production of saltpeter and gunpowder.

7. On the "little" declarations of independence see Pauline Maier, *American Scripture: Making the Declaration of Independence* (New York: Knopf, 1997), pp. 47–96. Gordon S. Wood, *The Creation of the American Republic 1776–1789* (Chapel Hill: University of North Carolina, 1969), pp. 127–61, describes the role played by state conventions in the run-up to independence and concludes that after May 15 the formal declarations of July 2 and 4, 1776, were derivative ("most explicit" and "the whole object," p. 130). The quote "for defense of their lives . . ." is from Adams' preamble cited by Robert Middlekauff, *The Glorious Cause: The American Revolution 1763–1789* (New York: Oxford University, 1982), p. 324.

8. The query was Samuel Johnson's in his 1775 pamphlet "Taxation No Tyranny," cited by Theodore Draper, *A Struggle for Power: The American Revolution* (New York: Times Books, 1996), p. 513. In his still classic *Jefferson* (New York: Harcourt, Brace, 1942), Saul K. Padover praised his subject for living up to his famous pledge ("I swear on the altar of God eternal hos-

tility against every sort of tyranny over the mind of man") and for the epitaph he wrote for his tombstone naming himself the author of the Declaration of Independence, the Virginia statute for religious freedom, and the University of Virginia. In fact, Jefferson believed in no god who required worship at altars, was not the sole author of the declaration, and followed Mason's lead on religious liberty. He did found the college in Charlottesville. Pauline Maier acknowledges Jefferson's positive qualities, but considers him the most overrated personage in American history in light of the hyperbolic adulation he has received. The most exhaustive biography is the six-volume *Jefferson and His Time* (Boston: Little, Brown, 1948–81) by Dumas Malone, and the latest and most balanced attempt to make sense of the man is Joseph J. Ellis, *American Sphinx: The Character of Thomas Jefferson* (New York: Knopf, 1997).

9. See Robert A. Rutland, ed., *The Papers of George Mason 1725–1792*, vol. 1: *1749–1778* (Chapel Hill: University of North Carolina, 1970), cxi–cxxvi, 276–78. Mason was a humble, crotchety, chronically ill planter from Fairfax County on the Northern Neck. Far from cavorting with other Cavaliers he lived quietly with his petite wife Ann and their children at Gunston Hall, attending his crops and slaves. Mason was almost as erudite as Jefferson, but entirely self-taught and free of ambition. He also declared as early as 1765 that slavery corrupted whites as well as oppressed blacks. He acknowledged 1776 was not the moment to address slavery, but later risked his health by traveling to the Constitutional Convention to promote abolition. Mason warned his sons not to wade into politics, but if they did he urged them to scorn all private interests and shelter the "sacred rights to which they themselves were born" (cxviii). Mason deserves more honor than his nation has given him. But then, he was never a hustler, his long, fruitless service as secretary to Virginia's Ohio Company notwithstanding.

10. Maier, *American Scripture*, is a work of exquisite research and style (for the editing of Jefferson's draft, pp. 97–153). Maier transcends the old debate between Carl Becker, *The Declaration of Independence: A Study in the History of Political Ideas* (New York: Harcourt, Brace, 1922) and Garry Wills, *Inventing America: Jefferson's Declaration of Independence* (Garden City, N.Y.: Doubleday, 1978) over the influence of Lockean and Scottish Enlightenment ideas on Jefferson by showing how little of the essence of the Declaration was original with Jefferson. On the drafting and editing of the Declaration see also Malone, *Jefferson and His Time*, vol. 1, *Jefferson the Virginian*, pp, 215–31 ("the Thing itself," p. 230) and Julian P. Boyd, *The Declaration of Independence: The Evolution of the Text* (Washington, D.C.: Library of Congress, 1943).

11. The complicated politics of Pennsylvania on the eve of independence are reconstructed, to the degree possible, in Richard Alan Ryerson, *The Revolution Is Now Begun: The Radical Committees of Philadelphia, 1765–1776* (Philadelphia: University of Pennsylvania, 1978) and adumbrated in Francis Jennings, *The Creation of America: Through Revolution to Empire* (Cambridge, U.K.: Cambridge University, 2000), pp. 172–79. On class conflict in Philadelphia see Gary B. Nash, *The Urban Crucible: The Northern Seaports and the Origins of the American Revolution*, 2 ed. (Cambridge, Mass.: Harvard University, 1986), pp. 244–45.

12. Delegate Thomas McKean started the legend that inspired the statue in Wilmington, Delaware. It shows Rodney charging on horseback through the downpour. Rodney's brother said he left home in a carriage and another witness said he arrived in one. But his dedication does not require embellishment. Rodney was fifty-seven years old, had skin cancer as well as asthma, and spent July 1 presiding over the assembly in New Castle, subduing a Tory mob at the head of Kent County's militia, then riding home to receive the desperate summons from McKean. He grabbed a quick bite and immediately set out for Philadelphia. See John A. Munroe, *Colonial Delaware: A History* (Millwood, N.Y.: KTO, 1978), pp. 250–52.

13. Morris later signed the Declaration of Independence, but Dickinson refrained.

Regarding the machinations that resulted in the Declaration's "unanimous" adoption, see Jennings, *Creation of America*, pp. 166–68, who suspects that pressure was secretly brought to bear, David McCullough, *John Adams* (New York: Simon & Schuster, 2001), pp. 126–30, who credits Adams' inspiring witness, and Jack N. Rakove, *The Beginnings of National Politics: An Interpretive History of the Continental Congress* (New York: Knopf, 1979), pp. 88–100, who argues that Congress by no means acted precipitously and had patiently waited for British outrages to do the work of converting most of the public to independence.

14. David Hackett Fischer, *Albion's Seed: Four British Folkways in America* (New York: Oxford University, 1989), pp. 827–30.

15. Washington's commitment to the Anglican faith he nominally confessed is a matter of dispute. But he clearly believed in Providence and—like so many military commanders subject to outrageous fortune—had a mystical belief that God spared him for some great destiny. For a sampling of his exhortations and prayers see Marvin Olasky, *Fighting for Liberty and Virtue: Political and Cultural Wars in Eighteenth-Century America* (Washington, D.C.: Regnery, 1995), pp. 161, 168–69. Middlekauff, *The Glorious Cause*, bucked historiographical trends by arguing anew that Washington was "the indispensable man" at the center of the American struggle for independence. The most detailed account of Washington's wartime career is still James Thomas Flexner, *George Washington in the American Revolution 1775–1783* (Boston: Little, Brown, 1967). A fine short summary of his legacy is Don Higginbotham's *George Washington and the American Military Tradition* (Athens: University of Georgia, 1985).

16. This is the approach taken by Charles Royster, *A Revolutionary People at War: The Continental Army and American Character, 1775–1783* (Chapel Hill: University of North Carolina, 1979), an extraordinary work.

17. The orotund, bookish Knox read up on gunnery, ballistics, tactics, and engineering before meeting Washington on the Roxbury road in 1775 and obtaining a Continental commission. But he was not without some hands-on experience. As early as 1765, the fifteen-year-old signed up for a militia artillery train in Boston, observing with care the procedures of a British battery that passed through in 1766. His first field pieces included just three three-pounder brass cannons the militia sneaked out of Boston to the American lines in Cambridge. Two of the little guns were still in service at the end of the war. Knox, then secretary of War, had them lovingly inscribed with the nicknames "Adams" and "Hancock." Knox was also one of few Americans sympathetic to Indians. He advised Washington: "A system producing the free operation of the mild principles of religion and benevolence toward an unenlightened race of men would at once be highly economical and honorable to the national character." See North Callahan, *Henry Knox: General Washington's General* (New York: Rinehart, 1958); quote, p. 316.

18. Royster, *Revolutionary People at War*, pp. 1–24 (quotes, pp. 10, 16); Allen quoted in Carl Bridenbaugh, *The Spirit of '76: The Growth of American Patriotism Before Independence* (New York: Oxford University, 1975), p. 144.

19. A lengthy, insightful account of Washington's self-presentation is Paul K. Longmore, *The Invention of George Washington* (Berkeley: University of California, 1988), especially pp. 137–83 (quotes, pp. 176, 182). See also Middlekauff, *The Glorious Cause*, pp. 293–96.

20. Flexner, *Washington in the American Revolution*, pp. 9–16 (quotes pp. 14, 16.).

21. Higginbotham, *Washington and the American Military Tradition*, pp. 44–61 ("a small knowledge," p. 89); Royster, *Revolutionary People*, pp. 51–126.

22. Higginbotham, *Washington and the American Military Tradition*, pp. 62–68.

23. Letter to Mercy Otis Warren, March 1776, cited by Benjamin W. Labaree, *Colonial Massachusetts: A History* (Millwood, N.Y.: KTO, 1979), p. 314.

24. Royster, *Revolutionary People at War*, pp. 127–51; slang words from Jennings, *Creation of America*, p. 198.

25. Trumbull served as Connecticut's governor throughout the war. A Harvard graduate, he gave up his religious calling to assist his father in business. In 1775 he was already sixty-five years old and would suffer the deaths of his wife, son, and daughter during the war. But like John Winthrop, Jr., long before, he personified the Nutmeg State's grit, telling recruits, "Play the man for God, and for the cities of our God. May the Hosts, the God of the armies of Israel, be your Captain." Connecticut sent the highest proportion of men into service and became known as the "provisions state" for the quality and quantity of the food, clothing, guns, powder, rum, tobacco, soap, and candles it supplied to the Continental army and navy. See Richard Buel, Jr., *Dear Liberty: Connecticut's Mobilization for the Revolutionary War* (Middletown, Conn.: Wesleyan University, 1980) and David M. Roth and Freeman Meyer, *From Revolution to Constitution: Connecticut 1763 to 1818* (Chester, Conn.: Pequot, 1975), pp. 30–41.

26. Higginbotham, *Washington and the American Military Tradition*, pp. 82–92 (quote, p. 87). John Hancock, sometimes touted as the first "president" of the United States, stepped down as president of the Continental Congress in 1777 and was succeeded in turn by Henry Laurens (S. C.), John Jay (N.Y.), Samuel Huntington (Conn.), Thomas McKean (Del.), John Hanson (Md.), Elias Boudinot (N.J.), and Thomas Mifflin (Penn.). Rakove, *Beginnings of National Politics*, pp. 119–32, also describes Congress' growing isolation and loss of prestige. In September 1777 Henry Laurens privately lamented the undistinguished men being sent to Congress and feared "this Assembly will be presently blown up" if the public lost confidence in it (p. 127).

27. Royster, *Revolutionary People at War*, p. 53. See also E. Wayne Carp, *To Starve the Army at Pleasure: Continental Army Administration and American Political Culture, 1775–1783* (Chapel Hill: University of North Carolina, 1984).

28. The campaigns of the war have inspired a library of excellent literature, but the best general accounts surely include Don Higginbotham, *The War of American Independence: Military Attitudes, Policies, and Practice 1763–1789* (Boston: Northeastern University, 1983), Piers Mackesy, *The War for America 1775–1783* (Cambridge, Mass.: Harvard University, 1964), George F. Scheer and Hugh F. Rankin, *Rebels and Redcoats* (Cleveland: World Publishing, 1957), and Christopher Ward, *The War of the Revolution*, 2 vols. (New York: Macmillan, 1952), as well as Middlekauff, *Glorious Cause*. For the British perspective see Jeremy Black, *War for America: The Fight for Independence 1775–1783* (New York: St. Martin's, 1991), H. T. Dickinson, ed., *Britain and the American Revolution* (London: Longman, 1998), and Michael Pearson, *Those Damned Rebels: The American Revolution as Seen Through British Eyes* (New York: Putnam, 1972).

29. Stephen Conway, "British Governments and the Conduct of the American War," in Dickinson, ed., *Britain and the American Revolution*, pp. 155–79. On the chimera of Irish troops, see also Thomas Bartlett, " 'A Weapon of War Yet Untried,': Irish Catholics and the Armed Forces of the Crown, 1760–1830," T. G. Fraser and Keith Jeffery, eds., *Men, Women and War* (Dublin: Lilliput, 1993).

30. British Major Patrick Ferguson is better known for inventing the breech-loading rifle, but his gentlemanly refusal to shoot an officer in the back, or so he said, permitted Washington to gallop away from the danger. Ferguson would be less gentlemanly in the North Carolina campaign of 1780. By the way, visitors to the Brandywine battlefield, hard by the George Wyeth Museum and Longwood Gardens, will discover a little gem of a National Historical Site.

31. The good folk of Philadelphia's Main Line suburbs honor Mad Anthony Wayne, and rightly so. But the Paoli attack caught him with his pants down—he was sleeping off a binge after Brandywine and failed to post pickets. When the British realized this they quietly fixed

bayonets and charged into the bivouac. Patriot propaganda called it a massacre, evidently on the theory no fight was fair unless Americans were allowed to hide behind trees and pick off soldiers marching in ranks.

32. Higginbotham, *War of American Independence,* pp. 216–22 (quote, p. 222), concludes that no evidence exists of a plot to remove Washington—it was all blown out of proportion. But Royster, *Revolutionary People at War,* pp. 255–56, is equally right to conclude that the crisis indicates how delicate civil-military relations were at this early stage of the United States. Many people feared that the commander might become a new Cromwell or king. What Americans really wanted was a sort of "high priest of the revolution" (p. 256). Washington rewarded their trust.

33. Again, Connecticut came to rescue. Governor Trumbull's son Epaphroditus and the state's commissary officer Henry Champion rounded up 300 head of cattle and drove them all the way to Valley Forge where the famished soldiers consumed the entire herd in five days.

34. See John M. Palmer, *General von Steuben* (New Haven: Yale University, 1937), Royster, *Revolutionary People at War,* pp. 190–254, and John Joseph Stoudt, *Ordeal at Valley Forge: A Day-to-Day Chronicle Compiled from the Sources* (Philadelphia: University of Pennsylvania, 1963). Steuben announced to Congress that his proper name was Friedrich Wilhelm Augustus Heinrich Ferdinand, Baron von Steuben, thereby cramming in just about every name prevalent among the members of Prussia's royal house of Hohenzollern. His grandfather had changed the spelling of the family name because an aristocratic line of Steubens existed, and Friedrich got himself knighted through the influence of the collateral Prince of Hohenzollern-Hechingen just before he and the prince left Germany in disguise to escape their debts. He did hold a commission in the Prussian army, but hardly the general's rank he claimed. Incidentally, the town of King of Prussia, Pennsylvania, lies next door to Valley Forge and is named for Frederick II. That obsessively frugal monarch attempted to outlaw coffee, sugar, and tobacco on the grounds they were bad for the people's health and the kingdom's balance of payments. He would spin in his grave to know King of Prussia boasts the largest pure shopping mall in America.

35. Stoudt, *Ordeal at Valley Forge,* p. 209.

36. Dull, *Diplomatic History of the American Revolution,* pp. 62–65, 75–78. Deane was also suspected of being a double agent and Congress pestered him so much about alleged irregularities in his accounts that he did begin to take British money in 1781. See Julian P. Boyd, "Silas Deane: Death by a Kindly Teacher of Treason?" *William and Mary Quarterly* 16 (1959): 165–87, 319–42. As for Lee, his obsession with security did not prevent a British embassy agent from stealing his entire cache of secret correspondence: Louis W. Potts, *Arthur Lee, a Virtuous Revolutionary* (Baton Rouge: Louisiana State University, 1981), pp. 173–78.

37. Paris went even more mad for Franklin and America in 1776–77 than in the late 1760s, as documented at length in Edward E. Hale and Edward E. Hale, Jr., *Franklin in France,* 2 vols. (Boston: Roberts Brothers, 1888), Carl Van Doren, *Benjamin Franklin* (New York: Viking, 1956 [1938]), and the latest biography by H. W. Brands, *The First American: The Life and Times of Benjamin Franklin* (New York: Doubleday, 2001). That French ladies could not keep their hands off him is well known, but the strangely erotic appeal of the American cause was more general. A joke made the rounds in Paris about a much desired young beauty who spurned "the call of love" in favor of reading about the exciting American "insurgents." At length, a clever suitor disguised himself as a Pennsylvania Quaker, confessing he burned for two things—liberty and madame—whereupon she succumbed (Echeverria, *Mirage in the West,* pp. 39–40). Franklin's own performance in Paris was acidly etched by Herman Melville in his novel *Israel Potter: His Fifty Years of Exile.* Israel, a lad from the "Promised Land" of the Berkshires, fights bravely at Bunker Hill only to be captured and transported to England. There he falls in with

"friends of America" who send him to Paris with secret papers inside his boot heel. He finds Franklin's study strewn with all manner of books, scientific instruments, and maps covered with lines as if the owner were busy dividing the world. Franklin wears a dressing gown, the "fanciful present from an admiring Marchesa, curiously embroidered with algebraic figures like a conjuror's robe." At first Franklin says "Bon jour," but when his visitor replies in a Yankee accent, he shifts into the role of rustic American: "Ah! I smell Indian corn." Potter is given a spare room and is promptly joined by a *jeune fille* expecting to meet Ben for a tryst. Melville's take on John Paul Jones is also not to be missed.

38. The half a million figure is from Paul H. Smith, "The American Loyalists: Notes on Their Organization and Numerical Strength," *William and Mary Quarterly* 25 (1968): 258–77. General studies include Robert McCluer Calhoon, *The Loyalists in Revolutionary America 1760–1781* (New York: Harcourt Brace Jovanovich, 1965), Wallace Brown, *The King's Friends: The Composition and Motives of the American Loyalist Claimants* (Providence: Brown University, 1965) and *The Good Americans: The Loyalists in the American Revolution* (New York: William Morrow, 1969), and William H. Nelson, *The American Tory* (Oxford: Clarendon, 1961).

39. Wood, *Creation of the American Republic*, pp. 127–161.

40. Maryland refused to ratify the Articles until early 1781 because it insisted that the seven states with claims to vast western lands first relinquish them to the Congress. Competition for western land thus continued even during the war. On the deliberations and politics eventuating in the Articles of Confederation see Rakove, *Beginnings of National Politics*, pp. 135–91.

41. Jennings, *Creation of America*, pp. 180–92; Sally Schwartz, *"A Mixed Multitude": The Struggle for Toleration in Colonial Pennsylvania* (New York: New York University, 1987), pp. 280–87. On the Pennsylvania constitution in theory and practice, see also Owen S. Ireland, *Religion, Ethnicity, and Politics: Ratifying the Constitution in Pennsylvania* (University Park: Pennsylvania State University, 1995).

42. Calhoon, *Loyalists in Revolutionary America*, pp. 397–414.

43. Carl Van Doren, *Secret History of the American Revolution* (New York: Viking, 1941), pp. 39–43. Washington forwarded Duché's letter to Congress and the good Anglican parson took ship for England. After 1783 he turned coat again and returned to America. The quotation is just one of scores of examples of vicious Tory abuse in Philip Davidson, *Propaganda and the American Revolution 1763–1783* (Chapel Hill: University of North Carolina, 1941), p. 317.

44. Longmore, *Invention of George Washington*, p. 193.

45. Higginbotham, *War of American Independence*, pp. 268–275; Brown, *The Good Americans*, pp. 126–46 (quote, p. 126).

46. Calhoon, *Loyalists in Revolutionary America*, pp. 257–58. Aside from being a profound insight into "democracy and its discontents," Wiswall's focus on happiness is a fascinating anticipation of Jefferson.

47. Venturi, *End of the Old Regime*, I: 144–199; Frank O'Gorman, "The Parliamentary Opposition to the Government's American Policy 1760–1782," James E. Bradley, "The British Public and the American Revolution," Neil Longley York, "The Impact of the American Revolution on Ireland," and John Cannon, "The Loss of America," in Dickinson, ed., *Britain and the American Revolution*, pp. 97–257 (George III quote, p. 234); Peter D. G. Thomas, *John Wilkes: A Friend to Liberty* (Oxford: Clarendon, 1996), pp. 169–75; Herbert Butterfield, *George III, Lord North, and the People 1779–80* (New York: Russell & Russell, 1968).

48. Thayendanega was an extraordinary cross-cultural product. Adopted in his teens by the great Indian agent Sir William Johnson, he was educated in Connecticut, christened in the Anglican Church with the name Joseph Brant, and ennobled for posterity by painters George

Romney and Gilbert Stuart. He even translated the Book of Common Prayer into Mohawk. After the war the British rewarded him for his services with land grants near what is now Brantford, Ontario. But he scalped prisoners in the usual Iroquois fashion and was all the more hated by Patriots for his civilized veneer. Of course, had American militias gotten their hands on Brant, they would given him the same treatment with relish. See Fon W. Boardman, Jr., *Against the Iroquois: The Sullivan Campaign of 1779 in New York State* (New York: David McKay, 1978), pp. 10–18.

49. An excellent monograph on Indians during the War of Independence is Colin G. Calloway, *The American Revolution in Indian Country* (New York: Cambridge University, 1995).

50. Boardman, Jr., *Against the Iroquois*, pp. 57–87 (quote, p. 87).

51. Scheer, *Rebels and Redcoats*, p. 398. The ordeal at Charleston and heartbreaking Franco-American assault against Savannah were by no means the fault of General Benjamin Lincoln, the middle-aged farmer from Hingham, Massachusetts, called upon to command southern planters, pioneers, and slave labor gangs. Though forced to surrender, he won the admiration of South Carolinians and General Washington alike, and would later serve as secretary of War. For a moving, yet scholarly account see David B. Mattern, *Benjamin Lincoln and the American Revolution* (Columbia: University of South Carolina, 1995).

52. John Shy, *A People Numerous and Armed: Reflections on the Military Struggle for American Independence* (Ann Arbor: University of Michigan, 1990), pp. 193–212 (quote, p. 209); Scheer, *Rebels and Redcoats*, pp. 389–400; Paul H. Smith, *Loyalists and Redcoats: A Study in British Revolutionary Policy* (Chapel Hill: University of North Carolina, 1964).

53. Paul David Nelson, *General Horatio Gates: A Biography* (Baton Rouge: Louisiana State University, 1976), pp. 236–39, defends Gates from insinuations of cowardice on the grounds that he could not have done anything to redeem the situation and would surely have been captured by Tarleton had he remained. But Nelson concurs that Gates' handling of the army was disastrous and due in large part to his lack of interest in the cavalry arm and excessive reliance on untried militia.

54. The legend of Marion as a chivalric knight of the boondocks and champion of American liberty was fashioned in 1808 by Mason Locke "Parson" Weems, who was looking to follow up his equally fanciful biography of Washington with another success. But the debunking of Weems' "Swamp Fox" should not erase the man's genuinely remarkable qualities. The youngest of five children of a middling planter, he was stunted in stature and born with malformed knees and ankles that caused him to walk with a limp. As a teenager Marion went to sea only to suffer terribly. A whale stove in his schooner. The crew drifted for days in a lifeboat, surviving only by slitting the throat of their beloved pet dog and drinking its blood. At age eighteen, when his father died, he took over management of the family farms and slaves. At age twenty-five he fought fierce battles against Cherokees in the French and Indian War. His service in the War of Independence was thus a sort of crescendo for this intense little man who refused to give up. After the war, although no one saw more plunder and rapine than Marion, he pleaded for mercy toward former Tories: "God has given us victory. Let us show our gratitude to Heaven, which we shall not do by cruelty to man." See Hugh F. Rankin, *Francis Marion: The Swamp Fox* (New York: Crowell, 1973), p. 292.

55. Elswyth Thane, *The Fighting Quaker: Nathanael Greene* (New York: Hawthorn, 1972), pp. 1–24 (quote, p. 20).

56. Franklin made his postmaster duties an excuse to pass through Rhode Island where he made ardent approaches to Catherine. Early in the affair Ben complained that her "favours come mixed with the snowy fleeces, which are pure as your virgin innocence, white as your

lovely bosom, and—as cold." But on another occasion they traveled together some distance by coach and when Franklin contrived to "get lost" they shared a room in a roadhouse. Letter of March 4, 1755, in William Greene Roelker, ed., *Benjamin Franklin and Catharine Ray Greene: Their Correspondence* (Philadelphia: American Philosophical Society, 1949), p. 10.

57. John F. Stegeman and Janet A. Stegeman, *Caty: A Biography of Catharine Littlefield Greene* (Athens: University of Georgia, 1977); quote, p. 10. Marvin Kitman, *The Making of the President 1789* (New York: Harper & Row, 1989) is a humorous book and hardly authoritative, but cites memoir evidence concerning "Kitty Greene's War Record." She certainly bestowed her favors on Anthony Wayne, probably on Lafayette, and possibly on other members of Washington's staff.

58. Greene bluntly informed Jefferson "the Army is all that the States have to depend upon for their political existence," but it would disintegrate if the southern states did not do their part. Jefferson, characteristically, was offended by the rebuke (Middlekauff, *The Glorious Cause*, pp. 463–64). Even the admiring Padover (*Jefferson*, p. 48) grants Jefferson was "psychologically unprepared to cope with the violent reality of war." As governor he acquiesced in legislative *cutbacks* of the state's war contributions, in part from fear of slave revolts if the militia left for the front. He did not shrink, however, from calling for the expulsion or extermination of all Indians on western lands claimed by Virginia (Calloway, *American Revolution in Indian Country*, p. 53).

59. An important ancillary effect of The Cowpens (and King's Mountain before it) was to keep the Indians quiet. In 1779 the Cherokees and Choctaws had sided with Britain. But Patriot militiamen made devastating raids on the Cherokees in late 1780, prompting the Indians to confess to Nathanael Greene's agent they had been "rogues" to align with the British. See James H. O'Donnell III, *Southern Indians in the American Revolution* (Knoxville; University of Tennessee, 1973), pp. 95–124.

60. Royster, *Revolutionary People at War*, p. 298; figures on currency and inflation from Thomas L. Purvis, *Revolutionary America 1763 to 1800* (New York: Facts on File, 1995), pp. 85, 104–5. Thorough treatments include E. James Ferguson, *The Power of the Purse: A History of American Public Finance, 1775–1790* (Chapel Hill: University of North Carolina, 1961) and Clarence L. Ver Steeg, *Robert Morris, Revolutionary Financier* (New York: Octogan, 1972 [1954]).

61. Arnold's defection was a psychological blow to the Continental Army, but had little strategic impact since his plan to deliver the American base at West Point to the British aborted. Arnold's go-between with Clinton, Major John André, was captured (and hanged), forcing Arnold to flee to the British with nothing to sell but his services. See James Kirby Martin, *Benedict Arnold, Revolutionary Hero: An American Warrior Reconsidered* (New York: New York University, 1997), Willard M. Wallace, *Traitorous Hero: The Life and Fortunes of Benedict Arnold* (New York: Harper, 1954), and Van Doren, *Secret History of the American Revolution*.

62. Tallmadge thus avenged the death of his Yale classmate and friend Nathan Hale, who was hanged by the British for espionage and said, in legend at least, "I regret that I have but one life to give for my country." A good account of the shadow war is John Bakeless, *Turncoats, Traitors & Heroes: Espionage in the American Revolution* (Philadelphia: Lippincott, 1960).

63. Who concocted the plan that won the battle that secured American independence? Not Washington, who expected to assault New York City, nor Rochambeau. Rather, Admiral de Grasse and Captain Francisco de Saavedra de Sangronis, commander of the Spanish Fleet based in Havana, imagined the bold stroke. Saavedra even raised money in Cuba and Santo Domingo to help pay for de Grasse's cruise. See Thomas E. Chávez, *Spain and the Independence of the United States: An Intrinsic Gift* (Albuquerque: University of New Mexico, 2002).

64. Why did the Americans win? Two analyses of the many "what if" scenarios in the war concur that the American cause might, and perhaps ought, to have aborted on numerous occasions. But luck, destiny, fate, or Providence aside, poor British leadership and strategy were what gave the Americans a chance for victory in the first place. During the critical early years, when they held all the initiative, the British wavered between trying to prod the colonists into negotiations, occupying their ports and suppressing commerce, striking inland in hopes of a climactic military victory, and recruiting Loyalist militia to overthrow Patriot governments. Contrast Thomas Fleming, "Unlikely Victory: Thirteen Ways the Americans Could Have Lost the Revolution," in Robert Cowley, ed., *What If? The World's Foremost Military Historians Imagine What Might Have Been* (New York: G. P. Putnam's Sons, 1999), pp. 155–86, and J. C. D. Clark, "British America: What If There Had Been No American Revolution?" in Niall Ferguson, ed., *Virtual History: Alternatives and Counterfactuals* (New York: Basic Books, 1999, pp. 125–74 (esp. 163–65).

65. Dull, *Diplomatic History of the American Revolution*, pp. 137–58, is the most recent and accurate account. But Richard B. Morris, *The Peacemakers: The Great Powers and American Independence* (New York: Harper & Row, 1965), tells the most detailed and colorful story of the American commissioners and their negotiations. Especially amusing are the contretemps between Adams and Franklin. The former abominated the latter's duplicity, not to mention his wanton lifestyle, while the latter shook his head over the former's self-defeating moralism. Someone unwilling to "dance, drink, game, flatter, promise, dress, swear with gentlemen, and small talk and flirt with the ladies" was not likely to accomplish much in Paris (p. 451).

66. Richard B. Morris, *The Forging of the Union 1781–1789* (New York: Harper & Row, 1987), pp. 42–54; Rakove, *Beginnings of National Politics*, pp. 297–329. On Morris' army plot and Washington's speech, see Richard H. Kohn, "The Inside History of the Newburgh Conspiracy: America and the Coup d'État," *William and Mary Quarterly* 27 (1970): 187–220. Hamilton, Gates, Lincoln, McDougall, and the other officers never intended to seize dictatorial power. They just wanted their rightful compensation from a nation that ducked the sacrifices they had made. But any military coercion would of course have set a disastrous precedent (see Mattern, *Benjamin Lincoln*, pp. 134–49).

67. Flexner, *Washington in the American Revolution*, pp. 516–18.

68. Morris, *Forging of the Union*, p. xi.

## FEDERALISTS, ANTIS, VESTALS, AND VICTIMS

1. The catalogue of brilliant works by the tightly knit community of Scottish philosophers is extensive, but its greatest achievements surely include Hume's *An Enquiry Concerning Human Understanding* (1748, rev. ed. 1758), Reid's *An Inquiry into the Human Mind on the Principles of Common Sense* (1764), Adam Ferguson's *Essay on the History of Civil Society* (1767), and Adam Smith's *Theory of Moral Sentiments* (1759) and *Inquiry into the Nature and Origins of the Wealth of Nations* (1776). The influence of these and other common sense philosophers on the ideas of America's founders was profound, though not so complete as argued by Garry Wills in *Inventing America: Jefferson's Declaration of Independence* (Garden City, N.Y.: Doubleday, 1978). The latest, most penetrating discussion of the Scottish enlightenment can be found in Arthur Herman, *How the Scots Invented the Modern World* (New York: Crown, 2001).

2. Mark A. Noll, *Princeton and the Republic: The Search for a Christian Enlightenment in the Era of Samuel Stanhope Smith* (Princeton: Princeton University, 1989), pp. 16–27 (quote, p. 24). Gilbert Tennent and Samuel Davies discovered Witherspoon during a fund-raising trip to Britain for the College of New Jersey. They mistook him for a New Light evangelist because of his opposition to the skeptical Hume.

3. Thomas Miller, ed., *The Selected Writings of John Witherspoon* (Carbondale, Ill.: Southern Illinois University, 1990), pp. 1–48 (quotes, p. 29); Noll, *Princeton and the Republic,* pp. 28–58. Of the twenty-five college men at the 1787 Constitutional Convention, nine were from Princeton, four from Yale, and just three from Harvard.

4. The orrery got its curious name from a London watchmaker hired by Charles Boyle, the earl of Orrery, to fashion a moving planetarium. It was later purchased by King George I for a thousand guineas. In 1761 the compiler of a biographical dictionary mistakenly named Orrery the inventor so his name was attached to the thing. The two Rittenhouse orreries (the other remained in Philadelphia) far surpassed anything else extant at the time and became famous tourist attractions. On Madison at Princeton see Virginia Moore, *The Madisons: A Biography* (New York: McGraw-Hill, 1979), pp. 20–45 (poem, p. 31; "great law," p. 99) and Jack N. Rakove, *James Madison and the Creation of the American Republic* (New York: HarperCollins, 1990), pp. 1–18.

5. See for instance John Chester Miller, *Alexander Hamilton: Portrait in Paradox* (Westport, Conn.: Greenwood, 1959) and Marie B. Hecht, *Odd Destiny: The Life of Alexander Hamilton* (New York: Macmillan, 1982). Forrest McDonald, *Alexander Hamilton: A Biography* (New York: W. W. Norton, 1979), calls Hamilton a Romantic (Necker anecdote, p. 85). Broadus Mitchell, *Alexander Hamilton,* 2 vols. (New York: Macmillan, 1957–62), is the most detailed account of his life albeit some of his details have since been corrected.

6. McDonald, *Hamilton,* pp. 3–50.

7. Letters to Lauren quoted in McDonald, *Hamilton,* pp. 19–22; "The Continentalist" articles, pp. 42–43; critique of lawyers, p. 50; Humean influence, p. 98. On Hamilton's philosophical views see also Gerald Stourzh, *Alexander Hamilton and the Idea of Republican Government* (Stanford, Calif.: Stanford University, 1970) and Harvey Flaumenhaft, *The Effective Republic: Administration and Constitution in the Thought of Alexander Hamilton* (Durham, N.C.: Duke University, 1992).

8. Richard B. Morris, *The Forging of the Union 1781–1789* (New York: Harper & Row, 1987), pp. 130–61; Lance Banning, "Political Economy and the Creation of the Federal Republic," in David Thomas Konig, ed., *Devising Liberty: Preserving and Creating Freedom in the American Republic* (Stanford, Calif.: Stanford University, 1995), pp. 11–49.

9. Pennsylvania adopted a scheme so complex that a newspaper claimed it took "Machiavellian shrewdness" to untangle. The brainchild of Charles Pettit, it began when speculators, back-country radicals, and even some Tories formed a junto to win control of the legislature and ram through a series of laws. Under them Pennsylvania revoked the charter for the Bank of North America, assumed all state debt and such national debt as was locally held, printed $400,000 in cash to issue new loans, and made wartime paper payable at par in the form of *land grants* in the west. Financial speculators were ecstatic because their bonds doubled and tripled in value. Land speculators were ecstatic because they could borrow against land they already held to buy securities at a discount, redeem them at par for more land, then sell enough to cover the original loan. Finally, state officials were ecstatic because they could retire $2 to $3 in debt for every $1 loaned out and put currency in circulation to boot. Hamilton paid close attention; he just wished Congress had the power to do something similar for the nation at large.

10. Under the Articles of Confederation agents of Congress concluded commercial treaties with the Netherlands, Sweden, Prussia, and Morocco, but those counted for little by comparison to Britain, France, and Spain.

11. Statistics from Thomas J. Purvis, *Revolutionary America 1763 to 1800* (New York: Facts on File, 1995), pp. 8, 123–25, 253. On pioneer farming, see Willard W. Cochrane, *The Development of*

*American Agriculture: A Historical Analysis,* 2 ed. (Minneapolis: University of Minnesota, 1993), pp. 37–56.

12. See Colin G. Galloway, *The American Revolution in Indian Country* (New York: Cambridge University, 1995), pp. 272–91 (quote, p. 282), Wilcomb E. Washburn, *The Indian in America* (New York: Harper & Row, 1975), pp. 146–69, and Bruce G. Trigger and Washburn, eds., *The Cambridge History of the Native Peoples of the Americas,* vol. 1: *North America* (Cambridge, U.K.: Cambridge University, 1996), pp. 462–98.

13. Morris, *Forging of the Union,* pp. 220–44; Daniel M. Friedenberg, *Life, Liberty, and the Pursuit of Land* (Buffalo, N.Y.: Prometheus, 1992), pp. 275–92.

14. By the 1780s the Spanish territories of Louisiana and West Florida (the Gulf Coast) contained about thirteen thousand Creoles, sixteen thousand enslaved and one thousand free Africans, and some thirty thousand Indians. The economy was still primitive, but the Indian trade in deerskins and exports of indigo, tobacco, and timber surpassed 5 million *livres* per year. See Daniel H. Usner, Jr., *Indians, Settlers, and Slaves in a Frontier Exchange Economy: The Lower Mississippi Valley Before 1783* (Chapel Hill: University of North Carolina, 1990).

15. Wilkinson was born in 1757 in Maryland and served as adjutant general for Horatio Gates during the War of Independence. In 1784 he sought his fortune in Kentucky, whose statehood he advocated whether inside or outside the American union. In 1787 he secretly swore allegiance to Spain and was on the Louisiana governor's payroll until 1800 under the code name "Number Thirteen." See James Ripley Jacobs, *Tarnished Warrior: Major-General James Wilkinson* (New York: Macmillan, 1938). McGillivray, the child of a British Indian agent, was accepted as a Creek under the tribe's matrilineal custom. His dual heritage and education in the ways of the whites made him extremely valuable to the Creeks. They soon bestowed on him an unprecedented leadership role. McGillivray deftly exploited the weakness of the United States by denying its claims under the white man's own laws and turning whites against whites (Spanish Florida vs. Georgia and Georgia vs. the Congress). The success of his brave fight on behalf of southern Indians depended, of course, on the Americans' *failing* to fix the Articles of Confederation. See John W. Caughey, *McGillivray of the Creeks* (Norman: University of Oklahoma, 1938).

16. Frederick W. Marks III, *Independence on Trial: Foreign Affairs and the Making of the Constitution* (Baton Rouge: Louisiana State University, 1973), pp. 3–95. Adding to the humiliations of Congress under the Articles were the Barbary pirates of North Africa, who captured several American merchant ships and sold their crews into slavery. Even America's French allies turned cold toward U.S. emissary Thomas Jefferson when Congress defaulted on servicing its wartime debt to France.

17. The famous Progressive accuser of the Framers was Charles A. Beard, *An Economic Interpretation of the Constitution of the United States* (New York: Macmillan, 1913), but his various hypotheses were decisively debunked by Forrest McDonald, *We the People: The Economic Origins of the Constitution* (Chicago: University of Chicago, 1958), especially pp. 21–92.

18. General Henry Knox damned the states with characteristic bluffness. "The vile state governments are sources of pollution which will contaminate the American name for ages," he wrote Rufus King. "Smite them, smite them, in the name of God and the people": William W. Crosskey and William Jeffrey Jr., *Politics and the Constitution in the History of the United States* (Chicago: University of Chicago, 1980), 20 vols., III: 420–21. On the Federalists see Stanley Elkins and Eric McKitrick, "The Founding Fathers: Young Men of the Revolution," in Jack P. Greene, ed., *The Reinterpretation of the American Revolution 1763–1789* (New York: Harper & Row, 1968), pp. 378–95, and the article they in turn credit by Cecilia Kenyon, "Men of Little

Faith: the Anti-Federalists on the Nature of Representative Government," *William and Mary Quarterly* 12 (1955): 3–43.

19. John F. Stegeman and Janet A. Stegeman, *Caty: A Biography of Catharine Littlefield Greene* (Athens: University of Georgia, 1977), pp. 113–33 (Wayne quote, p. 124); Elswyth Thane, *The Fighting Quaker: Nathaniel Greene* (New York: Hawthorn, 1972), pp. 277–79 (Washington quote, p. 279).

20. Adams and Lee quoted in Jack N. Rakove, *The Beginnings of National Politics: An Interpretive History of the Continental Congress* (New York: Knopf, 1979), pp. 383–91; quotes on small states in Catherine Drinker Brown, *Miracle at Philadelphia: The Story of the Constitutional Convention May to September 1787* (Boston: Little, Brown, 1966), p. 9.

21. Sorry to keep piling on Jefferson, but he was the one who called those measures (on the state level, mind you) the very foundations "for a government truly republican." In fact, entail was not widely practiced even in the Tidewater and where it did exist the inability to sell inherited land, far from creating a landed aristocracy, hurt planters desperate for cash. As for religious toleration, it was nearly universal (except for Catholics) for the simple reason that bans on dissenting sects and collection of Anglican tithes were unenforceable under American conditions. See Bernard Bailyn, "Political Experience and Enlightenment Ideas in Eighteenth-Century America," in Greene, ed., *Reinterpretation of the American Revolution*, pp. 283–84.

22. On Madison's "vices of the system" see Rakove, *Madison and the Creation*, pp. 30–52 and Gordon Wood, *The Creation of the American Republic 1776–1789* (Chapel Hill: University of North Carolina, 1969), pp. 393–429. Madison's belief that the weakness of the Confederation encouraged poorer rather than better state governments is explained by Lance Banning, *The Sacred Fire of Liberty: James Madison and the Founding of the Federal Republic* (Ithaca, N.Y.: Cornell University, 1995), pp. 66–75. A similar point is made by Colleen A. Sheehan, "The Politics of Public Opinion: James Madison's 'Notes on Government'," *William and Mary Quarterly* 49 (1992): 609–27. However important "checks and balances" were to Madison's thinking, he never ceased to believe in the importance of fostering a common republican opinion. Thus, his hope that a more elevated federal system would have benign effects on local government was an integral feature of his republican philosophy.

23. Morgan, *Birth of the Republic*, pp. 245–66; Middlekauff, *Glorious Cause*, pp. 582–601 (quote, p. 600).

24. The anger of farmers was even more justified than they knew. General Court in fact permitted payment of the new taxes in state securities to be honored at par, but collectors did not bother to inform rural folk. That permitted them to square their accounts with securities purchased for a pittance and pocket the hard cash they extracted from citizens. Happily, the Massachusetts affair ended peaceably when all fourteen of the leaders were pardoned or released after short terms in prison. The infamous General Sullivan, now governor of New Hampshire, was lenient toward "rebels" in his state as well. The Shaysite cause triumphed, moreover, when Massachusetts voters tossed out the hard-money elite in the spring. The assembly proceeded to abolish direct taxes and pass relief measures for debtors and veterans. See Forrest McDonald, *The Formation of the American Republic*, (Baltimore: Penguin, 1965), pp. 14–54. Congressional resolution quoted in George Brown Tindall, *America: A Narrative History*, 2 ed. (New York: W. W. Norton, 1988), p. 279 (italics added). On Shays' Rebellion see Van Beck Hall, *Politics Without Parties: Massachusetts, 1780–1791* (Pittsburgh: University of Pittsburgh, 1972) and Robert J. Taylor, *Western Massachusetts in the Revolution* (Providence: Brown University, 1954).

25. Madison knew how novel, hence controversial, his conception of federalism was. He

wrote Jefferson: "I admit the difference to be material. It presents the aspect rather of a feudal system of republics, if such a phrase may be used, than of a Confederacy of independent states" (quoted in William A. Williams, *The Contours of American History* (New York: Franklin Watts, 1973), p. 160). Madison's "middle way" thinking is described in Banning, *Sacred Fire of Liberty*, pp. 138–64. See also Rakove, *Madison and the Creation*, and William Lee Miller, *The Business of May Next: James Madison and the Founding* (Charlottesville: University of Virginia, 1992).

26. Wilson deserves to be ranked with Madison and Hamilton among the Framers. Born in 1742, he studied accounting at St. Andrews University, where his tutor marked him for greatness upon witnessing his natural talent for golf! Wilson emigrated in 1765 and tutored at the College of Philadelphia where he studied with Dickinson. But academics were a dead end, so Wilson practiced law in the frontier towns of Reading and Carlisle until he obtained the reputation and money to make it in Philadelphia, where he signed the Declaration of Independence. Staring from his portrait over small eyeglasses he looks both donnish and handsome. Wilson loved money and the good life, and drank and speculated with equal abandon, but was also a dogged Patriot and defender of the little man: in all things a complete American. His common sense philosophy persuaded him that the people at large were no more base—or elevated—than the high born, educated, and rich, and thus could be trusted with power. See Charles Page Smith, *James Wilson, Founding Father 1742–1798* (Chapel Hill: University of North Carolina, 1956) and Geoffrey Seed, *James Wilson* (Millwood, N.Y.: KTO, 1978).

27. McDonald, *Formation of the American Republic*, pp. 155–62; quotes from Moore, *The Madisons*, pp. 99–100. See also Rakove, *Madison and the Creation*, pp. 30–52. On Madison's constitutional thought see also Irving Brant, *James Madison: Father of the Constitution, 1787–1800* (Indianapolis: Bobbs-Merrill, 1950), Willi Paul Adams, *The First American Constitutions*, trans. Rita and Robert Kimber (Chapel Hill: University of North Carolina, 1980 [orig. 1973]), and Forrest McDonald, *Novus Ordo Seclorum: The Intellectual Origins of the Constitution* (Lawrence: University of Kansas, 1985).

28. McDonald, *Formation of the American Republic*, pp. 162–67.

29. Madison quoted in Max Farrand, ed., *The Records of the Federal Convention of 1787*, 3 vols. (New Haven: Yale University, 1911), I:471–72; "Emperors, kings" quote in a letter from Robert Osgood to John Adams, quoted in Rakove, *Beginning of National Politics*, p. 387; Hamilton quoted in Richard Brookhiser, *Alexander Hamilton: American* (New York: Free Press, 1999), pp. 64–67.

30. For southerners' positions at the convention see above all Don Fehrenbacher, *The Slaveholding Republic* (New York: Oxford University, 2001), as well as James Haw, *John and Edward Rutledge of South Carolina* (Athens: University of Georgia Press, 1997), pp. 198–215, and Frances Leigh Williams, *A Founding Family: the Pinckneys of South Carolina* (New York: Harcourt, Brace, Jovanovich, 1978), pp. 218–49.

31. Bowen, *Miracle at Philadelphia*, pp. 125–27.

32. McDonald, *Formation of the American Republic*, pp. 168–73; Morris, *Forging of the Union*, pp. 281–97 (quote pp. 296–97); Gerry quote from Bowen, *Miracle at Philadelphia*, p. 95. On Madison's and possibly Washington's opposition, see Stuart Leibinger, *Founding Friendship: George Washington, James Madison, and the Creation of the American Republic* (Charlottesville: University Press of Virginia, 1999), pp. 73–83. Luther Martin wrote "it did not appear to me that [Washington] was disposed to favor the claims of the *smaller states,* against the *undue superiority* attempted by the large states" (p. 76).

33. McDonald, *Formation of the American Republic*, pp. 176–78, surmised that Hugh Williamson's timely announcement of his intention to change North Carolina's vote facilitated a deal Rutledge and Sherman made over dinner on June 30. David Hackett Fischer exploded

this fanciful theory in *Historians' Fallacies: Toward a Logic of Historical Thought* (New York: Harper & Row, 1970), pp. 29–30, 77–78.

34. Why Hugh Williamson has attracted no biographers is a mystery. But see the eulogy delivered after his death by David Hosack, *A Biographical Memoir of Hugh Williamson, M.D., LL.D.* (New York: C. S. Van Winkle, 1820), John Washington Neal, "Life and Public Services of Hugh Williamson," *Trinity College Historical Society Papers*, series 13–15 (1919), pp. 62–111, Burton Craige, *The Federal Convention of 1787: North Carolina in the Great Crisis* (Richmond, Va.: Expert Graphics, 1987 [manuscript predates 1945]), pp. 131–67, and the excellent entry in the *Dictionary of American Biography*.

35. Quote from Williamson letter Governor Caswell (Aug. 20, 1787), in Max Farrand, ed., *The Records of the Federal Convention of 1787* (New Haven: Yale University, 1911), III: 70–71. Craige, *North Carolina in the Great Crisis*, pp. 35–45, attributes North Carolina's vote to Williamson's statesmanlike determination to compromise. Once satisfied with the plan to apportion seats in the first Congress and grant the House sole power to introduce money bills, he persuaded a wavering colleague to vote with him for the Connecticut Plan. Only one of North Carolina's four delegates, a die-hard Virginia follower, voted against. William S. Powell, *North Carolina Through Four Centuries* (Chapel Hill: University of North Carolina, 1989), pp. 221–25, is the latest to conclude North Carolina supported the compromise in the fear small states would explode the convention if their cause had been lost (p. 224). In the 1790s Williamson served in Congress where he took Jeffersonian positions. Upon marriage he moved to New York and resumed his scientific experiments. He died there in 1819, heralded as a Renaissance Man surpassed in America only by Franklin.

36. On Luther Martin's campaign see McDonald, *Formation of the American Republic*, pp. 179–84; Rutledge quote in Haw, *John and Edward Rutledge*, p. 210.

37. Jack N. Rakove, *Original Meanings: Politics and Ideas in the Making of the Constitution* (New York: Knopf, 1996), p. 366.

38. Morris was a snob, make no mistake. He insisted others pronounce his name "GouvernEUR" and bragged he was the only person on a first-name basis with Washington (Martha herself was not). He lost his leg in a riding accident, but according to society chatter the amputation had no effect on his romantic prowess. For his tinkering with the phraseology in the Constitution see McDonald, *Formation of the American Republic*, p. 187; for the debate over a bill of rights see Bowen, *Miracle in Philadelphia*, pp. 243–53 and McDonald, *States' Rights and the Union: Imperium in Imperio, 1776–1876* (Lawrence: University of Kansas, 2000), pp. 7–25.

39. Richard Hofstadter, "The Founding Fathers: An Age of Realism," in Robert H. Horwitz, ed., *The Moral Foundations of the American Republic*, 2 ed. (Charlottesville: University of Virginia, 1979), pp. 73–85; Middlekauff, *The Glorious Cause*, pp. 649–64.

40. McDonald, *Formation of the American Republic*, p. 188.

41. Bowen, *Miracle at Philadelphia*, pp. 50–53. Though they rebelled against Britain's "two-bottle tyrants" the delegates were not above indulging themselves: one receipt reveals that sixty bottles of madeira were ordered for a party of twelve. Dancing was another daily amusement, albeit European visitors complained no "libertine wives" could be found in the Quaker city.

42. Bowen, *Miracle at Philadelphia*, p. 13. In 1787 the Rhode Island supreme court ruled its currency law unconstitutional, an early example of judicial review.

43. See, for instance, Gordon S. Wood's discussions in *The Radicalism of the American Revolution* (New York: Vintage, 1993), pp. 368–69, "The Relevance and Irrelevance of John Adams" in *The Creation of the American Republic 1776–1789* (Chapel Hill: University of North Carolina, 1969), pp. 567–92, and "Interests and Disinterestedness in the Making of the

Constitution," in Richard Beeman, Stephen Botein, and Edward C. Carter III, eds., *Beyond Confederation: Origins of the Constitution and American National Identity* (Chapel Hill: University of North Carolina, 1987), pp. 69–109, and McDonald, *Formation of the American Republic*, pp. 194–95 (quote, p. 195). Of course, Adams and Jefferson went on to become chief executives under the Constitution, but later in life agreed the Founders had failed, or rather succeeded too well, by encouraging not virtue, but avarice and ambition masquerading as virtue.

44. Elkins and McKitrick, "The Founding Fathers," pp. 384–95.

45. See Richard D. Brown, "Shays's Rebellion and the Ratification of the Federal Constitution in Massachusetts," in Beeman, et al., *Beyond Confederation*, pp. 113–27.

46. Bowling was introduced to America by the Dutch in New Amsterdam, but spread quickly throughout the taverns of New England where it provided good winter sport and an occasion for gambling. Puritan fathers outlawed "ninepins" in the late 1600s, giving rise to the legend the contemporary game of ten-pin bowling was invented to circumvent the authorities.

47. On the Anti-Federalists see Herbert J. Storing, *The Complete Anti-Federalist*, 7 vols. (Chicago: University of Chicago, 1981), quote from "Essay of an Old Whig" in vol. 3: 44; Storing, *What the Anti-Federalists Were For* (Chicago: University of Chicago, 1981), Wood, "Interests and Disinterestedness," pp. 93–110 ("defraud" and "establish iniquity," pp. 107–8); Jackson Turner Main, *The Antifederalists: Critics of the Constitution* (Chapel Hill: University of North Carolina, 1961); and Christopher M. Duncan, *The Anti-Federalists and Early American Political Thought* (DeKalb: Northern Illinois University, 1995). Wood considers William Findley an excellent example of the Antis. A ruddy, pugnacious Scots-Irishman in an outlandish white hat, he settled in western Pennsylvania after 1763, fought in the militia, and though "middling" in every respect rose in politics by rousing the rabble and baiting the rich. When Hugh Henry Brackenridge, a Princeton man, sought to bring culture to Pittsburgh through a newspaper peppered with Latin quotations, Findley targeted him. Brackenridge played into his hands when he declared "the people are fools" for resisting Robert Morris' bank. Findley paraded the quote, setting back Brackenridge's career. The Antis lost the fight over the Constitution, but the future belonged to the Findleys.

48. The pitch and phrasing of Henry's orations tingle the spine even in print and are well worth a read. See volume III of Eliot, ed., *Debates in the Several State Conventions*, as well as Richard R. Beeman, *Patrick Henry: A Biography* (New York: McGraw-Hill, 1974), pp. 144–63. Beeman wryly notes Henry was on swampy turf when he extolled the virtue of state government: everyone knew Virginia's assembly was a comedy.

49. Clarence Eugene Miner, *The Ratification of the Federal Constitution by the State of New York* (New York: AMS, 1968 [1921]) and Elliot, *Debates on the Adoption*, II: 205ff. North Carolina, despite Williamson's crucial role at the Constitutional Convention, overwhelmingly opposed ratification, as did Rhode Island. They did not bow to the inevitable until November 1789 and May 1790, respectively, well after President Washington was in office.

50. According to the 1790 census, the thirteen states had a population of 3.92 million. Subtracting slaves, aliens, women, children, and those who failed to meet various state property requirements, about 640,000 adult white males were eligible to vote. But only about 120,000 went to the polls to choose state convention delegates. Assuming the vote broke 50–50 (Anti-Federalist New York had the highest turnout at 43.4 percent), that means about 60,000 people voiced approbation of the Philadelphia document. Good for them. On voting calculations for the period see Chilton Williamson, *American Suffrage from Property to Democracy, 1776–1865* (Princeton: Princeton University, 1962); some state data on turnout are provided in Purvis, *Revolutionary America 1763 to 1800*, p. 210.

51. Bowen, *Miracle at Philadelphia,* pp. 306–10 (quote, p. 310).

52. Check out the *Oxford English Dictionary* for its fascinating examples of usages from the 1500s forward.

53. This is the measure employed, quite rightly, by Wood in *The Radicalism of the American Revolution,* pp. 3–8.

54. Some readers may be surprised to learn this became the orthodox position in most American universities between the 1960s and 1980s, and was reflected in numerous high school textbooks. The controversial UCLA history standards proposed as national standards in the 1990s were not so dismissive of the changes wrought by the American Revolution, but their *idée fixe* was the "unfulfilled agenda" of equal rights for all regardless of race, class, creed, color, gender, or sexual orientation. The most virulent recent writer on the Founders is Larry E. Tise, *The American Counterrevolution: A Retreat from Liberty, 1783–1800* (Mechanicsburg, Pa.: Stackpole Books, 1998).

55. This paragraph shamelessly adumbrates some of the main contentions of Wood's chapters on hierarchy, republicanism, and democracy in *The Radicalism of the American Revolution.*

56. See especially Jon Butler, *Becoming America: The Revolution Before 1776* (Cambridge, Mass.: Harvard University, 2000).

57. Washington's lifelong endorsement of piety and his service on the vestry on his Anglican church are well known. Madison, an author of Virginia's act of toleration, wrote at length about the theological and political advantages of disestablishment. See John T. Noonan, Jr., *The Lustre of Our Country: The American Experience of Religious Freedom* (Berkeley: University of California, 1998), pp. 59–92. Less known are Franklin's views. When asked by Ezra Stiles about his beliefs Franklin replied in a letter he begged be kept secret. That proves his sincerity, because Franklin never lied *except* for public consumption. "I believe in one God, creator of the universe. That He governs it by His providence. That He ought to be worshiped. . . . That the soul of man is immortal, and will be treated with justice in another life. . . ." He expressed doubts about the divinity of Jesus, but thought his morals and religion "the best the world ever saw or is likely to see": Richard John Neuhaus, "The American Mind," *First Things* 118 (2001): 69–70. On the religious views of the Founders generally, see Melvin B. Endy, Jr., "Just War, Holy War, and Millenarianism in Revolutionary America," *William and Mary Quarterly* 42 (1985): 3–25.

58. To discern the importance of foreign policy in the thinking of Federalists one need only consult *The Federalist* papers, but a good overview is in Marks, *Independence on Trial,* pp. 167–206.

59. The classic study of American naturalization policy and its British and colonial antecedents is James H. Kettner, *The Development of American Citizenship, 1608–1870* (Chapel Hill: University of North Carolina, 1978).

60. See Barbara Clark Smith's rebuttal in "Forum: How Revolutionary Was the Revolution? A Discussion of Gordon S. Wood's *The Radicalism of the American Revolution,*" *William and Mary Quarterly* 51 (1994): 677–716.

61. Nancy Woloch, *Women and the American Experience,* 2 ed. (New York: McGraw-Hill, 1994), pp. 50–62. See also Frances Leigh Williams, *A Founding Family: The Pinckneys of South Carolina* (New York: Harcourt, Brace, Jovanovich, 1978).

62. Alice Hanson Jones, *Wealth of a Nation to Be: The American Colonies on the Eve of the Revolution* (New York: Columbia University, 1980), pp. 224–29.

63. Morris, *Forging of the Union,* p. 190.

64. See the excellent revisionist works by Mary Beth Norton, *Liberty's Daughters: The*

*Revolutionary Experience of American Women, 1750–1800* (Boston: Little, Brown, 1980), Linda K. Kerber, *Women of the Republic: Intellect and Ideology in Revolutionary America* (Chapel Hill: University of North Carolina, 1980), and Ronald Hoffman and Peter J. Albert, eds., *Women in the Age of the American Revolution* (Charlottesville: University of Virginia, 1989). A few women fought in the war by disguising themselves as men or serving guns on the ramparts in the heat of battle. A woman was killed at Québec and another, Margaret Corbin, took over her dead husband's place at Fort Washington: Don Higginbotham, *The War of American Independence: Military Attitudes, Policies, and Practice* (Boston: Northeastern University, 1983), pp. 262–63.

65. See Richard Godbeer, *Sexual Revolution in Early America* (Baltimore: Johns Hopkins University, 2002). Godbeer collects a mass of evidence (albeit few statistics) to argue for a "culture war" of sorts in eighteenth-century America. His discussion of New England is most enlightening. The early Puritans, far from being prudes, considered marital intercourse a spiritual, almost sacramental, affair. Believing women could not conceive without orgasm, Puritan manuals instructed husbands to engage in extended, wanton foreplay then take care to satisfy their wives' desires. All other sexual activity, of course, was proscribed. By the mid-eighteenth century, however, the kids on New England farms showed an alarming tendency to do what comes naturally behind the woodshed. So parents began letting sweethearts "bundle": that way they at least would know the father in case of a pregnancy.

66. Woloch, *Women and the American Experience*, pp. 63–97 (quotes, pp. 90–91). For a dissenting view see Joan Hoff Wilson, "The Negative Impact of the American Revolution on Women," in Mary Beth Norton and Ruth M. Alexander, eds., *Major Problems in American Women's History* (Lexington, Mass.: D. C. Heath, 1996): 83–103. Of course, any assessment of "negative" or "positive" impacts is by definition a presentist judgment.

67. The first campaign under General James Harmar lost 250 men killed in the Maumee Valley, 1790. He blamed "cowardly, untrained militia," but in fact walked into an ambush. General Arthur St. Clair returned the following year with 2,000 men, but was similarly trapped near Fort Wayne and lost 630 men killed. See Washburn, *Indian in America*, pp. 146–69 (quotes, p. 162); Trigger and Washburn, eds., *Cambridge History of the Native Peoples of the Americas*, vol. 1: *North America*, pp. 462–98. On Fallen Timbers see Paul D. Nelson, *Anthony Wayne: Soldier of the New Republic* (Bloomington: Indiana University, 1985).

68. William Peden, ed., *Notes on the State of Virginia* by Thomas Jefferson (Chapel Hill: University of North Carolina, 1955), p. 138.

69. Elliott, ed. *Debates in the Several State Conventions*, IV: 285–86.

70. Paul Finkelman, "Slavery and the Constitutional Convention: Making a Covenant With Death," in Beeman, et al., eds., *Beyond Confederation*, pp. 188–225 (quote, p. 193).

71. Passage of the bill, which awarded Mrs. Greene $47,000 to be paid in installments, was nevertheless delayed a year by her association with Anthony Wayne. It seems Wayne won himself a Georgia seat in Congress through an election so blatantly rigged even hardened politicians had to blush. When his feisty opponent James Jackson protested to his congressional colleagues they unseated Wayne by unanimous vote. Finally, in April 1792, the Greene indemnity passed 33 to 24 while Mrs. Greene sobbed in the gallery.

72. Stegeman and Stegeman, *Caty: A Biography*, pp. 156–66 (quotes, pp. 160–61); Constance McL. Green, *Eli Whitney and the Birth of American Technology* (Boston: Little, Brown, 1956), pp. 40–62.

73. Stegeman and Stegeman, *Caty: A Biography*, pp. 167–73 (quote, p. 172). Caty married Phineas Miller and moved with him and her surviving children (George, the oldest, died in an canoeing accident) to Cumberland Island, Georgia. After long legal tussles the Georgia legisla-

ture agreed to purchase the cotton gin patent from Whitney's company, enabling Caty at last to build her dream house "Dungeness" amidst the magnolias. But Whitney in turn sued his partners, returning Caty to the verge of bankruptcy. One of her last entrepreneurial efforts was a lumber company to harvest the island's live oak. Philadelphia shipbuilder Joshua Humphreys knew its strength and resilience, hence he purchased Cumberland oak for the hull of a new ship he was commissioned to build. She was christened the *U.S.S. Constitution*, but is better known as "Old Ironsides." Catherine Littlefield Greene Miller lived long enough to learn of the ship's victories in the War of 1812, then died at Dungeness, aged 61, in 1814.

74. Bowen, *Miracle at Philadelphia*, p. 42.

MASTER BUILDERS, PARTY MEN, AND A ROGUE

1.Whitehall Company, *The Presidents . . . Their Inaugural Addresses* (Chicago: Whitehall, 1968), pp. 47–53 (italics added).

2. The parenthetical "or vice versa" refers to the divide between pre- and post-millennialists, who argued whether the return of Christ would *begin* the thousand-year reign of the saints or whether the reign of the saints would *prepare* the way for the Second Coming.

3. Quotes from Holly A. Mayer, "Forging the Armor of Virtue," *Pennsylvania Legacies* 2:1 (May 2002): 13–17. An immense literature demonstrated how widespread was belief in the sacredness of America's cause and its millenarian associations even in the eighteenth century. See Ruth H. Bloch, *Visionary Republic: Millennial Themes in American Thought, 1756–1800* (New York: Cambridge University, 1985) as well as Ernest Lee Tuveson, *Redeemer Nation: The Idea of America's Millennial Role* (Chicago: University of Chicago, 1968), Nathan O. Hatch, *The Sacred Cause of Liberty: Republican Thought and the Millennium in Revolutionary New England* (New Haven: Yale University, 1977), John F. Berens, *Providence and Patriotism in Early America, 1640–1815* (Charlottesville: University of Virginia, 1978), and Mark Valeri, "The New Divinity and the American Revolution," *William and Mary Quarterly* 46 (Oct. 1989): 741–69.

4. This opinion was most recently advanced by Paul Johnson, *A History of the American People* (New York: HarperCollins, 1997), pp. 204–11.

5. Elmer T. Clark, et al., eds., *The Journal and Letters of Francis Asbury*, 3 vols. (Nashville: Abingdon Press, 1958), vol. 1, *The Journal 1771 to 1793*, pp. ix–xxiv, 3–6 ("The people God owns," p. 4); L. C. Rudolph, *Francis Asbury* (Nashville: Abingdon Press, 1966), pp. 13–20 ("God sent," p. 16).

6. Clark, *The Journal 1771 to 1793*, pp. 3–6 ("Whither am I going," p. 4); Rudolph, *Asbury*, pp. 71–79 ("hunger and cold," p. 72; doctor's report, p. 76).

7. Rudolph, *Asbury*, pp. 32–137 ("truly sorry," p. 33; "built plain," p. 105). An authoritative new study of the origins of American Methodism is Dee E. Andrews, *The Methodists and Revolutionary America, 1760–1800* (Princeton: Princeton University, 2000). See also John L. Peters, *Christian Perfection and American Methodism* (Nashville: Abingdon Press, 1956).

8. Thomas W. Spalding, *The Premier See: A History of the Archdiocese of Baltimore* (Baltimore: Johns Hopkins University, 1989), pp. 1–10 (quotes p. 9). See also John Tracy Ellis, *American Catholicism*, 2 ed. (Chicago: University of Chicago, 1969), Anabelle M. Melville, *John Carroll of Baltimore* (New York: Charles Scribner's Sons, 1955), and Charles H. Metzger, *Catholics in the American Revolution: A Study in Religious Climate* (Chicago: Loyola University, 1962).

9. Spalding, *Premier See*, pp. 11–34 (quotes pp. 12, 24, 32–33). Carroll also tried to appease the Philadelphia German by appointing him to a new parish in Baltimore. But the renegade caused more scandal by taking a parishioner's wife as a mistress. This time the wholly American bishop sued in *civil court* to evict him.

10. The widow of a New York merchant who lost his ships and fortune to French privateers and Barbary pirates, Seton grew up in a loveless home and was determined to spare other children, especially poor ones, that fate. Baptized by Carroll in 1805, she founded St. Joseph's Academy and the American Sisters of Charity, who extended her work throughout the new nation.

11. Sydney E. Ahlstrom, *A Religious History of the American People* (New Haven: Yale University, 1972), pp. 527–46; Spalding, *Premier See*, pp. 35–65 (quotes pp. 65, 59). On the strong Catholic presence in the District of Columbia, see William W. Warner, *At Peace with All Their Neighbors: Catholics and Catholicism in the National Capital 1787–1860* (Washington, D.C.: Georgetown University, 1994).

12. Raymond W. Albright, *History of the Protestant Episcopal Church* (New York: Macmillan, 1964); quote from Ahlstrom, *Religious History of the American People*, p. 370.

13. Ahlstrom, *Religious History of the American People*, pp. 375–84. One of the few issues among German churches was whether to begin the Lord's Prayer *Vater unser*, reflecting the Latin *Pater noster*, or to pray in good German *Unser Vater*. They agreed to disagree inasmuch as Martin Luther himself sternly opposed changing familiar and beloved liturgical language. Disestablishment of the old Puritan churches was achieved in 1818 in Connecticut and 1819 in New Hampshire, but not until 1833 in Massachusetts. See William G. McLoughlin, *New England Dissent*, 2 vols. (Cambridge, Mass.: Harvard University, 1971).

14. The literature on Freemasonry is vast and outrageously unreliable. Being a secret society that evolved over centuries and spread to many countries, its doctrines and rituals varied enormously, while its enemies made all manner of nefarious claims. The latest and most scholarly treatment, however, is Alexander Piatigorsky, *Freemasonry: The Study of a Phenomenon* (London: Harvill, 1999). For the early history of the English Grand Lodge, see pp. 37–97.

15. On the mystical letter see Paul F. Case, *The Masonic Letter "G"* (Richmond, Va.: Macoy, 1981).

16. Piatigorsky, *Freemasonry*, pp. 119–62 (Royal Arch ceremony, pp. 133–43).

17. Franklin quote in Steven C. Bullock, *Revolutionary Brotherhood: Freemasonry and the Transformation of the American Social Order 1739–1840* (Chapel Hill: University of North Carolina, 1996), p. 53; "ineffable" in Piatigorsky, *Freemasonry*, p. 141.

18. Bullock, *Revolutionary Brotherhood*, pp. 50–82; Piatigorsky, *Freemasonry*, pp. 163–97, and the case studies by Richard A. Rutyna and Peter C. Stewart, *The History of Freemasonry in Virginia* (Lanham, Md.: University Press of America, 1998), Dorothy Ann Lipson, *Freemasonry in Federalist Connecticut* (Princeton: Princeton University, 1977), and Wayne A. Huss, "Pennsylvania Freemasonry: An Intellectual and Social Analysis, 1727–1826" (PhD dissertation, Temple University, 1984).

19. On the Stars and Stripes as the holy totem of American civic religion, see the provocative book by Carolyn Marvin and David W. Ingle, *Blood Sacrifice and the Nation: Totem Rituals and the American Flag* (Cambridge, U.K.: Cambridge University, 1999). The legend that Betsy Ross sewed and perhaps designed the American flag was promulgated in 1870 by her grandson and is a matter of no little rancor. It is a matter of record, however, that Freemason Francis Hopkinson, the eminent Philadelphia lawyer, musician, and patriot, asked Congress to remunerate him for his artistic work on the American flag. Congress denied the claim on the grounds that "several" people had a hand in the design. On the Great Seal, see David Ovason, *The Secret Architecture of Our Nation's Capital: The Masons and the Building of Washington, D.C.* (New York: HarperCollins, 2000), pp. 217–40. The text of Virgil's *Aeneid*, book 9 line 625, was *audacibus annue coeptis* ("favor these audacious undertakings") and the text of Virgil's *Bucolics*,

eclogue 4 verse 5, was *magnus ab integro saeclorum nascitur ordo* ("a great series of ages begins anew"). The first phrase was thus shortened to thirteen letters and the second shortened to make twenty-six letters (twice thirteen) when combined with the Roman numerals for "1776."

20. Bullock, *Revolutionary Brotherhood*, pp. 184–219 on growth ("As Men from Brutes," p. 17; "republican machines," pp. 140–41; "unable to separate," p. 152). The web site of the Philadelphia Grand Lodge reveals its Grand Masters in the 1775–1815 era included two Episcopalians, a Presbyterian, a Baptist, and a Universalist Jew named Israel Israel.

21. Bullock, *Revolutionary Brotherhood*, pp. 150–53 (Revere); pp. 169–70 (Freemason's Heart).

22. Strangely, none of the excellent historians of American religion (e.g., Sidney Ahlstrom, Mark Noll, Martin Marty, Edwin Gaustad) seem to have anything to say about Freemasonry. Stranger still, historians focusing especially on American civic religion (e.g., Robert Bellah, Sidney Mead, Will Herberg, John F. Wilson, Leo Marx) overlook its roots in Freemasonry: see Russell E. Richey and Donald G. Jones, eds., *American Civil Religion* (New York: Harper & Row, 1974). Strangest of all, even critics who grasp the gnosticism in American civic religion (e.g., Harold Bloom, William Appleman Williams) miss the Freemasonic connection.

23. Len Travers, " 'In the Greatest Solemn Dignity': The Capitol Cornerstone and Ceremony in the Early Republic," and James Stevens Curl, "The Capitol in Washington, D.C., and Its Freemasonic Connections," in Donald Kennon, ed., *A Republic for the Ages: The United States Capitol and the Political Culture of the Early Republic* (Charlottesville: University of Virginia, 1999), pp. 155–76, 214–67. If the phrase "thirteenth year" on the silver plate was not a mistake, the engraver may have dated independence from the Battle of Yorktown in 1781 rather than July 4, 1776! If so, that not only allowed another invocation of the totemic 13, it made Washington's martial success, rather than Jefferson's literary one, the true birthday of the nation. Another theory for which I thank Steven Bullock is that the engraver may have dated the Union from ratification of the Articles of Confederation. Official sources on the Capitol's history all quote the text as "thirteenth" without even acknowledging, much less explaining, the apparent error. See for instance William C. Allen, *History of the United States Capitol: A Chronicle of Design, Construction, and Politics* (Washington, D.C.: G.P.O., 2001), pp. 23–24.

24. Christopher N. Klyza and Stephen C. Trombulak, *The Story of Vermont: A Natural and Cultural History* (Hanover, N.H.: University Press of New England, 1999), pp. 45–62; Michael A. Bellesiles, *Revolutionary Outlaws: Ethan Allen and the Struggle for Independence on the Early American Frontier* (Charlottesville: University of Virginia, 1993), pp. 6–24 (Dwight quote p. 7); Chilton Williamson, *Vermont in Quandary: 1763–1825* (Montpelier: Vermont Historical Society, 1949), pp. 1–34 ("most enterprising," p. 26).

25. "I was called by the Yorkers an outlaw, and afterwards, by the British, was called a rebel; and I humbly conceive that there was as much propriety in the one name as the other," boasted Ethan Allen in 1779: Bellesiles, *Revolutionary Outlaws*, p. 113; "Come York or come Hampshire," p. 187; "Blackguard Fellows" from Williamson, *Vermont in Quandary*, p. 36. He was indeed a scofflaw, rebel, hustler, and freebooter out to fashion a family empire. But he was Robin Hood to the smallholders of the New Hampshire Grants and the only executive authority in the vales and dells of Vermont.

26. On Allen's philosophy, Bellesiles, *Revolutionary Outlaws*, pp. 217–44.

27. The diplomacy of the Vermont republic and its path to statehood is described in detail by Williamson, *Vermont in Quandary*, pp. 90–184.

28. Whitehall Co., *Inaugural Addresses*, pp. 1–4.

29. Letter of May 5, 1789, in John Fitzpatrick, ed., *The Writings of George Washington*

(Washington, D.C.: G.P.O., 1931–44), vol. 30: 311. On Washington's character acting, Forrest McDonald, *The American Presidency: An Intellectual History* (Lawrence: University of Kansas, 1994), pp. 209–18.

30. John Jay was offered the State Department, but asked instead for the bench. So Washington named him Chief Justice and instead called Jefferson the Virginian home from Paris to become secretary of State. When Pennsylvania's Robert Morris turned down the Treasury, the President chose Alexander Hamilton of New York. New Englander Henry Knox carried over as secretary of War, fellow New Englander Samuel Osgood was named postmaster general, and Virginia's Edmund Randolph became attorney general. Associate justices of the Supreme Court included William Cushing of Massachusetts, James Wilson of Pennsylvania, John Blair of Virginia, and John Rutledge of South Carolina.

31. The literature on the precedents set by the Washington administration is immense, but useful summations can be found in James T. Flexner, *George Washington and the New Nation, 1783–1793* (Boston: Houghton Mifflin, 1969), Forrest McDonald, *The Presidency of George Washington* (Lawrence: University of Kansas, 1974), and *American Presidency*, pp. 209–44 ("squinted toward monarchy," p. 216), Glenn A. Phelps, "George Washington: Precedent Setter," in Thomas E. Cronin, ed., *Inventing the American Presidency* (Lawrence: University of Kansas, 1989), Mark J. Rozell, "Washington and the Origins of Presidential Power," in Gary L. Gregg II and Matthew Spalding, eds., *Patriot Sage: George Washington and the American Political Tradition* (Wilmington, Del.: ISI Books, 1999), and all the essays in Rozell, William D. Pederson, and Frank J. Williams, eds., *George Washington and the Origins of the American Presidency* (Westport, Conn.: Praeger, 2000).

32. R. B. Bernstein, "A New Matrix for National Politics: The First Federal Elections, 1788–90," in Kenneth R. Bowling and Donald R. Kennon, *Inventing Congress: Origins and Establishment of the First Federal Congress* (Athens: Ohio University, 1999), pp. 109–37 ("commencing," italics added, p. 119). On Madison's campaign, see Richard R. Beeman, *The Old Dominion and the New Nation, 1788–1801* (Lexington: University of Kentucky, 1972), pp. 23–27, and Jack N. Rakove, *James Madison and the Creation of the American Republic* (Glenview, Ill.: Little, Brown, 1990), pp. 78–79.

33. Charlene Bangs Bickford, "Public Attention Is Very Much Fixed. . . .": The First Federal Congress Organizes Itself," in Bowling and Kennon, *Inventing Congress*, pp. 138–65. In one important detail even the House of Representatives betrayed its role as the people's tribunes. It selected as clerk Virginian John Beckley, a conniving partisan under whose "care" all manner of documents were discarded. Any that might be put to later political use, however, Beckley carefully copied and kept in a private cache.

34. Leonard W. Levy, *Origins of the Bill of Rights* (New Haven: Yale University, 1999), pp. 1–43 (quotes pp. 33–36). One of those urging Madison to pass a Bill of Rights was the ever alert Hugh Williamson. He sensed North Carolina's Anti-Federalists did not really want a Bill of Rights lest it reconcile fence-sitters to the Constitution.

35. Levy, *Origins*, pp. 39–40.

36. Quotes from William P. Cohin, "The Invisible Smith: The Impact of Adam Smith on the Foundation of Early American Economic Policy," in Bowling and Kennon, *Inventing Congress*, pp. 280–81. For a full treatment of Hamilton's ideology and proposals see Stanley Elkins and Eric McKitrick, *The Age of Federalism* (New York: Oxford University, 1993), pp. 92–131.

37. James Jackson, whom Caty Greene described in a letter to Wadsworth as reputable and honest, if hotheaded, was the man defeated for re-election in that fraudulent contest waged by Caty's lover, Anthony Wayne. Jackson went on to become a two-term senator of Jeffersonian

persuasion and a leading proponent of Indian removal and states' rights. Four of his sons continued his legacy in the politics of antebellum Georgia. See Marie Sauer Lambremont, "Rep. James Jackson of Georgia and the Establishment of the Southern States' Rights Tradition in Congress," in Bowling and Kennon, *Inventing Congress*, pp. 191–207. Newspaper quotes from Claude G. Bowers, *Jefferson and Hamilton: The Struggle for Democracy in America* (Boston: Houghton Mifflin, 1966), pp. 50–51.

38. I reached this conclusion independently only to discover Elkins and McKitrick said it all in the introduction to their monumental *Age of Federalism*, pp. 18–29. See also Forrest McDonald, *Alexander Hamilton: A Biography* (New York: W. W. Norton, 1979), pp. 108–113, McDonald, *States' Rights and the Union: Imperium in Imperio, 1776–1876* (Lawrence: University of Kansas, 2000), p. 27–46, and Lance Banning, *The Sacred Fire of Liberty: James Madison and the Founding of the Federal Republic* (Ithaca, N.Y.: Cornell University, 1995), pp. 293–333.

39. Elkins and McKitrick, *Age of Federalism*, pp. 133–61 (Jefferson's account, pp. 155–56); Melvin Yazawa, "Republican Expectations: Revolutionary Ideology and the Compromise of 1790," in Donald R. Kennon, ed., *A Republic for the Ages: The United States Capitol and the Political Culture of the Early Republic* (Charlottesville University of Virginia, 1999), pp. 3–35. New Yorkers did scowl. When the capital moved to Philadelphia, the New York *Morning Post*, of Aug. 21, 1790, printed a "Valedictory" to the Pennsylvanians that did not even spare the popular Speaker Frederick Augustus Muhlenberg (cited by Charlene Bangs Bickford, " 'Throwing Open the Doors': The First Federal Congress and the Eighteenth-Century Media," in Bowling and Kennon, *Inventing Congress*, pp. 187–88.):

> Fred Augustus, God bless his red nose and fat head
> Has little more influence than a speaker of lead;
> And now sister Phila, we return you your clowns
> Transformed into shapes like bred in towns.
>
> When some of them made their 'pearance in York,
> They scarcely knew how to hold a knife or fork.
> But by living some time 'mongst people wellbred,
> They've learned to walk and to hold up a head.
>
> Our taylors and Sailors have learn'd them some taste
> Yet these wandering Members have departed in haste,
> Farewell silly Congress—repent all your lives,
> For following the devil wherever he Drives.

40. Elkins and McKitrick, *Age of Federalism*, pp. 223–44 (Jefferson quotes on scrippomania, pp. 243–44); Bray Hammond, *Banks and Politics in America from the Revolution to the Civil War* (Princeton: Princeton University, 1957), pp. 118–43; George Brown Tindall, *America: A Narrative History*, 2 ed. (New York: W.W. Norton, 1984), pp. 303–7 ("boundless field of power," p. 305). The dollar sign was already in use as a Spanish symbol of the peso.

41. On bounties, Elkins and McKitrick, *Age of Federalism*, pp. 276–77 ("aggregate prosperity," p. 261; Williamson quote, p. 276). On inventions, Doran Ben-Atar, "Alexander Hamilton's Alternative: Technological Piracy and the Report on Manufactures," *William and Mary Quarterly* 52 (1995): 389–414; Lance Banning, "Political Economy and the Creation of the Federal Republic," in David Thomas Konig, ed., *Devising Liberty: Preserving and Creating*

*Freedom in the New American Republic* (Stanford, Calif.: Stanford University, 1995), pp. 11–49; and Jacob E. Cooke, *Tench Coxe and the Early Republic* (Chapel Hill: University of North Carolina, 1978).

42. Lowell H. Harrison and James C. Klotter, *A New History of Kentucky* (Lexington: University of Kentucky, 1997), quotes on pp. 31, 5.

43. See John Mack Faragher, *Daniel Boone: The Life and Legend of an American Pioneer* (New York: Holt, 1992). But the classic by John Bakeless, *Daniel Boone: Master of the Wilderness* (Lincoln: University of Nebraska, 1989 [1939]) includes a beautiful summation of the pioneer from the point of view of Boone's first wife Rebecca (whose three daughters were kidnapped by Shawnees): "That, after all, was life as the wives of all the pioneers knew it. Marry your man and follow him. Bear his children. Feed him. Watch his cattle. Lend a hand with the farm at need. Milk, churn, weave, sew. Mold his bullets. Load his rifles when the shooting got rapid enough to demand it. Beat off the Indians yourself if need be. . . . Men, the great babies, must have their adventures; and perhaps—who knew?—there might be wealth at the end of it" (p. 69).

44. Malcolm J. Rohrbough, *The Trans-Appalachian Frontier: People, Societies, and Institutions 1775–1850* (New York: Oxford University, 1978), pp. 26–40 (quote p. 30); Daniel Blake Smith, " 'This Idea in Heaven': Image and Reality on the Kentucky Frontier," in Craig Thompson Friend, ed., *The Buzzel About Kentuck* (Lexington: University of Kentucky, 1999), pp. 77–98.

45. Harrison and Klotter, *History of Kentucky*, pp. 52–56 (quote p. 54).

46. On the struggle for statehood and state constitutions, see Joan Wells Coward, *Kentucky in the New Republic: The Process of Constitution Making* (Lexington: University of Kentucky, 1979), Harrison and Klotter, *History of Kentucky*, pp. 48–79, and Stephen Aron, *How the West Was Lost: The Transformation of Kentucky from Daniel Boone to Henry Clay* (Baltimore: Johns Hopkins University, 1996). Yet another convention in 1799 restored voice voting and direct election of the governor. But a motion to halt imports of slaves (supported by young Henry Clay) lost 14 to 37 and the new suffrage law excluded free blacks, mulattoes, and Indians. Kentucky emerged as a rough-hewn democracy, but only for whites, themselves divided into feuding factions.

47. Robert West Howard, *The Horse in America* (Chicago: Follett, 1965), pp. 103–15 (quotes pp. 105–6).

48. The account of the dinner (italics added) is in Franklin B. Sawvel, ed., *The Anas of Thomas Jefferson* (New York: Da Capo, 1970), pp. 36–37, discussed by McDonald, *American Presidency*, pp. 233–34.

49. Forrest McDonald, *Alexander Hamilton: A Biography* (New York: W. W. Norton, 1979), pp. 211–36.

50. Washington to Jefferson, Oct. 18, 1792, in John C. Fitzpatrick, ed., *The Writings of George Washington* (Washington, D.C.: G.P.O., 1931–44), vol. 35, pp. 185–86. He said the same to Hamilton.

51. Hamilton quoted by Tindall, *America: A Narrative History*, p. 311; Jefferson by Elkins and McKitrick, *Age of Federalism*, p. 289.

52. Conor Cruise O'Brien, *The Long Affair: Thomas Jefferson and the French Revolution, 1785–1800* (Chicago: University of Chicago, 1996), pp. 17–151 ("true god," pp. 67–68; "Adam and Eve," pp. 145–47). "Half-way house" cited by Elkins and McKitrick, *Age of Federalism*, p. 316.

53. Eugene P. Link, *The Democratic-Republican Societies, 1790–1800* (New York: Columbia University, 1942), Pennsylvania quote p. 42, and Philip S. Foner, ed., *The Democratic-Republican Societies, 1790–1800: A Documentary Sourcebook* (Westport, Conn.: Praeger, 1976).

54. Genêt's instructions are described in detail in Elkins and McKitrick, *Age of Federalism*, pp. 332–35. The standard account of his mission is Harry Ammon, *The Genet Mission* (New York: W. W. Norton, 1973). The affair ended in farce when Genêt begged permission to stay in the United States rather than risk the guillotine back in Paris. He then wooed and won the daughter of Governor Clinton and embraced the comfortable life of Hudson Valley society.

55. Adams in a letter to John Quincy Adams, cited by David McCullough, *John Adams* (New York: Simon & Schuster, 2001), p. 448.

56. Jerald A. Combs, *The Jay Treaty: Political Battleground of the Founding Fathers* (Berkeley: University of California, 1970).

57. Thomas P. Slaughter, *The Whiskey Rebellion: Frontier Epilogue to the American Revolution* (New York: Oxford University, 1986).

58. Arthur P. Whitaker, *The Spanish-American Frontier, 1783–1795: The Westward Movement and the Spanish Retreat in the Mississippi Valley* (Lincoln: University of Nebraska, 1969 [1927]) and Samuel Flagg Bemis, *Pinckney's Treaty: America's Advantage from Europe's Distress, 1783–1800* (New Haven: Yale University, 1960). Washington quotes on societies in Elkins and McKitrick, *Age of Federalism*, pp. 484–85.

59. McDonald, *Presidency of George Washington*, pp. 185–86, argues Washington failed to render the republic and executive branch secure from dangers and was not even the author of his administration's major achievements (Hamilton's financial program; Pinckney's Treaty, and Wayne's defeat of the Indians). Less debatable is McDonald's judgment regarding Washington's indispensable role as symbol of nation and its putative virtue. "He became a myth and legend, and those who knew better kept the secret to themselves. After all, other people had to be president, too."

60. The classic on the origin of Washington's testament is Felix Gilbert, *To the Farewell Address: Ideas of Early American Foreign Policy* (Princeton: Princeton University Press, 1961). For its place in the sweep of U.S. foreign policy, see Walter A. McDougall, *Promised Land, Crusader State: The American Encounter with the World Since 1776* (Boston: Houghton Mifflin, 1997), pp. 39–56.

61. That Jefferson did not want to prevail in 1796 is well documented by McCormick, *Presidential Game*, pp. 51–58, and Elkins and McKitrick, *Age of Federalism*, pp. 513–18. The last point, about Jefferson's desire to avoid the troubles brewing with France, is my insight (assuming it is one).

62. Robert E. Corlew, *Tennessee: A Short History*, 2 ed. (Knoxville: University of Tennessee, 1981), pp. 38–68 (Christian quote p. 43; Sevier's heroism pp. 66–67). The classic monograph is Thomas P. Abernethy, *From Frontier to Plantation in Tennessee: A Study in Frontier Democracy* (Chapel Hill: University of North Carolina, 1932).

63. William H. Masterson, *William Blount* (Baton Rouge: Louisiana State University, 1954); Rohrbough, *Trans-Appalachian Frontier*, pp. 21–32 (quote p. 29).

64. Corlew, *Tennessee: A Short History*, pp. 85–105 (quote p. 103).

65. Corlew, *Tennessee: A Short History*, pp. 106–25. Incidentally, *pace* Walt Disney, it was not Davy Crockett who inspired the legend of the Tennessee bear-hunting prodigy but rather Captain John Rains, who bragged of killing thirty-two bears with his unfailing musket named Betsy (p. 112).

66. Masterson, *William Blount*, pp. 286–347 (death scene p. 346).

67. Quote from Joseph J. Ellis, *Passionate Sage: The Character and Legacy of John Adams* (New York: W. W. Norton, 1993), p. 239. Thanks to Ralph Adams Brown, *The Presidency of John Adams* (Lawrence: University of Kansas, 1975), Peter Shaw, *The Character of John Adams* (Chapel Hill: University of North Carolina, 1976), Joseph Ellis, Stanley Elkins, and Eric

McKitrick, and most recently David McCullough, the second president's stock has risen sharply in the public's estimation. But however admirable his character, Adams never understood what the American people wanted or, when he did, deplored it. In that sense he was the first Mugwump. Such was his integrity Adams failed utterly to build a national Federalist coalition, as explained in "A National Experiment in Ordered Liberty: New England's Hegemony in the Adams Presidency," in David Hackett Fischer, *Albion's Seed: Four British Folkways in America* (New York: Oxford University, 1989), pp. 841–44.

68. The politics of the new model army in the 1790s is described at length by Richard H. Kohn, *Eagle and Sword: The Federalists and the Creation of the Military Establishment in America, 1783–1802* (New York: Free Press, 1975). Adams feared Hamilton intended nothing less than to ally with Britain, launch a campaign of imperial conquest against Spain and France, and seize control of the U.S. government. That, Adams believed, would provoke civil war at home and wreck the American union (pp. 256–73).

69. The standard (condemnatory) account is James Morton Smith, *Freedom's Fetters: The Alien and Sedition Laws and American Civil Liberties* (Ithaca, N.Y.: Cornell University, 1956). Elkins and McKitrick, *Age of Federalism*, pp. 590–93, show how disastrous the whole business was for Adams. On Matt Lyon's amazing career see Aleine Austin, *Matthew Lyon: "New Man" of the Democratic Revolution, 1749–1822* (University Park: Pennsylvania State University, 1981). Lyon later migrated to Kentucky, became a land speculator and slaveholder, and was elected to Congress again. In 1820 he won appointment as Indian factor in the Arkansas Territory and entered politics for a third time before dying alone at a remote trading post in 1821. It was said when mourners lifted the lid of his coffin, the skin on his face turned immediately into dust and "blew away to the four corners of the earth" (p. 151).

70. Levy, *Origin of the Bill of Rights*, pp. 108–111, shows Jefferson thought more deeply than any Founder about the press. But while he famously remarked he would unhesitatingly choose a free press over a free government, and swore "eternal hostility against any form of tyranny over the mind of man," the statutes he favored in Virginia only prohibited *prior* censorship. He always endorsed prosecution for "false facts affecting injuriously the life, liberty, property, or reputation of others or affecting the peace of the confederacy with foreign nations." His analogy was freedom of religion, which "does not give impunity to criminal acts dictated by religious error." Nor did he object to Virginia's 1792 law implying the truth of a published charge is not itself a defense. Call him a hypocrite, a thin-skinned gentleman, or just an eighteenth-century man whose views were rooted in Common Law, Jefferson was not quite the civil libertarian many like to believe he was.

71. Elkins and McKitrick, *Age of Federalism*, pp. 721–26; William W. H. Davis, *The Fries Rebellion, 1798–99* (New York: Arno Press, 1969 [1899]).

72. The official American memorial service for Washington was a suitably ecumenical affair held at Philadelphia's Zion Evangelical Lutheran Church and presided over by Episcopal Bishop White. It was there Henry Lee pronounced Washington "first in war, first in peace, and first in the hearts of his countrymen." But the brothers of Philadelphia's Grand Lodge were conspicuous in the parade by their numbers, regalia, and aprons edged in black. They had long since named Washington "The Great Master Builder (under the Supreme Architect) by whose Labours the Temple of Liberty hath been reared in the West, exhibiting to the Nations of the Earth a Model of Beauty, Order and Harmony worthy of their imitation and Praise." See Wayne A. Huss, *The Master Builders: A History of the Grand Lodge of Free and Accepted Masons of Pennsylvania*, 3 vols. (Philadelphia: Grand Lodge, 1986), I: 64–67.

73. This description of Republican ideology adumbrates Joyce Appleby's excellent

*Capitalism and a New Social Order: The Republican Vision of the 1790s* (New York: New York University, 1984) and *Inheriting the Revolution: The First Generation of Americans* (Cambridge, Mass.: Harvard University, 2000). She believes historians have missed the deeply capitalistic instincts of the Republicans because they forget it was a pre-industrial capitalism of the sort brought over from agrarian England. On that point see Allan Kulikoff, *The Agrarian Origins of American Capitalism* (Charlottesville: University of Virginia, 1992).

74. Barry Alan Shain, *The Myth of American Individualism: The Protestant Origins of American Political Thought* (Princeton: Princeton University, 1994) makes a powerful case for this.

75. Appleby, *Inheriting the Revolution*, p. 6.

76. Morris owned more ships and more land than any American, but he and his partners acquired their holdings by co-signing each other's notes and using one speculative acquisition as collateral for another. When at last three banks (all of which Morris helped found) called in some of his loans, his credit collapsed. For over a year he dared not leave his house for fear of process-servers, but his spirit broke in 1798 and the "financier of the Revolution" spent over three years in prison. Wilson fled south to escape debtor's prison, but caught malaria and seemingly went mad. A principal author of the Constitution, he died in an alcoholic miasma in 1798. The Welshman Nicholson was Pennsylvania's comptroller during the War of Independence, a major investor in Washington, D.C., and the Lancaster Pike, early industrialist, and angel to steamboat inventor John Fitch. But the collapse of his companies (which he claimed were worth exactly $4,000,627.23) landed him in prison in 1799. He died a year later at age forty-three, leaving a wife and eight children. Abigail Adams rued the distress caused to such men, their families, and thousands of small investors, noting, "We seldom learn experience until . . . too old to use it, or we grow callous to the misfortunes of the world by Reiterated abuse. . . . I have been led into these reflections in contemplating the unhappy situation of Mr. Morris, Nicolson, and others." See Bruce H. Mann, *Republic of Debtors: Bankruptcy in the Age of American Independence* (Cambridge, Mass.: Harvard University, 2002), Robert D. Arbuckle, *Pennsylvania Speculator and Patriot: The Entrepreneurial John Nicholson, 1757–1800* (University Park: Pennsylvania State University, 1975), Charles Page Smith, *James Wilson: Founding Father 1742–1798* (Westport, Conn.: Greenwood Press, 1973), and Daniel M. Friedenberg, *Life, Liberty, and the Pursuit of Land* (Buffalo: Prometheus Books, 1992), pp. 338–55.

77. A mere sketch cannot achieve what no ponderous biography, novel, or historical psychoanalysis has managed to do, which is to explain Aaron Burr to most people's satisfaction. Was he a creature of pure ambition like his contemporary, Napoleon, or a talented, brave man turned cynical by others' jealousy and his own bad luck? A thoroughly "modern" hustler or very old-fashioned man of honor? A "man who would be king" or the people's tribune? I am inclined to believe his sister when she says he was spoiled. Burr was raised with every advantage in life and no mentor, ideal, or personal trial was sufficient to knock him off his own pedestal. The only real passion he is known to have had was for his daughter, an extension of himself. Thus, even as Burr seemed Hamilton's double (both New York soldiers, lawyers, politicos, skirt-chasers, brilliant, and ambitious), he bears a strong resemblance to Jefferson, too. But Jefferson knew how to avoid mortal combat, whereas Burr fled toward it as if driven to kill the sources of his every frustration. See Jonathan Daniels, *Ordeal of Ambition: Jefferson, Hamilton, Burr* (Garden City, N.Y.: Doubleday, 1970) and Roger G. Kennedy, *Burr, Hamilton, and Jefferson: A Study in Character* (Oxford: Oxford University, 2000). For other opinions see Matthew L. Davis, *Memoirs of Aaron Burr* (New York: Harper & Bros., 1836–37), Herbert S. Parmet and Marie B. Hecht, *Aaron Burr: Portrait of an Ambitious Man* (New York: Macmillan, 1967), Philip Vail, *The Great American Rascal: The Turbulent Life of Aaron Burr* (New York: Hawthorn, 1973),

Gore Vidal, *Burr: A Novel* (New York: Random House, 1973), Milton Lomask, *Aaron Burr*, 2 vols. (New York: Farrar, Straus, & Giroux, 1979–83), Joanne B. Freeman, *Affairs of Honor: National Politics in the New Republic* (New Haven: Yale University, 2001), and Buckner F. Melton, Jr., *Aaron Burr: Conspiracy to Treason* (New York: John Wiley & Sons, 2002).

78. The Society of Saint Tammany dated from 1789 and was named after a legendary chief of the Lenape Indians. Hence its members aspired to the degrees of hunter, warrior, and sachem, and met at the Wigwam. Thanks to Burr it became the nucleus of New York's later Democratic party machine. The first "Tammany Hall" mayor was Fernando Wood in 1854, and the first to serve openly as chairman of the city's Democratic central committee and Grand Sachem of Tammany was William Marcy "Boss" Tweed in 1863 (Arthur Mann, introduction to William L. Riordon, *Plunkitt of Tammany Hall: A Series of Very Plain Talks on Very Practical Politics* [New York: E. P. Dutton, 1963], pp. vii–xxii).

79. Hammond, *Banks and Politics*, pp. 149–58, argues the populist political machine and bank of easy credit invented by Burr were not flukes but harbingers of the political and economic revolutions soon to spread and shape nineteenth-century American life.

80. On Republican party organization, see Noble E. Cunningham, *The Jeffersonian Republicans: The Formation of Party Organization, 1789–1801* (Chapel Hill: University of North Carolina, 1957), Roy F. Nichols, *The Invention of the American Political Parties* (New York: Macmillan, 1967), pp. 199–230; John C. Miller, *The Federalist Era 1789–1801* (New York: Harper & Row, 1960), pp. 251–77 ("every scoundrel" and "with Pennsylvania," p. 255); "crooked gun" and "great office" in Vail, *American Rascal*, p. 70.

81. Morton Borden, *The Federalism of James A. Bayard* (New York: AMS, 1968 [1955]), pp. 73–95, quotes Bayard's letters to illustrate the growing pressure he felt from public opinion to end the ordeal and save the Constitution. Miller, *The Federalist Era*, pp. 271–73, suggests Maryland Senator Samuel Smith was instrumental in getting the promise about officials from Jefferson's camp. Freeman, *Affairs of Honor*, pp. 241–53, argues Burr was both too ambitious to concede and too honorable to bargain with the enemy, hence he did nothing.

82. *Gazette of the United States*, cited by Sidney Warren, *The Battle for the Presidency* (Philadelphia: Lippincott, 1968), p. 48.

83. The Grand Lodge in Philadelphia has sponsored rigorous historical research and contains a gallery of presidential Freemasons. It used to include Jefferson and Madison, but since no incontrovertible evidence of their membership has been unearthed the scrupulous Freemasons have removed their portraits. It is known Jefferson participated in Masonic rites and it is hard to imagine he would have permitted the University of Virginia to fall so completely under Freemason influence were he not at least sympathetic.

## RELUCTANT NATIONALISTS, EAGER IMPERIALISTS

1. In *The Presidency of Thomas Jefferson* (Lawrence: University of Kansas, 1976), pp. 167–68, Forrest McDonald chides those of our profession who "cite but do not read" Adams' nine volumes. I shall accordingly evade his indictment by *not* citing Adams' original tomes. I relied instead on Ernest Samuels' abridged version, *The History of the United States of America During the Administrations of Jefferson and Madison* (Chicago: University of Chicago, 1967), which contains the most famous chapters *in toto* (city of Washington quote, pp. 26–27), as well as the indispensable corrective by Noble E. Cunningham, Jr., *The United States in 1800: Henry Adams Revisited* (Charlottesville: University of Virginia, 1988). For Adams' insights on Washington, D.C., and much else, see the brilliant essay by David Grimstead, " 'Conglomerate Rock': The American Nation and Capital in Its Greatest Work of History," in Donald R. Kennon, ed., *A*

*Republic for the Ages: The United States Capitol and the Political Culture of the Early Republic* (Charlottesville: University of Virginia, 1999), pp. 467–564 ("mud pie," p. 562).

2. I have as yet found no general U.S. histories that mention the influence of Freemasonry on the design of the nation's capital in spite of overwhelming evidence for it. See the essays of Len Travers, Steven C. Bullock, and James Stevens Curl on "Freemasonry and the Capitol" in Kennon, *Republic for the Ages*, pp. 155–267 ("as readable," p. 267) and David Ovason, *The Secret Architecture of Our Nation's Capital: The Masons and the Building of Washington, D.C.* (New York: HarperCollins, 2000). The "Federal Triangle," which still survives as the name of a district and two Metro stations, was originally described by equidistant lines among the Capitol, President's House, and Supreme Court, which was to be located north of Pennsylvania Avenue. But the central region of the city was not developed at all until the 1830s and the early Supremes held humble court in the Capitol's clammy (or stifling) basement.

3. C. M Harris, "Washington's Gamble, L'Enfant's Dream: Politics, Design, and the Founding of the National Capital," *William and Mary Quarterly* 56 (1999): 527–64; Kenneth Bowling, " 'The Year 1800 Will Soon Be Upon Us': George Washington and the Capitol," in Kennon, *Republic for the Ages*, pp. 55–63, James Sterling Young, *The Washington Community 1800–1828* (New York: Columbia University, 1966), pp. 1–10, Stanley Elkins and Eric McKitrick, *The Age of Federalism* (New York: Oxford University, 1993), pp. 163–93, William W. Warner, *At Peace with All Their Neighbors: Catholics and Catholicism in the National Capital 1787–1860* (Washington, D.C.: Georgetown University, 1994), and the Rochefoucauld quote from A. M. Sakolski, *The Great American Land Bubble* (New York: Harper & Bros., 1932), p. 168.

4. Quotes on Washington in Young, *The Washington Community*, pp. 22, 25, 33; poem cited by Warner, *At Peace with All Their Neighbors*, pp. 12–13.

5. Young, *The Washington Community*, pp. 41–64 (quote, p. 57).

6. In chronological order, Delaware's seat of government shifted from Newcastle to Dover in 1777, Virginia's from Williamsburg to Richmond in 1779, Georgia's from Savannah to Louisville in 1786 (and not Atlanta until 1877), South Carolina's from Charleston to Columbia in 1786, North Carolina's from New Bern to Raleigh in 1788, New Jersey's from Burlington/Perth Amboy to Trenton in 1790, New York's from the city to Albany in 1797, and Pennsylvania's from Philadelphia to Lancaster in 1799 (then Harrisburg in 1812).

7. David J. Jeremy, *Transatlantic Industrial Revolution: The Diffusion of Textile Technologies Between Britain and America, 1790–1830s* (Cambridge, Mass.: Harvard University, 1981) and Barbara M. Tucker, *Samuel Slater and the Origins of the American Textile Industry, 1790–1860* (Ithaca, N.Y.: Cornell University, 1984) describe the first factories in New England.

8. By the latter date American growers had captured 60 percent of the English mill market for cotton. Summaries of the unparalleled prosperity of the United States between 1790 and 1807 include Douglass C. North, *Growth and Welfare in the American Past: A New Economic History* (Englewood Cliffs, N.J.: Prentice-Hall, 1974), pp. 57–74, and *The Economic Growth of the United States 1790–1860* (New York: W. W. Norton, 1966), pp. 17–60; and the statistics in Thomas J. Purvis, *Revolutionary America 1763 to 1800* (New York: Facts on File, 1995). An insightful study of New England's demographics and adjustment to rural capitalism is Christopher Clark, *The Roots of Rural Capitalism: Western Massachusetts, 1780–1860* (Ithaca, N.Y.: Cornell University, 1990).

9. See Pauline Maier, "The Revolutionary Origins of the American Corporation," *William and Mary Quarterly* 50 (1993): 51–84 (quote, p. 84).

10. Bray Hammond, *Banks and Politics in America* (Princeton: Princeton University, 1957), pp. 144–71 (quote, p. 146); Thomas M. Doerflinger, *A Vigorous Spirit of Enterprise: Merchants*

*and Economic Development in Revolutionary Philadelphia* (Chapel Hill: University of North Carolina, 1986), pp. 335–44.

11. The same question could have been asked about law enforcement. In the 1790s the notorious Captain Sam Mason, a black sheep of the Virginia Masons, established a pirates' nest at Cave-in-Rock on the Illinois bank of the Ohio River. His men signed on as "pilots" to guide families in flatboats only to lure them to their deaths and sell their goods downriver. Years passed before vigilantes from as far afield as Louisville and Pittsburgh rousted them out. Mason's gang then set up shop on Stack Island near Natchez. This time it took Kentucky Rangers and a Spanish "posse" to scatter the cutthroats in 1802. The only *federal* official involved in the cleansing of this extensive crime ring was the Natchez customs agent on whose desk Mason's severed head was dumped from a gunny sack in 1803. Mason was betrayed by Wiley "Little" Harpe who hoped to claim a reward. But river men recognized Harpe as a serial murderer and horse thief from Kentucky. A Mississippi court ordered him hanged and his head impaled on a pole as "a warning to all outlaws." But so weak was federal authority, even after the Louisiana Purchase, that new gangs formed on the Natchez Trace. It is possible one of them murdered Meriwether Lewis in 1809 (Robert West Howard, *The Horse in America,* [Chicago: Follett, 1965], pp. 107–8).

12. On the last point see John C. Greene, *American Science in the Age of Jefferson* (Ames: University of Iowa, 1984).

13. These paragraphs on culture adumbrate Russell Blaine Nye, *The Cultural Life of the New Nation 1776–1830* (New York: Harper & Brothers, 1960), with quotes from pp. 43 (Webster), 111 (Ames).

14. Daniel Marder, *Hugh Henry Brackenridge* (New York: Twayne, 1967); Marder, *A Hugh Henry Brackenridge Reader 1770–1815* (Pittsburgh: University of Pittsburgh, 1970), quotes pp. 6, 244, 387–88); and Claude Milton Newlin, *The Life and Writings of Hugh Henry Brackenridge* (Princeton: Princeton University, 1932). He recorded the Indian affair in *The Trial of Mamachtaga* (1785) and his activities during the Whiskey Rebellion in *Incidents of the Insurrection in the Western Parts of Pennsylvania in the Year 1794.* His most important legal writings, gathered in *Law Miscellanies* (1814), amounted to commentaries on Blackstone's commentaries. On the origins of American humor see Kenneth S. Lynn, *Mark Twain and Southwestern Humor* (Boston: Little, Brown, 1959).

15. See Leigh Eric Schmidt, *Holy Fairs: Scottish Communions and American Revivals in the Early Modern Period* (Princeton: Princeton University, 1990).

16. The backgrounds of the revivalists and the events at Cane Ridge are reconstructed and critically analyzed by Paul K. Conkin, *Cane Ridge: America's Pentecost* (Madison: University of Wisconsin, 1990), pp. 26–114. The origins and effects of the broader revival receive expert treatment in John B. Boles, *The Great Revival 1787–1805* (Lexington: University of Kentucky, 1972).

17. Conkin, *Cane Ridge,* pp. 115–78; Boles, *Great Revival,* pp. 90–142 (McGready quote, pp. 128–29).

18. Reinhold Niebuhr and Alan Heimert, *A Nation So Conceived: Reflections on the History of America* (New York: Charles Scribner's Sons, 1963), pp. 20–21.

19. Rohrbough, *Trans-Appalachian Frontier,* pp. 63–87 ("birthday" and "good government," p. 69; "I hardly dared," p. 85), and R. Douglas Hurt, *The Ohio Frontier: Crucible of the Old Northwest, 1720–1830* (Bloomington: Indiana University Press, 1996), pp. 143–210 ("licentious," p. 188; "Three Kentucky boats," p. 189).

20. The Scioto settlements and Zane's Trace in Hurt, *Ohio Frontier,* pp. 190–92, 249–62; Cleaveland and the Western Reserve, pp. 197–210 (quotes pp. 197–98).

21. Jeffrey P. Brown, "The Political Culture of Early Ohio," in Jeffery P. Brown and Andrew R. L. Cayton, eds., *The Pursuit of Public Power in Ohio, 1787–1861* (Kent, Ohio: Kent State University, 1994), pp. 1–14; Hurt, *Ohio Frontier,* pp. 272–83 (St. Clair quotes p. 277; Worthington quote p. 280).

22. "Gain! Gain! Gain! is . . . the *alpha* and *omega* of the founders of American towns," a British visitor wrote, but at least they founded real towns. See Timothy J. Shannon, " 'This Unpleasant Business': The Transformation of Land Speculation in the Ohio Country, 1787–1820," Andrew R. L. Clayton, " 'Language Gives Way to Feelings': Rhetoric, Republicanism, and Religion in Jeffersonian Ohio," and Emil Pocock, " 'A Candidate I Shall Surely Be': Election Practices in Early Ohio, 1798–1825," in Brown and Cayton, *Pursuit of Public Power,* pp. 15–68 ("Gain" quote p. 29).

23. Ohio's presidential native sons included William Henry Harrison, Ulysses S. Grant, Rutherford B. Hayes, James Garfield, Benjamin Harrison, William H. McKinley, William Howard Taft, and Warren Gameliel Harding.

24. Excellent and mostly compatible treatments of the Jefferson presidency include Noble E. Cunningham, *The Jeffersonian Republicans in Power: Party Operations, 1801–1809* (Chapel Hill: University of North Carolina, 1963), Marshall Smelser, *The Democratic Republic 1801–1815* (New York: Harper & Row, 1968), the presidential chapters in Merrill D. Peterson, *Thomas Jefferson and the New Nation: A Biography* (New York: Oxford University, 1970), Robert M. Johnstone, Jr., *Jefferson and the Presidency: Leadership in the Young Republic* (Ithaca, N.Y.: Cornell University, 1978), McDonald, *Presidency of Thomas Jefferson* and *The American Presidency: An Intellectual History* (Lawrence: University of Kansas, 1994), pp. 245–74.

25. Whitehall Company, *The Presidents. . . . Their Inaugural Addresses* (Chicago: Whitehall, 1968), pp. 13–16.

26. James Madison of Virginia became secretary of State, Pennsylvania's Albert Gallatin got the Treasury, Henry Dearborn of Massachusetts became secretary of War and Maryland's Robert Smith, brother of Senator Samuel Smith, secretary of the Navy (after four other men turned down the job), Levi Lincoln of Massachusetts was named attorney general, and Gideon Granger of Connecticut postmaster general.

27. Three recent studies remind general readers (as opposed to law students) of Marshall's centrality in the process of nation-building. Jean Edward Smith, *John Marshall: Definer of a Nation* (New York: Henry Holt, 1996), R. Kent Newmyer, *John Marshall and the Heroic Age of the Supreme Court* (Baton Rouge: Louisiana State University, 2001), and James F. Simon, *What Kind of Nation? Thomas Jefferson, John Marshall, and the Epic Struggle to Create a United States* (New York: Simon & Schuster, 2002) describe how the Marshall Court prevented the nation from tilting too far toward states' rights as opposed to federal authority, or legislative authority as opposed to individual rights under Common Law. The exhaustive classic biography by a Progressive Republican Senator is Albert J. Beveridge, *The Life of John Marshall,* 4 vols. (Boston: Houghton Mifflin, 1916–19).

28. Gallatin at first rued the American Revolution and Constitution. When his land speculations on the Monongahela went awry and the Republican balloon began rising, Gallatin converted to the American civic religion and won Republican praise for writing two detailed critiques of Hamilton's financial projections. See Henry Adams' classic *The Life of Albert Gallatin* (New York: Peter Smith, 1943 [1879]), Raymond Walters, Jr., *Albert Gallatin: Jeffersonian Financier and Diplomat* (New York: Macmillan, 1957), and L. B. Kuppenheimer, *Albert Gallatin's Vision of Democratic Stability: An Interpretive Profile* (Westport, Conn.: Praeger, 1996).

29. James Ripley Jacobs, *The Beginning of the U.S. Army, 1783–1812* (Princeton: Princeton University, 1947), Sidney Foreman, *West Point: A History of the United States Military Academy* (New York: Columbia University, 1950), and Theodore J. Crackel, *West Point: A Bicentennial History* (Lawrence: University of Kansas, 2002) describe the founding of the academy; Francis Paul Prucha, *The Sword of the Republic: The United States Army on the Frontier 1783–1846* (New York: Macmillan, 1969) describes how the tiny professional army coped with its responsibilities in the west.

30. Rich detail and a feel for the early decades of the U.S. Navy may be gleaned from four books published by the U.S. Naval Institute, Annapolis, Md.: Christopher McKee, *Edward Preble: A Naval Biography 1761–1807* (1972); Leonard Guttridge and Jay Smith, *The Commodores,* 2 ed. (1986); James C. Bradford, ed., *Command Under Sail: Makers of the American Naval Tradition* (1985); and McKee, *A Gentlemanly and Honorable Profession: The Creation of the U.S. Naval Officer Corps, 1794–1815* (1991). See also Craig Symonds, *Navalists and Antinavalists: The Naval Policy Debate in the United States, 1785–1827* (Newark: University of Delaware, 1980).

31. On the first Barbary war see James A. Field, *America and the Mediterranean World 1776–1882* (Princeton: Princeton University, 1969), pp. 27–67, Louis B. Wright and Julia H. McLeod, *The First Americans in North Africa: William Eaton's Struggle for a Vigorous Policy Against the Barbary Pirates, 1799–1805* (Princeton: Princeton University, 1945), the essays by David F. Long (on Porter) and John H. Schroeder (on Decatur) in Bradford, *Command Under Sail,* pp. 173–219 (Nelson quote, p. 204), and Guttridge and Smith, *Commodores,* chapters 5–8.

32. Michael Zuckerman, "The Power of Blackness: Thomas Jefferson and the Revolution in Saint-Domingue," in his *Almost Chosen People: Oblique Biographies in the American Grain* (Berkeley: University of California, 1993). Zuckerman may exaggerate the factor of race in his account of Jefferson's motives, but it was certainly present as a source of his motivations toward Haiti since his days as secretary of State. For a few weeks in 1802 Jefferson even fantasized sparing America a mixture of races by shipping all slaves to Haiti. An analysis of the debate is in Conor Cruise O'Brien, *The Long Affair: Thomas Jefferson and the French Revolution, 1785–1800* (Chicago: University of Chicago, 1996), pp. 280–96.

33. For the diplomacy behind the Louisiana Purchase see especially the readable Alexander DeConde, *This Affair of Louisiana* (Baton Rouge: Louisiana State University, 1978); Jefferson quote, p. 113.

34. DeConde, *Affair of Louisiana,* pp. 102–3.

35. DeConde, *Affair of Louisiana,* pp. 144–45 ("federal maniacs") and Prucha, *Sword of the Republic,* p. 64 ("one of the most fortunate").

36. Wilkinson quoted by Prucha, *Sword of the Republic,* p. 77.

37. On Jefferson's policies, Spanish and British resistance to U.S. encroachments, and the first Oregon settlements see Donald Jackson, *Thomas Jefferson and the Stony Mountains: Exploring the West from Monticello* (Urbana: University of Illinois, 1981), Bernard DeVoto, ed., *The Journals of Lewis and Clark* (Boston: Houghton Mifflin, 1953), Warren L. Cook, *Flood Tide of Empire: Spain and the Pacific Northwest, 1543–1819* (New Haven: Yale University, 1973), John S. Galbraith, *The Hudson's Bay Company as an Imperial Factor, 1821–1869* (Berkeley: University of California, 1957), and James P. Ronda, *Astoria and Empire* (Lincoln: University of Nebraska, 1990). The tales are told briefly and elegantly, if I do say so myself, in Walter A. McDougall, *Let the Sea Make a Noise: A History of the North Pacific From Magellan to MacArthur* (New York: Basic Books, 1993), pp. 122–30, 146–51.

38. Ray Allen Billington and Martin Ridge, *Westward Expansion: A History of the American Frontier,* 5 ed. (New York: Macmillan, 1982), pp. 392–95; Prucha, *Sword of the Republic,* pp. 88–94

(quote, p. 93). The primary source is Donald Jackson, ed., *The Journals of Zebulon Montgomery Pike with Letters and Related Documents*, 2 vol. (Norman: University of Oklahoma, 1966); the best synthetic account of military exploration in the West is William H. Goetzmann, *Army Exploration in the American West, 1803–1863* (New Haven: Yale University, 1959).

39. On Federalist party organization see David Hackett Fischer, *The Revolution of American Conservatism: The Federalist Party in the Era of Jeffersonian Democracy* (New York: Harper & Row, 1965).

40. Mysteries still surround the Burr-Hamilton duel. To which of Hamilton's numerous denunciations did Burr choose to take mortal offense? One recent theory suggests Hamilton spread rumors alleging incest between Burr and his beautiful twenty-one-year-old daughter Theodosia, which would indeed have been unpardonable. See Arnold A. Rogow, *A Fatal Friendship: Alexander Hamilton and Aaron Burr* (New York: Hill & Wang, 1998), pp. 239–40, and Buckner F. Melton, Jr., *Aaron Burr: Conspiracy to Treason* (New York: John Wiley & Sons, 2002), pp. 47–48. Why did Hamilton not issue a retraction or apology, and then not defend himself? Joanne B. Freeman, *Affairs of Honor: National Politics in the New Republic* (New Haven: Yale University, 2001), pp. 187–98, suggests it was moral cowardice, not physical courage, that drove the men to their duel: both feared public disgrace more than death. (When Hamilton evinced on his deathbed he had acted to save the nation from Burr, the latter damned his hypocrisy.) Above all, what did Burr expect to gain from the duel save vengeance against a man he believed had stood in his way for twenty-five years?

41. The trial of Chase is briefly described in McDonald, *Presidency of Thomas Jefferson*, pp. 89–94 (quote p. 93) and Smelser, *Democratic Republic*, pp. 68–72, and covered at length in William H. Rehnquist, *Grand Inquests: The Historic Impeachment Trials of Samuel Chase and Andrew Johnson* (New York: Morrow, 1992). Jefferson was vexed by the acquittal of Chase, but Randolph felt downright humiliated. His efforts to block a bail-out for the fraudulent Yazoo land company had already cost him the speakership of the House. Now he began to court other Republican malcontents and speak of forming a *Tertium Quid*, or third party. It was the first serious bump for Jefferson's Congressional juggernaut.

42. Philip Vail, *The Great American Rascal: The Turbulent Life of Aaron Burr* (New York: Hawthorn, 1973), p. 107.

43. On the Burr Conspiracy, Melton, *Aaron Burr: Conspiracy to Treason*, is the latest scholarly treatment; Vail, *Great American Rascal* ("I am coy," p. 226) the best read; Thomas Perkings Abernethy, *The Burr Conspiracy* (New York: Oxford University, 1954), the classic. For my part, I think the shrewdest reading of Wilkinson's motives and acts is in Francis S. Philbrick, *The Rise of the West 1754–1830* (New York: Harper & Row, 1965), pp. 234–52 (Smelser, *Democratic Republic*, p. 112, even writes Wilkinson's "humbug and avarice may have saved his country") and the shrewdest reading of Jefferson's motives, acts, and failures to act is in McDonald, *Presidency of Thomas Jefferson*, pp. 109–30. I have followed their leads.

44. Nor would the United States recognize Haitian independence until 1862, after the slave states had seceded. See John Chester Miller, *The Wolf By the Ears: Thomas Jefferson and Slavery* (Charlottesville: University of Virginia, 1991), pp. 138–41.

45. Historians vary on how central a role Madison played in the run-up to the embargo. Burton Spivak, *Jefferson's English Crisis: Commerce, Embargo, and the Republican Revolution* (Charlottesville: University of Virginia, 1979) focuses on the President's leadership. But Dumas Malone, *Jefferson the President: Second Term, 1805–1809* (Boston: Houghton Mifflin, 1974), pp. 475–89, McDonald, *Presidency of Thomas Jefferson*, pp. 139–45 (quote, p. 140), J. C. A. Stagg, *Mr. Madison's War: Politics, Diplomacy, and Warfare in the Early American Republic 1783–1830*

(Princeton: Princeton University, 1983), pp. 3–22, and Robert Rutland, *The Presidency of James Madison* (Lawrence: University of Kansas, 1990) make strong cases for Madison's leadership and show the continuity of his economic theories before and after the embargo.

46. Samuels, ed., Adams' *History of the United States,* pp. 214–27 (quotes, pp. 214, 221, 216, 218); the passage is in volume IV, chapter XII in the original.

47. No party, economic interest, or region mourned the dead embargo except the 87 entrepreneurs who founded cotton mills to replace lost British imports. But the epitaphs penned by historians range from Henry Adams' "policy worth trying," to a heroic attempt to "combat war with instruments of peace" (Louis Martin Sears, *Jefferson and the Embargo* [Durham, N.C.: Duke University, 1927], p. 318), to a likely initiative by a "philosopher-king" who "asked too much of his people" (Bradford Perkins, *Prologue to War: England and the United States, 1805–1811* [Berkeley: University of California, 1961], p. 183), to a grotesque violation of civil rights attempting "enlightenment by force" (McDonald, *Presidency of Thomas Jefferson,* pp. 148–49). I like Smelser's last word in *Democratic Republic,* p. 180: "The embargo went against the grain by coercing Americans and demanding the subordination of grave economic interests to inglorious peace." But perhaps the most ingenious summation of the embargo is in Hiram Caton, *The Politics of Progress: The Origin and Development of the Commercial Republic, 1600–1835* (Gainesville: University of Florida, 1988), p. 510: "Jefferson was able to visit sublime and ridiculous absurdities on the nation because Federalists compromised the principle of equality by agreeing to countenance slavery. This was the root cause of the mendacity that took political life in its grip. A political culture whose logic system was wired to accept slave owners as spokesmen of liberty would probably exhibit a certain invincible ignorance about the elementary facts of national life, and a certain indecisiveness in affirming the basic conditions of modern political existence—a national government, an army and navy, roads and waterways, banks, education, protection for patents."

48. After 150 years of adulation by almost all schools of American thought, Jefferson has recently been under assault. He seems either too libertarian or not libertarian enough, too nationalist or not nationalist enough, too free-market capitalist or not capitalist enough, too backward-looking in his philosophy or too forward-looking, trusting too much in republican virtue or not practicing enough of it himself, and certainly no friend to women or red and black men. Thus, Leonard W. Levy, *Jefferson and Civil Liberties: The Darker Side* (Cambridge, Mass.: Harvard University Press, 1963) depicts a man highly selective in his respect for law and civil liberties. Bernard W. Sheehan, *Seeds of Extinction: Jeffersonian Philanthropy and the American Indian* (New York: W. W. Norton, 1973) and Anthony F. C. Wallace, *Jefferson and the Indians* (Cambridge, Mass.: Harvard University, 1999) argue the bankruptcy of his false or mistaken benevolence toward Native Americans. Miller, *Wolf By the Ears,* recounts how he consistently acted to perpetuate slavery even as he agonized in words over how to end it. Conor Cruise O'Brien, *The Long Affair: Thomas Jefferson and the French Revolution, 1785–1800* (Chicago: University of Chicago, 1996) thinks his stubborn faith in the French Revolution was a psychological purgation of his guilt over slavery at home. William Safire's novel *The Scandalmonger* (New York: Simon & Schuster, 2000) limns a distant and devious party boss countenancing betrayal, slander, blackmail, and possibly worse by his supporters. But let's not get carried away. Jefferson was a politician, narcissist, philosopher, and Virginia planter, and displayed the strengths and flaws of those ilks.

49. Lewis William Newton, *The Americanization of French Louisiana* (New York: Arno Press, 1980), pp. 1–5.

50. Bennett H. Wall, et al., *Louisiana: A History,* 2 ed. (Arlington Heights, Ill.: Forum

Press, 1990), pp. 18–87. The Baron de Carondelet saw the danger posed by Yankee frontiersmen in 1794 when he reported: "A carbine and a little maize in a sack are enough for an American to wander about in the forests alone for a whole month. With his carbine, he kills the wild cattle and deer for food and defends himself from the savages. The maize dampened serves him in lieu of bread. With some tree trunks crossed one above another in the shape of a square, he raises a house, and even a fort that is impregnable to the savages. . . . If such men succeed in occupying the shores of the Mississippi or the Missouri, or to obtain their navigation, there is, beyond doubt, nothing that can prevent them from crossing those rivers and penetrating into our provinces on the other side" ("Military Report on Louisiana and West Florida," Nov. 24, 1794, in James A. Robertson, *Louisiana Under the Rule of Spain, France, and the United States, 1785–1807*, 2 vols. [Cleveland: A. H. Clark, 1911], I: 298–99).

51. *Evangeline* tells of two Acadian lovers separated by the British expulsion and reunited only as the man, now old, lies dying. Like Longfellow's *Hiawatha* it educated Americans about a subculture ground under by the majority's progress, but less to affirm that culture than sentimentalize it. Albert Rhoads "cottoned on" to this American trick of waxing nostalgic for their victims after the fact in 1873: "The American is only satisfied when all foreign elements are thrown into the national turning shop and come out turned to his own exact proportions." All others succumbed, wrote Rhoads, but the Cajun resisted and "to the urgent demands of the Anglo-Saxon neighbor his '*Non, Monsieur,*' comes back as unerringly as the refrain of Poe's raven" (Carl A. Brasseaux, *Acadian to Cajun: Transformation of a People, 1803–1877* [Jackson: University of Mississippi, 1992], pp. 100–1).

52. Brasseaux, *Acadian to Cajun,* pp. 3–44.

53. Wall, *Louisiana: A History,* pp. 91–108; Newton, *Americanization of French Louisiana,* pp. 36–68 ("stranger in the country," p. 43); Rohrbough, *Trans-Appalachian Frontier,* pp. 128–33 ("uninformed, indolent," p. 128).

54. Quincy in *Annals of Congress,* 11th Cong., 3d Sess (1810–1811), pp. 524, 538, cited by Newton, *Americanization of French Louisiana,* pp. 86–87.

55. In appreciation of his patriotism and gallantry, Lafitte was granted a pardon for all his past felonies by President Madison. But after the war, like any boss of an organized crime ring, he "went back to business." At length the U.S. Navy expelled him from Barataria, but he simply removed his operation to Galveston Island, Texas. Blockaded again by the Navy, Lafitte decided henceforth to tangle only with Spaniards. He sailed away to South America, where he evidently continued his buccaneering exploits until death in 1825.

56. Wall, *Louisiana: A History,* pp. 109–37 (Twain quote, p. 126); Brasseaux, *Acadian to Cajun,* pp. 45–49.

57. Stagg, *Madison's War,* pp. 3–47; Jefferson quoted in Walter LaFeber, *The American Age: U.S. Foreign Policy at Home and Abroad 1750 to the Present,* 2 ed. (New York: W. W. Norton, 1994), p. 60.

58. Richard White, *The Middle Ground: Indians, Empire, and Republics in the Great Lakes Region, 1650–1815* (Cambridge, U.K.: Cambridge University, 1991), pp. 510–17; Andrew R. L. Cayton, *Frontier Indiana* (Bloomington: Indiana University, 1996), pp. 196–225 (quote, p. 219). The classic account is Benjamin Drake's *The Life of Tecumseh and of His Brother the Prophet* (1852), and John Sugden, *Tecumseh: A Life* (New York: Henry Holt, 1998) the latest and best.

59. Stagg, *Madison's War,* pp. 48–119, describes the fears for Republican party unity if the tensions with Britain were not leeched. Calhoun's War Report is quoted and interpreted in Steven Watts, *The Republic Reborn: War and the Making of Liberal America* (Baltimore: Johns

Hopkins University, 1987), pp. 263–74 (quotes, pp. 266, 271, 273). Calhoun's "second struggle" quoted in Perkins, *Prologue to War*, pp. 434–35; Clay quoted in Robert V. Remini, *Henry Clay, Statesman for the Union* (New York: W. W. Norton, 1991), p. 86; Randolph quoted in George Brown Tindall, *America: A Narrative History*, 2 ed. (New York: W. W. Norton, 1988), I: 365.

60. I adumbrate here and below the argument in Watts, *Republic Reborn* (Taylor quote, p. 23; Adams quotes, pp. 39, 42, 61; Breckenridge quote, p. 53; Rush quotes, pp. 139–41).

61. Watts, *Republic Reborn* (Clay quotes, pp. 86–92; Irving quote, p. 112) and Maurice G. Baxter, *Henry Clay and the American System* (Lexington: University of Kentucky, 1995), pp. 1–33. See also William Gribbin, *The Churches Militant: The War of 1812 and American Religion* (New Haven: Yale University, 1973).

62. At least seven (and possibly more) of the thirteen members of the war cabinet were Freemasons. The officer corps (especially the army) remained a bastion of the order, Andrew Jackson most prominently. In Congress, War Hawks Henry Clay, Felix Grundy, and Richard M. Johnson were all Freemasons, delegations from western states were at least 50 percent Masonic (and usually from the same lodge), and such promoters of national economic development as Hezekiah Niles and Mathew Carey were Freemasons. So was Parson Weems. A biographical dictionary of prominent political, commercial, legal, and military Freemasons in the decade of the 1810s would be a fat book, but an intriguing sampling may be found at http://politicalgraveyard.com/group/masons.html.

63. Charles Royster, *Light-Horse Harry Lee and the Legacy of the American Revolution* (Cambridge, U.K.: Cambridge University, 1981), pp. 117–85 (quotes, pp. 164, 168). After the war Lee went to West Indies for his health (and to flee creditors). But in 1818, near death, he begged transportation to American soil and spent his last days at the estate built by Caty Greene on Cumberland Island, Georgia. It was the last living link to the days when Light-Horse Harry Lee fought for American independence beside his adored commander Nathanael Greene; the days when his hopes for the new nation were still at flood tide.

64. Stagg, *Madison's War*, pp. 120–76 (quotes, pp. 163, 170). Irénée Du Pont, Pierre's son, was the founder of America's chemical industry and a great patriot. To meet the sudden demand for powder in the War of 1812 he ran round-the-clocks shifts in his Brandywine mill. That meant working at night with dangerous kerosene lamps. One touched off an explosion, killing nine men. It was, Du Pont consoled their wives, a sacrifice to the national cause as great as any soldier's death. See Marc Duke, *The Du Ponts: Portrait of a Dynasty* (New York: E. P. Dutton, 1976), pp. 98–106.

65. Stagg, *Madison's War*, pp. 227–69 (quote, p. 250); Prucha, *Sword of the Republic*, pp. 103–8; Alec R. Gilpin, *The War of 1812 in the Old Northwest* (East Lansing: Michigan State University, 1958), pp. 120–28. The pitiful Hull's personal maladies ought not obscure the impossible situation his orders put him in and the unpreparedness of the force he was obligated to lead. When a court martial sentenced him to death for cowardice, Madison to his credit pardoned him. The President also took some vengeance on New York by putting the governor of *New Jersey* in charge of New York City's defenses. That must have smarted!

66. Linda M. Maloney, "Isaac Hull: Bulwark of the Sailing Navy," in Bradford, *Command Under Sail*, pp. 251–72, tells of his origins in an impecunious Connecticut family and decision to go to sea as a boy just to make a living. But his uncle William (the driveling general in 1812) won young Isaac a commission. At Tripoli he became one of "Preble's Boys" and among the most skilled and daring officers of his generation. His victory over the *Guerrière* removed some of the sting from his uncle's defeat at Detroit. While it did not reconcile New England to the *fact* of

the war, it increased the will to wage it in Yankee ports and blew wind into the sails of southern Federalists (see James Broussard, *The Southern Federalists, 1800–1816* [Baton Rouge: Louisiana State University, 1978], p. 159). An old chanty captures the swelling American pride:

> The *Guerrière* a frigate bold on the foamy ocean rolled, commanded by proud Dacres, a
> grandee-o
> With as choice a British crew as they ever, ever drew. They could flog the Frenchmen two
> to one so dandy-o.
> The *Constitution* hove in view, said proud Dacres to his crew, come clear the ship for
> action and be handy-o.
> To the cannons, boys, now set her and to make our men fight better, mix gunpowder with
> their brandy-o.
> O, the cannon shot blew hot but the Yankees answered not til we got within a distance
> we called handy-o
> Then the broadsides we poured carried their mainmast by the board and made that lofty
> frigate look abandoned-o.

67. I am indebted to Harvey Sicherman for sharing his research in the Girard Papers in Philadelphia. For details on this little known millionaire-patriot see Harry E. Wildes, *Lonely Midas: The Story of Stephen Girard* (New York: Farrar & Rinehart, 1943) and Donald R. Adams, Jr., *Finance and Enterprise in Early America: A Study of Stephen Girard's Bank, 1812–1831* (Philadelphia: University of Pennsylvania, 1978).

68. Perry saw more action defending the Chesapeake in 1814, but what might have been a brilliant career was cut off in 1819. Ordered to negotiate a treaty with the new nation of Venezuela he sailed a gunboat into the Orinoco where real, not metaphorical, mosquitoes killed him and his crew with yellow fever. John K. Mahon, "Oliver Hazard Perry: Savior of the Northwest," in Bradford, *Command Under Sail*, pp. 126–46, describes the Battle of Lake Erie and contrasts the biographical literature on Perry. The most detailed account is David Curtis Skaggs, *A Signal Victory: The Lake Erie Campaign, 1812–1813* (Annapolis, Md.: U.S. Naval Institute, 1997).

69. For the other side in the Battle of the Thames see John Sugden, *Tecumseh's Last Stand* (Norman: University of Oklahoma, 1985). Shelby was known as "Kentucky's George Washington" for his military leadership over four decades and service as Kentucky's first governor. He returned to office in 1812 at age sixty-two to mobilize and command the most effective state militia in the northern theater. Indeed, it was Shelby who pressed Harrison into pursuing the Anglo-Indian forces retreating from Detroit and devised the victorious tactics on the Thames. Veterans of the battle included a future U.S. President, a vice president, four senators, and upwards of twenty congressmen.

70. "West Florida" comprised the strip of the Gulf Coast lying between the Apalachicola River and the Mississippi River. The Jefferson administration had claimed it was part of the Louisiana Purchase, but Spain continued to occupy it in defiance of the United States and Napoleon alike. In 1810 Madison and Congress simply annexed the territory after American "filibusters" rebelled against Madrid and set up a "free" government. The Creeks took due notice, concluding they must fight before all their refuges disappeared into the maw of the American behemoth. On West Florida and the Creek campaign: Thomas P. Abernethy, *The South in the New Nation* (Baton Rouge: Louisiana State University, 1961), pp. 330–72, and Robert V. Remini, *Andrew Jackson and the Course of American Empire 1767–1821* (New York: Harper & Row, 1977), pp. 187–233.

71. For British strategy (and excellent campaign histories) see John K. Mahon, *The War of 1812* (Gainesville: University of Florida, 1972) and Robert S. Quimby, *The U.S. Army in the War of 1812: An Operational and Command Study*, 2 vols. (East Lansing: Michigan State University, 1997).

72. Smelser, *Democratic Republic*, pp. 270–72. On Smith's role see Frank A. Cassell, *Merchant Congressman in the Young Republic: Samuel Smith of Maryland, 1752–1839* (Madison, University of Wisconsin, 1971). For a critique of the performance of Armstrong and Monroe alike as secretaries of War see Quimby, *U.S. Army in the War of 1812*. In addition to *The Star-Spangled Banner*, the War of 1812 gave the nation "Uncle Sam." He was Samuel "Uncle Sam" Wilson, an inspector of army provisions who had "U.S." stenciled on barrels approved for delivery.

73. Prevost was scalded in London for retreating before inferior force, but the Duke of Wellington himself judged offensive action fruitless without control of the interior waterways. For details on the battle and its hero, see Edward K. Eckert, "Thomas Macdonough: Architect of a Wilderness Navy," in Bradford, *Command Under Sail*, pp. 147–69, and David Curtis Skaggs, *Thomas Macdonough* (Annapolis, Md.: U.S. Naval Institute, 2002).

74. The Hartford Convention proposed repealing the three-fifths compromise for slave states' representation in Congress (take that, James Wilson and Hugh Williamson!), banning embargoes for more than sixty days and requiring a two-thirds majority in Congress to declare war or admit new states (take that, Republican Congress!), making foreign-born citizens ineligible for federal office (take that, Gallatin!), restricting presidents to one term (take that, Jefferson!), and disallowing two presidents in a row from the same state (take that, Madison!). The convention chose to ignore the fact four foreign-born businessmen (Astor, Girard, A. J. Dallas, and David Parish) kept the Treasury solvent.

75. Stagg, *Madison's War*, pp. 469–85 (quote, p. 473). A full-length study is James M. Banner, Jr., *To the Hartford Convention: the Federalists and the Origins of Party Politics in Massachusetts, 1789–1815* (New York: Knopf, 1970). A little maid's sampler stitched at the time expressed Yankee loyalties: "Amy Kittredge is my name, Salem is my dwelling place. New England is my Nation. And Christ is my salvation" (Samuel Eliot Morison, *The Maritime History of Massachusetts, 1783–1860* [Boston: Houghton Mifflin, 1979, orig. 1921], p. 211).

76. Abernethy, *The South in the New Nation*, pp. 367–402; Remini, *Jackson and the Course of American Empire*, pp. 255–97.

77. On the economic effects of the war and its aftermath: Stanley Lebergott, *The Americans: An Economic Record* (New York: Norton, 1984), pp. 95–130.

78. Richard White, *The Middle Ground: Indians, Empire, and Republics in the Great Lakes Region, 1650–1815* (Cambridge, U.K.: Cambridge University, 1991), pp. 510–17; Colin G. Galloway, *Crown and Calumet: British-Indian Relations, 1783–1815* (Norman: University of Oklahoma, 1987), pp. 24–57. All the British asked for at Ghent was an American promise to let Indians move back to the lands they occupied *ante bellum*. But the treaty did not say for how long. So Jackson and other U.S. authorities invited chiefs to parleys on their former land only to oust them in bilateral treaties. The Creeks and Seminoles appealed to London, but received a cold shoulder.

79. Hammond, *Banks and Politics*, pp. 229–41. Broussard, *Southern Federalists*, chapters 12–13 and Fischer, *Revolution of American Conservatism* analyze the collapse of the Federalist party.

80. Whitehall Company, *The Presidents . . . Their Inaugural Addresses*, pp. 29–36.

ENGINEERS, PIONEERS, PEDDLERS, AND DEMOCRATS

1. The Duke of Wellington referred to the Six Acts when he hoped "Our example will be of value in France and Germany": R. R. Palmer and Joel Colton, *A History of the Modern World*,

5 ed. (New York: Knopf, 1978), p. 441. Marshall quoted in R. Kent Newmyer, *John Marshall and the Heroic Age of the Supreme Court* (Baton Rouge: Louisiana State University, 2001), p. 331; *Niles' Weekly Register* (Dec. 2, 1815), pp. 238–39.

2. Bath is now known as Berkeley Springs, West Virginia. On Fulton's early life see Cynthia Owen Philip, *Robert Fulton: A Biography* (New York: Franklin Watts, 1985), pp. 1–13, and Wallace Hutcheon, Jr., *Robert Fulton: Pioneer of Undersea Warfare* (Annapolis, Md.: U.S. Naval Institute, 1981), pp. 4–17. On Fulton's place in the extraordinary evolution of submarine warfare generally see Alex Roland, *Underwater Warfare in the Age of Sail* (Bloomington: Indiana University, 1978).

3. George Rogers Taylor, *The Transportation Revolution 1815–1860* (New York: Holt, Rinehart, and Winston, 1964), pp. 56–73. On river transport generally before the era of steam, Leland D. Baldwin, *The Keelboat on Western Waters* (Pittsburgh: University of Pittsburgh, 1941). Fitch and Rumsey both applied for patents, then under the purview of the secretary of State. Jefferson could or would not determine who had priority—so many workable and unworkable innovations were involved—and instead issued patents to both on the same day. Fitch left his papers and autobiography with the Philadelphia Library against the day Jefferson should "ever be aiming for the President's chair," at which time he asked that his papers be shown to the Congress. See Frank D. Prager, ed., *The Autobiography of John Fitch* (Philadelphia: American Philosophical Society, 1976), quote above p. 208.

4. Philip, *Robert Fulton*, pp. 14–171; Hutcheon, *Undersea Warfare*, pp. 18–61.

5. Kirpatrick Sale, *The Fire of His Genius: Robert Fulton and the American Dream* (New York: Free Press, 2001), pp. 63–119; Philip, *Robert Fulton*, pp. 172–218 (quote, p. 204).

6. Sale, *Fire of His Genius*, 146–74; Philip, *Robert Fulton*, pp. 318–46 (quote, p. 346).

7. Taylor, *Transportation Revolution*, pp. 58–61; Wheaton J. Lane, *Commodore Vanderbilt: An Epic of the Steam Age* (New York: Knopf, 1942); Maurice G. Baxter, *The Steamboat Monopoly: "Gibbons v. Ogden," 1824* (New York: Knopf, 1972).

8. See Louis C. Hunter, *Steamboats on the Western Rivers: An Economic and Technological History* (Cambridge, Mass.: M.I.T., 1949), pp. 3–59; Marcus and Siegal, *Technology in America*, pp. 59–62; John H. Morrison, *History of American Steam Navigation* (New York: W. F. Sametz, 1903), pp. 191–264. On Shreve's contributions, see Edith McCall, *Conquering the Rivers: Henry Miller Shreve and the Navigation of America's Inland Waterways* (Baton Rouge: Louisiana State University, 1984), p. 158. Louis Hunter and David Freeman Hawke, *Nuts & Bolts of the Past: A History of American Technology 1776–1860* (New York: Harper & Row, 1988), pp. 82–87, think Shreve (after whom Shreveport, Louisiana, was named) gets too much credit for snag boats and incremental improvements in valves and tolerances on high-pressure engines. Many public and private agencies and "anonymous and unheroic craftsmen" contributed the ideas that opened the West's great waters. An interesting example of state involvement concerned the Steam Boat Company of Georgia, a monopoly granted Samuel Howard in 1816. Within five years the company owned six large steamboats, numerous lighters, real estate, facilities, and thirty-five slaves, for a total worth in excess of half a million dollars. Unfortunately, a drought limited service of its early, deep-draft boats upriver to Augusta. A South Carolina consortium bought out the company in order to deflect Georgia trade to Charleston. Henry Shultz, a hustling German immigrant, went so far as to leave Augusta and found a new town on the Carolina side of the Savannah River. He called it Hamburg after the great German port and won a $50,000 interest-free loan from the South Carolina legislature. Shultz was hailed as "manufacturer of cities" and "very useful citizen" until he failed to usurp Georgia's commerce. South Carolina then reneged on its promise to build him two big steamboats, while the Supreme Court ruling in 1825

brought the curtain down on his play. Free competition ensued. So, too, did the fierce rivalry between Charleston and Savannah, which survives to this day. See Ulrich Bonnell Phillips, *A History of Transportation in the Eastern Cotton Belt to 1860* (New York: Columbia University, 1908), pp. 70–82.

9. Taylor, *Transportation Revolution*, pp. 15–26; Alan I. Marcus and Howard P. Segal, *Technology in America: A Brief History* (New York: Harcourt Brace Jovanovich, 1989), pp. 52–59; Donald C. Jackson, "Roads Most Traveled: Turnpikes in Southeastern Pennsylvania," in Judith A. McGaw, ed., *Early American Technology: Making and Doing Things from the Colonial Era to 1850* (Chapel Hill: University of North Carolina, 1994), pp. 197–239.

10. Karl Raitz, ed., *The National Road* (Baltimore: Johns Hopkins University, 1996); especially Joseph S. Wood, "The Idea of the National Road," pp. 93–122; Billy Joe Peyton, "Surveying and Building the Road," pp. 123–158; and John A. Jakle, "Travelers' Impressions of the National Road," pp. 227–155 (quote, p. 233), and Philip D. Jordan, *The National Road* (Indianapolis: Bobbs-Merrill, 1948). The road petered out in Vandalia, Illinois, in 1850. Still, it stretched 750 miles west from Baltimore, and gave birth to many legends. Archer Butler Hulbert, *The Cumberland Road* (New York: AMS, 1971, orig. 1903), pp. 183–84, lists among its famous travelers Presidents Monroe, Jackson, Van Buren, Harrison, Polk, and Tyler, Henry Clay and Thomas Hart Benton, Lewis Cass, the Marquis de Lafayette, Mexican dictator Santa Anna, Illinois war chief Black Hawk, famed Swedish singer Jenny Lind, and the quintessential peddler of hokum, P. T. Barnum.

11. Taylor, *Transportation Revolution*, pp. 26–28.

12. Howard H. Peckham, *Indiana: A Bicentennial History* (New York: W. W. Norton, 1978), p. 1; Diane Carmony, "What's a Hoosier?" *University of Indiana Alumni Magazine* (July–August, 1992).

13. Ralph D. Gray, ed., *The Hoosier State: Readings in Indiana History* (Grand Rapids, Mich.: Eerdmans, 1980), pp. 10–11.

14. Andrew R. L. Cayton, *Frontier Indiana* (Bloomington: Indiana University, 1996), pp. 167–95, 228–35.

15. Cayton, *Frontier Indiana*, pp. 226–50 (quotes, pp. 227, 244, 247)

16. Gray, *Hoosier State*, pp. 142–47; Cayton, *Frontier Indiana*, pp. 251–60; Patrick J. Furlong, "Jennings, Jonathan," in *American National Biography Online* (Feb. 2000). There is no published biography of Jennings.

17. Roads described in Gray, *Hoosier State*, pp. 152–57 (quotes, pp. 154, 157); economics in Cayton, *Frontier Indiana*, pp. 267–87 (quote on towns, p. 273). A map in Byron L. Troyer, *Yesterday's Indiana* (Miami, Fla.: Seeman, 1975), p. 49, illustrates graphically how precocious was Indiana's network of roads, canals, and railroads c. 1840 by comparison to its neighbors.

18. Russell Bourne, *Floating West: The Erie and Other American Canals* (New York: W. W. Norton, 1992), pp. 13–18 (quotes, p. 18). Fulton's *A Treatise on the Improvement of Canal Navigation* was a precocious work conflating his observations of Bridgewater's canal, the ideas of utopian industrialist Robert Owen, the political economy of Adam Smith, and his own mechanical inventions. His preference for short canals was not well suited to American conditions and his fascination with inclines over locks was wrongheaded. But Fulton's belief in the power of engineering and free trade to end war for all time took root and grew into one of America's most abiding illusions.

19. Promotion of economic growth by Massachusetts General Court, and indeed by many other state governments, belies the notion the nineteenth-century United States was ever "laissez-faire." See Oscar Handlin and Mary Flug Handlin, *Commonwealth: A Study of the Role of*

*Government in the American Economy: Massachusetts, 1774–1861* (New York: Oxford University, 1947).

20. Ronald E. Shaw, *Canals for a Nation: The Canal Era in the United States 1790–1860* (Lexington: University of Kentucky, 1990), pp. 1–21; Elting E. Morison, *From Know-How to Nowhere: The Development of American Technology* (New York: Basic Books, 1974), pp. 16–39 (Knox quote, p. 21; Brindley quote, p. 28); Bourne, *Floating West*, pp. 36–51; Christopher Roberts, *The Middlesex Canal, 1793–1860* (Cambridge, Mass.: Harvard University, 1938). On Britain's canal mania from 1785 to 1795 and Brindley's extraordinary achievements see Per Sördom, ed., *Transport Technology and Social Change* (Stockholm: Tekniska Museet, 1980), pp. 67–89.

21. Bourne, *Floating West*, pp. 25–28, 70–93 (Jefferson quote, p. 27).

22. Why did Madison veto the Bonus Bill? Perhaps a Constitutional amendment empowering the federal government to fund public works would have eased delicate Jeffersonian consciences. But Jefferson and Madison had already presided over various projects, not least the National Road. Harry N. Scheiber, "The Transportation Revolution and American Law: Constitutionalism and Public Policy," in *Transportation and the Early Nation* (Indianapolis: Indiana Historical Society, 1982), pp. 1–29, suggests Madison's real concern was sectional. If Congress assumed power to vote improvements wherever it wished, the more populous northern states would funnel the lion's share to themselves. Shaw, *Canals for a Nation*, pp. 22–29 (Madison and Calhoun quotes, pp. 25–26) agrees constitutional arguments were a smokescreen behind which sectional interests haggled. On Clinton's extraordinary person and career, see Craig Hanyan, *De Witt Clinton and the Rise of the People's Men* (Montreal: McGill-Queen's University, 1996) and Evan Cornog, *The Birth of Empire: De Witt Clinton and the American Experience* (New York: Oxford University, 1998).

23. Bourne, *Floating West*, pp. 93–99 (West quote, p. 99). James Kent was known as "the American Blackstone" for his four volumes of commentaries on the Common Law published between 1826 and 1830. See John T. Horton, *James Kent, 1763–1847: A Study in Conservatism* (New York: Appleton, 1939).

24. After 1819, when malaria laid low hundreds of workers, contractors also distributed a folk remedy they called Jesuits' bark. It was quinine from South America, and provided an effective prophylactic against malaria even though nobody knew the anopheles mosquito was its carrier. Clinton quote in Bourne, *Floating West*, p. 103.

25. Lockport's well-preserved architecture, historical sites, and boat trips through the Erie Canal's greatest locks are thrills not to be missed by visitors to nearby Niagara Falls. New York's corruption is often on an imperial scale, but so, too, are its achievements. For the engineering of the Erie Canal see Shaw, *Canals for a Nation*, pp. 30–44, Bourne, *Floating West*, pp. 101–28, and the full-length treatments by Shaw, *Erie Water West: A History of the Erie Canal 1792–1854* (Lexington: University of Kentucky, 1966) and Noble E. Whitford, *History of the Canal System of New York*, 2 vols. (Albany: Brandow, 1906). Nathan Miller, *The Enterprise of a Free People: Aspects of Economic Development in New York State During the Canal Period, 1792–1838* (Ithaca, N.Y.: Cornell University, 1962) analyzes the canal's financing.

26. Quotes from Bourne, *Floating West*, pp. 123 (Freneau), 125 ("By the authority"), and Shaw, *Canals for a Nation*, p. 44 ("Holy cause").

27. Taylor, *Transportation Revolution*, pp. 32–55.

28. Daniel Hovey Calhoun, *The American Civil Engineer: Origins and Conflict* (Cambridge, Mass.: M.I.T., 1960), pp. 24–53 (Ellicott quote, p. 26). Calhoun confirms how engineers were made of lowly rodmen and axemen. For the rise of Jervis, after whom Port Jervis, New York, is

named, see Morison, *Know-How to Nowhere*, pp. 40–71 (Jervis quote, p. 48), Neil Fitzsimmons, *The Reminiscences of John B. Jervis, Engineer of the Old Croton* (Syracuse, N.Y.: Syracuse University, 1971), and F. Daniel Larkin, *John B. Jervis: An American Engineering Pioneer* (Ames: Iowa State University, 1990).

29. James P. Pate, ed., *The Reminiscences of George Strother Gaines: Pioneer and Statesman of Early Alabama and Mississippi, 1805–1843* (Tuscaloosa: University of Alabama, 1998), pp. 1–43 (quotes, pp. 42–43).

30. Malcom J. Rohrbough, *The Trans-Appalachian Frontier: People, Societies, and Institutions, 1775–1850* (New York: Oxford University, 1978), pp. 123–28; James J. Kirschke, "Sargent, Winthrop," *American National Biography Online* (Feb. 2000). A slave called Samson sued for fifteen years in Mississippi courts without winning freedom. An enslaved woman named Sue did win a writ of manumission in Virginia on the grounds she was part Indian, but before that judgment her master took her to Mississippi where a subsequent suit failed.

31. Rohrbaugh, *The Land Office Business: The Settlement and Administration of American Public Lands, 1789–1837* (New York: Oxford University, 1968), p. 45.

32. William Warren Rogers, et al., *Alabama: The History of a Deep South State* (Tuscaloosa: University of Alabama, 1994), pp. 61–65.

33. Rohrbough, *Trans-Appalachian Frontier*, pp. 192–217, Dabney quote, p. 403.

34. Pate, *Reminiscences of George Strother Gaines*, pp. 90–116.

35. Robert E. May, *John A. Quitman: Old South Crusader* (Baton Rouge: Louisiana State University, 1985); William Joseph Chute, *Damn Yankee! The First Career of Frederick A. P. Barnard: Educator, Scientist, Idealist* (Port Washington, N.Y.: Kennikat Press, 1978).

36. John Hebron Moore, *The Emergence of the Cotton Kingdom in the Old Southwest: Mississippi, 1770–1860* (Baton Rouge: Louisiana State University, 1988), pp. 1–17. New Orleans merchants marketed the new strain under the trade name Petit Gulf Cotton Seed. They also multiplied profits by re-selling seed every two or three years to planters in Alabama, Georgia, or overseas. That was because the new strain had to be continually cross-pollinated with Georgia seed lest it degenerate. The merchants and Natchez planters, of course, carefully guarded that secret.

37. Moore, *Emergence of the Cotton Kingdom*, pp. 73–115. Eugene D. Genovese, *Roll, Jordan, Roll: The World the Slaves Made* (New York: Vintage, 1974), pp. 49–70. Thus, Hugh Legaré's *Southern Agriculturalist* preached in the 1820s the master who practiced cruelty on slaves "violates the law of God and of humanity" and "endangers the institutions of his country" (p. 55).

38. Statistics on migrant slaves from J. D. B. DeBow, *Statistical View of the United States* (1854), cited by Allan Kulikoff, *The Agrarian Origins of American Capitalism* (Charlottesville: University of Virginia, 1992), p. 242. It was once thought almost all the slaves in the cotton belt were exported there by cynical Virginians breeding slaves on their played-out plantations. The statistical studies of Fogel and Engerman (see below) indicate to the contrary that literal cross-country migration was the norm and merchant transactions the exception. Data from New Orleans show only about a quarter of the slaves sold in its market were imported to the Delta.

39. Harold D. Woodman, *King Cotton and His Retainers: Financing and Marketing the Cotton Crop of the South, 1800–1925* (Lexington: University of Kentucky, 1968), pp. 5–195 (quote, p. 98)

40. James Oakes, *The Ruling Race: A History of American Slaveholders* (New York: Vintage, 1983), 37–68 (quote, p. 51). On Indian slave owners, see Theda Perdue, *Slavery and Evolution of Cherokee Society* (Knoxville: University of Tennessee, 1979) and R. Halliburton, *Red over Black:*

*Black Slavery Among the Cherokee Indians* (Westport, Conn.: Greenwood, 1977). On black slave owners, see Ira Berlin, *Slaves Without Masters: The Free Negro in the Antebellum South* (New York: Pantheon, 1974) and Kenneth W. Porter, *The Negro on the American Frontier* (New York: Arno, 1971).

41. The long debate over the character of Southern slavery is a prime example of Americans' capacity for self-delusion. In the next volume we must adumbrate the antebellum debates between southern sympathizers and northern abolitionists. For now, it is enough to cite the paragon of racial condescension that shaped a generation of Progressive historiography, Ulrich B. Phillips' *American Negro Slavery: A Survey of the Supply, Employment and Control of Negro Labor as Determined by the Plantation Regime* (New York: Appleton, 1918). Phillips accepted Southern paternalist stereotypes of "inert Negroes" so uncritically he depicted slavery as rather benign but utterly uneconomical. The critique of (then) Marxist Eugene D. Genovese, *The Political Economy of Slavery: Studies in the Economy & Society of the Slave South* (New York: Random House, 1961) granted the marginal profitability of slavery under certain conditions while damning the system as a pre-capitalist relic devoted to honor and power rather than money. The revisionist Kenneth M. Stampp, *The Peculiar Institution: Slavery in the Ante-Bellum South* (New York: Vintage, 1956), asserted the general profitability of slavery and suspected it was also relatively efficient, but (since he carried forward the assumption of slaves' diffidence and resistance) attributed its success to brutal coercion. Stanley M. Elkins, *Slavery: A Problem in American Institutional and Intellectual Life* (Chicago: University of Chicago, 1959), even likened plantations to totalitarian camps. Finally, Robert W. Fogel and Stanley L. Engerman, *Time on the Cross: The Economics of American Negro Slavery* and *Time on the Cross: Evidence and Methods* (Boston: Little, Brown, 1974), not only crunched the available statistics on the economics of slavery, but painted "by the numbers" the first fully human portrait of slaves and slave-owners.

42. In his later great work Genovese insightfully argues the Africans, not their masters, were the ones clinging to a "pre-industrial" work ethic. Like the first generation of English factory workers fresh from the farm, they resented regimens dictated by the clock or by piecework. Nor were they "draft animals." Genovese also grants Fogel's and Engerman's evidence regarding some masters' solicitousness toward black family ties, but believes the contrary evidence of divided families prevents generalization. A slave owner in financial straits or an inheritor of slave property or a court called to liquidate a plantation estate might find it impossible to keep enslaved families whole no matter how good their will. See "A 'Lazy' People" and "The Myth of the Absent Family," in *Roll, Jordan, Roll*, pp. 295–324, 450–58.

43. Leon Litwack, *North of Slavery: The Negro in the Free States, 1790–1860* (Chicago: University of Chicago, 1961); quote from *New London Gazette* (May 1, 1772), p. 11. Recent case studies include Joanne Pope Melish, *Disowning Slavery: Gradual Emancipation and "Race" in New England, 1780–1860* (Ithaca, N.Y.: Cornell University, 1998), Edgar J. McManus, *A History of Negro Slavery in New York* (Syracuse, N.Y.: Syracuse University, 2001), Gary B. Nash and Jean R. Soderlund, *Freedom by Degrees: Emancipation in Pennsylvania and Its Aftermath* (New York: Oxford University, 1991). Patience Essah, *A House Divided: Slavery and Emancipation in Delaware, 1683–1865* (Charlottesville: University of Virginia, 1996) examines the intriguing case of Delaware. At the Constitutional Convention James Madison excluded Delaware at the eastern end of the Mason-Dixon Line from his list of slave states, expecting the Swedish and Quaker elements north of Dover to abolish bondage. They tried repeatedly, but the southern counties settled from Maryland resisted (see also John A. Munroe, *Federalist Delaware 1775–1815* (New Brunswick, N.J.: Rutgers University, 1954), pp. 157–65). Thanks to widespread manumis-

sion free blacks came to outnumber enslaved ones three to one as early as 1810, yet the state legislature deadlocked over abolition. What is more, farmers and planters passed laws restricting mobility of free blacks so their labor was available at peak harvest time. Delaware remained a slave border state though the Civil War, then refused to ratify the 13th Amendment *until 1901* when a Quaker Republican governor won brief control of the state.

44. On playing the "race card" in northern politics see McManus, *Slavery in New York,* pp. 181–88 (quote, p. 187). On "The Slow Death of Slavery in the North" generally, Ira Berlin, *Many Thousands Gone: The First Two Centuries of Slavery in North America* (Cambridge, Mass.: Harvard University, 1998), pp. 228–55.

45. Statistics on the "insane" cited by Litwack, *North of Slavery,* pp. 40–41. The early abolitionist movements are summarized by Robert W. Fogel, *Without Consent or Contract: The Rise and Fall of American Slavery* (New York: W. W. Norton, 1989), pp. 238–54.

46. Litwack *North of Slavery,* pp. 18–29 ("is not the fault," pp. 21–22); Melish, *Disowning Slavery,* pp. 192–237 ("this is not their country" and "it will happen," pp. 195, 218). Liberia became an independent republic under a non-white president in 1847. Its history has been troubled ever since, American benevolence notwithstanding.

47. Etymologies are from George Stewart's classic *Names on the Land,* rev. ed. (Boston: Houghton Mifflin, 1967), pp. 85–86. On the French see James E. Davis, *Frontier Illinois* (Bloomington: Indiana University, 1998), pp. 14–64.

48. Victor Collot, an agent of the French Republic, visited the French settlers in 1796 and found them living like Indians albeit they still spoke with pride of their *patrie:* see Paul M. Angle, *Prairie State: Impressions of Illinois 1673–1967, By Travelers and Other Observers* (Chicago: University of Chicago, 1968), pp. 52–56. Chikagou, the future site of Fort Dearborn and America's "Second City," was first settled by a free Negro from San Domingue named Jean Baptiste Point du Sable, who built a trading post there c. 1779. On southerners in the early settlements, see Davis, *Frontier Illinois,* pp. 155–60. British colonel quoted by Theodore Calvin Pease, *The Story of Illinois,* 3 ed. (Chicago: University of Chicago, 1965, orig. 1925), pp. 66–67.

49. Lois A. Carrier, *Illinois: Crossroads of a Continent* (Urbana: University of Illinois, 1993), pp. 39–45; Davis, *Frontier Illinois,* pp. 161–71; Pease, *Story of Illinois,* pp. 68–81.

50. Carrier, *Crossroads,* pp. 46–59; Janet Cornelius, *A History of Constitution Making in Illinois* (Urbana: Institute of Government and Public Affairs, 1969).

51. Older accounts refer to the debate over slavery as a "good guys" and "bad guys" struggle, with Coles portrayed as a high-minded hero and the conventioneers as racist rednecks. James Simeone, *Democracy and Slavery in Frontier Illinois* (DeKalb: Northern Illinois University, 2000) depicts instead a complicated social and conceptual "culture war" among the factions disputing a second constitutional convention. See especially "How the People Became the White Folks" and "The White Folks Challenge the Big Folks," pp. 3–38. The "skeery" quote is cited in full in Carrier, *Crossroads,* p. 56.

52. Simeone, *Democracy and Slavery,* pp. 19–24. The scaremongers were wrong. Illinois grew 185 percent over the decade and Missouri 110 percent. What Illinois lost was an indeterminate number of southern immigrants while gaining northern ones, thus beginning the change in the overall complexion of the state.

53. This prejudice was returned. A Keesville, New York, girl who moved with her family to Illinois in 1833 wrote home about "a low set of people from Kentucky, Tennessee & thereabouts" (Davis, *Frontier Illinois,* pp. 2–4).

54. Coles later moved to Philadelphia where he became an abolitionist leader. But the son

he lost in the Civil War fought on the *Confederate* side (Davis, *Frontier Illinois,* p. 172). On the religious dimension of the conflict, see Simeone, *Democracy and Slavery,* pp. 166–96.

55. The German observer was Ferdinand Ernst, whose *Bemerkungen auf einer Reise* is excerpted in Angle, *Prairie State,* pp. 68–75. The Penn professor, William H. Keating, is excerpted on pp. 84–87. On the economic takeoff, see Pease, *Story of Illinois,* pp. 102–31.

56. John Woods, an Englishman, noted in 1819 how Illinoisans of high office spoke in the same rustic, complaining way as commoners. To all a wife was "woman," a horse "creature," a cow "the beef," and goods of any sort "plunder" or "truck" (Angle, *Prairie State,* pp. 82–83). Thus two Illinoisans conversed:

> "Well, Judge, how do you do? I hope you are well."
>
> "Well, Squire, I am tolerably bad. How do you do?"
>
> "Well, I am a heap better than I was; but I have been powerfully sick lately."
>
> "But, Squire, you have a powerful chance of plunder on your creature. What are you going to do with it?"
>
> "Well, I am going to town with a tolerable chance of plunder, to get it carded at the mill."
>
> "Well, so you have got your wool to be carded; I could not calculate what truck you had got."
>
> "Well, I fancy you have been to town. How goes times there?"
>
> "Times are dull; I calculated to trade my creature there. . . ."
>
> "Well, Judge, I must go on and toat my truck to mill, and then get right strait home."
>
> "Well, I must also get on, as my woman is powerfully sick and I am fetching her some whiskey."

57. "Not lofty, but pure" is how George Dangerfield's beautiful pencil sketch of Monroe characterizes his ambitions in *The Era of Good Feelings* (New York: Harcourt, Brace, & World, 1952), p. 95–104 (quotes, p. 97, 100). The title of biographer Harry Ammon, *James Monroe: The Quest for National Identity* (New York: McGraw-Hill, 1971) speaks for itself: in the decade after 1815 a new American nationalism was struggling for definition. Ralph Ketcham, *Presidents Above Party: The First American Presidency, 1789–1829* (Chapel Hill: University of North Carolina, 1984), pp. 124–40, speaks of Monroe's terms as "the ebb of the Republican presidency." Noble E. Cunningham, *The Presidency of James Monroe* (Lawrence: University of Kansas, 1996) sings his achievements in a minor key. He did not inspire adulation or condemnation; did not dominate Congress as Jefferson had; deferred to his cabinet; sought consensus. Given the potentially explosive issues his administration confronted, however, Monroe's temperament was a national boon (pp. 185–92). Finally, Richard P. McCormick, *The Presidential Game: The Origins of American Presidential Politics* (New York: Oxford University, 1982), pp. 106–16, describes the trends that seemed to ensure Monroe would lower the curtain on the Virginia dynasty.

58. Harry N. Scheiber, "The Transportation Revolution and American Law: Constitutionalism and Public Policy," and Douglas C. Clanin, "Internal Improvements in National Politics, 1816–1830," in *Transportation and the Early Nation,* pp. 1–60 (quote, p. 36).

59. Adams and Rush did not know it, but the 49th parallel settlement placed inside the United States the Wesabi Range, the richest iron deposits in North America, and the future site of Hibbing, Minnesota, birthplace of Bob Dylan. Adams did suspect the great value of the

Oregon Territory and was confident American pioneers would secure it for the United States over the course of a few decades.

60. These are the words picked by Jackson's most assiduous, perhaps most admiring, biographer Robert Remini, *Andrew Jackson and the Course of American Empire, 1767–1821* (New York: Harper & Row, 1977), pp. 1–2.

61. These are the words picked by that artist in ink Dangerfield in *Era of Good Feelings*, pp. 122–23.

62. These are the suppositions of James C. Curtis, *Andrew Jackson and the Search for Vindication* (Boston: Little, Brown, 1976), pp. 1–18. One need not go in for psychohistory to imagine Andy Jackson a driven, disturbed young man whose willpower and energy nonetheless hypnotized those around them. Controlled passion, even madness, is a valuable asset in a leader of men. "Conquer or die" (*buhidh no bas* in Gaelic, *vincere vel mori* in Latin) is inscribed on the coat of arms of Clan MacDougall.

63. The story of Jackson's marriage is complicated and not wholly untangled to this day. He took up lodgings near Nashville with the widow of John Donelson, a pioneer land baron in the Cumberland who was killed in an Indian war in 1785. Jackson revered the woman—she reminded him of his mother—and as so often happens when a young man falls for a matron he zeroed in on her daughter. Rachel was already married to Lewis Robards, but that did not deter Jackson. He wooed her until Robards' jealousy turned ugly, then came to her "rescue" and carried her off to wild Mississippi. Later, thinking Robards had obtained a divorce, Andrew and Rachel got married. But the divorce was not final, so they had to get married all over again. The stigma of being "home breakers" who "lived in sin" before legal marriage dogged the couple for the rest of their lives.

64. Quote from Worthington C. Ford, ed., *The Writings of John Quincy Adams*, 7 vols. (New York: Macmillan, 1913–17), IV: 474ff. Adams is considered by many the greatest U.S. secretary of state. For accounts of the American and Spanish sides in the negotiations see Charles Francis Adams, ed., *The Memoirs of John Quincy Adams*, 12 vols. (Philadelphia: Lippincott, 1874–77), vol. 2, Samuel Flagg Bemis, *John Quincy Adams and the Foundations of American Foreign Policy* (New York: Knopf, 1949), Warren L. Cook, *Flood Tide of Empire: Spain and the Pacific Northwest, 1543–1819* (New Haven: Yale University, 1973), and David M. Pletcher, *The Diplomacy of Annexation: Texas, Oregon, and the Mexican War* (Columbia: University of Missouri, 1973).

65. Bray Hammond, *Banks and Politics in America From the Revolution to the Civil War* (Princeton, N.J.: Princeton University, 1957), pp. 251–58; Dangerfield, *Era of Good Feelings*, pp. 175–90.

66. Rohrbough, *Land Office Business*, pp. 3–136 (quote, p. 46). A. M. Sakolski, *The Great American Land Bubble: The Amazing Story of Land-Grabbing, Speculations, and Booms from Colonial Days to the Present Time* (New York: Harper & Brothers, 1932) is an amusing example of a New Deal polemicist in high dudgeon.

67. Hammond, *Banks and Politics*, pp. 258–85 (quote, p. 259).

68. Several excellent studies of Marshall have recently appeared, including R. Kent Newmyer, *John Marshall and the Heroic Age of the Supreme Court* (Baton Rouge: Louisiana State University, 2001); James F. Simon, *What Kind of Nation: Thomas Jefferson, John Marshall, and the Epic Struggle to Create a United States* (New York: Simon & Schuster, 2002), Herbert A. Johnson, *The Chief Justiceship of John Marshall, 1801–1835* (Columbia: University of South Carolina, 1997) whose "A Marshall Vignette" includes the anecdotes mentioned above (pp. 13–21), Jean Edward Smith, *John Marshall: Definer of a Nation* (New York: Henry Holt, 1997), and G. Edward White,

*The Marshall Court and Cultural Change 1815–1835,* abridged edition (New York: Oxford University, 1991), an ambitious assessment of the Marshall Court's means of adjusting the Constitution to the changing realities of American life.

69. This paragraph summarizes White, *Marshall Court and Cultural Change,* pp. 1–10, 741–88.

70. On the curious origins of judicial review, see Shannon C. Stimson, *The American Revolution in the Law: Anglo-American Jurisprudence Before John Marshall* (Princeton, N.J.: Princeton University, 1990) and Alfred H. Kelly, Winfred A. Harbison, and Herman Belz, *The American Constitution: Its Origins and Development,* 6 ed. (New York: W. W. Norton, 1983), pp. 89–104, 176–82.

71. Newmyer, *John Marshall,* pp. 291–302 (quotes, pp. 296–98). Marshall's assertion about "the power to destroy" was no exaggeration. The legislatures of Maryland, Virginia, and Georgia *searched* for ways to expel the U.S. Bank from their midst. That of Ohio positively outlawed the Bank in 1821. The courts struck down all their laws.

72. Newmyer, *John Marshall,* pp. 245–46, 302–21; Johnson, *Chief Justiceship,* pp. 172–81 (quote, p. 176); White, *Marshall Court,* pp. 174–81.

73. This capsule is based on Thomas Perkins Abernethy, *The Formative Period in Alabama, 1815–1828* (Tuscaloosa: University of Alabama, 1965), J. Mills Thornton III, *Politics and Power in a Slave Society: Alabama, 1800–1860* (Baton Rouge: Louisiana State University, 1978), William Warren Rogers, et al., *Alabama: The History of a Deep South State* (Tuscaloosa: University of Alabama, 1994), pp. 3–150; and Rohrbough, *Trans-Appalachian Frontier* ("Alabama Feaver," p. 196). A representative pioneer of moderate means was Williamson Hawkins, who came to Alabama with the Tennessee militia in the Creek wars and returned in 1815 with a horse, a few cattle, and a slave couple. He staked out a homestead in Jones County (near present-day Birmingham) on the Cumberland Plateau, defended it with an axe against an angry bear, then cleared a field and planted corn. After roughing out a typical Alabama "dogtrot" log cabin (so named because pets and farm animals might have the run of its two open rooms), Hawkins left the slaves in charge while he fetched his wife, children, and household goods (Rogers, *Alabama,* p. 58). By next autumn he might have a small cotton crop to sell on the Cahaba or Black Warrior River and start to accumulate capital. In the South, all but the poorest hillbillies were capitalists from the "git-go."

74. Rogers, *Alabama,* pp. 54–89; Ruth Ketring Nuernberger, *The Clays of Alabama: A Planter-Lawyer-Politician Family* (Lexington: University of Kentucky, 1958). In his portrait pose Dixon Hall Lewis is not only wonderfully obese but rendered ridiculous by a tall black top hat. He traveled in a reinforced coach and carried his own outsized chair. But Lewis, who studied law under Judge Henry Hitchcock, was shrewd and eloquent. He represented the interests of the largest of large planters and slave owners, yet his stump speeches, girth, and common touch made him appealing to common folk. Alabama was in desperate need of roads, docks, flood control, and other projects only the federal government could afford. Yet Lewis won over the backcountry by warning that federal rule followed federal money. He was certainly right about that.

75. Rogers, *Alabama,* pp. 89–92; Thornton, *Politics and Power in a Slave Society,* pp. 26–29; Nuernberger, *Clays of Alabama,* p. 42 ("incalculable distress").

76. History books usually date the sectional crisis and beginnings of a separate southern identity from the Missouri dispute of 1819–21. Jesse T. Carpenter, *The South as a Conscious Minority, 1789–1861* (New York: New York University, 1930) long ago argued a southern consciousness dated from the Constitutional Convention. It just had little need to assert itself until northerners insisted on making slavery a national political issue.

77. Dangerfield, *Era of Good Feelings,* p. 217, describes the refurbished Capitol. On Tallmadge see Glover Moore, *The Missouri Controversy 1819–1821* (Lexington: University of Kentucky, 1953), pp. 33–40 (quotes pp. 35, 39, 43).

78. Don E. Fehrenbacher, *Sectional Crisis and Southern Constitutionalism* (Baton Rouge: Louisiana State University, 1995), pp. 9–23; Dangerfield, *Era of Good Feelings,* pp. 217–32; Moore, *Missouri Controversy,* pp. 41–64 (quotes, pp. 50–51).

79. Quotes from Moore, *Missouri Controversy,* pp. 92–93; Dangerfield, *Era of Good Feelings,* pp. 218–21. The most interesting conspiracy-monger was probably Mordecai M. Noah, Jewish editor of New York's *National Advocate.* A Tammany man, Noah supported Tallmadge until suspecting he had been put up to his crusade by Daniel Webster, Theodore Dwight, and other Yankees plotting to take the northeast out of the Union "under the garb of humanity." See Jonathan Sarna, *Jacksonian Jew* (New York: Holmes & Meyer, 1981) or the older Isaac Goldberg, *Major Noah: American-Jewish Pioneer* (New York: Knopf, 1937).

80. Cunningham, *Presidency of James Monroe,* pp. 87–104.

81. Robert V. Remini, *Henry Clay: Statesman for the Union* (New York: W. W. Norton, 1991), pp. 169–92.

82. John Quincy Adams thought Clay's sleight of hand an outrage. So did fiery Virginian John Randolph, who hoped to re-open debate on the Thomas Amendment. Randolph despised Clay for the rest of his life. In 1826 they fought one of the last formal duels in the United States. Clay shot to kill, but only damaged his enemy's cloak. Randolph, his honor established, shot at the sky.

83. Fehrenbacher, *Sectional Crisis,* pp. 17–23.

84. Edwin A. Churchill, "English Beachheads in Seventeenth-Century Maine," Alaric Faulkner and Gretchen Fearon Faulkner, "Acadian Settlement," Harald E. L. Prins, "Turmoil on the Wabanaki Frontier," David L. Ghere, "Diplomacy & War on the Maine Frontier," and James S. Leamon, "Maine in the American Revolution," in Richard W. Judd, Edwin A. Churchill, and Joel W. Eastman, eds., *Maine: The Pine Tree State from Prehistory to the Present* (Orono: University of Maine, 1995), pp. 51–168.

85. Ronald F. Banks, *Maine Becomes a State: The Movement to Separate Maine from Massachusetts, 1785–1820* (Middletown, Conn.: Wesleyan University, 1970), pp. 3–40 (quotes, pp. 29–30); James S. Leamon, Richard R. Wescott, and Edward O. Schriver, "Separation & Statehood," in Judd, et al., *Maine,* pp. 169–78.

86. Alan Taylor, *Liberty Men and Great Proprietors: The Revolutionary Settlement on the Maine Frontier, 1760–1820* (Chapel Hill: University of North Carolina, 1990), pp. 11–87 (quote, pp. 72–73).

87. Taylor, *Liberty Men,* pp. 89–153 (quote, p. 143). See also James B. Vickery, Richard W. Judd, and Sheila McDonald, "Maine Agriculture," in Judd, et al., *Maine,* pp. 242–61.

88. Banks, *Maine Becomes a State,* pp. 41–56; Taylor, *Liberty Men,* pp. 181–232. The first of these books deals exclusively with the politics of the pro-statehood elite, hence it ignores the social agitation just outside of Maine's towns. The latter book deals exclusively (albeit brilliantly) with the agitation, ignoring the concomitant battles over separation. No sources purport to read Maine farmers' minds, but adding 2 + 2 one may deduce the cause of the apparently contradictory 1807 votes as I have above.

89. Banks, *Maine Becomes a State,* pp. 57–149; Leamon, et al., "Separation & Statehood," pp. 178–92. The final push for Maine separation put Massachusetts Republicans in a quandary. They could hardly oppose their sister party in Maine, and statehood for them would increase Republican power nationally. But the loss of Maine's votes in Massachusetts elections might

give Federalists the upper hand in their own state, at least for a time. See Paul Goodman, *The Democratic Republicans of Massachusetts* (Cambridge, Mass.: Harvard University, 1964).

90. Banks, *Maine Becomes a State*, pp. 150–204 (quote, p. 189). For the overall context in Congress see Moore, *Missouri Controversy*. Maine voters also protested making Portland the capital. When at last Augusta won out in 1832, Maine's seat of government was established in the Kennebec Valley, heart of "white Indian" Country.

91. Richard R. Wescott and Edward O. Schriver, "Reform Movements & Party Reformation," in Judd, et al., *Maine*, pp. 193–216 ("acutely self-conscious, p. 194).

92. Moore, *Missouri Controversy*, pp. 129–69; Dangerfield, *Era of Good Feelings*, pp. 233–45; Monroe quote from *The Presidents. . . . Their Inaugural Addresses* (Chicago: Whitehall, 1968), p. 44. That Negro equality was an issue neither side wanted to raise is demonstrated by the 1820 law passed by Congress to restrict the mayoralty of the Federal City to white males. The one vote against Monroe was cast by William Plumer.

93. Douglas R. Egerton, *He Shall Go Out Free: The Lives of Denmark Vesey* (Madison: University of Wisconsin, 1999); David Robertson, *Denmark Vesey* (New York: Knopf, 1999); Edward A. Pearson, ed., *Designs Against Charleston: The Trial Record of the Denmark Vesey Slave Conspiracy of 1822* (Chapel Hill: University of North Carolina, 1999).

94. The critic Michael P. Johnson lit an historiographical firestorm when he published his findings in "Denmark Vesey and His Co-Conspirators," *William and Mary Quarterly* 58 (2001): 915–76. He returned to the sources after reading the three books, finding damning discrepancies between the *Official Report* and original court transcripts, noting as well Supreme Court Justice William Johnson, Jr., and Governor Thomas Bennett, Jr., condemned the secret proceedings at the time. Johnson's alternative theory of what happened focuses on rumors—one concerning an emancipation bill, the other a *white* plot to kill *blacks*—heard on the blacks' grapevine in 1821–22. Vesey, perhaps too outspoken in his Biblical condemnation of slavery, became a natural focus of attention among blacks and frightened whites alike. The authors Johnson criticized and other scholars of slave revolts responded in Robert A. Gross, ed., "Forum: The Making of a Slave Conspiracy, part 2," *William and Mary Quarterly* 59 (2002): 135–202. Johnson himself was already at work on a book, *Conjuring Insurrection*, showing Hamilton's fingerprints all over the "Vesey conspiracy."

95. Holland, *A Refutation of the Calumnies Circulated Against the Southern and Western States, Respecting the Institution and Existence of Slavery Among Them* (Charleston, 1822), quoted by Robert L. Paquette in Gross, ed., "Forum: The Making of a Slave Conspiracy, part 2," p. 185.

96. William E. Parrish, ed., *A History of Missouri*, 5 vols. (Columbia: University of Missouri, 1971), vol. I; Parish, et al., *Missouri: The Heart of the Nation* (St. Louis: Forum, 1980), pp. 1–36; William E. Foley, *The Genesis of Missouri: From Wilderness Outpost to State-hood* (Columbia: University of Missouri, 1989), pp. 1–79 (etymologies, p. 1; quotes, pp. 78–79).

97. Foley, *Genesis of Missouri*, pp. 80–158 (quote, p. 136). In the 1950s Walt Disney myth-makers made Mike Fink big, dumb, and lovable. He was really big, smart (when sober), and dangerous. Fink, Bill Carpenter, and their female companion "Pittsburg Blue," enjoyed shocking folks in town by shooting cups off each other's heads with their Kentucky rifles. In 1823 Fink accidentally killed Carpenter in this fashion and was himself killed by an angry boatman.

98. Dick Steward, *Frontier Swashbuckler: The Life and Legend of John Smith T* (Columbia: University of Missouri, 2000), pp. 1–154; Foley, *Genesis of Missouri*, pp. 162–69.

99. Parrish, *Missouri*, pp. 37–52; Foley, *Genesis of Missouri*, 203–59. On Clark's post-Pacific career see Jerome O. Steffin, *William Clark: Jeffersonian Man on the Frontier* (Norman:

University of Oklahoma, 1977); on Nathan Boone and his Rangers, R. Douglas Hurt, *Nathan Boone and the American Frontier* (Columbia: University of Missouri, 1998); on the earthquake, James L. Penick, Jr., *The New Madrid Earthquakes of 1811–1812* (Columbia: University of Missouri, 1976). Foley, p. 219, cites Boynton Merrill, Jr., *Jefferson's Nephews: A Frontier Tragedy* (Princeton: Princeton University, 1976) to the effect the temblor disgorged a buried skull in Kentucky belonging to a Negro murdered by none other than Thomas Jefferson's ne'er-do-well nephews.

100. Floyd Calvin Shoemaker, *Missouri's Struggle for Statehood 1804–1821* (New York: Russell & Russell, 1969, orig. 1916), pp. 37–80; Foley, *Genesis of Missouri*, pp. 283–98; Steward, *Frontier Swashbuckler*, pp. 155–63 (quote, p. 163) on Smith T and the abolitionist.

101. Shoemaker, *Missouri's Struggle*, pp. 114–34, 272–73; Perry McCandless, *History of Missouri*, vol. II: 1820 to 1860 (Columbia: University of Missouri, 1972), pp. 1–30.

102. McCandless, *History of Missouri*, pp. 67–126; also McCandless' 1953 dissertation "Thomas H. Benton: His Source of Political Strength in Missouri from 1815 to 1838" (Ann Arbor: University Microfilms, 1967); William N. Chambers, *Old Bullion Benton, Senator from the New West 1782–1858* (Boston: Little, Brown, 1956); Elbert B. Smith, *Magnificent Missourian: The Life of Thomas Hart Benton* (Westport, Conn.: Greenwood, 1973), and the classic biography by Theodore Roosevelt, *Thomas Hart Benton* (Boston: Houghton Mifflin, 1893).

103. Steward, *Frontier Swashbuckler*, pp. 164–93. Having helped to ruin Moses Austin, father of one of the founders of Texas, Smith T challenged Sam Houston to a duel in Nashville in 1826 and bragged Houston surrounded himself with armed men to avoid it. Houston denied the charge, insisting he was ready to slay the "butcher" Smith T like a dog should they meet.

104. For the saga of Spanish, British, Russian, and American competition see Walter A. McDougall, *Let the Sea Make a Noise. . . . A History of the North Pacific from Magellan to MacArthur* (New York: Basic Books, 1993).

105. Howard I. Kushner, *Conflict on the Northwest Coast: American-Russian Rivalry in the Pacific Northwest, 1790–1867* (Westport, Conn.: Greenwood, 1975), pp. 3–40 (quotes pp. 36, 40).

106. "Keep what is yours" in C. F. Adams, *Memoirs of John Quincy Adams*, 5: 252; "And is it not time" quoted in Bemis, *John Quincy Adams*, p. 515. On the Russo-American dispute and origins of the Monroe Doctrine see the summary in Walter A. McDougall, *Promised Land, Crusader State: The American Encounter with the World Since 1776* (Boston: Houghton Mifflin, 1997), pp. 57–75. On Adams' expansionism see Walter La Feber, *John Quincy Adams and American Continental Empire* (Chicago: Quadrangle Books, 1965).

107. Americans used the terms Holy Allies or Holy Alliance erroneously to refer to all the reactionary monarchies following the Congress of Vienna. The Holy Alliance was in fact a utopian Christian document drafted by Tsar Alexander and reluctantly adhered to by the Habsburg emperor and the Prussian king. The only powers capable of intervening in Latin America—France, Spain, and Britain—were not members of it. Quotes in this paragraph from Andrew A. Lipscomb and Albert E. Bergh, eds., *The Writings of Thomas Jefferson*, 20 vols. (Washington, D.C.: Jefferson Memorial Society, 1903–4), 15: 477–50; C. F. Adams, *Memoirs of John Quincy Adams*, 6: 1799, 186; John Quincy Adams, *An Address . . . on the Fourth of July 1821* (Washington, D.C.: David and Force, 1821), all cited in McDougall, *Promised Land, Crusader State*, pp. 68–72, 36.

108. Quotes from Chase C. Mooney, *William H. Crawford, 1772–1834* (Lexington: University of Kentucky, 1974), pp. 257–58, 287. On the collapse of the Virginia system of national politics and origins of the second American party system see McCormick, *Presidential Game*, pp. 117–63, and Roy F. Nichols, *The Invention of the American Political Parties* (New York:

Macmillan, 1967), pp. 262–95. For a narrative of the bizarre 1824 election see Dangerfield, *Era of Good Feelings*, pp. 331–45.

109. The conflicting accounts of Van Rensselaer's last-minute decision are from *The Autobiography of Martin Van Buren* (New York: Da Capo, 1973), 2: 152, and Margaret Bayard Smith, *The First Forty Years of Washington Society* (New York: Charles Scribner's Sons, 1906), p. 91.

110. Paul C. Nagel, *John Quincy Adams: A Public Life, a Private Life* (New York: Knopf, 1997), the latest biography, is valuable for its treatment of Adams' domestic politics and unhappy family life (quotes, pp. 266–67).

111. Adams quotes in Dangerfield, *Era of Good Feelings*, pp. 331, 348–49.

112. David A. Hounshell, *From the American System to Mass Production 1800–1932: The Development of Manufacturing Technology in the United States* (Baltimore: Johns Hopkins University, 1984), pp. 1–13, 25–32. Thanks to Jefferson's unwarranted praise, Whitney's alleged priority was taken for granted for over a century. See for instance the breathless Constance M. Green, *Eli Whitney and the Birth of American Technology* (Boston: Little, Brown, 1956). Robert S. Woodbury, "The Legend of Eli Whitney and Interchangeable Parts," *Technology and Culture* 1 (1960): 235–53, exploded the myth. Merritt Roe Smith, "John H. Hall, Simeon North, and the Milling Machine: The Nature of Innovation among Antebellum Arms Makers," *Technology and Culture* 14 (1973): 573–91, and *Military Enterprise and Technological Change: Perspectives on the American Experience* (Cambridge, Mass.: M.I.T., 1985), then reconstructed the true story. Whitney died in 1825, leaving his wife and four children the considerable sum of $130,000.

113. Hounshell, *American System*, pp. 28–46 (North quote, p. 28; Hall quote, pp. 40–41).

114. David Freeman Hawke, *Nuts and Bolts of the Past: A History of American Technology 1776–1860* (New York: Harper & Row, 1988), pp. 69–74; Hounshell, *American System*, pp. 51–61.

115. Nathan Rosenberg, "America's Rise to Woodworking Leadership," in Brooke Hindle, ed. *America's Wooden Age: Aspects of its Early Technology* (Tarrytown, N.Y.: Sleepy Hollow Restorations, 1975), pp. 37–62; Carolyn C. Cooper, "Patent Transformation: Woodworking Mechanization in Philadelphia, 1830–1856," in Judith A. McGaw, ed., *Early American Technology: Making and Doing Things from the Colonial Era to 1850* (Chapel Hill: University of North Carolina, 1994), pp. 278–327.

116. Stanley Lebergott, *The Americans: An Economic Record* (New York: W. W. Norton, 1984), pp. 124–38; John W. Oliver, *History of American Technology* (New York: Ronald, 1956), pp. 147–73 (Appleton quote, p. 159); Louis Hunter, "Waterpower in the Century of the Steam Engine," in Hindle, *America's Wooden Age*, pp. 160–90 (Merrimack quote, p. 181). E. I. Du Pont purchased America's first merino ram, the famous Dom Pedro, for $60 in 1801. Within a decade the domestic price for a fine merino soared above $300, causing Vermont's William Jarvis to ship 2,000 merino rams and ewes during his years as U.S. consul in Lisbon. See Carroll W. Pursell, Jr., "E. I. Du Pont and the Merino Mania in Delaware 1805–1815," *Agricultural History* 36 (1962): 91–100.

117. Robert B. Gordon, "Custom and Consequence: Early Nineteenth-Century Origins of the Environmental and Social Costs of Mining Anthracite," in McGaw, *Early American Technology*, pp. 240–77; Lebergott, *Americans: An Economic Record*, pp. 206–21; Judith McGaw, *Most Wonderful Machine: Mechanization and Social Change in Berkshire Paper Making, 1801–1885* (Princeton: Princeton University, 1987), pp. 3–89 (Melville quote, p. 9); Jack Larkin, *The Reshaping of Everyday Life 1790–1840* (New York: Harper & Row, 1988), concluding quote, p. 303.

118. Oliver, *American Technology*, pp. 144–56 (quote, p. 144); Bruce A. Sinclair,

*Philadelphia's Philosopher Mechanics: A History of the Franklin Institute, 1825–1865* (Baltimore: Johns Hopkins University, 1977).

119. The most recent debate on this era was kicked off by Charles G. Sellers, Jr., *The Market Revolution: Jacksonian America 1815–1846* (New York: Oxford University, 1991). Sellers argues American society was overwhelmingly composed of pre-capitalist subsistence farmers devoted to a moral economy and fearful of the insecurities and price fluctuations of the market. Capitalists and their legal "shock troops," he claims, attacked and conquered this society with dire results for liberty, equality, morality, and the environment. William E. Gienapp offers a withering critique of Sellers' book in "The Myth of Class in Jacksonian America," *Journal of Policy History* 6 (1994): 232–59.

120. Quotations cited by Gienapp, "Myth of Class," pp. 246–49.

121. For a lively and insightful account of the 1828 campaign see Robert V. Remini, *The Election of Andrew Jackson* (Philadelphia: Lippincott, 1963). The origins of the new politics symbolized by the rise of Jackson and founding of the Democratic Party are described in McCormick, *Presidential Game,* pp. 117–63, and Nichols, *Invention of American Political Parties,* pp. 279–95.

122. Remini, *Election of Jackson,* pp. 51–120. "My real friends" quoted in Stefan Lorant, *The Glorious Burden: The American Presidency* (New York: Harper & Row, 1968), p. 122; "primarily because" quoted in Dangerfield, *Era of Good Feelings,* p. 416.

123. On the national Republican effort see Remini, *Election of Jackson,* pp. 121–65, and Mary W. M. Hargreaves, *The Presidency of John Quincy Adams* (Lawrence: University of Kansas, 1985), pp. 281–303. Quote on "organization" in Robert V. Remini, *Andrew Jackson and the Course of American Freedom* (New York: Harper & Row, 1981), p. 148.

124. Glyndon G. Van Deusen, *The Rise and Decline of Jacksonian Democracy* (New York: Van Nostrand Reinhold, 1970), pp. 29–30. Another great Mason leaning to Adams was DeWitt Clinton. His death in February 1828 opened up the governorship, which Van Buren purloined thanks to the three-way split in the vote.

125. *Autobiography of Martin Van Buren,* 2: 255.

126. Bessie Rowland James, *Anne Royall's U.S.A.* (New Brunswick, N.J.: Rutgers University, 1972), pp. 246–50. Jackson speech in *The Presidents . . . Their Inaugural Addresses,* pp. 55–57.

TRAVELERS

1. Russell Blaine Nye, *The Cultural Life of the New Nation 1776–1830* (New York: Harper & Bros., 1960), pp. 235–67. Hawthorne quoted by George Brown Tindall, *America: A Narrative History,* 2 ed. (New York: W. W. Norton, 1988), I: 486.

2. Quotes in Nye, *Cultural Life,* pp. 244–46.

3. The tale is told in exquisite fashion by Alan Taylor, *William Cooper's Town: Power and Persuasion on the Frontier of the Early American Republic* (New York: Knopf, 1996).

4. The DeLanceys, being Loyalists, lost most of their property in the Revolution, hence his marriage did not enrich Cooper. On Cooper's background see Wayne Franklin, "Introduction," to James Fenimore Cooper, *The Spy: A Tale of the Neutral Ground* (New York: Penguin, 1997), pp. vii–xxx; Marcus Cunliffe, *The Literature of the United States,* 3 ed. (New York: Penguin, 1967), pp. 60–70. *The Spy* was the first American novel hailed in Britain, not least because of Cooper's sympathetic portrayal of officers in the service of King George.

5. Perry Miller, *The Life of the Mind in America from the Revolution to the Civil War* (New York: Harcourt, Brace, & World, 1965), pp. 99–104 (Bumppo quotes p. 101; "keened eligiacally"

are Miller's words, p. 99). It was Cooper's English fan Lord Edward Stanley (later the Earl of Derby and Conservative Prime Minister) who suggested a frontier romance set in Glens Falls near Lake George, hence *Mohicans.*

6. Taylor, *William Cooper's Town,* pp. 372–427 (quotes pp. 408, 423); James Fenimore Cooper, *Notions of the Americans: Picked up by a Travelling Bachelor,* 2 vols. (Philadelphia: Carey, Lea & Carey, 1828). For a good summary of *Notions,* see G. Edward White, *The Marshall Court and Cultural Change 1815–1835,* abridged edition (New York: Oxford University, 1991), pp. 12–39 ("emphatically an age of reading," p. 25).

7. See Bessie Rowland James, *Anne Royall's U.S.A.* (New Brunswick, N.J.: Rutgers University, 1972), Alice S. Maxwell and Marion B. Dunlevy, *Virago! The Story of Anne Newport Royall, 1769–1854* (Jefferson, N.C.: McFarland, 1985), the older George S. Jackson, *Uncommon Scold, the Story of Anne Royal* (Boston: B. Humphries, 1937), and Jeanne M. Malloy, "Royall, Anne Newport," *American National Biography Online,* Feb. 2000.

8. James, *Anne Royall's U.S.A.,* p. 88.

9. James, *Anne Royall's U.S.A.,* pp. 90–117 (quotes, pp. 97, 109, 112).

10. James, *Anne Royall's U.S.A.,* seriatim (quotes, in order of appearance, from pp. 179, 126, 133, 158, 140, 169, 274, 282). Major Mordecai M. Noah, the handsome Jewish diplomat, publisher, and erstwhile politician, was elected sheriff on the Tammany slate in 1822. He lost his reelection bid after making the unpopular decision to open New York's prisons during a yellow fever epidemic lest all the inmates perish. Royall was just as drawn to Jews as to Masons and Catholics. She thought Charleston's community of Portuguese Jews (dating from the seventeenth century) among the most upright and honorable of its citizens, noting also "All are Masons" (p. 277).

11. Malloy, "Royall" (including "the outpouring" and "vile speculations"); James, *Anne Royall's U.S.A.,* pp. 184–225 ("Under the name," p. 189; "The missionaries," p. 193; "But I am writing," p. 198).

12. The most complete account of the trial is in Maxwell and Dunlevy, *Virago!* The last issue of *The Huntress* is reproduced in James, *Anne Royall's U.S.A.,* pp. 385–87.

13. Nathan O. Hatch, *The Democratization of American Christianity* (New Haven: Yale University, 1989), pp. 3–16 (quote, p. 13). A massive, brilliant new study of Americans' flight from European theology is Mark A. Noll, *America's God: From Jonathan Edwards to Abraham Lincoln* (New York: Oxford University, 2002).

14. Thus, Richard Hofstadter concluded in *Anti-Intellectualism in American Life* (New York: Knopf, 1963) "revivalism succeeded where traditionalism had failed," as if American clergy shared some agenda with the wealthy to enlist the masses into the army of capitalism. But Paul E. Johnson, *A Shopkeeper's Millennium: Society and Revivals in Rochester, New York, 1815–1837* (New York: Hill and Wang, 1978) went all the way, describing urban revivals as "order-inducing, repressive, and quintessentially bourgeois." See Hatch's critique in *Democratization of American Christianity,* pp. 220–26.

15. The peculiar theology, methods, and reform agendas in the Second Great Awakening are summarized by Robert William Fogel, *The Fourth Great Awakening and the Future of Egalitarianism* (Chicago: University of Chicago, 2000), pp. 20–22, 68–107. Describing the revivalists' stress on the immanence of heavenly grace, Joyce Appleby writes: "For Christian leaders to embrace the very worldly aspirations evident in the larger culture involved a number of adjustments. . . . A more dramatic intellectual shift took place when thinkers started looking for God's will within the human lifetime rather than fixing exclusively on future rewards and punishments" (*Inheriting the Revolution: The First Generation of Americans* [Cambridge, Mass.:

Harvard University, 2000], pp. 250–51). She is precisely right: it was an *intellectual* (not anti-intellectual) shift.

16. R. Laurence Moore, *Selling God: American Religion in the Marketplace of Culture* (New York: Oxford University, 1994), pp. 13–39 (quotes, p. 21). See also Lewis G. Leary, *The Book Peddling Parson: An Account of the Life and Works of Mason Locke Weems, Patriot, Pitchman, Author, and Purveyor of Morality to the Citizenry of the Early United States of America* (Chapel Hill, N.C.: Algonquin Books, 1984) and David S. Reynolds, *Faith in Fiction: The Emergence of Religious Literature in America* (Cambridge, Mass.: Harvard University, 1981).

17. On the clerical-female alliance in older denominations, the cult of domesticity, and the power of female consumers in nineteenth-century America see the *tour de force* by Ann Douglas, *The Feminization of American Culture* (New York: Knopf, 1977), quotes, pp. 17, 8, 43. Douglas traces the metamorphosis in New England theology by contrasting the ways key figures of three successive generations explained the Atonement. In *True Religion Delineated* (1750), Joseph Bellamy described the God of Judgment as a stern, infinitely remote father demanding full retribution for his children's sins even though He himself made human beings incapable of meeting his standard of perfection. In the *Treatise on the Atonement* (1807), Universalist Hosea Ballou rejected Bellamy's prideful, vengeful God as profane. Instead, he depicted God as a kind, abiding father willing to sacrifice His own son that all people might at least have a chance to be saved. Finally, in *The Atoning Sacrifice, a Display of Love Not of Wrath* (1830), pacifist Noah Worcester wrote of the "dignity and sweetness" and "almost feminine gentleness" of a parental God unwilling to see *any* of his children condemned. Thus, Christ, the archetype Civilian, loves his enemies, turns the other cheek, and is butchered by soldiers so that men, heeding His example, might perfect human nature on their *own* (pp. 121–30). Douglas neatly entitles her chapter "The Loss of Theology."

18. Moore, *Selling God*, pp. 66–89; Douglas, *Feminization*, pp. 152–64 (quotes, p. 153); Mark A. Noll, *A History of Christianity in the United States and Canada* (Grand Rapids, Mich.: Eerdmans, 1992), pp. 174–78; Edwin S. Gaustad, *A Religious History of America*, rev. ed. (San Francisco: Harper & Row, 1990), pp. 128–44.

19. Tappan, *The Question Answered, Watchman, What of the Night?* (Salem, Mass., 1783) cited by Melvin B. Endy, Jr. "Just War, Holy War, and Millenarianism in Revolutionary America," *William and Mary Quarterly* 42 (1985): 3–25; Ernest Lee Tuveson, *Redeemer Nation: The Idea of America's Millennial Role* (Chicago: University of Chicago, 1968), pp. 53–54, lists just the most prominent among the clergy who wrote treatises on America's millennial destiny: Jonathan Edwards (pre-eminent American theologian), Joseph Bellamy (Edwards' prize pupil), Samuel Hopkins (founder of "New Light" theology), Joseph Priestley ("apostle of the American Revolution"), Richard Price (English friend of America whose later polemics inspired Burke's *Reflections on the Revolution in France*), Timothy Dwight (Congregational "Pope of Connecticut"), Alexander Campbell (principal western heir to Cane Ridge's McGready), Henry Boynton Smith (head of Union Theological Seminary), Lyman Beecher (Presbyterian revivalist, scourge of Unitarians, and "father of brains" including Henry Ward Beecher and Harriet Beecher Stowe), Horace Bushnell (Yale graduate, Hartford pastor, and "father of religious liberalism" spanning Puritanism and Transcendentalism), Enoch Pond (trainer of 700+ clergy at Bangor, Maine), Josiah Strong (founder of the Social Gospel movement), and so on and on.

20. Miller, *Life of the Mind*, pp. 3–14 (quotes, pp. 9, 24, 3); Noll, *History of Christianity*, pp. 174–78; Ahlstrom, *A Religious History of the American People* (New Haven: Yale University, 1972), pp. 458–61. The liveliest source for Finney's conversion and early preaching career is his own autobiography. See Garth M. Rosell and Richard A. G. Dupuis, eds., *The Memoirs of*

*Charles G. Finney, the Complete Restored Text* (Grand Rapids, Mich.: Academie Books, 1989), Keith Hardman, *Charles Grandison Finney, 1792–1875: Revivalist and Reformer* (Syracuse: Syracuse University, 1987), and Charles E. Hambrick-Stowe, *Charles G. Finney and the Spirit of American Evangelism* (Grand Rapids, Mich.: Eerdmans, 1996).

21. Miller, *Life of the Mind,* pp. 14–22; Fogel, *Fourth Great Awakening,* pp. 90–107 (quotes, p. 94).

22. Miller, *Life of the Mind,* pp. 22–35 (quotes, pp. 22, 23, 26, 31–32, 33). Noll, *History of Christianity,* pp. 174–78, believes a strong case can be made that Finney ranks with Jackson, Lincoln, and Andrew Carnegie as the most influential American of his century.

23. Tuveson, *Redeemer Nation,* pp. 79–82 (quotes, p. 81).

24. Ahlstrom, *Religious History,* p. 459; Miller, *Life of the Mind,* pp. 8–9.

25. Cunliffe, *Literature of the United States,* p. 70. Cooper's *The Crater* may have inspired some of Jules Verne's and Mark Twain's morbid allegories. It certainly influenced, and was influenced by, Herman Melville.

26. Hooper, one of the many Georgians who migrated to Alabama in search of his fortune, inspired later "western humorists" of whom Twain is most famous. Hooper became nationally known for *Some Adventures of Captain Simon Suggs, Late of the Tallapoosa Volunteers.* A traveling con man, Suggs exposes the hustling and hypocrisy prevalent in law, politics, religion, philanthropy, real estate, and just about every other pursuit in American frontier life. Unfortunately, Alabama voters so much identified the author with the japes of his character they repeatedly denied him the political career he desired! See W. Stanley Hoole, *Alias Simon Suggs: The Life and Times of Johnson Jones Hooper* (Tuscaloosa: University of Alabama, 1952). For Hooper's influence see Kenneth Lynn, *Mark Twain and Southwestern Humor* (Boston: Little, Brown, 1959).

# INDEX